SCOT McKN

THE *Second*

TESTAMENT

A NEW TRANSLATION

An imprint of InterVarsity Press
Downers Grove, Illinois

InterVarsity Press
P.O. Box 1400 | Downers Grove, IL 60515-1426
ivpress.com | email@ivpress.com

©2023 by Scot McKnight

All rights reserved. No part of this book may be reproduced in any form without written permission from InterVarsity Press.

InterVarsity Press® is the publishing division of InterVarsity Christian Fellowship/USA®. For more information, visit intervarsity.org.

All Scripture quotations, unless otherwise indicated, are translated by the author.

The publisher cannot verify the accuracy or functionality of website URLs used in this book beyond the date of publication.

Cover design and image composite: David Fassett
Interior design: Jeanna Wiggins
All figures copyright InterVarsity Press

ISBN 978-0-8308-4699-3 (print) | ISBN 978-0-8308-4700-6 (digital)

Printed in the United States of America ∞

Library of Congress Cataloging-in-Publication Data
A catalog record for this book is available from the Library of Congress.

CONTENTS

Preface	v
The Gospel of Matthew	1
The Gospel of Mark	37
The Gospel of Luke	59
The Gospel of John	96
The Acts of the Apostles	123
To the Romans	161
The First Letter to Corinth	176
The Second Letter to Corinth	191
To the Galatians	201
To the Ephesians	207
To the Philippians	213
To the Colossians	218
The First Letter to the Thessalonians	223
The Second Letter to the Thessalonians	227
The First Letter to Timothy	231
The Second Letter to Timothy	236
To Titus	240
To Philemon	243
To the Hebrews	245
The Letter of James	256
The First Letter of Peter	261
The Second Letter of Peter	266
The First Letter of John	270
The Second Letter of John	275
The Third Letter of John	277
The Letter of Jude	279
The Apocalypse of John	281
Glossary	301

PREFACE

A wonderful problem with translating the Bible, in my case only *The Second (or New) Testament*, is familiarity. Everyone's got a Bible, and everyone's also got an opinion of how it should sound or read, even when someone has no knowledge of the original languages. What sounds familiar and right in English might not sound like the Greek text itself at all, and when we translate into English, we can do a disservice to the original language and authors. This translation will do its best to make the text sound more like the Greek original, and sometimes it will not sound all that English-y. As such, "The Second Testament" is unlike any translation you have seen. Most translations take the original and convert it to something as close to English as possible. Most do this well, so well, in fact, that an alternative can be useful. My goal is to help English readers experience what the Greek reader experiences in reading the New Testament in Greek. If *The Second Testament* feels awkward and choppy and crunchy it is because the Greek feels that way. This translation is not correcting other translations but providing a supplement to our many fine translations.

Most of our translations are concerned with what the original text means in modern English, and they should be. But the moment we are most concerned with what the text means in our world, we shift into interpretation and into what makes most sense in English—that is, with natural, dynamic equivalents. Take 1 Petros (1 Peter) 1:13. Here are three equivalent, dynamic translations:

- "prepare your minds for action" (NRSV)
- "with minds that are alert" (NIV)
- "once you have your minds ready for action" (CEB)

Yes, those are fine English equivalents, but the Greek text literally reads something like "surrounding your waist mentally." By the way, the KJV has the much more literal "gird up the loins of your mind" and the translation in *The Second Testament* is "surrounding your mental waist [with your robe]." I don't claim that my translation is right and the others are wrong; I claim that something is regained with a more literal rendering. *The Second Testament* wants to preserve the kind of translation that is not as concerned with meaning or dynamic equivalence but that provides a more formal translation. I leave it to you, the reader, to make the meaning and sense.

I hope this translation will at times jar the reader enough to explore a more formal, literal rendering. There are two poles in translation, one that poses the differences as "formal" versus "dynamic" equivalence. This is a happy alternative, but what if we reframe those terms into "antiquating" (formal) versus "domesticating" (dynamic) and then suggest that the latter at times is colonizing? Dynamic equivalence can make the New Testament sound so much like our English that readers may well wonder whether the New Testament was written just after the century turned.

SOME PARTICULARS

It might be better English to say, "Jesus replied and said," but the original form is more literally "Replying, Jesus said." The formal rendering is not as smooth in English, but remember, our Second Testament was written in Greek, not English, and capturing more nuances of Greek is one of the major reasons for this translation.

The Second Testament takes some liberties with the Greek word *kai*. In English, a period at the end of a sentence with a capital letter starting the next sentence is more or less what *kai* often means, so in many cases I have chosen not to add "and." I have not done this every time because I want readers to remember that Greeks didn't have periods and capital letters ending and beginning sentences, so occasionally I begin a sentence with "And." Plus, the number of run-ons might tip even the most tolerant reader over if "and" appeared every time *kai* appeared. Translation, one recent translator has observed, is "an endless series of compromises."[1]

VOCABULARY

I have tried to use the same English word for the same Greek word, but sometimes this is impossible if one wants to make sense in English. Most of all, I have avoided what Robert Alter, a brilliant translator of what Christians call the Old Testament, calls the "rage to explain."[2] What Alter says about the KJV's translators and their theory can be repeated here: "They understood, at least intuitively, that a limited lexicon could work better than an expansive one, that repetition of terms could be a resource, that plain language could be better than highfalutin diction, and that the words of the Bible should be conveyed, not explained."[3] This translation's theory is perhaps best coined with the term *conveyed*. A translation that sticks to the original text conveys words and sentences to its readers.

The distinctive vocabulary of the first generation of Christians as found in the Second Testament was not new. Instead, the writers used mostly routine words that suddenly found themselves inside a new worldview. Those routine words became nothing less than entries in a new lexicon of meaning. The routine word *love* (*agapē*) shifted into pointing readers at living in the way of Jesus, what many today call a cruciform way of life. Examples could be multiplied for pages.

STYLE

Close your eyes, pinch the whole Second Testament between two fingers, approximate the middle, and where are you? In Acts. It's a problem for those who read its brilliant grammar and excellent variation in vocabulary and then want to communicate that higher level of Greek to English readers. The translator's calling is to convey that sense of elite accomplishment as well as possible. In translations, Acts ought not to sound like Mark, and neither should Mark sound like Paul, and Paul is not at all like John. At times I have elevated the vocabulary of Luke's two books because he is using words other authors in the New Testament don't use. If the term the Second Testament author uses is recondite and rare, it ought to be approximated in our English. Far too often translators take unusual terms such as "be *propitious* to me a sinner" (Luke 18:13, *The Second Testament*) and make them more understandable ("be *merciful* to me a sinner"), which robs us of hearing the author as he or she intended and of understanding how the original readers would have heard them (and perhaps asked others for the meaning of the term). Who decides that our translations must be at the level of a tenth-grade comprehension of English? Instead of answering that question, posing another one is better: What level is the language of the author, and ought we not to respect that by conveying that author's level of sophistication? Indeed.

Hebrews, too, is stylish, though most Bible readers today find it especially dense, filled as the text is with allusions to texts and practices most moderns don't care about. Nor do they matter to most people's faith. I've not tried to make the book relevant. Reading Hebrews is a bit like picking up Dickens and encountering the style well before last and wondering why he didn't write simpler prose. He didn't, and I do my best to make Hebrews sound as it did then.

I have occasionally mentioned some particulars of *The Second Testament* to friends, one of which is found in Luke 14:2, where I translate the passage as "a human with edema." One friend said, "I'd need a dictionary to know that means." Yes, and one suspects that Luke's readers at times asked others what he meant by such terms. But this next point is what makes this translation what it is: Why do we think we should reduce Lukan vocabulary to what we might understand? Why subject his vocabulary to ours? Why not, I contend, elevate our vocabulary to his? The man was a

---

[1] Robert Alter, *The Art of Bible Translation* (Princeton, NJ: Princeton University Press, 2019), ix.
[2] Alter, *Art of Bible Translation*, 7.
[3] Alter, *Art of Bible Translation*, 64.

doctor, and when he says *hyrdopikos* in Greek he is giving a medical diagnosis, which is what *edema* is (the swelling, probably, of legs due to poor blood circulation). The old, quaint term *dropsy* is common in translations, though both the NIV 2011 and NLT have suggested translations with the term *swelling*. I give Luke a chance to shine with his own medical terms. My doctor uses terms I don't understand, so I ask him what he means. Our way of asking is to look it up. If I were to say to my doctor, "I've got swollen legs," he might say, "Yes, you do; of a specific kind, called *edema*. Swelling can describe a variety of diagnoses."

NAMES

Place names in modern translations have acquired mostly Latin translations and transliterations, but this translation restores the Greek names in transliteration. Not Jerusalem but *Yierosoluma*, not Bethany but *Beth-Ania*, not Galilee but *Galilaia*, and so on.

Behind this translation is a concern about how English-y our translations are and thus how English-y our faith becomes. An example is the apostle "James." Herein lies a story: the word *James* is English. It derives from the Latin *Iacomus*, which is closer to the man's original name, often translated in English as "Jacob." However, the Hebrew is *Yakov* and the Greek is *Yakōbos*. The English "James" does not lead the reader to what is clearly a very important connection in the Bible: the apostle's name intentionally evokes the patriarch Jacob. There's more to say here: Rome, with its capacious Latin language, took over Europe (and plenty more in time) and in the process turned Greek names into Latin names, and our English names are Latin-based. It's the season to restore the original names—of people and places.

THEOLOGICAL TERMS

I have purposefully avoided common theological language—not "save" or "salvation" but "deliver" and "deliverance." Not "holy" but "devoted." As a young professor, I learned in reading linguistics scholars that a word has no more meaning in a given verse than it must have, and the opposite tendency sometimes rules our perceptions: we give to our special theological terms far more meaning than they can bear in a context. De-theologizing some of our pet terms might help us appreciate the ordinary roots of terms we treasure. I'm aware that changing special, conventional, sacred terms can unnerve readers, but I ask for patience. The aim is to provoke us to think again about the terms that have become too conventional. A different angle on a conventional term— such as *right* instead of *justification*—makes us think about it differently, and my prayer is that the change will fill in your conventional term with fuller meaning. At times you may feel you've never read a verse or passage, and I hope you feel that way. We all need this kind of experience with our Bible so we will think more deeply.

Translation at times cannot avoid some interpretation. A challenging term is normally translated as "law" (*nomos*, in Hebrew *torah*), which for this translator became a year-long vexation on how best to render the Greek term. Convinced "law" just doesn't get the job done, though it is a natural equivalent, I opted for "Covenant Code."

THANKS

I thank you, reader, for supplementing your regular translation(s) with *The Second Testament*. I can promise some surprises, and I hope some renewal of understanding. This project began with a comment I made to Jon Boyd at InterVarsity Press. When he asked whether I would like to translate *The Second Testament* as a companion to John Goldingay's *The First Testament*, I could not resist. I spent two years of long hours translating *The Second Testament*, but it could not have been completed without help from students who read it and made suggestions. Most of all I thank Jon Boyd, Anna Gissing, and Rachel Hastings for their efforts in bringing that conversation into book form.

INTRODUCTION TO THE GOSPEL OF MATTHEW

Four Gospels, three alike and one different. The three Gospels alike are Matthaios [Matthew], Markos [Mark], and Loukas [Luke], and they are called the "Synoptic" Gospels since they can be looked at together. The Gospel of Yōannēs [John] is noticeably different in themes, style, and content. All four of the Gospels are biographies of Yēsous and, as biographies, the content is Yēsous.

Each of the three Synoptic Gospels tells a similar biography of Yēsous but each also has its own style and his own plot and plan, and each develops distinctive themes. One of Matthaios's distinctive themes is the fulfillment of First Testament writings, and his favorite word is "to fill out" what was said in the First Testament. While some of these filling-out passages were First Testament predictions, others are theological explorations of the First Testament that are set into motion by something Yēsous actually said or did. Thus, Matthaios reads the First Testament both forward and at other seasons backward: that is, he starts in Genesis and shows how it leads to Yēsous, while at other times he starts with Yēsous and finds a text in the First Testament that fits something Yēsous says or does.

There are two major themes in the Synoptic Gospels: first, *Yēsous himself* and, second, *Empire of God* or, as Matthaios almost always phrases it, the "Heavens' Empire" or the "Empire of the heavens." Readers of the Gospel of Matthaios need to see that this text is called "the Gospel" of Matthaios because it's the gospel itself. The gospel of the Second Testament is that Yēsous is the long-awaited Messiah (here: Christos), the royal Son of God and Son of Dauid [David], who delivers Yisraēl [Israel] and others from their sins so they can live with and before God in a way that honors God and establishes God's Empire as society and culture. Empire, the second theme, highlights five convictions:

- that God alone is king in his Son Yēsous
- that this one true God rules by rescuing people from their wrongs and governing them
- that this king rules a people—in the First Testament called "Yisraēl," and in the Second Testament this people becomes the "church"
- that this people follows the will of God as taught by Yēsous
- that this people is governed by God in a now-universal land that has its own covenant in the pages of the Second Testament

One needs to note, too, that this Empire theme includes the very common theme in the Gospel of Matthaios of discipleship, Apprenticeship, or following Yēsous. It was impossible for Yēsous—and the Gospel authors—to have used this term *Empire* and have it not carry some notes of resistance to the all-too-common political empires of the day. You can't call the work of Yēsous "Empire" without raising eyebrows, without raising some blood pressure, and without awakening hopes for a new world.

Matthaios's Gospel alternates between narratives (chaps. 1–2, 3–4, 8–9, 11–12, 14–17, 19–22, 26–28) and speeches (chaps. 5–7, 10, 13, 18, 23–25). The collection of the teachings of Yēsous into speeches creates a Gospel that quickly became the "teacher's Gospel." Hence, his ethics, his missionary directions, his parables, his community's reconciliation, and his warnings about God's judgment on systemic corruption by political leaders—these are the topics in Yēsous' five speeches. A characteristic of Matthaios, Markos, and Loukas is Yēsous' telling of parables, which are *analogies* between the kingdom and elements in a very short story.

The gospel that gives rise to the Gospels is a story about Yēsous, and that means the Gospel of Matthaios will tell us about Yēsous' birth, his public teaching and mighty miracles, his healing people of diseases and disabilities, and his own Covenant Code (law) for his Apprentices. Running straight through that glamorous side of Yēsous' amazing deeds and profound wisdom is a set of figures—leaders in the system of Roman Galilaia and Youdaia [Galilee and Judea]—who are none too happy about Yēsous. In fact, early on we hear of their plots to get rid of him tempered only by their being afraid of his public approval. The last week of Yēsous, however, tilts the power away from Yēsous to the Roman leaders of Yierosoluma [Jerusalem] and their cooperatives, who arrest Yēsous and put him on trial that looks like nothing but a fraudulent sentence. Then he is publicly, unjustly crucified in a hideous manner. The story of Yēsous, however, knows both the death of Yēsous on a Friday and his resurrection on Easter Sunday. The reversal of reversals: what was clearly an injustice becomes the act whereby God establishes a new kind of gracious justice, or rightness, or making all things right. God's grace turns the injustice of a death into an atoning death, and the resurrection demonstrates that God's final word is life, not death, for those who enter into the life of this Christos. He is the son of Maria and Yōsef [Mary and Joseph], and the opening to Matthaios's Gospel is a geneaology that ties Yēsous' royal line to both Dauid and Abra'am [Abraham]—we are to read it forward from Abra'am on because we've learned to read it backward.

RELATIONSHIP OF MATTHAIOS, MARKOS, AND LOUKAS

Some think the canonical order is also the chronological order, while most, due to detailed analysis by way of comparing each Greek word in one Gospel with each Greek word in the other Gospels, conclude they are dependent on one another. The most common view, though contested at times, is that Markos is the earliest and that Matthaios and Loukas both used and copied from Markos while availing themselves of other sources as well. Many think Matthaios and Loukas used a common source independently that Markos did not have, and this source is often called Q (from the German word for "source," that is, *Quelle*).

THE GOSPEL OF MATTHEW

PROLOGUE

Yēsous' heritage

1 Book of the genesis of Yēsous Christos, descendant of Dauid [David], descendant of Abra'am.

²Abra'am gave a life to Yisa'ak [Isaac].
Yisa'ak gave a life to Yakōb [Jacob].
Yakōb gave a life to Youdas [Judah] and his siblings.
³Youdas gave a life to Phares [Perez] and to Zara [Zerah], son of Thamar [Tamar],
Phares gave a life to Hesrōm [Hezron].
Hesrōm gave a life to Aram.
⁴Aram gave a life to Amminadab.
Amminadab gave a life to Na'assōn [Nahshon].
Na'assōn gave a life to Salmōn.
⁵Salmōn gave a life to Boos [Boaz], son of Rachab [Rahab].
Boos gave a life to Yōbēd [Obed], son of Routh [Ruth].
Yōbēd gave a life to Yessai [Jesse].
⁶Yessai gave a life to Dauid, the king.

⁷Dauid gave a life to Solomōn, son of the wife of Ourias [Uriah].
Solomōn gave a life to Roboam [Rehoboam].
Roboam gave a life to Abia [Abijah].
Abia gave a life to Asaph.
⁸Asaph gave a life to Yōsaphat [Jehoshaphat].
Yōsaphat gave a life to Yōram [Joram].
Yōram gave a life to Ozia [Uzziah].
⁹Ozia gave a life to Yō'atham [Jotham].
Yō'atham gave a life to Achaz [Ahaz].
Achaz gave a life to Hezekias.
¹⁰Hezekias gave a life to Manassē [Manasseh].
Manassē gave a life to Amōs.
Amōs gave a life to Yōsiah [Josiah].
¹¹Yōsiah gave a life to Yechoniah [Jechoniah] and his siblings when they were deported to Babulōn [Babylon].

¹²After the Babulōn [Babylon] deportation:
Yechoniah gave a life to Salathiēl [Shealtiel].
Salathiēl gave a life to Zoro-babel [Zerubbabel].
¹³Zoro-babel gave a life to Abioud [Abiud].
Abioud gave a life to Eli-akim.
Eli-akim gave a life to Azōr.
¹⁴Azōr gave a life to Sadōk [Zadok].
Sadōk gave a life to Achim.
Achim gave a life to Eli-oud [Eliud].
¹⁵Eli-oud gave a life to Ele-azar.
Ele-azar gave a life to Matthan.
Matthan gave a life to Yakōb.
¹⁶Yakōb gave a life to Yōsēf [Joseph], the man of Maria [Mary], from whom Yēsous, who is called Christos, was given a life.

¹⁷Therefore, all the generations from Abra'am until Dauid: fourteen generations.
From Dauid until the Babulōn deportation: fourteen generations.
From the Babulōn deportation until the Christos: fourteen generations.

Yēsous born

¹⁸The genesis of Yēsous Christos was this: His mother, Maria, being engaged to Yōsēf, before they had assembled . . . she was found having a child in her womb of the Holy Spirit. ¹⁹Yōsēf, her man, being right and not wanting to exhibit her in public, decided to loosen her in secret. ²⁰Yōsēf musing on all these things . . . Look! The Lord's envoy appeared to him in his dream, saying, "Yōsēf, descendant of Dauid, don't be scared to receive Maria as your woman. For the one given life in her is from the Holy Spirit. ²¹She will birth a son, and you will call his name 'Yēsous,' for he will deliver his people from their sins."

²²This entire event occurred so what the Lord said through the prophet [Isaiah] would be filled out, saying,

²³"*Look! A virgin will have a child in her womb and will birth a son, and they will call his name "Emmanou-El,' which translated means, 'God with us.'*"

THE GOSPEL OF MATTHEW 1.24

^{24}Yōsēf, arising from the sleep, did as the Lord's envoy ordered him, and he received his woman, ^{25}and he did not know her until she birthed a son. He called his name "Yēsous."

Yēsous given gifts

2 Yēsous coming to life in Youdaian Bēth-le'em [Judean Bethlehem], in the days of King Hērōdēs [Herod] . . . Look! Diviners from the east arrived in Yierosoluma [Jerusalem], ^{2}saying, "Where is the one birthed to be king over the Youdaians? For we saw his star in the east and we came to bow down to him." ^{3}Hearing, King Hērōdēs was agitated and all Yierosoluma with him, ^{4}and assembling all the Senior Priests and the people's Covenant-Code scholars [scribes], he was inquiring from them where the Christos is given a life. ^{5}They said to him, "In Bēth-le'em of Youdaia, for thus it's written through the prophet:

> ^{6}You Bēth-le'em, land of Youdas [Judah],
> are in no way the least significant among
>   the governors of Youdas.
> A governor will exit from you,
> Who will pastor my people, Yisraēl [Israel]."

^{7}Then Hērōdēs, calling the diviners secretly, figured out from them the time of the star's appearing ^{8}and, sending them to Bēth-le'em, he said, "Journeying, search carefully [akribōs] for the child. Whenever you find, declare to me so I also, going, may bow down to him." ^{9}The ones hearing the king journeyed and Look! The star that they saw in the east was leading them until, coming, it sat over where the child was. ^{10}Seeing the star they rejoiced with a great, extreme joy. ^{11}Coming into the house, they saw the child with Maria, his mother, and falling down they bowed down to him and, opening their treasure chests, they offered to him gifts—gold and frankincense and ointment. ^{12}Being revealed in a dream not to return to Hērōdēs, they slipped out on a different path to their region.

Yēsous goes to Aiguptos

^{13}They slipped away . . . Look! The Lord's envoy appears in a dream to Yōsēf [Joseph], saying, "Being raised, take the child and his mother and flee to Aiguptos [Egypt], and be there until I tell you! For Hērōdēs is about to pursue the child to destroy it." ^{14}The one

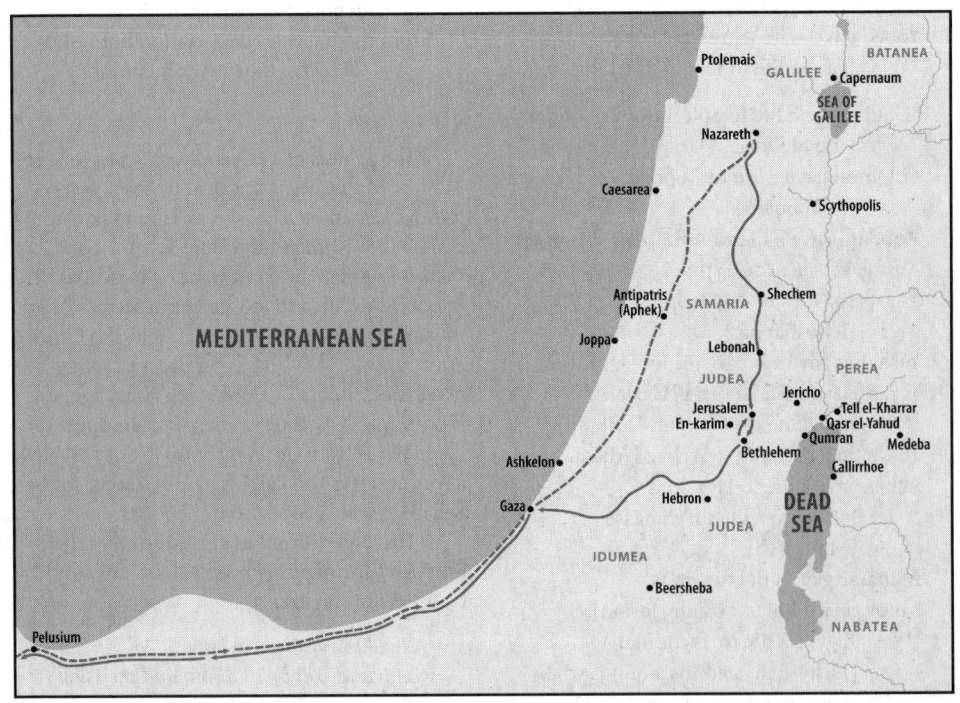

Figure 1. Jesus' journey to Egypt

being raised took the child and his mother at night and slipped away into Aiguptos, ¹⁵and it was there until the end of Hērōdēs so what was said by the Lord through the prophet may be filled out, saying,

> From Aiguptos I called my son.

Yēsous escapes murderers

¹⁶Then Hērōdēs, seeing that he had been mocked by the diviners, was enraged deeply and, commissioning, he did away with all the children in Bēth-le'em and all in its regions, from two years and younger, consistent with the time that he figured out from the diviners. ¹⁷Then what was said through the prophet Yeremias [Jeremiah] was filled out, saying,

> A voice in Rama was heard,
> Wailing and deep mourning;
> Rachēl wailing for her children,
> She did not want to be consoled,
> Because they are not.

Yēsous returns

¹⁹Hērōdēs's [life] ending . . . Look! The Lord's envoy appears in a dream to Yōsēf in Aiguptos, ²⁰saying, "Being raised, take the child and his mother, and journey to the land of Yisraēl, for the ones pursuing the child's self have died." ²¹The one being raised took the child and his mother and entered the land of Yisraēl.

Yēsous taken to safety

²²Hearing that Archelaos [Archelaus] rules over Youdaia instead of his father, Hērōdēs, he was scared to depart to there. Having been revealed in a dream, he slipped into the parts of the Galilaia [Galilee] ²³and, coming, he resided in a city called Nazara [Nazareth] so that what was said through the prophets would be filled out:

> He will be called a "Nazōraios [Nazarene]."

NARRATIVE ONE

Yēsous and a wilderness dipper

3 In those days Yōannēs the Dipper [John the Baptist] arrives announcing in the wilderness of Youdaias [Judea], saying, ²"Convert! The Heavens' Empire has come close!" ³For this is what is spoken about through Ēsaïas [Isaiah] the prophet, saying,

> A voice bellowing in the wilderness;
> "Get ready the Lord's path,
> Make his ways straight!"

⁴Yōannēs himself was having his clothing from camel's hairs and an animal skin belt around his waist, and his provision was locusts and wild syrup. ⁵Then Yierosouma [Jerusalem] and all Youdaia and all the Yordanēs [Jordan River] region was journeying out to him, ⁶and were being dipped in the Yordanēs River by him, publicly acknowledging their sins.

⁷Seeing many of the Observant [Pharisees] and Elites [Sadducees] coming to his dipping, he said to them,

> "Knot of vipers! Who exhibited to you to flee from the anger about to come? ⁸Therefore, make fruit deserving of conversion ⁹and don't think to say among yourselves, 'We have Abra'am as father,' for I say to you that 'God is able to raise up from these stones children for Abra'am.' ¹⁰Already the ax is laid on the trees' root. Therefore, every tree not making beautiful fruit is chopped down and tossed into fire. ¹¹I dip you in water for conversion, but the one coming after me is stronger than me— of him I am not adequate to carry the sandals. He will dip you in Holy Spirit-and-fire. ¹²His sifting shovel is in his hand and he will clear his floor and will collect his wheat into storage, but the husks he will burn in an inextinguishable fire."

Yōannēs dips Yēsous

¹³Then Yēsous arrives at the Yordanēs from the Galilaia [Galilee] to Yōannēs to be dipped by him. ¹⁴But Yōannēs was preventing him, saying, "I have a need to be dipped by you, and come to me?" ¹⁵Responding, Yēsous said to him, "Release this for now, for so it's appropriate for us to fill out all rightness." Then he releases him. ¹⁶Being dipped, Yēsous suddenly ascended from the water, and Look! The heavens were opened, and he saw God's Spirit descending as a dove, coming upon him. ¹⁷Look! A voice from the heavens, saying, "This

is my royal Son,[a] the one loved, in him I was delighted."

Yēsous tested

4 Then Yēsous was led into the wilderness by the Spirit to be tested by the Accuser. ²Fasting forty days and forty nights, afterwards he hungered. ³Coming, the testing one said to him, "If you are God's royal Son, tell these stones to become breads." ⁴Responding, he said, "It's written: *The human will live not only on bread but on every utterance journeying out through God's mouth.*" ⁵Then the Accuser takes him with him to the devoted city and stood him on the temple's turret ⁶and says to him, "If you are God's royal Son, toss yourself down, for it's written that *He will command his envoys about you and they will lift you in their hands, so you will not stub your foot on a stone.*" ⁷Yēsous said to him: "Again it's written, *You will not test out the Lord your God.*" ⁸Again the Accuser takes him to an exceedingly high mountain and exhibits to him all the empires of the Kosmos and their splendor ⁹and said to him, "I will give you all these if, falling, you bow down to me." ¹⁰Then Yēsous says to him, "Go away! Satanas [Satan], for it's written, *You will bow down to the Lord God and you will venerate only him.*" ¹¹Then the Accuser releases him, and Look! Envoys came and were serving him.

Yēsous announces in the Galilaia

¹²Hearing that Yōannēs [John] had been given over, he slipped into the Galilaia [Galilee]. ¹³Abandoning Nazara [Nazareth], coming, he resided in Kaphar-Naoum [Capernaum] next to the Sea, in the regions of Zaboulōn [Zebulun] and Nephthalim [Naphtali], ¹⁴so what was said through Ēsaïas [Isaiah], the prophet, might be filled out, saying,

> ¹⁵*Land of Zaboulōn* and *land of Nephthalim,*
> *path by the Sea,*
> *Beyond the Yordanēs* [Jordan]
> *The Galilaia of the ethnic groups.*
> ¹⁶*The people sitting in darkness saw a great light,*
> *and for the ones sitting in the region and in death's shadow a light rose for them.*

Yēsous' first disciples

¹⁷From then Yēsous began to announce and to say, "Convert! The Heavens' Empire has come close!"
¹⁸Walking around along the Sea of the Galilaia, he saw two brothers, Simōn (called Petros [Peter]) and Andreas [Andrew] his brother, tossing a fish net into the Sea. (They were fishers.) ¹⁹He says to them, "Come behind me! I will make you into human-fishers." ²⁰Immediately, releasing the nets, they followed him. ²¹Proceeding from there, he saw another two brothers, Yakōbos [James]—son of Zebedaios [Zebedee]—and Yōannēs [John]—his brother, in the boat with Zebedaios their father, preparing their nets, and he called them. ²²Immediately, the boat- and father-releasers followed him.

Yēsous described: A summary

²³He was leading around the whole of the Galilaia, teaching in their assembly halls, announcing the gospel about the Empire, and healing every illness and every malady among the people. ²⁴His report departed into the whole of Suria [Syria]. They offered to him all those who were in a bad way, those absorbed by various illnesses and pains, and the demonized, those with seizures, the paralyzed—and he healed them. ²⁵A large crowd followed him from the Galilaia and the Ten Cities [Decapolis] and Yerosoluma [Jerusalem] and Youdaia [Judea] and Beyond the Yordanēs.

SPEECH ONE

Yēsous on the mountain

5 Seeing the crowds, he ascended into the mountain and . . . he sat down . . . his Apprentices approached him. ²Opening his mouth, he was teaching them, saying,

Yēsous announces who is blessed

> ³God blesses the beggars in spirit
> because theirs is Heavens' Empire.

---

[a] "Son of God," as seen in Psalm 2, was a Hebrew and Jewish expression for the king of Israel, and thus especially for the Messiah/Christos.

⁴God blesses the grievers because they will be consoled. ⁵God blesses the meek because they will inherit the land. ⁶God blesses the ones hungering and thirsting for the rightness because they will be satisfied. ⁷God blesses the compassionate because they will be shown compassion. ⁸God blesses the clean in the heart because they will see God. ⁹God blesses the peacemakers because they will be called 'God's descendants.' ¹⁰God blesses the ones who have been chased for rightness because theirs is Heavens' Empire. ¹¹God bless you whenever they degrade you and chase you and say every evil thing against you, falsifying, because of me. ¹²Be joyful and be overjoyed because your wage will be much in the heavens, for so they chased the prophets before you.

Yēsous and mission

¹³You are the land's salt. If the salt becomes foolish, with what will it become salty? It no longer has strength except, being tossed outside, to be trampled on by humans. ¹⁴You are Kosmos's light. A city laid on a mountain isn't able to be hidden, ¹⁵nor do they enflame a lamp and place it under a measuring basket but on a lampstand, and it shines for everyone in the house. ¹⁶So shine your light before humans so they may see your beautiful works and splendor your Father in the heavens.

Yēsous as Moses 2.0

¹⁷Don't think that I came to destroy the Covenant Code or the Prophets. I did not come to demolish but to fill out. ¹⁸For this is true to say to you: Until the heaven and the land pass away, one letter or one stroke will never pass away from the Code, until all things will happen. ¹⁹Therefore, whoever loosens one of least of these orders, and teaches such to humans, will be called 'Least' in the Heavens' Empire; but whoever observes and teaches, this person will be called 'Great' in the Heavens' Empire. ²⁰For I say this: if your rightness doesn't flow over that of the Code Scholars [scribes] and the Observant [Pharisees], you will never ever enter the Heavens' Empire.

Yēsous versus the Interpreters: Seven cases

²¹You heard that it was said to the Ancients, *You will not murder*, and 'Whoever murders will be guilty before the judgment.' ²²But I say this to you, that the one angry with his sibling will be guilty before the judgment. Anyone who says to his sibling with 'Fool!'[b] will be guilty before the Central Council. Whoever says, 'Idiot!' will be guilty before the Valley of Destructive Fire [Gehenna]. ²³Therefore, if you offer your donation at the sacrificial altar and there remember that your sibling has something against you, ²⁴release there your donation before the sacrificial altar, first go away, be reconciled with your sibling, and then, coming, offer your donation. ²⁵Become friends with your adversary quickly—while you are on the path with him—or else your adversary may give you over to the judge and the judge to the subordinate, and you will be tossed into prison. ²⁶This is true to say to you: you will never exit from there until you have paid off the last copper coin.

²⁷You heard that it was said, *You will not be adulterous.* ²⁸But I say this to you that anyone looking at a woman to desire her already adulterated in his heart. ²⁹If your right eye trips you, pull it out and toss it from you, for it's to your benefit that one of your [body] parts is destroyed and your whole body not be tossed into the Valley of Destruction. ³⁰If your right hand trips you up, chop it off and toss it from you, for it's to your benefit that one of your body parts is destroyed and your whole body not depart into the Valley of Destruction.

³¹It was said, 'Whoever loosens his woman let him give to her a legal dismissal.' ³²But I say this to you: Anyone loosening his woman—an exception for the case of sexual immorality—makes her to adulterate, and whoever marries the woman loosened adulterates.

---

[b] An Aramaic term roughly equivalent to the Greek term *Mōre* to follow; both terms roughly mean "Stupid!" or "Idiot!" or "Fool!" and are contemptuous condemnations.

³³Again, you heard that it was said to the Ancients, 'You will not perjure, but you will give back to the Lord your oath.' ³⁴But I say this to you: Don't make oaths at all—not by heaven because it's God's Throne, ³⁵not by the land because it's his footstool for his feet, not in Yierosoluma [Jerusalem] because it's the great king's city, ³⁶nor are you to make oaths by your head because you aren't able to make one hair white or black. ³⁷Let your word be yes, yes; no, no. Anything bounding beyond this is from the evil one.

³⁸You heard that it was said, *Eye for eye* and *tooth for tooth*. ³⁹But I say this to you: Not to resist the evil person. But whoever slaps your right jaw turn even the other jaw to him. ⁴⁰And for the one wanting you to be judged and to take your shirt, release also your robe to him.ᶜ ⁴¹Whoever conscripts you for one mile, go away with him for two. ⁴²Give to the one asking, and don't turn away from the one who asks to borrow from you.

⁴³You have heard that it was said, *You will love your neighbor* and you will hate your enemy. ⁴⁴But I say this to you: Love your enemies and pray for the ones chasing you, ⁴⁵so that you become children of your Father in the heavens, because his sun rises on evil persons and the good persons, and it rains on the right ones and the wrongdoers. ⁴⁶For if you love the ones loving you, what wage do you have? Don't even tax agents do the same? ⁴⁷If you greet only your siblings, what have you done that abounds? Don't even the ethnic groups do the same? ⁴⁸Therefore, you will be complete as your Father, the Heavenly One, is complete.

Yēsous versus stereotypical religious folk

6 Beware not to do rightness before humans to be observed by them. Otherwise you have no wage from your Father in the heavens.

²Whenever you do a donation, don't trumpet as the masked ones do in the assembly halls and on streets so they may be splendored by humans. This is true to say to you: They've got their wage. ³You are doing a donation . . . don't let your right hand know what your left hand is doing ⁴so that your donation is in the hidden place, and your Father who sees in the hidden place will pay you back.

⁵Whenever you pray, you will not be like the masked ones because they love to pray standing in the assembly halls and on the corners of the plazas so they will be apparent to humans. This is true to say to you: They've got their wage. ⁶Whenever you pray, enter into your private place and, shutting your door, pray to your Father who is in the hidden place, and your Father who sees in the hidden place will pay you back.

⁷Praying, don't jabber along like the ethnic groups, for they think they will be heard in their endless words. ⁸Therefore, don't be comparable to them, for your Father knows of what you have a need before you ask him. ⁹Therefore, pray like this:

> Our Father who is in the heavens:
> Your Name be devoted,
> ¹⁰Your Empire come,
> Your will become reality—as in heaven
>   so on the land,
> ¹¹Give to us our bread, for existence, for
>   a day,
> ¹²Release us from our debts as we also
>   released the ones indebted to us,
> ¹³Don't enter us into the test but rescue
>   us from the Evil One.

(¹⁴For if you released humans from their wrongs, your Father, the Heavenly One, will release you too. ¹⁵But if you did not release humans, neither will your Father release you from your wrongs.)

¹⁶Whenever you fast don't become like the masked ones, grim ones, for they make their faces disappear so that they will be apparent, fasting, to humans. This is true to say to you: They've got their wage. ¹⁷You, fasting, oil your head and wash your face ¹⁸so that you will not appear to humans, fasting, but to your Father who is in the secret place, and your Father who sees in the secret place will pay you back.

Yēsous versus this world's lords

¹⁹Don't treasure for yourselves treasure chests on the land, where moth and rust make them disappear and where thieves break in and

---

ᶜThe "robe" could not be requisitioned in court and was thus an act of extravagance; see Ex 22:25-27; Deut 24:12-13.

thieve. ²⁰Treasure for yourselves heavenly treasure chests, where neither moth nor rust make them disappear and where thieves don't break in or thieve. ²¹For where your treasure chest is, there will also be your heart.

²²The body's lamp is the eye. Therefore, if your eye is healthy, your whole body will be illumined. ²³But if your eye is evil, your whole body will be darkened. Therefore, if the light that is in you is dark, how great is the darkness!

²⁴No one is able to slave for two lords, for either he will hate one and love the other, or he will stick to one and snub the other. You aren't able to slave for God and accumulations [Mammon].

Yēsous versus anxieties

²⁵Because this is true, I say to you: Don't disturb your self—what you might eat or what you might drink—or your body—what to put on. Isn't the self more than provision and the body more than clothing? ²⁶Observe the heaven's birds, that they don't plant seeds, they don't harvest, and they don't assemble into storage, and your Father, the Heavenly One, nurtures them. Are you not superior to them? ²⁷Who among you, disturbing, is able to add one length to one's life? ²⁸And why disturb yourself about clothing? Consider the lilies in the field—how they grow: they neither labor nor spin. ²⁹I say this to you, that not even Solomōn in all his splendor was covered like one of these. ³⁰If God so outfits the grass of the field—here today and tossed into the clay oven tomorrow—how much more [will he] not [outfit] you, little believers? ³¹Therefore, don't disturb yourselves, saying, 'What might we eat?' Or, 'What might we drink?' Or, 'With what might we cover ourselves?' ³²These are all things the ethnic groups pursue. For your Father, the Heavenly One, knows you require all these things. ³³Pursue first God's Empire and his rightness, and all these things will be added for you. ³⁴Therefore, don't disturb yourselves about tomorrow, for tomorrow will disturb itself. The evil of that day is enough for the day.

Yēsous versus chips

7 Don't judge so you will not be judged. ²For you will be judged by the judgment by which you judge, and it will be measured to you by the measure by which you measure. ³Why do you see the chip in your sibling's eye but don't ponder the stick in your eye? ⁴Or, how will you say to your sibling, 'Release me to toss away the chip from your eye,' and Look! A stick is in your eye! ⁵Masked one! First toss away the stick from your eye, and then you will clearly see to toss out the chip of your sibling's eye.

Yēsous versus the dogs and hogs

⁶Don't give the devoted item to dogs nor toss your pearls before the hogs, or the hogs will trample them with their trotters and the dogs, returning, will tear you into pieces.

Yēsous' Father versus human fathers

⁷Ask—God will give it to you.
Pursue—you will find.
Knock—God will open the door for you.
⁸For everyone who asks receives and the one who pursues finds and for the one who knocks God will open the door. ⁹Or, which human is among you whose son will ask him for bread: Will he ever give him a stone? ¹⁰Or, if his son will ask for a fish, will he ever give him a snake? ¹¹Therefore, if you, being evil, know to give good gifts to your children, how much more will your Father, the one in the heavens, give good gifts to the ones asking him!

Yēsous versus human morals

¹²Therefore, everything—whatever you would want that the humans do to you—so also you do to them! This is the Covenant Code and the Prophets.

Yēsous versus easy morality

¹³Enter through the tight gate because wide is the gate and roomy is the leading-to-destruction path, and many are the entrants through that gate. ¹⁴But tight is the gate and troubled is the leading-to-life path, and few are the ones finding it.

Yēsous versus the false prophets

¹⁵Beware the false prophets! Who come to you in the sheep's clothing but inside they are snatching wolves. ¹⁶You will perceive them from their fruits. Do they collect grapes from thorns, or figs from thistles? ¹⁷Thus, every good tree makes beautiful fruit, but a diseased tree makes evil fruit. ¹⁸A good tree isn't able to make evil fruit, nor is a diseased tree [able] to make beautiful fruit. ¹⁹Every tree not making beautiful

fruit is chopped down and tossed into fire. ²⁰So then, you will perceive them from their fruits.

Yēsous versus cheap grace

²¹Not everyone saying 'Lord, Lord' to me will enter the Heavens' Empire but the one doing my Father's will, the one in the heavens. ²²On that Day many will say to me, 'Lord, Lord, but we prophesied in your name and we tossed out demons in your name, and we did many powers in your name.' ²³Then I will openly agree about them, 'I have never known you. *You separate from me, Covenant-breakers!*' ²⁴Therefore, whoever listens to these my words and observes them will be compared to a prudent man who formed his house on the rock. ²⁵The rain descended and the rivers came and the winds blew and they all fell down on that house, and it did not fall for it was founded on the rock. ²⁶Everyone who hears these my words, and not observing them, will be compared to an idiot who formed his house on the sand. ²⁷The rain descended and the rivers came and the winds blew and they fell down on that house, and it fell and its disaster was great."

End of Speech One

²⁸It happened: when Yēsous completed these words, the crowds were shocked at his teaching, ²⁹for he was teaching them as one having authority and not as their Covenant-Code scholars [scribes].

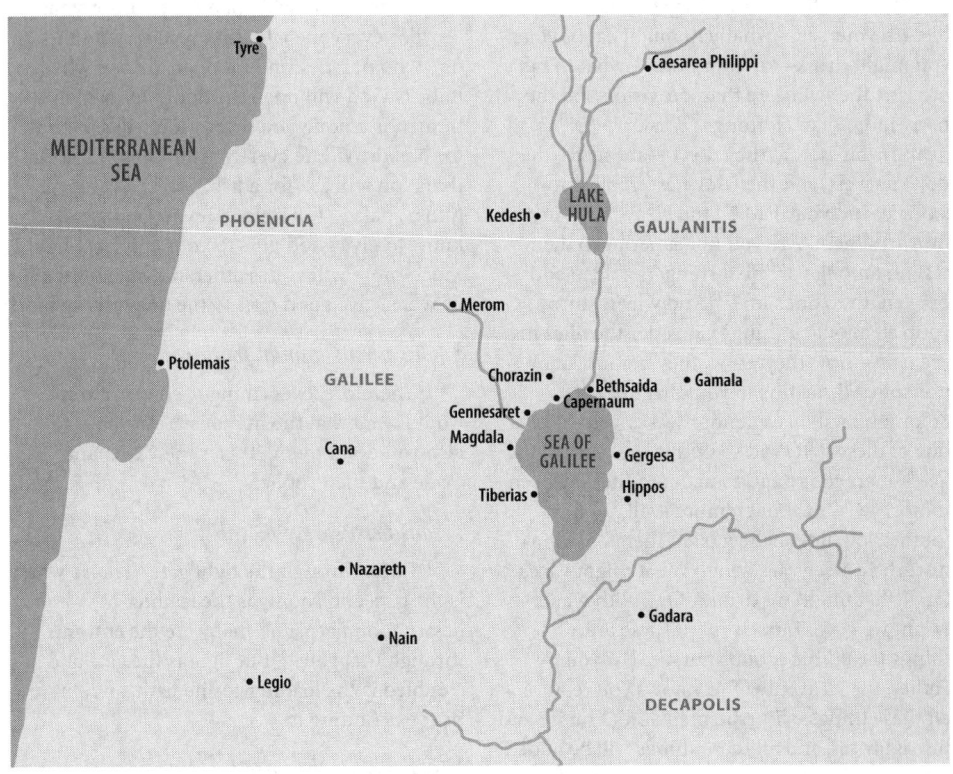

Figure 2. Jesus' ministry in Galilee

NARRATIVE TWO

Yēsous cures

8 He's descending from the mountain . . . a large crowd followed him. ²Look! A scaly-skin man, approaching, bows down to him, saying, "Lord, if you want you are able to clean me." ³Extending the hand, he touched him, saying, "I want to. Be cleaned." Immediately, his scaliness was cleaned. ⁴Yēsous says to him, "See that you tell no one but go away *exhibit* yourself *to the priest* and offer the gift that Mōūsēs [Moses] ordered as witness to them."

⁵He's entering Kaphar-Naoum [Capernaum] . . . a leader of a hundred soldiers approached him, begging him ⁶and saying, "Lord, my young servant is tossed down in the house, paralyzed, tortured terribly." ⁷He says to him, "Should I, entering, heal him?" ⁸Responding, the leader said, "Lord, I am inadequate for you to come under my roof, but only say with a word and my young servant will be cured. ⁹For even I am a human under authority, having soldiers under me, and I say to this one 'Journey!' and he journeys, and to another 'Come!' and he comes, and to my slave 'Do this!' and he does it." ¹⁰Hearing, Yēsous was stunned and said to the ones following, "This is true to say to you: I found in no one in Israel such trust. ¹¹I say this to you: Many from east and west will come and recline with Abra'am and Yisa'ak [Isaac] and Yakōb [Jacob] in Heavens' Empire, ¹²but the Empire's sons will be tossed out to outer darkness. There will be weeping and teeth grinding." ¹³Yēsous said to the leader, "Go away! As you trusted it will happen to you." His young servant was cured at that very hour.

Yēsous heals

¹⁴Yēsous, entering Petros's [Peter's] house, saw Petros's mother-in-law tossed down and fevering. ¹⁵He touched her hand and the fever released her, and she arose and was serving him.

¹⁶It was evening . . . they offered to him many demonized persons and he tossed out the spirits with a word, and all those in a bad way were healed. ¹⁷So that what was said through Ēsaïas [Isaiah], the prophet, might be filled out, saying,

> Our weaknesses he took,
> and our maladies he carried.

Yēsous calls

¹⁸Seeing a crowd around him, Yēsous signaled to depart to Beyond [the Yordanēs]. ¹⁹Approaching, one Covenant-Code scholar [scribe] said to him, "Teacher, I will follow you wherever you go away." ²⁰Yēsous says to him, "Foxes have dens and birds of the heaven nests, but the Son of Humanity[d] doesn't have a place to recline the head." ²¹Another of the Apprentices said to him, "Lord, permit me first to go away and to bury my father." ²²Yēsous says to him, "Follow me and release the dead to bury their own dead."

Yēsous, what kind of man is he?

²³In boarding down into the boat, his Apprentices followed him. ²⁴Look! A great commotion occurred in the Sea so that the boat was covered by the waves, but he was sleeping. ²⁵They, approaching, raised him, saying, "Lord, deliver! We are being destroyed." ²⁶He says to them, "Why are you cowardly, little believers?" Then, being raised, he rebuked the winds and the Sea, and a great calm occurred. ²⁷The humans were stunned, saying, "What kind of man is this that even the winds and the Sea heed him?"

Yēsous liberates

²⁸He was coming to Beyond [the Yordanēs] into the region of the Gadarēnes . . . two demonized men—exiting the tombs, deeply dangerous, so that no one was strong enough to pass by on that path—came out to meet him. ²⁹Look! They cried out, saying, "What is there between us and you, royal Son of God? Did you come here to torture us before the season?" ³⁰Far from them there was a large herd of hogs feeding. ³¹The demons were begging him, saying, "If you toss us out, commission us into the herd of hogs." ³²He said to them, "Go away!" They, exiting, departed into the hogs. Look! The whole herd dashed down the cliff into the sea and died in the waters. ³³The feeders fled and, departing into the city, they announced everything and the events about the demonized. ³⁴Look! The whole city exited to meet Yēsous and, seeing him, they begged that he shift from their region.

Yēsous releases a man from sins

9 And boarding down into the boat, he crossed back [over the Sea] and came to his city. ²Look! They were offering to him a paralyzed man tossed down on a cot. Yēsous, seeing their trust, said to the paralyzed man, "Be

---

[d] The expression "Son of Humanity," if it comes from Daniel 7:13 (*First Testament* has "one like a human being"), is a title (Son of Humanity), while if this Greek expression translates a common Aramaic expression it means "a human."

courageous, child! Your sins are released." ³Look! Some Covenant-Code scholars [scribes] said among themselves, "This man insults [God]." ⁴Yēsous, seeing their musings, he said, "Why do you muse with evil ideas in your hearts? ⁵For which is easier? To say 'Your sins are released' or to say 'Rise and walk around'? ⁶But so you might know that the Son of Humanity has authority in the land to release sins"—then he says to the paralyzed man, "Being raised, lift your cot and go away to your house!" ⁷Being raised, he went away to his house. ⁸The crowds, seeing, were awed and splendored the God who gave such authority to humans.

Yēsous calling

⁹Yēsous, passing on from there, saw a human sitting at the tax booth—he was called Matthaios [Matthew]—and says to him, "Follow me!" Arising, he followed him. ¹⁰It happened: he was reclining in his house . . . Look! Many tax agents and sinners, coming, were reclining with Yēsous and his Apprentices. ¹¹The Observant [Pharisees], seeing, were saying to his Apprentices, "For what reason is your teacher eating with tax agents and sinners?" ¹²Hearing, he said, "The strong have no need of a doctor, but those in a bad way [do]. ¹³Go be apprenticed to what this is: *I want compassion not sacrifice*, for I did not come to call 'right ones' but sinners."

Yēsous suspends fasting

¹⁴Yōannēs's [John's] apprentices approach him, saying, "Why do we and the Observant fast but your Apprentices don't fast?" ¹⁵Yēsous said to them, "Are the groom's sons able to grieve as long as the groom is with them? The days will come whenever the groom is taken away from them, and then they will fast. ¹⁶No one tosses a patch of unshrunk cloth on an ancient robe. For its fullness pulls from the robe and the rip becomes worse. ¹⁷Nor do they toss new wine into ancient wineskins. Otherwise, the wineskins break apart and the wine pours out and the wineskins are destroyed. But they toss new wine into fresh wineskins, and both are preserved."

Yēsous touches

¹⁸He's speaking these things to them . . . Look! One leader, coming, bows down to him, saying, "My daughter's life has just now ended but, coming, lay your hand on her and she will live." ¹⁹Being raised, Yēsous followed him, and his Apprentices.

²⁰Look! A twelve-year-blood-flowing woman, approaching him from behind, touched the tassels of his robe. ²¹For she was saying in herself, *if only I can touch his robe, I will be delivered.* ²²Yēsous, turning around and seeing her, said, "Be courageous, daughter! Your trust has delivered you." The woman was delivered from that hour.

²³Yēsous, coming into the leader's house and seeing the persons playing recorders and the disturbed crowd, ²⁴was saying, "Slip out of here! For the girl did not die but sleeps." They were laughing at him. ²⁵When the crowd was tossed out, entering, he grabbed her hand and the girl was raised. ²⁶This report exited into that whole land.

Yēsous gives sight to the sightless

²⁷Two sightless men followed Yēsous, going on from there, crying out and saying, "Show some compassion on us, son of Dauid [David]." ²⁸The sightless approached him, entering the house, and Yēsous says to them: "Do you trust that I am able to do this?" They say to him: "Yes, Lord." ²⁹Then he touched their eyes, saying, "May it be done for you consistent with your trust." ³⁰Their eyes were opened. Yēsous snorted at them, saying, "See! Let no one know!" ³¹They, exiting, advertised him in that whole land.

Yēsous exorcises

³²They're exiting . . . Look! They offered a speechless, demonized man to him. ³³The demon being tossed out . . . the sightless man spoke. The crowds were stunned, saying, "Never has something like this appeared in Yisraēl [Israel]." ³⁴But the Observant were saying, "The demons are tossed out by the leader of the demons."

Yēsous re-described: Repeating the summary (cf. 4:23-25)

³⁵Yēsous was leading around all the cities and villages, teaching in their assembly halls, announcing the gospel about the Empire, and healing every illness and every malady.

SPEECH TWO

Yēsous spots the problem: Pastoral abuse

³⁶Seeing the crowds, he empathized with them because they were—as sheep not having a shepherd—disturbed and dejected. ³⁷Then he says to his Apprentices: "The harvest is great, the workers are few. ³⁸Therefore, plead to the harvest's Lord that he toss out workers into his harvest."

Yēsous commissions

10 Calling his twelve Apprentices, he gave them authority over contaminating spirits so they could toss them out and heal every illness and every malady.

²These are the names of the twelve Commissioners:

first, Simōn—who is called Petros
    [Peter]—and Andreas [Andrew],
    his brother;
Yakōbos [James]—who is from
    Zebedaios [Zebedee]—and
    Yōannēs [John], his brother;
³Philippos [Philip] and Bar-Tholomaios
    [Bartholomew];
Thōmas and Matthaios [Matthew]—the
    tax agent;
Yakōbos—who is from Halphaios
    [Alphaeus]—and Thaddaios
    [Thaddaeus];
⁴Simōn Kananaios [Simon the
    Canaanite] and Youdas the
    Dagger Man [Judas Iscariot], the
    one who gave him over.

⁵Yēsous commissioned these twelve, ordering them, saying,

"Don't go out on the path to the ethnic groups and don't enter into a city of the Samaritōn [Samaritans]. ⁶Instead, journey to the sheep—the destroyed ones—of Yisraēl's [Israel's] house. ⁷Journeying, announce, saying that 'The Heavens' Empire has come close.'

⁸Heal the weak,
Raise the dead,
Clean the scaly,
Toss out demons.
You received as a gift, give as a gift.

⁹Don't acquire gold or silver or bronze
    in your belts,
¹⁰nor a bag for the path,
    nor two shirts, nor sandals,
    nor a walking stick.
The worker deserves one's provision.

¹¹Into whatever city or village you enter, search in it for someone who is deserving and remain there until you exit. ¹²Entering into the house, greet it. ¹³If the house is deserving, let your peace come upon it, but if the house isn't deserving, let your peace return to you. ¹⁴Whoever doesn't receive you or hear your words, exiting out of the house or that city, shake off the dust from your feet. ¹⁵This is true to say to you: It will be lighter for the land of Sodoma [Sodom] and Gomorra [Gomorrah] on the day of judgment than for that city.

¹⁶Look! I commission you as sheep in the middle of wolves. Therefore, be both prudent as snakes and innocent as doves.

¹⁷Beware of humans! They will give you over to the Central Councils and in their assembly halls they will lash you. ¹⁸You will be led before governors and kings because of me—as a witness to them and to the ethnic groups. ¹⁹Whenever they give you over, don't be disturbed how or about what you might say, for what you are to say in that hour will be given to you. ²⁰For you are not the ones speaking but the Spirit of your Father that is speaking in you.

²¹Sibling will give over sibling and a father a child, and children will rise up in rebellion against parents and they will kill them. ²²You will be hated by all because of my name, but the one resilient to the completion—this person will be delivered. ²³Whenever they chase you in this city, flee to another. This is true to say to you: You will never complete the cities of Yisraēl before the Son of Humanity[e] comes.

²⁴An apprentice isn't above the teacher, nor is a slave above the lord. ²⁵It's adequate for an apprentice to become as one's teacher, and a slave as one's lord. If they called the master of the house 'master of demons' [Beelzeboul], how much more his house members.

---

[e] This echoes Daniel 7:13, so "Son of Humanity" is a title for the coming king.

²⁶Therefore, don't be scared of them. For there is nothing covered that will not be apocalypsed, and hidden that will not be known. ²⁷What I say to you in the darkness, say in the light! What you hear in the ear, announce on terraces! ²⁸Don't be scared of ones killing the body but not ones able to kill the self. Instead, be awed of the one able to destroy both self and body in the Valley of Destructive Fire [Gehenna]. ²⁹Are not two little sparrows sold for an assarion[f]? Not one of them falls on the land apart from your Father. ³⁰Even your head's hairs are all numbered. ³¹Therefore, don't be scared. You are superior to all the little sparrows.

³²Therefore, everyone who openly agrees with me before humans I will also openly agree about that person before my Father in the heavens. ³³Whoever denies me before humans, I will also deny that person before my Father in the heavens.

³⁴Don't think that I came to toss peace on the land. I did not come to toss peace but a long knife. ³⁵For, I came to split *a man against his father* and *a daughter against her mother* and *a bride against her mother-in-law* ³⁶and *a human's enemies—his own house members*.

³⁷The one loving father or mother more than me doesn't deserve me, and the one loving son or daughter more than me doesn't deserve me, and ³⁸the one who doesn't take his cross and follow behind me doesn't deserve me. ³⁹The one finding one's self will destroy it, and the one destroying one's self—because of me—will find it.

⁴⁰The one receiving you receives me, and the one receiving me receives the one who commissioned me. ⁴¹The one receiving a prophet in the name of a prophet will receive the prophet's wage, and the one receiving a right one in the name of a right one will receive the right one's wage. ⁴²Whoever gives a cup of cold water to one of these little ones in the name of an apprentice—this is true to say to you—will never destroy one's wage."

11 It happened: when Yēsous completed ordering his twelve Apprentices, he shifted from there to teach and to announce in their cities.

NARRATIVE THREE

Yēsous sends a message back to Yōannēs

²Yōannēs [John], hearing in confinement about the Christos's works, sending through his own Apprentices, ³said to him, "Are you the Coming One or are we anticipating someone different?" ⁴Responding, Yēsous said to them, "Journeying, declare to Yōannēs what you hear and see:

> ⁵*The sightless see again,*
> The lame walk around,
> The scaly are cleaned,
> *The deaf hear,*
> *The dead arise,*
> The beggars are gospeled.

⁶God blesses whoever isn't tripped up by me."

Yēsous explains Yōannēs to the crowds

⁷These are journeying . . . Yēsous began to speak to the crowds about Yōannēs. "What did you exit into the wilderness to observe? A reed shaken by wind? ⁸But what did you exit to see? A human outfitted in delicate clothing? Look! The ones wearing delicate things are in the houses of kings. ⁹But what did you exit to see? A prophet? Yes, I say this to you: And exceeding a prophet. ¹⁰This is the person about whom it's written:

> *Look! I commission my envoy before* your face,
> *Who will prepare your path before* you.

¹¹This is true to say to you: No one greater than Yōannēs the Dipper has been raised among the ones given life by women. Yet, the smallest in the Heavens' Empire is greater than him. ¹²From days of Yōannēs the Dipper until now—the Heavens' Empire is forcefully advancing, and the enforcers snatch it. ¹³For all the Prophets and the Covenant Code prophesied until Yōannēs. ¹⁴If you want to accept it, he is Ēlias [Elijah] who is to come. ¹⁵The one who has ears—let that person hear.

Yēsous describes this generation

¹⁶To what will I compare this generation? It's comparable to children sitting in the squares, who are voicing out to the others; ¹⁷they say,

---

[f] An assarion is a copper coin and one-sixteenth of a Roman denarius, a day's pay.

'We played the recorder for you and you
    did not dance;
We lamented and you did not strike
    yourselves.'

¹⁸For Yōannēs came neither eating nor drinking, and they say, 'He has a demon.' ¹⁹The Son of Humanity came eating and drinking, and they say, 'Look! A human who is a glutton and a winedrinker, a friend of tax agents and sinners.' Wisdom was righted by her works."

Yēsous describes Gentile cities

²⁰Then he began to degrade the cities in which most of his powers happened because they did not convert. ²¹"Oy! on you, Chorazin! Oy! on you, Bēth-saïda! Because—if the powers that happened in your cities had been done in Tyros [Tyre] and Sidōn—long ago they would have converted in sack and soot. ²²However, I say this to you: It will be lighter for Tyros [Tyre] and Sidōn on the Judgment Day than for you. ²³As for you, Kaphar-Naoum [Capernaum], *will you be raised in status as far as heaven? You will descend into Hadēs.* Because if the powers that happened in you had happened in Sodoma [Sodom], it would remain until this day. ²⁴However, I say this to you: It will be lighter on the Judgment Day for Sodoma than for you."

Yēsous praises the Father

²⁵At that season, responding, Yēsous said, "I publicly acknowledge You, Father, Lord over heaven and the land because you hid these things from the wise and understanding ones, and apocalypsed these things to the childlike. ²⁶Yes, Father, because this is what becomes a delight before you. ²⁷All things have been given over to me by my Father, and no one perceives the Son but the Father, nor does any perceive the Father but the Son—and the one to whom the Son decides to apocalypse."

Yēsous invites

²⁸Come to me—all the laboring and loaded—and I will [provide] rest [for] you. ²⁹Lift my yoke upon you and be apprenticed by me, because I am meek and impoverished in heart, and *you will find rest for your selves.* ³⁰For my yoke is gracious and my load is light."

Yēsous, Lord over the Sabbath

12 At that season, Yēsous journeyed on Sabbaths through the grain fields. His Apprentices hungered and began to pick heads of grain and to eat. ²Seeing, the Observant [Pharisees] said to him: "Look! Your Apprentices do what isn't observant to do on a Sabbath."

³He said to them,

"Did you not read what Dauid [David] did when he hungered—including those with him? ⁴How he entered into God's house and they ate the Presence Breads, which was not observant for him to eat—nor for those with him—but only for the priests? ⁵Or, did you not read in the Covenant Code that the priests in the temple on Sabbaths defile the Sabbath, and they are innocent? ⁶I say this to you, that something greater than the temple is here. ⁷If you had known what this means—*I want compassion, not sacrifice*—you would not have condemned the innocent. ⁸For the Son of Humanity is Lord over the Sabbath."

⁹Shifting from there, he came into their assembly hall. ¹⁰Look! A human, having a stiff hand. They questioned him, saying, "Is it observant to heal on the Sabbaths?" so they might accuse him. ¹¹He said to them, "Which human among you, who has one sheep and if it falls into a pot bunker on the Sabbaths, will he not grab it and raise it?" ¹²Therefore, how much superior is a human to a sheep. So, it's observant to do beautifully on the Sabbaths. ¹³Then he says to the human, "Extend your hand!" He extended and it was restored—as healthy as the other. ¹⁴Exiting, the Observant took council against him so they could destroy him.

Yēsous fills out Ēsaïas

¹⁵Yēsous, knowing, slipped away from there. Great crowds followed him, and he healed them all ¹⁶and rebuked them not to make him apparent, ¹⁷so to fill out what was said through Ēsaïas [Isaiah], the prophet, saying,

¹⁸*Look! My young servant whom I chose
    him,*

My loved one, in whom my self was
    delighted.
I will place my Spirit on him,
He will declare justice for the ethnic
    groups.
¹⁹He will neither strive nor make a racket,
Nor will anyone hear his voice in the
    plazas.
²⁰He will not snap a broken reed
And he will not snuff out a smoking
    wick . . .
Until he tosses out justice for conquering.
²¹And in his name ethnic groups will
    hope.

Yēsous versus Beelzeboul

²²Then a demonized man was offered to him—sightless and speechless—and he healed him so to speak and to see. ²³All the crowds were beside themselves and saying, "This can't be the son of Dauid, can it?" ²⁴Hearing, the Observant said, "This man doesn't toss out demons except by Beelzeboul, the leader of the demons."

²⁵Recognizing their musings, he said to them, "Every empire parted against itself becomes wilderness, and every city or house parted against itself will not stand up. ²⁶If the Satanas [Satan] tosses out the Satanas, he is parted against himself! Therefore, how will his empire stand up?

²⁷If I toss out demons by Beelzeboul, by what do your sons toss out? Because this is true they will be your judges.

²⁸If I toss out demons by the Spirit of God, then God's Empire arrived upon you.

²⁹Or, how is someone able to enter into the strong one's house and snatch his vessels if he doesn't, first, bind the strong one? Then he will seize his house.

³⁰The one not with me is against me,
and the one not assembling with me
    scatters.

³¹Because of this I say to you: Every sin and insult will be released for humans, but insulting the Spirit will not be released. ³²And whoever says a word against the Son of Humanity—it will be released for him. But whoever says [something] against the Holy Spirit, it will not be released from him—neither in this Era nor [the Era] to Come.

Yēsous and the final judgment

³³Either make a beautiful tree and its fruit beautiful, or make a diseased tree and its fruit diseased. For the tree is known from the fruit. ³⁴Knot of vipers! How are you, being evil, able to speak good things? For the mouth speaks from the overflow of the heart. ³⁵The good human tosses out good things from a good treasure chest, and an evil human tosses out evil things from an evil treasure chest. ³⁶I say this to you, Every workless utterance that humans speak will be given over to his word on the Judgment Day. ³⁷For you will be righted from your words and you will be judged wrong from your words."

Yēsous and this generation

³⁸Then some of the Covenant-Code scholars [scribes] and Observant responded to him, saying, "Teacher, we want to see an authenticating sign from you." ³⁹Responding, he said to them,

"An evil-and-philandering generation pursues an authenticating sign, and an authenticating sign will not be given to it—except the authenticating sign of Yōnas [Jonah], the prophet. ⁴⁰For just as *Yōnas was in the belly of the big fish for three days and three nights,* so the Son of Humanity will be in the heart of the land for three days and three nights. ⁴¹The Nineuitēs [Ninevites] men will rise up with this generation at the judgment and they will condemn it, because they converted at the Yōnas announcement. Look! Greater than Yōnas is here. ⁴²The Queen of the East will be raised with this generation at the judgment and will condemn it, because she came from over the land to hear Solomōn's wisdom. Look! Greater than Solomōn is here.

⁴³Whenever the contaminating spirit exits from the human, it crosses through parched places pursuing rest and doesn't find it. ⁴⁴Then it says, 'I will return to my house from where I exited.' Entering, it finds it unoccupied, swept clean, and decorated. ⁴⁵Then it journeys and takes along with himself seven other spirits more evil than itself and, entering, resides there. The last things of that human become worse than the first things. Thus it will be for this evil generation."

Yēsous and his family

⁴⁶While he was still speaking to the crowds . . . Look! The mother and his brothers had been standing outside pursuing to speak with him. ⁴⁷Someone said to him, "Look! Your mother and your siblings have been standing outside pursuing to speak with you." ⁴⁸Responding, he said to the one speaking to him, "Who is my mother and who are my siblings?" ⁴⁹Extending his hand on his Apprentices, he said, "Look! My mother and my siblings! ⁵⁰For whoever does the will of my Father, who is in the heavens, that person is my brother and sister and mother."

SPEECH THREE

Yēsous tells the analogy of the planter and the seeds

13 On that day, Yēsous, exiting the house, was sitting next to the Sea. ²Many crowds assembled to him so that he, boarding down into the boat, sat, and the whole crowd had been standing on the shore. ³He spoke many things to them in analogies, saying, "Look! A planter exited for planting. ⁴In his planting, some seeds fell next to the path and, coming, the birds gobbled them. ⁵Others fell on rocky ground where it did not have much land and immediately it rose up because they did not have depth of land. ⁶The sun arose . . . it was scorched and, because it did not have root, it was stiffened. ⁷Others fell on the thorns, and the thorns ascended and suffocated them. ⁸Others fell on the beautiful land and it was giving fruit—one a hundred, one sixty, and one thirty. ⁹The one who has ears—let that person hear."

Yēsous explains his analogies

¹⁰His Apprentices, approaching, said to him, "Why do you speak to them in analogies?" ¹¹He, responding, said to them, "Because to you is given to know the secrets of the Heavens' Empire, but to them it has not been given. ¹²For whoever has, it will be given to the person and it will flow over. But whoever doesn't have, even what that person has will be lifted from the person. ¹³Because this is true I speak to them in analogies—because, seeing, they don't see and, hearing, they don't hear or understand, ¹⁴and the prophecy of Ēsaïas [Isaiah] is filled up for them—which is saying,

> In hearing you will hear and never understand,
> And, seeing, you will see and never perceive.
> ¹⁵For this people's heart has thickened
> And they hear with dull ears
> And they shut their eyes . . .
> So that they may never perceive with eyes
> And hear with ears
> And understand with heart
> And return . . .
> And I will cure them.

¹⁶Your eyes are blessed by God because they see and your ears because they hear. ¹⁷This is true to say to you, that many prophets and right ones desired to see what you see and did not see, and to hear what you hear and did not hear.

Yēsous explains the analogy with the planter

¹⁸Therefore, hear the analogy about the planter:
¹⁹Everyone hearing the word about the Empire and not understanding . . . the Evil One comes and snatches what is planted in the person's heart—this is the one planted next to the path.
²⁰The one planted on rocky ground—this is the one hearing the word and suddenly accepts it with joy, ²¹but the person did not have root within oneself but is momentary . . . trouble and pursuit come because of the word . . . suddenly they are tripped.
²²The one planted in the thorns—this is the one hearing the word, and the Era's anxiety and wealth's delusion suffocate the word and the person becomes fruitless.
²³The one planted on beautiful land—this is the one hearing the word and understanding—who also bears fruit and makes: one a hundred, one sixty, and one thirty."

Yēsous gives more analogies

²⁴He presented another analogy to them, saying, "The Heavens' Empire can be compared to a human planting beautiful seed in his field.

²⁵While the humans were sleeping his enemy came and overplanted zizania [weeds] in the middle of the wheat and departed. ²⁶When the stalk sprouted and made fruit, then also the zizania appeared. ²⁷Approaching, the slaves of the master's household said to him, 'Lord, did you not plant beautiful seed in your field? How therefore does it have zizania?' ²⁸He responded to them, 'A human enemy did this.' The slaves say to him, 'Therefore, do you want, departing, that we gather them up?' ²⁹But he said, 'No, for in gathering the zizania you might uproot the wheat with them. ³⁰Release them to grow together until the harvest, and at the harvest season I will say to the harvesters, 'Gather first the zizania and bind them into bundles to burn them up, but assemble the wheat into my storage barn.'"

³¹He presented another analogy to them, saying, "The Heavens' Empire is comparable to a mustard seed, which, taking, a human planted in his field. ³²Which is the smallest of all seeds, but whenever it grows it's larger than leafy vegetables and becomes a tree, so that *the birds of the heaven* come *and nest in its branches.*"

³³He spoke another analogy to them, "The Heavens' Empire is comparable to yeast, which a woman, taking, hid in three portions of flour until it leavened the whole."

Yēsous' rationale for analogies

³⁴Yēsous spoke all these things to the crowds in analogies, and spoke nothing to them apart from an analogy, ³⁵so that what was said through the prophet might be filled out, saying,

I will open my mouth in analogies,
I will pour out things buried from the Kosmos's origin.

Yēsous explains the story of the wheat and zizania

³⁶Then, releasing the crowds, he came into the house. His Apprentices approached him, saying, "Clarify for us the analogy about the zizania of the field." ³⁷Responding, he said,

"The Planter of the beautiful seed is the Son of Humanity,
³⁸the field is the Kosmos,
the beautiful seed, these are the Empire's descendants,
but the zizania are the evil one's descendants,
³⁹the enemy who planted them is the Accuser,
and the harvest is the completion of the Era,
and the harvesters are the envoys.

⁴⁰Therefore, just as the zizania are gathered and burned in fire so it will at the completion of the Era: ⁴¹the Son of Humanity will commission his envoys and they will gather from his Empire all those tripped up and the Covenant-breakers, ⁴²and *they will be tossed into the fiery furnace.* There will be weeping and grinding teeth. ⁴³Then the right ones will, like the sun, shimmer in their Father's Empire. The one who has ears—let that person hear.

Yēsous gives more analogies

⁴⁴"The Heavens' Empire is comparable to a treasure chest hidden in the field, which a human, finding, hid and out of his joy goes away and sold whatever he has and purchases that field.

⁴⁵Again, the Heavens' Empire is comparable to a human conducting business pursuing beautiful pearls. ⁴⁶Finding one priceless pearl, going away, he has sold everything he had and purchased it.

⁴⁷Again, the Heavens' Empire is comparable to a seine, tossed into the sea and assembles from all sorts [of fishes], ⁴⁸which when it was filled out, hauling to the shore and sitting down, he gathered the beautiful into a container but the bad he tossed out. ⁴⁹So it will be at the completion of the Era: the envoys will exit and isolate the evil out of the presence of the right ones, ⁵⁰and *they will toss them into the fiery furnace.* There will be weeping and grinding teeth."

Yēsous and his Covenant-Code expert Apprentices

⁵¹"Have you understood all these?" They say to him, "Yes." ⁵²He said to them, "Because this is true: Every Covenant-Code scholar [scribe], apprenticed in Heavens' Empire, is comparable to a human house master who tosses out from his treasure chest new and ancient things."

⁵³It happened: when Yēsous completed these analogies, he moved on from there.

NARRATIVE FOUR

Yēsous rejected at home

⁵⁴Coming into his ancestral village, he was teaching them in their assembly hall, so that they were shocked and saying, "What's the source for this man—this wisdom and the powers? ⁵⁵Isn't he the artisan's son? Isn't his mother called 'Mariam' [Mary] and his brothers 'Yakōbos [James], Yōsēf [Joseph], Simōn, and Youdas [Judas]'? ⁵⁶Are not his sisters all with us? Therefore, what's the source for this man—all these things?" ⁵⁷They were tripped up by him. Yēsous said to them, "A prophet isn't dishonored except in one's ancestral village and house."

⁵⁸He did not do there many powers because of their anti-trust.

Yēsous told about Yōannēs

14 At that season, Hērōdēs [Herod] the tetrarch, heard the report about Yēsous ²and said to his young servants, "This is Yōannēs the Dipper [John the Baptist]. He has been raised from among the dead and because of this the powers are working in him." ³Hērōdēs, grabbing Yōannēs, bound him and placed him in a prison because of Hērōdias, Philippos [Philip] his brother's woman. ⁴For Yōannēs was saying to him: "It isn't observant for you to have her." ⁵Wanting to kill him, he was scared of the crowd because they had him as a prophet. ⁶On Hērōdēs's birthday Hērōdias's daughter danced in the middle and she pleased Hērōdēs ⁷so he openly agreed to her with an oath to give her whatever she asked. ⁸She, being instigated by her mother, said, "Give to me here Yōannēs the Dipper's head on a tray." ⁹Being grieved, because of the oath and the ones reclining together, the king signaled it to be given, ¹⁰and, sending, they decapitated Yōannēs in the prison. ¹¹His head was carried on a tray and was given to the young woman, and she carried it to her mother. ¹²Approaching, his Apprentices lifted the corpse and buried him, and coming, they declared [this] to Yēsous.

Yēsous feeds more than five thousand

¹³Yēsous, hearing, slipped away from there in a boat to a wilderness place by himself. The crowds, hearing, followed him on foot from the cities. ¹⁴Exiting, he saw a large crowd and he empathized with them and healed their ill ones.

¹⁵It was evening . . . the Apprentices approached him, saying, "This is a wilderness location and the hour has already passed by. Loosen the crowds so that, departing to the villages, they can purchase for themselves foods." ¹⁶Yēsous said to them, "They don't have a need to depart. You give them [something] to eat." ¹⁷They say to him, "We don't have [anything] here but five breads and two fishes." ¹⁸Yēsous said, "Bring them to me—here." ¹⁹Signaling the crowds to recline on the grass, taking the five breads and the two fishes, looking up to heaven, he blessed and, cracking, he gave the breads to the Apprentices. The Apprentices to the crowds. ²⁰They all ate and were satisfied, and they lifted the overflow of the broken pieces—twelve full baskets. ²¹The ones eating were about five thousand men, apart from the women and children.

Yēsous walks on water, Petros sinks in water

²²Immediately he compelled the Apprentices to board down into the boat and to go ahead to Beyond the Yordanēs [Jordan] while he loosened the crowds. ²³Loosening the crowds, he ascended the mountain by himself—to pray . . . it was evening . . . he was there alone. ²⁴The boat was already many stades[g] from the land, tortured by the waves—for the wind was contrary. ²⁵At the fourth watch of the night [early a.m.], he came to them, walking around on the Sea. ²⁶The Apprentices, seeing him walking around on the Sea, were agitated, saying that "It's a phantom!" They cried out from being scared. ²⁷Suddenly, Yēsous spoke to them, saying, "Be courageous! I am. Don't be scared!"

²⁸Responding to him, Petros [Peter] said, "Lord, if you are, signal me to come to you on the waters." ²⁹He said, "Come!" Petros, descending from the boat, walked around on

---

[g] One "stade" is about two hundred yards.

the waters and came to Yēsous. ³⁰Seeing the strong wind, he was scared and, beginning to be submerged, he cried out, saying, "Lord, deliver me!" ³¹Immediately, Yēsous, extending the hand, took hold of him and says to him, "Little believer! Why did you doubt?" ³²[They] ascended into the boat . . . the wind ceased. ³³Those in the boat bowed down to him, saying, "You are truly Son of God."

³⁴Crossing to Beyond the Yordanēs [Jordan], they came on the land to Gennēsaret. ³⁵The men of that location, perceiving him, commissioned into that whole area and they carried to him all who were in a bad way, ³⁶and they were begging him that they might only touch the tassels of his robe, and those who touched were delivered.

Yēsous and human conventions

15 Then Observant [Pharisees] and Covenant-Code scholars [scribes] from Yierosoluma [Jerusalem] approach Yēsous, saying, ²"Why do your Apprentices violate the convention of the elders? For they don't wash their hands whenever they eat bread." ³Responding, he said to them, "Why do you also violate God's order because of your convention? ⁴For God said, *Honor the father and the mother*, and *the denouncer of father or mother—let his life end in death*, ⁵but you say, 'Whoever says to father or mother—"what you gain from me is a donation," ⁶won't honor his father.' You invalidate God's word because of your convention. ⁷Masked ones! Ēsaïas [Isaiah] prophesied beautifully about you, saying,

> ⁸*This people honors me with the lips
> But their heart is a far distance from me.
> ⁹They revere me in vain
> Teaching teachings that are human
>   prescriptions.*

¹⁰Calling the crowd, he said to them, "Listen and understand: ¹¹what enters the mouth doesn't make a human common, but what comes out of the mouth—this makes the human common."

¹²Then the Apprentices, approaching, say to him, "Do you know that the Observant, hearing the word, were tripped up?" ¹³Responding, he said, "Every plant that my Father, the Heavenly One, doesn't plant will be uprooted. ¹⁴Release them! They are sightless guides of sightless. If the sightless guide the sightless, both will fall into a pot bunker."

¹⁵Responding, Petros said to him: "Explain to us this analogy." ¹⁶He said,

> "Are you also still ignorant? ¹⁷Do you not know that everything journeying into the mouth makes space in the stomach and is tossed out into the sewer? ¹⁸But what journeys out of the mouth exits from the heart—these matters make the human common. ¹⁹For from the heart exit
> evil deliberations,
> murders,
> adulteries,
> sexual immoralities,
> thefts,
> false witnesses,
> insults.
> ²⁰These are what make a human common, but to eat with unwashed hands doesn't make the human common."

Yēsous and a Gentile woman

²¹Exiting from there, Yēsous slipped away into the region of Tyros [Tyre] and Sidōn. ²²Look! A Kananaia [Canaanite] woman from that region, exiting, cried out, saying, "Show some compassion on me, Lord, son of Dauid [David]. My daughter is demonized terribly." ²³He did not respond to her with a word. His Apprentices, approaching, were asking him, saying, "Loosen her! Because she's crying out from behind us." ²⁴Responding, he said, "I was not commissioned except to the sheep—the destroyed ones—of Yisraēl's [Israel's] house." ²⁵The woman, coming, was bowing down to him, saying, "Lord, help me!" ²⁶Responding, he said, "It isn't beautiful to take the children's bread and toss it to the puppies." ²⁷She said, "Yes, Lord, for even the puppies eat crumbs falling from their lord's table." ²⁸Then, responding, Yēsous said to her, "Wow, woman! Your trust is great. It will be done to you as you want." Her daughter was cured from that hour.

Yēsous heals

²⁹Shifting from there, Yēsous came along the Sea of Galilaia [Galilee] and, ascending into the mountain, he was sitting down there. ³⁰Many crowds approached him, having with them persons who were lame, sightless,

impaired, speechless, and many others, and they dropped them off at his feet, and he healed them ³¹so that the crowd was stunned, seeing the speechless speaking, the impaired healthy, and the lame walking around and the sightless seeing, and they splendored the God of Israel.

Yēsous feeds more than four thousand

³²Yēsous, calling his Apprentices, said, "I empathize with this crowd. They are attached to me already for three days and they don't have anything they can eat. I don't want to loosen them fasting, or they might faint on the path." ³³The Apprentices say to him, "From what source, in a wilderness, is there such breads so to satisfy such a crowd?" ³⁴Yēsous says to them, "How many breads do you have?" They said, "Seven and a few small fishes." ³⁵Ordering the crowd to lie down on the land, ³⁶he took the seven breads and the fishes and, giving thanks, he cracked [it] and was giving [them] to the Apprentices, and the Apprentices to the crowds. ³⁷Everyone ate and was satisfied. They lifted the overflow of the broken pieces, seven full big baskets. ³⁸The ones eating were four thousand men, apart from women and children.

³⁹Loosening the crowds, he boarded the boat and came to the region of Magadan.

Yēsous and an authenticating sign

16 Approaching, the Observant [Pharisees] and Elites [Sadducees], testing, asked him to demonstrate an authenticating sign from heaven for them. ²Responding, he said to them, "It's evening . . . you say, 'Good weather for the heaven reddens,' ³and in the morning, 'Today is stormy for the heaven reddens, threatening.' You know how to discriminate the heaven's face, but the authenticating signs of the seasons you aren't able. ⁴An evil-and-philandering generation pursues an authenticating sign, and an authenticating sign will not be given to it—except the authenticating sign of Yōnas [Jonah]." Abandoning them, he departed.

Yēsous and breads

⁵The Apprentices, coming to Beyond the Yordanēs [Jordan], forgot to take breads. ⁶Yēsous said to them, "See! Beware the yeast of the Observants and Elites!" ⁷They were deliberating among themselves, saying that "We did not take breads." ⁸Knowing, Yēsous said, "Why deliberate among yourselves, little believers, that you don't have breads? ⁹Don't you know yet nor remember the five breads of the five thousand and how many baskets you received? ¹⁰Nor the seven breads of the four thousand and how many big baskets you received? ¹¹How do you not know that I spoke to you not about breads? Beware the yeast of the Observants and Elites!" ¹²Then they understood that he spoke to them not about the yeast of breads but of the teachings of the Observants and Elites.

Yēsous confessed as Christos

¹³Yēsous, coming to the region of Kaisareia Philippos [Caesarea Philippi], was asking his Apprentices, saying, "Who do humans say the Son of Humanity is?" They said, "Some [say] Yōannēs the Dipper [John the Baptist], others Ēlias [Elijah] and yet others Yieremias [Jeremiah] or one of the prophets." ¹⁵He says to them, "But you, who do you say I am?" ¹⁶Responding, Simōn Petros [Simon Peter] said, "You are the Christos, the living God's royal Son." ¹⁷Responding, Yēsous said him, "God blesses you, Simōn Bar-Yōnas [Simon son of Jonah], because flesh-and-blood did not apocalypse to you but my Father, the one in the heavens. ¹⁸So I say to you, that you are the Rock [Petros] and on this rock [petra] I will form my assembly, and the gates of Hadēs will not prevail over it. ¹⁹I will give you keys to the Heavens' Empire, and whatever you bind on the land will be bound in the heavens, and whatever you loosen on the land will be loosened in the heavens."

²⁰Then he ordered the Apprentices that they tell no one that he is the Christos.

Yēsous calls to the cross-life

²¹From then Yēsous began to demonstrate for his Apprentices that it's necessary for him to depart to Yierosoluma [Jerusalem] and to suffer much from the Elders and Senior Priests and Covenant-Code scholars [scribes], and to be killed, and on the third day to be raised. ²²Petros, taking him in, began to rebuke him, saying, "Mercy for you, Lord! Never will this be for you!" ²³He, turning, said to Petros, "Go

away behind me, Satanas [Satan]! You are a trip for me because you are not thinking God's ways but the ways of humans."

²⁴Then Yēsous said to his Apprentices, "If anyone wants to come behind me, let that person renounce oneself, lift up one's cross, and let the person follow me. ²⁵For whoever wants to deliver one's self, the person will destroy it; but whoever destroys one's self because of me, the person will find it. ²⁶For what can a human gain if one takes advantage of the whole Kosmos but damages one's self? Or, what will a human give in compensation for one's self? ²⁷For the Son of Humanity is about to come in the splendor of his Father with his envoys, and then *he will pay back to each person consistent with one's practice*. ²⁸This is true to say to you, that there are some standing here who will not taste death before they see the Son of Humanity coming in his Empire."

Yēsous glows

17 After six days, Yēsous takes Petros [Peter] and Yakōbos [James] and Yōannēs [John], his brother, and he guides them up on a high mountain by themselves, ²and he was metamorphosed before them, and his face shone like the sun, his robes became white as light. ³Look! Mōüsēs [Moses] and Ēlias [Elijah] appeared to them—conversing with him. ⁴Responding, Petros said to Yēsous, "Lord, it's beautiful for us to be here. If you want, I will make here three tents, one for you, one for Mōüsēs, one for Ēlias." ⁵While he was speaking . . . Look! A cloud full of light enveloped them, and Look! A voice out of the cloud saying,

> "This is my royal Son, the one loved, in him I was delighted. Listen to him!"

⁶Hearing, the Apprentices fell on their faces and they were extremely scared. ⁷Yēsous approached and, touching them, said, "Be raised! Don't be scared!" ⁸Lifting up their eyes, they saw no one but Yēsous alone.

Yēsous and Ēlias

⁹They're descending from the mountain . . . Yēsous ordered them, saying, "Tell no one about the vision—until the Son of Humanity has been raised from among the dead." ¹⁰The Apprentices asked him, saying, "Therefore, why do the Covenant-Code scholars [scribes] say that *it's necessary first for Ēlias to arrive*?" ¹¹Responding, he said, "*Ēlias comes and will restore* all things, ¹²but I say this to you, Ēlias already came, and they did not perceive him but they did with him whatever they wanted. So also the Son of Humanity is about to suffer by them." ¹³Then the Apprentices understood that he spoke to them about Yōannēs the Dipper [John the Baptist].

Yēsous heals a man's son

¹⁴They're approaching the crowd . . . a human, genuflecting before him, approached him, ¹⁵saying, "Lord, show some compassion on my son because he has seizures and suffers terribly, for he often falls into the fire and often into the water. ¹⁶I offered him to your Apprentices, and they weren't able to heal him." ¹⁷Responding, Yēsous said, "Wow, anti-trust and distorted generation! How long will I be with you? How long will I put up with you? Bring him here to me." ¹⁸Yēsous rebuked, it and the demon exited from him and the child was healed from that hour. ¹⁹Then approaching Yēsous privately, the Apprentices said to him, "Why weren't we able to toss it out?" ²⁰He says to them, "Because of your little trust. This is true to say to you: If you have trust like a mustard seed, you will say to this mountain, 'Shift from there to here,' and it will shift. Nothing will be impossible for you."

Yēsous predicts his death

²²They're coming together in the Galilaia [Galilee] . . . Yēsous said to them: "The Son of Humanity is about to be given over into human hands, ²³and they will kill him, and on the third day he will be raised." They grieved extremely.

Yēsous on the temple tax

²⁴They're coming into Kaphar-Naoum [Capernaum] . . . the collectors of the two-drachma tax approached Petros and said, "Does your teacher not pay the two-drachma tax?" ²⁵He says, "Yes." Yēsous anticipated him, the one entering into the house, saying, "What does it look like to you, Simōn? The kings of the land receive tax and custom from whom?

From their own descendants or from outsiders?" ²⁶Saying, "From outsiders" . . . Yēsous said to him, "Then the descendants are liberated. ²⁷But so we don't trip them, journeying to the sea, toss a hook and take the first fish ascending, and opening its mouth, you will find a statēr.ʰ Taking that, give to them for me and for you."

SPEECH FOUR

Yēsous instructs on status in God's Empire

18 In that hour the Apprentices approached Yēsous, saying, "Who, then, is the greatest in the Heavens' Empire?" ²Calling a child, he stood it in their middle ³and said, "This is true to say to you: If you don't convert and become as the children, you can never enter into the Heavens' Empire. ⁴Therefore, whoever impoverishes oneself as this child—this person is the greatest one in the Heavens' Empire. ⁵Whoever receives one such child in my name, receives me.

⁶Whoever trips one of these little ones who trust in me—it would be to that person's benefit if a donkey-driving grinding-stone were hung around the person's neck and plunged in the deeps of the sea. ⁷Oy! to the Kosmos because of tripping! It's compulsory for trippings to come—however, Oy! to the human through whom the trip comes. ⁸If your hand or your foot trips you, chop it off and toss it away from you. It's beautiful for you to enter life impaired or sightless than, having two hands or two feet, to be tossed into the Era's Fire. ⁹If your eye trips you, pull it out and toss it from you. It's beautiful for you to enter single-eyed into life than, having two eyes, to be tossed into the Valley of Destructive Fire [Gehenna]. ¹⁰See! Don't snub one of these little ones. For I say this to you that their envoys in heavens through all [time] see the face of my Father in the heavens.

Yēsous tells a story about a wandering sheep

¹²What does it look like to you? If one hundred sheep are some human's and one of them wanders off, will he not release the ninety-nine on the mountains and, journeying, pursue the wanderer? ¹³If he happens to find it—this is true to say to you that he has more joy over the one than over the ninety-nine who are not wandering. ¹⁴So, it isn't the will in the presence of your Father, who is in the heavens, that one of these little ones be destroyed.

Yēsous and community reconciliation

¹⁵If your sibling sins against you, go away, convince the person—between you and that person alone. If the person hears you, you have an advantage with your sibling. ¹⁶If the person won't hear [you], take one or two with you—so *in the mouth of two witnesses—or three—every utterance may stand.* ¹⁷If the person won't listen to them, tell the assembly. If that person won't listen to the assembly, let the person be just as the ethnic and tax agent. ¹⁸This is true to say to you: whatever you bind on the land will be bound in heaven and whatever you loosen on the land will be loosened in heaven. ¹⁹Again, this is true to say to you that if two of you concur on the land about any matter about which you ask, it will happen for them with my Father who is in the heavens. ²⁰For where there are two or three assembled in my name, I am there in the middle of them."

Yēsous responds to Petros with a story

²¹Then Petros [Peter], approaching, said to him, "Lord, how often will my sibling sin against me and I will release him? Up to seven times?" ²²Yēsous says to him:

> "I don't say to you 'up to seven times,' but 'up to seventy times seven!' ²³Because this is true the Heavens' Empire can be compared to a human king, who wanted to settle an account with his slaves. ²⁴He began to settle . . . one debtor with an inestimable debtⁱ was brought to him. ²⁵He doesn't have [funds] to pay back . . . the lord signaled for him to be sold, along with the woman and the children and everything he had, and to be paid back. ²⁶Therefore, the slave, falling down,

---

ʰA coin of much value, paying the temple tax for two.

ⁱTen thousand talents is equivalent to sixty million days of labor! The debt there (a "loan" in v. 27) is hyperbolic.

was bowing down to him, saying, 'Show patience on me, and I will pay everything back.' ²⁷Empathizing, the slave's lord loosened him and released the loan for him.

²⁸Exiting, that slave found one of his co-slaves, who owed him ten dēnaria,ʲ and, grabbing, he was suffocating him, saying, 'Pay back what you owe!' ²⁹Therefore, falling down, his co-slave was begging him, saying, 'Show patience on me, and I will pay back.' ³⁰He didn't want to but, departing, tossed him into prison until he paid back the indebtedness. ³¹Therefore, his co-slaves, seeing what happened, were extremely grieved and, coming, clarified for their lord everything that happened. ³²Then his lord, calling him, says to him, 'Evil slave! I released you from that whole debt—since you begged me. ³³Is it not necessary also for you to show compassion with your co-slave, as I showed compassion with you?' ³⁴His lord, angered, gave him over to the tormentors until he could pay back everything indebted.

³⁵So also, my Father—the Heavenly One—will do to you if you don't release—each of you—one's siblings from your hearts."

19 It happened: when Yēsous completed these words, he moved on from the Galilaia [Galilee] and came into the regions of Youdaia [Judea] Beyond the Yordanēs [Jordan River]. ²Many crowds followed him, and he healed them there.

NARRATIVE FIVE

Yēsous instructs about divorce and celibacy

³The Observant [Pharisees] approached him, testing him and saying, "Is it observant for a man to loosen his woman for every cause?" ⁴Responding, he said, "Do you not know that the one who created at the beginning *made them male and female?*" ⁵And he said, "*Because of this a human will abandon the father and the mother and will be united with his woman, and the two will be one flesh.* ⁶So that they are no longer two but one flesh. Therefore, what God connected let not a human separate."

⁷They say to him: "Why therefore did Mōusēs [Moses] command to give *a divorce document* and to loosen her?" ⁸He says to them, "Because Mōusēs permitted you to loosen your women because of your hard-heartedness, but from the beginning it was not so. ⁹I say this to you that, Whoever loosens his woman—except in a case of sexual immorality—and marries another, adulterates."

¹⁰His Apprentices say to him, "If the cause of humans with women is like this, it's not to one's benefit to marry." ¹¹He said to them, "Not everyone creates space for this word, but those to whom it's given. ¹²For there are celibates who were given life like this from their mother's belly, and there are celibates who were made celibates by humans, and there are celibates who made themselves celibates because of the Heavens' Empire. The one capable of creating space, let that person create space."

Yēsous blesses children

¹³Then children were offered to him so he could place hands on them and pray. The Apprentices rebuked them. ¹⁴But Yēsous said, "Release the children and don't prohibit them to come to me, for the Heavens' Empire is of such ones." ¹⁵Placing the hands on them, he journeyed from there.

Yēsous challenges a life of possessions

¹⁶Look! Someone approaching him said, "Teacher, what good might I do so I might have Era Life?" ¹⁷He said to him: "Why do you ask me about the good? One is the good. If you want to enter into the Life, observe the orders." ¹⁸He says to him, "Which ones?" Yēsous said,

"The *You will not murder,*
You will not adulterate,
You will not thieve,
You will not false witness,
¹⁹*Honor the father and the mother* and
You will love your neighbor as yourself."

ʲTen dēnaria, or ten days of labor.

²⁰The youth says to him: "I guarded all these. What do I still lack?" ²¹Yēsous said to him: "If you want completion, go away, sell your possessions and give to the beggars, and you will have a treasure chest in heavens, and come follow me!" ²²The youth, hearing the word, departed, grieving, for he was one having many acquisitions.

²³Yēsous said to his Apprentices, "This is true to say to you, that the wealthy with difficulty will enter into the Heavens' Empire. ²⁴Again, I say this to you: It's easier for a camel to cross through a needle's eye than for the wealthy to enter into God's Empire." ²⁵The Apprentices, hearing, were shocked extremely, saying, "Who then is able to be delivered?" ²⁶Yēsous, observing, said to them, "With humans this is impossible, but with God all things are possible."

²⁷Then responding, Petros said to him, "Look! We released all things and we followed you. What then will there be for us?" ²⁸Yēsous said to them: "This is true to say to you that you, the ones following me, at the Restoration, when the Son of Humanity sits on his splendor's throne, will also be seated on twelve thrones judging Yisraēl's [Israel's] twelve tribes. ²⁹Anyone who released houses or brothers or sisters or father or mother or children or fields—because of my name, will receive one hundred times more and will inherit the Era Life.

³⁰Many first ones will be last [ones] and last [ones] first [ones].

Yēsous tells a story about vineyard workers

20 The Heavens' Empire is comparable to a human house master who exited early in the day to hire workers for his vineyard. ²Concurring with the workers for a dēnarion a day, he commissioned them into his vineyard. ³Exiting about the third hour, he saw others standing workless in the squares ⁴and to them he said, 'You also go away into the vineyard and I will give to you what would be right.' ⁵They went away. Again, exiting about the sixth and ninth hour he did similarly. ⁶About the eleventh hour, exiting, he found others standing and says to them, 'Why have you stood here the whole day workless?' ⁷They say to him, 'Because no one hired us.' He says to them, 'You also go away into the vineyard.'

⁸It was evening . . . the lord of the vineyard says to his supervisor, 'Call the workers and give back to them the wage, beginning from the last until the first.' ⁹Coming, the eleventh-hour ones received one dēnarion. ¹⁰Coming, the first-hour ones thought that they would receive more. They also received one denarius each. ¹¹Receiving, they murmured against the house master, ¹²saying, 'These last ones did one hour, and you made them equal to us, those who carried the load of the day and the scorching heat.'

¹³Responding, he said to one of them, 'Friend! I didn't wrong you. Did you not concur with me for a dēnarion? ¹⁴Take yours and go away! I want to give to this last one as to you. ¹⁵Or, is it not observant for me to do what I want with what is mine? Or, is your eye evil because I am good? ¹⁶So the last ones will be first [ones] and the first ones last [ones].'"

Yēsous predicts his death again

¹⁷Yēsous, ascending into Yierosoluma [Jerusalem], took the twelve Apprentices by himself and on the path said to them, ¹⁸"Look! We are ascending into Yierosoluma, and the Son of Humanity will be given over to the Senior Priests and Covenant-Code scholars [scribes], and they will condemn him to death, ¹⁹and they will give him over to the ethnic groups to mock and to lash and to crucify, and on the third day he will be raised."

Yēsous and a mother with high hopes

²⁰Then the mother of Zebedaios's [Zebedee's] sons approached him with her sons, bowing down and asking for something from him. ²¹He said to her, "What do you want?" She says to him, "Say that these my two sons may sit, one on your right and one on your left, in your Empire." ²²Responding, Yēsous said, "You don't know what you ask. Are you able to drink the cup that I am about to drink?" They said to him, "We are able." ²³He says to them, "You will indeed drink my cup, but the sitting at my right and left isn't mine to give, but for those whom it's prepared by my Father."

²⁴The ten, hearing, were angered with the two brothers. ²⁵Calling them, Yēsous said, "You know that the leaders of the ethnic groups overrule them and the great ones overpower

them. ²⁶It will not be so among you: Instead, whoever wants to become great among you will be your servant, ²⁷and whoever wants to be first among you will be your slave. ²⁸Just as the Son of Humanity did not come to be served but to serve and to give his self as liberation price for many."

Yēsous gives sight to the sightless

²⁹They're journeying out of Yierichō [Jericho] . . . a large crowd followed him. ³⁰Look! Two sightless men, sitting along the path, hearing that Yēsous is going by, cried out, saying, "Show compassion on us, Lord, Dauid's [David's] son!" ³¹The crowd rebuked them so they might be silenced. But they cried out all the more, saying, "Show compassion on us, Lord, Dauid's son!" ³²Standing, Yēsous voiced to them and said, "What do you want that I do for you?" ³³They say to him, "Lord, that our eyes may be opened." ³⁴Empathizing, Yēsous touched their eyes, and immediately they saw again and they followed him.

Yēsous enters Yierosoluma

21 When they came close to Yierosoluma [Jerusalem], and they came to Bēth-Phagē [Bethphage] to the mountain of olives [Mount Olivet], then Yēsous commissioned two Apprentices, ²saying to them, "Journey into the village opposite of you, and immediately you will find a tied-up donkey and a foal with her. Loosening, bring to me. ³If anyone says to you, 'Why?' you will say that 'The Lord has a need for them.' Suddenly he will commission them." ⁴This occurred to fill out what was said through the prophet, saying,

> ⁵*Tell Daughter Siōn* [Zion],
> *Look! Your king comes to you*
> *Meek and mounted on a donkey,*
> *On a foal, male of a pack animal.*

⁶The Apprentices, journeying and doing just as Yēsous ordered them, ⁷led the donkey and foal, and placed their robes on them, and he sat upon them.

⁸The very numerous crowd spread their robes in the path, and others snapped branches from the trees and were spreading in the path. ⁹The crowds—the ones leading him and the ones following—were crying out, saying,

> *Hosanna to Dauid's* [David's] *son!*
> *Blessed is the one coming in the Lord's name.*
> *Hosanna* in the highest levels.

¹⁰He enters into Yierosoluma . . . the whole city was shaken, saying, "Who is this?" ¹¹The crowds were saying, "This is the prophet Yēsous—the man from Nazara [Nazareth] of the Galilaia [Galilee]."

Yēsous in the temple

¹²Yēsous entered into the temple and tossed out all the sellers and purchasers in the temple, and he tipped over the tables of the moneychangers and the chairs of those selling doves. ¹³He says to them,

> "It's written: *My house will be called a prayer house,* but you have made it a *bandits' cave.*"

Yēsous heals the sightless and lame

¹⁴Sightless and lame in the temple approached him, and he healed them. ¹⁵The Senior Priests and Covenant-Code scholars [scribes]—seeing the wonders that he did and the young servants crying out "Hosanna to Dauid's son!" in the temple—were angered ¹⁶and said to him, "Do you hear what these are saying?" Yēsous says to them, "Yes. Have you never read that *From the mouth of infants and the nursing I have prepared praise?*" ¹⁷Abandoning them, he exited out of the city into Bēthania [Bethany] and overnighted there.

Yēsous dries out a fig tree

¹⁸At dawn, returning into the city, he hungered. ¹⁹Seeing one fig tree on the path, he came to it and found nothing in it but only leaves, and he says to it, "May there be no fruit from you into the Era!" Instantly, the fig tree dried out. ²⁰The Apprentices, seeing, were stunned, saying, "How did the fig tree dry out so instantly?" ²¹Responding, Yēsous said to them, "This is true to say to you: If you have trust and don't mentally waver, you will not only do what occurred to the fig tree, but even if you say to this mountain, 'Be lifted and be tossed into the sea,' it will happen. ²²Whatever you ask in prayer, trusting, you will receive."

Yēsous and authority

²³He's entering into the temple... the Senior Priests and the people's Elders approached him [as he was] teaching, saying, "By what sort of authority do you do these things? Who gave to you this authority?" ²⁴Responding, Yēsous said to them, "I will also ask you one word, which if you tell me I will also tell you by what sort of authority I do these things: ²⁵The dipping, Yōannēs's [John's]—what is its origin? From heaven or from humans?" They were deliberating among themselves, saying, "If we say 'From heaven,' he will ask us, 'Why then did you not declare allegiance to him?' ²⁶If we say, 'From humans'—we are scared of the crowd. (For everyone has Yōannēs as a prophet.) ²⁷Responding to Yēsous, they said, "We don't know." He said to them, "Neither do I say to you by what sort of authority I do these things."

Yēsous tells a story about two children

²⁸"What does it look like to you? A human had two children. Approaching the first, he said, 'Child, go away, work today in the vineyard.' ²⁹But, responding, he said, 'I will not.' But later, regretting, went away. ³⁰Approaching the other, he said similarly. But, responding, he said, 'I [will], Lord,' but did not go away. ³¹Which of the two did the father's will?" They say, "The first." Yēsous says to them, "This is true to say to you: The tax agents and the prostitutes go ahead of you into God's Empire. ³²For Yōannēs came to you in the path of rightness, and you did not declare allegiance to him, but the tax agents and prostitutes declared allegiance to him. You, seeing, did not later regret it so to declare allegiance to him.

Yēsous tells an analogy about bad vineyard workers

³³Listen to another analogy! [There was] a human, a house master, who planted a vineyard and encircled it with a hedge and dug a winepress in it and formed a tower and gave it out to farmers and traveled abroad. ³⁴When the fruit season came close, he commissioned his slaves to the farmers to take his fruit. ³⁵The farmers, taking the slaves—one they beat, one they killed, and one they stoned. ³⁶Again, [the house lord] commissioned other slaves, more than the first ones, and they did similarly to them. ³⁷Finally, he commissioned to them his son, saying, 'They will defer to my son.' ³⁸The farmers, seeing the son, said among themselves, 'This is the heir. Come! Let us kill him and we may have his inheritance,' ³⁹and, taking him, they tossed him out of the vineyard and killed him. ⁴⁰Therefore, when the vineyard's lord comes, what will he do to those farmers?" ⁴¹They say, "He will destroy badly those bad ones and he will give the vineyard out to other farmers, who will pay back to him the fruit in their season." ⁴²Yēsous says to them, "Have you never read in the writings?

A stone the formers rejected...
This [stone] became the foundation stone.
This happened from the Lord
And it's a stunner in our eyes?

⁴³Because this is true, I say this to you: God's Empire will be lifted from you and it will be given to an ethnic group doing its fruits. ⁴⁴The Faller on this stone will be shattered, but upon whom it falls, it will pulverize the person." ⁴⁵The Senior Priests and Observant [Pharisees], hearing his analogy, knew that he is speaking about them. ⁴⁶They, pursuing him to grab [him], were scared of the crowds, since they had him as a prophet.

Yēsous tells a story about a marriage

22 Responding, Yēsous again spoke to them in analogies, saying, ²"The Heavens' Empire may be compared to a human king, who made a marriage for his son. ³He commissioned his slaves to call the ones called to the marriage, and they did not want to come. ⁴Again, he commissioned other slaves, saying, 'Say to the called: Look! I have prepared the luncheon, my bulls and the fattened [calves] are slaughtered and everything is prepared. Come to the marriage!' ⁵The ones neglecting went away, one to his own field, and one to his business. ⁶The ones remaining, grabbing, assaulted and killed the slaves. ⁷The king was angered and, sending his troops, destroyed those murderers and set their city on fire. ⁸Then he says to his slaves, 'The marriage is prepared, the ones called are not deserving. ⁹Therefore, journey to the path's exits and call whomever you find to the marriage.' ¹⁰Exiting to the paths, those slaves assembled everyone they found—both evil and good. The marriage was full of reclining ones. ¹¹The king, entering to observe the ones reclining, saw there a human not having put on in marriage clothes, ¹²and says to him, 'Friend! How did you enter here not having marriage clothes?' He was silenced. ¹³Then the king said to his servants, 'Binding his feet and hands, toss him out to the dark edges, where there will be weeping and teeth grinding. ¹⁴Many are the called, few are the elect.'"

Yēsous and Kaisar

¹⁵Then, journeying on, the Observant [Pharisees] took a council so they might trap him in a word. ¹⁶They commissioned to him their Apprentices with the Hērodianoi [Herodians], saying, "Teacher, we know that you are true and you teach God's path in truth and no one is a worry to you, for you don't see into the face of humans. ¹⁷Therefore, tell us, what does it look like to you? Is it observant to give a tax to Kaisar [Caesar] or not?" ¹⁸Knowing their evil, Yēsous said, "Why do you test me? Masked ones! ¹⁹Demonstrate to me the coin for the tax!" They offered to him a dēnarion. ²⁰He says to them, "This image and inscription—whose is it?" ²¹They say to him, "Kaisar's." Then he says to them, "Therefore, pay back to Kaisar what is Kaisar's, and to God what is God's." ²²Hearing, they were stunned and, releasing him, they went away.

Yēsous and Elites

²³On that day Elites [Sadducees] approached him—those claiming there is no resurrection—and they asked him, ²⁴saying, "Teacher, Mōüsēs [Moses] said, *If someone ends life without children, his brother will marry his woman and will raise up seed for his brother.* ²⁵There were seven brothers among us. The first, marrying, [his life] ended, and not having a seed, he released his wife to his brother. ²⁶Likewise for the second and the third until the seventh. ²⁷After all of them, the wife died. ²⁸Therefore, in the resurrection, of which of the seven will she be a woman?" (All of them had her.) ²⁹Responding, Yēsous said to them, "You are deceived, understanding neither the writings nor God's power. ³⁰At the resurrection they don't marry or get married, but they are like envoys in heaven. ³¹Concerning the resurrection from among the dead . . . did you not read what was said to you by God, saying, *I am the God of Abra'am and the God of Yisa'ak and the God of Yakōb*? He isn't the God of the dead ones but of the living ones." ³³Hearing, the crowds were shocked by his teaching.

Yēsous—his creed

³⁴The Observant, hearing that he silenced the Elites, were assembled at the same place, ³⁵and one of their Covenant-Code experts, testing him, asked, ³⁶"Teacher, which is the great order in the Code?" ³⁷He said to him, "*You will love the Lord, your God, in your whole heart and in your whole self and in your whole intelligence.* ³⁸This is the great and the first order. ³⁹The second is comparable: *You will love your neighbor as yourself.* ⁴⁰The whole Code and the prophets hang on these two orders."

Yēsous as Dauid's son

⁴¹The Observant assembled together . . . Yēsous asked them, ⁴²saying, "What does it look like to you about the Christos? Whose son is he?" They say to him, "Of Dauid [David]." ⁴³He says to them, "Therefore, how does Dauid, in Spirit, call him 'Lord,' saying, ⁴⁴*The Lord said to my Lord: Sit from my right until I place your enemies under your feet*? ⁴⁵If, therefore, Dauid calls him 'Lord,' how is he his son?" ⁴⁶No one was able to respond a word to him, and neither did anyone dare—from that day on—to question him about anything.

SPEECH FIVE

Yēsous unmasks the masked

23 Then Yēsous spoke to the crowds and to his Apprentices, ²saying, "The Covenant-Code scholars [scribes] and the Observant [Pharisees] sat on the teaching chair of Mōüsēs [Moses]. ³Therefore, do and observe whatever they say, but don't do consistent with their works, for they say and don't do. ⁴They bind heavy and difficult-to-bear burdens, and they place them on the shoulders of humans, but they, with their finger, don't want to move them. ⁵They do all their works to be observed by humans. For they widen their prayer straps and they magnify their prayer tassels, ⁶they love the first-status positions at banquets and the first-status seats in the assembly halls ⁷and the greetings in the squares and to be called 'My Greatness [Rabbi]' by humans.

⁸But you are not to be called 'My Greatness,' for your teacher is one, and you are all siblings. ⁹Don't call your father on the land because one is your Father—the Heavenly One. ¹⁰Nor are you to be called 'Instructor' because your instructor is one, the Christos. ¹¹The greatest of you will be your servant. ¹²Whoever raises one's own status will be impoverished and whoever impoverishes oneself will be raised in status.

Yēsous warns

¹³Oy! on you, Covenant-Code scholars and Observant, masked ones! Because you lock the Heavens' Empire in front of humans. For you are not entering, nor do you release those entering to enter.ᵏ

¹⁵Oy! on you, Covenant-Code scholars and Observant, masked ones! Because you lead around sea and dry ground to make one convert and, whenever it happens, you make the person twice the descendant of the Valley of Destruction [Gehenna] as you are.

¹⁶Oy! on you, sightless guides, who say, 'Whoever makes an oath by the sanctuary, it's nothing, but whoever makes an oath by the gold of the sanctuary is obligated.' ¹⁷Idiot and Sightless! For which is greater, the gold or the temple, which makes the gold devoted? ¹⁸And, 'whoever makes an oath by the sacrificial altar, it's nothing, but whoever makes an oath by the donation on it is obligated.' ¹⁹Sightless! Which is greater, the gift or the sacrificial altar that makes the gift devoted? ²⁰Therefore, the one who makes an oath by the sacrificial altar makes an oath by it and everything on it. ²¹The one who makes an oath by the sanctuary makes an oath by it and by the one who resides in it. ²²The one who makes an oath by the heaven makes an oath by God's throne and by the one who sits on it.

²³Oy! on you, Covenant-Code scholars and Observant, masked ones! Because you donate a tenth of mint and dill and cumin and released the heavier things of the Code—justice and compassion and allegiance. It's necessary to do these without releasing those. ²⁴Sightless guides! Those sifting out the gnat but swallowing the camel.

²⁵Oy! on you, Covenant-Code scholars and Observant, masked ones! Because you clean the exterior of the cup and the saucer, but inwardly are filled with extortion and the absence of control. ²⁶Sightless Observant one! Clean first the inside of the cup so its outside also becomes clean.

²⁷Oy! on you, Covenant-Code scholars and Observant, masked ones! Because you can be compared to plastered tombs, which outside appear to be elegant but inside are full of bones of the dead and every kind of uncleanness. ²⁸So also you—outside you appear to humans as right ones but inside you are full of mask-wearing and Code-breaking.

²⁹Oy! on you, Covenant-Code scholars and Observant, masked ones! Because you form the prophets' graves and decorate the memorials of the right ones, ³⁰and say, 'Had we been alive in the days of our fathers, we would not have had in common the murder-blood of the prophets.' ³¹So that you witness to yourselves that you are descendants of prophet-murderers. ³²You—fill out the standard [established by] your fathers! ³³Snakes! Knot of vipers! How are you to flee from the judgment of the Valley of Destruction?

³⁴Because this is true, Look! I commission prophets and wise ones and Code Scholars to you. [Some] of them you will kill and crucify, and some of them you will lash in your assembly halls and chase from city to city, ³⁵so will come down on you all the right, poured-out-on-the-land blood—from the blood of Abel—the one who did what was right—up to the blood of Zacharias, son of Barachias, whom you murdered between the sanctuary and the sacrificial altar. ³⁶This is true to say to you: All these things will fall upon this generation.

³⁷Yierousalēm Yierousalēm [Jerusalem], killer of the prophets and stoner of those commissioned to her! How many times have I wanted to assemble your children—the way a hen assembles her chicks under the wings—and you did not want [this]. ³⁸Look! Your house is released to you as wilderness.

ᵏMatthaios 23:14 isn't found in the best manuscripts.

³⁹For I say this to you, You will never see me from now until you say, *Blessed is the one coming in the Lord's name.*"

Yēsous and the coming disaster

24 Exiting, Yēsous was journeying from the temple, and his Apprentices approached him to demonstrate to him the formations of the temple. ²Responding, he said to them, "Do you not see all these things? This is true to say to you: Stone on stone here will never be released that will not be demolished."

³He was sitting on the mountain of olives [Mount Olivet] . . . the Apprentices approached him by himself, saying, "Tell us, when will these things occur? What is the authenticating sign of your Parousia and the completion of the Era?" ⁴Responding, Yēsous said to them, "Beware that someone not deceive you! ⁵For many will come in my name, saying, 'I am the Christos,' and they will deceive many. ⁶You are about to hear of wars and war reports. See! Don't be alarmed! For it's necessary to happen, but this isn't yet the completion. ⁷For ethnic group will be raised against ethnic group and empire against empire, and there will be famines and earthquakes from place to place. ⁸All these are the beginning of labor pains.

⁹Then they will give you over into the troubles and they will kill you, and you will be hated by all the ethnic groups because of my name. ¹⁰Then many will be tripped up and they will give over one another and they will hate one another. ¹¹Many false prophets will be raised up and they will deceive many. ¹²Because Covenant-breaking will be abounding, the love of many will become cold. ¹³The one resilient to the completion—this person will be delivered. ¹⁴This gospel of the Empire will be announced in the whole inhabited world as a witness to all the ethnic groups. Then the completion will come.

¹⁵Therefore, whenever you see *the desecrating abomination*, what was said through Daniēl [Daniel], the prophet, standing in the Devoted Place—let the lector know— ¹⁶then let those who are in Youdaia [Judea] flee to the mountains, ¹⁷let not the one on the terrace descend to lift things from his house, ¹⁸and let not the one in the field return back to lift his robe. ¹⁹Oy! for women who have a child in the womb and nursing in those days! ²⁰Pray that your flight occurs neither in stormy season nor on a Sabbath. ²¹For then there will be great trouble such that has not occurred from the beginning of the Kosmos until now nor that ever may be. ²²If those days were not cut short, all flesh could not be delivered. For the elect ones, those days will be cut short.

²³Then, if someone says to you, 'Look! The Christos is here, or here,' don't trust. ²⁴For false Christoses and false prophets will be raised, and they will give great authenticating signs and omens so to deceive—if possible—even the elect ones. ²⁵Look! I have told you in advance. ²⁶Therefore, if they say to you, 'Look! In the wilderness,' don't exit. 'Look! In a private room,' don't trust. ²⁷For just as the lightning exits from the east and appears to the west, so will be the Parousia of the Son of Humanity. ²⁸Wherever the corpse is, there the eagles will be assembled.

²⁹Immediately after the troubles of those days,

> *The sun will be darkened,*
> *And the moon will not give its light,*
> *And the stars will fall* from the heaven,
> *And the heavens' powers* will be shaken.

³⁰Then the authenticating sign—the Son of Humanity—will appear in heaven, and then all the tribes of the land will strike themselves, and they will see *the Son of Humanity coming on the clouds of heaven* with power and much splendor. ³¹He will commission his envoys with a great trumpet blast, and they will assemble his elect ones from the four winds—from the ends of the heavens until their ends.

³²Be apprenticed about an analogy from the fig tree: Whenever its branch is already tender and the leaves sprout, you know the summer is close. ³³So also you—whenever you see all these things, you know that it's close, at the doors. ³⁴This is true to say to you: this generation will never pass away until all these events occur. ³⁵The heaven and the land will pass away, but my words will never pass away.

Yēsous and the time

³⁶About that day and hour, no one knows—neither the heavens' envoys nor the royal Son, except only the Father. ³⁷For as the days of Nōe [Noah], so will be the Parousia of the Son of Humanity. ³⁸For as in those days,

the ones before the flood, chewing and drinking, marrying and receiving marriage until the day Nōe entered into the chest [ark], ³⁹and they did not know until the flood came and all of them were lifted: So will be the Parousia of the Son of Humanity. ⁴⁰Then two will be in the field, one received and one released; ⁴¹two grinding meal in the mill, one received and one released. ⁴²Therefore, be awake! Because you don't know on what day your Lord comes. ⁴³Know this: If the house master had known on which night-watch the thief comes, he would have been awake and would not have permitted [the thief] to break into his household. ⁴⁴Because this is true, you also be prepared because at an hour you don't seem [to know] the Son of Humanity comes.

⁴⁵Who then is the allegiant and prudent slave, whom the Lord established over his domestics to give them provision at the season? ⁴⁶Blessing on that slave who, coming, his lord will find doing so. ⁴⁷This is true to say to you that he will establish him over all his possessions. ⁴⁸But if that bad slave says in his heart, 'My lord is taking a long time,' ⁴⁹and begins to beat his fellow slaves, and eats and drinks with the boozers, ⁵⁰that slave's lord will come on a day that he doesn't anticipate and at an hour that he doesn't know, ⁵¹and he will cut him in half and place his part among the masked ones, where there will be weeping and teeth grinding.

Yēsous tells an analogy with ten virgins

25 Then the Heavens' Empire will be compared to ten virgins, who, taking their lamps, exited for the official welcome of the bridegroom. ²Five of them were idiots and five prudent. ³For the idiots, taking their lamps, did not take olive oil with them, ⁴but the prudent took olive oil in containers with their own lamps. ⁵The bridegroom taking a long time . . . all got drowsy and were sleeping. ⁶In the middle of the night, a shout occurred. 'Look! The bridegroom! Exit for the official reception!' ⁷Then all those virgins were raised and decorated their lamps. ⁸But the idiots said to the prudent, 'Give us of your olive oil because our lamps are snuffing out.' ⁹The prudent responded, saying, '[We can't] in the event there may not be enough for us and for you. Instead, journey to sellers and purchase for yourselves.' ¹⁰They go away to purchase . . . the bridegroom came and the prepared ones entered with him into the marriage and the door was shut. ¹¹Later the remaining virgins come saying, 'Lord, lord, open for us.' ¹²Responding, he said, 'This is true to say to you: I don't know you.' ¹³Therefore, be awake! because you don't know the day or the hour.

Yēsous tells a story about investments

¹⁴For just as a human, traveling abroad, called his own slaves and gave over his possessions: ¹⁵To one he gave five measures of silver [*talanta*], to one two, to another one—to each consistent with his own power, and he traveled abroad.

Immediately, ¹⁶journeying, the five-measures slave, taking, worked with them and got the advantage of five more. ¹⁷Similarly, the two-measures slave got the advantage of two more. ¹⁸But the one-measure slave, taking, departing, dug the land and hid his lord's silver.

¹⁹After a long time, those slaves' lord came and settled a word with them. ²⁰Approaching, the five-measures slave, taking, offered five more measures of silver, saying, 'Lord, you gave over to me five measures of silver. Look! I got the advantage of five more measures.' ²¹His lord said to him, 'Well done, good and allegiant slave. You were allegiant over a few, I establish you over many. Enter into your lord's joy.' ²²Also approaching, the two-measures slave said, 'Lord, you gave over to me two measures of silver. Look! I got the advantage of two more measures.' ²³His lord said to him, 'Well done, good and allegiant slave. You were allegiant over a few, I establish you over many. Enter into your lord's joy.' ²⁴Also approaching, the one who had received the one measure said, 'Lord, I know you—that you are a harsh human, harvesting where you did not plant and assembling where you did not scatter, ²⁵and, being scared, departing, I hid your measure of silver in the land. Look! You have your [measure].' ²⁶Responding, his lord said to him, 'Evil and timid slave! Did you know that I harvest where I did not plant and assemble where I did not scatter? ²⁷Therefore, it was necessary for you to toss my silver to the table managers and, coming, I would have obtained mine with interest. ²⁸Therefore, lift the measure of silver from him and give to the ten-measures slave.

²⁹To the one having much will be given and it will flow over, but from the one not having even what the person has will be lifted from him. ³⁰Toss this unprofitable slave to the dark edges, where there will be weeping and teeth grinding.'

Yēsous tells a story about goats and sheep

³¹Whenever the Son of Humanity comes in his splendor and all the envoys with him, then he will sit on his splendorous throne, ³²and all the ethnic groups will be assembled before him, and he will isolate them from one another, just as a shepherd removes sheep from goats, ³³and he will locate the sheep at his right but the goats at his left.

³⁴Then the king will say to those at his right, 'Come! Blessed ones by my Father. Inherit the Empire prepared for you from the Kosmos's origin. ³⁵For I hungered and you gave me to eat, I thirsted and you gave me to drink, I was an outsider and you assembled me, ³⁶naked and you covered me, I was weak and you cared for me, I was in prison and you came to me.' ³⁷Then the righteous ones will respond to him, saying, 'Lord, when did we see you hungering and nurture you, or thirsting and we gave you a drink? ³⁸When did we see you as an outsider and assemble you, or naked and cover you? ³⁹When did we see you weak or in prison and came to you?'

⁴⁰Responding, the king will say to them, 'This is true to say to you: Whatever you did to one of these my siblings, the least, you did it to me.' ⁴¹Then he will say also to those at his left, 'Journey from me—cursed ones. You are prepared for the Era's fire, what is prepared for the Accuser and his envoys. ⁴²For I hungered and you didn't give me to eat, I thirsted and you didn't give me to drink, ⁴³I was an outsider and you didn't assemble me, naked and you didn't cover me, weak and in prison and you didn't care for me.' ⁴⁴Then they will also respond, saying, 'Lord, when did we see you hungering or thirsting or an outsider or naked or weak or in prison and we did not serve you?' Then he will respond to them, saying, 'This is true to say to you: Whenever you didn't do to one of these least, neither did you do it to me.'

⁴⁶These will go away into the Era's chastisement, but the righteous ones into the Era's Life."

NARRATIVE SIX

Yēsous' death indicated

26 It happened: when Yēsous completed all these words, he said to his Apprentices, ²"You know the Pascha [Passover] comes after two days, and the Son of Humanity is given over to be crucified."

³The Senior Priests and the people's Elders were assembled into the enclosure of the Senior Priest, who is called Kaiaphas [Caiaphas], ⁴and they planned together to grab Yēsous in disguise and kill him, ⁵but they were saying, "Not at the feast so there won't be a disturbance among the people."

⁶Yēsous was in Beth-Ania [Bethany] in scaly Simōn's house . . . ⁷a woman with an alabaster vase of very expensive fragrant ointment approached him and poured it on his head as he is reclining. ⁸Seeing, the Apprentices were angry, saying, "Why this destruction? ⁹For it was possible for this to have been sold for much and to be given to the beggars." ¹⁰But knowing, Yēsous, said to them, "Why present labor for this woman? For she has worked a beautiful work for me. ¹¹For you always have beggars with you, but you don't always have me. ¹²For tossing this ointment on my body: she did this to prepare to bury me. ¹³This is true to say to you to you: Wherever this gospel is announced in the whole Kosmos, what she did will be spoken about in her memory."

Yēsous' betrayal plotted

¹⁴Then, one of the Twelve, who is called Youdas the Dagger Man [Judas Iscariot], having journeyed to the Senior Priests, ¹⁵said, "What do you want to give to me, and I will give him over to you?" They established thirty coins of silver for him. ¹⁶From then he was pursuing a good time that he might give him over.

Yēsous' Pascha celebrated

¹⁷On the first of Flatbreads [Unleavened Bread], the Apprentices approached Yēsous, saying, "Where do you want that we prepare for you to eat the Pascha?" ¹⁸He said, "Go away into the city to a specific person and say to him, 'The Teacher says, My season is close, I do the Pascha at your [house] with my Apprentices.'"

¹⁹The Apprentices did as Yēsous ordered them and they prepared the Pascha.

²⁰It was evening . . . he was reclining with the Twelve. ²¹They're eating . . . he said, "This is true to say to you, that one of you will give me over." ²²Grieving extremely, they began to say to him—each one of them, "I am not the one, Lord, am I?" ²³Responding, he said, "The one who dips the hand with me in the bowl—this person will give me over. ²⁴The Son of Humanity goes away as it's written about him, but Oy! on that human through whom the Son of Humanity is given over. It was beautiful for him if that human was not given a life." ²⁵Responding, Youdas, the one who gave him over, said, "I am not the one, My Greatness [Rabbi], am I?" He says to him, "You said [it]."

²⁶They're eating . . . Yēsous, taking bread and blessing, cracked [it] and, giving to the Apprentices, said, "Take. Eat. This is my body." ²⁷Taking a cup and thanking, he gave to them, saying, "Drink of it, all. ²⁸For this is my Covenant blood that is poured out for many to release from sins. ²⁹I say to you: I will not drink from now on of the produce of the vine until that day whenever I drink it with you anew in my Father's Empire." ³⁰Singing a hymn, they exited to the mountain of olives [Mount Olivet].

Yēsous' denials predicted

³¹Then Yēsous says to them, "You all will be tripped up on this night, for it's written,

> I will beat the shepherd,
> And the flock's sheep will be scattered.

³²After my arising, I will proceed you to the Galilaia [Galilee]."

³³Responding, Petros [Peter] said to him, "If all are tripped up by you, I will never be tripped up." ³⁴Yēsous said to him, "This is true to say to you, that: On this night, before the voicing of the rooster you will deny me three times." ³⁵Petros says to him, "If it's necessary for me to die with you, I will never deny you." All the Apprentices said likewise.

Yēsous given over in Gethsēmani

³⁶Then Yēsous comes with them to an area called Gethsēmani [Gethsemane] and says to the Apprentices, "Sit here while, departing, I pray there." ³⁷Taking Petros and the two sons of Zebedaios, he began to grieve and to be discomforted. ³⁸Then he says to them, "*My self is deeply grieved* to the point of death. Remain here and be awake with me." ³⁹Proceeding a little ways, he fell on his face, praying and saying, "My Father—if it's possible—may this cup pass me by. However—not as I want but as you [want]." ⁴⁰He comes to the Apprentices and finds them sleeping, and he says to Petros, "Are you [pl.] then not strong enough to be awake with me for one hour? ⁴¹Be awake and pray so that you don't enter into the test. The spirit's eager, but the flesh is weak." ⁴²Again, departing a second time, he prayed, saying, "My Father, if it isn't possible for this to pass me by unless I drink it, may your will be." ⁴³Coming again, he found them sleeping—for their eyes were heavy. ⁴⁴Releasing them, again departing, he prayed a third time, saying the same word again. ⁴⁵Then he comes to the Apprentices and he says to them, "Sleep the remaining [time] and rest yourselves! Look! The hour has come close and the Son of Humanity is given over into the hands of sinners. ⁴⁶Be raised, let's go. Look! The one giving me over has come close."

⁴⁷He's still speaking . . . Look! Youdas, one of the Twelve, came and with him a large crowd with long knives and clubs—from the Senior Priests and the people's Elders. ⁴⁸The one giving him over gave to them an authenticating sign, saying, "The one I kiss—he is the one. Grab him." ⁴⁹Immediately approaching Yēsous, he said, "Rejoice, My Greatness!" He kissed him. ⁵⁰Yēsous said to him, "Friend—you are here for this." Then, approaching, they tossed hands on Yēsous and grabbed him. ⁵¹Look! One of those with Yēsous, extending the hand, removed his long knife, and striking the Senior Priest's slave, he sliced off his ear. ⁵²Then Yēsous says to him, "Return the long knife into its place, for all taking a sword will be destroyed by a sword. ⁵³Do you not think I am not able to beg my Father and he will present to me now more than twelve battalions of envoys? ⁵⁴How then will the writings be filled out that so this is necessary to occur?"

⁵⁵At that hour Yēsous said to the crowds, "You exit with long knives and clubs to take me as if for a bandit. Daily in the temple I was

sitting teaching and you did not grab me. ⁵⁶All this happened so the writings of the prophets may be filled out." Then all the Apprentices, releasing him, fled.

Yēsous, Petros, and a trial before the Senior Priest

⁵⁷Those who grabbed Yēsous led to Kaiaphas, the Senior Priest, where the Covenant-Code scholars [scribes] and the Elders were assembled. ⁵⁸Petros was following him at a distance up to the Senior Priest's enclosure and, entering inside, he was sitting with the subordinates to see the completion. ⁵⁹The Senior Priests and the whole Central Council were pursuing a false witness against Yēsous so they could kill him, ⁶⁰and they did not find . . . many false witnesses approaching. Finally, two approaching ⁶¹said, "This man said, 'I am able to demolish God's sanctuary and to form [another] after three days.'" ⁶²Rising up, the Senior Priest said to him, "Do you have nothing to respond about what these are accusing you?" ⁶³Yēsous was silent. The Senior Priest said to him, "I make an oath before the Living God that you tell us if you are the Christos, God's royal Son." ⁶⁴Yēsous says to him, "You said. However, I say to you: From now on you will see *the Son of Humanity* sitting at the Power's right and *coming on heaven's clouds*." ⁶⁵Then the Senior Priest ripped his robes, saying, "He insults [God]. Why do we still have a need for witnesses? Look! Now you heard the insult of God. ⁶⁶What does it look like to you?" The ones responding said, "He is guilty of death." ⁶⁷Then they spit in his face and beat him, but others slapped him, ⁶⁸saying, "Prophesy to us, Christos—who is the one who hit you?"

⁶⁹Petros was sitting outside in the enclosure. One servant-girl approached him, saying, "You were with Yēsous of the Galilaia." ⁷⁰He denied [him] before everyone, saying, "I don't know what you are saying." ⁷¹Exiting to the gate, another [servant-girl] saw him and says to them there, "This man was with Yēsous the Nazōraios [Nazarene]." ⁷²Again, he denied [him] with an oath, that "I don't know the man." ⁷³After a little while, the ones standing, approaching, said to Petros, "Truly you are one of them, for your speech makes it clear." ⁷⁴Then he began to curse and to make an oath that "I don't know the human." Immediately, the rooster voiced. ⁷⁵Petros remembered the utterance Yēsous had spoken, that "Before the rooster voices you will deny me three times." Exiting outside, he wailed bitterly.

Yēsous on trial before Pilatos

27 It was early in the morning . . . all the Senior Priests and the people's Elders took a council against Yēsous so to put him to death. ²Binding him, they led him out and gave him over to Pilatos [Pilate], the Governor.

³Then Youdas [Judas], the one who gave him over, seeing that he had been condemned, regretting, returned the thirty coins of silver to the Senior Priests and Elders, ⁴saying, "I sinned giving over innocent blood." But they said, "What is that to us? You will see." ⁵Throwing the silver coins into the sanctuary, he slipped away; departing, he hanged himself. ⁶The Senior Priests, taking the silver coins, said, "It isn't observant to toss these into the temple donation box, since it's the price of blood." ⁷Taking a council, they purchased with them the potter's field for burying outsiders. (⁸That is why that field is called "Field of Blood" to this day.) ⁹Then what was said through Yieremias [Jeremiah], the prophet, was filled out, saying, *I took thirty silver coins, the price of one on whom a price was set, which they— descendants of Yisraēl —priced.* ¹⁰They gave them [silver coins] for the Field of Blood, *as the Lord ordered* me.

¹¹Yēsous was stood before the Governor. The Governor asked him, saying, "Are you the king over the Youdaians?" Yēsous said, "You say." ¹²In his accusations by the Senior Priests and Elders, he did not respond a thing. ¹³Then Pilatos says, "Do you not hear how much they accuse you?" ¹⁴He did not respond to him, not even one utterance, so that the Governor is deeply stunned.

¹⁵At each feast, the Governor was accustomed to loosen for the crowd one prisoner whom they wanted. ¹⁶They had then a known prisoner named Yēsous Bar-Abbas [Barabbas, "son of the father"]. ¹⁷Therefore, they're assembling together . . . Pilatos said to them, "Whom do you want that I should loosen for you, Yēsous Bar-Abbas or Yēsous, the one called Christos?" (¹⁸For he knew that they gave him over because of envy.)

[19]He's seated on the Bēma [judgment seat] . . . his woman commissioned to him, saying, "Let there be nothing between you and that right one for I suffered many things today in a dream because of him."

[20]The Senior Priests and the Elders persuaded the crowds that they might ask for Bar-Abbas, but that they destroy Yēsous. [21]Responding, the Governor said to them, "Which of the two do you want that I loosen for you?" They said, "Bar-Abbas." [22]Pilatos says to them, "Therefore what am I to do with Yēsous, the one called Christos?" They all say, "Let him be crucified." [23]He said, "For what? What bad thing did he do?" They loudly cried out, saying, "Let him be crucified!" [24]Pilatos, seeing that he was gaining nothing but instead a disturbance is occurring, taking water, he washed the hands in front of the crowd, saying, "I am innocent of this blood. You will see." [25]Responding, the whole crowd said, "His blood is on us and our children." [26]Then he loosened for them Bar-Abbas but, whipping Yēsous, he gave him over that he would be crucified.

Yēsous degraded

[27]Then the Governor's soldiers, taking Yēsous to the soldiers' headquarters, assembled the whole cohort upon him. [28]Stripping him, they covered him with a scarlet mantle [29]and, weaving a crown out of thorns, they placed it on his head and a reed in his right hand, and genuflecting before him, they mocked him, saying, "Rejoice! King over the Youdaians [Judeans, Jews]!" [30]Spitting at him, they took the reed and were beating on his head. [31]Then they mocked him, they stripped him of the mantle and put on his robes and led him out to be crucified.

Yēsous crucified

[32]Exiting, they found a Kurēnaion [Cyrenian] human, with the name Simōn, whom they conscripted that he might lift his cross. [33]Coming to a place called "Golgota," which is called "Skull Place," [34]they gave him wine—mixed with bile—to drink. Tasting, he did not want to drink. [35]Crucifying him, *they split his robes, tossing the die* [36]and, sitting, they were keeping watch over him there. [37]Over his head they placed his inscribed cause:

| This is Yēsous, the king over the Youdaians.

[38]Then they crucify him with two bandits, one from the right and one from the left. [39]The ones journeying by were insulting him, wagging their heads [40]and saying, "The one demolishing the sanctuary and forming in three days—deliver yourself! If you are God's royal Son, descend from the cross!" [41]Likewise and the Senior Priests, mocking with the Covenant-Code scholars [scribes] and Elders, were saying, [42]"He delivered others, but isn't able to deliver himself. King of Yisraēl [Israel], he is, now let him descend from the cross and we will trust in him. [43]*He was persuaded in God—let him now be rescued if he wants him*, for he said, 'I am God's royal Son.'" [44]The bandits, who were co-crucified with him, were degrading him the same.

[45]From the sixth hour [noon] darkness came over all the land—until the ninth hour. [46]About the ninth hour, Yēsous bellowed in a loud voice, saying,

"*Ēli, Ēli, lema sabachthani?*"

That is,

"*My God, my God, why did you abandon me?*"

[47]Some bystanders there, hearing, were saying, "This one voices for Ēlias [Elijah]." [48]Immediately, one of them, running and taking a sponge, filling it with sour wine, and placing it on a reed, was giving him a drink. [49]But the remaining ones were saying, "Release [him], let us see if Ēlias comes delivering him." [50]Yēsous again, crying in a loud voice . . . released the spirit.

[51]Look! The sanctuary's inner curtain was split from top to bottom, in two, and the land was shaken and the rocks were split, [52]and the tombs were opened and many bodies of sleeping devoted ones were raised, [53]and, exiting the tombs after his resurrection, they entered into the Devoted City and appeared to many.

[54]The leader of a hundred soldiers and with him those keeping watch over Yēsous, seeing the authenticating sign and what happened,

were extremely scared, saying, "Truly this was God's royal Son!"

⁵⁵Many women were there observing at a distance—they followed Yēsous from the Galilaia [Galilee] to serve him. ⁵⁶Among whom was Maria, the Magdalēnē [Mary Magdalene], and Maria [Mary], the mother of Yakōbos [James] and Yōsēf [Joseph], and the mother of the sons of Zebedaios [Zebedee].

Yēsous buried

⁵⁷It was evening . . . a wealthy human from Arimathaia, named Yōsēf, who was himself apprenticed to Yēsous, came. ⁵⁸Approaching Pilatos, this one pleaded for Yēsous' body. Then Pilatos signaled for [it] to be given over. ⁵⁹Taking the body, Yōsēf wrapped it in clean linen ⁶⁰and placed it in his new tomb, which he cut in the rock and, rolling a great stone at the tomb's door, he departed.

⁶¹Mariam, the Magdalēnē, was there and the other Maria, sitting in front of the tomb.

Yēsous guarded

⁶²On the next day, which is the day after [Pascha] Preparation, the Senior Priests and the Observant [Pharisees] were assembled to Pilatos, ⁶³saying, "Lord, we remember what that deceiver said while living, 'After three days I arise.' ⁶⁴Therefore, signal for the tomb to be secured until the third day, just in case, coming, his Apprentices steal him and say to the people, 'He has been raised from among the dead.' The last deception will be greater than the first." ⁶⁵Pilatos said to them, "You have a custodian. Go away, secure as you know." ⁶⁶The ones journeying secured the tomb, sealing the stone—with the custodian.

Yēsous raised

28 After the Sabbaths, at dawn, on day one of the Sabbaths, Mariam, the Magdalēnē, and the other Maria came to observe the tomb. ²Look! A great earthquake occurred for the Lord's envoy, descending from heaven and approaching, rolled the stone and was sitting on it. ³His appearance was like lightning and his clothing white as snow. ⁴The ones keeping watch were shaken out being scared of him [the envoy], and they became like dead men. ⁵Responding, the envoy said to the women, "You, don't be scared, for I know that you are pursuing Yēsous, the crucified. ⁶He isn't here, for he has been raised as he said. Come! Look at the place where he was laying. ⁷Quickly journeying, tell his Apprentices that he has been raised from among the dead! Look! He goes ahead of you into the Galilaia [Galilee], there you will see him. Look! I told you."

⁸Departing quickly from the tomb with awe and great joy, they ran to declare [it] to his Apprentices. ⁹Look! Yēsous went out to meet them, saying, "Rejoice!" But the approaching women grabbed his feet and bowed down to him. ¹⁰Then Yēsous says to them, "Don't be scared! Go away, announce to my brothers that they depart into the Galilaia, they will see me there."

Yēsous' resurrection distorted

¹¹They're journeying . . . Look! Some of the custodian [soldiers], coming into the city, announced to the Senior Priests everything that happened. ¹²Being assembled with the Elders, taking council, they gave adequate silver coins to the soldiers, ¹³saying, "Say that his Apprentices, coming at night, stole him . . . we're sleeping. ¹⁴If this is heard before the Governor, we will persuade him and we will keep you from concern." ¹⁵The ones taking the silver coins did as they were taught. This word was advertised among Youdaians [Judeans, Jews] to this day.

Yēsous commissions

¹⁶The eleven Apprentices journeyed into the Galilaia to the mountain where Yēsous ordered them. ¹⁷Seeing him, they bowed down, but some doubted.

¹⁸Yēsous, approaching, spoke to them, saying, "All authority in heaven and on the land has been given to me. ¹⁸Therefore, journeying, make all the ethnic groups into Apprentices, dipping them in the name of the Father and the Son and the Holy Spirit, ²⁰teaching them to observe everything I ordered you. Look! I am with you every day—until the completion of the Era."

INTRODUCTION TO THE GOSPEL OF MARK

In the Hebrew Bible, or the First (or Old) Testament, the last book is the Chronicles, famous for its lengthy geneaology. Matthaios's [Matthew's] Gospel comes first in the traditional Second Testament most likely because, like the Chronicles, it has a geneaology. When it comes to the chronology of when the Gospels were written, however, Markos's [Mark's] Gospel is most likely the earliest of our Second Testament Gospels to have been written. Both Matthaios and Loukas [Luke] availed themselves of Markos when they drafted their biographies of Yēsous, at times copying straight out of Markos. I have tried to reproduce their exact wording in Greek with exact wording in English.

Notice where Markos opens: with Yōannēs the Dipper [John the Baptist]. Notice, too, how abruptly it ends—"for they were scared." Markos's Gospel is filled with short, abrupt, almost incomplete sentences. If this Gospel's wording isn't as smooth flowing as Matthaios or Loukas, there remains a more or less seamless flow in the narrative from the early days with Yōannēs the Dipper through various records of the teachings and actions of Yēsous, who is thematically the subject and center of this (and the other) Gospels. A high point in the narrative is the confession of Petros [Peter], and the narrative from that point on keeps the reader/listener aware of the impending death of Yēsous.

Along with Matthaios and Loukas, the focal themes are God's Empire and the story about Yēsous, who is God's royal Son and the Son of Humanity. Like Matthaios's Gospel, the Empire theme is all about God as king, God ruling over God's people, God's will expressed in the teachings of Yēsous, and all this occurs in the land of Yisraēl [Israel] and the Galilaia [Galilee]. Discipleship, or apprenticeship, is the appropriate response to Yēsous, which involves listening to his teachings, doing what he says, and, even more importantly, following him and his pattern of life. Noticeably, in Markos 8, 9, and 10 we hear Yēsous announce his death and then call the Apprentices to live into that death. The Gospel of Markos announces the gospel itself. In other words, it tells us that the story of Yisraēl has found its fulfillment in the very story of Yēsous as its Christos, its royal Son of God, and its Deliverer from sin and systemic evils.

An early Christian tradition said Markos's Gospel was Markos's record of the apostle Petros's preaching in Rome. Like pinning down the date of Markos's Gospel (some say the 50s, some the 60s, others the 70s), we don't have enough information to know. The author, Markos, if he is the one who traveled with Paulos [Paul], could inform us of the Yēsous comparisons Paulos knew and taught.

Markos's biography of Yēsous is vivid—he wants his readers to experience the analogies as if they were going on in front of them as they are hearing them read. His account is also seemingly in a hurry to get Yēsous to the cross, and this hurry can be found in the constant use of "suddenly" (*euthys*). Yet, for all his vividness and hurry, Markos also uses irony: telling people not to tell others who he is becomes the way to make him known, the crucified one is the Son of God, the one rejected by Roman and Jewish leaders is announced as God's Son by a Roman military leader, and the abrupt and seeming nonending is actually the beginning of telling others that the crucified one has been raised.

THE GOSPEL OF MARK

The Yēsous gospel begins with Ēsaïas

1 The gospel's origin about Yēsous Christos, God's royal Son: ²Just as it's written in Ēsaïas [Isaiah], the prophet:

> Look! I commission my envoy before your face,
> Who will prepare the path before you.
> ³A voice bellowing in the wilderness:
> "Get ready the way for the Lord,
> Make his ways straight!"

Yēsous and a wilderness dipper

⁴It happened: Yōannēs [John], the one dipping in the wilderness and announcing a conversion dip for releasing sins. ⁵The whole Youdaian [Judean] region and all Yierosolumitēs [Jerusalemites] were journeying out to him, and they were being dipped by him in the Yordanēs [Jordan] River, publicly acknowledging their sins. ⁶Yōannēs had put on camel hairs and an animal-skin waistband around his waist and [he was] eating locusts and wild syrup.

⁷He announced, saying, "The one stronger than me is following me—of him I am inadequate, stooping [down] to loosen the strap of his sandals. ⁸I dipped you in water, he will dip you in the Holy Spirit."

⁹And it happened: in those days Yēsous came from the Galilaian Nazara [Galilean Nazareth] and was dipped into the Yordanēs by Yōannēs. ¹⁰Suddenly, ascending from the water, he saw the heavens splitting and the Spirit as a dove descending to him, ¹¹and a voice happened from the heavens: "You are my royal Son, the one loved, in you I was delighted."

¹²Suddenly, the Spirit tossed him out into the wilderness. ¹³He was in the wilderness forty days, being tested by the Satanas [Satan], and he was with the wild things and the envoys were serving him.

Yēsous announcing God's Empire

¹⁴After Yōannēs was given over, Yēsous came into the the Galilaia [Galilee], announcing God's gospel and ¹⁵saying that "The season is filled out and the Empire has come close! Convert and be allegiant to the gospel!"

Yēsous' first followers

¹⁶Going along the Sea of the Galilaia, he saw Simōn and Andreas [Andrew], Simōn's brother, casting a fish net in the Sea. (They were fishers.) ¹⁷Yēsous said to them, "Come behind me! I will make you become human-fishers." ¹⁸Suddenly, releasing the nets, they followed him. ¹⁹Proceeding a little ways, he saw Yakōbos [James]—son of Zebedaios [Zebedee]—and Yōannēs [John]—his brother, [and he saw] them in the boat preparing the nets. ²⁰Suddenly he called them. And, releasing their father Zebedaios in the boat with the wage laborers, they departed behind him.

Yēsous silences a contaminated spirit

²¹They journey into Kaphar-Naoum [Capernaum] and, suddenly, entering the assembly hall on the Sabbaths, he was teaching. ²²They were shocked at his teaching, for he was teaching them as one having authority and not as the Covenant-Code scholars [scribes]. ²³Suddenly, in their assembly hall was a human with a contaminating spirit and he yelled, ²⁴saying, "What is there between us and you, Yēsous Nazarēnos [Nazarene]? Have you come to destroy us? I know you—who you are: God's devoted one!" ²⁵Yēsous rebuked it, saying, "Be silenced! Exit out of him!" ²⁶Rocking him, the contaminating spirit, voicing in a loud voice, exited from him. ²⁷All were amazed—disputing with themselves, saying, "What is this? A new teaching with authority! He orders contaminating spirits and they heed him!" ²⁸His report exited suddenly everywhere in the whole Galilaia region.

Yēsous heals

²⁹Suddenly, exiting from the assembly hall, he came into Simōn and Andreas's house with Yakōbos and Yōannēs. ³⁰Simōn's mother-in-law was laid out, fevering. Suddenly, they speak to him about her. ³¹Approaching, he raised her,

grabbing the hand. The fever released her, and she was serving them. ³²It was evening ... when the sun set they were carrying to him all those in a bad way and the demonized. ³³The whole city was assembled together at the door. ³⁴He healed many in a bad way with various maladies, and he tossed out many demons. He was not releasing the demons to speak because they had known him.

Yēsous prays and proclaims and tosses demons

³⁵Rising early, in deep darkness, he exited and went out into a wilderness place, and there he was praying. ³⁶Simōn (and those with him) chased after him, ³⁷and they found him and say to him that "All are pursuing you." ³⁸He says to them, "Let us go somewhere else, to the nearby smaller cities, so I may announce there. For I have exited for this."

³⁹He came announcing in their assembly halls in the whole Galilaia and tossing out demons.

Yēsous heals a scaly-skin man

⁴⁰A scaly-skin man comes to him, begging him and genuflecting and saying to him that, "If you want you are able to clean me." ⁴¹Empathizing, extending his hand, he touched and says to him, "I want to. Be cleaned." ⁴²Suddenly, the scaliness departed from him, and he was cleaned. ⁴³Snorting at him, suddenly he tossed him out. ⁴⁴He says to him, "See that you say nothing to anyone. Go away, *exhibit* yourself *to the priest*, and offer the matters Mōüses [Moses] ordered for your cleansing as witness to them." ⁴⁵He, exiting, began to announce many things and to advertise the word, so that he was no longer able to enter a city openly, but was outside in wilderness locations. They were coming to him from all directions.

Yēsous releases a man from sins

2 Entering again after some days into Kaphar-Naoum [Capernaum], it was heard that he is in a house. ²Many were assembled together so that there was no longer space, not even spaces at the door, and he was speaking the word to them. ³They came, carrying to him a paralyzed man, lifted by four. ⁴Not being able to offer [him] to him [Yēsous] because of the crowd, they unroofed the roof where he was and, ripping out, they lower the mat on which the paralyzed man was lying. ⁵Seeing their trust, Yēsous says to the paralyzed man, "Child, your sins are released." ⁶There were some Covenant-Code scholars [scribes] sitting there and deliberating in their hearts, ⁷"Why does this man speak like this? He insults [God]. Who is able to release sins except one—God?" ⁸Suddenly, Yēsous, perceiving in his spirit that they were deliberating like this among themselves, says to them, "Why do you deliberate these things in your hearts? ⁹Which is easier? To say to the paralyzed man, 'Your sins are released' or to say 'Rise up! and lift your mat and walk'? ¹⁰But so you might know that the Son of Humanity has authority in the land to release sins"—he says to the paralyzed man—¹¹"I say to you, Rise up! Lift your mat and go away to your house!" ¹²He was raised and, suddenly lifting the mat, he exited before all so all were beside themselves and splendored God, saying that "We never saw such a thing!"

Yēsous calling

¹³He exited again to the Sea shore. The whole crowd was coming to him, and he was teaching them. ¹⁴Passing on, he saw Leui [Levi], Alphaios's [Alphaeus's] son, sitting at the tax booth, and he says to him, "Follow me!" Arising, he followed him. ¹⁵It happens that he is reclining in his house, and many tax agents and sinners were reclining with Yēsous and his Apprentices. (For there were many, and they were following him.) ¹⁶The Observants' [Pharisees'] Code scholars, seeing that he is eating with sinners and tax agents, were saying to his Apprentices, "Why is he eating with tax agents and sinners?" ¹⁷Hearing, Yēsous says to them, "The strong have no need of a doctor, but those in a bad way do. I did not come to call 'right ones' but sinners."

Yēsous suspends fasting

¹⁸Yōannēs's Apprentices and the Observant were fasting. They come and say to him, "Why do Yōannēs's Apprentices and the Observants' Apprentices fast, and your Apprentices don't

fast?" ¹⁹Yēsous said to them, "Are the groom's sons able to fast when the groom is with them? So long as they have the groom with them they are not able to fast. ²⁰The days will come whenever the groom is taken away from them, and then they will fast on that day. ²¹No one sews a patch of unshrunk cloth on an ancient robe. Otherwise, the fullness pulls from it—the new from the ancient—and the rip becomes worse. ²²No one tosses new wine into ancient wineskins. Otherwise, the wine tears the wineskins and the wine is destroyed—and the wineskins. But new wine [is] for fresh wineskins."

Yēsous, Lord over the Sabbath

²³It happened: he is journeying along on Sabbaths through the grain fields. His Apprentices began to make a path, picking heads of grain. ²⁴The Observant were saying to him, "Look! Why do they do on the Sabbath what isn't observant?" ²⁵He says to them, "Did you not once read what Dauid [David] did when he had a need and hungered—he and those with him? ²⁶How he entered into God's house—at the [time of the] Senior Priest Abiathar—and he ate the Presence Breads, which was not observant to eat . . . but for the priests? And [how] he gave [some] also to those who were with him?" ²⁷He was saying to them, "The Sabbath happened because of the human, and not the human because of the Sabbath. ²⁸So that, the Son of Humanity is Lord even over the Sabbath."

3 Again, he entered into the assembly hall. There was a human, having a stiffened hand. ²Some were spying on him—if he will heal him on the Sabbaths—so they might accuse him. ³He says to the human having the stiff hand, "Arise in the center!" ⁴He says to them, "Is it observant on the Sabbaths to do good or to do evil, to deliver a self or to kill?" They went silent. ⁵Looking around at them with anger, grieving at their heart's hardness, he says to the human, "Extend the hand!" He extended and his hand was restored. ⁶Exiting, the Observant [Pharisees] suddenly were giving council against him with the Hērōdianoi [Herodians] so they could destroy him.

Yēsous heals

⁷Yēsous with his Apprentices slipped away to the Sea. A great mass from the Galilaia followed—and from Youdaia [Judea] ⁸and from Yierosoluma [Jerusalem] and from Idoumaia [Idumea] and Beyond the Yordanēs [Jordan River] and around Turos [Tyre] and Sidōn—a great mass, hearing what he was doing, came to him. ⁹He said to his Apprentices that a small boat might be prepared because of the crowd, that they might not trouble him. ¹⁰For he healed many—so they fell down on him so they could touch him—who were afflicted. ¹¹The contaminating spirits, whenever they were observing him, fell before him and were crying out, saying that "You are God's royal Son." ¹²He was rebuking them often not to make him apparent.

Yēsous calls twelve

¹³He ascends to the mountain and he calls those whom he wanted, and they departed to him. ¹⁴He made twelve, whom he named "Commissioners," that they would be with him, and that he would commission them to announce ¹⁵and to have authority to toss out demons. ¹⁶He made the Twelve,

> and he placed the name "Petros [Peter]" on Simōn,
> ¹⁷and on Yakōbos [James], son of Zebedaios [Zebedee], and Yōannēs [John], his brother, he placed the names "Boanērges" (which is "Thunder's Sons"),
> ¹⁸and Andreas [Andrew] and Philippos [Philip] and Bar-Tholomaios [Bartholomew] and Matthaios [Matthew] and Thōmas and Yakōbos, son of Alphaios [Alphaeus] and Thaddaios [Thaddaeus] and Simōn Kananaios [Simon the Zealot]
> ¹⁹and Youdas the Dagger Man [Judas Iscariot], who also gave him over.

Yēsous, his family, and Beelzeboul

²⁰He comes into a house. Again, the crowd comes together so they are not able even to eat bread. ²¹Hearing, those alongside him exited to

grab him, for they were saying that "He was beside himself."

²²The Covenant-Code scholars [scribes], those from Yierosoluma, descending, were saying that "He has Beelzeboul!" and that "He tosses out demons by the leader of demons!" ²³Calling them, he was speaking to them in analogies:

"How is Satanas [Satan] able to toss out Satanas?

²⁴If an empire is parted in itself, that empire isn't able to stand.

²⁵If a house is parted in itself, that house will not be able to stand.

²⁶If Satanas rose up against himself and was parted, he isn't able to stand but he has [come to] the end.

²⁷But no one, entering into the strong one's house, is able to seize his vessels if he doesn't, first, bind the strong one, and then he will seize his house.

²⁸This is true to say to you, that: All things will be released for human descendants—their sin-acts and insults, whatever they might insult, ²⁹but whoever insults the Holy Spirit doesn't have release into the Era, but is guilty of the Era's sin-act."

(³⁰Because they were saying, "He has a contaminating spirit.")

³¹His mother and his brothers come and, having stood outside, they commissioned to him, calling him. ³²A crowd was sitting around him, and they say to him, "Look! Your mother and your brothers and your sisters are outside pursuing you." ³³Responding to them, he says: "Who is my mother and my siblings?" ³⁴Looking around at those sitting in a circle around him, he says, "Look! My mother and my siblings! ³⁵For whoever does God's will, this person is my brother and sister and mother."

Yēsous tells the story of the planter and the seeds

4 Again, he began to teach next to the Sea. The largest crowd assembles to him so that he, boarding down into the boat, sat in the Sea, and the whole crowd was along the Sea on the land. ²He was teaching them many things in analogies, and he was saying to them in his teaching: ³"Hear! Look! The planter exited to plant. ⁴It happened in his planting a seed fell next to the path and the birds came and gobbled it. ⁵Another fell on rocky ground where it did not have much land and suddenly it rose up because it did not have depth of land. ⁶When the sun rose up it was scorched and, because it did not have root, it was stiffened. ⁷Another fell in the thorns and the thorns ascended and suffocated it, and it did not give fruit. ⁸Others fell in the beautiful land and it was giving fruit, ascending and growing, and it was bearing [fruit], one thirty, one sixty, and one one hundred."

⁹He was saying, "Whoever has ears to hear, let the person hear."

Yēsous explains his analogies

¹⁰When it happened [that] he was alone, those around him with the Twelve were asking about the analogies, ¹¹and he says to them, "To you is given the secret of God's Empire, but to those outside all matters come in analogies, ¹²so,

> seeing, they may see and not perceive
> and, hearing, they may hear and not understand—
> otherwise they might return and it be released for them."

Yēsous explains the story about the planter

¹³He says to them, "Do you not understand this analogy? How will you know all the analogies?

¹⁴The planter plants the word. ¹⁵These are those next to the path, where the word is planted and, whenever they hear, suddenly Satanas comes and lifts the word planted in them.

¹⁶These are like those being planted on rocky ground, those who whenever they hear the word, suddenly with joy they receive it, ¹⁷and they don't have root within themselves and are momentary . . . then trouble and pursuit come because of the word . . . suddenly they are tripped.

¹⁸Others are those being planted in the thorns—these are the ones hearing the word, ¹⁹and the Era's anxieties and wealth's delusion and the desires for remaining matters, journeying in, suffocate the word, and the person becomes fruitless.

²⁰These are the ones planted on beautiful land, who hear the word and welcome [it] and they bear fruit: one thirty, one sixty, and one one hundred."

Yēsous says clever things

21 He was saying to them, "Does the lampstand come so it may be placed under a measuring basket or under a cot? No, so it may be placed on a lampstand. **22** For nothing hidden will not be apparent, nothing concealed will not come into appearance. **23** If someone has ears to hear, let the person hear."

24 He says to them, "See what you are hearing! You will be measured by the measure by which you measure, and it will be added to you. **25** For whoever has, it will be given to the person. Whoever doesn't have, even what the person has will be lifted from the person."

Yēsous tells the story of the growing seed

26 He was saying, "God's Empire is like this: as a human might toss seed on the land, **27** and sleeps and arises night and day, and the seed sprouts and elongates—he doesn't know how. **28** The land spontaneously yields fruit—first a blade, then a grain head, then a full grain in the head. **29** Whenever the fruit is given over, suddenly [the farmer] commissions the sickle because the harvest is present."

Yēsous tells the story of the mustard seed

30 He was saying, "How do we compare God's Empire? Or, by which analogy do we place it [the Empire]?

31 Like a mustard seed, which, whenever it's planted on the land—the smallest of all seeds on the land—**32** and whenever it's planted, it ascends and becomes larger than all leafy vegetables and it makes great branches, so that *heaven's birds* are able *to nest* under its shadow."

33 He was speaking the word to them in many such analogies as they were able to hear. **34** He was not speaking to them apart from an analogy, but by himself he unraveled all matters for his own Apprentices.

Yēsous, who is he?

35 He says to them on that day . . . it was evening . . . "Let us cross to Beyond the Yordanēs [Jordan River]." **36** Releasing the crowd, they receive him as he was in the boat, and other boats were with him. **37** A great gale of wind comes, the waves were tossing over into the boat so that the boat is already filled. **38** He was in the stern on the pillow sleeping. They raise him and say to him, "Teacher, is it no concern to you that we are being destroyed?" **39** Being raised awake, he rebuked the wind and said to the Sea, "Be silent! Be stilled!" The wind died down and there was a great calm. **40** He said to them, "Why are you so cowardly? How do you not yet have trust?" **41** They were scared with a great scare, and they were saying to one another, "Who then is this that even the wind and the Sea heeds him?"

Yēsous liberates

5 He came to Beyond the Yordanēs [Jordan], into the region of the Gerasēnos [Gerasenes]. **2** He was exiting from the boat . . . suddenly, a human with a contaminating spirit came out of the tombs to meet him, **3** who had a dwelling in the tombs, and—not even with a chain—was anyone any longer able to bind him **4** because he had often been bound with shackles and chains, and the chains and shackles had been broken by him, and no one was strong enough to tame him. **5** During every night and day in the tombs and in the mountains he was crying out and cutting himself with stones.

6 Seeing Yēsous from a distance, he ran and bowed down to him **7** and, crying in a great voice, says, "What is there between me and you, Yēsous, Highest God's royal Son? I implore you by God, don't torture me!" **8** For he was saying to him, "Exit from the human, contaminating spirit!" **9** He was asking him, "What is your name?" He says to him, "*Legion* is my name because we are many." **10** He begged him many times not to commission them out of the region.

11 There was there at the mountain a great herd of hogs feeding. **12** They begged him, saying, "Send us into the hogs so we may enter into them!" **13** He permitted them. The exiting contaminating spirits entered into the hogs. The herd dashed down the cliff into the sea, about two thousand, and were suffocating in the Sea.

14 The ones feeding them fled and declared in the city and in the fields. They exited to see what it is that happened. **15** They come to Yēsous and they observe the demonized person sitting, robed and sensible—the one who had the Legion—and they were scared. ⁱ⁶The ones seeing narrated to them how it happened to the demonized person and about the hogs. ¹⁷They began to beg him to depart from their region.

¹⁸He's boarding down into the boat . . . the one demonized begs him that he might be with him. ¹⁹He did not release him, but says to him, "Go away into your house to yours and declare to them whatever the Lord has done for you, and he has been compassionate to you." ²⁰He departed and began to announce in the Dekapolis [Decapolis] whatever Yēsous did for him, and everyone was stunned.

Yēsous heals more

²¹Yēsous was crossing back in the boat again to the other side . . . a large crowd was assembled to him, and was along the Sea. ²²One of the assembly hall leaders, with the name Yaïros [Jairus], comes and, seeing him, falls at his feet ²³and begs him many times, saying that "My little daughter has come to the end—so you, coming, [please] place the hands on her so she may be delivered and live." ²⁴He departed with him. A great crowd followed him, and they were jostling him.

²⁵A woman being in a twelve-year blood flow ²⁶and who suffered much from many doctors and exhausted everything she had and gained nothing but coming rather into worse [shape], ²⁷hearing about Yēsous, coming behind in the crowd, touched his robe. ²⁸For she was saying that "if I can touch his robe, I will be delivered." ²⁹Suddenly, her blood spring dried up, and she knew in the body that she had been cured from the affliction. ³⁰Suddenly, Yēsous, perceiving in himself the power exiting from him, being turned in the crowd, was saying, "Who touched my robe?" ³¹His Apprentices were saying to him, "Do you see the crowd jostling you and you say, 'Who touched me?'" ³²He was looking around to see the woman who did this. ³³The woman, being scared and trembling, knowing what had happened to her, came and fell before him and said to him the whole truth.

³⁴He said to her, "Daughter, your trust has delivered you. Go away in peace and be healthy from your affliction."

³⁵While he was speaking . . . some come from the assembly hall leader, saying that "Your daughter died. Why still disturb the teacher?" ³⁶Yēsous, overhearing the word spoken, says to the assembly hall leader, "Don't be scared! Just trust!" ³⁷He did not release anyone with him to follow with him except Petros [Peter], Yakōbos [James], Yōannēs [John], Yakōbos's brother. ³⁸They come into the leader of the assembly hall's house and he is observing the clamor, and much wailing and shrieking ³⁹and, entering, he says to them, "Why are you disturbed and wailing? The child did not die but sleeps." ⁴⁰They were laughing at him but he, tossing everyone out, receives the child's father and mother and those with him and journeys into where the child was. ⁴¹Grabbing the child's hand, he says to her, "*Talitha koum*" (which translated [is]) "Girl, I say to you, rise up!" ⁴²Suddenly the girl arose and was walking around. (For [she] was twelve years old.) They were suddenly beside themselves with great ecstasy. ⁴³He ordered them many times that no one could know this, and he said [something] be given to her to eat.

Yēsous rejected at home

6 He exited there and comes to his ancestral village, and his Apprentices follow him. ²It was a Sabbath . . . he began to teach in the assembly hall. The many listening were shocked, saying, "What's the source for these things for him? What is the wisdom that is given to this man and these powers being done through his hands? ³Isn't this the artisan, Maria's [Mary's] son and Yakōbos's [James's] and Yōsēs's [Joseph's] and Youda's [Judah's] and Simōn's brother? Are not his sisters here with us?" They were tripped up by him. ⁴Yēsous says to them that "A prophet isn't dishonored except in one's ancestral village and among one's relatives and in one's house." ⁵He was not able there to do any power, except, placing the hands on a few ill ones, he healed. ⁶He was stunned because of their anti-trust.

He was leading around the encircling villages teaching.

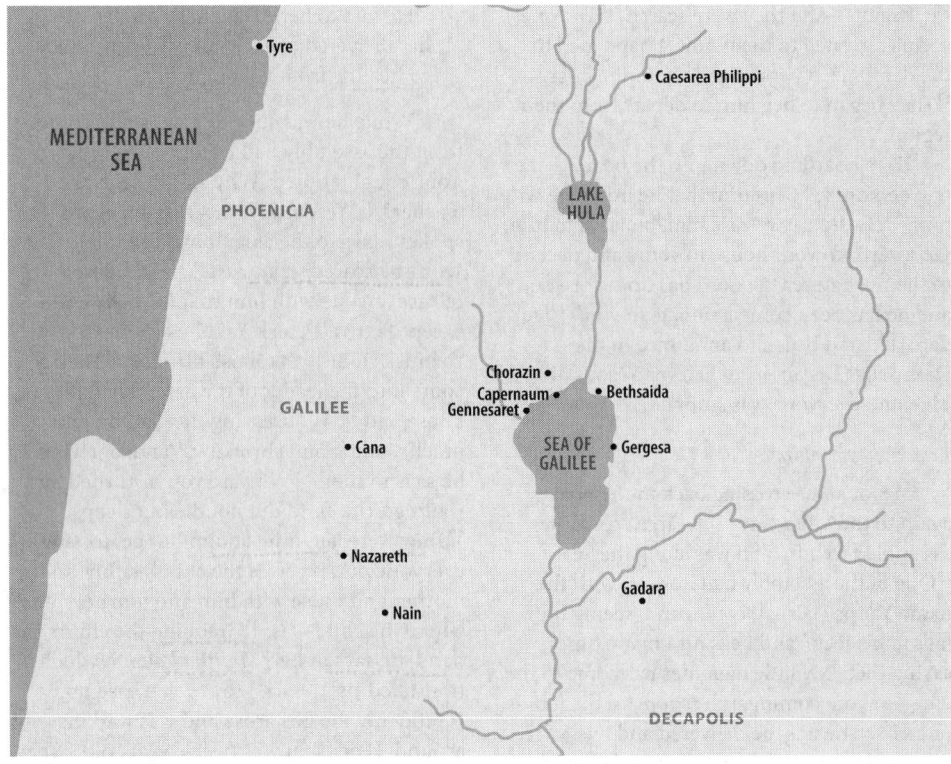

Figure 3. Jesus's Ministry in Palestine

Yēsous commissions twelve

⁷He calls the Twelve. He began to commission them two by two. He was giving to them authority over contaminating spirits. ⁸He ordered them that they not lift anything for the path—

> except only a walking stick,
> not bread,
> not a bag,
> not bronze in the belt
> ⁹but [wear] bound sandals,
> and don't put on two shirts!

¹⁰He was saying to them, "Wherever you enter into a house, remain there until you exit from there. ¹¹Whatever place doesn't receive you nor hear you, journeying from there, shake off the soil that is under your feet—as a witness to them." ¹²Exiting, they announced that they should convert, ¹³and they were tossing out many demons, and they were oiling with oil many ill ones and they were healing.

Yēsous told about Yōannēs

¹⁴King Hērōdēs [Herod] heard, for his name became apparent. They were saying that "Yōannēs the Dipper [John the Baptist] had been raised from among the dead ones and because of this the powers are working in him." ¹⁵But others were saying that it's Ēlias [Elijah]. Others were saying that "A prophet like one of prophets." ¹⁶Hērōdēs, hearing, was saying, "The one I decapitated, Yōannēs—this man has been raised."

¹⁷For Hērōdēs himself, commissioning, grabbed Yōannēs and bound him in prison because of Hērōdias, Philippos [Philip] his brother's woman—because he married her. ¹⁸For Yōannēs was saying to Hērōdēs that "It is not observant for you to have your brother's woman." ¹⁹Hērōdias had it in for him and was wanting to kill him and wasn't able. ²⁰For Hērōdēs was scared of Yōannēs, knowing him to be a right and devoted man, and was preserving him and, hearing him many times, he was perplexed, and he was hearing him with pleasure.

²¹A good season happened . . . when Hērōdēs made a banquet on his birthday with the Galilaia's [Galilee's] magnates and leaders of a thousand and first men. ²²His daughter, Hērōdias, entering and dancing . . . she pleased Hērōdēs and the ones reclining together. The king said to the girl, "Ask me whatever you want, and I will give to you." ²³He made an oath to her that "Whatever you ask, I will give to you up to half my empire." ²⁴Exiting, she said to her mother, "What am I to ask?" She said, "[Ask for] the Yōannēs the dipping one's head." ²⁵Entering suddenly with seriousness to the king, she asked, saying, "I want—right now—that you give to me on a tray Yōannēs the Dipper's head."

²⁶Being grieved, the king, because of the oath and the reclining ones, did not want to reject her. ²⁷Suddenly, commissioning, the king ordered the executioner to bring his head. Departing, he decapitated him in the prison. ²⁸He brought his head on a tray and gave it to the girl, and the girl gave it to her mother.

²⁹Hearing, his Apprentices came and lifted his corpse and placed it in a tomb.

³⁰The Commissioners assembled with Yēsous, and they declared to him everything whatever they did and whatever they taught.

Yēsous feeds more than five thousand

³¹He says to them, "You yourselves come by yourselves to a wilderness place and rest a little." For there were many coming and going away, and they did not even have a good season to eat. ³²They departed in the boat to a wilderness place by themselves. ³³They saw them going away, and many perceived and were running there on foot from all the cities and they approached him.

³⁴Exiting [the boat], he saw a large crowd and he empathized with them because they were *like sheep without a shepherd* and he began to teach them many things. ³⁵The hour was already late . . . approaching him, his Apprentices were saying that "This is a wilderness place and the hour is already late. ³⁶Loosen them so that, departing to the encircling fields and villages, they can purchase for themselves something they may eat." ³⁷Responding, he said to them, "You give them [something] to eat." They say to him, "Departing, how are we to purchase two hundred dēnaria worth of bread? Are we to give to them to eat?" ³⁸He says to them, "You have how many breads? Go away, see!" Knowing, they say, "Five and two fishes." ³⁹He ordered them all to recline, dining-group by dining-group, on the green grass. ⁴⁰They sat down, group by group, by ten and by fifty. ⁴¹Taking the five breads and the two fishes, looking up to heaven, he blessed and snapped the breads and he was giving to the Apprentices so they might present [the pieces] before them, and he divided the two fishes for all. ⁴²They all ate and were satisfied, ⁴³and they lifted the broken pieces—twelve flowing-over baskets and [they lifted what was left] from the fishes. ⁴⁴The ones eating the breads were five thousand men.

Yēsous walks on water

⁴⁵Suddenly, he compelled his Apprentices to board down into the boat and to go ahead to Beyond the Yordanēs to Bēthsaïda until he loosens the crowd. ⁴⁶Saying farewell to them, he departed to the mountain to pray. ⁴⁷It was evening . . . the boat was in the middle of the Sea, and he was alone on the land. ⁴⁸Seeing them tortured in the driving—for the wind was against them—about the fourth watch of the night [early a.m.] he comes to them, walking around on the Sea. He wanted to pass them by. ⁴⁹Seeing him walking around on the Sea, they thought that it was a phantom, and they yelled. ⁵⁰For they all knew him and were agitated. Suddenly, he spoke with them and says to them, "Be courageous! I am. Don't be scared!" ⁵¹He ascended to them into the boat. The wind ceased. They were greatly, aboundingly beside themselves among themselves. ⁵²(For they did not understand the breads, but their hearts were petrified.)

Yēsous delivers

⁵³Crossing to Beyond the Yordanēs on the land they came to Gennēsaret, and they were anchored. ⁵⁴They exited from the boat . . . suddenly, perceiving him, ⁵⁵they were running around that whole region and they began to carry on mats those who were in a bad way—where they were hearing he is. ⁵⁶Wherever he was journeying into villages or into cities or into fields, they placed the weak ones in the squares, and they were begging him that they might even touch the tassels of his robe, and whoever touched him they were being delivered.

Yēsous and human conventions

7 The Observant [Pharisees] and some of the Covenant-Code scholars [scribes] assemble to him, coming from Yerosoluma [Jerusalem]. ²Seeing some of his Apprentices eating the breads with common hands, that is, unwashed ...

(³For the Observant and all the Youdaians [Judeans, Jews]—if they don't wash the hands "cupped" they don't eat, grabbing the convention of the Elders. ⁴[Returning] from the square, if they don't dip, they don't eat. And many other [conventions] they received to grab—dipping cups and measuring vessels and copper kettles.)

⁵... the Observant and Code scholars were asking him, "Why do your Apprentices not walk around consistent with the convention of the Elders, but are eating the bread with common hands?" ⁶He said to them, "Ēsaïas [Isaiah] prophesied beautifully about you masked ones, as it's written that,

> This people honors me with the lips
> But their heart is a far distance from me.
> ⁷They revere me in vain
> Teaching teachings that are human
>   prescriptions.

⁸Releasing God's command, they grab the convention of humans." ⁹He was saying to them, "You 'beautifully' reject God's command so you may keep your convention. ¹⁰For Mōüses [Moses] said, *Honor your father and your mother*, and *the denouncer of father or mother—let his life end in death*. ¹¹You say, 'If a human says to father or mother, *Korban* (which is *donation*) what you gain from me,' ¹²you no longer release him to do anything for the father or the mother—¹³annulling God's word for your convention which you have given over. You do many similar conventions."

¹⁴Again calling the crowd, he was saying to them, "All hear me and understand! ¹⁵There is nothing outside a human journeying into the person that is able to make the person common. But the matters journeying out of a human are matters that make a human common."ᵃ

¹⁷When he entered into a house from the crowd, his Apprentices were asking him about the analogy, ¹⁸and he says to them, "So, are you also ignorant? Do you not know that everything from the outside journeying into the human isn't able to make the person common—¹⁹because it doesn't journey into his heart but into the stomach and journeys out into the sewer?" (Cleaning all foods.)

²⁰He was saying that

> "What journeys out of the human, that makes the human common. ²¹For from within the heart of the human bad deliberations journey out—
>
> sexual immoralities,
> thefts,
> murders,
> ²²adulteries,
> wanting more and more,
> evils,
> disguise,
> flaunting sensuality,
> evil eye,
> insult,
> status-mongering,
> imprudence.
>
> ²³All these evils journey out from within and make the human common."

Yēsous and a Gentile woman

²⁴From there, arising, he departed into the regions of Turos [Tyre]. Entering into a house, he did not want anyone to know and was unable to escape notice. ²⁵But suddenly, a woman hearing about him, whose little daughter was having a contaminated spirit, coming, fell down at his feet. ²⁶(The woman was a Hellēnis [Hellene, Greek], Surophoinikissa [Syro-Phoenician] by family.) She was asking him that he might toss out the demon from her daughter. ²⁷He says to her, "Permit the children first to be satisfied, for it isn't beautiful to take the children's bread and toss it to the puppies." ²⁸She responded and says to him, "Lord, even the puppies below the table eat from the children's crumbs." ²⁹He said to her, "Because of this word, go away; the demon has exited from your daughter."

³⁰Departing into her house, she found the child, tossed down on the cot, and the demon had exited.

ᵃThe good manuscripts don't include 6:16.

Yēsous heals

31 Again exiting from the regions of Turos, he came through Sidōn to the Galilaia Sea [Sea of Galilee]—into the middle of the Dekapolis [Decapolis]. **32** They carry to him a deaf and aphasic man, and they beg him to place the hand on him. **33** Taking him by himself away from the crowd, he tossed his fingers into his ears and, spitting, touched his tongue **34** and, looking into the heaven, he groaned and says to him, "*Ephphatha!*" that is, "Be opened!" **35** Immediately, his hearing was opened and his tongue's bond was loosened and he was speaking properly. **36** He ordered them that they tell no one. The more he was ordering them, the more excessively they were announcing. **37** They were being shocked beyond excess, saying, "He has done all things beautifully. He makes the deaf ones to hear and the aphasic to speak."

Yēsous feeds more than four thousand

8 In those days, again . . . there is a large crowd and not have anything they may eat . . . calling the Apprentices, he says to them, **2** "I empathize with this crowd. They are attached to me already for three days and they don't have anything they can eat. **3** If I loosen them fasting to their house, they will faint on the path, and some of them have come from afar." **4** His Apprentices responded to him that "From what source is someone here able to satisfy these with breads in the wilderness?" **5** He was asking them, "How many breads do you have?" They said, "Seven." **6** He orders the crowd to lie down on the land. Taking the seven breads, giving thanks, he cracked [it] and was giving [them] to his Apprentices so they could present [them], and they presented [them] to the crowd. **7** They were having some little fishes and, blessing them, he said to present these also. **8** They ate and were satisfied, and they lifted an overflow of pieces, seven big baskets. **9** There were about four thousand. He loosened them.

10 Suddenly, boarding down into the boat with his Apprentices, he came to the area of Dalmanoutha [Dalmanutha].

Yēsous and an authenticating sign

11 The Observant [Pharisees] exited and began to dispute with him, pursuing from him an authenticating sign from heaven, testing him. **12** Groaning in his spirit, he says, "Why does this generation pursue an authenticating sign? This is true to say to you: if an authenticating sign will be given to this generation." **13** Releasing them, again boarding, he departed to Beyond the Yordanēs [Jordan].

Yēsous and breads

14 They forgot to take breads—except for one bread, they did not have [any] with them in the boat. **15** He ordered them, saying, "See! Beware the Observants' yeast and Hērōdēs' yeast!" **16** They were deliberating to one another that they don't have breads. **17** Knowing, he says to them, "Why deliberate that you don't have breads? Do you not yet know nor understand? Do you have your heart petrified? **18** *Having eyes do you not see? Having ears do you not hear?* Do you not remember **19** when I cracked the five breads for five thousand—how many baskets full of pieces you lifted?" They say to him, "Twelve." **20** "When [I broke] the seven for four thousand, how many big baskets of overflowing pieces did you lift?" They say, "Seven." **21** He was saying to them, "Do you not yet understand?"

Yēsous heals a sightless man

22 They come into Bēthsaïda. They bring to him a sightless man and beg him to touch him. **23** Taking hold of the sightless man's hand, he brought him outside the village and, spitting into his eyes, placing the hands on him, he was asking him, "Do you see anything?" **24** Looking up, he was saying, "I see humans, that I see [them] as trees walking." **25** Then again he placed the hands on his eyes, and he looked intently, and he was restored and he was observing all things distinctly. **26** He commissioned him to his house, saying, "Don't enter into the village."

Yēsous confessed as Christos

27 Yēsous and his Apprentices exited into the villages of Kaisareia Philippos [Caesarea Philippi]. On the path he was asking his Apprentices, saying to them, "Who do humans say I am?" **28** They said to him, saying that "Yōannēs the Dipper [John the Baptist], others Ēlias [Elijah], and others that [you are] one of the prophets." **29** He asks them, "But you, who do you say I am?" Petros [Peter] responding, says to him, "You are the Christos." ³⁰He rebuked them not to say anything about him.

Yēsous calls to the cross-life

³¹He began to teach them that "It's necessary for the Son of Humanity to suffer much, and to be rejected by the Elders and the Senior Priests and Covenant-Code scholars [scribes], and to be killed, and after three days to rise." ³²He was speaking the word frankly. Petros, taking him in, began to rebuke him. ³³He, turning around and seeing his Apprentices, rebuked Petros and says, "Go away behind me, Satanas [Satan]!, because you are not thinking God's ways but the ways of humans."

³⁴Calling the crowd with his Apprentices, he said to them, "If anyone wants to follow behind me, let the person renounce oneself, lift up one's cross, and let the person follow me. ³⁵For whoever wants to deliver one's self, the person will destroy it; but whoever destroys one's self because of me and the gospel will deliver it. ³⁶For what can a human gain to take advantage of the whole Kosmos and for the person's self to be damaged? ³⁷Or, what does a human give in compensation for one's self? ³⁸For whoever is degraded by me and my words in this adulterous and sinful generation, the Son of Humanity will degrade the person whenever he comes in his Father's splendor with the holy envoys."

9 He was saying to them, "This is true to say to you that: There are some having stood here who will not taste death before they see God's Empire having come in power."

Yēsous glows

²After six days, Yēsous takes Petros [Peter] and Yakōbos [James] and Yōannēs [John] and he guides them up on a high mountain by themselves alone, and he was metamorphosed before them, ³and his robes became glowing bright white—such as a bleacher in the land isn't able so to whiten. ⁴Ēlias [Elijah] with Mōūsēs [Moses] appeared to them, and they were conversing with Yēsous. ⁵Petros, responding, says to Yēsous, "My Greatness [Rabbi], it's beautiful for us to be here. Let us make three tents, one for you, one for Mōūsēs, one for Ēlias." (⁶For he did not know what to respond. For they became scared.) ⁷A cloud came enveloping them, and a voice came out of the cloud, "This is my royal Son, the one loved. Listen to him!" ⁸Unexpectedly, looking around, they no longer saw anyone except Yēsous alone with them.

Yēsous and Ēlias

⁹They're descending from the mountain . . . he ordered them that they narrate what they saw to no one—except when the Son of Humanity arises from among the dead ones. ¹⁰They grabbed the word, disputing among themselves what is "To arise from among the dead ones." ¹¹They were asking him, saying, "Why do the Covenant-Code scholars [scribes] say, 'It's necessary first for Ēlias to come'?" ¹²He said to them, "Indeed, Ēlias, coming first, *restores* all things, yet how is it written about the Son of Humanity that he might suffer many things and be devalued? ¹³But I say this to you, both that Ēlias has come and that they did to him whatever they wanted, just as it's written about him."

Yēsous heals a man's son

¹⁴Coming to the Apprentices, they saw a great crowd around them and Covenant-Code scholars disputing with them. ¹⁵Suddenly, the whole crowd, seeing him, was amazed and, running forward, they were greeting him. ¹⁶He asked them, "Why are you disputing with them?" ¹⁷One from the crowd responded to him, "Teacher, I brought my son to you, having an aphasic spirit. ¹⁸Wherever it prevailed over him, it breaks him apart, and he froths [at the mouth] and grinds the teeth and he stiffens. I said to your Apprentices that they might toss it out, and they did not have strength." ¹⁹Responding, he says to them, "Wow, anti-trusting generation! How long will I be with you? How long will I put up with you? Bring him to me." ²⁰They brought him to him. Seeing him, the spirit suddenly rocked him and, falling on the land, he was rolling, frothing [at the mouth]. ²¹He asked his father, "How long is it since this has happened?" He said, "From childhood. ²²Often it tossed him into fire and into waters to destroy him. But, if you are able, help us, empathizing with us." ²³Yēsous said to him, "That—'if you are able'—all things are able for

the trusting one!" ²⁴Suddenly, crying out, the child's father was saying, "I trust. Help me in my anti-trust!" ²⁵Yēsous, seeing that a crowd is running together, rebuked the contaminating spirit, saying to it, "Aphasic and deaf spirit, I order you: Exit from him and no longer enter into him!" ²⁶Crying out and rocking him often, it exited. He became as a dead man so that many say that he died. ²⁷Yēsous, grabbing his hand, raised him and he rose up. ²⁸[Yēsous] entering into a house . . . his Apprentices were asking him by himself, "Why were we unable to toss it out?" ²⁹He said to them, "This type isn't able to exit in any way except in prayer."

Yēsous predicts his death

³⁰Exiting from there, they were journeying through the Galilaia [Galilee], and he was not wanting that any might know. ³¹For he was teaching his Apprentices and was saying to them that "The Son of Humanity is being given over into human hands, and they will kill him and, being killed, after three days will rise." ³²They were uninformed about the utterance, and they were scared to ask him.

Yēsous instructs on Empire status

³³They came into Kaphar-Naoum [Capernaum]. Being in the house, he was asking them, "What were you deliberating on the path?" ³⁴They were silent, for they were deliberating with one another on the path, "Who is greatest?" ³⁵Sitting, he voiced to the Twelve and says to them, "If someone wants to be first, he will be last of all and servant of all." ³⁶Taking a child, he stood it in their middle and, hugging it, he said to them, ³⁷"Whoever welcomes one of these children in my name, welcomes me. Whoever welcomes me doesn't welcome me but the one who commissioned me."

Yēsous and other exorcists

³⁸Yōannēs said to him, "Teacher, we saw someone tossing out demons in your name and we were prohibiting him because he wasn't following us." ³⁹Yēsous said, "Don't prohibit him. For there is no one who will do power in my name and, quickly, will be able to denounce me. ⁴⁰For the one isn't against us is for us. ⁴¹For whoever gives a cup of water in a name—because you are Christos's—this is true to say that the person will never destroy his wage.

Yēsous and tripping

⁴²Whoever trips one of these little ones who trusts in me . . . it would be beautiful for that person if instead a donkey-driving grinding-stone were draped around that person's neck and tossed into the sea. ⁴³If your hand trips you up, chop it off. It's beautiful for you to enter into life impaired than, having two hands, to depart into the Valley of Destructive Fire [Gehenna], into the Inextinguishable Fire.ᵇ ⁴⁵If your foot trips you up, chop it off. It's beautiful for you to enter into life lame than, having two feet, to be tossed into the Valley of Destructive Fire.ᶜ ⁴⁷If your eye trips you up, toss it out. It's beautiful for you to enter into God's Empire single-eyed than, having two eyes, to be tossed into the Valley of Destructive Fire. ⁴⁸*Where their worm doesn't end a life and the fire isn't snuffed out.*

Yēsous likes salt

⁴⁹For everyone will be salted in fire. ⁵⁰Salt is beautiful, but if salt becomes unsalty, how will it be seasoned? Have salt among yourselves. Be at peace with one another.

Yēsous instructs about divorce

10 Arising from there, he comes into the regions of Youdaia [Judea] and Beyond the Yordanēs [Jordan River], again the crowds journey to him and, as was custom, again he was teaching them. ²The Observant [Pharisees], approaching, were asking him, "Is it observant for a man to loosen his wife," testing him. ³Responding, he said to them, "What did Mōüsēs [Moses] order for you?" ⁴They said, "Mōüsēs permitted [for us] to write *a divorce document* and to loosen." ⁵Yēsous said to them, "He wrote to you this order because of your hard-heartedness. ⁶From the beginning of creation he *made them male and female.* ⁷*Because of this a human will abandon his father and the mother and will be joined to his*

ᵇThe good manuscripts don't include 9:44.
ᶜThe good manuscripts don't include 9:46.

woman, ⁸*and the two will be one flesh*. So that they are no longer two but one flesh. ⁹Therefore, what God connected let not a human separate."

¹⁰Again, in the house, the Apprentices were asking him about this. ¹¹He says to them, "Whoever loosens his woman and marries another, adulterates against her. ¹²If she, loosening her man, marries another, she adulterates [against him]."

Yēsous blesses children

¹³They were presenting children to him so he might touch them. The Apprentices rebuked them. ¹⁴Yēsous, seeing, was angered and said to them, "Release the children to come to me, don't prohibit them, for God's Empire is of such ones. ¹⁵This is true to say to you: Whoever doesn't welcome God's Empire as a child, cannot ever enter into it." ¹⁶Hugging them, he was blessing [them], placing the hands on them.

Yēsous challenges a life of possessions

¹⁷He is journeying out into the path . . . a person, running to him and genuflecting to him, was asking him, "Good Teacher, what might I do so I might inherit Era Life?" ¹⁸Yēsous said to him, "Why do you call me 'good'? No one is 'good' except the one God. ¹⁹You know the orders,

> Don't murder,
> Don't adulterate,
> Don't thieve,
> Don't false witness,
> Don't deprive,
> Honor your father and mother."

²⁰He said to him, "Teacher, I myself guarded all these from youth." ²¹Yēsous, gazing at him, loved him and said to him, "One thing lacks for you: Go away! Whatever you have, sell! Give to the beggars and you will have a treasure chest in heaven. Come follow me!" ²²He, growing gloomy at the word, departed, grieving, for he was one having many acquisitions.

²³Yēsous, looking around, says to his Apprentices, "How difficult [will it be for] those having monies to enter into God's Empire!" ²⁴The Apprentices were amazed at his words. Yēsous, again responding, says to them, "Children, how difficult it is to enter into God's Empire! ²⁵It's easier for a camel to cross through a needle's eye than for the wealthy to enter God's Empire." ²⁶They were exceedingly shocked, saying to themselves, "Who is able to be delivered?" ²⁷Yēsous, observing them, says, "With humans this is impossible, but not with God. For all things are possible with God."

²⁸Petros [Peter] began to say to him, "Look! We released all things and have followed you." ²⁹Yēsous said, "This is true to say to you: There is no one who released house or brothers or sisters or mother or father or children or fields—because of me and because of the gospel . . . ³⁰if that person doesn't receive one hundred times more now, in this season— houses and brothers and sisters and mothers and children and fields with chasings, and [will receive] in the Coming Era, Era Life.

³¹Many first ones will be last [ones] and the last [ones] first [ones]."

Yēsous predicts his death again

³²They were in path ascending into Yierosoluma [Jerusalem], and Yēsous was leading them, and they were amazed, and the Apprentices were scared. Again, taking along the Twelve, he began to tell them the things about to coalesce for him, that: ³³"Look! We are ascending into Yierosoluma, and the Son of Humanity will be given over to the Senior Priests and to the Covenant-Code scholars [scribes], and they will condemn him to death, and they will give him over to the ethnic groups ³⁴and they will mock him and they will spit on him and they will lash him and they will kill, and after three days he will arise."

Yēsous and the mother of two Apprentices

³⁵Yakōbos [James] and Yōannēs [John], Zebedaios's [Zebedee's] sons, journey to him, saying to him, "Teacher, we want that whatever we ask you, you may do for us." ³⁶He said to them, "What do you want that I may do for you?" ³⁷They said to him, "Give to us that we may sit in your splendor, one at your right and one at your left." ³⁸Yēsous said to them, "You don't know what you ask. Are you able to drink the cup that I drink, or to be dipped with the dipping in which I am dipped?" ³⁹They said to him, "We are able." Yēsous said to them, "You will indeed drink the cup that I drink, and you

will be dipped in the dipping that I am dipped. ⁴⁰But this sitting at my right or my left isn't mine to give, but for whom it has been prepared."

⁴¹The ten, hearing, began to be angered about Yakōbos and Yōannēs. ⁴²Calling them, Yēsous says to them, "You know that the ones seeming to rule the ethnic groups overrule them, and their great ones overpower them. ⁴³It will not be so among you: Instead, whoever wants to become great among you will be your servant, ⁴⁴and whoever wants to be first among you will be everyone's slave. ⁴⁵For the Son of Humanity did not come to be served but to serve and to give his self as liberation price for many."

Yēsous gives sight to a sightless man

⁴⁶They come into Yiericho [Jericho]. He and his Apprentices and an adequate crowd were journeying from Yerichō . . . the son of Timaios, Bar-Timaios [Bartimaeous], sightless, a supplicant, was sitting along the path. ⁴⁷Hearing that it's Yēsous, the Nazarēnos [Nazarene], he began to cry out and to say, "Dauid's [David's] Son, Yēsous, show compassion on me!" ⁴⁸Many were rebuking him so he might be silenced. He was crying out all the more, "Dauid's Son, show compassion on me!" ⁴⁹Standing, Yēsous said, "Call him!" They called the sightless man, saying to him, "Be courageous! Rise up! He calls you." ⁵⁰Tossing away his robe, leaping up, he came to Yēsous. ⁵¹Yēsous, responding to him, said, "What do you want that I do for you?" The sightless man said to him, "My Greatness [Rabbi], that I may see again." ⁵²Yēsous said to him, "Go away! Your trust has delivered you." Suddenly he saw again and he was following him on the path.

Yēsous enters Yierosoluma

11 When they're coming close to Yierosoluma [Jerusalem], to Bēth-Phagē [Bethphage] and Bēth-Ania [Bethany],ᵈ to the mountain of olives [Mount Olivet], he commissions two of his Apprentices ²and says to them, "Go away into the village opposite of you, and suddenly, journeying into it, you will find a tied-up foal, upon which no human has yet sat. Loosen it and bring. ³If someone says to you, 'Why do you do this?' say, 'The Lord has a need for it. Suddenly, he commissions him [back] here again.'" ⁴They departed and found a tied-up foal at the door outside at the street, and they loosen it. ⁵Some of those standing there were saying to them, "What are you doing, loosening the foal?" ⁶They said to them just as Yēsous said, and they released them. ⁷They bring the foal to Yēsous, and they toss their robes on it, and he sat on it. ⁸Many spread their robes into the path, others [spread on the path] straw, cut from the fields. ⁹The ones leading and the ones following were crying out,

> *Hosanna!*
> *Blessed is the one coming in name of Lord.*
> ¹⁰*Blessed is the coming Empire of Dauid,*
>   *our father.*
> *Hosanna in the highest levels.*

Yēsous in the temple

¹¹He entered into Yierosoluma, into the temple and, looking around at everything . . . being already the evening hour . . . he exited to Bēth-Ania with the Twelve.

¹²On the next day . . . they're exiting from Bēth-Ania . . . he hungered. ¹³Seeing from a distance a fig tree having leaves, he came [to it to see] then if he will find something [growing] on it and, coming, he found nothing on it except leaves. (For the season for figs was not [yet].) ¹⁴Responding, he said to it, "May no one any longer eat fruit from you into the Era!" His Apprentices were listening.

¹⁵They come into Yierosoluma. Entering into the temple he began to toss out the sellers and the purchasers in the temple, and he overturned the tables of the moneychangers and the chairs of those selling doves. ¹⁶He was not releasing so that anyone could carry a vessel through the temple. ¹⁷He was teaching and saying to them, "Is it not written that *My house will be called a prayer house for all the ethnic groups*? But you have made it a *bandits' cave*." ¹⁸The Senior Priests and the Covenant-Code scholars [scribes] heard and were pursuing how they might destroy him. For they were scared of him, for the crowd was shocked at his teaching. ¹⁹Whenever it became evening, he journeyed outside the city.

ᵈBeth-Phage means "House of Unripe Figs" and Beth-Ania probably "House of the Poor."

[20]Journeying early, they saw the fig tree dried from the root. [21]Petros [Peter], having remembered, says to him, "My Greatness [Rabbi], Look! The fig tree that you cursed has dried out." [22]Responding, Yēsous says to them, "Have trust in God. [23]This is true to say, that whoever says to this mountain, 'Be lifted and be tossed into the Sea,' and doesn't mentally waver in his heart but trusts that what he speaks occurs, it will be for him. [24]Because this is true I say to you, Whatever you pray and ask, trust that you received, and it will be for you. [25]Whenever you stand praying release what you have against someone so also your Father, the one in the Heavens, may release you from your wrongs."[e]

Yēsous and authority

[27]They come again into Yierosoluma . . . he's walking around in the temple . . . the Senior Priests and the Covenant-Code scholars and the Elders come to him [28]and they were saying to him, "By what sort of authority do you do these things? Or, who gave to you this authority that you do these things?" [29]Yēsous said to them, "I will also ask you one word, and you respond to me, and I will also tell you by what sort of authority I do these things: [30]The dipping, Yōannes's [John's]—was it from heaven or from humans? Respond to me!" [31]They were deliberating with themselves, saying, "If we say 'From heaven,' he will say, 'Why then did you not declare allegiance to him?' [32]But if we say 'From humans'?" . . . they were scared of the crowd. (For everyone held that Yōannēs really was a prophet.) [33]Responding to Yēsous, they say, "We don't know." Yēsous says to them, "Neither do I say to you by what sort of authority I do these things."

Yēsous tells a story about bad vineyard workers

12 He began to speak to them in analogies. "A human planted a vineyard and encircled it with a hedge and dug a winepress and formed a tower and leased it to farmers and traveled abroad. [2]He commissioned a slave to the farmers at the season so he could take the vineyard's fruit from the farmers. [3]Taking him, they beat and commissioned him away empty. [4]Again, he commissioned another slave to them. That one they beat on the head and dishonored. [5]He commissioned another. That one they killed. [He sent] many others—beating some, killing some. [6]He still had one, a son, one loved. He commissioned him last to them, saying that 'They will defer to my son.' [7]Those farmers said to themselves that 'This is the heir. Come! Let us kill him and the inheritance will be ours.' [8]Taking, they killed him and tossed him out of the vineyard. [9]What, therefore, will the vineyard's lord do? He will come and destroy the farmers and he will give the vineyard to others. [10]Have you not read this writing:

A stone the formers rejected . . .
This [stone] became the foundation stone.
[11]*This happened from the Lord*
And it's a stunner in our eyes?"

[12]They were pursuing to grab him, and they were scared of the crowd, for they knew that he told this analogy about them. Releasing him, they departed.

Yēsous and Kaisar

[13]They commission to him some of the Observant [Pharisees] and Hērōdianoi [Herodians] that they might to catch him in a word. [14]Coming, they say to him, "Teacher, we know that you are true and no one is a worry to you, for you don't see into the face of a human but you teach God's path in truth. Is it observant to give a tax to Kaisar [Caesar] or not? Do we give or not give?" [15]He, knowing their mask-wearing, said to them, "Why do you test me? Bring to me a dēnarion that I may see." [16]They brought, and he says to them, "This image and inscription—whose is it?" They said to him, "Kaisar's." [17]Yēsous said to them, "Pay back to Kaisar what is Kaisar's, and to God what is God's." They were stunned at him.

Yēsous and Elites

[18]Elites [Sadducees] come to him—who say there is no resurrection—and were asking him, saying, [19]"Teacher, Mōüsēs [Moses] wrote to us that *If a brother of someone dies and abandons a woman and doesn't release a child,* that *his*

---

[e]The good manuscripts don't include 14:26.

brother receives the woman and raises up seed for his brother. ²⁰There were seven brothers. The first received a woman and, dying, did not release seed. ²¹The second received her and he died, not abandoning seed. The third similarly. ²²The seventh did not release seed. Last of all the woman also died. ²³In the resurrection, whenever they arise, of which of them will she be a woman?" (The seven had her as a woman.) ²⁴Yēsous said to them, "Because this is true, are you not deceived, understanding neither the writings nor God's power? ²⁵For whenever they arise from among the dead ones, they don't marry or get married, but they are like envoys in the heavens. ²⁶Concerning the dead ones, that they are raised, have you not read in Mōūsēs's book: at the bush how God said to him, saying, *I am the God of Abra'am and God of Yisa'ak* [Isaac] *and the God of Yakōb* [Jacob]? ²⁷He isn't God of the dead ones but of the living ones. You are much deceived."

Yēsous—his creed

²⁸Approaching, one of the Covenant-Code scholars [scribes], hearing them disputing, knowing that he responded beautifully to them, asked him, "Which is the first order of all?" ²⁹Yēsous responded that "The first is *Hear, Yisraēl* [Israel], *the Lord our God is one Lord.* ³⁰*You will love the Lord, your God, from your whole heart and from your whole self and from your whole intelligence and from your whole strength.* ³¹The second is this: *You will love your neighbor as yourself.* Greater than these isn't another order." ³²A Code scholar said to him, "Beautiful, Teacher. You said in truth that *One is* [God] *and there isn't another aside from him.* ³³And, *to love him from the whole heart and from the whole understanding and from the whole strength*, and *to love the neighbor as oneself*—[this is] abounding beyond all burnt offerings and sacrifices." ³⁴Yēsous, seeing him, that he responded intelligently, said to him, "You are not far from God's Empire." No one dared any longer to ask him.

Yēsous as Dauid's son

³⁵Responding, Yēsous was saying, teaching in the temple. "How do the Covenant-Code scholars say that the Christos is Dauid's [David's] son? ³⁶Dauid himself said in the Holy Spirit, *The Lord said to my Lord: Sit from my right until I place your enemies under your feet.* ³⁷Dauid himself calls him 'Lord,' and how then can he be his son?" The large crowd was hearing him with pleasure.

Yēsous warns about the Covenant-Code scholars

³⁸In his teaching he was saying, "Beware the Covenant-Code scholars, those wanting to walk around in stoles and [wanting] greetings in the squares ³⁹and first-status seats in the assembly halls and first-status positions at the banquets . . . ⁴⁰the ones gobbling up widows' houses and praying at length in pretension . . . these will receive 'abundance' in judgment."

Yēsous, speaking of widows

⁴¹Sitting across from the treasury box, he was observing how the crowd tosses bronze into the treasury box. Many wealthy were tossing many [coins]. ⁴²Coming, one begging widow tossed two lepta [small copper coins], which is a kodrantēs [bronze coin]. ⁴³Calling his Apprentices, he said to them, "This is true to say to you that, this widow, the begging one, tossed more than all those tossing into the treasury box. ⁴⁴For they all tossed from their overflow, but she tossed all she had from her lack—her whole life."

Yēsous and the coming disaster

13 He's journeying out of the temple . . . one of his Apprentices says to him, "Teacher, Look! What stones and what formations!" ²Yēsous said to him, "Do you see these great formations? Stone on stone will never be released that will not be demolished."

³He's sitting in the mountain of olives [Mount Olivet] across from the temple . . . Petros [Peter] and Yakōbos [James] and Yōannēs [John] and Andreas [Andrew] were asking him by himself, ⁴"Tell us, when will these things be? What is the authenticating sign when all these things are about to be completed?"

⁵Yēsous began to say to them, "Beware that someone not deceive you! ⁶Many will come in my name, saying that 'I am,' and they will deceive many. ⁷Whenever you hear about wars and war reports, don't be alarmed! It's

necessary to happen, but [this is] not yet the completion. ⁸For ethnic group will be raised against ethnic group and empire against empire, and there will be earthquakes from place to place and there will be famines. These are the beginning of labor pains.

⁹You beware of yourselves! They will give you over to the Central Councils, and you will be beaten in assembly halls and you will be stood up before governors and kings because of me—as a witness to them. ¹⁰First it's necessary for the gospel to be announced to all the ethnic groups. ¹¹Whenever they lead you, giving over, don't be pre-disturbed what you might say, but whatever is given to you in that hour—this you speak. For you are not the ones speaking but the Holy Spirit. ¹²Sibling will give over sibling, and a father a child; and children will rise up in rebellion against parents and they will kill them. ¹³You will be hated by all because of my name, but the one resilient to the completion—this person will be delivered.

¹⁴Whenever you see *the desecrating abomination* standing where it isn't necessary—let the reader know—then let those who are in Youdaia [Judea] flee to the mountains, ¹⁵let not the one on the terrace descend nor let the person enter anything to lift [things] from his house, ¹⁶and let not the one in the field return back to lift his robe. ¹⁷Oy! for women who have a child in the womb and ones nursing in those days! ¹⁸Pray that it not be in a stormy season! ¹⁹For those days will be trouble such that have not so occurred from the beginning of the creation, that God created, until now and that ever may be. ²⁰Unless the Lord cuts short those days, all flesh could not be delivered. But because of the elect ones, whom he elected, he cut short those days.

²¹Then, if someone says to you, 'Look! The Christos is here, or look there,' don't trust! ²²False christoses and false prophets will be raised, and they will give authenticating signs and omens for deceiving—if possible—even the elect ones. ²³You beware! I have told you all things in advance.

²⁴But in those days after that trouble,

*The sun will be darkened,
And the moon will not give its light,*

²⁵*And the stars will be falling* from the heaven,
And the powers, the ones in the heavens,
   will be shaken.

²⁶Then they will see *the Son of Humanity coming on the clouds* with much power *and splendor*. ²⁷Then he will commission the envoys, and he will assemble his elect from the four winds—from the end of the land to the end of the heaven.

²⁸Be apprenticed about an analogy from the fig tree: Whenever its branch is already tender and the leaves sprout, you know the summer is close. ²⁹So also you—whenever you see these things happening, you know that it's close, at the doors. ³⁰This is true to say to you: this generation will never pass away until all these events occur. The heaven and the land will pass away, but my words will not pass away. ³²About that day or hour, no one knows—neither the envoys in heaven nor the royal Son, except the Father. ³³Beware! Watch! For you don't know when it's the season. ³⁴As a traveling human, releasing his household and giving authority to his slaves, to each his work, ordered his doorkeeper that he stay awake. ³⁵Therefore, be awake! For you don't know when the house lord comes—at evening or at midnight or when the cock crows or early. ³⁶May he, coming unexpectedly, not find you sleeping. ³⁷What I say to you, I say to all: Be awake!"

Yēsous predicts his death

14 The Pascha [Passover] and the Flatbreads [Unleavened Bread] Feast are after two days. The Senior Priests and the Covenant-Code scholars [scribes] were pursuing how, grabbing him in disguise, they might kill him, ²for they were saying, "Not at the Feast so there will not be a clamor from the people."

³He's in Beth-Ania [Bethany] in Simōn the scaly's house, he's reclining . . . a woman came, having an alabaster vase of fragrant ointment—pure and costly, breaking the vase, she poured it on his head. ⁴Some were angry among themselves: "Why has this destruction of fragrance happened? ⁵For it was possible for the fragrance to have been sold for above three hundred dēnaria and to be given to the beggars."

They snorted at her.

⁶Yēsous said, "Release her. Why present labor for her? She has worked a beautiful work in me, ⁷for you always have beggars with you, and whenever you want you are able to do good for them, but you don't always have me. ⁸She did what she had. She 'fragranced' my body beforehand to prepare me for burial. ⁹This is true to say to you: Wherever the gospel is announced into the whole Kosmos, what she did will be spoken about in her memory."

¹⁰Youdas the Dagger Man [Judas Iscariot], who is one of the Twelve, departed to the Senior Priests so he could give him over to them. ¹¹The ones hearing [this] rejoiced and pledged to give silver to him. He was pursuing how he might give him over at a good season.

Yēsous celebrates Pascha

¹²On the first day of Flatbreads, when the Pascha [lamb] was being slaughtered, his Apprentices say to him, "Where do you want that we, departing, prepare that you may eat the Pascha?" ¹³He commissions two of his Apprentices and says to them, "Go away into the city. A human will meet you carrying a water jug. Follow him. ¹⁴Wherever he enters, say to the house master that 'The Teacher says, Where is my guest room where I may eat the Pascha with my Apprentices?' ¹⁵He will exhibit to you a large upper room, having been already furnished. Prepare [it] there for us." ¹⁶The Apprentices exited and came to the city and found [it] just as he said to them, and they prepared the Pascha.

¹⁷It was evening . . . he comes with the Twelve. ¹⁸They're reclining and eating . . . Yēsous said, "This is true to say to you: One of you will give me over, the one eating with me." ¹⁹They began to grieve and to say to him one by one: "It isn't I, is it?" ²⁰He said to them, "One of the Twelve, the one dipping in with me into the bowl. ²¹Because the Son of Humanity goes away as it's written about him, but Oy! on that human through whom the Son of Humanity is given over. It would be beautiful for him if that human was not given a life."

²²They're eating . . . taking bread, blessing, he cracked [it] and gave to them and said, "Take. This is my body." ²³Taking a cup, thanking, he gave to them, and they all drank from it. ²⁴He said to them, "This is my Covenant blood, poured out for many. ²⁵This is true to say to you: I will no longer drink of the produce of the vine until that day whenever I drink it anew in God's Empire." ²⁶Singing a hymn, they exited to the mountain of olives [Mount Olivet].

Yēsous predicts Petros's denials

²⁷Yēsous says to them that "You all will be tripped up because it's written,

> I will beat the shepherd,
> And the shepherd's sheep will be scattered.

²⁸But after my arising, I will precede you to the Galilaia [Galilee]." ²⁹Petros [Peter] said to him, "Even if all are tripped up—but not I." ³⁰Yēsous says to him, "This is true to say to you that: You, today, on this night, before the voicing twice by the rooster you will deny me three times." ³¹He was speaking excessively, "If it's necessary for me to die with you, I will never deny you." All were saying similarly.

Yēsous given over in Gethsēmani

³²They come into an area, of which the name is Geth-sēmani [Gethsemane], and he says to his Apprentices, "Sit here while I pray." ³³He takes Petros and Yakōbos [James] and Yōannēs [John] with him, he began to be amazed and discomforted. ³⁴He says to them, "*My self is deeply grieved* to the point of death. Remain here and be awake." ³⁵Proceeding a little ways, he was falling on the land and he was praying that, if possible, the hour might pass him by. ³⁶He was saying, "Abba, the Father, all things are possible for you. May this cup be taken from me. But not want I want but what you [want]." ³⁷He comes and finds them sleeping, and he says to Petros, "Simōn, are you sleeping? Are you not strong enough to be awake for one hour? ³⁸Be awake and pray so that you don't come into the test. The spirit is eager but the flesh is weak." ³⁹Again, departing, he prayed, saying the same word. ⁴⁰Coming again, he found them sleeping—their eyes were very heavy—and they did not know what they might respond to him. ⁴¹He comes the third time and says to them, "Sleep the remaining [time] and rest yourselves! Stay away. The hour came. Look! The Son of Humanity is given over into the hands of

sinners. ⁴²Be raised, let's go. Look! The one giving me over has come close."

⁴³Suddenly, he's still speaking . . . Youdas [Judas], one of the Twelve, arrives and with him a crowd with long knives and clubs—from the Senior Priests and the Covenant-Code scholars [scribes] and the Elders. ⁴⁴The one giving him over had given to them a signal, saying, "The one I kiss—he is the one. Grab him and lead him away securely." ⁴⁵Coming suddenly, approaching him, he says, "My Greatness [Rabbi]," and he kissed him. ⁴⁶They tossed hands on him and grabbed him. ⁴⁷One of those who had been standing there, drawing the long knife, struck the Senior Priest's slave and sliced off his ear.

⁴⁸Responding, Yēsous said to them, "You exit with long knives and clubs to take me as if for a bandit. ⁴⁹Daily I was in the temple teaching and you did not grab me—but that the writings may be filled out." ⁵⁰Releasing him, they all fled. ⁵¹Some young man was following with him, covering his nakedness with a fine cloth, and they grab him. ⁵²Abandoning his fine cloth, he fled naked.

Yēsous, Petros, and a trial before the Senior Priest

⁵³They led Yēsous away to the Senior Priest, and all the Senior Priests and the Elders and the Covenant-Code scholars assemble together. ⁵⁴Petros followed him at a distance into the Senior Priest's inner enclosure and was sitting with the subordinates and warming himself in the light.

⁵⁵The Senior Priests and the whole Central Council were pursuing witness against Yēsous to kill him, and they were not finding. ⁵⁶For many were false witnessing against him, and the witnesses were not equal. ⁵⁷Some, standing up, were falsely witnessing against him, saying ⁵⁸that "We heard him saying that 'I will demolish this handmade sanctuary and I will form another not handmade after three days.'" ⁵⁹Not even in this manner was their witness equal. ⁶⁰Rising up in the middle, the Senior Priest asked Yēsous, saying, "Do you have nothing to respond about what these are accusing you?" ⁶¹He was silent and did not respond anything. Again, the Senior Priest was asking him and says to him, "Are you the Christos, the Son of the Blessed One?"

⁶²Yēsous said, "I am. You will see *the Son of Humanity sitting at the Power's right and coming with heaven's clouds.*" ⁶³The Senior Priest, ripping his shirts, says, "Why do we still have a need of witnesses? ⁶⁴You heard the insult [of God]. What does it appear to you?" All condemned him to be guilty of death. ⁶⁵Some began to spit at him and to cover his face and to beat him and to say to him, "Prophesy!" The subordinates took him with slaps.

⁶⁶Petros is below in the enclosure . . . one of the Senior Priest's servant-girls comes ⁶⁷and, seeing Petros warming himself, observing him says, "You were with Yēsous the Nazarēnos [Nazarene]." ⁶⁸He denied, saying, "You neither know nor comprehend what you are saying." He exited out into the enclosure foyer [and the rooster voiced]. ⁶⁹The servant-girl, seeing him, began again to say to the ones standing near that "This man is of them." ⁷⁰Again, he was denying. After a little while, again, the ones standing near were saying to Petros, "Truly, you are of them. For you are a Galilaios [Galilean]." ⁷¹He began to curse and to make an oath that "I don't know this man of whom you speak." ⁷²Suddenly, the rooster voiced a second time. Petros remembered the utterance as Yēsous said to him that "Before the rooster's voicing twice you will deny me three times." Tossing [himself] down, he was wailing.

Yēsous on trial before Pilatos

15 Suddenly, early in the morning, the Senior Priests with the Elders and the Covenant-Code scholars [scribes] and the whole Central Council making a council, binding Yēsous, they led him out and handed him over to Pilatos [Pilate]. ²Pilatos asked him, "Are you the king over the Youdaians [Judeans, Jews]?" Responding, he says to him, "You say." ³The Senior Priests were accusing him of many things. ⁴Pilatos, again, was asking him, saying, "Do you not respond anything? Look how much they are accusing you!" ⁵Yēsous no longer responded anything, so that Pilatos was stunned.

⁶At each feast, he loosened to them one prisoner whom they requested. ⁷There was one named Bar-Abbas [Barabbas, "son of the father"], bound with the anarchists—who in the anarchy had done murder.

⁸Ascending, the crowd began to ask just as he was doing for them. ⁹Pilatos responded to them, saying, "Do you want that I should loosen for you the king over the Youdaians?" (¹⁰For he knew that the Senior Priests had handed him over because of envy.) ¹¹The Senior Priests agitated the crowd that, instead, he would loosen Bar-Abbas to them. ¹²Pilatos, again, responding, was saying to them, "Therefore, what do you want that I to do with him you call 'King over the Youdaians'?" ¹³They again cried out, "Crucify him!" ¹⁴Pilatos was saying to them, "For what? What bad thing did he do?" They loudly cried out, "Crucify him!" ¹⁵Pilatos, deciding what was adequate to do for the crowd, loosened Bar-Abbas to them, and they handed Yēsous over, whipping, that he would be crucified.

Yēsous degraded

¹⁶The soldiers led him out into the enclosure, that is, the soldiers' headquarters, and they call together the whole cohort, ¹⁷and they dress him up in purple and they place on him, weaving a crown of thorns. ¹⁸They began to greet him, "Rejoice! King over the Youdaians!" ¹⁹They were beating on his head with a reed and were spitting at him and, placing their knees, they were bowing down to him. ²⁰When they mocked him, they stripped him of the purple and put on his robes, and they lead him out so that they crucified him. ²¹They conscripted someone passing by, Simōn Kurēnaion [Cyrenian] coming from the field—Alexandros [Alexander] and Rouphos's [Rufus's] father—that he might lift his cross.

Yēsous crucified

²²They bring him to the "Golgota" place, which being interpreted [is] "Skull Place." ²³They were giving him myrrh-flavored wine, which he did not take. ²⁴They crucify him and *they split his robes, tossing the die for them—* who would take what. ²⁵It was the third hour [around 9 a.m.] and they crucified him. ²⁶His cause-epigraph was inscribed:

| The king over the Youdaians

²⁷With him they crucify two bandits, one from his right and one from his left.ᶠ ²⁹The ones journeying by insulted him, wagging their heads and saying, "Oy! The one demolishing the sanctuary and forming in three days— ³⁰deliver yourself, descending from the cross!" ³¹Likewise also the Senior Priests, mocking among themselves with the Covenant-Code scholars, were saying, "He delivered others, but isn't able to deliver himself. ³²Christos, King of Yisraēl—now let him descend from the cross so we can see and trust him." The ones co-crucified with him were degrading him.

³³It's the sixth hour [around noon] . . . darkness came over the whole land until the ninth hour. ³⁴At the ninth hour, Yēsous bellowed in a loud voice,

"*Elōi, Elōi, lama sabachthani?*"

Which being translated, "*My God, my God, for what did you abandon me?*"

³⁵Some bystanders, hearing, were saying, "Look! He voices for Ēlias [Elijah]." ³⁶Someone, running, filling a sponge with sour wine, placing it on a reed, was giving him a drink, saying, "Release [him], let us see if Ēlias comes to take him down." ³⁷Yēsous, releasing a loud voice, expired. ³⁸The sanctuary's inner curtain was split in two from top to bottom. ³⁹The leader of a hundred soldiers, who had been standing opposite him, seeing that he expired that way, said, "Truly, this human was God's royal Son!"

⁴⁰There were also women observing at a distance, among whom [was] Maria the Magdalēnē [Mary Magdalene], and Maria, mother of Yakōbos [James] the Smaller and Yōsēs [Joseph], and Salōmē ⁴¹—who were following him and serving him when he was in the Galilaia [Galilee], and many others who ascended with him into Yierosoluma [Jerusalem].

Yēsous buried

⁴²It was already evening . . . since it was Preparation Day [Friday], the day before Sabbath, ⁴³coming, Yōsēf [Joseph], the one from Arimathaia, a respected councilor, who was also himself attending to God's Empire, daring to enter to Pilatos, and pleaded for Yēsous' body. ⁴⁴Pilatos was stunned he had already died and, calling the leader of a

---

ᶠThe good manuscripts don't include 15:28.

hundred soldiers, asked him how long ago he died. ⁴⁵Knowing from the leader of a hundred soldiers, he granted the corpse to Yōsēf. ⁴⁶Purchasing linen, taking him down, he wrapped the linen [around him] and placed him in the tomb that had been cut from rock and rolled a stone at the tomb's door. ⁴⁷Maria the Magdalēnē and Maria, mother of Yōsēs, were observing where it was placed.

Yēsous announced as raised by a young man

16 The Sabbath's elapsing . . . Maria the Magdalēnē [Mary Magdalene] and Maria of Yōsēs [Joseph] and Salōmē purchased spices so, coming, they might oil him. ²Very early on one of the Sabbaths, they come to the tomb . . . the sun's rising. ³They were saying to themselves, "Who will roll the stone away from the tomb's door for us?" ⁴Looking up, they observe that the stone had been rolled away, for it was extremely large. ⁵Entering into the tomb, they saw a young man seated on the right, covered with a white stole, and they were amazed. ⁶He says to them, "Don't be amazed! You pursue Yēsous the Nazarēnos, the crucified. He has been raised. He isn't here. Look! The place where they placed him. ⁷But go away, say to his Apprentices and to Petros [Peter] that 'He precedes you into the Galilaia [Galilee], there you will see him, just as he said to you.'" ⁸Exiting, they fled from the tomb, for they had tremble and ecstasy, and they said nothing to no one, for they were scared.[g]

---

[g] Mark ends at this point in the good manuscripts, though others have attempted to write other completions to the Gospel.

INTRODUCTION TO THE GOSPEL OF LUKE

By far the most sophisticated of the four Gospels, the Gospel of Loukas [Luke] reveals vocabulary not seen in other Gospels, subtle revisions of the other Gospels, and structural moves unseen in the Second Testament up to this point.

Like Matthaios [Matthew], Loukas begins his biography before Markos's [Mark's] opening with Yōannēs the Dipper [John the Baptist] by taking us back into the days of Jesus' father and mother, Maria [Mary]. In its opening two chapters this Gospel contains some Christian favorites, but what pulls us into the text are the poetic, song-like compositions. It also contains genuine comparisons of the birth of Yōannēs and Yēsous. Loukas's knack for the great anecdote includes the good Samaritan, Martha and Mary, the rich fool, the prodigal son, the rich man and Lazarus, Zacchaeus, and others.

When it comes to themes, salvation—or deliverance and liberation—rules in all its comprehensiveness: spiritual, physical, and social. The opening lines of the Gospel of Loukas reveal this author to be self-consciously a historian of Yēsous and his world, an articulate writer, and one concerned with composing a reliable record of value to those who love and fear God. Loukas also brings into his story the themes of Matthaios and Mark: history as governed by God's redemptive plan, God as Father, Yēsous as Lord and Deliverer, and the kingdom of God inaugurated by Yēsous. But Loukas gives an emphasis to the Spirit and has his eye on the poor and marginalized, including the many unlikely people who repent and are converted to follow Yēsous. Running from the opening line of the Second Testament to the last is the constant reminder that the Yēsous movement continues the Israel movement as it claims its Yēsous is the Christos/Messiah of that story. A tradition has it that Loukas was a doctor. If so, that explains his interest in healing and liberation from sins, sicknesses, and various disabilities.

Loukas isn't alone as this biography, unlike Matthaios, Markos, or Yōannēs [John], has a sequel in Acts, which itself tells us this Gospel begins with Yōannēs and Yēsous but continues through the story of Yēsous into a biography of the church expanding through the apostles Petros [Peter] and Paulos [Paul]. It's also the story from Bet-lehem [Bethlehem] to Rome, from the Galilaia [Galilee] and Youdaia [Judea] all the way to Italia [Italy]. The two books combined are over one-quarter of the entire Second Testament. As such, one has to think there is a strong apologetic reason for this Gospel and its sequel: Paulos in prison may well need a defense, and who better to show the peacefulness of the Yēsous movement than Paulos's sophisticated companion, Loukas.

Loukas's Gospel has an introduction that focuses on the birth of Yēsous (1:1-4, 1:5–2:52); the ministry of Yēsous is prepared (3:1–4:13) and then launched in the Galilaia (4:14–9:50), after which Yēsous is determined to accomplish his mission in Yierosoluma [Jerusalem] itself (9:51–19:48). Yēsous teaches in the city (20:1–21:38), and then we read of his suffering, death, and resurrection/exaltation (22:1–24:53).

THE GOSPEL OF LUKE

1 ¹Inasmuch as many have put their hand to order a narrative concerning the matters that are fully assured among us, ²Just as the eyewitnesses from the beginning and those who became the word's subordinates gave over to us, ³It seemed to me, one who has carefully followed everything from above to write for you, Exceptional God-Lover, a sequentially ordered [narrative] ⁴So you may perceive with security the words into which you have been catechized.

Yōannēs's birth predicted

⁵It happened in the days of Hērōdēs [Herod], Youdaia's [Judea's] king, a priest, with the name Zacharias [Zechariah], of Abia's [Abijah's] [temple] shift, and his woman was of A'arōn's [Aaron's] daughters and her name was Eli-sabet [Elizabeth].ᵃ ⁶They were both right before God, journeying as infallibles in all the Lord's orders and right rules. ⁷A child was not [given] to them because Eli-sabet was sterile and both were advanced in their days.

⁸It happened in priesting in his shift's order before God, ⁹consistent with the priest's custom, he was designated to burn incense, entering into the Lord's sanctuary, ¹⁰and the whole mass of people was praying outside at the hour for incense. ¹¹Lord's envoy appeared to him standing at the incense altar's right. ¹²Zacharias was agitated, seeing, and awe fell upon him. ¹³The envoy said to him:

> "Don't be scared, Zacharias,
> Because your request has been listened to,
> And your woman Eli-sabet will give a
>   son's life to you,
> And you will call his name Yōannēs
>   [John].
> ¹⁴And he will be joy for you and overjoy,
> And many will be joyed at his genesis.
> ¹⁵For he will be great before the Lord,
> *And he will never drink wine and liquor,*
> And he will be filled with Holy Spirit—
>   even from his mother's belly.
> ¹⁶And he will turn back many of
>   Yisraēl's [Israel's] descendants to
>   their Lord God.
> ¹⁷And [God] will proceed before him in
>   Ēlias's [Elijah's] spirit and power,
>   to turn back fathers' hearts to
>   children and the unpersuaded in
>   the right ones' prudence,
>   to get ready for Lord a people fully
>   prepared."

¹⁸Zacharias said to the envoy, "How will I know this? For I am old and my woman is advanced in her days." ¹⁹Responding, the envoy said to him, "I am Gabri-ēl, the one standing before God, and I was commissioned to speak to you and to gospel these things to you. ²⁰Look! You will be silent and unable to speak until the day these matters occur because you did not trust my words, which will be filled out in their season." ²¹The people was anticipating Zacharias and they were stunned at the time he was in the sanctuary. ²²Exiting, he was not able to speak to them. They perceived that he had seen a vision in the sanctuary. He was nodding to them and he persisted as speechless.

²³It happened as his temple service's days were filled, he departed to his house. ²⁴After those days, Eli-sabet, his woman, conceived and sequestered herself for five months, saying ²⁵that "Lord has done so for me in the days that he looked upon me to lift away my accusation among humans."

Yēsous' birth predicted

²⁶In the sixth month, the envoy Gabri-ēl was commissioned by God to a Galilaian city to which [was given] the name Nazara [Nazareth] ²⁷to a virgin engaged to a man to

---

ᵃIn modern Hebrew, *Elisheva*, and pronounced "Eli-shéva." "Eli" means "My God," and "sheva" could mean "to whom I make an oath" or "is my fortune."

whom [was given] the name Yōsēf [Joseph], from Dauid's [David's] house, and the virgin's name [was] Mariam [Mary]. ²⁸Entering to her, he said, "Rejoice! One who has been graced! The Lord [be] with you!" ²⁹She was disturbed at the word and deliberating what sort of greeting this might be. ³⁰The envoy said to her,

"Don't be scared, Mariam, for you have found grace with God.
³¹Look! You will conceive in womb and will birth a son,
And call his name 'Yēsous.'
³²This one will be great and will be called 'Highest One's Son,'
And the Lord God will give to him his father Dauid's throne,
³³And he will rule Yakōb's [Jacob's] house to the Eras
And there will not be completion of his Empire."

³⁴Mariam said to the envoy, "How will this be since I don't know a man?" ³⁵Responding, the envoy said to her,

"Holy Spirit will come upon you
And Highest One's power will envelop you.
Therefore also, the devoted one who is given life will be called 'God's Son.'

³⁶Look! Eli-sabet, your relative, also has conceived a son in her old age, and this is the sixth month for her who was called 'Sterile' ³⁷because every utterance from God will not be impossible." ³⁸Mariam said, "Look! The Lord's slave! May it be for me consistent with your utterance!" The envoy departed from her.

Mariam to Eli-sabet

³⁹Arising, Mariam journeyed in those days to the hill country with seriousness to a Youdas [Judah] city, ⁴⁰and entered into Zacharias's house and greeted Eli-sabet. ⁴¹It happened as Eli-sabet heard Maria's greeting the infant in her belly jumped and Eli-sabet was filled with the Holy Spirit, ⁴²and she voiced up in a great shout and said, "You are blessed among women and blessed is your stomach's fruit! ⁴³For what reason [has this occurred] to me—that my Lord's mother came to me? ⁴⁴For Look! As your greeting's voice came into my ears, the infant in my belly jumped in over-joy. ⁴⁵God's blessing on her who trusts that there will be completion regarding what has been spoken to her by Lord."

Mariam's song

⁴⁶Mariam said,

"My self magnifies the Lord,
⁴⁷My spirit was overjoyed in God, my Deliverer,
⁴⁸Because he looked upon his impoverished slave.
For Look! From now all generations will bless me,
⁴⁹Because the Powerful One did greatnesses for me,
his name is devoted.
⁵⁰His compassion is for generations and generations who are awed at him.
⁵¹He made a grip with his right arm,
he scattered status-mongers in their hearts' intelligence.
⁵²He took down the powerful ones from thrones
and raised the status of the impoverished.
⁵³He filled in the hungering ones with goods
and commissioned the rich ones away hollow.
⁵⁴He attached himself to his young servant, Yisraēl [Israel], to remember compassion,
⁵⁵just as he spoke to our fathers,
to Abra'am and to his seed to the Era."

⁵⁶Mariam remained with her about three months and returned to her house.

Yōannēs's birth announced

⁵⁷For Eli-sabet the time was full for her to birth, and she gave life to a son. ⁵⁸The neighborhood and her relatives heard that Lord magnified his compassion with her and they co-rejoiced with her. ⁵⁹It happened on the eighth day: they came to circumcise the child and were calling it by the name of his father, Zacharias. ⁶⁰Responding, his mother said, "No, but he will be called 'Yōannēs.'" ⁶¹They said to her that no one is from your relatives by that name. ⁶²They were nodding to his father what he might want for it to be called. ⁶³Asking for a small tablet, he wrote,

saying, "Yōannēs is his name." All were stunned. ⁶⁴His mouth was opened instantly and his tongue, and he was speaking, blessing God. ⁶⁵It happened: fear on all those neighboring them, and in the whole Youdaian [Judean] hill country they were speaking about all these utterances, ⁶⁶and all the ones hearing placed in their hearts, saying, "What then will this child be?" For even Lord's hand was with him.

⁶⁷Zacharias, his father, was filled with Holy Spirit and prophesied, saying,

> ⁶⁸"Blessed the Lord God of Yisraēl,
> because he cared for and did liberation
>   for his people,
> ⁶⁹he raised deliverance's horn for us in
>   his young servant Dauid's house,
> ⁷⁰just as he spoke through the mouth of
>   his devoted prophets of [the
>   former] Era,
> ⁷¹deliverance from our enemies and
>   from the hand of all who hate us,
> ⁷²to do compassion with our fathers and
>   to remember his devoted
>   Covenant,
> ⁷³the oath that he made with our father
>   Abra'am to give to us
> ⁷⁴fearlessly—being rescued from
>   enemies' hand—to venerate him
> ⁷⁵in piety and rightness before
>   him all our days.
> ⁷⁶And you, child, will be called 'Highest
>   One's prophet,' for you will journey
>   before Lord to prepare his paths,
> ⁷⁷to give deliverance's knowledge to his
>   people in release from their sins,
> ⁷⁸through the empathies of our God's
>   compassion,
> in which [empathies] he will care for
>   us—the rising from the heights,
> ⁷⁹to manifest to those sitting in darkness
>   and death's shadow,
> to straighten for our feet peace's path.

⁸⁰The child grew and was strengthened in spirit and was in the wilderness until his day of showing to Yisraēl.

Yēsous born

2 It happened in those days: A decree exited from Kaisar [Caesar] Augoustos for all the inhabited world to be registered. ²This was the first registration during Kurēnios's [Quirinius's] governing of Suria. ³All journeyed to be registered, each to his own city. ⁴Yōsēf [Joseph] also ascended from the Galilaia [Galilee] from the city of Nazara [Nazareth] to Youdaia [Judea] to Dauid's [David's] city, which is called Bēth-le'em [Bethlehem], because he is from Dauid's house and paternity ⁵to register with Mariam [Mary], who was engaged to him, being pregnant. ⁶It happened while they were there: the days were filled for her to birth, ⁷and she birthed her son, the firstborn, and she swaddled him and reclined him in a feeding trough because there was no place in the guest room.

⁸Shepherds were in that region, living outdoors and staying on guard at night over their flock, ⁹and Lord's envoy stood over them and Lord's splendor shone around them, and they were awed with great awe. ¹⁰The envoy said to them, "Don't be scared, for Look! I gospel to you great joy that will be for all the people ¹¹because today a Deliverer, who is Lord Christos, has been birthed for you in Dauid's city. ¹²This will be the authenticating sign for you: you will find an infant swaddled and lying in a feeding trough." ¹³Unexpectedly, it happened with the envoy: a mass, a heavenly army, praising God and saying,

> ¹⁴"Splendor in the highest places to God,
> and on the land, peace among God-
> pleased humans."

¹⁵It happened as the envoys departed from them into the heaven: the shepherds were speaking to one another, "Let us then cross through to Bēth-le'em that we may see this utterance that has been done that the Lord made known to us." ¹⁶They went, hurrying, and discovered both Mariam and Yōsēf and the infant lying in the feeding trough. ¹⁷Seeing, they made known [to the family] about the utterance that was spoken to them about this child. ¹⁸All those who heard were stunned about what was spoken by the shepherds to them. ¹⁹Mariam maintained all these matters, engaging [them] in her heart. ²⁰The shepherds returned, splendoring and praising God for all that they heard and saw—just as it was spoken to them.

Yēsous enters the Covenant

21 When eight days were filled up to circumcise him and his name was called "Yēsous," which he was called by the envoy before he was conceived in the belly. **22** When their cleansing days—consistent with Mōüsēs' [Moses'] Covenant Code—were filled up, they led him up to Yierosalēm [Jerusalem] to be presented to the Lord, **23** just as it's written in the Lord's Code that *every male that opens a mother will be called "Devoted to the Lord,"* **24** and to give a sacrifice consistent with what has been said in the Lord's Code, *a pair of doves or two new pigeons.*

Yēsous announced by Sumeōn

25 And Look! A human was in Yierosoluma, to whom [was given] the name Sumeōn [Simeon], and this human was right and of good regard, attending to Yisraēl's [Israel's] encouragement, and the Spirit on him was devoted. **26** It was revealed by the Holy Spirit that he would not see death before he saw the Lord's Christos. **27** He came in the Spirit into the temple. In the parents' leading in the child Yēsous so they could do to him [what is] consistent with the Code's custom, **28** and he received it into his arms and blessed God and said,

> **29** "Now you loosen your slave,
> Emperor—
> consistent with your utterance—in
> peace,
> **30** Because my eyes saw your deliverance,
> **31** which you prepared in the presence of
> all peoples,
> **32** a light to apocalypse to the ethnic
> groups
> and splendor for your people, Yisraēl."

33 His father and mother were stunned at what is being said about him. **34** Sumeōn blessed them and said to his mother Mariam: "Look! This one will be laid out for disaster and rising up of many in Yisraēl and for a contradicted authenticating sign— **35** and a sword will cross through your own self—so that the deliberations of many hearts will be apocalypsed."

Yēsous announced by Anna

36 Anna, Phanou-ēl's daughter, from Asēr's [Asher's] tribe, was a prophet. She was well advanced in many days, living with a man [as wife] seven years from her virginity, **37** and she was a widow until eighty-four years [of age], who was not removing herself from the temple, venerating in fasts and requests night and day. **38** At that hour, standing over [the family], she was acknowledging God and was speaking about him to all those attending to Yierosalēm's liberation.

Yēsous returns to Nazara

39 As they completed all observances consistent with Lord's Code, they returned to the Galilaia to their own city, Nazara. **40** The child grew and was strengthening, being filled with wisdom, and God's grace was on the child.

Yēsous returns to the temple

41 His parents were journeying each year to Yierosalēm for the feast of Pascha [Passover]. **42** When he was twelve years . . . they're ascending consistent with their feast-custom . . . **43** [they're] completing the days . . . in their returning, the young servant Yēsous remained in Yierosalēm, and his parents did not know. **44** Thinking him to be in the caravan they went on the path for a day, and they were inquiring about him among their relatives and the ones knowing [him], **45** and not finding, they returned to Yierosalēm, inquiring about him. **46** It happened after three days: they found him in the temple, sitting in the middle of the teachers and listening to them and questioning them. **47** All the ones hearing him were beside themselves at his understanding and his responses. **48** Seeing him, they were shocked, and his mother said to him, "Child, why did you do like this to us? Look! Your father and I, sorrowing, were pursuing you." **49** He said to them, "Why were you pursuing me? Have you not known that it's necessary for me to be among those of my Father?" **50** They did not understand the utterance that he spoke to them. **51** He descended with them and came to Nazara and was ordering himself under them. His mother was retaining these utterances in her heart. **52** Yēsous was advancing in the wisdom and maturity and grace—with God and humans.

Yēsous and a wilderness prophet

3 In the fifteenth year of Tiberios Kaisar's [Caesar's] governorship, Pontios Pilatos [Pontius Pilate] governing Youdaia [Judea] . . . and Hērōdēs [Herod] tetrarching over the Galilaia [Galilee] . . . his brother Philippos [Philip] tetrarching over the Itouraios [Ituraea] and Trachōnitis region . . . and Lusianias tetrarching over Abilēnē, ²with Hannas [Annas] and Kaīaphas [Caiaphas] Senior Priest . . . God's utterance came upon Yōannēs [John], Zacharias's [Zechariah's] son, in the wilderness. ³He came into all the Yordanēs [Jordan River] region, announcing a conversion dip for releasing sins, ⁴as it's written in the book of Ēsaïas [Isaiah] the prophet's words,

> *A voice bellowing in the wilderness;*
> *"Prepare the Lord's path,*
> *Make his ways straight!"*
> ⁵*Every ravine will be filled,*
> *And every mountain and hill will be impoverished [lowered],*
> *And the crooked will be straight,*
> *And the rugged into smooth paths.*
> ⁶*All flesh will see God's deliverance.*

⁷Therefore, he was saying to the crowds journeying out to be dipped by him,

"Knot of vipers! Who divulged to you to flee from the anger about to come? ⁸Therefore, make fruits deserving of conversion and don't begin to say among yourselves, 'We have Abra'am as father,' for I say to you that God is able to raise up from these stones children for Abra'am. ⁹Already the ax is laid on the trees' root. Therefore, every tree not making beautiful fruit is chopped down and tossed into fire."

¹⁰The crowds were asking him, saying, "What therefore should we do?" ¹¹Responding, he was saying to them, "The one who has two shirts, let that person distribute to the one who doesn't have, and the one having foods, let that person do likewise." ¹²The tax agents came to be dipped and said to him, "Teacher, what should we do?" ¹³He said to them, "Don't collect more taxes than what has been ordered for you." ¹⁴The ones soldiering were asking him, saying, "And what should we do?" He said to them, "Don't shake anyone down or commit fraud, and consider your fees enough." ¹⁵The people are anticipating and all deliberating in their hearts about Yōannēs—if he might not be the Christos.

¹⁶Yōannēs responded, saying to all,

"I dip you in water, but the one stronger than me comes, of him I am inadequate to loosen the strap of his sandals. He will dip you in Holy Spirit-and-fire; ¹⁷his sifting shovel is in his hand to clear his floor and to assemble the wheat into his storage, but the husks he will burn in an inextinguishable fire."

¹⁸Therefore, begging [to do] many other [instructions], he was gospeling the people. ¹⁹Hērōdēs, the tetrarch, being convinced by him about Hērōdias, his brother's woman, and about all the evil Hērōdēs did, ²⁰also added this upon all: he confined Yōannēs in prison.

²¹It happened in all the people being dipped . . . Yēsous was being dipped and was praying . . . the heaven was opened ²²and the Holy Spirit descending in body-form as a dove upon him, and a voice coming from heaven, "You are my royal Son, the one loved, in you I was delighted."

The sons in the line of Yēsous

²³Yēsous was himself, beginning, about thirty years, being a son (as was thought) . . .
of Yōsēf [Joseph],
of Ēli,
²⁴of Maththat,
of Leui [Levi],
of Melchi,
of Yannai [Jannai],
of Yōsēf,
²⁵of Mattathias,
of Amōs,
of Naoum [Nahum],
of Hesli,
of Naggai,
²⁶of Maath,
of Mattathias,
of Semeïn,
of Yōsēch [Josech],
of Yōda [Joda],
²⁷of Yōanan [Joannen],
of Rēsa,
of Zorobabel [Zerubbabel],
of Salathiēl [Shealtiel],
of Nēri,
²⁸of Melchi,
of Addi,
of Kōsam [Cosam],

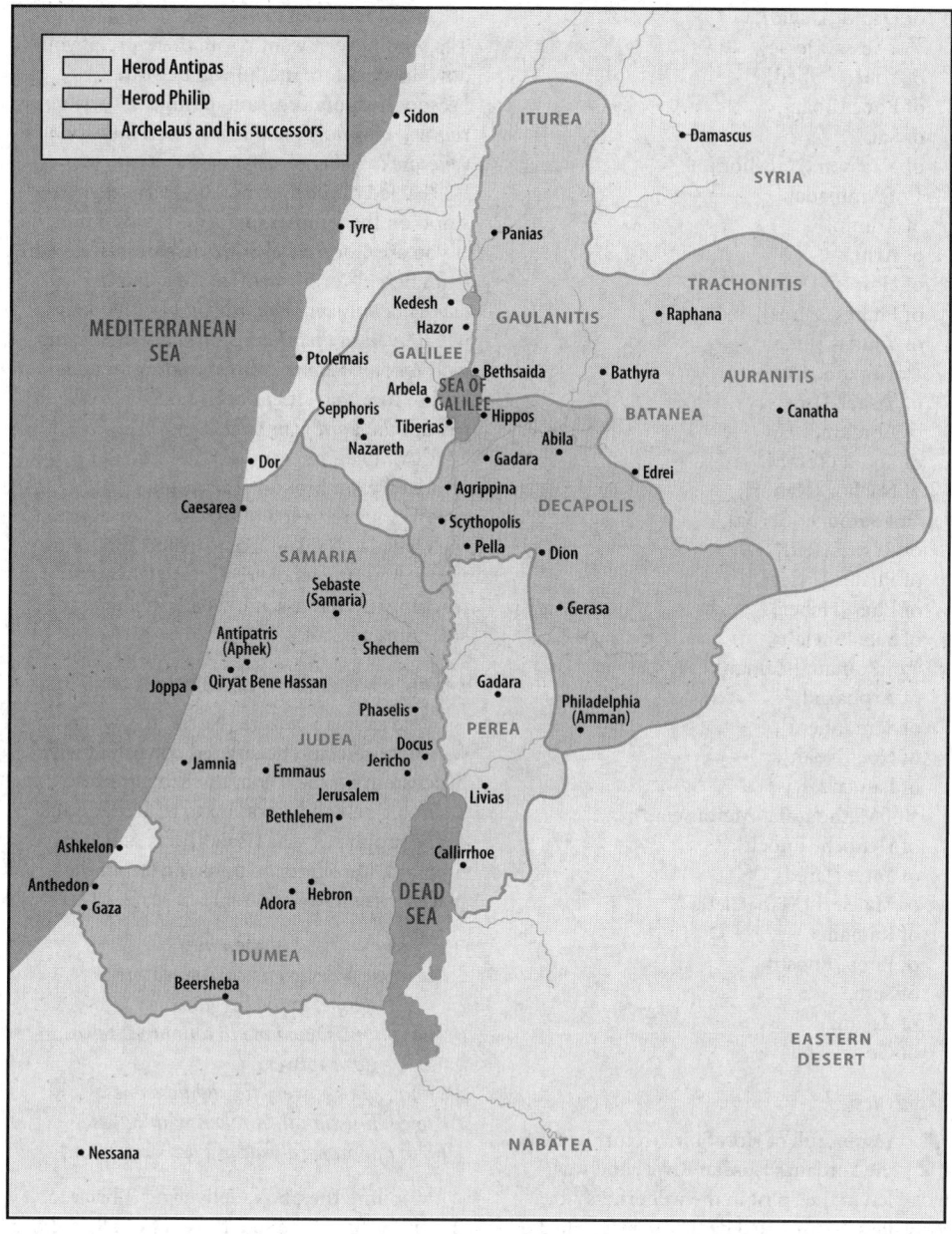

Figure 4. Map of the Herods

of Elmadam,
of Ēr,
²⁹of Yēsous,
of Eliezer,
of Yōrim [Jorim],
of Maththat,
of Leui [Levi],
³⁰of Sumeōn [Simeon],

of Youdas [Judah],
of Yōsēf,
of Yōnam [Jonam],
of Eliakim,
³¹of Melea,
of Menna,
of Mattatha,
of Natham [Nathan],

of Dauid [David],
³²of Yessai [Jesse],
of Yōbēd [Obed],
of Boos [Boaz],
of Sala,
of Na'assōn [Nahshon],
³³of Aminadab,
of Admin,
of Arni,
of Hesrōm [Hezron],
of Phares [Perez],
of Youdas [Judah],
³⁴of Yakōb [Jacob],
of Yisa'ak [Isaac],
of Abra'am,
of Thara [Terah],
of Nachōr [Nahor],
³⁵of Serouch [Serug],
of Raga'u [Reu],
of Phalek [Peleg],
of Eber [Heber],
of Sala [Shelah],
³⁶of Kaïnam [Cainan],
of Arphaxad,
of Sēm [Shem],
of Nōe [Noah],
of Lamech,
³⁷of Mathousala [Methuselah],
of Henōch [Enoch],
of Yaret [Jared],
of Maleleēl [Mahalalel],
of Kaïnam
of Enōs [Enosh],
of Sēth,
of Adam,
of God.

Yēsous tested

4 Yēsous, full of Holy Spirit, returned from the Yordanēs [Jordan River] and was being led in the Spirit in the wilderness ²for forty days, being tested by the Accuser. He did not eat anything in those days . . . they were completed . . . he hungered.

³The Accuser said to him, "If you are God's royal Son, tell this stone to become bread." ⁴Yēsous responded to him, "It's written that *The human will live not on only bread*."

⁵Leading him up, he exhibited to him all the inhabited world's empires in a moment of time ⁶and the Accuser said to him, "I will give you all this authority and their splendor, because it has been given over to me and I give it to whomever I want. ⁷You, therefore, if you bow down before me, all will be yours." ⁸Yēsous, responding, said to him, "It's written: *You will bow down to the Lord God and you will venerate only him.*"

⁹He led him to Yierosalēm [Jerusalem] and stood on the temple's turret and said to him, "If you are God's royal Son, toss yourself down from here, ¹⁰for it's written: *He will order his envoys about you to guard you and* that *they will lift you in their hands, so you will not stub your foot on a stone.*" ¹²Responding, Yēsous said to him that "It has been said, *You will not test out the Lord your God.*"

¹³Completing every test, the Accuser removed from him until a season.

¹⁴Yēsous returned in the Spirit's power to the Galilaia [Galilee]. Fame exited about him throughout the whole region. ¹⁵He was teaching in their assembly halls, being splendored by all.

Yēsous in Nazara's assembly hall

¹⁶He came to Nazara [Nazareth], where he was nurtured, and he entered consistent with his custom on the day of the Sabbaths into the assembly hall and stood up to read. ¹⁷A book of the prophet Ēsaias [Isaiah] was delivered to him and, unrolling the book, he found the place where it was written:

> ¹⁸*Spirit of Lord is upon me,*
> *because of which he christened me to*
>   *gospel to the beggars,*
> *he commissioned me to announce release*
>   *for captives,*
> *and sight-recovery for sightless ones,*
> *to commission the broken with release,*
> ¹⁹*to announce a year of Lord's reception.*

²⁰Rolling the book, delivering it back to the subordinate, he sat. The eyes of all in the assembly hall were gazing at him. ²¹He began to say to them that "Today this writing has been filled out in your ears." ²²All were witnessing him and were stunned at his gracious words journeying from his mouth and they were saying, "Isn't this Yōsēf's [Joseph's] son?" ²³He said to them, "Always you will say this analogy to me: 'Doctor, heal yourself! What we heard that happened in Kaphar-Naoum [Capernaum], do also here in

your ancestral village!'" ²⁴He said, "This is true to say to you: That no prophet is received in one's ancestral village. ²⁵I say this to you on the basis of truth: There were many widows in Ēlias's [Elijah's] day in Yisraēl [Israel], when the heaven was shut for three years and six months, as a great famine happened on all the land, ²⁶and to none of them was Ēlias sent except to Sidōn's Sarepta [Zarephath] to a widow woman. ²⁷And many scaly-skinned were in Yisraēl at [the days of] the prophet Elisaios [Elisha], and not one of them was cleared except the Suros Naiman [Naaman the Syrian]."

²⁸All in the assembly hall were filled out with fury, hearing these things ²⁹and, rising up, they tossed him out of the city and led him to the bank of the mountain on which their city had been formed so they could throw him down. ³⁰But he, crossing through the middle of them, was journeying on.

Yēsous relocates to Kaphar-Naoum

³¹He went down to Kaphar-Naoum, a Galilaian city. He was teaching them on the Sabbaths,ᵇ ³²and they were shocked at his teaching because his word was with authority. ³³In the assembly hall was a human having a contaminating demonic spirit, and he yelled in a loud voice, ³⁴"Ach! What is there between us and you, Yēsous Nazarēnos [Nazarene]? Have you come to destroy us? I know you—who you are: God's devoted one!" ³⁵Yēsous rebuked it, saying, "Be silenced! Exit from him!" The demon, dropping him into the middle [of them], exited from him, not harming him. ³⁶A shock happened to all and they were conversing with one another, saying, "What is this word that with authority and power he orders the contaminating spirits and they come out?" ³⁷An echo journeyed out about him into every place of the region.

Yēsous heals

³⁸Arising from the assembly hall, he entered into Simōn's house. Simōn's mother-in-law was absorbed by a great fever, and they asked him about her. ³⁹Standing over her, he rebuked the fever and it released her. Instantly arising, she was serving them.

⁴⁰The sun is setting . . . all those having weak ones with various maladies led them to him. The one who laid hands on each one of them healed them. ⁴¹Demons exited from many, making a racket and saying that "You are God's royal Son!" Rebuking, he did not permit them to speak because they had known he is the Christos.

Yēsous gospels

⁴²The day's happening . . . exiting, he journeyed into a wilderness place. The crowds were pursuing him and they came to him and they were possessing [him] not to journey away from them. ⁴³He said to them that "It's also necessary for me to gospel other cities about God's Empire, because for this I was commissioned." ⁴⁴He was announcing in the Youdaian [Judean] assembly halls.

Yēsous' first follower

5 It happened: in the crowd's imposing on him and hearing God's word, and he was standing along Gennēsaret's lake ²and he saw two boats standing along the lake. The fishermen, getting out of them, were rinsing their nets. ³Boarding down into one of the boats, which was Simōn's, he asked him to return [the boat back] a little from the land. Sitting, he was teaching crowds from the boat. ⁴As he paused speaking, he said to Simōn, "Return to the deep and lower your nets for a catch." ⁵Responding, Simōn said, "Superintendent, laboring through a whole night, we took nothing, but at your word I will lower the nets." ⁶Doing this, they enclosed a great mass of fishes, and their nets were ripping. ⁷They nodded to their associates in another boat to come assist them. They came and they filled both boats so that they're sinking. ⁸Simōn Petros [Peter], seeing, fell at Yēsous' knees, saying, "Exit from me because I am a sinful man, Lord." ⁹For a shock contained him and all those with him in the catch of fishes which they took, ¹⁰and likewise with Yakōbos [James] and Yōannēs [John], Zebedaios's [Zebedee's] sons, who were in common with Simōn. Yēsous said to Simōn, "Don't be scared! From now on you will be catching humans."

ᵇGospel writers use "Sabbath" and "Sabbaths" interchangeably.

[11] Leading the boats onto the land, releasing everything, they followed him.

Yēsous heals a scaly-skin man

[12] It happened that he was in one of the cities, and Look! A man full of scaliness. Seeing Yēsous, falling upon face, he pleaded with him, saying, "Lord, if you want to, you have the ability to clean me." [13] Extending the hand, he touched him, saying, "I want to. Be cleansed." Immediately, the scaliness departed from him. [14] He ordered him to speak to no one but "departing, *exhibit* yourself *to the priest* and present for your cleansing as Mōūsēs [Moses] ordered, as testimony to them." [15] Rather, the word about him was crossing over, and many crowds were gathering to hear and to be healed from their weaknesses. [16] He was retreating in the wilderness and praying.

Yēsous releases a man from sins

[17] It happened on one of the days and he was teaching, and the Observant [Pharisees] and Covenant-Code teachers were sitting—those who had come from all villages of the Galilaia [Galilee] and Youdaia [Judea] and Yierosalēm [Jerusalem]—and Lord's power was for his curing. [18] Look! Men carrying a human on a cot who had been disabled and they were pursuing him to enter him in and to place him before him. [19] Not finding any way that they might enter him in because of the crowd, ascending onto the terrace, through the tiles they lowered him with his little cot into the middle before Yēsous. [20] Seeing their trust, he said, "Human, your sins are released for you." [21] The Covenant-Code scholars [scribes] and Observant began to deliberate, saying, "Who is this who is speaking insults? Who is able to release sins except only God?" [22] Yēsous, perceiving their deliberations, responding, said to them, "Why deliberate in your hearts? [23] Which is easier? To say 'Your sins are released for you' or to say 'Rise up and walk around!'? [24] But so you might know that the Son of Humanity has authority on the land to release sins," he said to the one disabled, "I say to you, Rise up! Taking up your little cot, journey to your house!" [25] Instantly standing up before them, taking up what he was reclining on, he departed to his house, splendoring God. [26] Ecstasy took all and they were splendoring God and they were filled up with awe, saying that "We saw beyond-splendor today."

Yēsous calling

[27] After these things he exited and he observed a tax agent, by name Leui [Levi], sitting at the tax booth, and said to him, "Follow me!" [28] Abandoning everything behind, arising, he was following him. [29] Leui did a great reception for him in his house, and it was a big crowd of tax agents and other sorts who were reclining with them. [30] The Observant and their Covenant-Code scholars were murmuring to his Apprentices, saying, "For what reason do you eat and drink with tax agents and sinners?" [31] Responding, Yēsous said to them, "The healthy have no need of a doctor, but those in a bad way do. [32] I have not come to call 'right ones' but sinners to conversion."

Yēsous suspends fasting

[33] Some said to him, "The Apprentices of Yōannēs [John] fast frequently and make requests, also likewise do those of the Observant, but those belonging to you eat and drink." [34] Yēsous said to them, "You aren't able to make the groom's sons fast when the groom is with them, are you? [35] The days will come, and whenever the groom is taken away from them then they will fast in those days."

[36] He was telling an analogy to them, that: "No one, splitting a patch from new cloth, tosses it on ancient cloth. Otherwise, the new will also split and the patch that is from the new [cloth] will not concur with the ancient. [37] No one tosses new wine into ancient wineskins. Otherwise, the new wine tears the wineskins and it will be spilled out and the wineskins will destroy. [38] Instead, new wine must be tossed into fresh wineskins. [39] No one drinking ancient [wine] wants new. For he says, 'The ancient is gracious.'"

Yēsous, Lord over the Sabbath

6 It happened on a Sabbath: he journeys through grain fields, and his Apprentices were picking and eating heads of grain, hulling with the hands. [2] Some of the Observant [Pharisees] said, "Why do what isn't observant for Sabbaths?" [3] Responding to them, Yēsous said, "Have you not read this, what Dauid [David] did when he hungered—and those who were with him? ⁴As he entered into God's house and, taking the Presence Breads, he ate and gave to those with him, which was not observant to eat . . . but only for the priests?" ⁵He was saying to them, "The Son of Humanity is Lord over the Sabbath."

⁶It happened on another Sabbath: he entered into the assembly hall and was teaching. A human was there and his hand, the right one, was stiff. ⁷The Covenant-Code scholars [scribes] and the Observant were spying on him—if he heals on the Sabbath—so they might find [grounds] to accuse him. ⁸He had known their deliberations and he said to the man who has the stiff hand, "Arise and stand in the center!" Arising, he stood. ⁹Yēsous said to them, "I ask you if it's observant on the Sabbath to do good or to do evil, to deliver a self or to destroy?" ¹⁰Looking around at them all, he said to him, "Extend your hand!" He did and his hand was restored. ¹¹They were filled up with ignorance and were discussing with one another what they might do with Yēsous.

Yēsous calls twelve

¹²It happened on those days: he exited to the mountain to pray, and he was over-nighting in prayer to God, ¹³and when day happened, he addressed his Apprentices, and selecting twelve from them, whom he named "Commissioners."

¹⁴Simōn, whom he also named Petros [Peter],
and Andreas [Andrew], his brother,
and Yakōbos [James]
and Yōannēs [John]
and Philippos [Philip]
and Bar-Tholomaios [Bartholomew]
¹⁵and Matthaios [Matthew]
and Thōmas
and Yakōbos of Alphaios [Alphaeus]
and Simōn, called "Zealot"
¹⁶and Youdas the Dagger Man [Judas Iscariot], who became a traitor.

Yēsous heals

¹⁷Descending with them, he stood on a plain place, and a great crowd of his Apprentices, a great mass of people from all Youdaia [Judea] and Yierosalēm [Jerusalem] and the coast of Turos [Tyre] and Sidōn— ¹⁸who came to hear him and to be cured from their illnesses. The disturbed from contaminating spirits were being healed, ¹⁹and the whole crowd was pursuing to touch him, because power exited from him and cured all.

Yēsous teaches on the plain

²⁰He, lifting his eyes up toward his Apprentices, was saying,

"God blesses the beggars because yours is
     God's Empire.
²¹God blesses the ones hungering now
     because you will be satisfied.
God blesses the ones wailing now
     because you will laugh.
²²God blesses you whenever the humans
     hate you
and when they isolate you and degrade
     you and toss out your name as
     evil because of the Son of
     Humanity.
²³Rejoice in that day and jump in joy for
     Look! Your wage is great in
     heaven. Their fathers were doing
     things consistent with these acts
     to the prophets.
²⁴However, Oy! to you, the wealthy,
     because you've got your
     encouragement.
²⁵Oy! to you, the now-filled-up, because
     you will hunger.
Oy! to you, the now-laughers, because
     you will grieve and wail.
²⁶Oy! whenever all the humans speak
     beautifully about you. For the
     fathers were doing things
     consistent with these acts to the
     false prophets.

²⁷But to you I say to those who are hearing:

Love your enemies!
Do beautifully to the ones hating you!
²⁸Bless the ones cursing you!
Pray for the ones mistreating you!
²⁹To the one who beats you on the
     cheek—present the other, and
     from the one who takes your robe,
     don't prohibit your shirt!
³⁰Give to everyone requesting, and don't
     make claims from the one taking
     your things!

³¹And just as you want that humans do to you, you do likewise to them!
³²If you love the ones loving you, what grace is it to you? For even the sinners love the ones loving them.
³³For even if you do good to the ones doing good to you, what grace is it to you? Even the sinners do the same.
³⁴And if you lend from whom you hope to receive, what grace is it to you? Even sinners lend to sinners that they might receive back equal things.
³⁵However, love your enemies and do good and lend, hoping for nothing back! Your wage will be great, and you will be descendants of the Highest One, because he is gracious on the ungracious and evil.
³⁶Be sympathetic as your Father is sympathetic!
³⁷Don't judge, and you will never be judged!
Don't condemn, and you will never be condemned!
Loosen, and you will be loosened!
³⁸Give, and it will be given to you! A beautiful measure—pressed down, shaken, overflowing—will be given into your garment's fold. For you will be re-measured by the measure by which you measure."
³⁹He also told them an analogy:
"Is a sightless person able to guide a sightless person? [No.] Will they not both fall into a pot bunker?
⁴⁰An apprentice isn't above the teacher. Everyone prepared will be as one's teacher.
⁴¹Why do you see the chip in your sibling's eye but don't ponder the stick in your own eye? ⁴²Or, how are you able to say to your sibling, 'Sibling, release so I may toss away the chip that is in your eye,' when you yourself aren't seeing the stick that is in your eye! Masked one! First toss away the stick from your eye, and then you will clearly see to toss away the chip that is in your sibling's eye.

⁴³For a beautiful tree doesn't make diseased fruit, nor again does a diseased tree make beautiful fruit. ⁴⁴For you will know each tree from its own fruit. For they don't collect figs from thorns, nor do they pick a grape from a wild blackberry bush. ⁴⁵The good human produces the good from the heart's good treasure chest, and the evil [human] produces evil from [the heart's] evil [treasure chest]. For the person's tongue speaks from the heart's overflow.

⁴⁶Why do you call me 'Lord, Lord' and not do what I say?

⁴⁷Everyone coming to me and hearing my words and doing them, I will show to you what is comparable: ⁴⁸the person is comparable to a human forming a house who dug, and deepened, and placed a foundation upon rock. A water surge's happening . . . the river drove to that house and it was not strong [enough] to shake it because it was formed beautifully. ⁴⁹But the one hearing and not doing is comparable to a human who formed a house on the land without foundation—the river drove into it, and immediately collapsed and that house became a mega-ruin."

Yēsous heals

7 Since he filled out all his utterances in the people's hearing, he entered into Kaphar-Naoum [Capernaum]. ²A leader of a hundred soldiers' slave, being in a bad way, was about to end life—he was honorable to him. ³Hearing about Yēsous, he commissioned Youdaian [Judean, Jewish] Elders to him, asking him that, coming, he might preserve his slave. ⁴The ones coming near to Yēsous were begging him with commitment, saying that "He deserves you to perform this for him ⁵for he loves our ethnic group and he formed the assembly hall for us." ⁶Yēsous was journeying with them. Already . . . he was not far from the house . . . the leader sent friends, saying to him, "Lord, don't be disturbed, for I am inadequate that you enter under my roof. ⁷Therefore, neither did I myself deserve to come to you. But, say a word, and my young servant will be cured. ⁸For even I am a human under authority, ordering, having soldiers under me. I say to one, 'Journey!' and he journeys, and to another, 'Come!' and he comes, and to my slave, 'Do this!' and he does it." ⁹Hearing these things, Yēsous was stunned at him and, turning, said to the crowd following him: "I say to you: I did not find such trust in Yisraēl." ¹⁰Returning to the house, those sent found the slave healthy.

Yēsous raises a dead widow's son

¹¹It happened next: He journeyed into a city called Naïn and his Apprentices were journeying with him and a large crowd. ¹²As he came close to the city's gate, and Look! One dead was being transported, the only son to his mother and she was a widow, and an adequate crowd from the city was with her. ¹³Seeing her, the Lord empathized with her and said to her, "Don't wail!" ¹⁴Approaching, he touched the bier, and the carriers stood, and he said, "Young man, I say to you, Be raised!" ¹⁵The dead man sat up and began to speak, and he gave him to his mother. ¹⁶Fear took all and they splendored God, saying that "A great prophet has been raised among us" and that "God has cared for his people." ¹⁷This word about him exited in the whole Youdaia [Judea] and in all the region.

Yēsous sends a message back to Yōannēs

¹⁸His Apprentices declared to Yōannēs [John] about all these matters. Calling two of his Apprentices, Yōannēs ¹⁹sent to the Lord, saying, "Are you the Coming One or are we anticipating another?" ²⁰Coming near to him, the men said, "Yōannēs the Dipper [John the Baptist] commissioned us to you, saying, 'Are you the Coming One or are we anticipating another?'" ²¹On that hour he healed many from maladies and afflictions and evil spirits, and many sightless persons he graced to see. ²²Responding, he said to them,

> "Journeying, declare to Yōannēs what
>   you saw and heard:
> *The sightless see again,*
> The lame walk around
> *The scaly are cleaned and*
> *The deaf hear,*
> *The dead arise,*
> The beggars are gospeled.

²³God blesses whoever isn't tripped up by me."

Yēsous explains Yōannēs to the crowds

²⁴Yōannēs's envoys departed . . . he began to speak to the crowds about Yōannēs. "What did you exit into the wilderness to observe? A reed shaken by wind? ²⁵But what did you exit to see? A human outfitted in delicate robes? Look! The ones in splendorous robes and luxury are among the empire-ish. ²⁶But what did you exit to see? A prophet? Yes, I say this to you: And exceeding a prophet. ²⁷This is the person about whom it's written:

> *Look! I commission my envoy before* your
>   face,
> *Who will prepare your path before* you.

²⁸I say to you: No one greater than Yōannēs is among the ones given life by women. Yet, the smallest in God's Empire is greater than him. ²⁹All the people hearing, even the tax agents, [said] God [is] right, being dipped with Yōannēs's dip. ³⁰The Observant [Pharisees] and the Covenant-Code experts rejected God's plan for themselves, not being dipped by him.

³¹Therefore to what will I compare the humans of this generation? To what are they comparable? ³²They are comparable to children sitting in the square and voicing out one another, saying,

> 'We played the recorder for you and you
>   did not dance;
> We lamented and you did not wail.'

³³Yōannēs the Dipper has come neither eating bread nor drinking wine, and you say: 'He has a demon.' ³⁴The Son of Humanity has come eating and drinking, and you say, 'Look! A human who is a glutton and a winedrinker, a friend of tax agents and sinners.' ³⁵Wisdom was righted by all of her descendants."

Yēsous and a sinful woman

³⁶One of the Observant was asking him if he [Yēsous] might eat with him and, entering into the Observant's house, he reclined. ³⁷Look! A woman in the city, a sinner, and perceiving that he was reclining in the Observant's house, obtaining an alabaster vase of fragrant ointment, ³⁸and standing behind at his feet, wailing, began to rain tears on his feet and she dried [them] with her head's hair and kissed his feet and oiled them with fragrant ointment.

³⁹The Observant, the one who called him, seeing, saying in himself, "This man, if he was a prophet, he would have known who and what sort of woman who is touching him, that she is a sinner." ⁴⁰Yēsous, responding, said to him, "Simōn, I have something to say to you." He said, "Teacher, speak!"

⁴¹"Two debtors were indebted to a certain lender. One owed five hundred dēnaria, the other fifty. ⁴²They, not having [a way] to repay . . . he graced both. Therefore, which of them will love him more?"

⁴³Responding, Simōn said, "I suppose that the one to whom the most was graced." He said to him, "You judged properly."

⁴⁴Turning to the woman, he said to Simōn, "Do you see this woman? I entered your house, you did not give water for feet, but she rained tears on my feet and dried [them] with her hair. ⁴⁵You did not give a kiss to me, but she, from the time she entered, did not cease kissing my feet. ⁴⁶You did not oil my head with oil, but she oiled my feet with fragrant ointment. ⁴⁷Because of which I say to you: Her sins, [of which] are many, have been released because she loved much. To the one little is released—loves little." ⁴⁸He said to her, "Your sins have been released." ⁴⁹The co-recliners began to say in themselves, "Who is this who even releases sins?" ⁵⁰He said to the woman, "Your trust delivered you. Journey in peace!"

Yēsous with the Twelve and some women

8 It happened in sequence: He was traversing city to city and village to village, announcing and gospeling God's Empire, and the Twelve were with him ²and some women who had been healed from evil spirits and weaknesses—Maria [Mary], the one called Magdalēnē, from whom seven demons had come out, ³and Yōanna [Joanna], Chouza's (Hērōdēs's supervisor) woman, and Sousanna [Susanna] and many other women, who were serving them from their own possessions.

Yēsous tells the analogy of the planter and the seeds

⁴A large crowd gathers together and journeys to him city by city . . . he spoke through analogy:

⁵"The planter exited to plant his seed. In his planting, a seed fell next to the path and it was trampled and the birds of the heaven gobbled it. ⁶Another fell down on the rock, and growing, it stiffened because it did not have moisture. ⁷Another fell in the middle of the thorns and, growing with it, suffocated it. ⁸Another fell in the good land and, growing, made fruit multiplied one hundred times."

Saying these things, he voiced: "The one who has ears to hear—let that person hear."

⁹His Apprentices were asking him what this analogy might be. ¹⁰He said, "To you is given to know the secrets of God's Empire, but to the remaining [I speak] in analogies so, seeing, they may not see and, hearing, they may not understand.

¹¹This is the analogy: The seed is God's word.

¹²Those next to the path are those who hear, then the Accuser comes and lifts the word from their heart so they may not, trusting, be delivered.

¹³Those on the rock are those who, whenever they hear, they receive the word with joy, and these don't have root, they trust for a season and in time of testing they remove themselves.

¹⁴The one who fell in the thorns, these are the ones who hear and, journeying, are suffocated by anxieties and wealth and life's pleasures and don't carry on to completion.

¹⁵The one in the beautiful land, these are the ones who, hearing the word in a beautiful and good heart, possess and yield fruit with resilience.

Yēsous says clever things

¹⁶No one, touching a lamp, covers it with a vessel or places it under a cot, but places it on a lampstand so the ones journeying in may see the light. ¹⁷For nothing hidden that will not become apparent, nothing concealed that will not be known and come into manifest. ¹⁸Therefore, see how you hear! For whoever has, it will be given to the person, and whoever doesn't have, even what the person seems to have will be lifted from the person."

Yēsous and his family

¹⁹The mother and his brothers came next to him and they were not able to come together with him because of the crowd. ²⁰It was declared to him, "Your mother and your

brothers have been standing outside, wanting to see you." ²¹Responding, he said to them, "My mother and my brothers, these are the ones hearing God's word and doing."

Yēsous, who is he?

²²It happened on one of the days: he boarded down into a boat—and his Apprentices, and he said to them, "Let us cross over Beyond the Lake." They were led up [by the winds]. ²³They're sailing . . . he fell asleep. A gale of wind descended to the lake and they were filling up and were endangered. ²⁴Approaching, they raised him, saying, "Superintendent, superintendent! We are perishing." He, being raised awake, rebuked the wind and the water's waves. They stopped and there was calm. ²⁵He said to them, "Where is your trust?" Being awed, they were stunned, saying to one another, "Who then is this that he even orders the winds and the water and they heed him?"

Yēsous liberates

²⁶They sailed down into the Gerasēnes' region, which is opposite the Galilaia [Galilee]. ²⁷Some man from the city—having a demon and for an adequate time he did not put on a robe, and he was not remaining in a house but in the tombs—met him exiting onto the land. ²⁸Seeing Yēsous, yelling, he fell before him and said in a loud voice, "What is there between me and you, Yēsous, Highest God's royal Son? I plead with you, Don't torture me!" ²⁹(For he ordered the contaminating spirit to exit from the human. For many times it had seized him, and he was bound with chains and shackles, being guarded, and ripping apart the bonds, he was driven by the demon into the wildernesses.) ³⁰Yēsous asked him, "What is your name?" He said, "Legion," because many demons entered into him ³¹and they were begging him not to order them to depart into the abyss. ³²There was there an adequate herd of hogs feeding on the mountain. They begged him that he might permit them to enter those. He permitted them. ³³The demons, exiting from the human, entered into the hogs, and the herd dashed down the cliff into the lake and were suffocated.

³⁴The feeders, seeing what happened, fled and declared in the city and in the fields. ³⁵They exited to see what happened, and they came to Yēsous and they found, sitting, the human from whom the demons exited, robed and sensible, at Yēsous' feet, and they were scared. ³⁶The ones seeing declared to them how the one demonized was delivered. ³⁷The whole mass from the Gerasēnes' region asked him to depart from them because they were absorbed with a great scare. He, boarding down into a boat, returned. ³⁸The man from whom the demons had exited begged him to be with him. He loosened him, saying, ³⁹"Return to your house and narrate whatever God did for you." He departed, announcing to the whole city whatever Yēsous did for him.

Yēsous touches

⁴⁰In Yēsous' returning, the crowd welcomed him. For they were anticipating him. ⁴¹Look! A man, with a name Yaïros [Jairus], came, and this man was the assembly hall leader, and falling before Yēsous' feet, he was begging him to enter into his house ⁴²because his only daughter was about twelve years old and she was dying. In his departing the crowds were suffocating him.

⁴³A woman being in a twelve-year blood flow, who—expending on doctors [her] whole livelihood—was not strong enough to be healed by anyone, ⁴⁴approaching from behind, touched his robe's tassels and instantly her blood flow stood [still]. ⁴⁵Yēsous said, "Who is the one who touched me?" Everyone's denying [it] . . . Petros [Peter] said, "Superintendent, the crowds are absorbing and pressing you." ⁴⁶Yēsous said, "Someone touched me, for I knew a power had exited from me." ⁴⁷The woman seeing that she could not escape notice, trembling, came and, falling before him, declared before all the people the cause for her touching him and how she was cured instantly. ⁴⁸He said to her, "Daughter, your trust has delivered you. Journey in peace!"

⁴⁹While he's speaking . . . someone from the assembly hall leader comes, saying that "Your daughter has died. No longer disturb the

teacher." ⁵⁰Yēsous, hearing, responded to him, "Don't be scared! Just trust! And she will be delivered." ⁵¹Coming into the house, he did not release anyone to enter with him except Petros and Yōannēs [John] and Yakōbos [James] and the child's[c] father and mother. ⁵²All were wailing and striking themselves for her. He said, "Don't wail, for she did not die but sleeps." ⁵³They were laughing at him, knowing that she died. ⁵⁴He, grabbing her hand, voiced, saying, "Child, Rise up!" ⁵⁵Her spirit returned and she arose instantly, and he ordered [that something] be given to her to eat. ⁵⁶Her parents were beside themselves. He declared to them not to tell anyone what happened.

Yēsous commissions

9 Calling together the Twelve, he gave to them power and authority over all demons and to heal all illnesses. ²He commissioned them to announce God's Empire and to cure the weak, ³and he said to them,

"Don't lift anything for the path:
no walking stick,
nor a bag,
nor a bread,
nor silver,
nor to have two shirts per person.

⁴Whatever house you enter, remain there and exit from there. ⁵Whoever doesn't welcome you, exiting from that city, shake off the dust from your feet—as a witness to them."

⁶Exiting, they went through village by village, gospeling and healing everywhere.

Yēsous and Hērōdēs

⁷Hērōdēs [Herod], the tetrarch, heard all that happened and was getting perplexed because it was being said by some that Yōannēs [John] was raised from among the dead ones, ⁸by some that Ēlias [Elijah] had appeared, and by others that one prophet of the ancients arose. ⁹Hērōdēs said, "I decapitated Yōannēs. Who is this about whom I hear these things?" He was pursuing to see him.

Yēsous feeds more than five thousand

¹⁰Returning, the Commissioners narrated to him whatever they did. Taking them, he retreated by himself into a city called Bēthsaïda [Bethsaida]. ¹¹The crowds, knowing, followed him and, receiving them, he spoke to them about God's Empire, and he was curing those having a need for healing.

¹²The day began to recline. The Twelve, approaching, said to him, "Loosen the crowd so, journeying to the encircling villages and fields, they may lodge and find provisions because we are here in this wilderness place." ¹³He said to them, "You give them [something] to eat." They said, "There are not with us more than five breads and two fishes, unless perhaps we, journeying, purchase foods for all this people." ¹⁴For they were about five thousand men. He said to his Apprentices, "Have them recline in groups of fifty." ¹⁵They did so and they had them all recline. ¹⁶Taking the five breads and the two fishes, looking up to heaven, he blessed them and snapped [them] and was giving [them] to the Apprentices to present to the crowd. ¹⁷All ate and were satisfied, and the overflow for them was lifted—twelve baskets of broken pieces.

Yēsous calls to the cross-life

¹⁸It happened in his praying alone, the Apprentices were with him, and he asked them, saying, "Who do the crowds say I am?" ¹⁹They, responding, said, "Yōannēs the Dipper [John the Baptist], others Ēlias, others that one prophet of the ancients arose." ²⁰He said to them, "But you, who do you say I am?" Petros [Peter], responding, said, "God's Christos." ²¹Rebuking them, he ordered to say this to no one, ²²saying that it's necessary for the Son of Humanity to suffer much, and to be rejected from the Elders and Senior Priests and Covenant-Code scholars, and to be killed, and on the third day to be raised.

²³He was saying to all, "If one wants to come after me let the person deny oneself, lift up one's cross day by day, and let the person follow me. ²⁴For whoever wants to deliver one's self, the person will destroy it; whoever destroys one's self because of me, this person will deliver it. ²⁵For what can a human gain, taking advantage of the whole Kosmos and destroying oneself or being damaged? ²⁶For whoever is degraded by me and my words the

---

[c]Greek is *pais* and is feminine, hence it could be rendered "girl."

Son of Humanity will degrade that person whenever he comes in his splendor and the Father's and the devoted envoys.' ²⁷I say to you truly: there are some having stood here who will not taste death before they see God's Empire."

Yēsous glows

²⁸It happened after these words, about eight days: Taking Petros and Yōannēs [John] and Yakōbos [James], he ascended into the mountain to pray. ²⁹It happened in his praying: his face's form [was] another and his robe [was] white, dazzling. ³⁰Look! Two men were conversing with him, who were Mōūsēs [Moses] and Ēlias, ³¹who, appearing in splendor, were talking about his exodus, which he was about to fill out in Yierosalēm [Jerusalem]. ³²Petros and those with him were heavy in sleep. Being fully awake, they saw his splendor and the two men standing with him. ³³It happened in their separating from him, Petros said to Yēsous, "Superintendent, it's beautiful for us to be here. Let us make three tents, one for you, one for Mōūsēs, one for Ēlias." (Not knowing what he is saying.) ³⁴Saying these things . . . a cloud came and it enveloped them. They were scared in their entering into the cloud. ³⁵A voice came from the cloud, saying,

> "This is my royal Son, elected. Listen to him!"

³⁶In the voice having occurred, Yēsous was found alone. They were silent and declared to no one in those days nothing of what they had seen.

Yēsous heals a man's son

³⁷It happened on the next day, they're coming down from the mountain . . . a large crowd met him. ³⁸Look! A man from the crowd bellowed, saying, "Teacher, I plead with you to look upon my son because he is my only son." ³⁹Look! A spirit takes him and unexpectedly it cries out and it convulses him with froth and rarely separates from him, breaking him. ⁴⁰I pleaded with your Apprentices that they toss it out, and they were not able." ⁴¹Responding, Yēsous said, "Wow, anti-trust and distorted generation! How long will I be with you and put up with you? Lead your son here." ⁴²He's still approaching . . . the demon tore and convulsed him. Yēsous rebuked the contaminating spirit and cured the child and gave him back to his father. ⁴³All were shocked at God's magnificence.

Yēsous predicts his death

All are amazed at all that he was doing . . . he said to his Apprentices, ⁴⁴"You place these words in your ears: For the Son of Humanity is about to be given over into human hands." ⁴⁵They were uninformed about this utterance, and [it] was hidden from them that they might perceive it. They were scared to ask him about this utterance.

Yēsous instructs on Empire status

⁴⁶A deliberation entered among them, namely, who of them might be greatest. ⁴⁷Yēsous, knowing their heart's deliberation, taking hold of a child, stood it alongside himself ⁴⁸and said to them, "Whoever welcomes this child in my name, welcomes me. Whoever welcomes me welcomes the one who commissioned me. For the one who is least among all of you—this person is great."

Yēsous and other exorcists

⁴⁹Responding, Yōannēs said, "Superintendent, we saw someone tossing out demons in your name and we were prohibiting him because he wasn't following with us." ⁵⁰Yēsous said to him, "Don't prohibit. For the one who isn't against us is for us."

Yēsous rejected by a Samaritēs village

⁵¹It happened with the days of his assumption being completed that he fixed his face to journey to Yierosalēm. ⁵²He commissioned envoys before his face. Journeying, they entered into a Samaritēs [Samaritan] village as to prepare for him. ⁵³They did not welcome him because his face was journeying to Yierosalēm. ⁵⁴Knowing, the Apprentices Yakōbos and Yōannēs said, "Lord, do you want that we say *Fire to descend from the heaven and consume them*?" ⁵⁵Turning, he rebuked them. ⁵⁶They journeyed to another village.

Yēsous calls

⁵⁷They're journeying on the path. . . . Someone said to him, "I will follow you wherever you depart." ⁵⁸Yēsous said to him,

"Foxes have dens and birds of the heaven nests, but the Son of Humanity doesn't have a place where he might recline the head." ⁵⁹He said to another, "Follow me!" But he said, "Permit me, departing, first to bury my father." ⁶⁰He said to him, "Release the dead to bury their own dead, but you, departing, announce God's Empire!" ⁶¹Another also said, "I will follow you, Lord. First permit me to say farewell to those in my house." ⁶²Yēsous said to him, "No one, tossing down the hand on a plow and looking to what is behind, is well-placed for God's Empire."

Yēsous commissions seventy-two

10 After these things the Lord elevated seventy-two others and commissioned them two by two before his face into every city and place where he was about to come. ²He was saying to them,

"The harvest is great, the workers are few. Therefore, plead to the harvest's Lord that he toss out workers into his harvest. ³Go away! Look! I commission you as lambs in the middle of wolves.

⁴Don't carry a sack,
Nor a bag,
Nor sandals,
And don't greet anyone on the path.

⁵Whatever house you enter, say first: 'Peace to this house.' ⁶If there be a person of peace there, your peace will come to rest upon it. Otherwise it will return upon you. ⁷Remain in the same house, eating and drinking what is before you, for the worker deserves one's wage. Don't shift from house-to-house. ⁸Whatever city you enter and they receive you, eat what is presented to you. ⁹Heal the weak in it and say to them, 'God's Empire has come close upon you.' ¹⁰Whatever city you enter and they don't receive you, exiting into its plazas, say, ¹¹'Even the dust that was united to us on our feet from your city we will wipe away for you. However, know this: that God's Empire has come close.' ¹²I say to you, 'It will be lighter on that Day for Sodoma [Sodom] than for that city.'

¹³Oy! on you, Chorazin! Oy! on you, Bēth-saïda [Bethsaida]! Because if the powers that happened in your cities had happened in Tyros [Tyre] and Sidōn, long ago they would have converted sitting in sack and soot. ¹⁴However, it will be lighter for Tyros and Sidōn at the judgment than for you. ¹⁵And you, Kaphar-Naoum [Capernaum], will you be *raised in status as far as heaven? You will descend into Hadēs.*

¹⁶The one hearing you hears me. The one rejecting you rejects me. The one rejecting me rejects the one who commissioned me."

¹⁷The seventy-two returned with joy, saying, "Lord, even the demons were ordered under by us in your name." ¹⁸He said to them, "I was observing the Satanas [Satan] falling as lightning from the heaven. ¹⁹Look! I have given to you the authority to trample on snakes and scorpions, and [I have given to you] all power over the enemy, no one will ever wrong you. ²⁰However, don't rejoice in this, that the spirits are ordered under by you—rejoice that your names have been written in the heavens."

Yēsous praises the Father

²¹In that hour he was overjoyed in the Holy Spirit and said, "I publicly acknowledge You, Father, Lord over heaven and the land because you hid these things from the wise and understanding ones, and apocalypsed these things to the childlike. Yes, Father, because this is what becomes a delight before you. ²²All things have been given over to me by my Father, and no one knows who the Son is but the Father, nor who the Father is but the Son—and the one to whom the Son decides to apocalypse."

Yēsous blesses his Apprentices

²³Turning to his Apprentices he said privately, "The eyes—the ones seeing what you see—are blessed by God. ²⁴For I say to you, that many prophets and kings wanted to see what you see and did not see, and to hear what you hear and did not hear."

Yēsous tells a story about trauma

²⁵Look! Some Covenant-Code expert stood up, testing him out, saying, "Teacher, by doing what will I inherit Era Life?" ²⁶He said to him, "What is written in the Code? How do you read?" ²⁷Responding, he said, *"You will love the Lord, your God, from your whole heart and in your whole self and in your whole strength and in your whole intelligence and your neighbor as yourself."* ²⁸He said to him, "You have responded properly. Do this and you will live."

²⁹Wanting to right himself he said to Yēsous, "And who is my neighbor?"

³⁰Yēsous, taking up [the question], said, "Some human was descending from Yierosalēm [Jerusalem] to Yiericho [Jericho] and he fell among bandits, who also stripping him and putting plagues [on him], departed, releasing him half-dead. ³¹Serendipitously, some priest was descending on that path and, seeing him, passed by avoiding [him]. ³²Likewise, also a Leuitēs [Levite], coming upon that place, and seeing, passed by avoiding [him]. ³³But some Samaritēs [Samaritan], walking the path, came upon him, and seeing, empathized ³⁴and, approaching, bandaged his trauma, pouring oil and wine [on him], hoisting him up on his own animal, led him to an 'All Are Welcome' place and managed his care. ³⁵On the next day, tossing out, he gave two dēnars to the 'Welcomer of All' and said, "Manage his care, and whatever more you spend I, in my returning, will pay you back."

³⁶Which of these three looks to you like one who became a neighbor for the one who fell among bandits?" ³⁷He said, "The one doing mercy with him." Yēsous said to him, "Go and you do likewise."

Yēsous with Martha and Mariam

³⁸In their journeying, he entered into some village. Some woman, by name Martha, welcomed him. ³⁹She had a sister named Mariam [Mary], and sitting alongside at the Lord's feet, she was hearing his word. ⁴⁰Martha was annoyed over so much service. Standing over [him], she said, "Lord, is it not a concern for you that my sister abandoned me alone to serve? Therefore, tell her to assist me." ⁴¹The Lord, responding, said to her, "Martha Martha, you are disturbed and agitated over many things ⁴²but one is a need, for Mariam chose the good part, which will not be lifted away from her."

Yēsous teaches about prayer

11 It happened: in his praying in some place, as he stopped, one of his Apprentices said to him, "Lord, teach us to pray just as Yōannēs [John] also taught his Apprentices." ²He said to them, "Whenever you pray, say [this]:

> Father,
> Your name be devoted,
> Your Empire come,
> ³Give our bread to us, for our existence,
>   day by day,
> ⁴Release from us our sins, for we ourselves
>   release those indebted to us,
> Don't guide us into the test."

⁵He said to them, "Which of you [Knocker] will have a friend and will journey to him [Resident Friend] in the middle of the night and say to him: 'Friend, lend me three breads ⁶since my friend came to me from the path and I don't have something that I may present to him.' ⁷That person inside [Resident Friend], responding, said, 'Don't present labor for me. Already the door has been closed and my children are with me in the bed. I am unable, arising, to give [anything] to you.'

⁸I say this to you: "Even if he [Resident Friend] will not, arising, give [breads] to him [Knocker] because he is his [Resident's] friend, yet because of his [Knocker's] impudence,ᵈ being raised, he will give to him whatever he requires."

⁹"And I say this to you:
> Ask—God will give it to you.
> Pursue—you will find.
> Knock—God will open the door for you.

¹⁰For everyone who asks receives and the one who pursues finds and for the one who knocks God will open the door. ¹¹Or, which father among you whose son will ask for a fish: Will he ever give him a snake instead of a fish? ¹²Or, he will ask for an egg: Will he give him a scorpion? ¹³Therefore, if you, existing as evil, know to give good gifts to your children, how much more will your Father, the one of heaven, give the Holy Spirit to the ones asking him!"

Yēsous versus Beelzeboul

¹⁴He was tossing out a demon and it was speechless. It happened . . . the demon's exiting . . . the speechless person spoke and the crowd

---

ᵈEverything in this parabolic story hangs on the meaning of "impudence," one viable translation of *anaideia*. The term can mean "shamelessness" but not "persistence" or "avoidance of shame." It counters friendship in this verse.

was stunned. ¹⁵Some of them said, "By Beelzeboul, the leader of demons, he tosses out demons." ¹⁶Others, testing, were pursuing an authenticating sign from heaven from him. ¹⁷He, knowing their notions, said to them, "Every empire split in itself becomes wilderness and house falls upon house. ¹⁸If the Satanas [Satan] is split against himself, how will his empire stand up? (Because you say I toss out the demons by Beelzeboul.) ¹⁹If I toss out demons by Beelzeboul, by what do your sons toss [them] out? Because this is true, they will be your judges. ²⁰If I toss out demons by God's finger, then God's Empire arrived upon you.

²¹Whenever the fully armed strong one guards his enclosure his possessions are in peace. ²²When one stronger than him, coming upon, conquers him, lifts his panoply of weapons upon which he is fully persuaded and distributes his plunder.

> ²³The one not with me is against me,
> and the one not assembling with me scatters.

²⁴Whenever the contaminating spirit exits from the human, it crosses over parched places pursuing rest and not finding [it]. Then it says: 'I will return to my house from which I exited.' ²⁵Entering, it finds it swept clean and decorated. ²⁶Then it journeys and takes along seven other spirits more evil than itself and, entering, resides there. The last things of that human become worse than the first things."

Yēsous blesses

²⁷It happened in his saying these things, some woman, lifting up [her] voice from the crowd, said to him, "God blesses the belly that carried you and the breasts you nursed." ²⁸He said, "Rather, God blesses the ones hearing and guarding God's word."

Yēsous and this generation

²⁹The crowds are thronging around him . . . he began to say, "This generation is an evil generation. It pursues an authenticating sign, and an authenticating sign will not be given to it—except the authenticating sign of Yōnas [Jonah]. ³⁰For just as Yōnas became an authenticating sign to the Nineuitēs [Ninevites] so also will the Son of Humanity be to this generation. ³¹The Queen of the East will be raised with this generation of men at the judgment and will condemn them because she came from over the land to hear Solomōn's wisdom. Look! Greater than Solomōn is here. ³²The Nineuitēs men will rise up with this generation at the judgment and they will condemn it because they converted at the Yōnas announcement. Look! Greater than Yōnas is here.

Yēsous on light and darkness

³³No one holding a lamp places it in hiding nor under a basket, but on a lampstand so ones journeying in may see the light. ³⁴The body's lamp is your eye. Whenever your eye is healthy, your whole body is also illumined. If it's evil, your body is also darkened. ³⁵Therefore, watch that the light in you isn't darkness. ³⁶Therefore, if your whole body is illumined, not having a part that is darkened, it will be wholly illumined—as whenever the lamp illumines you in lightning."

Yēsous unmasks the Observant

³⁷In speaking, an Observant [Pharisee] asks him that he might lunch with him. Entering, he lay down. ³⁸The Observant, seeing, was stunned that [his hands] were not first dipped [washed] before the luncheon. ³⁹The Lord said to him, "Now you Observant clear the exterior of the cup and the tray, but your interior is filled with extortion and evil. ⁴⁰Imprudent! Did not the maker of the exterior make the interior? ⁴¹Rather, give what's inside [the cup] as donation and, Look! all is clean for you.

⁴²But Oy! on you Observant! Because you donate a tenth of mint and rue and every leafy vegetable and bypass justice and love for God. It was necessary to do these not dropping those.

⁴³Oy! on you Observant! Because you love first-status seats in the assembly halls and greetings in the squares.

⁴⁴Oy! on you! Because you are like obscure tombs, and humans walking around on them and don't know."

⁴⁵Responding, one of the Covenant-Code experts says to him, "Teacher, saying these things and you assault us."

⁴⁶He said, "Oy! on you Code experts! Because you burden humans with double-burdens, and you yourselves don't touch the burdens with one of your fingers.

⁴⁷Oy! on you because you form the prophets' tombs, but your fathers killed them. ⁴⁸Therefore, you are witnesses and you are pleased with your fathers' works because they themselves killed them and you are forming [their tombs]. ⁴⁹Because this is true, and God's wisdom said, 'I commission to them prophets and Commissioners.' [Some] of them they will kill and chase ⁵⁰so all the prophets' blood—what was poured from the Kosmos's foundation—will be searched out from this generation ⁵¹—from Habel's [Abel's] blood to Zacharias's [Zechariah's] blood (who was destroyed between the sacrificial altar and the house). Yes, I say to you, it will be searched out from this generation.

⁵²Oy! on you Code experts! Because you lift knowledge's keys, and you yourselves did not enter [into such knowledge] and you prohibited those entering."

⁵³He's exiting from there . . . the Code scholars [scribes] and the Observant began to have it in badly [for him] and to interrogate him concerning many things, ⁵⁴lying in ambush to catch something from his mouth.

12

During which . . . a crowd of myriads was assembling so that [they] are trampling on one another . . . he began to say to his Apprentices first, "Beware among yourselves from the Observants' [Pharisees'] leaven, which is mask-wearing.

Yēsous urges public fearlessness

²There is nothing covered up that will not be apocalypsed, and hidden that will not be known. ³Because, whatever you said in the dark will be heard in the light, and what you spoke to ears in the private rooms will be announced on terraces.

⁴I say to you my friends: Don't be scared of ones killing the body and, after these things, not doing what abounds. ⁵I will show you what to be scared of: Be scared of the one who, after the killing, having authority to toss you into the Valley of Destructive Fire [Gehenna]. Yes, I say to you: Be scared of this person. ⁶Are not five little sparrows sold for two assaria[e]? And not one of them is forgotten before God. ⁷But even your head's hairs have all been numbered. Don't be scared. You are superior to all the little sparrows.

⁸I say to you: Everyone who openly agrees with me before humans, the Son of Humanity will openly agree about the person before God's envoys. ⁹The one who denies [me] before humans will be denied before God's envoys.

¹⁰Anyone who will say a word against the Son of Humanity, it will be released for him. But the one insults the Holy Spirit it will not be released.

¹¹Whenever they guide you to the assembly halls and the leaders and authorities, don't be disturbed how or about what you might defend or what you might say. ¹²For the Holy Spirit will teach you in that hour what is necessary to say."

Yēsous tells a story about an imprudent rich man

¹³Someone from the crowd said to him, "Teacher, tell my brother to part the inheritance with me." ¹⁴He said to him, "Human, who appointed me as judge or part-er over you?" ¹⁵He said to them, "See and guard yourself from all wanting more and more, because one's life isn't in the overflow of one's possessions."

¹⁶He told an analogy to them, saying, "The region of some rich human propagated well. ¹⁷He was deliberating in himself, saying, 'What am I to do because I don't have somewhere I might assemble my fruits?' ¹⁸He said, 'I will do this: I will pull down my storages and I will form greater ones, and I will assemble there all my wheat and my good things, ¹⁹and I will say to my self, Self, you have laid up many good things for many years. Rest. Eat. Drink. Be glad.' ²⁰God said, 'Imprudent one, on this night they request your self from you. The things you prepared, for whom will they be?' . . . ²¹so . . . the one treasuring for himself and not being rich to God."

Yēsous teaches the Apprentices

²²He said to his Apprentices:

"Because this is true, I say to you: Don't disturb your self—what you might eat, or the body—what to put on. ²³For the self is more than provision and the body more than clothing. ²⁴Ponder the crows that they neither plant seeds nor do they harvest, for whom there isn't a private room nor storage, and God

---

[e] An assarion is a copper coin and one-sixteenth of a Roman denarius, a day's pay.

nurtures them. How much more superior are you than the birds! ²⁵Who among you, disturbing, is able to add a length to one's life? ²⁶Therefore, if you are not able [to provide] for the least matter, why disturb yourselves about what remains? ²⁷Ponder the lilies—how they grow: they neither labor nor spin. I say to you: not even Solomōn in all his splendor was covered like one of these. ²⁸If in the field God so outfits the grass—here today and tossed into the clay oven tomorrow—how much more [will he outfit] you, little believers? ²⁹You: don't pursue what you might eat and what you might drink, and don't be presumptuous. ³⁰For these are all things the Kosmos's ethnic groups pursue, and your Father knows you require all these things. ³¹However, pursue his Empire and these things will be added for you.

³²Don't be scared, my little flock, because your Father delighted to give you the Empire. ³³Sell your possessions and give a donation. Make for yourselves non-aging sacks, an inexhaustible treasure chest in the heavens, where a thief doesn't get close nor does a moth abominate. ³⁴For where your treasure chest is there also will be your heart.

³⁵Let *your waists be wrapped* and your lamps be aflame! ³⁶You: be comparable to humans attending to their lord when he leaves the marriage so, coming and knocking, immediately they open for him. ³⁷God blesses those slaves whom the lord, coming, finds awake. This is true to say to you: He will wrap himself and he will recline [with] them and, passing by, will serve them. ³⁸If he comes in the second or if in the third night-watch and finds them so—they are blessed by God.

³⁹Know this, that if the house master had known on which hour the thief comes, he would not release his house to be broken into. ⁴⁰You: be prepared because on an hour you don't seem [to know] the Son of Humanity comes."

⁴¹Petros [Peter] said to him, "Lord, are you telling this analogy for us or also for all?" ⁴²The Lord said,

"Who then is the allegiant administrator, the prudent one, whom the Lord will appoint over his service personnel to give in season the food allotment? ⁴³God blesses that slave whom his lord, coming, will find doing so. ⁴⁴Truly, I say to you that he will appoint him over all his possessions. ⁴⁵But if that slave says in his heart, 'My lord is taking a long time to come,' and begins to beat the servant-boys and servant-girls, and to eat and drink and to booze, ⁴⁶that slave's lord will come on a day that he doesn't anticipate and at an hour that he doesn't know, and he will bisect him and place his part among the anti-trusting ones. ⁴⁷That slave, the one knowing his lord's will, and not preparing or doing his will, will be beaten many times. ⁴⁸The [slave], the one not knowing but doing what deserved plagues, will be beaten a few times. To all to whom much has been given, will be pursued for much from him, and to whom much is presented, they will ask him for what abounds.

⁴⁹I came to toss fire on the land, and how I want that it had already been kindled! ⁵⁰I have a dipping to be dipped, and how absorbed I am until it's completed! ⁵¹Does it seem to you that I have come to give peace on the land? No, I say to you, but rather dissension. ⁵²For from now on five in one house will be split, three-on-two and two-on-three, ⁵³a father will be split against a son and *a son* against *a father*, a mother against the daughter and *a daughter against the mother*, a mother-in-law against her daughter-in-law and *a daughter-in-law against the mother-in-law*."

Yēsous speaks to the crowds

⁵⁴He was saying to the crowds,

"Whenever you see the cloud rising in the west, immediately you say that a squall comes and so it happens. ⁵⁵Whenever [you see] a south wind blowing, you say that it will be scorching heat and it happens. ⁵⁶Masked ones! You know to judge the land's and heaven's face, but how do you not know to judge this season? ⁵⁷And why do you not also judge from yourselves what is right? ⁵⁸For as you go away with your adversary before the leading one, on the path give effort to be liberated from him, or else he may drag you to the judge, and the judge will give you over to the bailiff and the bailiff will toss you into the prison. ⁵⁹I say this to you: You will never exit from there until you pay back the last leptos [smallest coins]."

Yēsous' call to conversion

13 In that season, some were present declaring to him about the Galilaioi

[Galileans] whose blood Pilatos [Pilate] mixed with their sacrifices. ²Responding, he said to them, "Does it seem that these Galilaioi were sinners beyond all the Galilaioi because they have suffered these things? ³No, I say to you: If you don't convert, all of you will be destroyed likewise. ⁴Or, those eighteen upon whom the tower in Silōam fell and killed them, does it seem that they were debtors beyond all humans who were inhabiting Yierosalēm [Jerusalem]? ⁵No, I say to you: If you don't convert, all of you will be destroyed similarly."

Yēsous gives an analogy about a viticulturist

⁶He was telling this analogy:
"Someone had a fig tree planted in his vineyard, and he came pursuing fruit in it and did not find [fruit]. ⁷He said to the viticulturist: 'Look! For three years I come pursuing fruit in this fig tree and I don't find [fruit]. Therefore, chop it down. Why should it undo the land?' ⁸He, responding, says to him, 'Lord, release it for this year until I dig around it and toss manure [around it], ⁹and it might make fruit in the future. Otherwise, you will chop it down.'"

Yēsous liberates a woman's body

¹⁰He was teaching in one of the assembly halls on the Sabbaths. ¹¹Look! A woman having a spirit-based weakness for eighteen years and was stooped and unable to stand completely erect. ¹²Seeing her, Yēsous voiced and said to her, "Woman, you have been loosened from your weakness," ¹³and he placed hands on her. Instantly, she was straightened up and splendored God. ¹⁴The assembly hall leader, responding, being angered that Yēsous healed on the Sabbath, was saying to the crowd that "There are six days in which it's necessary to work. Therefore, coming on those days be healed and not on a Sabbath day." ¹⁵The Lord responded to him and said, "Masked ones! Doesn't each of you, on the Sabbath, loosen his ox or donkey from the feeding trough, and leading it out, give it a drink? ¹⁶Is it not necessary for this [woman], being Abra'am's daughter, whom the Satanas [Satan] bound—Look! for eighteen years—to be loosened from this bond on a Sabbath day?" ¹⁷He's saying these things . . . all the ones opposing him were degraded [in honor], and the whole crowd was rejoicing about all the splendorous doings by him.

Yēsous provides two short comparisons

¹⁸Therefore he was saying, "To what is God's Empire comparable and to what will I compare it? ¹⁹It's comparable to a mustard seed which a human, taking, tossed into his own garden, and it grew and became a tree, and *the birds of the heaven nested in its branches*."
²⁰Again he said, "To what will I compare God's Empire? ²¹It's comparable to yeast, which a woman, taking, hid in three portions of flour until it leavened the whole."

Yēsous on "Who makes it?"

²²He was journeying through city by city and village by village, teaching and making a journey to Yierosoluma [Jerusalem]. ²³Someone said to him, "Lord, are the ones being delivered few?" He said to them, ²⁴"Be a contestant to enter through the tight door because many, I say to you, pursue to enter and will not have the strength. ²⁵From the time when the house master is raised and blocks the door, and you begin to stand outside and knock on the door, saying, 'Lord, open to us,' and responding he will say to you, 'I don't know where you are from.' ²⁶Then you will begin to say, 'We ate and drank before you, and you taught in our plazas.' ²⁷He will say, saying to you, 'I don't know where you are from. *Depart from me, all workers of wrongdoing!*' ²⁸There will be weeping and teeth grinding whenever you see Abra'am and Yisa'ak [Isaac] and Yakōb [Jacob] and all the prophets in God's Empire, but yourselves tossed out outside. ²⁹They will come from east and west and from north and south and they will recline in God's Empire. ³⁰Look! There are last who will be first, and first who will be last."

Yēsous determined to go to Yierosalēm

³¹On that hour some Observant [Pharisees] approached, saying to him, "Exit and journey from this place because Hērōdēs [Herod] wants to kill you." ³²He said to them, "Journeying, tell that fox, 'Look! I toss out demons and I accomplish cures today and tomorrow, and I will be finished on the third day. ³³However, it's necessary for me today and tomorrow and on the coming [day] to journey

on because it isn't appropriate for a prophet to be destroyed outside Yierosalēm.'

³⁴Yierosalēm Yierosalēm, the one killing prophets and stoning ones commissioned to her! How many times I wanted to assemble your children—the way a hen [assembles] her chicks under the wings, and you did not want [this]. ³⁵Look! Your house is released from you. I say this to you: You will never see me until [the day] comes when you say, *God's blessing on the one coming in the Lord's name.*"

Yēsous heals on a Sabbath

14 It happened in his coming into the house of one of the leaders of the Observant [Pharisees] on a Sabbath to eat bread and they were spying on him. ²Look! A human with edema, in front of him. ³Yēsous, responding, said to the Covenant-Code experts and Observant, saying, "Is it observant to heal on the Sabbath or not?" ⁴They went quiet. Taking hold [of him], he cured him and he loosened him. ⁵He said to them, "Who among you whose son or ox falls into a cistern, and does he not immediately extract him on the Sabbath day?" ⁶They went quiet on countering these [words].

Yēsous subverts the status system

⁷He was telling an analogy to the called ones, clinging to how they were selecting the first-status seats, saying to them,

⁸"Whenever you are called by someone to a marriage, don't recline at the first-status seats so if one more publicly honorable than you is called by him ⁹and, coming, the one who called you and him will say to you, 'Give [your] place to this person,' and then you will begin to have shame about the last place. ¹⁰But, whenever you are called, journey [and] fall down at the last place so whenever the one who has called you comes he will say to you, 'Friend, ascend to a higher [status seat].' Then for you it will be splendor before all those reclining with you. ¹¹Because everyone who raises his own status will be impoverished and the one who impoverishes himself will be raised in status."

¹²He was saying also to the one had called him, "Whenever you do a luncheon or banquet, don't call your friends, not your siblings, not your relatives, not the next-door wealthy, since they also may call you in turn and there may be reciprocation for you. ¹³But whenever you do a reception, call beggars, disabled, lame, sightless [persons]. ¹⁴God will bless you because they don't have [a way] to reciprocate to you, for you will be reciprocated at the right ones' resurrection."

Yēsous tells a story about a great banquet

¹⁵One of the recliners, hearing these things, said to him, "God blesses whoever eats bread in God's Empire!"

¹⁶He said to him, "A human was making a great banquet and he called many ¹⁷and he commissioned his slave at the banquet's hour to say to the called, 'Come because it's already prepared.' ¹⁸They all, as one, began to request [an excused absence]. The first said to him, 'I purchased a field and I have a compulsion, exiting, to see it. I ask you, have me excused.'ᶠ ¹⁹Another said, 'I purchased five yokes of oxen and I am journeying to approve them. I ask you, have me excused.' ²⁰Another said, 'I married a woman and because of this I am unable to come.' ²¹The slave, being present, declared to his lord these things. Then the house master, being angry, said to his slave, 'Exit quickly into the plazas and city streets and lead here the beggars and disabled and sightless and lame.' ²²The slave said, 'Lord, what you have ordered is done, and there is still place.' ²³The lord said to the slave, 'Exit to the paths and walls and compel [more] to enter so my house may be filled. ²⁴For I say to you that none of these men who have been called will taste my banquet.'"

²⁵Many crowds were journeying with him and, turning, he said to them,

²⁶"If someone comes to me and doesn't hate one's own father and mother and woman and children and brothers and sisters—indeed, even one's own self, isn't able to be my apprentice. ²⁷Whoever doesn't carry one's own cross and come after me, isn't able to be my apprentice.

²⁸For who among you, wanting to form a tower, doesn't first, sitting, estimate the expense, if he has [enough] for accomplishment? ²⁹So that all those observing

---

ᶠTwice in 14:18 and once in 14:19 the same term is used: "request" means "request an excused absence."

him laying a foundation and not having strength to complete [the task] begin to mock him, ³⁰saying, 'This human began to form and did not have strength to complete.'

³¹Or what king, journeying to engage another king in war, does he not, sitting down first, take counsel if he is able with ten thousand to meet the one with twenty thousand coming upon him? ³²Otherwise, while being far away, commissioning an embassy, he asks [terms] for peace.

³³Thus, therefore, anyone of you who doesn't say farewell to all his possessions, isn't able to be my apprentice.

³⁴Therefore, salt is beautiful, but if salt becomes foolish, with what will it be seasoned? ³⁵It's well-placed neither for the land nor for manure. They toss it outside. The one having ears to hear, let the person hear."

Yēsous tells three more analogies

15 All the tax agents and sinners were getting close to him to hear him, ²yet the Observant [Pharisees] and Covenant-Code scholars [scribes] were grumbling, saying, "This one attends to 'sinners' and eats with them."

³He told them this analogy, saying, ⁴"Which human among you, having a hundred sheep and losing one of them, doesn't abandon the ninety-nine in the wilderness and journey for the one lost until he finds it? ⁵And, finding, one places [the sheep] on his shoulders, rejoicing ⁶and coming to his house, he calls together the male friends and those next door, saying to them, 'Rejoice with me because I found my sheep, the one lost.' ⁷I say to you that so there will be more joy in heaven about one converting sinner than about ninety-nine right ones who don't need conversion.

⁸Or which woman, having ten drachmas^g and if she loses one drachma, does she not touch a lamp and sweep the house and pursue intensively until she finds [it]? ⁹And, finding [it], she calls together the female friends and those next door, saying, 'Rejoice with me because I found the drachma that I lost.' ¹⁰So, I say to you, there is joy before God's envoys about one converting sinner."

¹¹He said, "Some human had two sons. ¹²The younger of them said to the father, 'Father, give me the portion of the estate tossed [toward me].' He apportioned the property to them. ¹³Not many days after, assembling everything, the younger son traveled abroad to a far-off region and there scattered his estate, living un-redemptively. ¹⁴He's exhausting everything . . . a strong famine came against that region, and he began to lack. ¹⁵Journeying, he united himself to one of that region's citizens, and he [citizen] sent him into his fields to feed hogs, ¹⁶and he was desiring to be satisfied from the carob pods that the hogs were eating, and no one was giving [any] to him. ¹⁷Coming to himself, he said, 'How many of my father's hired servants flow over with breads and I am being destroyed here in a famine. ¹⁸Arising, I will journey to my father and I will say to him, Father, I sinned toward heaven and before you, ¹⁹I no longer deserve to be called your son. Make me as one of your hired servants.' ²⁰Arising, he came to his own father. While he was far away . . . his father saw him and empathized and, running, fell upon his neck [hugged] and kissed him. ²¹The son said to him, 'Father, I sinned toward heaven and before you, I no longer deserve to be called your son.' ²²The father said to his slaves, 'Quickly, carry out the first stole and put it on him, and give a ring for his finger and sandals for the feet, ²³and bring the fat-calf, slaughter and, eating, let us be glad ²⁴because this my son was dead and lived again, was lost and now has been found.' They began to be glad.

²⁵His older son was in the field. As coming, he came close to the house, he heard harmony and dancing, ²⁶and calling one of the young servants, he was inquiring what these things might be. ²⁷He said to him that your brother has come and your father slaughtered the fat-calf because he received him back healthy. ²⁸He was angered and did not want to enter. His father, exiting, encouraged him. ²⁹He, responding, said to his father, 'Look! All these years I slave for you and not once did I pass by your order, and not once did you give for me a goat that I could be glad with my male friends. ³⁰When this your son, the one gobbling up

---

^gCoins and their comparable purchasing capacities are nearly impossible to compare to our economy. A drachma was a silver coin. 100 drachmas = a mina; 6,000 drachmas = a talent.

your property with prostitutes, came, you slaughtered for him the fat-calf.' ³¹He said to him, 'Child, you are always with me and all my things are your things. ³²It's necessary to be glad and to rejoice because this your brother was dead and lived, and lost and has been found.'"

Yēsous teaches about accumulations

16 He was saying to the Apprentices, "Some human was rich who had an administrator, and this person was discredited to him [the rich man] as one scattering his possessions. ²Voicing him, he said to him, 'What is this I hear about you? Give back your administration's account, for you are no longer able to administrate.' ³The administrator said to himself, 'What will I do because my lord has carried away the administration from me? I'm not strong [enough] to dig, I'm ashamed to beg. ⁴I know what I'll do so that, whenever I'm removed from the administration, they'll receive me in their houses.' ⁵Calling each one of his own lord's debtors, he was saying to the first, 'How much do you owe my lord?' ⁶He said, 'A hundred vats of olive oil.' He said to him, 'Receive your bill, quickly sitting, write [the bill for] fifty.' ⁷Then he said to another [debtor], 'You, how much do you owe?' He said, 'A hundred containers of wheat.' He says to him, 'Receive your bill and write eighty.'

⁸The wrongdoing administrator's lord praised [him] because he did [such things] prudently—because this Era's descendants are more prudent than the Light's descendants in their own generation. ⁹I say this to you: Make friends for yourselves out of wrongdoing's accumulations [Mammon] so that when it's eclipsed you may be received into the Eras'ʰ tents.

¹⁰The allegiant one in least matters is allegiant in many matters, and the wrongdoer in least matters is a wrongdoer in many matters. ¹¹If therefore you don't become trustworthy with unjust accumulations, who will trust you with true [accumulations]? ¹²If you don't become allegiant with an outsider's [accumulations], who will give to you your own?

¹³No domestic is able to slave for two lords. For either he will hate the one and love the other, or he will stick to one and snub the other.

You are not able to slave for God and accumulations."

Yēsous teaches

¹⁴The Observant [Pharisees], being silver-lovers, were hearing all these things and they snorted at him. ¹⁵He said to them, "You are the ones righting yourselves before humans, but God knows your hearts. Because what is high status among humans is an abomination before God.

¹⁶The Covenant Code and the Prophets [were preached] until Yōannēs [John]. Since then God's Empire is being gospeled and everyone forcefully tries to enter into it.

¹⁷It's easier for the heaven and the land to pass away than for one stroke of the Code to fall.

¹⁸Anyone loosening his woman and marrying another, adulterates, and [anyone] marrying one loosened from a man, adulterates."

Yēsous tells a story about providing for the poor

¹⁹"Some human was rich and he was dressing himself in purple and linen, gladdened daily ostentatiously. ²⁰Some beggar, with the name 'God Helps [Lazarus],' had been tossed at his gate with ulcerated sores, ²¹desiring to be satisfied with what falls from the rich man's table, but instead the dogs, coming, were licking his sores. ²²The beggar happened to die and was carried by the envoys to Abra'am's garment's fold. The rich man also died and was buried. ²³In Hadēs, lifting up his eyes, being in pains, [the rich man] saw Abra'am from a distance and 'God Helps' in his garment's fold. ²⁴He, voicing, said, 'Father Abra'am, show me compassion and send "God Helps" so he may dip his finger's tip in water and refresh my tongue, because I am sorrowing in this flame.' ²⁵Abra'am said, 'Child, remember that you received your good things in your life and "God Helps" likewise [received his] bad things. Now here he is encouraged and you are

---

ʰLoukas shifts from the singular "this Era" (the present time) to the plural "the Eras" (era of eras, that is, eternity).

pained. ²⁶In all these things a great chasm supports [the distance] between us and you so that those wanting to come over from here to you are not able and neither may they cross over from there to us.' ²⁷He said, 'Therefore, I ask you, father, that you send him to my father's house, ²⁸for I have five brothers, so that he may witness to them so they may not come into this painful place.' ²⁹Abra'am says, 'They have Mōüsēs [Moses] and the prophets—let them hear them.' ³⁰He said, 'No, father Abra'am, but if someone journeys to them from among the dead ones they will convert.' ³¹He said to him, 'If they don't hear Mōüsēs and the prophets, neither will they be persuaded if someone arises from among the dead.'"

Yēsous teaches some more

17 He said to his Apprentices, "It's unavoidable for trippings not to come, but Oy! on the one through whom they come. ²It would be a better end for him if a grinding-stone were draped about his neck and dropped into the sea than a person trip up one of these little ones. ³Beware among yourselves.

If your sibling sins, rebuke the person; if the person converts, release the person. ⁴If [that sibling] sins against you seven times a day, and turns back to you seven times, saying, 'I convert,' release the person."

⁵The Commissioners said to the Lord, "Add trust in us." ⁶The Lord said, "If you have trust like a mustard seed, you would say to this mulberry tree, 'Be uprooted and be planted in the sea!' and it would heed you.

⁷Which of you, having a slave plowing or shepherding, who, entering from the field, will say to him, 'Immediately, passing by, lie down [at the table]!' ⁸but will he not say to him, 'Prepare what I may eat and, wrapping yourself, serve me until I eat and drink, and after these things you will eat and drink'? ⁹He doesn't have a grace for the slave because he did what he was ordered, does he? ¹⁰Thus also you, whenever you do all that was ordered for you, you say that 'We are useless slaves, we have done what we are indebted to do.'"

Yēsous heals a grateful Samaritēs

¹¹It happened in journeying to Yierosalēm [Jerusalem] and he was going through border of Samareia [Samaria] and the Galilaia [Galilee]. ¹²He's entering into some village . . . ten scaly men met him, who stood at a distance. ¹³They lifted a voice, saying, "Yēsous, Superintendent, have compassion on us." ¹⁴Seeing, he said to them, "Journeying, demonstrate yourselves to the priests." It happened in their departing, they were cleaned. ¹⁵One of them, seeing that he was cured, returned, with a great voice splendoring God, ¹⁶and he fell on [his] face at his feet, thanking him. (He was a Samaritēs [Samaritan].) ¹⁷Responding, Yēsous said, "Weren't ten cleaned? Where are the nine? ¹⁸They were not found returning to give splendor to God, except this other-ethnic one, were they?" ¹⁹He said to him, "Arising, journey. Your trust has delivered you."

Yēsous predicts

²⁰Being asked by the Observant [Pharisees] when God's Empire comes, he responded to them and said, "God's Empire doesn't come by calculation, ²¹nor will they say, 'Look here or there!' For Look! God's Empire is among you."

²²He said to the Apprentices: "Days are coming when you will desire to see one of the Son of Humanity's days and you will not see [one]. ²³They will say to you, 'Look there or look here!' Don't depart nor chase [their ideas]. ²⁴Just as the lightning, lightening, shines from the heaven to the heaven, so will be the Son of Humanity on his Day. ²⁵First it's necessary for him to suffer many things and to be rejected by this generation. ²⁶Just as it happened in Nōe's [Noah's] days, so it will be also in the Son of Humanity's days. ²⁷They were eating, drinking, marrying, receiving marriage until the day Nōe entered into the chest [ark], and the flood came and destroyed all things.

²⁸Likewise, just as it happened in Lōt's days. There were eating, drinking, purchasing, selling, planting, building. ²⁹On the day Lōt exited from Sodoma [Sodom], fire and sulfur rained down from heaven and destroyed all things. ³⁰Consistent with these things will be the Day on which the Son of Humanity is apocalypsed. ³¹On that Day: the one will be on the housetop with vessels in the house, let that one not descend to lift these things, and the one in the field, likewise, let that one not return back. ³²Remember Lōt's woman. ³³Whoever pursues to secure one's self will destroy it, and whoever

destroys [one's self] generates it. ³⁴I say to you, on that night there will be two men on one cot—one man will be received and the other man released. ³⁵There will be two women grinding meal together—one woman will be received, the other woman released."ⁱ
³⁷Responding, they say to him, "Where, Lord?" He said to them, "Where the body [is], there also the eagles will be assembled on it."

Yēsous tells an analogy about a widow and a judge

18 He was telling an analogy to them— that it was necessary for them always to pray and not to neglect [prayer], ²saying, "Some judge was in some city, having no awe for God and no deference for a human. ³A widow was in that city and was coming to him, saying, 'Make it right for me against my adversary.' ⁴He did not want [to] for a time but after these things he said in himself, 'Although I neither awe God nor defer to a human, ⁵yet because this widow presents labor to me, I will make it right for her so she will not pound my reputation, coming to me until the completion.'" ⁶The Lord said, "Hear what the wrongdoing judge says. ⁷Will not God surely make it right for his elect who bellow out to him day and night? Is he not patient with them? ⁸I say to you that he will make it right for them quickly. However, the Son of Humanity, coming, will he then find allegiance on the land?"

Yēsous tells an analogy about an Observant and a tax agent

⁹He also told—to some who were persuaded among themselves that they are the right ones and devalued the remaining ones— this analogy: ¹⁰"Two humans ascended to the temple to pray, one an Observant [Pharisee] and the other a tax agent. ¹¹The Observant, standing up, was praying about himself: 'God, I thank you that I am not as the remaining humans—rapacious, wrongdoers, adulterers— or even as this tax agent. ¹²I fast twice per Sabbath, I donate a tenth of everything I acquire.' ¹³The tax agent, having stood at a distance, did not even want to lift up his eyes to heaven but beat his breast, saying, 'God, be propitious to me a sinner.' ¹⁴I say to you, This [tax agent] descended fully right to his house rather than that [Observant one] because everyone who raises his status will be impoverished, and the one who impoverishes himself will be raised in status."

Yēsous blesses children

¹⁵They were presenting to him even infants so he might touch them. The Apprentices, seeing, rebuked them. ¹⁶But Yēsous called them, saying, "Release the children to come to me and don't prohibit them, for God's Empire is of such ones. ¹⁷This is true to say to you: whoever doesn't welcome God's Empire as a child will never enter into it."

Yēsous challenges a life of possessions

¹⁸Some leader asked him, saying, "Good teacher, What, in doing, so I may inherit Era Life?" ¹⁹Yēsous said to him, "Why do you call me 'good'? No one is 'good' except the one God. ²⁰You know the orders,

Don't adulterate,
Don't murder,
Don't thieve,
Don't false witness,
Honor your father and mother."

²¹He said, "I guarded all these from youth." ²²Yēsous, hearing, said to him, "One [order] still remains for you. Everything whatever you have, sell and distribute to the beggars! You will have a treasure chest in heavens. Come follow me!" ²³He, hearing these things, became grief-stricken, for he was extremely rich.
²⁴Seeing him [become grief-stricken], Yēsous said, "How difficult [will it be for] those having monies to journey into God's Empire! ²⁵For it's easier for a camel to enter through a small needle's eye than for the wealthy to enter God's Empire." ²⁶The hearers said, "Who is able to be delivered?" ²⁷He said, "The powerlessnesses with humans are powers with God."
²⁸Petros [Peter] said, "Look! We, releasing our stuff, followed you." ²⁹He said to them, "I tell you the truth, that there is no one who released house or woman or siblings or parents or children because of God's Empire, ³⁰who

---

ⁱThe best manuscripts don't have verse 36.

won't receive back many times as much in this season and, in the Coming Era, Era Life."

Yēsous predicts his death again

³¹Taking along the Twelve, he said to them, "Look! We are ascending into Yierosalēm [Jerusalem], everything written through the prophets about the Son of Humanity will be completed. ³²For he will be given over to the ethnic groups and mocked and assaulted and spat upon ³³and, lashing, they will kill him, and on the third day he will arise." ³⁴They understood nothing of these [words], and this utterance was hidden from them, and they were not knowing what is being said.

Yēsous heals a sightless man near Yierichō

³⁵It happened in his getting close to Yierichō [Jericho], someone sightless was sitting along the path begging. ³⁶Hearing a crowd journeying by, he inquired what might this be. ³⁷They declared to him that Yēsous, the Nazōraios [Nazarene], was passing by. ³⁸He bellowed, saying, "Yēsous, Dauid's [David's] Son, show compassion on me!" ³⁹The ones leading were rebuking him so he would be silent, but he was crying out all the more, "Dauid's Son, show compassion on me!" ⁴⁰Standing up, Yēsous signaled for him to be led to him. He's getting close . . . [Yēsous] asked him, ⁴¹"What do you want that I do for you?" He said, "Lord, that I may see again." ⁴²Yēsous said to him, "See again! Your trust has delivered you." ⁴³Instantly he saw again and was following him, splendoring God. All the people, seeing, gave praise to God.

Yēsous and Zakchaios

19 Entering, he was going through Yierichō. ²Look! A man who was called by the name "Zakchaios [Zacchaeus]," and he was a leading tax agent and he was rich. ³He was pursuing to see who Yēsous is and he was not able to from [where he was in] the crowd, because he was little^j in measurement. ⁴Running to the front, he ascended on a sycamore tree so he might see him because he was about to go through that [path]. ⁵As he came to that place, looking up, Yēsous said to him, "Zakchaios, hurrying, descend! For today it's necessary for me to remain in your house." ⁶Hurrying, he descended and welcomed him, rejoicing. ⁷Seeing, all were grumbling, saying, "He entered to lodge with a sinful man." ⁸Standing up, Zakchaios said to the Lord, "Look! Half of my possessions, Lord, I am giving to the beggars, and if I defrauded someone, I am giving back four times." ⁹Yēsous said to him that "Today deliverance has happened in this house because he is also Abra'am's descendant. ¹⁰For the Son of Humanity came to pursue and deliver what is lost."

Yēsous tells an analogy about investments

¹¹They're hearing these things . . . adding on, he told an analogy because he was close to Yierosalēm [Jerusalem] and it seemed to them that God's Empire is about to appear instantly. ¹²Therefore, he said, "Some noble human journeyed to a far country to take for himself a kingdom and to return. ¹³Calling his ten slaves he gave to them ten minas^k and said to them, 'Negotiate [with these] while I go.' ¹⁴His citizens were hating him and they commissioned a delegation after him, saying, 'We don't want this [noble human] to rule over us.' ¹⁵It happened in his returning, having taken the kingdom, and he said for these slaves—to whom the silver had been given—to be voiced to him so he might know what they negotiated. ¹⁶The first appeared, saying, 'Lord, your one mina worked into ten minas.' ¹⁷He said to him, 'Well done, good slave! Because you were allegiant in little matters you are to have authority over ten cities.' ¹⁸The second came, saying, 'Your one mina, Lord, made five minas.' ¹⁹He said also to this one, 'You are to be over five cities.' ²⁰The other came, saying, 'Lord, Look! Your one mina, which I was laying up in a kerchief, ²¹for I was scared of you because you are an austere human: you lift what you did not place down and you harvest what you did not plant.' ²²He says to him, 'I will judge you on the basis of your mouth, evil slave! Do you know that I am an austere human, lifting what I did not place down and harvesting what I did not plant? ²³Why did you not give my

---

^j Or "young."
^k A mina is 100 drachma, about four months' wages.

silver on the table? I, coming [back], could put it into practice with interest.' ²⁴To those standing near he said, 'Lift the mina from him and give to the one having ten minas.' (²⁵They said to him, 'Lord, he has ten minas.') ²⁶I say this to you that 'It will be given to everyone who has, from the one who doesn't have, even what that person has will be lifted. ²⁷However, these my enemies who did not want me to rule over them: lead them here and slaughter them before me!'"

²⁸Saying these things, he was journeying ahead, ascending to Yierosoluma [Jerusalem].

Yēsous enters Yierosoluma

²⁹It happened as he was getting close to Bēth-Phagē [Bethphage] and Bēth-Ania [Bethany], to the mountain called "Of the Olives" [Mount Olivet], he commissioned two of his Apprentices, ³⁰saying, "Go away into the village opposite [of you], in which, journeying into, you will find a tied-up foal, upon which no human has ever sat and, loosening it, lead [it to me]. ³¹If someone asks you, 'Why are you loosening?' Say thus 'That the Lord has a need for it.'" ³²Departing, the commissioned ones found [it] as he said to them. ³³They're loosening the foal . . . its lords said to them, "Why are you loosening the foal?" ³⁴They said, "Because the Lord has a need for it." ³⁵They led it to Yēsous and, throwing their robes on the foal, they sat Yēsous on it. ³⁶He's journeying . . . they were spreading their robes in the path. ³⁷He's already getting close to the descent of the mountain of olives . . . the whole mass of Apprentices, rejoicing, began to praise God in a great voice for all the powers they saw, ³⁸saying,

> *"God is blessing the one coming, the King,*
> *   in name of Lord.*
> Peace in heaven and splendor in the
>   highest levels."

Yēsous weeps and predicts

³⁹Some of the Observant [Pharisees] from the crowds said to him, "Teacher, rebuke your Apprentices!" ⁴⁰Responding, he said, "I say this to you: If these will be silent, the stones will cry out." ⁴¹As he got close [to Jerusalem], seeing the city, he wept over it, ⁴²saying that "If you [only] knew on this day, even you, the matters [leading] to peace—but now it has been hidden from your eyes ⁴³because days will come on you and your enemies will set up ramparts against you, and they will encircle you and they will absorb you from all sides, ⁴⁴and they will raze you and your children among you, and they will not release stone upon stone among you—because you did not know your mentorship's season!"

Yēsous in the temple

⁴⁵Entering into the temple, he began to toss out the sellers, ⁴⁶saying to them, "It's written:

> *My house will be a prayer house,*
> You made it a *bandits' cave."*

⁴⁷He was teaching daily in the temple. The Senior Priests and the Covenant-Code scholars were pursuing to destroy him—also the first ones of the people, ⁴⁸and they were not finding what they might do, for all the people were hanging on to him, listening.

Yēsous and authority

20 It happened on one of the days, he's teaching the people in the temple and gospeling . . . The Senior Priests and Covenant-Code scholars with the Elders stood over [them] ²and said, saying to him, "Tell us: By what sort of authority do you do these things? Or, who is the one who gave to you this authority?" ³Responding, he said to them, "I will also ask about a word, and you tell me! ⁴The Yōannēs's [John's] dipping—was it from heaven or from humans?" ⁵They were co-deliberating with themselves, saying, "If we say 'From heaven,' he will say, 'Why did you not declare allegiance to him?' ⁶If we say 'From humans,' the whole people will pelt us with stones, for it's persuaded Yōannēs is a prophet." ⁷They responded [that they] did not know from where [the authority came]. ⁸Yēsous said to them, "Neither do I say to you by what sort of authority I do these things."

Yēsous tells an analogy about bad vineyard workers

⁹He began to tell the people this analogy: "Some human planted a vineyard, and leased it to farmers, and traveled abroad for an adequate time. ¹⁰In season he commissioned a slave to the farmers so they will give to him [what he wanted] from the vineyard's fruit. The

farmers commissioned him away empty, beating [him]. ¹¹He added another to send another slave. Beating that one and dishonoring [him], they commissioned [him] away empty. ¹²He added to send a third. The inflicters-of-wounds also tossed this one out. ¹³The vineyard's lord said, 'What will I do? I will send my son, the loved one. They will defer to him as an equal.' ¹⁴Seeing him, the farmers were deliberating among one another, saying, 'This is the heir! Let us kill him so the inheritance may be ours.' ¹⁵Tossing him out of the vineyard, they killed [him].

Therefore, what will vineyard's lord do to them? ¹⁶He will come and destroy those farmers and he will give the vineyard to others." Hearing, they said, "May that never happen!" ¹⁷The one observing them said, "What therefore is this that is written:

A stone the formers rejected . . .
This [stone] became the foundation stone?

¹⁸All who fall on this stone will be smashed; on whomever [this stone] falls, it will crush him." ¹⁹The Code scholars [scribes] and the Senior Priests pursued to toss their hands on him on that hour, and they were scared of the people, for they knew he told this analogy about them.

Yēsous and Kaisar

²⁰Spying, they commissioned moles, wearing the mask of the right ones so they might take hold of him with a word so to give him over to the Governor's rule and authority. ²¹They asked him, saying, "Teacher, we know that you speak properly, and you teach and don't respect a face [show deference], but you teach God's path in truth. ²²Is it observant for us to give tribute to Kaisar [Caesar] or not?" ²³Pondering their trickery, he said to them, ²⁴"Exhibit for me a dēnarion. It has the image and inscription of whom?" They said, "Kaisar's." ²⁵He said to them, "Then pay back to Kaisar what are Kaisar's, and to God what are God's." ²⁶They did not have strength before the people to take hold of him in an utterance and, being stunned at his response, they were silenced.

Yēsous and Elites

²⁷Some of the Elites [Sadducees], approaching—the ones contradicting [saying] there is no resurrection—asked him, ²⁸saying, "Teacher, Mōusēs [Moses] wrote to us that *If a brother of someone dies having a woman* and this man *is childless,* that *his brother receives the woman and raises up seed for his brother.* ²⁹Therefore, there were seven brothers. The first received a woman and died childless. ³⁰The second ³¹and the third received her, likewise also the seven did not leave [her] with children and died. ³²Finally, the woman also died. ³³Therefore, the woman, in the resurrection, is a woman for which one of them?" (For the seven had her as a woman.) ³⁴Yēsous said to them, "This Era's descendants marry and are being married, ³⁵and the ones deserving to attain that Era and the resurrection from among the dead ones neither marry nor are being married. ³⁶For they are no longer able to die, for they are equal-to-envoys and God's descendants, being the resurrection's descendants. ³⁷That the dead ones are raised, Mōusēs divulged at the bush, as he says, *Lord God of Abraʾam and God of Yisaʾak* [Isaac] *and God of Yakōb* [Jacob]. ³⁸He isn't God of the dead ones but of living ones, for to him all are living." ³⁹Responding, some of the Code scholars said, "Teacher, you spoke beautifully." ⁴⁰For they were no longer daring to ask him anything.

Yēsous and Dauid's son

⁴¹He said to them, "How do they say the Christos is Dauid's [David's] son? ⁴²For Dauid says in the book of Psalms, *The Lord said to my Lord: Sit from my right* ⁴³*until I place your enemies under your feet.* ⁴⁴Therefore, Dauid calls him Lord, and how is he his son?"

Yēsous warns about the Covenant-Code scholars

⁴⁵All the people are listening . . . he said to his Apprentices, ⁴⁶"Beware the Code scholars, ones wanting to walk around in stoles and loving greetings in the squares and first-status seats in the assembly halls and first-status positions in the banquets, ⁴⁷who gobble up widows' houses and pray at length in pretension. These will receive a more abundant judgment."

Yēsous, speaking of widows

21 Looking up, he saw the rich tossing their donations into the treasury box, ²and he saw some indigent widow there tossing two lepta [small copper coins], ³and he said, "Truly, I say this to you that this widow, the begging one, tossed more than all. ⁴For these all tossed from their overflow into [the treasury box as] donations, but she tossed from her lack all that she had from her life."

Yēsous and the coming disaster

⁵Some are speaking about the temple, that it was decorated with beautiful stones and ornaments . . . he said, ⁶"These things you are observing—days are coming in which stone upon stone will not be released that will not be demolished." ⁷They asked him, saying, "Teacher, therefore when will these things happen? What is the authenticating sign when these are about to happen?" ⁸He said, "Beware you are not deceived! For many will come in my name, saying, 'I am,' and 'The time is close.' Don't journey after them! ⁹Whenever you hear about wars and anarchies, don't be terrified! For it's necessary for these things to happen first, but the completion will not [be] immediately."

¹⁰Then he was saying to them,

"Ethnic group will be raised against ethnic group and empire against empire, ¹¹there will be mega-earthquakes and famines and pestilences from place to place, and there will be frightening events and great authenticating signs from heaven.

¹²Before all these [signs happen] they will lay their hands on you and chase [you], giving [you] over to the assembly halls and prisons, being led on to kings and governors because of my name. ¹³This will turn out for you as a witness. ¹⁴Therefore place in your hearts not to prepare in advance to be defended. ¹⁵For I will give to you a mouth and wisdom which all those contradicting you will not be able to be resist or counter. ¹⁶You will even be given over by parents and siblings and relatives and friends, and they will kill [some] of you. ¹⁷You will be hated by all because of my name. ¹⁸Not a hair from your head will be destroyed. ¹⁹In your resilience acquire your selves!

²⁰Whenever you see Yierosalēm [Jerusalem] encircled by armed encampments then you know that her desolation is close. ²¹Then let those in Youdaia [Judea] flee to the mountains, and let those in her inside get out, and let those on the outside not enter into her, ²²because these are the days of right-making to fill up all what has been written. ²³Oy! on women who have a child in the womb and on those nursing in those days! For there will be a great compulsion on the land and anger for this people, ²⁴and they will fall by the long knife's mouth and will be taken captive to all the ethnic groups, and Yierosalēm will be walked on by ethnic groups until seasons of ethnic groups are filled out.

²⁵There will be authenticating signs in sun and moon and stars, and on the land ethnic groups' anguish—in perplexity over [the] roaring of the sea and waves. ²⁶Humans fainting away from fear and expectation of what is coming on the inhabited world for *the heavens' powers* will be shaken. ²⁷Then they will see *the Son of Humanity coming on a cloud* with power and much splendor. ²⁸These things are beginning to happen . . . stand erect and lift up your heads because your liberation is close."

²⁹He told them an analogy: "Look at the fig tree and all the trees! ³⁰Whenever they already sprout, seeing for yourselves, you know already the summer is close. ³¹So also you, whenever you see these things happening, you know that God's Empire is close. ³²This is true to say to you: this generation will never pass away until all events occur. ³³The heaven and the land will pass away, but my words will never pass away.

³⁴Beware among yourselves so that your hearts may not be depressed in a hangover and drinking and life's anxieties and that Day stand over you unexpectedly, ³⁵like a trap. For it will come upon all those sitting on the face of all the land. ³⁶Be alert in every season, pleading that you might prevail to flee from all these events about to happen and to stand before the Son of Humanity."

³⁷He was teaching days in the temple and exiting nights, he overnighted on the mountain called "[the mountain] of Olives [Mount Olivet]." ³⁸All the people were rising early [to come] to him to hear him in the temple.

Yēsous predicts his death

22 The Flatbreads [Unleavened Bread] Feast, which is called "Pascha [Passover]," was close. ²The Senior Priests and the Covenant-Code scholars [scribes] were pursuing how they might do away with him, for they were scared of the people. ³Satanas [Satan] entered into Youdas [Judas], who is called "Dagger Man [Iscariot]," being among the Twelve's number. ⁴Departing, he spoke with the Senior Priests and police about how he might give him over to them. ⁵They rejoiced and agreed to give to him silver, ⁶and he publicly acknowledged [the offer] and he was pursuing the right time to give him over to them—apart from a crowd.

⁷The Flatbreads Day came, on which [day] it was necessary to sacrifice the Pascha [lamb]. ⁸He commissioned Petros [Peter] and Yōannēs [John], saying, "Journeying, prepare the Pascha for us so we may eat." ⁹They said to him, "Where do you want us to prepare [the Pascha]?" ¹⁰He said to them, "Look! You're entering into the city . . . a human will meet you carrying a water jug. Follow him into the house to which he journeys, ¹¹and you will say to the house's housemaster, 'The Teacher says to you, "Where is the guest room where I may eat the Pascha with my Apprentices?"' ¹²That person will exhibit to you a large upper room, furnished. Prepare [Pascha] there." ¹³Departing, they found [it] just as he had said to them, and they prepared the Pascha.

¹⁴When the hour occurred, he lay down and the Commissioners with him. ¹⁵He said to them, "I desired with desire to eat this Pascha with you before my suffering, ¹⁶for I say to you that I will never eat it until [it] is filled out in God's Empire." ¹⁷Receiving a cup, thanking, he said, "Take this and split [it] among yourselves, ¹⁸for I say to you that I will never drink from now [on] of the produce of the vine until God's Empire comes." ¹⁹Taking bread, thanking, he cracked it and gave to them, saying, "This is my body, which is given for you. Do this in my memory." ²⁰The cup, likewise, after the eating, saying, "This cup is the new covenant in my blood, which is poured out for you. ²¹However, Look! The hand of the one who gives me over is on the table with me ²²because the Son of Humanity journeys consistent with what is established. However, Oy! on that human through whom he is given over." ²³They began to dispute among themselves who among them was about to practice this.

Yēsous and "greatness"

²⁴A rivalry happened among them: who of them seems to be greater. ²⁵He said to them, "The ethnic groups' kings rule them and those overpowering them are called 'benefactors.' ²⁶You are not so. Instead, let the great one among you be as the young one, and the leading one as the serving one. ²⁷For who is greater? The one reclining or the one serving? Is it not the reclining one? I am in your midst as the one serving. ²⁸You are the ones who have persisted with me in my tests. ²⁹I arrange for you as my Father arranged for me—an Empire, ³⁰so you may eat and drink at my table in my Empire, and will be seated on thrones judging Yisraēl's [Israel's] twelve tribes.

Yēsous speaks with Simōn

³¹Simōn Simōn, Look! Satanas called out for [all of] you to sift [you] as wheat. ³²I have pleaded for you that your allegiance doesn't eclipse and you, when turning back, strengthen your siblings." ³³He said to him, "Lord, I am prepared to journey with you even to prison and to death." ³⁴He said to him, "I say to you, Petros, a rooster will not voice today until you deny you know me three times."

Yēsous and swords

³⁵He said to them, "When I commissioned you apart from a sack, bag, and sandals, you did not lack anything, did you?" They said, "Not a thing." ³⁶He said to them, "But now: the one having a sack, let the person lift it. Likewise also a bag. The one not having [sack or bag¹], let the person sell his shirt and purchase a long knife. ³⁷For I say this to you, that it's necessary for this that has been written to be finished in me, namely this: *he was calculated with non-Covenanted*. For what [is written] about me has a completion." ³⁸They

---

¹The object here is unstated and could be either "sack or bag" or "long knife."

said, "Lord, Look! Here are two long knives." He said to them, "It's adequate."

Yēsous prays on Mount Olivet

⁹⁹Exiting, he journeyed consistent with the custom to the mountain of olives [Mount Olivet], and the Apprentices followed him. ⁴⁰Being at the place, he said to them, "Pray not to enter into the test." ⁴¹He was removed from them about a stone's toss and, placing his knees [down], was praying, ⁴²saying, "Father, if you decide, may this cup pass by from me. However, let not what I want but [what] you [want] be done." [⁴³An envoy from heaven appeared to him, strengthening him. ⁴⁴Being in agony, he was praying stretchingly. His sweat became like blood drops, descending onto the land.ᵐ] ⁴⁵Arising from the prayer, coming to the Apprentices, he found them sleeping from the pain, ⁴⁶and said to them, "Why are you sleeping? Arising, pray so you may not enter into the test."

Yēsous given over

⁴⁷While he's speaking . . . Look! A crowd, and the one called Youdas, one of the Twelve, was leading them and he got close to Yēsous to kiss him. ⁴⁸Yēsous said to him, "Youdas, are you giving over the Son of Humanity with a kiss?" ⁴⁹The ones around him, seeing what will happen, said, "Lord, should we beat with a long knife?" ⁵⁰Someone of them beat the Senior Priest's slave and sliced off his right ear. ⁵¹Responding, Yēsous said, "Take leave of this!" Touching the ear, he cured him. ⁵²Yēsous said to the ones coming upon him, Senior Priests and temple police and Elders: "Do you exit with long knives and clubs as if for a bandit? ⁵³Daily I'm with you in the temple . . . you did not extend the hand on me—but this is your hour and darkness' authority."

Yēsous, Petros, and a trial before the Central Council

⁵⁴Taking him, they led and led into the Senior Priest's house. Petros was following at a distance. ⁵⁵Having lit a fire in the middle of the enclosure, sitting together . . . Petros was sitting in the middle of them. ⁵⁶Some servant-girl seeing him sitting in the light and gazing at him, said, "This man was with him." ⁵⁷He denied, saying, "I don't know him, woman." ⁵⁸After a short time, another, seeing him, said, "You are also one of them." Petros said, "Human, I am not." ⁵⁹About one hour interval later . . . some other person was insisting, saying, "In truth, this man was also with him, for he is also a Galilaios [Galilean]." ⁶⁰Petros said, "Human, I don't know what you are saying." Instantly, while he's speaking . . . the rooster voiced. ⁶¹The Lord, turning, observed Petros, and Petros remembered the Lord's utterance—as he said to him that you will deny me three times before the rooster voices today. ⁶²Exiting outside, he wailed bitterly.

⁶³The men who were absorbed with him were mocking him, beating [on him]. ⁶⁴Covering him, they were asking, saying, "Prophesy! Who is the one who beat you?" ⁶⁵Many others, insulting, were speaking against him.

⁶⁶As day came, the people's eldership, both Senior Priests and Covenant-Code scholars, were assembled and led him out to their Central Council, ⁶⁷saying, "If you are the Christos, tell us." He said to them, "If I say to you, you will never trust. ⁶⁸If I ask, you will never respond. ⁶⁹From now on the Son of Humanity will be seated at the right hand of God's Power." ⁷⁰All said, "Are you therefore God's Son?" He said to them, "You say that I am." ⁷¹They said, "Why do we still have a need of a witness? For we ourselves heard from his mouth."

Yēsous on trial before Pilatos, then Hērōdēs, then Pilatos again

23 The entire mass of them, arising, led him to Pilatos [Pilate]. ²They began to accuse him, saying, "We found this person distorting our ethnic group, preventing to give tribute to Kaisar [Caesar], and saying he is Christos, a king." ³Pilatos asked him, saying, "Are you the king over the Youdaians [Judeans, Jews]?" Responding, he said to him, "You say." ⁴Pilatos said to the Senior Priests and the crowds, "I don't find any ground [for legal accusation] in this human." ⁵They were insisting, saying that "He is agitating the people,

---

ᵐThese two verses are not in all the good manuscripts.

teaching throughout the whole of Youdaia [Judea], beginning from the Galilaia [Galilee] until here." ⁶Pilatos, hearing, asked if the human is a Galilaios [Galilean] ⁷and, perceiving that he was of Hērōdēs's [Herod's] authority, he sent him to Hērōdēs, being himself in Yierosoluma [Jerusalem] in those days.

⁸Hērōdēs, seeing Yēsous, rejoiced deeply, for he was wanting for an adequate time to see him because of hearing about him and he was hoping to see some authenticating sign occur by him. ⁹He was asking him in adequate words, but he responded nothing to him. ¹⁰The Senior Priests and Covenant-Code scholars had been standing [near], vigorously accusing him. ¹¹Devaluing him, even Hērōdēs with his troops also mocking, covering [him] with radiant clothing, sent him up to Pilatos. (¹²Both Hērōdēs and Pilatos became friends with one another on that day for previously they were in enmity with themselves.)

¹³Pilatos, calling together the Senior Priests and leaders and the people, ¹⁴said to them, "You presented me this human as one agitating the people, and Look! I, examining [him] before you, found no ground [of accusation] in this human, of which you are accusing him. ¹⁵Neither did Hērōdēs, for he sent him up to us, and Look! Nothing deserving death has been performed by him. ¹⁶Therefore, disciplining, I will loosen him."ⁿ

¹⁸They yelled as an entire mass, saying, "Lift [away] this person, loosen to us Bar-Abbas [Barabbas]!" (¹⁹Who was tossed into prison because of some anarchy that happened in the city and a murder.) ²⁰Again, Pilatos voiced out to them, wanting to loosen Yēsous. ²¹They were voicing back, saying, "Crucify! Crucify him!" ²²A third time he said to them, "For what? What bad thing did this person do? I found no ground for death in him. Therefore, disciplining, I will loosen him." ²³They were pressing with great voices, pleading for him to be crucified, and their voices prevailed.

²⁴Pilatos rendered judgment that their accusation would be met. ²⁵He loosened the one tossed in prison for anarchy and murder, for whom they pleaded, and he gave over Yēsous to what they wanted.

Yēsous crucified

²⁶As they were leading him away, taking hold of some Simōn Kyrēnaios [Cyrenian] coming from the field, they placed on him the cross to carry [it] behind Yēsous. ²⁷A great mass of the people and women, who were striking themselves and lamenting him, were following him. ²⁸Turning to the women, Yēsous said, "Yierosalēm's daughters, don't wail for me. However, wail for yourselves and for your children, ²⁹because Look! The days are coming in which you will say, 'God blesses the sterile, and the bellies that did not give life and breasts that did not nurture.' ³⁰Then they began *to say to the mountains, 'Fall on us! and to the hills, Cover us!'* ³¹Because if they do these things with green wood, what happens with dry [wood]?"

³²Two others, bad guys, were led with him to be put away. ³³When they came to the place called "Kranion" [Skull], there they crucified him and the bad guys, one on his right and one on his left. [³⁴Yēsous was saying, "Father, release them, for they don't know what they are doing."]ᵒ *Splitting his robes, they tossed the die.* ³⁵The people had been standing, observing. The leaders were snorting, saying, "He delivered others, let him deliver himself, if this person is God's Christos, the Elect One." ³⁶They mocked him and the soldiers, approaching, offering to him sour wine ³⁷and saying, "If you are the king over the Youdaians, deliver yourself!" ³⁸There was also an inscription above him:

| This is the king over the Youdaians

³⁹One of the bad guys hanging was insulting him, saying, "Are you not the Christos? Deliver yourself and us!" ⁴⁰Responding, the other one, rebuking him, said, "Do you not have awe for God because you are in the same judgment? ⁴¹We [are judged] rightly, for we are receiving a deserving [judgment] for what we practiced, but this person practiced nothing out of place." ⁴²He was saying, "Yēsous, remember me whenever

---

ⁿSome manuscripts read verse 17 as "He had a necessity to release one [prisoner] at each feast."
ᵒSome manuscripts don't have this half of the verse.

you come into your Empire." ⁴³He said to him, "This is true to say to you: Today you will be with me in Paradise."

⁴⁴It was already about the sixth hour [noon] and darkness came over the whole land until the ninth hour ⁴⁵. . . the sun's eclipsed . . . the sanctuary's inner curtain was split in the middle. ⁴⁶Voicing in a loud voice, Yēsous said, "Father, *into your hands I present my spirit.*" Saying this, he expired. ⁴⁷The leader of a hundred soldiers, seeing what occurred, splendored God, saying, "Really, this human was right." ⁴⁸All the crowds who gathered at this observance, observing what occurred, smiting the breasts, returned [home]. ⁴⁹All those who knew him and the women from the Galilaia who follow him together had been standing at a distance to see these things.

Yēsous buried

⁵⁰Look! A man with the name Yōsēf [Joseph], being a councilor and a good and right man—⁵¹this man had not consented to their plan and practice—from Arimathaia [Arimathea], a city of the Youdaians, was attending to God's Empire, ⁵²this man, approaching Pilatos, pleaded for Yēsous' body ⁵³and, taking [it] down, wrapped it in linen and placed him in a carved tomb, where no one had ever been laid. ⁵⁴It was the Day of Preparation, and Sabbath was dawning.

⁵⁵Following closely, the women who had come together from the Galilaia with him observed the tomb and as they had laid his body, ⁵⁶returning, prepared spices and fragrant ointment. They quieted on the Sabbath consistent with the order.

Yēsous announced as raised by women to the apostles

24 On the first [day] of the Sabbaths, during deep dawn, they came to the tomb carrying the spices they prepared. ²They found the stone rolled away from the tomb, ³and entering, they did not find the Lord Yēsous' body. ⁴It occurred in their perplexity about this, and Look! Two men in radiant clothing stood over them ⁵. . . they're over-awed and reclining [their] faces to the land . . . they said to them [the women], "Why pursue the living with the dead? ⁶He isn't here but has been raised. Remember, as he spoke to you while in the Galilaia [Galilee], ⁷saying it's necessary for the Son of Humanity to be given over into the hands of human sinners and to be crucified and on the third day to rise up." ⁸They remembered his utterances, ⁹and returning from the tomb, they declared all these things to the Eleven and to all the remaining. ¹⁰(They were Maria the Magdalēnē [Mary Magdalene] and Yōanna [Joanna] and Maria [Mary], mother of Yakōbos [James], and the women remaining with them.) They were saying these things to the Commissioners, ¹¹and these utterances appeared before them as nonsense, and they were not trusting the women. ¹²Petros [Peter], arising ran to the tomb and, peering, sees only the linen cloths, and he departed, stunned in himself about what had happened.

Yēsous walks to Emmaous

¹³Look! Two of them on the same day were journeying to a village sixty stades [7 miles] from Yierosalēm [Jerusalem], whose name is Emmaous [Emmaus]. ¹⁴They were sharing with one another about all these things that had coalesced. ¹⁵It happened during their sharing and disputing [about how to understand what happened], and Yēsous himself, coming close, was journeying with them. ¹⁶Their eyes were being grasped so they would not perceive him. ¹⁷He said to them, "What are these words you, walking, are tossing back and forth with one another?" They, grim ones, stood still. ¹⁸Responding, one by name Kleopas [Cleopas], said to him, "Are you the only one inhabiting Yierosalēm and don't know the things that happened in it in these days?" ¹⁹He said to them, "What things?" They said to him, "The things about Yēsous Nazarēnos [Nazarene], who was a man—a prophet, powerful in work and word before God and all the people, ²⁰such that the Senior Priests and our leaders gave him over to death-judgment and they crucified him. ²¹We were hoping that he is the one coming to liberate Yisraēl [Israel] but instead with all these [events] it leads to this third day since all these things happened. ²²But also, some women among us were beside themselves with us, being at the tomb at dawn, ²³and not finding his body, saying to have seen a vision of envoys who say he lives. ²⁴Some of those with us departed to the tomb and found it so, just as

the women said, and they did not see him." ²⁵He said to them, "O brainless and heavy in heart to trust in everything that the prophets spoke! ²⁶It was necessary for the Christos to suffer these things and to enter his splendor, was it not?" ²⁷Beginning from Mōüsēs [Moses] and from all the prophets, he interpreted for them the events about himself in all the writings.

²⁸They came close to the village where he was journeying, and he made like he was to journey farther. ²⁹They urged him, saying, "Remain with us because it is nearly evening and the day has already reclined." He entered to remain with them. ³⁰It happened in his reclining with them, taking the bread, he blessed and, cracking, was giving [some] to them, ³¹their eyes were opened and they perceived him. He became invisible from them. ³²They said to one another, "Was not our heart aflame in us as he was speaking to us in the path as he opened the writings for us?"

³³Arising at that hour, they returned to Yierosoluma and found the Eleven and those with them now clustered, ³⁴saying that "The Lord has really been raised and has been seen by Simōn." ³⁵They expounded the matters in the path and as he was made known to them in cracking the bread.

Yēsous appears to them

³⁶They're speaking these things . . . he stood in the middle of them and says to them, "Peace to you!" ³⁷Being terrified and becoming over-awed, they were thinking they were observing a spirit. ³⁸He said to them, "Why have you become disturbed? Why are deliberations ascending in your [pl.] heart? ³⁹See my hands and my feet—that I am he. Feel me and see that a spirit doesn't have flesh and bones—as you observe me having." ⁴⁰Saying this, he showed them the hands and the feet. ⁴¹While they're not trusting from the joy and being stunned . . . he said to them, "Do you have any edible food here?" ⁴²They gave to him a piece of roasted fish ⁴³and, taking, he ate before them.

⁴⁴He said to them, "These [are] my words that I spoke to you while being with you, that it's necessary to fill out about me all that is written in Mōüsēs' Covenant Code and in the Prophets and Psalms." ⁴⁵Then he opened their mind to understand the writings ⁴⁶and said to them that "Thus it's written for the Christos to suffer and to rise up from the dead ones on the third day ⁴⁷and for repentance to be announced in his name for release from sins for all the ethnic groups. Beginning from Yierosalēm ⁴⁸you are witnesses of these things. ⁴⁹Look! I commission upon you the Father's pledge. Sit in the city until you put on power from the heights."

⁵⁰He led them out until Bēth-Ania [Bethany] and, lifting his hands, he blessed them. ⁵¹It happened in his blessing them he separated from them and was being guided into the heaven.

⁵²They, bowing down before him, returned into Yierosalēm with great joy ⁵³and they were always in the temple, blessing God.

INTRODUCTION TO THE GOSPEL OF JOHN

The Fourth Gospel shows how Yēsous is put on trial, and then in turn, he puts the Kosmos on trial. Hence, as 15:26-27 makes clear, there is a witness theme running throughout this Gospel in which the Spirit as Illuminator [Paraklētos] prosecutes the world for Yēsous. In chapter 20 we are explicitly told why this Gospel was written, and we would do well to let its witness theme inform our every reading: "Therefore, Yēsous did many other authenticating signs before his Apprentices, which are not written in this book, but these things have been written so you may trust that Yēsous is the Christos, God's Son, and so trusting, you may have Life in his name" (20:30–31). This biography of Yēsous was written to spread trust in Yēsous so people could have genuine Life, and this means it's both for those who are allegiant and for those who are yet in the Kosmos. It enhances existing faith as well as opens the door for new followers.

This longtime favorite of the Gospels combines a presentation of Yēsous as God's only Son with a rich exploration of simple terms such as Life (Era Life) and Light and Darkness and especially Faith (trust, allegiance). What was so typical for the Synoptic Gospels—the expression "God's Empire" (kingdom of God)—has mutated into "Life," and the deity of the Christos is far more explicit in this Gospel than in the first three. What was also typical—paragraph-length episodes of Yēsous' teaching and actions—has become long, speech-like explorations of themes.

This Gospel has a one-of-a-kind prologue (1:1-14) followed by four chapters that witness to who Yēsous is (1:15–4:54), where the focus is on Yōannēs the Dipper's [John the Baptist's] witness along with the witness of authenticating signs (such as turning water into wine). Chapters 5–12 are about the Life that Yēsous provides: through who he is, through trusting him, and through his authenticating signs. Yōannēs 13–17 is Yōannēs's version of the last events of Yēsous with his disciples, while 18–21 cover the customary terrain of his arrest, trials, death-by-crucifixion, resurrection, and appearances.

It's customary to say there are seven authenticating signs and seven "I am" sayings.

The signs:

1. Water to wine (2:1-11)
2. Healing the official's son (4:46-54)
3. Healing the man at the pool (5:1-9)
4. Feeding 5,000 (6:1-13)
5. Walking on water (6:16-21)
6. Healing a sightless man (9:1-12)
7. Raising Lazaros (11:1-44)

The "I am" sayings:

1. Life's Bread (6:35)
2. Kosmos's Light (8:12)
3. Door for Sheep (10:9)
4. Good Shepherd (10:11)
5. Path, Truth, and Life (14:6)
6. Resurrection and Life (11:25)
7. True Vine (15:1)

Each of these is a witness to who Yēsous is as God's Son who brings Life to the Kosmos through his death and resurrection. Each of these, then, unpacks what Yōannēs means by the word *Logos* in the prologue. He is the Truth, the Life, the Path to God, and he gives this Life because he has been sent by the Father.

Based on style (simple vocabulary, straightforward sentences, Hemingway-like rigor), the author of the Gospel of Yōannēs is the author of the letters of Yōannēs, and whoever wrote the Gospel had an intentionally unstated relationship to the apprentice Yēsous loved (e.g., Yōannēs 13:23-25). The author of the letters refers to himself as the "Elder," but in this Gospel that Elder Yōannēs appears to be one of the Commissioners (apostles) who was at the Last Supper and who appears to be the Apprentice Yēsous loved, and so many think it's probable that the author is the apostle Yōannēs (in our translation, "Commissioner Yōannēs"), the son of Zebedaios [Zebedee] and brother of Yakōbos [James]. It's possible the Elder Yōannēs was someone other than the Commissioner Yōannēs and that both of them were at the Last Supper, in which case the author could be the Apprentice Yēsous loved who is the Elder Yōannēs, not the Commissioner Yōannēs. That the "other Apprentice" had not known Yēsous' statement about a resurrection on the third day (20:9) suggests the author is not one of the Commissioners.

THE GOSPEL OF JOHN

Pro-logos

1 ¹In the beginning was the Logos,
and the Logos was with God,
and the Logos was God.
²This one was in the beginning with God.
³All things were through him,
and apart from him there was not one thing.
What was ⁴in him was Life,
and the Life was the Light for humans.
⁵The Light appears in the Darkness,
and the Darkness did not prevail against it.

⁶There was a human, commissioned from God, the name for him was Yōannēs [John]. ⁷This person came for witness so he might witness about the Light, so all could trust through him. ⁸That person was not the Light, but so he might witness about the Light.

⁹He was the true Light (which enlightens every human) coming into the Kosmos. ¹⁰He was in the Kosmos, and the Kosmos came through him, and the Kosmos did not know him. ¹¹He came to his own and his own did not receive him. ¹²Whoever received him, he gave to them authority to become God's children, to those trusting in his name, ¹³who are given life not from blood, not from flesh's will, and not from man's will but from God. ¹⁴The Logos became flesh and pitched a tent among us, and we observed his splendor, the splendor as from the only Son from the Father, full of grace and truth. (¹⁵Yōannēs witnesses about him and has cried out, saying, "This was [the one] of whom I said, 'The one coming after me has been before me, because he was first before me.'") ¹⁶Because we all received from his completeness and grace after grace. ¹⁷Because the Covenant Code was given through Mōūsēs [Moses], grace and truth came through Yēsous Christos. ¹⁸No one has seen God once. The only [Son], God, who being in the Father's garment-fold, that one expounded [God].

Yōannēs witnesses about Yēsous

¹⁹This is Yōannēs' witness when the Youdaians [Judeans, Jews] from Yierosoluma [Jerusalem] commissioned priests and Leuitēs [Levites] to him so they could ask him, "Who are you?" ²⁰He openly agreed and did not deny, and openly agreed that "I am not the Christos." ²¹They asked him, "Who then? Are you Ēlias [Elijah]?" and he says, "I am not." "Are you the prophet?" and he responded, "No." ²²Therefore, they said to him, "Who are you? So we may give a response to the ones who sent us. What do you say about yourself?" ²³He said,

"I am *a voice bellowing in the wilderness,
Make straight the Lord's path*,"

just as Ēsaïas [Isaiah] the prophet said.

²⁴They were commissioned from the Observant [Pharisees]. ²⁵They asked him and said to him, "Why, therefore, do you dip if you are not the Christos or Ēlias or the prophet?" ²⁶Yōannēs responded to them, saying, "I dip in water. In the middle of you has stood one whom you did not know, ²⁷the one coming after me, of whom I am not deserving that I loosen the strap of his sandals." (²⁸These things happened in Bēth-Ania [Bethany] Beyond the Yordanēs [Jordan River], where Yōannēs was dipping.)

²⁹On the next day, he sees Yēsous coming to him and says,

"Look! God's Lamb who lifts the Kosmos's sin! ³⁰This is for whom I said, 'After me a man comes who was before me, because he was first before me.' ³¹I had not known him, but—that he might appear to Yisraēl [Israel]—because of this I came dipping in water."

³²Yōannēs witnessed, saying that

"I have observed the Spirit descending as a dove from heaven and it remained on him. ³³I had not known him, but the one who sent me to dip in water, that one said to me, 'Upon whomever you saw the Spirit descending and remaining on him, this person is the one dipping in Holy Spirit.' ³⁴I have seen and I have witnessed that this is God's Son."

³⁵On the next day again Yōannēs had been standing, and two of his Apprentices, ³⁶and observing Yēsous walking around, says, "Look, God's Lamb!" ³⁷The two Apprentices heard him speaking and they followed Yēsous. ³⁸Yēsous, turning and observing them following, says to them, "What are you pursuing?" They said to him, "My Greatness [Rabbi] (which translated says, 'Teacher'), where are you remaining?" ³⁹He says to them, "Come and see." Therefore, they came and saw where he remains and they were remaining with him that day. It was about the tenth hour [4 p.m.]. ⁴⁰One of the two who heard from Yōannēs and followed him was Andreas [Andrew], Simōn Petros's [Simon Peter's] brother. ⁴¹This one first finds his own brother, Simōn, and says to him, "We have found the Messias [Messiah] (which translated is 'Christos')." ⁴²They led him to Yēsous. Yēsous, observing him, said, "You are Simōn, Yōannēs's son, you will be called 'Kēphas' (which is translated 'Petros' [Rock])."

Yēsous in the Galilaia with more Apprentices

⁴³On the next day he wanted to exit to the Galilaia [Galilee] and he finds Philippos [Philip]. Yēsous says to him, "Follow me." ⁴⁴Philippos was from Bēthsaida, from Andreas's and Petros's city. ⁴⁵Philippos finds Nathana-ēl [Nathanael] and says to him, "We have found [the one] about whom Mōusēs wrote in the Code and the prophets, Yēsous, son of Yōsēf [Joseph], who is from Nazara [Nazareth]." ⁴⁶Nathana-ēl said to him, "Is it possible for something good to be from Nazara?" Philippos says to him, "Come and see." ⁴⁷Yēsous saw Nathana-ēl coming to him and says about him, "Look! Truly, an Yisraēlites [Israelite] in whom there isn't a disguise." ⁴⁸Nathana-ēl says to him, "From where do you know me?" Yēsous responded and said to him, "Before Philippos's voicing to you, being under the fig tree, I saw you." ⁴⁹Nathana-ēl responded to him, "My Greatness, you are God's Son, you are Yisraēl's king." ⁵⁰Yēsous responded and said to him, "Because I said to you that I saw you underneath the fig tree, do you trust? You will see greater than these." ⁵¹He says to him, "This is especially true that I say to you: You will see *heaven having been opened and God's envoys ascending and descending* upon the Son of Humanity."

Yēsous in Kana of the Galilaia

2 On the third day there was a marriage in Kana of the Galilaia [Cana of Galilee], and Yēsous' mother was there. ²Both Yēsous and his Apprentices were called to the marriage. ³Wine's lacking . . . Yēsous' mother says to him, "They do not have wine." ⁴Yēsous says to her, "What is there to me and to you, woman? My hour has not yet come." ⁵His mother says to the servants, "Whatever he says to you, do." ⁶There were lying there six stone water vessels consistent with Youdaian [Judean] cleansing [rites], each making space for two or three measures [c. 20–30 gallons each]. ⁷Yēsous says to them, "Fill the vessels with water," and they filled them to the top, ⁸and he says to them, "Now draw out and carry to the *maître d'*." They carried. ⁹As the *maître d'* tasted the water-become-wine and had not known where it came from—but the servants who drew [it] had known—the *maître d'* voiced to the groom ¹⁰and says to him, "Every human places the beautiful wine first and whenever they are boozed the lesser. You have kept the beautiful wine until now."

¹¹Yēsous did this first of authenticating signs in Kana of the Galilaia and he made apparent his splendor, and his Apprentices trusted in him. ¹²After this, he descended to Kaphar-Naoum [Capernaum]—and his mother and his brothers and his Apprentices, and they remained there not many days.

Yēsous and Pascha

¹³The Youdaians' Pascha [Passover] was close, and Yēsous ascended to Yierosoluma [Jerusalem], ¹⁴and he found in the temple persons selling oxen, sheep, and doves, and seated moneychangers. ¹⁵Making a whip from ropes, he tossed all out from the temple (both the sheep and oxen), and he poured out the moneychangers' coins and turned over the

tables, ¹⁶and to the sellers of doves he said, "Lift these things from here, do not make my Father's house a business house!" (¹⁷His Apprentices remembered that it's written, *Zeal for your house gobbles me up.*)

¹⁸The Youdaians, therefore, responded and said to him, "What authenticating sign do you demonstrate for us that you do these things?" ¹⁹Yēsous responded and said to them, "Loosen this sanctuary and on third day I will raise it." ²⁰The Youdaians therefore said, "This sanctuary was formed over forty-six years, and you will raise it in three days?" (²¹But that one was saying [this] about his body's sanctuary. ²²Therefore, when he was raised from among the dead ones, his Apprentices remembered that he was saying this, and they trusted in the writing and in the word Yēsous said.)

²³As he was in the Yierosolumas^a in the Pascha at the feast, many trusted in his name, observing his authenticating signs that he was doing. ²⁴Yēsous himself did not trust himself to them because he knew all, ²⁵and because he was having no need that someone witness about a human, for he knew what was in the human.

Yēsous and Nikodēmos

3 There was a human of the Observant [Pharisees], Nikodēmos [Nicodemus] a name for him, leader of the Youdaians [Judeans, Jews]. ²This person came to him at night and said to him, "My Greatness [Rabbi], we know that you have come from God [as a] teacher. For no one is able to do these authenticating signs that you do unless God be with him." ³Yēsous responded and said to him, "This is especially true to say to you: Unless someone is given a life from above, one isn't able to see God's Empire." ⁴Nikodēmos says to him, "How is a human able to be given a life, being old? Is one able to enter into one's mother's stomach a second time and to be given a life?" ⁵Yēsous responded, "This is especially true to say to you: Unless someone is given Life from water and Spirit, one isn't able to enter into God's Empire. ⁶What has been given Life from the Flesh is flesh, and what has been given Life from the Spirit is spirit. ⁷Don't be stunned that I said to you, 'It's necessary to be given Life from above.' ⁸The Spirit spirits where it wants and you hear its voice, but you do not know from where it comes and where it goes out. So it is for everyone given life from the Spirit." ⁹Nikodēmos responded and said to him, "How is it possible for these to happen?" ¹⁰Yēsous responded and said to him, "You are Yisraēl's [Israel's] teacher and you do not know these things? ¹¹This is especially true to say to you that: We speak what we know and we witness what we have seen, and you do not receive our witness. ¹²If I say earthly things to you and you do not trust, how will you trust if I say heavenly things to you? ¹³No one has ascended into the heaven except the one descended from the heaven, the Son of Humanity. ¹⁴Just as Mōüsēs [Moses] raised the status of the snake in the wilderness, so it's necessary for the Son of Humanity to be raised up in status, ¹⁵so that everyone trusting in him may have Era Life. ¹⁶For God loved the Kosmos in such a way that he gave his only Son so everyone trusting in him may not be destroyed but have Era Life. ¹⁷For God did not commission the Son into the Kosmos so he might judge the Kosmos but so the Kosmos might be delivered through him. ¹⁸The one trusting in him isn't judged, and the one not trusting has already been judged, because the person has not trusted in the name of God's only Son. ¹⁹This is the judgment: that Light has come into the Kosmos and humans loved instead the Darkness rather than the Light. For their works were evil. ²⁰For everyone practicing foul [works] hates the Light and doesn't come to the Light so one's works may be convicted. ²¹The one doing the Truth comes to the Light so his works may become apparent, having been worked in God."

Yēsous dips

²²After these Yēsous and his Apprentices came into Youdaian [Judean] land and spent time there and were dipping. ²³Yōannēs [John] was dipping in Ainōn [Aenon] close to Saleim [Salim] because there was much water there, and they were coming and were being dipped. ²⁴For Yōannēs had not yet been tossed into prison.

²⁵Therefore, a dispute came from Yōannēs's Apprentices with a Youdaian about cleansing [rites]. ²⁶They came to Yōannēs and said to

---

^aPlural here.

him, "My Greatness, the one who was with you Beyond the Yordanēs [Jordan], to whom you have witnessed, Look! this one is dipping and all are coming to him." ²⁷Yōannēs responded and said, "A human isn't able to receive, not even one thing, unless it be given to the person from heaven. ²⁸You yourselves witness about me that I said, 'I am not the Christos but that I am commissioned before that one.' ²⁹The one having the bride is the groom. The groom's friend, the one standing and hearing him, joys in joy because of the groom's voice. Therefore, this my joy is filled out. ³⁰It's necessary for that one to grow but for me to diminish.

³¹The one coming from above is above all. The one being from the land is from the land and speaks from the land. The one coming from the heaven is above all. ³²What we have seen and heard, this we witness, and no one receives his witness. ³³The one receiving his witness sealed that God is true. ³⁴For the one God commissioned speaks God's utterances, for he doesn't give the Spirit from a measure. ³⁵The Father loves the Son and gave all things in his hand. ³⁶The one trusting in the Son has Era Life. The one unpersuaded by the Son will not see Life, but God's anger remains on the person."

Yēsous and the woman from Samareia

4 Therefore, as Yēsous knew that the Observant [Pharisees] heard that "Yēsous was making and dipping more Apprentices than Yōannēs [John]" ²—although Yēsous himself was not dipping but his Apprentices [were]—³he released Youdaia [Judea] and departed again to the Galilaia [Galilee].

⁴It was necessary for him to go through Samareia [Samaria]. ⁵Therefore, he comes into a city of Samareia, called Suchar, a neighbor to the region that Yakōb [Jacob] gave to his son Yōsēf [Joseph]. ⁶Yakōb's spring was there. Therefore, Yēsous, being labored from the journey's path, so sat down at the spring. It was about the sixth hour [noon].

⁷A woman from Samareia comes to draw water. Yēsous says to her, "Give me to drink." ⁸For his Apprentices had departed to the city so they might purchase provisions. ⁹Therefore, the Samaratis woman says to him, "How do you, being Youdaian, ask to drink from me, being a Samaritis woman?" (For Youdaians do not deal with Samaritēs.) ¹⁰Yēsous responded and said to her, "If you had known God's gift and who the one is who says to you, 'Give me to drink,' you would have asked him and he would have given you living water." ¹¹The woman says to him, "Lord, you do not even have a drawing bucket and the cistern is deep. Therefore, where do you have this living water? ¹²You aren't greater than our father Yakōb who gave the cistern to us and he himself and his sons and livestock were drinking from it, are you?" ¹³Yēsous responded and said to her, "Everyone who drinks from this water will thirst again, ¹⁴but whoever drinks from the water that I will give to the person, will never ever thirst into the Era, but the water that I will give to the person will become in the person a spring of water leaping into Era Life." ¹⁵The woman says to him, "Lord, give to me this water so I may not thirst nor come through here to draw."

¹⁶He says to her, "Go away, voice your man and come here." ¹⁷The woman responded and said to him, "I do not have a man." Yēsous says to her, "You have said beautifully that 'I do not have a man.' ¹⁸For you had five men and now the one you have isn't your man. You have spoken truly." ¹⁹The woman says to him, "Lord, I observe that you are a prophet. ²⁰Our fathers bowed down on this mountain, and you [pl.] say that the place where it's necessary to bow down is Yierosolumas [Jerusalem]." ²¹Yēsous says to her, "Trust me, woman, that the hour comes when you will bow down to the Father neither on this mountain nor in Yierosolumas. ²²You bow down to what you do not know. We bow down to what we know because deliverance is from the Youdaians. ²³But an hour comes and is now when true bowing-downers will bow down to the Father in spirit-and-truth. For the Father pursues such bowing-downers to him. ²⁴God is spirit, and it necessary for the bowing-downers to bow down in spirit-and-truth." ²⁵The woman says to him, "I know that Messias [Messiah] (who is called Christos) comes. Whenever that one comes, he will announce all things to us." ²⁶Yēsous says to her, "I am [he], the one speaking to you."

²⁷At this [moment] his Apprentices came and were stunned that he was speaking with a woman. No one, however, said, "What are you pursuing or why do you speak with her?" ²⁸Therefore, the woman released her water vessel and departed

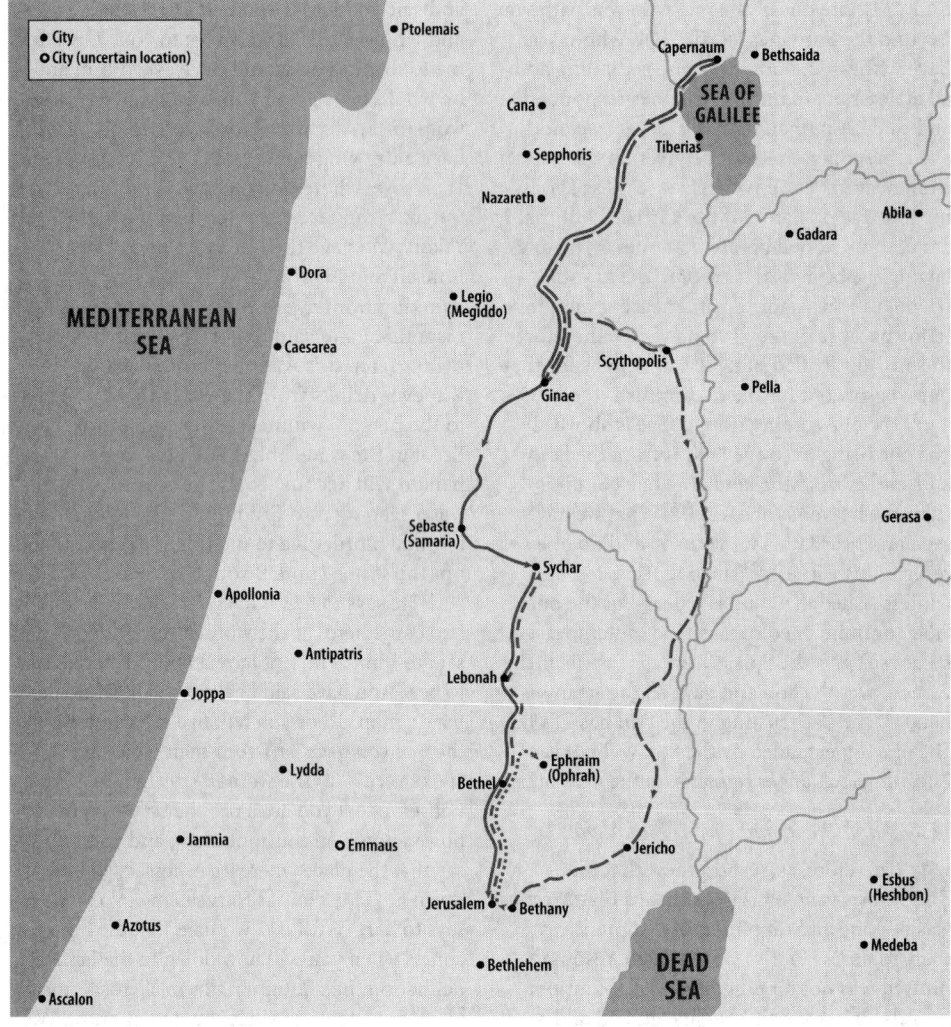

Figure 5. Jesus' journeys to Jerusalem

into the city and says to the humans, "Come! Look at a human who said to me everything I did. Is this one not the Christos?" ³⁰They exited from the city and were coming to him.

³¹Meanwhile, the Apprentices were asking him, saying, "My Greatness [Rabbi], eat!" ³²He said to them, "I have food to eat that you do not know." ³³Therefore, the Apprentices were saying to one another, "Someone has not brought food to him to eat, have they?" ³⁴Yēsous says to them, "My food is that I may do the will of the one who sent me, and I will complete his work. ³⁵Do you not say that 'There is still four months and the harvest comes?' Look! I say to you, Lift up your eyes and observe the fields that are white for harvest. Already ³⁶the one harvesting receives a wage and assembles fruit for Era Life, so the one planting may rejoice and the one harvesting may rejoice together. ³⁷For in this the word is true that 'One is planter and another is harvester.' ³⁸I commissioned you to harvest for what you have not labored. Others have labored and you have entered into their labor."

³⁹From that city many of the Samaritēs trusted in him through the woman's word, witnessing that "He said to me everything I did." ⁴⁰Therefore, as the Samaritēs came to him, they were asking him to remain with them. He remained there two days. ⁴¹Many more trusted

through his word, ⁴²and they were saying to the woman, "It's no longer through your speaking that we trust, for we ourselves have heard and we know that this one is truly the Kosmos's Deliverer."

Yēsous goes to the Galilaia

⁴³After two days he exited from there into the Gailaia [Galilee], ⁴⁴for Yēsous himself witnessed that a prophet doesn't have honor in one's ancestral village. ⁴⁵Therefore, when he came into the Galilaia, the Galilaioi [Galileans] received him, all having seen whatever he did in Yierosolumas at the feast. For they also went to the feast. ⁴⁶ᵃTherefore, he came again to Kana [Cana] of the Galilaia, where he made the water wine.

⁴⁶ᵇThere was some empire person whose son was weakening in Kaphar-Naoum [Capernaum]. ⁴⁷This person, hearing that Yēsous had come from Youdaia into the Galilaia, departed to him and was asking that he might descend and cure his son, for he was about to die. ⁴⁸Therefore, Yēsous said to him, "Unless you [pl.] see authenticating signs and omens, you will never trust." ⁴⁹The empire person says to him, "Lord, descend before my child dies." ⁵⁰Yēsous says to him, "Journey! Your son lives." The human trusted the word that Yēsous said to him, and he was journeying. ⁵¹Already he's descending . . . his slaves met him, saying that his child lives. ⁵²He inquired, therefore, about the hour from them on which he had recovery. Therefore they said to him that yesterday at the seventh hour [1 p.m.] the fever released him. ⁵³Therefore the father knew on that hour in which Yēsous said to him, "Your son lives." He trusted and his whole household. ⁵⁴This, again, was the second authenticating sign Yēsous did, coming from Youdaia into the Galilaia.

Yēsous and Sabbath

5 After these there was a Youdaian [Judean] feast and Yēsous ascended into Yierosoluma [Jerusalem]. ²There is in Yierosolumas, at [the gate] for the sheep, a pool that is been called in Hebraïsti [Hebrew], "Bēth-Zatha [Bethesda]," having five porches. ³In these were laying a mass of weak ones: sightless, lame, stiffened.ᵇ ⁵Some human was there, having his weakness for 38 years. ⁶Yēsous, seeing this person lying there and knowing that he already had [been there] many years, says to him, "Do you want to become healthy?" ⁷The weakening one responded to him, "Lord, I don't have a human that, whenever the water is agitated, can toss me into the pool, at which [time] I come, another descends before me." ⁹Yēsous says to him, "Rise! Lift your mat and walk around." ⁹Immediately the human became healthy and he lifted his mat and was walking around.

It was Sabbath on that day. ¹⁰Therefore the Youdaians were saying to the one healed, "It's Sabbath, and it isn't observant for you to lift your mat." ¹¹He responded to them, "The one who made me healthy, that person said to me, 'Lift your mat and walk around.'" ¹²They asked him, "Who is the human who said to you, 'Lift and walk around'?" ¹³The one who had been cured did not know who it is, for Yēsous slipped away . . . a crowd's in that place . . . ¹⁴After these Yēsous finds him in the temple and said to him, "Look! You have become healthy. Sin no longer so that something worse doesn't happen to you." ¹⁵The human departed and announced to the Youdaians that it was Yēsous who made him healthy.

Yēsous and the Father and Son

¹⁶Because of this the Youdaians were chasing Yēsous because he was doing these things on Sabbath. ¹⁷Yēsous responded to them, "My Father works until now and I work." ¹⁸Because of this, therefore, the Youdaians were rather pursuing him to kill [him], because not only was he loosening the Sabbath but also he was saying his own Father was God, making himself equal to God.

¹⁹Therefore, Yēsous responded and was saying to them, "This is especially true to say to you: The Son isn't able to do anything from himself except what he sees the Father doing. For whatever that one [Father] does these things and the Son likewise does. ²⁰For the Father loves the Son and exhibits all things to him that he does, and greater works than these he will exhibit to him, so you may be stunned. ²¹For just as the Father raises the dead ones and makes life, so also the Son makes life for

---

ᵇSome manuscripts mention here occasional descents of an angel to heal.

those he wants. ²²For the Father doesn't judge anyone but gave all judgment to the Son, ²³so all may honor the Son as they honor the Father. The one who doesn't honor the Son doesn't honor the Father who sent him.

²⁴This is especially true to say to you, that: The one who hears my word and trusts in the one who sent me has Era Life and does not come into judgment but has shifted from Death into Life. ²⁵This is especially true to say to you that: The hour comes and now is when the dead ones will hear God's Son's voice and the hearing ones will live. ²⁶For just as the Father has Life in himself, so also he gave to the Son to have Life in himself. ²⁷He gave authority to him to make judgment, because he is Son of Humanity. ²⁸Do not be stunned at this because the hour comes at which [time] all who are in tombs will hear his voice, ²⁹and the ones who did good works will journey out into Life's resurrection, but the ones who practiced foul works into judgment's resurrection.

³⁰I am not able to do anything from myself. Just as I hear, I judge. My judgment is right because I do not pursue my will but the one who sent me's will.

³¹If I witness about myself my witness is not true. ³²Another is the one who witnesses about me, and I know that the witness that he witnesses about me is true. ³³You [pl.] have commissioned to Yōannēs [John] and he has witnessed to the Truth. ³⁴I do not receive the witness from a human but I say these things so you may be delivered. ³⁵That one was a lamp aflame and appearing but you chose to be overjoyed for an hour in his light.

³⁶I have the witness that is greater than Yōannēs.' For the works that the Father gave to me, so I may complete them, these works that I do witness about me that the Father has commissioned me. ³⁷The Father who sent me, that one has witnessed about me. You have never heard his voice, nor have you seen his form, ³⁸and you don't have his word remaining in you, because the one whom he commissioned, you do not trust in this one. ³⁹Explore the writings because you think in them to have Era Life. These are the ones witnessing about me. ⁴⁰You do not want to come to me so you may have Life.

⁴¹I do not receive splendor from humans, ⁴²but I have known you that you do not have God's love in yourselves. ⁴³I have come in my Father's name and you do not receive me. If another comes in one's own name, you will receive that one. ⁴⁴How are you able to trust, receiving splendor from one another, and do not pursue the splendor that is from the only God?

⁴⁵Don't think that I will accuse you to the Father. The one accusing you is Mōūsēs [Moses], in whom you have hoped. ⁴⁶For if you trusted in Mōūsēs, you would have trusted in me, for that one wrote about me. ⁴⁷If you do not trust in that one's writings, how will you trust in my utterances?"

Yēsous and bread

6 After these Yēsous departed to Beyond the Galilaia Sea [Sea of Galilee], the Tiberias [Sea]. ²A big crowd was following him because they were observing the authenticating signs that he was doing for the weakened ones. ³Yēsous went up into the mountain and was sitting there with his Apprentices. ⁴The Pascha [Passover] was close, the Youdaians' [Judeans', Jews'] feast.

⁵Therefore, Yēsous, lifting up the eyes and observing that a big crowd comes to him, says to Philippos [Philip], "From where can we purchase breads so these may eat?" ⁶This he was saying, testing him, for he knew what he was about to do. ⁷Philippos responded to him, "Breads worth two hundred denaria would not be sufficient for them so that each may take a little." ⁸One of his Apprentices, Andreas [Andrew], brother of Simōn Petros [Peter], says to him, ⁹"There is a small child here who has five barley breads and two little fishes, but what are these for so many?" ¹⁰Yēsous said, "Make the humans lie down." There was much grass in the place. Therefore, the men laid down—in number about five thousand. ¹¹Therefore, Yēsous received the breads and, thanking, distributed to the ones reclining, likewise also from the fishes, as much as they wanted. ¹²As they were filled up, he says to his Apprentices, "Assemble the abounding broken pieces so there may not be any destroyed." ¹³Therefore, they assembled and filled twelve baskets of broken pieces from the five barley breads that were abounding for those who had eaten. ¹⁴Therefore, the humans, seeing the authenticating sign he did, were saying that "This is truly the prophet who comes into the Kosmos." ¹⁵Therefore, Yēsous, knowing that

they were about to come and snatch him to make him king, slipped out again into the mountain by himself.

¹⁶As evening came, his Apprentices descended to the sea ¹⁷and, getting down into a boat, they began [to cross] Beyond the Sea to Kaphar-Naoum [Capernaum]. Darkness had already come and Yēsous had not yet come to them, ¹⁸and the sea . . . a great wind's blowing . . . was roused. ¹⁹Therefore, having driven about twenty-five or thirty stades [3–4 miles], they observe Yēsous walking around on the sea and coming close to the boat, and they were scared. ²⁰He says to them, "I am. Do not be scared." ²¹Therefore, they were wanting to take him into the boat, and immediately the boat came upon the land toward which they were going away.

²²On the next day, the crowd that had been standing Beyond the Sea saw that another little boat was not there except the one, and that Yēsous did not go with his Apprentices into the boat but his Apprentices departed alone. ²³But some little boats from Tiberias came close to the place where they ate the bread, thanking the Lord. ²⁴Therefore, when the crowd saw that Yēsous is not there nor his Apprentices, they themselves got down into the small boats and came to Kaphar-Naoum, pursuing Yēsous. ²⁵Finding him Beyond the Sea, they said to him, "My Greatness [Rabbi], when did you come here?"

²⁶Yēsous responded to them and said, "This is especially true to say to you: You pursue me not because you saw authenticating signs but because you ate from the breads and were satisfied. ²⁷Work not for destructible food but for food that remains into Era Life, which the Son of Humanity will give to you. For God, the Father, sealed this one." ²⁸Therefore, they said to him, "What may we do that we may work God's works?" ²⁹Yēsous responded and said to them, "This is God's work, that you trust in whom that one commissioned."

³⁰Therefore, they said to him, "Therefore, what authenticating sign do you do that we may see and trust you? What do you work? ³¹Our ancestors ate manna in the wilderness, just as it's written: *He gave bread from the heaven to them to eat.*" ³²Therefore, Yēsous said to them, "This is especially true to say to you: Mōūsēs [Moses] has not given to you bread from the heaven, but my Father gives to you the true bread from the heaven. ³³For God's bread is the one who descends from the heaven and gives Life to the Kosmos." ³⁴Therefore, they said to him, "Lord, always give to us this bread."

³⁵Yēsous said to them, "I am Life's bread. The one who comes to me will never hunger and the one who trusts in me will never thirst ever. ³⁶But I said to you that you both have seen me and do not trust. ³⁷All whom the Father gives to me will come to me, and I will never toss away the one coming to me, ³⁸because I have descended from the heaven not that I may do my will but the one who sent me's will. ³⁹This is the one who sent me's will: that I may not destroy any person of all whom he has given to me, but I will raise it up on the Last Day. ⁴⁰For this is my Father's will, that everyone who observes the Son and trusts in him may have Era Life, and I will raise him up on the Last Day."

⁴¹Therefore, the Youdaians were grumbling about him because he said, "I am the bread that descended from the heaven," ⁴²and they were saying, "Is this not Yēsous, Yōsēf's [Joseph's] son, whose father and mother we know? How now does he say that 'I have descended from the heaven'?"

⁴³Yēsous responded and said to them, "Do not grumble with one another. ⁴⁴No one is able to come to me unless the Father, who sent me, pulls him, and I will raise him up on the Last Day. ⁴⁵It's written in the prophets: *All will be God-taught.* Everyone who heard and was apprenticed from the Father comes to me— ⁴⁶not that someone has seen the Father except the one is with God—this one has seen the Father. ⁴⁷This is especially true to say to you: The one who trusts has Era Life. ⁴⁸I am Life's bread. ⁴⁹Your ancestors ate manna in the wilderness and they died. ⁵⁰This is the bread, the one descending from the heaven so someone eats of it and does not die. ⁵¹I am the bread, the living one, the one who descended from the heaven. If someone eats of this bread the person will live into the Era, and also the bread that I give for the Kosmos's life is my flesh."

⁵²Therefore, the Youdaians were warring with one another, saying, "How is this person able to give his flesh to eat?" ⁵³Therefore, Yēsous said to them, "This is especially true that I say to you: If you do not eat the Son of Humanity's flesh and drink his blood, you do not have Life in yourselves. ⁵⁴The one chewing my flesh and

drinking my blood has Era Life, and I will raise him up on the Last Day. ⁵⁵For my flesh is true food, and my blood is true drink. ⁵⁶The one chewing my flesh and drinking my blood remains in me and I in the person. ⁵⁷Just as the living Father commissioned me and I live because of the Father, so the one chewing me, that one will live because of me. ⁵⁸This is the bread that descended from heaven—not as the ancestors ate and died. The one chewing this bread will live into the Era."

⁵⁹He said these things, teaching in an assembly hall in Kaphar-Naoum.

⁶⁰Therefore, many of his Apprentices hearing, said, "This word is harsh. Who is able to hear it?" ⁶¹Yēsous, knowing in himself that his Apprentices were grumbling about this, said to them, "Are you tripping over this? ⁶²Therefore, if you were observing the Son of Humanity ascending where he was at first . . . ? ⁶³The Spirit is the Life-maker, the flesh gains nothing. The utterances that I have spoken to you are Spirit and are Life. ⁶⁴But there are among you some who are not trusting." (For Yēsous had known from the beginning some were not trusters and who the one who gives him over is.) ⁶⁵He was saying, "Because of this I have said to you that no one is able to come to me unless it be given to the person from the Father."

⁶⁶From this many of his Apprentices departed to the things that were behind and no longer were walking around with him. ⁶⁷Therefore, Yēsous said to the Twelve, "You do not want to go away also, do you?" ⁶⁸Simōn Petros responded to him, "Lord, to whom will we depart? You have utterances of Era Life. ⁶⁹We have both trusted and we have known that you are God's Devout One." ⁷⁰Yēsous responded to them, "Did I not select you Twelve? And from you one is an accuser." (⁷¹He was speaking about Youdas [Judas], son of Simōn the Dagger Man [Iscariot], for this one was about to give him over—one of the Twelve.)

Yēsous, his brothers, a feast, and controversy

7 After these Yēsous was walking around in the Galilaia [Galilee], for he did not want to walk around in Youdaia [Judea] because the Youdaians [Judeans, Jews] were pursuing to kill him.

²The feast of the Youdaians, the [feast] of Bivouacs [Booths], was close. ³Therefore, his brothers said to him, "Shift from here and go away into Youdaia so your Apprentices also will observe your works that you do, ⁴for no one does something in hiding and himself pursues to be in frankness. If you do these things, make yourself apparent to the Kosmos." (⁵For even his brothers were not trusting in him.) ⁶Therefore, Yēsous says to them, "My season is not yet present, but your season is always prepared. ⁷The Kosmos isn't able to hate you, but it hates me because I witness about it that its works are evil. ⁸You ascend to the feast, and I don't ascend to this feast because my season is not yet filled out." ⁹He, saying these things, was remaining in the Galilaia.

¹⁰As his brothers ascended to the feast, then he also ascended—not apparently but as in hiding. ¹¹Therefore, the Youdaians were pursuing him at the feast and were saying, "Where is that one?" ¹²And there was much grumbling about him in the crowds. Some were saying, "he is good" but others were saying, "no, but he deceives the crowd." ¹³No one, although, was speaking about him in frankness because they were scared of the Youdaians.

¹⁴The feast was already in its middle . . . Yēsous ascended to the temple and was teaching. ¹⁵Therefore, the Youdaians were stunned, saying, "How does this person know the grammar, not having been apprenticed?" ¹⁶Therefore, Yēsous responded and said to them, "My teaching is not mine but [from] the one who sent me. ¹⁷If someone wants to do his will, he will know about the teaching, whether it's from God or I speak from myself. ¹⁸The one speaking from oneself pursues his own splendor, but the one pursuing the one who sent him's splendor—this person is true and there is no wrongdoing in him. ¹⁹Has not Mōusēs [Moses] given to you the Covenant Code? No one from you does the Code. Why do you pursue to kill me?"

²⁰The crowd responded, "You have a demon. Who is pursuing to kill you?" ²¹Yēsous responded and said to them, "I did one work and everyone is stunned. ²²Because of this Mōusēs has given to you the circumcision—not that it's from Mōusēs but from the ancestors—and you circumcise a human on a Sabbath. ²³If a human receives circumcision on a Sabbath so the Code of Mōusēs is not loosened—[why] are you so choleric with me because I made a

whole human healthy on a Sabbath? ²⁴Do not judge consistent with visage but judge the right judgment."

²⁵Therefore, some of the Yierosolumites [Jerusalemites] were saying, "Is this one not the one whom they are pursuing to kill? ²⁶Look! he speaks frankly and they say nothing to him. Did perhaps the leaders truly know that this person is the Christos? ²⁷But we know where this person comes from. The Christos, whenever he comes, no one knows where he is from." ²⁸Therefore, Yēsous cried out in the temple, teaching and saying, "You both know me and know where I am from. I have not come from myself, but the one who sent me is true, whom you do not know. ²⁹I know him because I am from him and that one commissioned me." ³⁰Therefore, they were pursuing to catch him, and no one tossed the hand on him because his hour had not yet come.

³¹Many from the crowd trusted in him and were saying, "The Christos, whenever he comes, Will he not do greater authenticating signs that this person did?" ³²The Observant [Pharisees] heard the crowd grumbling these things about him; the Senior Priests and Observant commissioned subordinates so they might catch him. ³³Therefore, Yēsous said, "I am with you for yet a little time and I go away to the one who sent me. ³⁴You will pursue me and you will not find me, and where I am you aren't able to come." ³⁵Therefore, the Youdaians said to themselves, "Where is this person about to journey that we will not find him? He is not about to journey into the Hellēne [Greek] diaspora and to teach the Hellēnes, is he? ³⁶What is this word that he said, 'You will pursue me and you will not find me' and 'Where I am you aren't able to come'?"

³⁷On the last day of the great feast Yēsous had stood and cried out, saying, "If someone thirsts, let the person come to me and I will give the person a drink. ³⁸The one trusting in me, just as the writing said, 'Rivers of living water will flow from his stomach.'" (³⁹This he said about the Spirit whom the ones who trusted in him were about to receive. For the Spirit was not yet, because Yēsous had not yet been splendored.)

⁴⁰Therefore, the ones from the crowd who heard these words were saying, "This person is truly the prophet." ⁴¹Others were saying, "This person is the Christos." But some were saying, "The Christos does not come from the Galilaia, does he? ⁴²Did not the writing say that 'The Christos comes from Dauid's [David's] seed and from Bēth-leʿem [Bethlehem], the village where Dauid was from'?" ⁴³Therefore, a rip happened in the crowd because of him. ⁴⁴Some of them wanted to catch him, but no one tossed the hands on him.

⁴⁵Therefore, the subordinates came to the Senior Priests and Observant, and those said to them, "Why did you not lead him [here]?" ⁴⁶The subordinates responded, "No one ever spoke like this human." ⁴⁷Therefore, the Observant responded to them, "You are not being deceived, too, are you? ⁴⁸Someone from the leaders or the Observant did not trust in him, did they? ⁴⁹But this crowd, not knowing the Covenant Code, are deplorables." ⁵⁰Nikodēmos [Nicodemus] (the one who came to him first, being one of them) says to them, ⁵¹"Our Code does not judge a human unless it hears first from him and knows what he does, does it?" ⁵²They responded and said to him, "You also aren't from the Galilaia, are you? Explore and Look! because a prophet does not arise from the Galilaia."ᶜ

Yēsous, the Kosmos's light, and disputes with the Youdaians

8 ¹²Therefore, again Yēsous spoke to them, saying, "I am the Kosmos's Light. The one following me never walks around in the Darkness but will have the Life's Light." ¹³Therefore, the Observant [Pharisees] said to him, "You are witnessing about yourself. Your witness is not true." ¹⁴Yēsous responded and said to them, "Even if I witness about myself, my witness is true because I know where I come from and where I go away, but you don't know from where I come from and where I go away. ¹⁵You judge consistent with the flesh; I do not judge anyone. ¹⁶If I judge, my judgment is true because I am not alone but I and also the one the Father sent [are judging]. ¹⁷In your own Code it's written that a two-human

---

ᶜSome manuscripts contain a wonderful story about Jesus offering grace to a woman caught in the act adultery, but the evidence against it being part of the original Gospel of Yōannēs is overwhelming.

witness is true. ¹⁸I am the one witnessing about myself, and the Father who sent me witnesses about me."

¹⁹Therefore, they were saying to him, "Where is your Father?" Yēsous responded, "You know neither me nor my Father. If you had known me, you would also have known my Father." ²⁰He spoke these utterances in the treasury, teaching in the temple. No one caught him because his hour had not yet come.

²¹Therefore, he again said to them, "I go away and you will pursue me, and you will die in your sin. Where I go away you aren't able to come." ²²Therefore, the Youdaians were saying, "He won't kill himself, will he?" because he says, "'Where I go away you are not able to come'?" ²³He was saying to them, "You are from 'the below,' I am from 'the above.' You are from this Kosmos, I am not from this Kosmos. ²⁴Therefore I said to you that 'you will die in your sins.' For if you do not trust that 'I am,' you will die in your sins." ²⁵Therefore, they were saying to him, "Who are you?" Yēsous said to them, "What can I speak to you from the beginning? ²⁶I have many things to speak about you and to judge, but the one who sent me is true, and I speak the things I heard from him into the Kosmos." (²⁷They did not know that he was speaking to them about the Father.) ²⁸Therefore, Yēsous said to them, "Whenever you raise the status of the Son of Humanity, then you will know that 'I am,' and I do nothing from myself, but just as the Father taught me, I speak these things. ²⁹The one who sent me is with me. He did not release me alone because I always do pleasing acts for him." ³⁰He's speaking these things . . . many trusted in him.

Yēsous responding to former Apprentices

³¹Therefore, Yēsous was saying to the Youdaians who had trusted in him, "If you remain in my word, you are truly my Apprentices, ³²and you will know the Truth, and the Truth will liberate you."

³³They responded to him, "We are Abra'am's seed and we have never been enslaved to anyone. How do you say that you will become liberated ones?" ³⁴Yēsous responded to them, "This is especially true to say to you, that everyone doing sin is Sin's slave. ³⁵The slave does not remain in the house into the Era, the son remains into the Era. ³⁶Therefore, if the Son liberates you, you will be really liberated ones. ³⁷I know that you are Abra'am's seed, but you pursue to kill me because my word doesn't have space in you. ³⁸What I have seen with the Father, I speak. Therefore, you do what you heard from the 'father.'" ³⁹They responded and said to him, "Our father is Abra'am." Yēsous says to them, "If you are Abra'am's children, you would be doing Abra'am's works, ⁴⁰but you now pursue to kill me, a human who—I have spoken the Truth to you that I heard from God. This Abra'am did not do. ⁴¹You do your 'father's' works." Therefore, they said to him, "We have not been given life from sexual immorality, we have one Father, God."

⁴²Yēsous said to them, "If God were your Father, you would love me, for I exited and I came from God. For I have not come from myself, but that one commissioned me. ⁴³Why do you not know my speaking? Because you aren't able to hear my word. ⁴⁴You are of the father-Accuser and you want to do your 'father's' desires. That one was a human-killer from the beginning and was not standing in the Truth because there is no truth in him. Whenever he speaks falsehoods, he speaks from himself, because he is a false speaker and its father. ⁴⁵But because I say the truth, you do not trust me. ⁴⁶Who from you demonstrates me with respect to sin? If I say truth, why do you not trust me? ⁴⁷The one from God hears God's utterances. Because of this you do not hear because you are not from God."

⁴⁸The Youdaians responded and said to him, "Do we not say beautifully that you are a Samaritēs and you have a demon?" ⁴⁹Yēsous responded, "I don't have a demon, but I honor my Father and you dishonor me. ⁵⁰I do not pursue my splendor. There is one who pursues and judges. ⁵¹This is especially true to say to you: If someone observes my word, that one will not observe death into the Era."

⁵²Therefore, the Youdaians said to him, "Now we have known that you have a demon. Abra'am and the prophets died, and you say, 'If someone observes my word, the person will never taste death into the Era.' ⁵³You are not greater than Abra'am our father (who died), are you? And the prophets died. Who do you make yourself [to be]?" ⁵⁴Yēsous responded, "If I

splendor myself, my splendor is nothing. It's my Father who splendors me, about whom you say that 'He is our God,' ⁵⁵and you have not known him, but I know him. If I say that I do not know him, I will be like you, a false speaker. But I know him and I observe his word. ⁵⁶Your father Abra'am was overjoyed that he might see my day, and he saw and rejoiced." ⁵⁷Therefore, the Youdaians said to him, "You have not yet had fifty years, and you have seen Abra'am?" ⁵⁸Yēsous said to them, "This is especially true to say to you: Before Abra'am was, 'I am.'" ⁵⁹Therefore, they lifted stones that they might toss at him, but Yēsous was hidden and exited from the temple.

Yēsous and sightlessness

9 Going along, he saw a human, sightless from the moment of life. ²His Apprentices asked him, saying, "My Greatness [Rabbi], who sinned, this person or his parents that he was given life sightless?" ³Yēsous responded, "Neither this person sinned nor his parents, but that God's works may appear in him. ⁴It's necessary for us to work the works of the one who sent me while it's day. Night comes when no one is able to work. ⁵Whenever I am in the Kosmos, I am the Kosmos's Light." ⁶Saying these things, he spit on the ground and made a lump from the spit and smeared the lump on the eyes, ⁷and said to him, "Go away! Wash in the pool of Silōam (which translated is 'commissioned')." Therefore, he departed and washed and he came [back] seeing.

⁸Therefore, the ones next door and the ones observing him formerly, that he was a supplicant, were saying, "Is this person not the one sitting and supplicating?" ⁹Some were saying "This person is [he]," and others were saying, "No, but someone comparable to him." That person was saying that "I am." ¹⁰Therefore, they were saying to him, "Therefore, how were your eyes opened?" ¹¹That person responded, "The human who is called 'Yēsous' made a lump and smeared my eyes and said to me that, 'Go away to Silōam and wash.' Therefore, departing and washing, I saw again." ¹²They said to him, "Where is that person?" He says, "I do not know."

¹³They lead him to the Observant [Pharisees], the one once sightless. ¹⁴It was a Sabbath on which day Yēsous made a lump and opened his eyes. ¹⁵Therefore, again the Observant were asking him how he saw again. He said to them, "He placed a lump on my eyes and I washed and I see." ¹⁶Therefore, some from the Observant were saying, "This person is not from God—this human, because he does not observe the Sabbath." Others were saying, "How is a sinful human able to do such authenticating signs?" A rip was among them. ¹⁷Therefore, they say to the sightless man again, "What do you say about him because he opened your eyes?" He said that "He is a prophet."

¹⁸Therefore, the Youdaians did not trust about him, that he was sightless and saw again until they voiced the parents of the one who saw again, ¹⁹they asked them, saying, "Is this your son, whom you say that he was given life sightless? Therefore, how does he see now?" ²⁰Therefore, his parents responded and said, "We know this is our son and that he was given life sightless. ²¹How he now sees we do not know, or who opened his eyes we do not know. Ask him, he has age, he will speak for himself." (²²His parents said these things because they were scared of the Youdaians. For already the Youdaians had agreed that if someone openly agreed he was the Christos, they would be de-assembled. ²³Because of this, his parents said that "He has age, ask him.")

²⁴Therefore, they voiced the human who was sightless a second [time] and said to him, "Give splendor to God. We know that this human is a sinner." ²⁵Therefore, that person responded, "If he is a sinner, I do not know. One thing I know, that being sightless I now see." ²⁶Therefore, they said to him, "What did he do to you? How did he open your eyes?" ²⁷He replied to them, "I told you already and you did not hear. Why do you want to hear again? You also don't want to become his Apprentices, do you?" ²⁸They beat him and said, "You are an Apprentice of that person, but we are Apprentices of Mōüsēs [Moses]. ²⁹We know that God has spoken in Mōüsēs but we do not know where this person is from." ³⁰The human responded and said to them, "For there is something stunning in this: that you don't know where he is from and he opened my eyes. ³¹We know that God does not hear sinners, but if someone is God-reverent and does his will, he hears this person. ³²From the Era it has not been heard that someone opened

the eyes of someone given life sightless. ³³Unless this person was from God, he wouldn't be able to do anything." ³⁴They responded and said to him, "You were given life wholly in sins, and you are teaching us?" They tossed him out.

³⁵Yēsous heard that they tossed him out and, finding him, said, "Do you trust in the Son of Humanity?" ³⁶That person responded and said, "And who is he, Lord, that I may trust in him?" ³⁷Yēsous said to him, "And you have seen him and the one speaking with you is that person." ³⁸He said, "I trust, Lord." He bowed down to him.

³⁹Yēsous said, "I came into this Kosmos for judgment so that the ones not seeing may see and the ones seeing may become sightless." ⁴⁰The ones who are with him of the Observant heard these things and said to him, "We are not also sightless, are we?" ⁴¹Yēsous said to them, "If you were sightless, you would not have sin, but now you say that 'We see'—your sin remains.

Yēsous, the good shepherd

10 This is especially true to say to you: The one not entering through the door into the sheep's enclosure but ascending from another place, that person is a thief and bandit. ²The one entering through the door is the sheep's shepherd. ³The doorkeeper opens for this one and the sheep hear his voice and he voices his own sheep by name and he leads them out. ⁴Whenever he tosses out all his own, he journeys before them, and the sheep follow him because they know his voice. ⁵They will never follow an outsider but will flee from him because they do not know the outsider's voice." (⁶Yēsous said this proverb to them but they did not know what it was he was speaking to them.)

⁷Therefore, Yēsous said again, "This is especially true to say to you, that: I am the door for the sheep. ⁸All who came before me are thieves and bandits, but the sheep did not hear them. ⁹I am the door. If someone enters through me, the person will be delivered and will enter and will exit and will find pasture. ¹⁰The thief does not come except to thieve and slaughter and destroy. I came that they may have Life and have [it] abundantly. ¹¹I am the beautiful shepherd. The beautiful shepherd places his self for his sheep. ¹²The wage-taker, and not being a shepherd, whose sheep are not his own, observes the wolf coming and releases the sheep and flees, and the wolf snatches them and scatters [them], ¹³because he is the wage-taker and there is no concern for him about the sheep. ¹⁴I am the beautiful shepherd and I know mine and mine know me, ¹⁵just as the Father knows me and I know the Father, and I place my self for the sheep. ¹⁶I have other sheep that are not of this enclosure. It's necessary for me also to lead those and they will hear my voice, and they will become one flock, one shepherd. ¹⁷Because of this, the Father loves me because I place my self so I may receive it again. ¹⁸No one lifts it from me but I place it from myself. I have authority to place it, and I have authority again to receive it. I received this order from my Father."

¹⁹Again, there was a rip among the Youdaians [Judeans, Jews] because of these words. ²⁰Many of them were saying, "He has a demon and is frenzied. Why hear him?" ²¹Others were saying, "These utterances are not from one demonized. A demon isn't able to open eyes for the sightless, is he?"

Yēsous and the Renewal Feast

²²Then Renewal Feast [Hanukkah] happened in Yierosolumas [Jerusalem] . . . it was a stormy season, ²³and Yēsous was walking around in the temple, in Solomōn's porch. ²⁴Therefore, the Youdaians encircled him and were saying to him, "For how long will you lift up our selves [in suspense]? If you are the Christos, say [it] to us frankly." ²⁵Yēsous responded to them, "I said to you, and you do not trust. The works that I do in my Father's name, these witness about me, ²⁶but you do not trust because you are not of my sheep. ²⁷My sheep hear my voice, and I know them and they follow me, ²⁸and I give to them Era Life and they will never be destroyed into the Era and someone will not snatch them from my hand. ²⁹What my Father has given to me is greater than all, and no one is able to snatch from my Father's hand. ³⁰I and the Father, we are one."

³¹Again, the Youdaians carried stones so they could stone him. ³²Yēsous responded to them, "I exhibited many beautiful works to you from my Father. For which work of these do

you stone me?" ³³The Youdaians responded to him, "We do not stone you for the beautiful work but for insult [of God] and because you, being a human, make yourself God." ³⁴Yēsous responded to them, "Is it not written in your Covenant Code that *I said, You are gods*? ³⁵If he said *gods* to those to whom God's word came—and the writing is not able to be loosened—³⁶do you say about the one the Father devoted and commissioned into the Kosmos that he is insulting because I said, 'I am God's Son'? ³⁷If I do not do my Father's works, do not trust in me. ³⁸If I do, even if you do not trust in me, trust in the works so you may know and may continue knowing that the Father is in me and I in the Father." (³⁹Therefore, they were pursing to catch him, and he exited from their hand.)

⁴⁰He departed again Beyond the Yordanēs [Jordan River] into the place where Yōannēs [John] was first dipping, and he was remaining there. ⁴¹Many came to him and were saying that "Whereas Yōannēs did no authenticating sign, yet everything Yōannēs said about this one was true." ⁴²Many trusted in him there.

Yēsous, Lazaros, and Martha—with the aftermath

11 Someone was weakening—Lazaros [Lazarus] from Bēth-Ania [Bethany], from the village of Mariam [Mary] and Martha her sister. ²Maria, the one who oiled the Lord with ointment and who wiped his feet with her hair—her brother Lazaros was weakening. ³Therefore, the sisters commissioned [someone] to him, saying, "Lord, Look! The one you love is weakening." ⁴Yēsous, hearing, said, "This weakness is not to death but for God's splendor, so God's Son may be splendored through it." ⁵Yēsous was loving Martha and her sister and Lazaros. ⁶Therefore, as he heard that he's weakening, then he remained in the place in which he was for two days. ⁷Then after this he says to the Apprentices, "Let us go into Youdaia [Judea] again." ⁸The Apprentices say to him, "My Greatness [Rabbi], the Youdaians [Judeans, Jews] now were pursuing to stone you, and again you go away there?" ⁹Yēsous responded, "Are there not twelve hours of the day? If someone walks around in the day, one does not fall down because one sees this Kosmos's light. ¹⁰If someone walks around in the night, one falls down because the light is not in the person."

¹¹He said these things and after this he says to them, "Our friend Lazaros has fallen asleep but I journey so I may awaken him." ¹²Therefore, the Apprentices said to him, "Lord, if he has fallen asleep, he will be delivered." (¹³Yēsous had spoken about his death but they thought that he is speaking about the dream-sleep.) ¹⁴Therefore, then Yēsous said to them frankly, "Lazaros died, ¹⁵and I rejoice because of you so you may trust because I was not there. But let us go to him." ¹⁶Therefore, Thōmas, the one called Twin [Didymos], said to the co-Apprentices, "Let us also go so we may die with him."

¹⁷Therefore, going, Yēsous found him, having been already four days in the tomb. ¹⁸Bēth-Ania was close to Yierosolumas [Jerusalem], about fifteen stades [2 miles] away. ¹⁹Many of the Youdaians had come to Martha and Maria so they might soothe them about the brother. ²⁰Therefore, Martha, as she heard that Yēsous comes, met him. Maria was sitting in the house. ²¹Therefore, Martha said to Yēsous, "Lord, if you had been here my brother would not have died, ²²but also now I know that whatever you ask God, God will give to you." ²³Yēsous says to her, "Your brother will arise." ²⁴Martha says to him, "I know that he will arise in the resurrection on the last day." ²⁵Yēsous said to her, "I am the Resurrection and the Life. The one who trusts in me, if the person dies, will live, ²⁶and everyone who lives and trusts in me will never die into the Era. Do you trust this?" ²⁷She says to him, "Yes, Lord, I have trusted that you are the Christos, God's Son, the one coming into the Kosmos."

²⁸The one who said this departed and voiced Maria her sister, saying secretly, "The Teacher is here and voices you." ²⁹That one, as she heard, arose quickly and was coming to him. ³⁰Yēsous had not yet come into the village but was still in the place where Martha met him. ³¹Therefore, the Youdaians, the ones being with her in the house and soothing her, seeing Maria that she arose quickly and exited, followed her, thinking that she goes away to the tomb so she may wail there.

³²Therefore, Maria, as she came to where Yēsous was, seeing him, fell at his feet, saying to

him, "Lord, if you had been here my brother would not have died." ³³Therefore, Yēsous, as he saw her wailing and the Youdaians coming with her wailing, he snorted in spirit and agitated himself. ³⁴He said, "Where have they placed him?" They say to him, "Lord, come and see." ³⁵Yēsous teared up. ³⁶Therefore, the Youdaians were saying, "Look! How he was loving him!" ³⁷Some of them said, "Was this person, the one who opened the sightless man's eyes, unable to do [something] so this person would not die?"

³⁸Therefore, Yēsous, again snorting in himself, comes to the tomb. It was a cave and a stone was placed against it. ³⁹Yēsous says, "Lift the stone." Martha, the sister of the one whose life had ended, says to him, "Lord, it already stinks for it's the fourth." ⁴⁰Yēsous says to her, "Did I not say to you that if you trust you will see God's splendor?" ⁴¹Therefore, they lifted the stone. Yēsous lifted the eyes up and said, "Father, I thank you that you heard me. ⁴²I have known that you always hear me but because of the crowd standing around, I said so they may trust that you have commissioned me." ⁴³Saying these things in a great voice, he made a racket, "LAZAROS, COME OUT!" ⁴⁴The one who had been dead exited, bound feet and hands in strips and his visage was wrapped in a head-kerchief. Yēsous says to them, "Loosen him and release him to go away!"

⁴⁵Therefore, many of the Youdaians who came to Maria and who observed what he did trusted in him, ⁴⁶but some of them departed to the Observant [Pharisees] and said to them what Yēsous did.

⁴⁷Therefore, the Senior Priests and the Observant assembled the Central Council and were saying, "What do we do because this human is doing many authenticating signs? ⁴⁸If we release him [to continue doing] so, all will trust in him and the Romaioi [Romans] will come and will lift us away us and our place and our ethnic group." ⁴⁹One of them, Kaïaphas [Caiaphas], being the Senior Priest that year, said to them, "You don't know anything, ⁵⁰and neither do you calculate that it's a benefit for you that one human die for the people and that the whole ethnic group not be destroyed." (⁵¹This he did not say from himself but being Senior Priest that year he prophesied that Yēsous was about to be die for the ethnic group, ⁵²and not for the ethnic group alone but so also that he could assemble God's children, the scattered ones, into one [group]. ⁵³Therefore, from that day, they decided that they would kill him.)

⁵⁴Therefore, Yēsous no longer walked around frankly among the Youdaians but departed from there into a region close to the wilderness, to a city called Ephraim, and remained there with the Apprentices.

⁵⁵The Youdaians' Pascha [Passover] was close, and many ascended to Yierosolumas from the region before the Pascha so they may devote themselves. ⁵⁶Therefore, they were pursuing Yēsous and were saying with one another, standing in the temple, "What does it seem to you? He will never come to the feast, will he?" ⁵⁷The Senior Priests and the Observant had given orders that if someone knew where he is, one divulge [it] so they might catch him.

Yēsous and Mariam

12 Therefore, Yēsous, six days before the Pascha [Passover], came into Bēth-Ania [Bethany], where Lazaros [Lazarus] was, whom Yēsous raised from among the dead ones. ²Therefore, they did supper with him there. Maria [Mary] was serving and Lazaros was one of the ones reclining with him.

³Therefore, Mariam, taking a pound of costly, pure fragrant ointment, oiled Yēsous' feet and wiped his feet with her hair. The house was filled out from the ointment's fragrance. ⁴Youdas the Dagger Man [Judas Iscariot], one of his Apprentices, who being about to give him over, says, ⁵"Why was this ointment not sold for three hundred denaria and given to beggars?" (⁶He said this not because there is a concern in him about the beggars but because he was a thief and, having the money bag, he was carrying [away] what was tossed [in it].) ⁷Therefore, Yēsous said, "Release her so she may keep it for the day of my entombment. ⁸For you have the beggars with you always, but you do not have me always."

⁹Therefore, the great crowd from the Youdaians [Judeans, Jews] knew he is there and they came not because of Yēsous only but so also they might see Lazaros, whom he raised

from among the dead ones. ¹⁰The Senior Priests decided that they would also kill Lazaros, ¹¹because many of the Youdaians were going away because of him and were trusting in Yēsous.

Yēsous' entry into Yierosolumas

¹²On the next day, the great crowd, the one coming to the feast, hearing that Yēsous comes into Yierosolumas, ¹³took the date-palm branches and exited for a meeting with him and they were making a racket,

> "Hosanna!
> God's blessing on the one coming in the
>   Lord's name,
> Yisraēl's [Israel's] king."

¹⁴Yēsous, finding a young donkey, sat on it, just as it's written,

> ¹⁵*Do not be scared Siōn's* [Zion's]
>   *daughter,*
> *Look! your king comes,*
> *Sitting on a colt of a donkey.*

¹⁶His Apprentices did not know these things at first, but when Yēsous was splendored, then they remembered that these things were written about him and they did these things for him. ¹⁷Therefore, the crowd, the one being with him when he voiced Lazaros from the tomb and raised him from among the dead ones, was witnessing [this]. ¹⁸Because of this also the crowd met him because they heard about this authenticating sign he had done to him. ¹⁹Therefore, the Observant [Pharisees] said to themselves, "Observe that you gain nothing. Look! The Kosmos departs after him."

Yēsous and the Hellēnes

²⁰There were some Hellēnes [Greeks] ascending [up to Jerusalem] so they might bow down at the feast. ²¹Therefore, these came to Philippos [Philip], the one from the Galilaian Bēth-saïda [Galilean Bethsaida], and they were asking him, saying, "Lord, we want to see Yēsous." ²²Philippos comes and says to Andreas [Andrew], Andreas comes—and Philippos, and they say to Yēsous. ²³Yēsous replies to them, saying, "The hour has come so the Son of Humanity may be splendored. ²⁴This is especially true to say to you: Unless the wheat-grain (falling into the land) dies, it remains alone, but if it dies, it carries much fruit. ²⁵The one who loves one's self destroys it; the one who hates one's self in this Kosmos will guard it into Era Life. ²⁶If someone serves me, let the person follow me, and where I am my servant will also be there. If someone serves me, the Father will honor the person. ²⁷Now *my self has been agitated*, and what do I say? 'Father, *deliver me* from this hour'? But because of this I came into this hour. ²⁸Father, splendor your name."

Therefore, a voice came from heaven, "I both splendored and I will splendor again." ²⁹Therefore, the crowd that was standing and hearing was saying, "Thunder happened," but others were saying, "An envoy has spoken to him." ³⁰Yēsous responded and said, "This voice has not come because of me but because of you. ³¹Now is judgment for this Kosmos, now the one who leads this Kosmos will be tossed outside, ³²and I, if I am raised in status from the land, I will pull all to myself." (³³He was saying this, signifying what kind of death he was about to die.)

³⁴Therefore, the crowd responded to him, "We heard from the Covenant Code that the Christos remains into the Era, and how do you say that it's necessary for the Son of Humanity to be raised in status? Who is this Son of Humanity?" ³⁵Therefore, Yēsous said to them, "For a little more time the Light is among you. Walk around as you have the Light so the Darkness may not prevail against you. The one walking around in the Darkness does not know where one is going away. ³⁶As you have the Light, trust in the Light so you may become the Light's children."

Yēsous spoke these things and, departing, was hid from them.

Yēsous not trusted

³⁷He had done such [stunning] authenticating signs before them . . . they were not trusting in him, ³⁸so Ēsaias [Isaiah] the prophet's word might be filled out that said,

> *Lord, who trusted our report?*
> *The Lord's arm has been apocalypsed to*
>   *whom?*

³⁹Because of this they weren't able to trust because again Ēsaias said,

⁴⁰*He has sightlessed their eyes,*

And hardened their *heart*,
So they may not see with the eyes,
And may not know with the heart,
And turn,
and I will cure them.

⁴¹Ēsaias said these because he saw his splendor, and he spoke about him. ⁴²Despite that, many from the leaders trusted in him but weren't openly agreeing because of the Observant so they would not become de-assemblied, ⁴³for they loved human splendor more than God's splendor.

⁴⁴Yēsous cried out and said, "The one trusting in me does not trust in me but in the one who sent me, ⁴⁵and the one observing me observes the one who sent me. ⁴⁶I, Light, have come into the Kosmos, so that everyone trusting in me may not remain in the Darkness. ⁴⁷If someone hears my utterances and does not guard [them], I do not judge the person, for I did not come so I might judge the Kosmos, but so I might deliver the Kosmos. ⁴⁸The one rejecting me and not receiving my utterances has one judging the person. The word that I spoke, that will judge the person on the last day, ⁴⁹because I didn't speak from myself but the Father who sent me, he gave to me an order what I may say and what I may speak. ⁵⁰I know that his order is Era Life. Therefore, what I speak—just as the Father has said to me, so I speak."

Yēsous at supper

13 Before the Pascha [Passover] feast Yēsous, knowing that his hour came that he would be shifted from this Kosmos to the Father, loving his own in this Kosmos, he loved them to completion.

²Supper happening . . . the Accuser already having tossed into the heart that Youdas [Judas], [son of] Simōn the Dagger Man [Iscariot], would give him over . . . ³[Yēsous], knowing that the Father gave all things to him into the hands and that he exited from God and goes away to God, ⁴arose from the dinner and placed the robes and, taking a towel, he wrapped himself. ⁵Then he tosses water into the wash bowl and began to wash the Apprentices' feet, and he wiped [them] with the towel with which he was wrapped.

⁶Therefore, he comes to Simōn Petros [Peter]. He says to him, "Lord, are you washing my feet?" ⁷Yēsous responded and said to him, "What I do you don't now know, but you will know after these things." ⁸Petros says to him, "You will never wash my feet into the Era!" Yēsous responded to him, "If I don't wash you, you have no part with me." ⁹Simōn Petros says to him, "Lord, not only my feet but also my hands and my head!" ¹⁰Yēsous says to him, "The one being washed doesn't have a need (except for feet) to be washed but is completely clean. You [pl.] are clean, but not all." (¹¹For he knew the one giving him over. Because of this he said that "Not all are clean.")

¹²Therefore, when he washed their feet and took his robes and lay down [at table] again, he said to them, "Do you know what I have done to you? ¹³You voice me 'the Teacher' and 'the Lord,' and you speak beautifully, for I am. ¹⁴If therefore I washed your feet—the Lord and the Teacher—you also are obligated to wash one another's feet, ¹⁵for I gave to you a model that, just as I did to you, also you do. ¹⁶This is especially true to say to you: A slave is not greater than one's lord, nor is the commissioner greater than the one who sent the person. ¹⁷If you know these things, you are God-blessed if you do them. ¹⁸I speak not about all of you. I know the ones I elected. But so the writing may be filled out: *The one chewing my bread lifted up* his *heel against me.* ¹⁹From now I say to you before it happens so you may trust (whenever it happens) that 'I am.' ²⁰This is especially true to say to you: The one receiving whomever I send receives me, and the one receiving me receives the one who sent me."

²¹Saying these things, Yēsous was agitated in spirit and witnessed and said, "This is especially true to say to you, that one of you will give me over." ²²The Apprentices were looking into one another, being perplexed about whom he is speaking. ²³One of the Apprentices was reclining on Yēsous' garment-fold, whom Yēsous was loving. ²⁴Therefore, Simōn Petros nods to this one to inquire [of Yēsous] who it may be about whom he speaks. ²⁵Therefore, that one, lying down against Yēsous' breast, says to him, "Lord, who is [it]?" ²⁶Yēsous replies, "The one for whom I will dip the piece of bread and to whom I will give it." Therefore, dipping the piece of bread,

he takes and gives to Youdas, [son] of Simōn the Dagger Man. ²⁷After the piece of bread, then Satanas [Satan] entered into that one. Therefore, Yēsous says to him, "What you do, do quickly." ²⁸No one of the recliners knew this, why he said [this] to him. ²⁹For some where thinking, since Youdas had the money bag, that Yēsous says to him, "Purchase what we have need for the feast" or that he might give something to the beggars. ³⁰Therefore, taking the piece of bread, that one exited immediately. It was night.

³¹Therefore, when he exited, Yēsous says, "Now the Son of Humanity has been splendored and God has been splendored in him. ³²If God has been splendored in him, and God will splendor him in himself, and immediately he will splendor him. ³³Children, for a little while I am with you. You will pursue me, and just as I said to the Youdaians [Judeans, Jews] that where I go away you aren't able to come, also I say now to you. ³⁴I give to you a new order, that you love one another. Just as I loved you so also you love one another. ³⁵In this all will know that you are my Apprentices: if you have love among one another."

³⁶Simōn Petros says to him, "Lord, where do you go away?" Yēsous responded to him, "Where I go away you aren't able to follow me now, but later you will follow me." ³⁷Petros says to him, "Lord, why am I unable to follow you now? I will place my self for you." ³⁸Yēsous replies, "Will you place your self for me? This is especially true to say to you [sg.], the rooster will never voice until you deny me three times.

Yēsous, the Path to the Father

14 Let your [pl.] heart not be agitated. Trust in God and trust in me. ²In my Father's house are many rooms. If it were not so, would I have said to you that I journey to prepare a place for you? ³If I journey and prepare a place for you, I come again and I will take you to myself so where I am you may also be ⁴and where I go away, you know the path."

⁵Thōmas says to him, "Lord, we do not know where you go away. How are we able to know the path?" ⁶Yēsous says to him, "I am the Path and the Truth and the Life. No one comes to the Father except through me. ⁷If you have known me, you will know my Father. From now you know him and have seen him."

⁸Philippos [Philip] says to him, "Lord, exhibit for us the Father and it's enough for us." ⁹Yēsous says to him, "I am with you for so much time and you have not known me, Philippos? The one who has seen me has seen the Father. How do you say, 'Exhibit to us the Father'? ¹⁰Do you not trust that I am in the Father and the Father is in me? The utterances that I say to you I do not speak from myself but the Father remaining in me does his works. ¹¹Trust me that I am in the Father and the Father in me. If not, trust because of the works themselves.

¹²This is especially true to say to you: The one trusting in me, that person will do the works that I do and will do greater than these, because I journey to the Father. ¹³Whatever you ask in my name, this I will do so the Father may be splendored in the Son. ¹⁴If you ask me for something in my name, I will do [it].

¹⁵If you love me, you will observe my orders. ¹⁶I will request the Father and he will give another Illuminator [*Paraklētos*] to you, so he may be with you to the Era, ¹⁷the Truth-Spirit, whom the Kosmos isn't able to receive because it does not observe it nor know it. You know it because it remains with you and will be in you. ¹⁸I will not release you as orphans; I come to you. ¹⁹For a little while and the Kosmos no longer observes me, but you observe me because I live and you will live. ²⁰On that day you will know that I am in my Father and you in me and I also in you. ²¹The one having my orders and observing them, that person is the one loving me. The one loving me will be loved by my Father, and I will love the person and will make myself apparent to the person."

²²Youdas [Judas]—not the Dagger Man [Iscariot]—says to him, "Lord, what has happened that you are about to make yourself apparent to us and not to the Kosmos?" ²³Yēsous responded and said to him, "If someone loves me, the person will observe my word, and my Father will love the person and we will come to the person and we will make a room along with the person. ²⁴The one not loving me does not observe my words, and the word that you hear isn't from me but from the Father who sent me.

²⁵I have spoken these things to you remaining along with you. ²⁶The Illuminator, the Holy Spirit, whom the Father will send in

my name, that one will teach you all things and will remember all things for you that I said to you. ²⁷I release peace for you, my peace I give to you, not as the Kosmos gives I give to you. May your [pl.] heart not be agitated nor frightened. ²⁸You heard that I said to you, 'I go away and I come to you.' If you were loving me, you would rejoice that I journey to the Father because the Father is greater than I. ²⁹Now I have spoken to you before it happens so whenever it happens, you may trust. ³⁰I will no longer speak many things with you, for the Kosmos's leader comes. He doesn't have anything in me, ³¹but so the Kosmos may know that I love the Father, and just as the Father ordered me, so I do.

Arise!
Let us lead on from here.

Yēsous the vineyard

15 I am the true vineyard and my Father is the farmer. ²Every vine in me not carrying fruit, he lifts it. Every [vine] carrying fruit, he cleans it so it may carry more fruit. ³You are already clean because of the word that I have spoken to you. ⁴Remain in me, and I in you. Just as the vine isn't able to carry fruit from itself unless it remain in the vineyard, so neither [are] you unless you remain in me. ⁵I am the vineyard, you are the vines. The one remaining in me and I in the person, this person carries much fruit, because apart from me you aren't able to do anything. ⁶If someone doesn't remain in me, [that person] is tossed outside as the vine and is stiffened and they assemble them and toss into the fire and is enflamed. ⁷If you remain in me and my utterances remain in you, you may ask whatever you want and it will happen for you. ⁸In this my Father is splendored, that you carry much fruit and you become Apprentices to me.

Yēsous loves his friends

⁹Just as the Father loved me, I loved you. Remain in my love. ¹⁰If you observe my orders, you will remain in my love just as I have observed my Father's orders and I remain in his love. ¹¹I have spoken these things to you so my joy may be in you and your joy may be filled out. ¹²This is my order, that you love one another as I loved you. ¹³No one has greater love than this, that someone places one's self for one's friends. ¹⁴You are my friends if you do the things I order you. ¹⁵I no longer say you [are] 'slaves' because the slave does not know what one's lord is doing. I have called you 'friends' because I made known to you everything I heard from my Father. ¹⁶You did not elect me, but I elected you and placed you that you go away and carry fruit and your fruit remains, so whatever you ask the Father in my name, he may give to you. ¹⁷I order these things for you, that you love one another.

Yēsous and the Kosmos

¹⁸If the Kosmos hates you, know that it has hated me before you. ¹⁹If you were of the Kosmos, the Kosmos would love its own. Because you are not of the Kosmos, but I elected you from the Kosmos—because of this the Kosmos hates you. ²⁰Remember the word that I said to you: A slave is not greater than one's lord. If they chased me, they also will chase you. If they observed my word, they also will observe yours. ²¹They will do all these things to you because of my name, because they don't know the one who sent me. ²²If I did not come and speak to them, they would not have sin, but now they do not have pretension about their sins. ²³The one hating me also hates the Father. ²⁴If I did not do works among them that no other person did, they would not have sin, but now both have seen and have hated both me and my Father. ²⁵But, so the word written in their Covenant Code may be filled out, that [says] *They hated me 'as a gift.'* ²⁶Whenever the Illuminator [*Paraklētos*] comes, whom I will send to you from the Father, the Truth-Spirit who journeys out from the Father, that [Spirit] will witness about me. ²⁷You also witness, because you are with me from the beginning.

16 These things I have spoken to you so you may not be tripped. ²They will make you de-assemblied, but the hour comes that all who killed you may think one is offering veneration to God. ³They will do these things because they didn't know either the Father or me. ⁴But I have spoken these things to you so whenever their hour comes you may remember them—that I told you. I did not say these things to you from the beginning because I was with you. ⁵Now I go away to the one who sent me, and not one of you asks me, 'Where are you going away?' ⁶But because I have spoken to you, pain has filled out your [pl.] heart. ⁷But I say the Truth to you: It's to your benefit that I depart. For, if I do not depart the Illuminator [*Paraklētos*] will not come to you. If I journey, I will send him to you. ⁸Coming, that one will convince the Kosmos about sin and about rightness and about judgment:

> ⁹about sin, because they did not trust in me;
> ¹⁰about rightness, because I go away to the Father and you observe me no longer;
> ¹¹about judgment, because this Kosmos's leader has been judged.

¹²I still have many things to say to you, but you aren't able to carry [them] now. ¹³Whenever that one comes, the Truth-Spirit, he will make a path for you in all the Truth, for he will not speak from himself, but whatever he hears he will speak and will declare the coming things to you. ¹⁴That one will splendor me because he takes from me and will declare [them] to you. ¹⁵Everything the Father has is mine. Because of this I said that he takes from me and will declare [it] to you.

Yēsous goes away to the Father

¹⁶A little while and you no longer observe me, and again a little while and you will see me." ¹⁷Therefore, [some] of his Apprentices said to one another, "What is this that he says to us, 'A little while and you don't observe me,' and 'again a little while and you will see me'? And, 'Because I go away to the Father'?" ¹⁸Therefore, they were saying, "What is this that he says 'a little while'? We do not know what he is saying." ¹⁹Yēsous knew that they wanted to ask him, and he said to them, "Are you pursuing about this with one another because I said, 'A little while and you don't observe me,' and 'Again a little while and you will see me'? ²⁰This is especially true to say to you that you will wail and lament, but the Kosmos will rejoice. You will be pained, but your pain will become joy. ²¹Whenever the woman births, she has pain because her hour came. Whenever she gives life to the child, she no longer remembers the trouble because of the joy that a human was given life into the Kosmos. ²²Therefore, you now have pain but I will see you again and your [pl.] heart will rejoice, and no one lifts your joy from you. ²³On that day you will ask me for nothing. This is especially true to say to you: whatever you ask the Father in my name he will give to you. ²⁴Until now you did not ask for anything in my name. Ask and you will receive so your joy may be filled out. ²⁵I have spoken these proverbs to you: The hour comes when I will no longer speak to you in proverbs but I will declare to you frankly about the Father. ²⁶On that day you will ask in my name. I do not say to you that I will ask the Father about you. ²⁷For the Father himself loves you because you have loved me and have trusted that I exited from God. ²⁸I exited from the Father and I have come into the Kosmos. Again, I release the Kosmos and journey to the Father."

²⁹His Apprentices say, "Look! Now you speak frankly and you say no longer in proverbs. ³⁰Now we know that you know all things and you have no need that someone ask you. In this we trust that you exited from God." ³¹Yēsous responded to them, "Do you now trust? ³²Look! The hour comes and has come that each may be scattered to his own home and you will release me alone. I am not alone because the Father is with me. ³³I have spoken these things to you so in me you may have peace. You have trouble in the Kosmos, but be courageous! I have conquered the Kosmos."

Yēsous prays

17 Yēsous spoke these things and, lifting his eyes to the heaven, he said, "Father, the hour has come. Splendor your Son so your Son may splendor you, ²just as you gave to him authority over all flesh, so—all that you gave to him—he may give to them Era Life. ³This is Era Life, that they may know you (the only true God) and him you commissioned (Yēsous Christos). ⁴I splendored you on the land, completing the work that you have given to me that I may do. ⁵Now you splendor me, Father, by your side with the splendor that I had by your side before the Kosmos was.

⁶I made your name apparent to humans that you gave me from the Kosmos. They were yours and you gave them to me and they have observed your word. ⁷Now they have known that everything that you gave to me is from you

⁸because the utterances that you gave me I have given to them and they received and knew truly that I exited from you, and they trusted that you commissioned me.

⁹I ask for them, I do not ask for the Kosmos but for the ones you have given to me because they are yours, ¹⁰and all who are mine are yours and yours mine, and I have been splendored in them. ¹¹I am no longer in the Kosmos, and they are in the Kosmos, and I come to you. Devoted Father, keep them in your name that you have given to me so that they may be one just as we [are one]. ¹²When I was with them, I was keeping them in your name that you have given to me, and I guarded, and not one of them is destroyed except Destruction's son—so that the writing may be filled out. ¹³Now I come to you and I speak these things in the Kosmos so they may have my joy filled out in them. ¹⁴I have given your word to them, and the Kosmos hated them because they are not of the Kosmos just as I am not of the Kosmos. ¹⁵I do not ask that you lift them from the Kosmos but that you keep them from the Evil One. ¹⁶They are not from the Kosmos just as I am not from the Kosmos. ¹⁷Devote them in the Truth. Your word is the Truth. ¹⁸Just as you commissioned me into the Kosmos, so I commissioned them into the Kosmos. ¹⁹I devote myself for them so they may also be devoted in Truth.

²⁰I do not ask for these alone but also for the ones trusting in me because of their word, ²¹so all may be one, just as you, Father, are in me and I in you so also they may be in us so that the Kosmos may trust that you commissioned me. ²²I have given to them the splendor that you have given to me so they may be one just as we are one—²³I in them and you in me—so they may be completed into one so the Kosmos may know that you commissioned me and loved them just as you loved me.

²⁴Father—what you have given to me—I want that where I am they also may be with me so they may observe my splendor that you have given to me because you loved me before the Kosmos's origin. ²⁵Right Father, and the Kosmos did not know you, but I knew you, and these knew that you commissioned me. ²⁶I made known to them your name and I will make [it] known so that the love with which you loved me may be among them and I also in them."

Yēsous betrayed and arrested

18 Saying these things, Yēsous exited with his Apprentices beyond the Kedrōn [Kidron] Brook where there was a garden, into which he entered and his Apprentices. ²And now Youdas [Judas], who gave him over, had also known about the place because Yēsous was often assembled there with his Apprentices. ³Therefore, Youdas, taking a cohort and subordinates from the Senior Priests and from the Observant [Pharisees], comes there with torches and lamps and weapons. ⁴˙Therefore, Yēsous, having known all that was coming upon him, exited and says to them, "Whom are you pursuing?" ⁵They responded to him, "Yēsous the Nazōraios [Nazarene]." He says to them, "I am." Youdas, who gave him over, had been standing with them. ⁶Therefore, as he said to them "I am," they went backward and fell to the ground. ⁷Therefore, again he asked them, "Whom are you pursuing?" They said, "Yēsous the Nazōraios." ⁸Yēsous responded, "I said to you that I am. Therefore, if you pursue me, release these to go away. ⁹So that the word that he said might be filled out, that 'The ones you have given to me I did not destroy any of them.'" ¹⁰Therefore, Simōn Petros [Peter], having a long knife, pulled it and beat the Senior Priest's slave and chopped off his right ear. (The slave's name was Malchos.) ¹¹Therefore, Yēsous said to Petros, "Toss the long knife into its place. The cup that the Father has given to me, will I not drink it?"

¹²Therefore, the cohort and the leader of a thousand and the Youdaians' [Judeans', Jews'] subordinates took Yēsous and bound him and ¹³led to Hannas [Annas] first, for he was Kaïaphas's [Caiaphas's] father-in-law, who was Senior Priest that year. ¹⁴Kaïaphas was planning together with the Youdaians that, "It was beneficial for one human to die for the people."

Yēsous before Hannas, Petros denies Yēsous three times

¹⁵Simōn Petros was following Yēsous and another Apprentice. That Apprentice was known to the Senior Priest and entered with Yēsous into the Senior Priest's enclosure, ¹⁶but

Petros had stood outside at the door. Therefore, the other Apprentice, the one known by the Senior Priest, exited and spoke to the female porter and led in Petros. ¹⁷Therefore, the female servant, the porter, says to Petros, "Are you not also of this human's Apprentices?" That one says, "I am not." ¹⁸The slaves and subordinates had been standing, having made a charcoal fire because it was cold, and they were warming themselves. Petros was also with them, standing and warming himself.

¹⁹Therefore, the Senior Priest asked Yēsous about his Apprentices and about his teaching. ²⁰Yēsous responded to him, "I have spoken frankly to the Kosmos; I always taught in assembly hall and in the temple, where all the Youdaians come together, and I spoke nothing in hiding. ²¹Why do you ask me? Ask the ones who have heard what I spoke to them. Look! These know what I said." ²² . . . He's saying these things . . . one who had been standing near the subordinates gave a slap to Yēsous, saying, "Do you respond this way to the Senior Priest?" ²³Yēsous responded to him, "If I have spoken badly, witness about what is bad. If beautifully, why do you beat me?" ²⁴Therefore, Hannas [Annas] commissioned him bound to Kaïaphas the Senior Priest.

²⁵Simōn Petros was standing and warming himself. Therefore they said to him, "Are you not also of his Apprentices?" That one denied and said, "I am not." ²⁶One of the Senior Priest's slaves, being a relative of the one whose ear Petros chopped off, says, "Did I not see you in the garden with him?" ²⁷Again therefore, Petros denied, and immediately the cock voiced.

Yēsous before Pilatos and the decision to crucify

²⁸Therefore, they led Yēsous from Kaïaphas to the soldiers' headquarters. It was early, and they did not enter into the Praitōrion [Praetorium] so they may not be soiled but could eat the Pascha [Passover]. ²⁹Therefore, Pilatos [Pilate] exited outside to them and said, "What category do you carry against this human?" ³⁰They responded and said to him, "If this person were not doing bad we would not have given him over to you." ³¹Therefore, Pilatos said to them, "You take him and you judge him consistent with your Covenant Code." The Youdaians said to him, "It's not observant for us to kill anyone." (³²So Yēsous' word may be filled out that said, "signifying by what kind of death he was about to be killed.")

³³Therefore, Pilatos entered again into the soldiers' headquarters and voiced Yēsous and said to him, "Are you the king over the Youdaians?" ³⁴Yēsous responded, "Do you say this from yourself or did others talk about me to you?" ³⁵Pilatos responded, "I'm not a Youdaian, am I? Your ethnic group and Senior Priests gave you over to me. What did you do?" ³⁶Yēsous responded, "My Empire is not of this Kosmos. If my Empire were of this Kosmos, my subordinates would be contesting so I would not be given to the Youdaians. But now my Empire is not from here." ³⁷Therefore, Pilatos said to him, "Accordingly, are you a king?" Yēsous responded, "You say that I am a king. I have been given life for this and for this I have come into the Kosmos, that I may witness to the Truth. Everyone who is of the Truth hears my voice." ³⁸Pilatos says to him, "What is Truth?"

Saying this, he again exited to the Youdaians and says to them, "I find in him no cause. ³⁹It's a custom for you that I loosen one to you at Pascha. Therefore, do you choose [that] I loosen to you the king over the Youdaians?" ⁴⁰Therefore, again they made a racket, saying, "Not this one but Bar-Abbas [Barabbas]." (Bar-Abbas was a bandit.)

19 Therefore, then Pilatos [Pilate] took Yēsous bandit and lashed [him]. ²The soldiers, weaving a crown out of thorns, placed it on his head and wrapped around him a purple robe ³and were coming to him and saying, "Rejoice! King over the Youdaians [Judeans, Jews]!" They were giving slaps to him. ⁴Again, Pilatos exited outside and says to them, "Look! I lead him outside to you so you may know that I find in him no cause." ⁵Therefore, Yēsous exited outside, wearing the thorn-crown and the purple robe. He says to them, "Look! The Human!"

⁶Therefore, when the Senior Priests and subordinates saw him they made a racket, saying, "Crucify! Crucify!" Pilatos says to them, "You take him and crucify! For I do not find a cause in him." ⁷The Youdaians responded to him, "We have a Covenant Code and

consistent with the Code it's an obligation to kill [him] because he made himself God's Son." [8]Therefore, when Pilatos heard this word he was more scared [9]and entered into the soldiers' headquarters again and says to Yēsous, "Where are you from?" Yēsous did not give a response to him. [10]Therefore, Pilatos says to him, "Do you not speak to me? Do you not know that I have authority to release you and I have authority to crucify you?" [11]Yēsous responded to him, "You would not have any authority against me unless it had been given to you from above. Because of this the one who gave me over to you has a greater sin." [12]From this [moment] Pilatos was pursuing to release him, but the Youdaians made a racket, saying, "If you release this person, you are not Kaisar's [Caesar's] friend. Everyone making oneself king contradicts Kaisar." [13]Therefore, Pilatos, hearing these words, led Yēsous outside and sat on the Bēma [judgment seat] in a place called "Lithostrōtos" [Stone Pavement], in Hebraïsti [Hebrew] "Gabbatha." [14]It was Pascha's [Passover's] preparation day, it was about the sixth hour [noon]. He says to the Youdaians, "Look! Your king." [15]Therefore, they made a racket. "Lift! Lift! Crucify him!" Pilatos says to them, "Should I crucify your king?" The Senior Priests responded, "We have no king except Kaisar." [16]Therefore, then he gave him over to them so he might be crucified.

Yēsous crucified

Therefore, they took Yēsous along [17]and, carrying by himself the cross, he exited to the place called "Skull's Place," which is said in Hebraïsti "Golgotha," [18]where they crucified him and with him two others one here and one there, Yēsous in the middle. [19]Pilatos wrote also a title and placed it on the cross. It was written,

> Yēsous the Nazōraios [Nazarene], the king over the Youdaians.

[20]Therefore, many of the Youdaians read this title because the place was close to the city where Yēsous was crucified. It was written in Hebraïsti, Rōmaïsti [Latin], Hellēnisti [Greek]. [21]Therefore, the Youdaian Senior Priests were saying to Pilatos, "Do not write 'the king over the Youdaians' but that 'this person said "I am the king over the Youdaians."'" [22]Pilatos responded, "What I have written, I have written."

[23]Therefore, the soldiers, when they crucified Yēsous, took his robes and made four parts, a part for each soldier, and [they also took] the shirt. The shirt was seamless—woven from the top throughout. [24]Therefore, they said to one another, "Let us not rip it but designate for whose it will be." So the writing might be filled out that says,

> They split my robes for themselves,
> And they tossed the die for my shirt.

Therefore, the soldiers did these things. [25]His mother and his mother's sister, Maria of Klōpas [Mary of Clopas], and Maria, the Magdalēnē, had been standing near Yēsous' cross. [26]Therefore, Yēsous, seeing the mother and the Apprentice he loved standing near, says to the mother, "Woman, Look! Your son." [27]Then he says to the Apprentice, "Look! Your mother." (From that hour the Apprentice took her into his own [home].)

[28]After this, Yēsous, knowing that already all things had been completed, so the writing may be completed, says, "I thirst." [29]A vessel was lying there full of sour wine. Therefore, poking a sponge full of sour wine with a hyssop [stick], they offered to his mouth. [30]Therefore, when he took the sour wine, Yēsous said, "It's completed," and leaning his head, he gave over the spirit.

[31]Therefore, the Youdaians—since it was Preparation [Day], so the bodies might not remain on the cross on the Sabbath, for that Sabbath was a great day—asked Pilatos that they might snap their legs and be lifted. [32]Therefore, the soldiers came and snapped the legs of the first one and of the other who had been crucified with him. [33]Coming upon Yēsous, as they saw him already having died, they did not snap his legs, [34]but one of the soldiers stabbed his side with a spear, and immediately blood and water exited. ([35]The one who has seen has witnessed, and his witness is true, and that one knew that he speaks truly so also you may trust.) [36]For these things happened so the writing may be filled out, *His bones will not be broken*. [37]Again, another writing says, *They will see one they pierced*.

Yēsous entombed

38After these things, Yōsēf [Joseph], the one from Arimathaia (being Yēsous' Apprentice, having been hidden because he was scared of the Youdaians) asked Pilatos that he might lift Yēsous' body. Pilatos permitted. Therefore, he came and lifted his body. **39**Also, Nikodēmos [Nicodemus], the one who came to him first at night, came, carrying a mixture of ointment and aloes, each about a hundred pounds. **40**Therefore, they took Yēsous' body and bound it with linen cloths with the spices, just as it was a custom for burying among the Youdaians. **41**There was a garden in the place where he was crucified, and in the garden was a new tomb in which no one was ever placed. **42**There, therefore, because it was Preparation for the Youdaians, because the tomb was close, they placed Yēsous.

Yēsous raised

20 On the first day of the Sabbaths, Maria [Mary], the Magdalēnē, comes early . . . being still darkness . . . to the tomb and sees the stone having been lifted from the tomb. **2**Therefore, she runs and comes to Simōn Petros [Peter] and to the other Apprentice whom Yēsous was loving, and says to them, "They lifted the Lord from the tomb and we do not know where they placed him." **3**Therefore, Petros exited and the other Apprentice, and they were coming to the tomb. **4**The two were running together and the other Apprentice ran quickly ahead of Petros and came first to the tomb. **5**Peering, he sees linen cloths laid out, nevertheless he did not enter. **6**Therefore, Simōn Petros comes following him and entered into the tomb and observes the linen cloths laid out, **7**and the kerchief, which was on his head, not laid out with the linen cloths but apart, wrapped up in one place. **8**Therefore, then also the other Apprentice, who came first to the tomb, entered and he saw and trusted. (**9**For he had not yet known the writing that it's necessary for him to arise from among the dead ones.) **10**Therefore, the Apprentices departed again to them [their homes].

11Maria had stood outside the tomb wailing. Therefore, as she was wailing, she peered into the tomb **12**and observes two envoys in whites sitting, one at the head and one at the feet, where Yēsous' body was lying. **13**Those say to her, "Woman, why wail?" She says to them that "They lifted my Lord and I do not know where they placed him." **14**Saying these things, she was turned to what was behind her and she observes Yēsous standing and she had not known that it's Yēsous. **15**Yēsous says to her, "Woman, why wail? Whom do you pursue?" That woman, thinking it's the gardener, says to him, "Lord, if you carried him tell me where you placed him, and I will lift him." **16**Yēsous says to her, "Mariam." Turning, that woman says to him in Hebraïsti [Hebrew], "My Greatness [Rabbi]," (which is saying "Teacher"). **17**Yēsous says to her, "Do not touch me, for I have not yet ascended to the Father. Journey to my siblings and say to them, 'I ascend to my Father and your Father and my God and your God.'" **18**Mariam the Magdalēnē comes, declaring to the Apprentices that "I have seen the Lord" and the things he said to her.

Yēsous appears to the Apprentices

19Therefore . . . it was evening on that day, the first day of the Sabbaths and the door had been shut where the Apprentices were because they were scared of the Youdaians . . . Yēsous came and stood in the middle and says to them, "Peace to you." **20**Saying this, he exhibited the hands and the side to them. Therefore, the Apprentices rejoiced, seeing the Lord. **21**Therefore, Yēsous said to them again, "Peace to you. Just as the Father has commissioned me, I also send you." **22**Saying this, he blew and says to them, "Receive Holy Spirit. **23**Whose sins you release have been released to them; whose you grab, have been grabbed."

24Thōmas, one of the Twelve, who is called "Twin [Didymos]," was not with them when Yēsous came. **25**Therefore, the other Apprentices were saying to him, "We have seen the Lord." He said to them, "If I do not see in his hands the nails' type and toss my finger into the nails' type and toss my hand into his side, I will never trust." **26**After eight days the Apprentices were again inside and Thōmas with them. Yēsous comes . . . the doors were shut . . . and he stood in the middle and said, "Peace to you." **27**He says to Thōmas, "Carry your finger here and look at my hands, and carry your hand and toss into my side. Do not be anti-trusting but trusting." **28**Thōmas responded and said to him, "My Lord and my God." ²⁹Yēsous says to him, "Because you have seen me you have trusted? God's blessing on the ones not seeing and trusting."

Why this book was written

³⁰Therefore, Yēsous did many other authenticating signs before his Apprentices, which are not written in this book, ³¹but these things have been written so you may trust that Yēsous is the Christos, God's Son, and so, trusting, you may have Life in his name.

Yēsous appears in the Galilaia

21 After these things, Yēsous made himself apparent again to the Apprentices at the Tiberias Sea. He manifested [himself] like this: ²Simōn Petros [Peter] and Thōmas (who is called "Twin" [Didymos]) and Nathan-aēl (who is from the Galilaia's Kana [Cana of Galilee]) and the [sons] of Zebadaios [Zebedee] and two others of his Apprentices were together. ³Simōn Petros says to them, "I am going away to fish." They say to him, "We also are going with you." They exited and got down into the boat, and in that night they caught nothing. ⁴It's already early . . . Yēsous stood on the shore. The Apprentices, however, did not know that it's Yēsous. ⁵Therefore, Yēsous says to them, "Children, you don't have something for eating, do you?" They responded to him, "No." ⁶He said to them, "Toss the net over the boat's right side, and you will find." Therefore, they were tossing and no longer were strong enough to pull it from the mass of fishes. ⁷Therefore, that Apprentice whom Yēsous was loving says to Petros, "It's the Lord." Therefore, Simōn Petros, hearing that it's the Lord, wrapped on the shirt, for he was [all but] naked, and he tossed himself into the Sea, ⁸but the other Apprentices came in the small boat, for they were not far from the land but about two hundred yards, dragging the net of fishes. ⁹Therefore, as they went away into the land, they see a charcoal fire laid out and fish laid on top and bread. ¹⁰Yēsous says to them, "Carry from the fishes that you caught now." ¹¹Therefore, Simōn Petros ascended and pulled the net into the land, full of great fishes—153! Being so many . . . the net was not ripped. ¹²Yēsous says to them, "Come, dine!" No one of the Apprentices was daring to scrutinize him, "Who are you?" knowing that it's the Lord. ¹³Yēsous comes and takes the bread and gives to them, and likewise the fish. ¹⁴This was already the third [time] Yēsous was made apparent to the Apprentices, having risen from among the dead ones.

¹⁵Therefore, when they dined Yēsous says to Simōn Petros, "Simōn of Yōannēs [John], do you love me more than these?" He says to him, "Yes, Lord, you know that I love you." He says to him, "Feed my lambs." ¹⁶He says to him again a second time, "Simōn of Yōannēs, do you love me?" He says to him, "Yes, Lord, you know that I love you." He says to him, "Pastor my sheep." ¹⁷He says to him a third time, "Simōn of Yōannēs, do you love me?" Petros was pained that he said to him a third time 'Do you love me?' and he says to him, "Lord, you know all things, you know that I love you." Yēsous says to him, "Feed my sheep. ¹⁸This is especially true to say to you: when you were young, you wrapped yourself and you walked around where you wanted. Whenever you get old, you will extend your hands, and another will wrap you and will carry you where you do not want." (¹⁹He said this signifying by what kind of death he will splendor God.) Saying this, he says to him, "Follow me!"

²⁰Petros, turning around, sees the Apprentice whom Yēsous was loving following—who also at dinner lay upon his breast—and said, "Lord, who is the one who gives you over?" ²¹Therefore, Petros seeing this one, says to Yēsous, "Lord, what about this one?" ²²Yēsous says to him, "If I want him to remain until I come, what is [that] to you? You follow me!" ²³Therefore, this word exited to the siblings that that Apprentice does not die, but Yēsous did not say to him that he does not die but "If I want him to remain until I come, what is that to you?"

The ending

²⁴This is the Apprentice who witnesses about these and who wrote these things, and we know that his witness is true. ²⁵There are also many other things that Yēsous did, which if one were to write each one, I suppose the Kosmos itself would not make space for the books written.

INTRODUCTION TO THE ACTS OF THE APOSTLES

The Acts of the Apostles tells the story of God empowering the apostles (Commissioners)—Petros [Peter], then Paulos [Paul], or Petros and Paulos—to spread the gospel to Rome and to expand the people of God (Yisraēl) to include the ethnic groups of the Roman Empire. Acts 1:8 is thus the theme of Acts. As such, this biography of the early church tells the story of the mighty power of the Holy Spirit. Even with this emphasis on God and the Spirit the book remains a fine example of early Christian history, and the preface to Acts (1:1-4) echoes ancient texts of history.

A significant category for understanding God's acts of the Spirit through the apostles is *witness*. There are plenty of sermons or speeches or addresses or talks in Acts, and each of them exemplifies in its own way early Christian witness to God's redemptive work in Christ (Acts 2; 3; 4; 10; 11; 13; 14; 17; 21; 22; 23; 24; 25; 26; 27; 28). It must not be forgotten that Acts is designed to take the Gospel of Loukas [Luke] into the next chapters of the story of God's redemption in the world. Loukas-Acts, then, is a narrative of God's work from the Messiah's announcements and birth to his death, resurrection, and ascension, along with this sending of the Spirit to empower the apostles. Loukas's purpose in the Loukas-Acts narrative is to encourage the church to faithfulness because it knows the God of all creation is at work for redemption of the whole world. This plan of God continues the story of Israel but expands it through the Messiah, Yēsous, through the Spirit's anointings, and through the Commissioners' preaching of the gospel from [Jerusalem] to Rome.

The major theme of Loukas-Acts is salvation or redemption, which means salvation from sins, liberation to Spirit-filled living and power and into a new community that transcends ethnic groups. This community of the allegiant ones challenges in many ways the dominant ethos of Rome and Jerusalem, not least in its vision of economic generosity. Sometimes this ethos is called "the Path," or the "Way," in Acts.

Authorship of the book of Acts has been debated, but the "we" sections (16:10-17; 20:5-15; 21:1-18; esp. 27:1–28:16) mean the author wanted readers to think of himself as present on those occasions, and the traditional answer has much in its favor, namely, Loukas the physician and companion of Paulos. As for dating Acts, it can't have happened prior to Paulos's arrest and time in Rome in the early to mid-60s. One could suggest, then, that it was written while Paulos was in prison in Rome.

THE ACTS OF THE APOSTLES

1 ¹I did my first word about all the events,
O Theophilos,
That Yēsous began both to do and to teach,
²Ordering the Commissioners,
Through the Holy Spirit,
Whom he elected,
Until the day he was taken up,
³To whom also he presented himself living
(After his suffering) by many proofs,
Appearing to them through forty days,
And saying things about God's Empire.
⁴Gathering with them,
He declared for them not to separate themselves
From Yierosoluma [Jerusalem]
But "to wait around for the Father's pledge,
Which you heard from me:
⁵Because Yōannēs [John] dipped in water,
But you will be dipped in Holy Spirit
Not after many [of] these days."

Yēsous commissions and ascends

⁶Therefore, the ones coming together were asking him, saying, "Lord, [are you] at this time restoring the empire to Yisraēl [Israel]?" ⁷He said to them,

"It isn't for you to know the times or seasons that the Father placed in his own authority, ⁸but you will receive power . . . the Holy Spirit's coming upon you . . . and you will be my witnesses in both Yierousalēm and in all Youdaia [Judea] and Samareia [Samaria], and even to the last of the land."

⁹Saying these things . . . they're seeing . . . he was taken up and a cloud took him from their eyes. ¹⁰As they were gazing into the heaven . . . he's journeying . . . and Look! Two men had been standing next to them in white clothing, ¹¹and who said, "Galilaioi [Galilean] people, why do you stand looking into the heaven? This Yēsous, who has been taken up from you into the heaven, will so come in the manner you observed him journeying into the heaven."

Gathering for prayer

¹²Then they returned to Yierousalēm from the mountain called "Olive Grove," which is close to Yierousalēm, a Sabbath's path away.

¹³When they entered, they ascended to the upper room where they were staying—Petros [Peter] and Yōannēs [John] and Yakōbos [James] and Andreas [Andrew], Philippos [Philip] and Thōmas, Bar-Tholomaios [Bartholomew] and Matthaios [Matthew], Yakōbos of Halphaios [James of Alphaeus] and Simōn the Zealot and Youda of Yakōbos [Judas of James]. ¹⁴All these were persisting with shared passion in prayer with women and Mariam [Mary], mother of Yēsous, and his siblings.

Replacing Youdas

¹⁵In those days, Petros rising up in the middle of the siblings—now there was a crowd of names altogether about 120—said, ¹⁶"Siblings, it was necessary for the writing to be filled out that the Holy Spirit, through Dauid's [David's] mouth, said previously about Youdas . . . who's a guide to those who took in Yēsous . . . ¹⁷that he was numbered among us and designated for this service's portion. ¹⁸This man, therefore, acquired a field from his wrongdoing's wage, going head first, the middle burst open, and all his belly poured out. ¹⁹This became known to all those residing in Yierousalēm, so that that field was called, in their dialect, 'Akeldamach,' which is 'Blood Field.' ²⁰For it's written in the book of Psalms,

Let his property become a wilderness,
And may there be no inhabitants in it.

And

Let another receive his mentorship.

²¹,²²Therefore, from the men who came with us during all the time in which the Lord Yēsous entered and exited from us—beginning from Yōannēs's dipping until the day on which he was taken up from us—it's necessary for one of these to be a witness of his resurrection with us." ²³They stood two, Yōsēf [Joseph], who is called Bar-Sabbas [Barsabbas] (who was called Youstos [Justus]), and Matthias. ²⁴Praying, they said, "You, Lord, knower of all hearts, show the one you elect from these two ²⁵to take this service's and commission's place, which Youdas violated to journey to his own place." ²⁶They gave portions for them, and the portion fell upon Matthias, and he was admitted with the eleven Commissioners.

Holy Spirit on Pentēkostē

2 When the Day of Pentēkostē [Pentecost] [Fifty-Day Celebration] was filled up, they were all joined together. ²Unexpectedly, an echo came from heaven, like a strong rushing wind, and it filled out the whole house where they were sitting ³and split tongues—like fire—appeared to them and sat on each one of them, ⁴and they were all filled with Holy Spirit and they began to speak in other tongues as the Spirit was giving them to enunciate.

⁵Youdaians [Judeans, Jews] were residing in Yierousalēm [Jerusalem], people of good regard from all the ethnic groups under heaven. ⁶This voice's occurring... the mass came together and were stirred up because each one of them was hearing their speaking in their own dialect. ⁷They were beside themselves and were stunned, saying, "Look! Are not all these who are speaking Galilaioi [Galileans]? ⁸How do we each hear in our own dialect in which we were given life? ⁹Parthoi [Parthians] and Mēdoi [Medes] and Elamitēs and those residing in the Mesopotamia, both Youdaia [Judea] and Kappadokia [Cappadocia], Pontos [Pontus] and the Asia, ¹⁰both Phrugia and the Pamphulia, Aiguptos [Egypt] and parts of Libyē [Libya], which is Cyrēnē, and Roman visitors, ¹¹both Youdaians and converts, Krētes [Cretes] and Arabes [Arabs]: we hear their speaking in other tongues about God's magnificences." ¹²They were all beside themselves and perplexed, saying one to another, "What does this [event] want to be?" ¹³Others, deriding, were saying that "They have been filled with sweet wine."

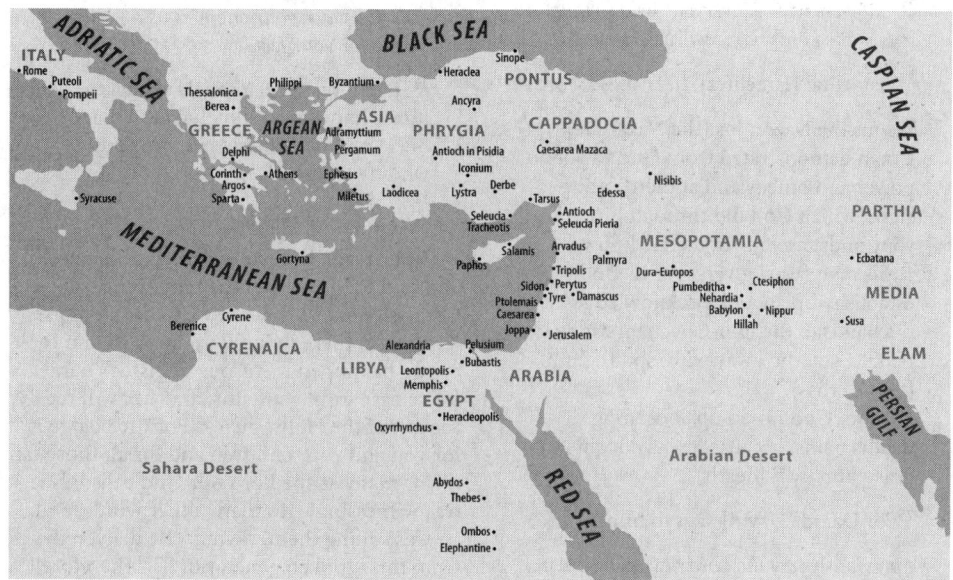

Figure 6. Jewish Diaspora

Petros preaches on Pentēkostē

14 Petros [Peter], having stood with the Eleven, lifted up his voice and enunciated to them, "Youdaians and all Yierousalēm residents, may this be known to you and give ear to my utterances. **15** For these persons are not boozing as you suppose, for it's the day's third hour [9 a.m.], **16** but this is what has been spoken through the prophet Yōēl [Joel]:

17 *It will be* in the last days, God says,
I will pour out from my Spirit on all flesh
And your sons and your daughters will prophesy,
And your young men will see visions,
And your elders will be dreaming dreams.
18 And on both my male slaves and my female slaves in those days,
I will pour out my Spirit, and they will prophesy.
19 *I will give omens in the heaven* above
And *authenticating signs on the land* below—
Blood and fire and smoky vapor.
20 The sun will twist into darkness,
And the moon into blood.
Before the Lord's great and appearing Day's coming.
21 And there will be: Everyone who calls upon the Lord's name will be delivered.

22 Yisraēlitai [Israelites], hear these words:

Yēsous the Nazōraios [the Nazarene], a man demonstrated from God to you in power and omens and authenticating signs, which God did through him in your midst as you yourselves know, **23** this man [was] given over in God's established plan and foreknowledge by the hands of the non-Covenant-Code people, you did away with, spiking him [to the cross], **24** whom God raised up, loosening death's pains, because it was not able to grasp him by it [death].

25 For Dauid [David] says to him,

I previously saw the Lord always before me,
Because he is from my right [hand] so that I will not be shaken.
26 *Because of this, my heart is gladdened and my tongue overjoyed,*
Indeed, my flesh also nests in hope.
27 *Because you will not abandon my self in Hades,*
Nor will you give your saint to see desecration.
28 *You made known to me life's paths,*
You filled me out with gladness with your face.

29 Siblings, it's observant to say with frankness to you about the patriarch Dauid that both his life ended and he was buried, and his tomb is among us to this day. **30** Therefore, being a prophet and having known that God made an oath with him to set on his throne [one] of his waist's fruit, **31** foreknowing, he spoke about the Christos's resurrection that he would not be abandoned in Hades, nor would his flesh see desecration. **32** God raised up this Yēsous, of whom we are all witnesses. **33** Therefore, his status being raised to God's right hand, and receiving from the Father the pledge, the Holy Spirit, he has poured this [Spirit] out, which you see and hear. **34** For Dauid didn't ascend into the heavens, he himself says,

The Lord said to my Lord, Sit at my right hand,
35 *until I place your enemies as a footstool for your feet.*

36 Therefore, let all Yisraēl's [Israel's] house know assuredly that God made him Lord and Christos, this Yēsous whom you crucified."

Responding to Petros's gospel

37 Hearing, they were pierced to the heart, and said to Petros and the remaining Comissioners, "What are we to do, siblings?" **38** Petros to them, "Convert," he said "and each of you be dipped in Yēsous Christos's name for release from your sins, and you will receive the gift of the Holy Spirit. **39** For the pledge is for you and your children and for all those far off, as many as the Lord our God calls." **40** He was witnessing with many other words, and he was calling them, saying, "Be delivered from this crooked generation!" **41** Therefore, those receiving his word were dipped and they added about three thousand selves on that day.

Forming a common life

⁴²They were persisting in the Commissioners' teaching and in the common life, in cracking the bread and in the prayers. ⁴³Fear came to all selves, many omens and authenticating signs were done through the Commissioners. ⁴⁴All the allegiant ones were together and had all possessions in common. ⁴⁵They were selling their acquisitions and properties, and these things were split as anyone had need. ⁴⁶Daily persisting in shared passion in the temple, cracking bread in houses, they were sharing provision in over-joy and heart-simplicity, ⁴⁷praising God and having grace with the whole people. The Lord was adding to those being delivered daily in that place.

Petros heals

3 ¹Petros [Peter] and Yōannēs [John] were ascending into the temple at the prayer hour, the ninth [3 p.m.]. ²Some man, being lame from his mother's belly, was being carried, whom they placed daily at the temple's door, which is called Elegant, to ask for a donation from those journeying into the temple, ³who seeing Petros and Yōannēs about to be in the temple, was asking to take a donation. ⁴Petros (with Yōannēs), gazing at him, said, "Look at us!" ⁵He was clinging to them, anticipating to take something from them. ⁶Petros said, "Silver and gold are not possessed by me, but what I have, this I give to you: In Yēsous Christos of Nazōraios's [of Nazareth's] name, rise and walk around!" ⁷Catching him by the right hand, he raised him. Instantly, his feet and ankles were reinvigorated ⁸and, leaping up, he stood and was walking around and entered with them into the temple, walking around and leaping and praising God. ⁹All the people saw him walking around and praising God. ¹⁰They were perceiving him that he was the one sitting for a donation at the temple's Elegant Gate and they were filled with shock and ecstasy at what things coalesced for him.

Petros preaches

¹¹He's grasping Petros and Yōannēs . . . the whole crowd, totally shocked, was running together to them at the porch that is called "Solomōn's." ¹²Petros, seeing, responded to the crowd,

> "Yisraēlitai [Israelites], why are you shocked at this or why gaze at us as those who have made him walk in our own power or civilized piety? ¹³Abra'am's and Yisa'ak's [Isaac's] and Yakōb's [Jacob's] God, our fathers' God, splendored his young servant Yēsous, whom you gave over and denied before Pilatos [Pilate] . . . he's judging to loosen him. ¹⁴You denied the Devout and Right One and asked for a murderous man to be given to you. ¹⁵You killed Life's Originator, whom God raised from among the dead ones, of whom we are witnesses. ¹⁶By trusting in his name, this one whom you observe and know . . . [whom] his name reinvigorated . . . and the trust that, through him, he gave to him this complete health before all of you. ¹⁷Now, siblings, I know that you practiced consistent with ignorance, just as your leaders [practiced], ¹⁸but God so filled out the events he pre-proclaimed through the mouth of all the prophets—that his Christos is to suffer. ¹⁹Therefore, convert and turn back so your sins are wiped off, ²⁰so that revival seasons may come from the Lord's face, and that he may commission the hand-selected Christos for you, Yēsous, ²¹for whom it's necessary for heaven to receive until times of complete restitution of all [humans], about which God spoke from the Era through the mouth of the devoted prophets. ²²Mōüsēs [Moses] said that *the Lord your God will raise up a prophet for you from your siblings like me. Hear him consistent with everything he speaks* to you. ²³*It will be [that] every self who, if he doesn't hear that prophet, will be destroyed from the people.* ²⁴All the prophets who spoke, from Samouēl [Samuel] and those in sequence, proclaimed these days. ²⁵You are the descendants of the prophets and Covenant that God arranged for your fathers, saying to Abra'am, *And in your seed all the land's peoples will be blessed.* ²⁶To you first, God, raising up his young servant, commissioned him, blessing you, to turn each back from your evil ways."

Petros and Yōannēs gospeling

4 ¹They're speaking to the people . . . the priests and the temple police and the Elites [Sadducees] stood over [them], ²exercising themselves because of their teaching the people and [their] proclaiming in Yēsous the resurrection that is from among the dead ones, ³and they tossed the hands on them and placed them under observation until the next day, for it was already evening. ⁴Many of the ones who listened to the word trusted, and the number of the men was about five thousand.

⁵It happened on the next day their leaders and Elders and Covenant-Code scholars [scribes] were assembled in Yierousalēm [Jerusalem]—⁶and the high priest Hannas [Annas] and Kaïaphas [Caiaphas] and Yōannēs [John] and Alexandros [Alexander] and whoever was part of the high priestly family—⁷and, standing them in the middle, they were inquiring [of them], "In what power or in what name did you do this?" ⁸Then Petros [Peter], being filled with Holy Spirit, said to them,

> "Ones leading the people and Elders: ⁹if we today are being examined for this good work for a weakened human, by which this man is delivered, ¹⁰let it be known to you all and to all Yisraēl's [Israel's] people that in the name of Yēsous Christos
> —whom you crucified,
> whom God raised from among the dead ones—
> in this [name] this person has stood before you healthy.
> ¹¹*This* [one] *is the stone,*
> *the one devalued by you (the builders),*
> *the one who became the corner's head* [cornerstone].
> ¹²Deliverance is in no other for there is no other name under heaven that is given to humans in which it's necessary for us to be delivered."

¹³Observing Petros and Yōannēs's frankness (and [mentally] prevailing that they are uneducated and novices), they were stunned and were perceiving them that they were with Yēsous, ¹⁴and seeing with them the human standing, who had been healed, they had nothing to contradict. ¹⁵Signaling them to depart outside the Central Council, they were engaging with one another, ¹⁶saying, "What are we to do with these humans? For it's evident for all those residing in Yierousalēm that a known authenticating sign happened through them, and we are not able to deny. ¹⁷But, that [this story] not spread any further to the people—let us threaten them to speak no longer in this name to any humans." ¹⁸Calling them, they ordered entirely not to utter a peep nor teach in Yēsous' name.

¹⁹Petros and Yōannēs, responding, said to them, "Before God, is it right to listen to you rather than God? You judge! ²⁰For we are incapable of not speaking about what we saw and heard."

²¹Threatening, they loosened them, not finding, because of the people, how they might chastise them, because all were splendoring God about what happened. ²²For he had been [weakened] more than forty years—the human upon whom this authenticating sign of curing happened.

Praying about the city

²³Being loosened, they came to their own and declared what the High Priests and the Elders said to them. ²⁴The ones hearing lifted in shared passion a voice to God and said, "Emperor, *you, the one who made the heaven and the land and the sea and everything in them,* ²⁵who through the Holy Spirit by the mouth our father Dauid [David], your young servant, saying,

> *Why were the ethnic groups arrogant,*
> *And why did the peoples focus on vanities?*
> ²⁶*The land's kings took a stand*
> *And the leaders assembled together*
> *Against the Lord and against his Christos.*

²⁷For in truth, in this city, against your devoted young servant Yēsous (whom you christened), both Hērōdēs [Herod] and Pontios Pilatos [Pontius Pilate] were assembled with ethnic groups and Yisraēl's people, ²⁸to do whatever your hand and your plan predetermined to be done. ²⁹Now, Lord, look upon their threats and give your slaves to speak your word with all frankness, ³⁰in extending your hand for curing and authenticating signs and omens to be one through your devoted young servant Yēsous' name."

³¹They're asking . . . the place in which they were assembled was shaken, and they were all filled up with the Holy Spirit and they were speaking God's word with frankness.

Gathering in the city

³²The mass of the allegiant ones was one in heart and self, and not one of them was saying

any of their possessions was theirs but was all common for them. ³³With great power the Commissioners were giving witness about the Lord Yēsous' resurrection, and great grace was upon all of them. ³⁴For there was no one deprived among them. For those who had ownership of fields or houses, selling, they were carrying the price of what is sold ³⁵and they were placing [the money] at the Commissioners' feet, and it was distributed to each according to who had need.

Bar-Nabas, Hananias and Sapphira

³⁶Yōsēf [Joseph], who was called Bar-Nabas [Barnabas] by the Commissioners, which translated is "Consolation's Son," a Leuitēs [Levite], Kyprios [Cypriot] by family, ³⁷selling a field owned by him, brought the money and placed [it] at the Commissioners' feet.

5 Some man, Hananias [Ananias] by name, with Sapphira his woman, sold an acquisition ²and purloined for himself from the price . . . and his wife fully knowing . . . carrying some part [of it], placed [it] at the Commissioners' feet. ³Petros [Peter] said, "Hananias, why has the Satanas [Satan] filled out your heart to falsify to the Holy Spirit and to purloin for yourself from the field's price? ⁴Remaining, was [the property] not remaining with you? Having been sold, was it not in your authority? Why [is it] that you placed this matter in your heart? You did not falsify to humans but to God!" ⁵ Hananias, hearing these words, falling, expired, and great fear happened on all those hearing. ⁶Arising, the young men tightened him [in burial clothing] and, carrying [him] out, buried [him].

⁷An interval of about three hours happened and his woman, not having known what happened, entered. ⁸Petros responded to her, "Tell me, if you sold [the acquisition] for such [an amount]?" She said, "Yes, such [an amount]." ⁹Petros to her, "Why [is it] that you both concurred to test the Lord's Spirit? Look! Your man's buriers' feet are at the door and they will carry you out." ¹⁰Instantly, she fell at his feet and expired. The young men, entering, found her dead and carrying [her] out, buried [her] next to her man, ¹¹and great fear came upon the whole assembly and upon all hearing these things.

Commissioners healing

¹²Authenticating signs and many omens occurred through the Commissioners' hands among the people. They were all in a shared passion in Solomōn's porch, ¹³yet none of the remaining dared to unite with them, but the people magnified them—¹⁴rather, allegiant ones were being added to the Lord, a mass of both men and women—¹⁵so that they even carried out the weak into the plazas and placed [them] on stretchers and mats so . . . Petros's coming . . . if even the shadow may envelop one of them. ¹⁶And also the mass of the cities around Yierousalēm [Jerusalem] were assembling, carrying the weak and those being crowded by contaminating spirits—who were all being healed.

Commissioners persecuted

¹⁷Arising, the High Priest and all those with him, that is, of the Elites [Sadducees] faction, were filled with zeal ¹⁸and tossed hands on the Commissioners and placed them under a public observation. ¹⁹The Lord's envoy, during the night, opening the prison's gates, leading them out, said, ²⁰"Journey and, standing, speak to the people in the temple all the utterances of this life." ²¹Hearing, they entered at dawn into the temple and were teaching.

Arriving, the High Priest and the ones with him called together the Central Council and all the Senate of Yisraēl's [Israel's] descendants and commissioned to the confinement for them to be led [there]. ²²The arriving subordinates did not find them in the prison. Returning, they declared, ²³saying that "We found the confinement shut down with all security and the prison guards standing at the doors, but opening, we found no one inside." ²⁴As the temple police and the High Priests heard these words, they were perplexed about them—what this might be. ²⁵Someone arriving, he declared to them that "Look! The men whom you placed in the prison are in the temple, standing and teaching the people." ²⁶Then departing, the police with the subordinates led them without force, for they were scared of the people—that they might be stoned.

²⁷Leading them, they stood [them] in the Central Council, and the High Priest asked them,

[28]saying, "We ordered you with an order not to teach in this name, didn't we? Look! You have filled out Yierousalēm with your teaching and you decide to bring upon us this man's blood." [29]Responding, Petros and the Commissioners said, "It's necessary to consent willingly to God rather than to humans. [30]Our fathers' God raised Yēsous, to whom you administered death, hanging on a tree. [31]God raised the status of this man to his right [hand] as Originator and Deliverer to give conversion to Yisraēl and release from sins. [32]We are witnesses of these utterances, and the Holy Spirit whom God gave to those who willingly consent to him."

[33]The ones who heard were cut in two and were deciding to do away with them. [34]Arising, an Observant one [Pharisee] in the Central Council, by the name Gamali-ēl, a Covenant-Code teacher, honored by all the people, ordered the humans to be put outside for a short period, [35]and said to them,

> "Yisraēlitai [Israelites], beware among yourselves what you are about to practice with these men, [36]for before these days Theudas rose up, saying he was himself someone [special], on whom a number of men (about four hundred) leaned. He was done away with, and all who were persuaded by him dissolved and became nothing. [37]After this, Youdas the Galilaios [Judas the Galilean] arose in those registration days and he removed a people [to come] after him. He too was destroyed, and all who were persuaded by him were scattered. [38]Now I say these things to you: Remove from these humans and release them, because if it—this plan or this work—is from humans, it will be demolished. [39]If it's of God, you will not be able to demolish them—in which case you will be found as a God-fighter."

They were persuaded by him [40]and, summoning the Commissioners, beating, they ordered [them] not to speak in Yēsous' name and they loosened [them]. [41]Therefore, rejoicing, they journeyed from the Central Council's face because they deserved to be dishonored for the Name, [42]yet every day in the temple and house-to-house they were not ceasing, teaching and gospeling Christos Yēsous.

COMPARISONS ABOUT SPIRIT-FILLED DEACONS

Deacons appointed

6 In those days the Apprentices were abounding . . . a grumbling from Hellenists occurred against the Hebraioi [Hebrews] because their widows were unnoticed in the daily service. [2]The Twelve, summoning the mass of Apprentices, said, "It isn't pleasing for us, abandoning God's word, to serve tables. [3]You then look out for seven witnessed men from among you, full of Spirit and wisdom, whom we may establish for this need, [4]and we will persist in prayer and in the word's service." [5]The word was pleasing before the whole mass, and they elected Stephanos [Stephen], a man full of allegiance and Holy Spirit, and Philippos [Philip] and Prochoros and Nikanōr [Nicanor] and Timōn and Parmenas and Nikolaos [Nicolas], an Antiochian convert [6]—whom they stood before the Commissioners and, praying, they placed the hands on them. [7]God's word grew, and the number of Apprentices in Yierousalēm [Jerusalem] abounded extremely. A large crowd of priests heeded the faith.

Diakonos Stephanos

[8]Stephanos, full of grace and power, was doing omens and great authenticating signs among the people. [9]Some of the assembly hall called Libertinos [Freedmen]—Kurēnaioi [Cyrenians] and Alexandreis [Alexandrians] and those from Kilikia [Cilicia] and Asia—arose, disputing Stephanos, [10]and they were not strong to resist the wisdom and the Spirit by which he was speaking. [11]Then they suborned men who were saying, "We have heard him speaking insulting utterances against Mōusēs [Moses] and God." [12]They incited the people and the Elders and the Covenant-Code scholars [scribes] and, standing over [them], they seized him and led him to the Central Council, [13]and false witnesses stood [up], saying, "This human isn't ceasing speaking utterances against this devoted place and the Code, [14]for we have heard him saying that this Yēsous, the Nazōraios [Nazarene], will demolish this place and change the customs that Mōusēs gave

over to us." ¹⁵Gazing at him, all those sitting in the Council saw his face as an envoy's face.

7

The High Priest said, "Are these things so?" ²He said, "Siblings and fathers, listen!

LAND

The splendorous God was seen by our father Abra'am, being in Mesopotamia, before he resided in Charran [Haran], ³and he said to him, *Exit from your land and from your relatives, and come to the land that I will exhibit to you!* ⁴Then, exiting from the land of the Chaldaioi [Chaldeans], he resided in Charran. From there, after his father died, God migrated him to this land in which you now reside, ⁵and did not give to him an inheritance in it, not even a footrest, and pledged *to give it for his possession and to his seed after him* . . . he's not with a child. ⁶God spoke thus, that '*his seed will be temporary residents in an outsider's land and they will be enslaved to it and they do bad things [to them] for four hundred years* ⁷*and I will judge the ethnic group to whom they are enslaved*,' God said, '*and after these things they will exit* and they will venerate me in this place.' ⁸He gave him a Circumcision-Covenant. Thus he gave a life to Yisa'ak [Isaac] and circumcised him on the eighth day, and Yisa'ak [gave a life to] Yakōb [Jacob], and Yakōb [gave a life to] the twelve patriarchs.

EXILE

⁹The patriarchs, being zealous for Yōsēf [Joseph], sold him to Aiguptos [Egypt]. God was with him ¹⁰and pulled him out of all his troubles and gave to him grace and wisdom before Pharaō, king of Aiguptos, and established him leader over Aiguptos and over his whole house. ¹¹A famine came over the whole Aiguptos and Chana'an [Canaan] and great trouble, and our ancestors were not finding sustenance. ¹²Yakōb, hearing grain being in Aiguptos, commissioned our ancestors out for a first [visit]. ¹³In the second [visit] Yōsēf was recognized by his brothers and it became apparent to Pharaō [that this] was Yōsēf's family. ¹⁴Comissioning, Yōsēf called back Yakōb his father and all his relatives, seventy-five selves. ¹⁵Yakōb descended to Aiguptos and he ended his life [there] and all our ancestors, ¹⁶and they were shifted to Sychem [Shechem] and placed in the tomb that Abra'am obtained for a price of silver from Hemmōr's [Hamor's] sons in Sychem.

RETURN TO LAND

¹⁷As the pledged time God openly agreed upon with Abra'am got close, the people grew and abounded in Aiguptos ¹⁸until *another king arose over Aiguptos who did not know Yōsēf.* ¹⁹This one, deceiving our family, did bad things to our ancestors—[he] making [them] expose their infants so as not to be kept alive. ²⁰In which season, Mōüsēs [Moses] was given a life and was attractive to God, who was nourished for three months in the father's house ²¹. . . he's exposed . . . Pharaō's daughter lifted him up and nurtured him as a son for herself. ²²Mōüsēs was educated in all of Aiguptos' wisdom and was powerful in his words and deeds.

²³As a time of forty years was filled out for him, it ascended in his heart to care for his brothers, Yisraēl's [Israel's] sons. ²⁴Seeing one of them being wronged, he protected [him] and made it right for the exhausted one, beating the Aiguptios. ²⁵He was thinking that his siblings would understand that God is giving them deliverance through his hand, but they did not understand. ²⁶On the next day he appeared to them warring and conciliated them for peace, saying, 'Men, you are brothers. Why do you wrong one another?' ²⁷The one wronging the neighbor repelled him, saying, '*Who established you as leader and judge over us?* ²⁸*Do you not want to do away with me in the manner yesterday you did away with the Aiguptios?*' ²⁹Mōüsēs was fleeing at this word and became a temporary resident in Madiam [Midian], where he gave a life to two sons.

³⁰Forty years were filled out . . . an envoy, in a bush's fiery flame, appeared to him in Mount Sina's [Sinai's] wilderness. ³¹Mōüsēs, seeing, was stunned at the vision . . . he's approaching to ponder . . . the Lord's voice came, ³² '*I am your ancestors' God, Abra'am's and Yisa'ak's and Yakōb's God.*' Mōüsēs, a-trembling, was not daring to ponder. ³³The Lord said to him, '*Loosen the sandals from your feet, for the place on which you have stood is devoted land.* ³⁴*Looking, I saw the mistreatment of my people who were in Aiguptos and I heard their groaning,*

and I descended to pull them out. Now come, I commission you to Aiguptos.' ³⁵It was this Mōüsēs whom they denied, saying, *'Who established you to be leader and judge?'* and God has commissioned this one to be leader and liberator with the hand of an envoy who appeared to him in the bush.

COVENANT CODE

³⁶This [Mōüsēs] led them out, doing omens and authenticating signs in Aiguptos in the Red Sea and in the wilderness for forty years. ³⁷This is the Mōüsēs, the one who said to Yisraēl's descendants, *'God will raise up a prophet from your siblings like me.'* ³⁸This is the one who was in the church in the wilderness with the envoy who is speaking to him at Mount Sina, and with our ancestors, who received living sayings to give to us, ³⁹to whom our ancestors did not want to be obedient ones but repelled [him] and turned back in their hearts to Aiguptos, ⁴⁰saying to A'arōn [Aaron], *'Make gods for us, who journey before us, for this Mōüsēs, who led us out from the land of Aiguptos, we don't know what became of him.'* ⁴¹In those days they made a calf and they led it up as a sacrifice to the demon-idol and they were gladdened with their own hands' works. ⁴²God turned [away] and gave them over to venerate heaven's army as it's written in the prophets' book:

> *Did you not offer to me beasts and sacrifices*
> *For forty years in the wilderness, Yisraēl's house?*
> ⁴³*You took up Molochs tent*
> *And your god's star, Raïphan [Rephan],*
> *The types that you made* to bow down to them,
> *And I will migrate you beyond* Babulōn [Babylon].

WITNESS TENT AND TEMPLE

⁴⁴The witness tent was for our ancestors in the wilderness as [God], who speaks to Mōüsēs, ordered to make it consistent with the type that he had seen, ⁴⁵which [tent] also our ancestors, inheriting, led in with Yēsous [Joshua] in dispossessing the ethnic groups, whom God expelled from our ancestors' face until Dauid's [David's] days, ⁴⁶who found grace before God and asked to find a tenting place for Yakōb's house. ⁴⁷Solomōn formed a house for him, ⁴⁸but the Highest One doesn't reside in handmade places, as the prophet says,

> ⁴⁹*Heaven is throne for me,*
> *The land is a footstool for my feet.*
> *What sort of house will you form for me, says the Lord,*
> *Or, what place is for my resting?*
> ⁵⁰*Did not my hand make all these things?*

STEPHANOS'S PROPHETIC REBUKE

⁵¹Stiffnecks! Uncircumcised in hearts and ears! You always object to the Holy Spirit—as your ancestors, so you! ⁵²Which of the prophets did your ancestors not chase away? They killed the one who previously proclaimed the coming of the Right One, whose betrayers and murderers you have now become, ⁵³who received the Covenant Code in decrees by envoys and did not guard [it]."

⁵⁴Hearing these things, they were cut in two in their hearts and were grinding the teeth at him. ⁵⁵Being full of Holy Spirit, gazing into heaven, he saw God's splendor and Yēsous standing at God's right hand ⁵⁶and said, "Look! I observe the heavens opened and the Son of Humanity standing at God's right hand." ⁵⁷Crying out in a loud voice, they covered their ears and rushed with a shared passion at him ⁵⁸and, tossing him out of the city, they were stoning [him]. The witnesses placed their robes at the feet of a young man called Saulos [Saul]. ⁵⁹They were stoning Stephanos, who is calling out and saying, "Lord Yēsous, receive my spirit." ⁶⁰Placing his knees [down], he cried out in a loud voice, "Lord, may this sin not stand against them." Saying this, he went to sleep.

8 ᵃSaulos [Saul] was co-pleased with killing him.

STORIES ABOUT SPIRIT-FILLED GOSPEL AGENTS

Saulos persecuting and his mission

ᵇA great chasing happened in those days against the assembly that was in Yierosoluma [Jerusalem] and all were scattered by region— Youdaia [Judea] and Samareia [Samaria]—except the Commissioners. ²Men of good regard buried Stephanos [Stephen] and had great grief over him. ³Saulos was ruining the assembly, journeying into house by house and, dragging men and women, he was giving [them] over to prison.

But first . . . Deacon Philippos

⁴Therefore, the scattered ones crossed through [the region] gospeling the word.

⁵Philippos [Philip], going down to the city of Samareia [Samaria], announced the Christos to them. ⁶The crowds, with a shared passion, became aware of what's said by Philippos—when they heard and saw the authenticating signs he was doing, ⁷for many of those having contaminating spirits were exiting, bellowing in a loud voice, and many disabled and lame were healed. ⁸Much joy happened in that city.

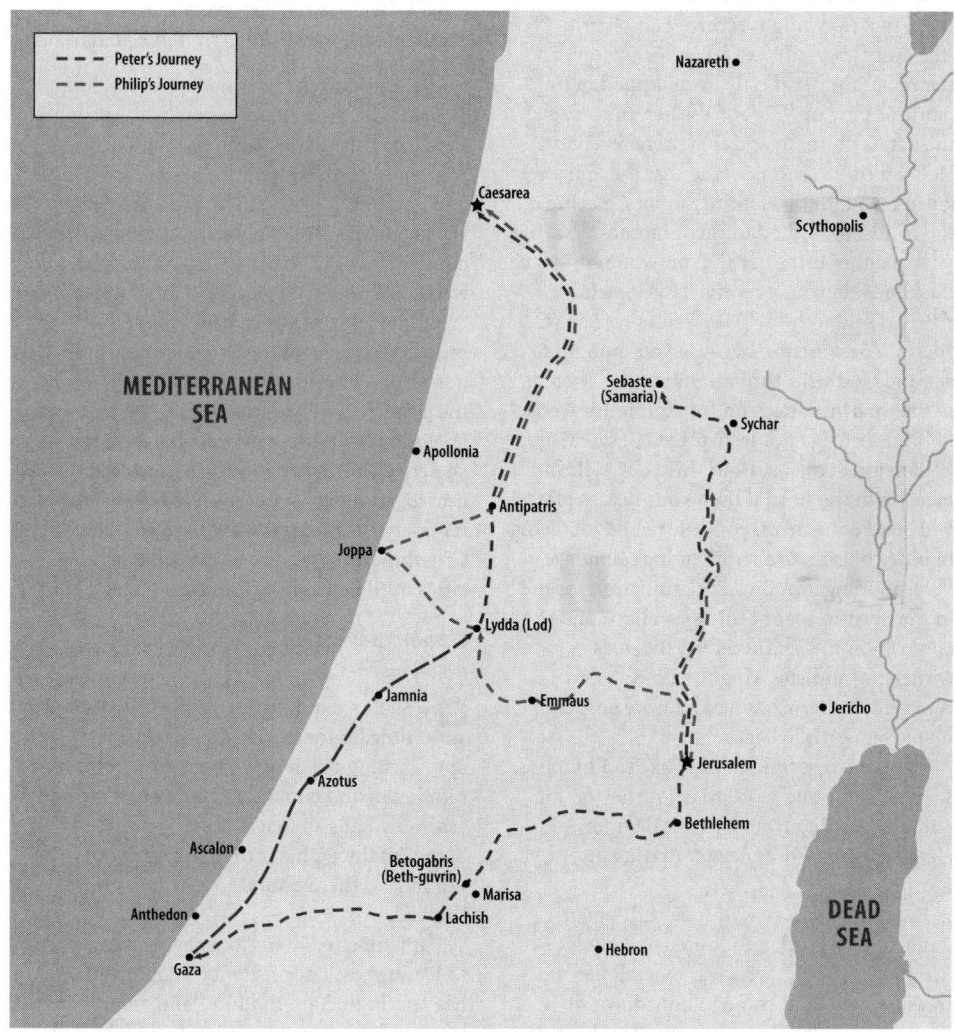

Figure 7. Ministry of Peter and Philip

⁹Some man by the name of Simōn was previously practicing magic in the city and the Samareia ethnic group was beside itself. He was saying he was himself someone great. ¹⁰All were absorbed by him, from little to great, saying, "This person is God's power, the one called 'Great.'" ¹¹They were absorbed by him because for adequate time his magic made them beside themselves. ¹²When they trusted Philippos's gospeling about God's Empire and

Yēsous Christos's name, both men and women were being dipped. ¹³Even Simōn himself trusted and, being dipped, was persisting with Philippos and was beside himself, observing both authenticating signs and great powers being done.

¹⁴The Commissioners in Yierosoluma, hearing that Samareia had received God's word, commissioned to them Petros [Peter] and Yōannēs [John], ¹⁵who, descending, prayed for them that they might receive Holy Spirit. ¹⁶For [the Spirit] had not yet fallen on any one of them, but they had only been dipped in the name of the Lord Yēsous. ¹⁷Then they placed the hands on them and they were receiving Holy Spirit. ¹⁸Simōn, seeing that the Spirit was given through the Commissioners' placing of the hands, presented to them monies, ¹⁹saying, "Give me this authority that on whom if I place the hands they may receive Holy Spirit." ²⁰Petros said to him, "May your silver be with you into destruction because you thought to acquire God's gift through monies! ²¹There is neither part nor portion for you in this word for your heart is not well-placed before God. ²²Therefore, convert from this your evil, and plead with the Lord if then your heart's plot will be released from you, ²³for I see you being in bitter poison and wrongdoing's bondage." ²⁴Responding, Simōn said, "You plead for me to the Lord so that nothing you have said may come upon me." ²⁵Therefore, the ones witnessing and speaking the Lord's word returned to Yierosoluma and were gospeling many Samaritēs villages.

²⁶An envoy of the Lord spoke to Philippos, saying, "Arise and at midday journey on the path descending from Yierousalēm to Gaza"—this is wilderness. ²⁷Arising, he journeyed.

Look! A man, an Aithiops [Ethiopian] eunuch (powerful with Kandakē [Candace], Aithiops's Queen), who was over all her treasure, who had come to bow down in Yierousalēm, ²⁸and was returning and sitting on his chariot and was reading the prophet Ēsaïas [Isaiah]. ²⁹The Spirit said to Philippos, "Approach and unite with this chariot." ³⁰Running toward it, Philippos heard him reading the prophet Ēsaïas and said, "Do you then know what you are reading?" ³¹He said, "For how am I able if someone doesn't guide me?" So he encouraged Philippos, ascending, to sit with him. ³²The writing's lection that he was reading was this:

As a sheep is led to slaughter,
And as a lamb before its shearer is
speechless,
So he did not open his mouth.
³³In his impoverishment his judgment
was lifted away.
Who will narrate his generation?
Because his life is lifted from the land.

³⁴Responding, the eunuch said to Philippos, "I plead with you: About whom is the prophet speaking this? About himself or about someone else?" ³⁵Philippos, opening his mouth and beginning from this writing, gospeled Yēsous to him. ³⁶As he was journeying consistent with the path, they came upon some water, and the eunuch said, "Look! Water! What prevents me from being dipped?" ³⁸He ordered the chariot to stand and they both descended into the water, both Philippos and the eunuch, and he dipped him. ³⁹When they ascended from the water, the Lord's Spirit snatched Philippos, and the eunuch did not see him any longer, for he was journeying his path rejoicing. ⁴⁰Philippos was found in Azōtos. Crossing through, he was gospeling all the cities until he came to Kaisareia [Caesarea].

Commissioner Saulos, who becomes a gospeler

9 Saulos [Saul], still smelling threats and murder for the Lord's Apprentices, approaching the Senior Priest, ²asked from him letters to Damaskos [Damascus] to the assembly halls so that if some were found being "of the Path," both men and women, he might lead them bound to Yierousalēm [Jerusalem].

³It happened in his journeying, he is close to Damaskos, unexpectedly a light from heaven flashed around him ⁴and, falling on the land, he heard a voice saying to him, "Saoul, Saoul, why do you chase me?" ⁵He said, "Who are you, Lord?" He said, "I am Yēsous, whom you are chasing. ⁶But, arise and enter into the city and it will be spoken to you what it's necessary for you to do." ⁷The men who were on the path with him stood stupefied, hearing the voice but observing nothing.

⁸Saulos was raised from the land, his eyes being opened, he was seeing nothing. Leading by hand, they led him into Damaskos. ⁹He was not seeing for three days and he did not eat or drink.

¹⁰There was some apprentice in Damaskos by the name of Hananias [Ananias], and the Lord said to him in a vision, "Hananias." He said, "Look! [It is] I, Lord." ¹¹The Lord to him, "Arising, journey to the street called Straight and pursue in Youdas's [Judas's] house the Tarseus-man named Saulos. For Look! He is praying ¹²and he saw in a vision a man named Hananias entering and placing the hands on him so that he might see again." ¹³Hananias responded, "Lord, I heard from many about this man about whatever evil he did to your devoted ones in Yierousalēm. ¹⁴He has here authority from the Senior Priests to bind all those called by your name." ¹⁵The Lord said to him, "Journey because this man is an elected vessel for me to carry my name before both ethnic groups and kings as well before Yisraēl's [Israel's] children. ¹⁶For I will exhibit to him whatever it's necessary for him to suffer for my name." ¹⁷Hananias departed and entered into the house and, placing the hands on him, he said, "Saoul, sibling, the Lord has commissioned me—Yēsous, the one who appeared to you on the path on which you were going, so that you might see again and be filled with Holy Spirit." ¹⁸Immediately, something like scales fell from his eyes, and he both saw again and, arising, was dipped ¹⁹and, taking provision, he was restrengthened.

It happened after some days with the Apprentices in Damaskos ²⁰and immediately he was announcing Yēsous in the assembly halls, that this one is God's Royal Son. ²¹All the ones hearing were beside themselves and were saying, "Is this not the one devastating in Yierousalēm the ones called by this name? Has he come here for this, that binding them, he may lead [them] to the Senior Priests?" ²²Saulos, instead, was being empowered and stirring up the Youdaians [Judeans, Jews] who reside in Damaskos, inferring that this one is the Christos.

²³As adequate days were filled out, the Youdaians planned together to do away with him. ²⁴Their plan became known to Saulos. They were also keeping the gates both day and night so that they might do away with him. ²⁵His Apprentices, taking him, at night, let him down through the wall, lowering him in a basket.

Commissioner Saulos in Yierousalēm

²⁶Appearing in Yierousalēm, he was testing uniting with the Apprentices, and all were scared of him, not trusting that he is an Apprentice. ²⁷Bar-Nabas [Barnabas], taking hold, led him to the Commissioners and narrated for them how on the path he saw the Lord and that he spoke to him and how in Damaskos he spoke frankly in Yēsous' name. ²⁸He was with them, journeying in and out of Yierousalēm, speaking frankly in the Lord's name. ²⁹He was both speaking and disputing with Hellenists, but they were laying hands [on him] to do away with him. ³⁰The siblings, perceiving, led him down to Kaisareia [Caesarea] and they commissioned him away to Tarsos.

Big picture

³¹Therefore, the assembly of the whole Youdaia [Judea] and the Galilaia [Galaliee] and Samareia [Samaria] had peace, forming and journeying in the Lord's awe, and it was abounding in the Holy Spirit's encouragement.

Commissioner Petros and Aineas

³²It happened: Petros [Peter], crossing through all [places], went down to the devoted ones residing in Ludda [Lydda]. ³³He found there some human by the name Aineas [Aeneas], reclining on a mat for eight years, who was disabled. ³⁴Petros said to him, "Aineas, Yēsous Christos cures you. Arise and spread [a bed now] for yourself." Immediately, he arose. ³⁵They saw him, all residents of Ludda and Sarōn [Sharon] who turned to the Lord.

Commissioner Petros and Tabitha

³⁶In Yoppē [Joppa], there was some Apprentice named Tabitha, which being interpreted says "Dorkas" [gazelle, deer]. She was full of good works and donations that she was doing. ³⁷It happened in those days: weakening, she died. Washing, they placed her in an upper room.

³⁸Ludda's close to Yoppē . . . the Apprentices, hearing that Petros is in it, commissioned two men to him, encouraging [him]: "Don't delay to cross through to us." ³⁹Arising, Petros came with

them and, appearing, they led him, who is appearing, to the upper room, and all the widows stood next to him, wailing and exhibiting whatever robes and clothing that Dorkas, being with them, was making. ⁴⁰Petros, tossing all outside and placing the knees [down], prayed and, turning to the body, said, "Tabitha, rise up!" She opened her eyes and, seeing Petros, sat up. ⁴¹Giving to her a hand, he raised her up. Voicing the devoted ones and widows, he presented her living. ⁴²It became known through the whole of Yoppē, and many trusted on the Lord. ⁴³It happened for adequate days [that he] remained in Yoppē with some Simōn the leather worker.

Commissioner Petros and Kornēlios

10 Some man in Kaisareia [Caesarea], by the name Kornēlios [Cornelius], leader of a hundred of a cohort called "Italikos," ²with a civilized piety and in awe of God with all his house, making all donations for the people and pleading with God always. ³He saw manifestly in a vision—about the ninth hour of the day [3 p.m.]—God's envoy entering to him and saying to him, "Kornēlios." ⁴Gazing at him and being in awe, he said, "What is it, Lord?" He said to him, "Your prayers and your donations ascended into memory before God. ⁵Now, send men to Yoppē [Joppa] and send back some Simōn, who is called 'Petros [Peter].' ⁶This one is receiving hospitality from some Simon the tanner, for whom a house is next to the sea." ⁷As the envoy speaking to him departed, calling for two of the domestics and a pious soldier, who persistently served him ⁸and, expounding everything to them, he commissioned them to Yoppē.

⁹On the next day . . . they're journeying on the path and coming close to the city . . . Petros ascended on the house to pray about the sixth hour [noon]. ¹⁰It happened he was hungry and wanted to taste [some food]. They're preparing [the food] . . . an ecstasy happened to him ¹¹and he observes heaven opened and some vessel descending (like a great sheet with four corners), lowering on the land, ¹²in which were all the quadrupeds and the land's reptiles and heaven's birds. ¹³A voice happened to him, "Arising, Petros, slaughter and eat!" ¹⁴Petros said, "Absolutely not, Lord! Because I never ate any common or contaminating [food]." ¹⁵A voice, again, a second time, to him, "What God cleaned, don't [call] common!" ¹⁶This happened a third time and, suddenly, the vessel was taken up into the heaven.

¹⁷As Petros was perplexed in himself—what the vision he saw might be—Look! The men commissioned by Kornēlios, asking about Simōn's house, stood at the gate ¹⁸and, voicing, they were inquiring if Simōn, who was called Petros, was receiving hospitality there. ¹⁹Petros is interpreting the vision . . . the Spirit said to him, "Look! Three men [are] pursuing you ²⁰but, arising, descend and journey with them, not mentally wavering, because I have commissioned them." ²¹Descending, Petros said to the men, "Look! I am the one you pursue. What is the cause for which you stand [here]?" ²²They said, "Kornēlios—the leader of a hundred, a right man and one who is in awe of God, witnessed to by the whole Youdaians [Judeans, Jews] ethnic group—it was revealed by a devout envoy to send you back to his house and to hear utterances from you." ²³Therefore, calling them in, he gave hospitality to them.

On the next day, arising, he exited with them, and some of the siblings from Yoppē went with him. ²⁴On the next day, he entered into Kaisareia. Kornēlios was anticipating them, calling together his relatives and necessary friends. ²⁵As Petros happened to enter, Kornēlios met him, falling at his feet he bowed down. ²⁶Petros raised him, saying, "Be raised up! I am a human myself." ²⁷Conversing with him, he entered and he finds many assembled ones ²⁸so he said to them, "You comprehend how it's non-observant for a Youdaian man to be joined with or to approach [a person from] another tribe. God exhibited to me to call no human 'common' or 'contaminating.' ²⁹So, without uttering a word, I, being sent back, came. Therefore I inquire, for what word I am being sent back?"

³⁰Kornēlios said,

"Four days ago, at this hour, I was praying at the ninth hour [3 p.m.] in my house, and Look! A man stood before me in radiant clothing ³¹and said, 'Kornēlios, your prayer has been heard and your donations have been remembered before God. ³²Therefore, send to Yoppē to call back Simōn called Petros. This one is receiving hospitality in the house of Simōn the leather worker next to the sea.' ³³Therefore, instantly, I sent to you; doing beautifully, you have arrived. Therefore, now we all are before God to hear all that has been ordered for you by the Lord." ³⁴Opening his mouth, Petros said, "I prevail truthfully that God doesn't respect a face [show deference], ³⁵but in every ethnic group the one in awe of him and who works rightness is receivable to him. ³⁶⁻³⁷The word that he commissioned to Yisraēl's [Israel's] descendants, gospeling peace through Yēsous Christos—this one is Lord over all—you know the utterance that happened through the whole of Youdaia (beginning from the Galilaia [Galilee] after the dipping that Yōannēs [John] announced), ³⁸[the utterance about] Yēsous the one from Nazara [Nazareth], as God christened him with Holy Spirit and power, who crossed through [the land] doing good works and curing all those over-ruled by the Accuser because God was with him. ³⁹We are witnesses of all that he did, both in the Youdaian region and in Yierousalēm, whom they also did away with, hanging [him] on a tree. ⁴⁰God raised this man on the third day and gave him to become apparent, ⁴¹not to all the people but to witnesses, who were previously handpicked by God—to us, who ate and drank with him after his arising from among the dead ones. ⁴²He ordered us to announce to the people and to become witnesses that this man is established by God as judge of the living and the dead. ⁴³All the prophets witness to this man— that everyone who trusts in him receives release from sins through his name."

⁴⁴While Petros is speaking these utterances . . . the Holy Spirit fell on all hearing the word. ⁴⁵The circumcised allegiant ones, who came along with Petros, were beside themselves because the Holy Spirit gift had also been poured out on the ethnic groups. ⁴⁶For they were hearing them speaking in tongues and magnifying God. Then Petros responded, ⁴⁷"Is anyone able to prohibit water for their being dipped, who received the Holy Spirit as also we [did]? (No.)" ⁴⁸He ordered them to be dipped in the name of Yēsous Christos. Then they asked him to remain for some days.

Commissioner Petros and Yierousalēm

11 The Commissioners and the siblings who were throughout Youdaia [Judea] heard that the ethnic groups received God's word. ²When Petros [Peter] ascended into Yierousalēm [Jerusalem], those of the circumcision [faction] mentally wavered about him, ³saying that "You entered into [fellowship] with the foreskin [people] and you ate with them." ⁴Beginning, Petros, laid things out sequentially, saying,

⁵"I was in the Yoppē [Joppa] city praying and saw a vision in an ecstasy, some descending vessel, like a large sheet with four corners lowering from heaven, and it came as far as me. ⁶Gazing into it, I was pondering and saw the land's quadrupeds and wild things and reptiles and heaven's birds. ⁷I heard also a voice saying to me, 'Arise, Petros, slaughter and eat!' ⁸I said, 'Absolutely not, Lord! Because what is common or contaminating has never entered into my mouth.' ⁹He responded a second time from heaven, 'What God cleaned, don't [call] common!' ¹⁰This happened a third time, and everything was again pulled up into heaven.
¹¹Look! Instantly, three men stood at the house in which we were [staying], having been commissioned from Kaisareia [Caesarea] to me. ¹²The Spirit said to me to come with them, not mentally wavering. They came with me and these six siblings and we entered into the man's house. ¹³He declared to us how he saw an envoy in his house standing and saying, 'Commission to Yoppē and send back Simōn, who is called Petros, ¹⁴who will speak utterances to you by which you will be delivered and all your house.'
¹⁵In my beginning to speak, the Holy Spirit fell upon them as also on us in the beginning. ¹⁶I remembered the Lord's utterance as he was saying, 'Yōannēs dipped with water, but you will be dipped in Holy Spirit.' ¹⁷Therefore, if God gave the equal gift to them as to us who trusted on the Lord Yēsous Christos, who was I? Was I able to

prevent God?" ¹⁸Hearing these things, they were silent and splendored God, saying, "God, then, gave conversion to life also to the ethnic groups."

The assembly in Antiocheia

¹⁹The ones scattered from the trouble that happened to Stephanos [Stephen] crossed through to Phoinikē [Phoenicia] and Kypros [Cyprus] and Antiocheia [Antioch], speaking the word to no one except Youdaiaoi [Judeans, Jews] only. ²⁰Some of them were men from Kyprios and Kyrēnaios [Cyrene] who, coming to Antiocheia, were speaking also to the Hellēnists, gospeling the Lord Yēsous. ²¹The Lord's hand was with them, and a large number trusting, turned to the Lord. ²²The word was heard in the ears of the assembly that is in Yierousalēm about them, and they commissioned Bar-Nabas [Barnabas] to cross through to Antiocheia, ²³who, coming and seeing God's grace, was joyed and encouraged all with the heart's intention to be attached to the Lord, ²⁴because he was a good man and full of Holy Spirit and allegiance. An adequate crowd was added to the Lord.

²⁵Then he [Bar-Nabas] exited to Tarsos to inquire for Saulos [Saul] ²⁶and, finding, he led [him] to Antiocheia. It happened to them: for a whole year they were assembled in the assembly and they taught an adequate crowd; the Apprentices were revealed firstly in Antiocheia as "Christianoi [Christians]."

²⁷In those days, prophets from Yierosoluma came down to Antiocheia. ²⁸Arising, one of them, by the name Hagabos [Agabus], made a signal through the Spirit that there was about to be a great famine on the whole inhabited world, which happened under Klaudios [Claudius]. ²⁹Of the Apprentices, just as any was prospering, each of them established for a service to send to those siblings residing in Youdaia. ³⁰Which also they did, commissioning to the Elders through the hand of Bar-Nabas and Saulos.

Commissioners Yakōb and Petros

12 Consistent with that season, Hērōdēs [Herod] the king tossed hands to do bad things to some of those from the assembly. ²He did away with Yōannēs's [John's] brother Yakōbos [James] with a long knife. ³Seeing that it was delightful for the Youdaians [Judeans, Jews], he added to take in Petros [Peter] also—it was Days of Flatbread [Unleavened Bread]—⁴whom, also catching, he placed in a prison, giving over four squads of soldiers to guard him, deciding to lead him up [for judgment] to the people after the Pascha [Passover]. ⁵Therefore Petros was being observed in prison, and prayer was [made] stretchingly by the assembly to God for him.

⁶When Hērōdēs about to lead him out, on that night Petros was sleeping between two soldiers, bound with two chains, and guards before the door were observing the prison. ⁷Look! The Lord's envoy stood over them, and light radiated in the building. Beating on Petros's side, he raised him, saying, "Rise up quickly!" His chains fell off from the hands. ⁸The envoy said to him, "Dress and bind on your sandals!" He did so. [The envoy] says to him, "Wrap on your robe and follow me!" ⁹Exiting, he was following and did not know it was true what was happening through the envoy. He was thinking he's seeing a vision. ¹⁰Crossing through the first prison and second, they came upon the iron gate carrying them into the city, which spontaneously was opened for them and, exiting, they approached one street, and immediately the Lord's envoy moved away from him. ¹¹Petros, coming to himself, said, "Now I know truly that the Lord commissioned out his envoy and it lifted me out from Hērōdēs' hand and from all the Youdaian people's expectation."

¹²Recognizing, he came to Maria's [Mary's] house, mother of Yōannēs [John], the one called Markos [Mark], where an adequate [number] were joined together and praying. ¹³He's knocking the gate's door . . . a servant-girl, by the name Rodē [Rhoda], approached to heed [the knocking]. ¹⁴Perceiving Petros's voice, out of joy she did not open the gate but, running in, she declared Petros was standing before the gate. ¹⁵They said to her, "Are you frenzied?" She was insisting to have it so. They were saying, "This is his envoy." ¹⁶Petros was remaining [at the gate] knocking. Opening, they saw him and were beside themselves. ¹⁷Gesturing to them with his hand to be silent, he narrated for them how the Lord led him out of the prison, and said, "Declare to

Yakōbos and to the siblings these things." Exiting, he journeyed to another place.

18A day's happening . . . there was no small agitation among the soldiers about what became of Petros. **19**Hērōdēs, pursuing him and not finding, examining the guards, he ordered them to be led away [for death].

Going down from Youdaia, he [Hērōdēs] spent time in Kaisareia [Caesarea].

Hērōdēs struck down

20He was hostile with ones in Tyrios [Tyre] and Sidōnios [Sidon]. With a shared passion they became present to him and, persuading Blastos, the king's valet, they asked for peace because their region was nurtured by the king. **21**Hērōdēs, on an appointed day, having put on kingly clothing and, sitting on the Bēma [judgment seat], gave a public speech to them, **22**and the public was voicing up, "God's voice, not a human's!" **23**Instantly, the Lord's envoy beat him because he did not give splendor to God, and, being consumed by worms, he expired. **24**God's word was growing and abounding. **25**Filling out their service in Yierousalēm, Bar-Nabas [Barnabas] and Saulos [Saul] returned from Yierousalēm, taking along Yōannēs, who was also called Markos.

Bar-Nabas and Saulos commissioned

13 There were in Antiocheia [Antioch], consistent with the assembly there, prophets and teachers: Bar-Nabas [Barnabas], Sumeōn [Simeon] (who is called "Black"), Loukios the Kyrēnaios [Lucius the Cyrenian], Manaēn (reared with Hērōdēs [Herod] the Tetrarch[a]), and Saulos [Saul]. **2**They're performing a religious service to the Lord and fasting . . . the Holy Spirit said, "Isolate for me Bar-Nabas and Saulos for the work for which I have called them." **3**Then, fasting and praying and placing on them hands, they loosened them.

Figure 8. Paul's first missionary journey

Comissioners on mission in Kypros

4Therefore they, being sent out by the Holy Spirit, went down to Seleukeia [Seleucia], and from there they sailed to Kypros [Cyprus] **5**and, being in Salamis, they proclaimed God's word in the Youdaians' [Judeans', Jews'] assembly halls. They were having Yōannēs [John] as a subordinate.

6Crossing through the whole island until Paphos, they found some man, a diviner, a Youdaian false prophet, by the name Bar-

---

[a]Herod Antipas.

Yēsous [Bar-Jesus], ⁷who was with Proconsul Sergios Paulos, an understanding man. This one, calling Bar-Nabas and Saulos, pursued to hear God's word. ⁸The diviner "Elumas [Elymas]" (for so his name is translated), resisted, pursuing to turn the Proconsul away from the faith. ⁹Saulos, who is also "Paulos [Paul]," filled with the Holy Spirit, gazing at him, ¹⁰said, "O full of all deceit and all evil-working, descendant of the Accuser, enemy of all rightness, will you not stop turning [people] away from the Lord's straight paths? ¹¹Now Look! The Lord's hand is on you and you will be sightless, not seeing the sun for a season." Instantly, a mist and a darkness fell upon him and, going around, he was pursuing someone to be a hand-leader. ¹²Then the Proconsul, seeing what happened, trusted, shocked by the teaching about the Lord.

Commissioners on mission in Pisidian Antiocheia

¹³Being led up [by the wind] from Paphos, the ones around Paulos came into Pamphilia's Pergē [Perga], but Yōannēs, separating from them, returned to Yierosoluma [Jerusalem]. ¹⁴They, crossing through from Pergē, arrived in Pisidian Antiocheia [Antioch] and, entering into the assembly hall on the Sabbaths' day, they sat down. ¹⁵After the reading of the Covenant Code and the Prophets, the synagogue leader commissioned [an invitation] to them, saying, "Siblings, if there is some encouraging word for the people, say [so]." ¹⁶Paulos, arising and gesturing with the hand, said,

> "Yisraēlitai [Israelites] and those in awe of God, listen! ¹⁷The God of this people, Yisraēl [Israel], elected our ancestors and raised the people's status in the exile in Aiguptos [Egypt] and with a raised-up arm he led them out from it, ¹⁸and for about forty years he tolerated them in the wilderness ¹⁹and, taking down seven ethnic groups in Chana'an land [Canaan], he gave their land as inheritance—²⁰about four hundred and fifty years. After these things, he gave judges until Samou-ēl [Samuel] the prophet. ²¹Then they asked for a king and God gave to them Saoul [Saul], son of Kis [Kish], a man from Ben-Yamin's [Benjamin's] tribe, [for] forty years. ²²Removing him, he raised up Dauid [David] for them to be a king, to whom he said, witnessing, 'I found Dauid, son of Yessai [Jesse], a man consistent with my heart, who will do all my will.' ²³Of this man's seed, consistent with the pledge, God led the Deliverer Yēsous to Yisraēl. ²⁴Yōannēs, announcing in advance, before the face of [Yēsous'] path-entry, a conversion dip for all the people of Yisraēl. ²⁵As Yōannēs was filling out his course, he was saying, 'Who do you suppose I am? I am not [that one] but Look! He comes after me, of whom I am not deserving to loosen the sandals on his feet.' ²⁶Siblings, descendants of Abra'am's family and ones among us who are in awe of God, to us this deliverance's word has been commissioned. ²⁷For Yierousalēm's residents and the ones ruling them, not being informed of this [Yēsous] and the prophets' voices—the ones they are reading every Sabbath—they filled out [what was predicted], judging [him] ²⁸and, finding not even one cause for death, they asked Pilatos [Pilate] to do away with him. ²⁹As they finished all that was written about him, taking [him] down from the tree, they placed [him] in a tomb. ³⁰God raised him from among the dead ones, ³¹who appeared for many days to those who ascended with him from the Gailaia [Galilee] to Yierousalēm, who are now his witnesses to the people.
> ³²We are gospeling you about the pledge that came to the ancestors, ³³that God has fulfilled this [pledge] for us, the children, raising up Yēsous as also it's written in the second psalm,
>
> *My son you are,*
> *I have given life to you today.*
>
> ³⁴Because he raised him up from among the dead ones that will no longer return to desecration—thus he has said that I will give *to you the saintly, allegiant Dauid*. ³⁵Because also in another place it says, *You will not give your saintly one to see desecration*. ³⁶For Dauid, domestically serving his own generation

in God's plan, was put to sleep, and they added [him] to his ancestors and he saw desecration. ³⁷But the one God raised did not see desecration.

³⁸Therefore, let it be known to you, siblings, that, through this one, release from sins is proclaimed for you—from all [the sins] from which you are not able to be righted in Mōūsēs' [Moses'] Covenant Code—³⁹in this one everyone who is allegiant is righted. ⁴⁰Therefore, look that what has been written in the Prophets not come upon you:

⁴¹*Look, you despisers!*
Be stunned and disappear!
Because I work a work in your days,
A work that you would not trust
If someone rehearsed [it] to you."

⁴²They're going out [of the assembly hall] . . . they [the people] were calling [them] for these utterances to be spoken to them on the next Sabbath. ⁴³The assembly hall's loosened . . . many of the Youdaians and the reverent converts followed Paulos and Bar-Nabas, who, speaking with them, were persuading them to be attached to God's grace.

⁴⁴On the coming Sabbath, almost all the city was assembled to hear the Lord's word. ⁴⁵Seeing the crowds, the Youdaians were filled with zeal and were contradicting what is spoken by Paulos, insulting [them]. ⁴⁶Being frank, Paulos and Bar-Nabas said, "It was necessary first for God's word to be spoken to you. Since you repelled it and you judge yourselves not deserving of the Era Life, Look! We are turning to the ethnic groups! ⁴⁷For so the Lord has ordered us,

I have placed you for a light to the ethnic groups,
So you are for deliverance to the end of the land."

⁴⁸The ethnic groups, hearing, were rejoicing and splendoring the Lord's word, and the ones who were ordered for Era Life trusted. ⁴⁹The Lord's word carried through the whole region. ⁵⁰The Youdaians were inciting the reverent women of good standing and the city's first [status], and they raised up trouble against Paulos and Bar-Nabas, and they tossed them out from their region. ⁵¹The ones shaking dust from the feet against them came to Yikonion [Iconium]. ⁵²The Apprentices were filled out with joy and Holy Spirit.

Commissioners on mission in Yikonion

14 It happened in Yikonion [Iconium] the same way: they entered into the Youdaians' [Jews'] assembly hall and they spoke thus so that a great mass of Youdaians and Hellēnes [Greeks] trusted. ²The unpersuaded Youdaians rose up and did bad things to the ethnic groups's selves [so they would be] against the siblings. ³Therefore, they spent adequate time speaking frankly about the Lord who witnesses to the word about his grace, giving to do authenticating signs and omens through their hands. ⁴The city's mass was split, and some were with the Youdaians and some with the Commissioners. ⁵As a surge happened—by both the ethnic groups and the Youdaians, with their leaders—to assault and stone them, they, ⁶discovering, fled into the Lukaonia [Lycaonia] cities—Lustra [Lystra] and Derbē and the surrounding area—⁷and there they were gospeling.

Commissioners in Lukaonia

⁸Some man, powerless in feet, in Lystra was sitting who, lame from his mother's womb, had never walked around. ⁹This one heard Paulos [Paul] speaking who, gazing at him and seeing that he had trust to be delivered, ¹⁰said in a great voice, "Rise up straight on your feet!" He leaped up and was walking around. ¹¹The crowds, seeing what Paulos did, raised up their voice, in Lukaonisti [Lycaonian] saying, "The gods, being like humans, descended to us." ¹²They were calling Bar-Nabas "Dia" [Zeus] and Paulos "Hermēs," since he was the one leading the word. ¹³Dia's priest [of the temple], which was before the city, carrying bulls and garlands to the gates with the crowds, wanted to sacrifice [to them]. ¹⁴Hearing, the Commissioners Bar-Nabas and Paulos, ripping their robes, leaped out into the crowd, crying out ¹⁵and saying, "Men, why do you do these things? We are also men with like-passions to you, gospeling you to turn away from these useless [gods] to the living [one], *who made the heaven and the land and the sea and all things in them,* ¹⁶who in the elapsed generations permitted all the ethnic groups to journey in their own paths, ¹⁷yet he has not released

himself witnessless, doing good—giving you rains from heaven and fruitful seasons, filling [you] up with provision and your hearts with gladness." ¹⁸Saying these things, they barely rested the crowds from sacrificing to them.

¹⁹Youdaians exited from Antiocheia [Antioch] and Yikonion and, persuading the crowds and stoning Paulos, they were dragging [him] outside the city, thinking him to have died. ²⁰The Apprentices gathering around him . . . rising up, he entered into the city. On the next day, he exited with Bar-Nabas to Derbē.

²¹Gospeling that city and apprenticing an adequate number, they returned to Lustra and to Yikonion and to Antiocheia, ²²strengthening the Apprentices' selves, encouraging to remain in the faith and because it's necessary for us through many troubles to enter God's Empire. ²³Laying hands on Elders for them from assembly to assembly, praying with fastings, they presented them to the Lord to whom they had become allegiant.

²⁴Crossing through Pisidia, they came to Pamphulia [Pamphylia] ²⁵and, speaking in Pergē [Perga] the word, they descended to Attaleia [Attalia], ²⁶and from there they sailed to Antiocheia, where they had been given over by God's grace to the work that they filled out. ²⁷Arriving and assembling the assembly, they announced whatever God did with them and that he opened a door of allegiance for the ethnic groups. ²⁸They spent not a little time with the Apprentices.

Commissioners Council in Yierousalēm

15 Some, coming down from Youdaia [Judea], were teaching the siblings that, "If you are not circumcised by Mōüsēs' [Moses'] custom, you are not able to be delivered." ²Anarchy and dispute happening—not a little—by Paulos [Paul] and Bar-Nabas [Barnabas] with them . . . they ordered Paulos and Bar-Nabas and some others among them to ascend to the Commissioners and Elders in Yierousalēm [Jerusalem] concerning this dispute. ³Therefore, the ones sent ahead by the assembly were crossing through both Phoinikē [Phoenicia] and Samareia [Samaria], narrating the turning around by the ethnic groups, and they were making great joy for all the siblings. ⁴Arriving in Yierousalēm, they were welcomed by the assembly and the Commissioners and the Elders, and they announced whatever God did with them. ⁵Some from the Observant [Pharisees] faction, who had trusted, stood out, saying that "It's necessary to circumcise them and to order [them] to observe Mōüsēs' Covenant Code."

PETROS

⁶The Commissioners and the Elders were assembled to see about this word. ⁷Much dispute is happening . . . arising, Petros said to them,

> "Siblings, you comprehend that from ancient days God elected for the ethnic groups to hear through my mouth the word about the gospel and to trust. ⁸God the heart-knower witnessed to them, giving [to them] the Holy Spirit as also to us, ⁹and no one mentally wavered between us and them, by faith cleaning their hearts. ¹⁰Therefore, now why test God to place a yoke on the Apprentices' neck that neither our ancestors nor we were strong to carry? ¹¹But, we trust that we are delivered through the Lord Yēsous Christos's grace consistent with the manner that these are."

BAR-NABAS AND PAULOS

¹²The whole mass was silenced, and they were hearing Bar-Nabas and Paulos expounding whatever authenticating signs and omens God did among the ethnic groups through them.

YAKŌBOS

¹³After their silencing, Yakōbos [James] responded, saying, "Siblings, listen to me.

¹⁴Sumeōn [Simeon] expounded how God first superintended to receive a people from the ethnic groups for his name. ¹⁵The Prophets' words concur with this as it's written:

> ¹⁶*After these things I will return*
> *And I will re-form Dauid's* [David's] *tent*
> *   that is fallen,*
> *And what has been razed of it*
> *I will re-form and straighten it back up,*
> ¹⁷*So that the remaining humans may*
> *   pursue the Lord*
> *Even all the ethnic groups upon whom my*
> *   name has been invoked upon them,*
> *Says the Lord who does these things—*
> ¹⁸*things known from* [the] *Era.*

[19] Therefore I judge not to make it difficult for those who have turned back from the ethnic groups to God, [20] but to send a letter to them to stay away from demon-idol pollutions and from sexual infidelity and from what is strangled and from blood. [21] For since ancient generations, city by city, Mōüsēs has ones announcing him, being read in the assembly halls on every Sabbath."

DECISION

[22] Then it seemed to the Commissioners and the Elders, with the whole assembly, to send elected men from them to Antiocheia [Antioch] with Paulos and Bar-Nabas, Youdas [Judas] who is called Bar-Sabbas [Barsabbas], and Silas, leading men among the siblings, [23] writing through their hand,

The Commissioners and the Elders, siblings,

To the siblings in Antiocheia and Suria [Syria] and Kilikia [Cilicia] who are of the ethnic groups,

Greetings!

[24] Since we heard that some of us (whom we did not order), exiting, disturbed you with words, devastating your selves, [25] it seemed to us, being in a shared passion, electing men, to send to you with our loved Bar-Nabas and Paulos, [26] humans who have given over their selves for our Lord Yēsous Christos' name. [27] Therefore, we have commissioned Youdas and Silas, themselves declaring the same things through a [personal] word. [28] For it seemed to the Holy Spirit and to us not to place on you any more burden that these necessities: [29] to stay away from what is presented to demons and from blood and from what is strangled and from sexual infidelity. You will practice good, keeping yourselves from these.

Be strong!

[30] Therefore, the ones loosened went down to Antiocheia and, assembling the mass, they passed on the letter. [31] Reading, they rejoiced at the encouragement. [32] Both Youdas and Silas, being themselves prophets, encouraged and strengthened the siblings through many words. [33] Doing time, they were loosened away with peace from the siblings to those who commissioned them. [35] But Paulos and Bar-Nabas spent time in Antiocheia, teaching and gospeling with many others the Lord's word.

Figure 9. Paul's second missionary journey

36 After some days, Paulos said to Bar-Nabas, "Returning then, let's care for the siblings, in every city in which we proclaimed the Lord's word, [and see] how they are." 37 Bar-Nabas was deciding to take along also Yōannēs [John], who is called Markos [Mark]. 38 Paulos did not think he deserved to take this one along, the one who removed from them from Pamphulia [Pamphylia] and not coming along with them for the work. 39 An incitement happened so that they separated from one another, Bar-Nabas taking along Markos to sail off to Kypros [Cyprus]. 40 Paulos, choosing Silas, exited, being given over to the Lord's grace by the siblings. 41 He was crossing through Suria and Kilikia, strengthening the assemblies.

Commissioner Paulos and Timotheos

16 He arrived in Derbē and in Lustra [Lystra]. Look! Some Apprentice was there by the name Timotheos [Timothy], son of an allegiant Youdaian [Judean] woman and a Hellēn [Greek] father, 2 who was witnessed to by the siblings in Lustra and Yikonion [Iconium]. 3 Paulos [Paul] wanted this person to exit with him and, taking, he circumcised him because of the Youdaians who were in that place, for they all knew that his father was a Hellēn.

4 As they were journeying through the cities, they were giving over to them to guard the decrees that had been judged by the Commissioners and Elders who are in Yierosoluma [Jerusalem]. 5 Therefore, the assemblies were being strengthened in allegiance and abounding in numbers daily.

Commissioner Paulos guided to Makedōn

6 They crossed through the Phrugia-Galatikos [Phrygia-Galatian] region, being prevented by Holy Spirit to speak the word in Asia. 7 Coming along Musia [Mysia], they were tempted to journey into Bithunia [Bithynia], and Yēsous' Spirit did not permit them. 8 Passing by Mysia, they descended to Trōas. 9 A vision during the night appeared to Paulos, some Makedōn [Macedonian] man was standing and encouraging him and saying, "Crossing over to Makedonia, help us!" 10 As he saw the vision, immediately we pursued to exit to Makedonia, inferring that God had called us to gospel them.

Commissioner Paulos in Phillipoi

11 Being led up from Trōas, we ran straight to Samothrakē [Samothrace] and on the next day to New City [Neapolis], 12 from there to Philippoi [Philippi], which is the First City of the Makedonian territory, a colony [of Rome]. We were spending some days in that city.

13 On the day of the Sabbaths, we exited out the gate along the river where we were thinking there is a Prayer House and, sitting, we were speaking with the women who gathered [there]. 14 Some woman by name Ludia [Lydia], a seller of purple cloth, from the city of Thuateira [Thyatira], a God-reverer, was listening, whose heart the Lord opened to absorb what was spoken by Paulos. 15 As she was dipped (and her house), she encouraged [Paulos], saying, "If you have judged me to be allegiant to the Lord, entering in my house, remain." She urged us.

16 It happened: we're journeying to the Prayer House . . . a servant-girl with a clairvoyant spirit met us, who acquired much work for her lords, conjuring oracles. 17 She, following Paulos and us, was crying out, saying, "These men are slaves of the Highest God, who proclaim to you the path of deliverance." 18 She was doing this for many days. Being exercised, Paulos, turning to the spirit, said, "I order you in Yēsous Christos' name to exit from her." It exited that hour. 19 Her lords, seeing that their work's hope exited, taking hold of Paulos and Silas, they pulled [them] into the square before the leaders 20 and, leading them to the police, said, "These men are disturbing our city, being Youdaians, 21 and are proclaiming customs that are not observant for us to receive or to do, being Romaioi [Romans]." 22 The crowd joined the attack on them, and the police, ripping off their robes, were signaling to flog [them], 23 and laying many plagues on them, they tossed [them] into prison, ordering the prison guard to keep them assuredly. 24 Receiving such an order, taking, he tossed them into the inner prison and secured their feet into the wood [stocks].

25 About midnight, Paulos and Silas, praying, were singing a hymn to God, and the prisoners were turning their ears to them. 26 Unexpectedly, a great earthquake happened so that the confinement's foundations were shaken. Instantly, all the doors were opened,

and the bonds of all came off. ²⁷The prison guard came awake and, seeing the opened prison doors, drawing the long knife, was about to do away with himself, thinking the prisoners to have fled. ²⁸Paulos voiced in a great voice, saying, "Don't practice a bad thing to yourself, for we are all in here!"

²⁹Asking for lights, he hoofed it in and, trembling, fell before Paulos and Silas ³⁰and, leading them outside, said, "Lords, what is necessary for me to do that I may be delivered?" ³¹They said, "Trust in the Lord Yēsous and you and your house will be delivered." ³²They spoke the Lord's word to him and all those in his house. ³³Receiving them in that hour of the night, he washed [them] from their plagues, and instantly he was dipped (and all of his [household]). ³⁴Leading them into the house, he presented before them a table [of food] and he, having trusted in God, was glad with the whole house.

³⁵The day comes . . . the police commissioned the floggers, saying, "Loosen those men!" ³⁶The prison guard declared these words to Paulos that "The police have commissioned that you be loosened. Therefore, now, exiting, journey in peace!" ³⁷But Paulos said to them, "Beating us in public without a judgment, being Romaios men, they tossed [us] into prison, and now secretly they toss us out? For no! But coming, let them lead us out themselves." ³⁸The floggers declared these words to the police. They were scared, hearing that they are Romaios ³⁹and, coming, they encouraged them and, leading them out, they were asking them to go away from the city. ⁴⁰Exiting from the prison, they entered Ludia's [house] and, seeing, encouraged the siblings and exited.

Commissioner Paulos and Silas in Thessalonikē

17 Taking the path through Amphipolis and Apollōnia, they came to Thessalonikē [Thessalonica], where there was a Youdaian [Jewish] assembly hall. ²Consistent with Paulos's [Paul's] custom, he entered with them and on three Sabbaths he deliberated with them from the writings, ³opening and presenting that it is necessary for the Christos to suffer and to be raised up from among the dead ones and that this is the Christos, Yēsous whom I proclaim to you. ⁴Some of them were persuaded and were affixed to Paulos and Silas, so too did a great mass of Hellēn [Greek] reverers, as well as First Women—not a few. ⁵The Youdaians [Jews], being zealous and welcoming some bad loitering men of the city squares, and making a crowd, were disturbing the city and, standing over the house of Yasōn [Jason], were pursuing them to lead them into the public. ⁶Not finding them, they were dragging Yasōn and some siblings before the politarchs, bellowing out that "These are anarchists [causing trouble] to the inhabited world, and are now present here, ⁷whom Yasōn has welcomed. All these practice against the Kaisar's [Caesar's] decrees, saying there's another emperor—that is, Yēsous." ⁸They agitated the crowd and the politarchs, hearing these things ⁹and, taking adequate [bond] from Yasōn and the remaining, they loosened them.

Commissioner Paulos and Silas in Beroia

¹⁰Immediately, the siblings sent both Paulos and Silas out during the night to Beroia [Berea] who, arriving, they went away into the Youdaians' assembly hall. ¹¹These were nobler than those in Thessalonikē, who received the word with all ardor, daily examining the writings—if [Paulos] might have these things so. ¹²Therefore, many of them trusted, that is, good-standing Hellēn women and men—not a few. ¹³As the Youdaians from Thessalonikē knew that also in Beroia God's word was being proclaimed by Paulos, they came there, shaking and agitating the crowds. ¹⁴Immediately then, the siblings commissioned out Paulos to journey as far as the sea, but both Silas and Timotheos [Timothy] remained there. ¹⁵The ones establishing Paulos led [him] to Athēnai [Athens] and they, taking an order to Silas and Timotheos that as soon as possible they might come to him, went away.

Commissioner Paulos in Athēnai

¹⁶Paulos is awaiting them in Athēnai . . . the spirit in him was provoked, observing the city being demon-full. ¹⁷Therefore, he was deliberating in the assembly hall with Youdaians and reverent ones, and in the square every day with those who happened to be present. ¹⁸Also some of the Epikoureioi [Epicureans] and Stoïkoi [Stoic] philosophers were engaging him,

and some were saying, "Whatever might this scrounger want to say?" Others, "He seems to be a proclaimer of foreign demons." (Because he was gospeling Yēsous and the resurrection.) ¹⁹Taking hold of him, they led him onto Mars Hill [Areopagus], saying, "Are we able to know what this new teaching is that is spoken by you? ²⁰For you are bring into our hearing some foreign [ideas]. Therefore, we want to know what these things mean." ²¹(All the Athēnaioi [Athenians] and visiting foreigners were looking for a good moment to say or to hear the newest thing.) ²²Paulos, being stood up in the middle of Mars Hill, said,

> "Athēnaioi, in all things I observe you as ones devoted-to-the-demonic, ²³for, going through and clearly observing your places for reverence, I even found a platform on which is inscribed, 'To Unknown God.' Therefore you revere [what is] not known. This I proclaim to you: The God who made the Kosmos and all things that are in it, this one being Lord of heaven and land, doesn't reside in handmade sanctuaries, ²⁵nor is he served by human hands, asking to receive something—he giving to all [created] things life and breath and all things. ²⁶He made from one [human] every ethnic group of humans to reside on the whole face of the land, establishing ordered seasons and their residences' boundaries, ²⁷that [they would] pursue God, if only they might feel him and might find [him], and indeed being not far from each one of us. ²⁸For in him we live and we move and we are—as also some poets consistent with you have said.
>
> | For we are also given a life from him.ᵇ

²⁹Therefore, being ones given life by God, we ought not to decree the divine to be analogous to gold or silver or stone, an artisan's mark and a human's musings. ³⁰Therefore God, looking beyond the times of the unknowing, now orders all humans in all places to convert. ³¹Just as he stood a day on which he is about to judge the inhabited world in rightness, in the Man whom he established, presenting [a reason for] faith for all, raising him up from among the dead ones."

³²Hearing about resurrection from among the dead ones, some were deriding [him], but some said, "We will hear from you about this again."

³³Thus, Paulos exited from their middle. ³⁴Some men, joining to him, trusted, among whom was Dionysios, a Mars Hillian, and a women named Damaris and others with them.

Commissioner Paulos in Korinthos

18 After these things, being separated from Athēnai [Athens], he came into Korinthos [Corinth]. ²Finding some Youdaian [Jew] by the name Akulas [Aquila], Pontikos [Pontus] by family, having recently come from Italia [Italy], and Priskilla [Priscilla], his woman, because Klaudios [Claudius] ordered all Youdaians to be separated from Rōmē, he approached them ³and, because he had the same skill, he was remaining with them and he was working. For they were tentmakers by skill. ⁴He was deliberating in the assembly hall every Sabbath and he was persuading both Youdaians and Hellēnes [Greeks].

⁵As both Silas and Timotheos [Timothy] went down from Makedonia [Macedonia], Paulos [Paul] was absorbed with the word, witnessing to the Youdaians that Yēsous is the Christos. ⁶They're counter-ordering and insulting . . . shaking out his robes, he said to them, "Your blood on your head. I am clean. From now I will journey to the ethnic groups." ⁷Shifting from there, he entered into the house of someone by the name of Titios Youstos [Titius Justus], a God-reverer, whose house was formed with the assembly hall. ⁸Krispos [Crispus], leader of the assembly hall, trusted the Lord with his whole house, and many of the Korinthioi [Corinthians], hearing, were trusting and were being dipped.

⁹The Lord said at night through a vision to Paulos, "Don't be scared, but speak and don't go silent ¹⁰because I am with you and no one will place on you to do bad things to you because there is a great people for me in this city." ¹¹He sat for a year and six months, teaching among them God's word.

ᵇQuoting a Stoic named Aratos.

¹²Galliōn is Proconsul of Achaïa . . . the Youdaians rose up against Paulos with shared passion and they led him to the Bēma [judgment seat], ¹³saying that "Against the Covenant Code, this man dissuades humans to revere God." ¹⁴Paulos is about to open his mouth . . . Galliōn said to the Youdaians, "If there were some wrongdoing or disloyal act, O Youdaians, I would put up with you in this word [of complaint], ¹⁵but if this is a dispute about a word and names and your own Code—you yourselves will see [to it]. I don't want to be judge of these matters." ¹⁶He expelled them from the Bēma. ¹⁷All, taking hold of Sōsthenēs, the leader of the assembly hall, were pounding him before the Bēma, and none of these was a concern to Galliōn.

Commissioner Paulos circles back

¹⁸Paulos, being attached there adequate days, saying farewell to the siblings, was sailing to Suria [Syria], and with him Priskilla and Akulas, shaving the head in Kenchreai [Cenchreae]—for he was formulating a vow. ¹⁹They arrived in Ephesos [Ephesus]; there he abandoned them and he, entering into the assembly hall, deliberated with the Youdaians. ²⁰They're asking [him] to remain for more time . . . he did not consent ²¹but, saying farewell and saying "Again I will return to you . . . God willing" . . . he was led up from Ephesos ²²and, coming down to Kaisareia [Caesarea], ascending and greeting the assembly [in Jerusalem], he descended to Antiocheia [Antioch].

Figure 10. Paul's third missionary journey

²³Doing some time [there], he exited, going through the Galatikos-Phrugia [Galatian Phrygia] region sequentially, strengthening all the Apprentices.
²⁴Some Youdaian, by name Apollōs, Alexandreus [Alexandria] by family, a word-gifted man, arrived in Ephesos, being powerful in the writings. ²⁵This man was catechized in the Lord's Path and, zesty in the Spirit, he was speaking and teaching carefully the matters about Yēsous, comprehending only Yōannēs's [John's] dipping. ²⁶This man began to speak frankly in the assembly hall. Hearing him, Priskilla and Akulas welcomed him and laid out God's Path more carefully.
²⁷He's wanting to go through to Achaïa . . . the siblings, directing, wrote to the Apprentices to receive him who, arriving, engaged much with the ones who had trusted through grace. ²⁸For he was vigorously refuting the Youdaians in public, exhibiting through the writings that Yēsous is the Christos.

Commissioner Paulos in Ephesos

19 It happened in Apollōs's being in Korinthos [Corinth], Paulos's [Paul's] going through the interior areas coming down to Ephesos [Ephesus] and finding some Apprentices, ²he said to them, "Did you receive the Holy Spirit—believing?" They said to him, "But we did not even hear there is a 'Holy Spirit.'" ³He said, "Into what, therefore, were you dipped?" They said, "Into Yōannēs's [John's] dipping." ⁴Paulos said, "Yōannēs dipped with a conversion dipping, saying to the people that they are to trust in the one who comes after him—that is, in Yēsous." ⁵Hearing, they were dipped in the Lord Yēsous' name ⁶. . . Paulos's placing hands on them . . . the Holy Spirit came on them, they were speaking in tongues and they were prophesying. ⁷They were about a total of twelve men.

⁸Entering into the assembly hall, he was speaking frankly for three months, deliberating and persuading matters about God's Empire. ⁹As some became stubborn and were persuading, speaking bad about the Path before the mass [of people], isolating, he separated the Apprentices from them, daily deliberating in Turannos's [Tyrannus's] lecture hall. ¹⁰This happened for two years so that all Asian residents heard the Lord's word, both Youdaians [Jews] and Hellēnes [Greeks]. ¹¹God was doing powerful things—not at all ordinary—through Paulos's hands ¹²so that even upon the weak headkerchiefs and handcloths, carried away from his skin, [were placed] and the illnesses were liberated from them and the evil spirits journeyed away.

¹³Even some of Youdaian itinerant exorcists attempted to name the Lord Yēsous upon those having evil spirits, saying, "I implore you by the 'Yēsous' whom Paulos announces [to leave]." ¹⁴Seven sons of some Skeuas [Sceva], a Youdaian Senior Priest, were doing this. ¹⁵Responding, the evil spirit said to them, "Yēsous I know and Paulos I comprehend, but who are you?" ¹⁶Springing upon them, the human in whom there was the evil spirit, ruled over all of them, strong-armed them so that [they] fled from that house naked and traumatized. ¹⁷This became known to all the Youdaians and Hellēnes who reside in Ephesos, and awe fell on all of them and the Lord Yēsous' name was magnified. ¹⁸Many of the ones who had trusted were coming [forward], publicly acknowledging and announcing their practices. ¹⁹An adequate number of the ones practicing marginal deeds, pulling together, were burning the books before all, and they tallied up their prices and they found fifty thousand silver [coins]. ²⁰So, consistent with the Lord's grip, the word was growing and strengthening.

²¹As these things were filled out, Paulos placed in the Spirit, crossing through Makedonia [Macedonia] and Achaïa, to journey to Yierosoluma [Jerusalem], saying that "After I have been there it's necessary for me to see Rōmē." ²²Commissioning two of those serving him, Timotheos [Timothy] and Erastos [Erastus], to Makedonia, he held back for a time in Asia.

²³Consistent with that season an agitation—not small—happened concerning the Path. ²⁴For someone, Dēmētrios [Demetrius] by name, a silversmith, a maker of silver shrines for Artemis, was presenting to the artisans work—no small amount, ²⁵whom, joining together—as well as workers of such things—said,

> "Men, you comprehend the prosperity for us from this work ²⁶and you observe and hear—not only in Ephesos but almost all of Asia—that this Paulos, persuading, shifted an adequate crowd, saying that 'The ones coming through hands are not gods.' ²⁷Not only is there a danger for us that our part comes to disrepute, but also for the great goddess Artemis's temple to be calculated as nothing—indeed, the one whom all Asia and the inhabited world reveres is about to be taken down from her magnificence!"

²⁸Hearing and being filled with fury, they were crying out, saying, "Great is Artemis of the Ephesioi [Ephesians]!" ²⁹The city was filled with confusion, and they rushed with shared passion into the theater, seizing Gaïos [Gaius] and Aristarchos [Aristarchus], Paulos's fellow travelers from Makedonia. ³⁰Paulos's wanting to enter into the public, the Apprentices aren't permitting him . . . ³¹even some of the Asiarchs, being friends to him, sending to him, were begging [him] not to give himself into the theater. ³²Therefore, some were crying out other things, for the assembly was confused

and the many did not know even why they had come together. ³³Youdaians are tossing him forward . . . [some] from the crowd instructed Alexandros [Alexander]. Alexandros, gesturing with the hand, wanted to defend himself in the public. ³⁴Perceiving that he is Youdaios, one voice of all was for about two hours, crying out, "Great is Artemis of the Ephesioi!"

³⁵The legal expert, soothing the crowd, said,

"Ephesioi, for who is there among humans who doesn't know [that] the city of the Ephesioi is sanctuary keeper of the great Artemis and of what fell from the sky? ³⁶These things being therefore indisputable . . . it being necessary for you to be soothed and not to practice something precipitous. ³⁷For you led these men [here, who are] neither temple-robbers nor insulters of our God. ³⁸If therefore Dēmētrios and the artisans with him have a word against anyone, the courts are leading on and there are Proconsuls, let them call in one another. ³⁹If you pursue something further, it will be explained in the legal assembly. ⁴⁰For we are in danger of being called in for anarchy for this day . . . there's no charge about which we will be able to hand over a word concerning this conspiracy."

⁴¹Saying these things, he released the assembly.

Commissioner Paulos circles over and back

20 After the clamor stopped, Paulos [Paul]—sending for and encouraging the Apprentices, greeting [them], he exited to journey to Makedonia [Macedonia]. ²Going through those parts and encouraging them with much [preaching of the] word, he came into Hellas [Greece], ³doing three months. A plot by the Youdaians [Jews] was against him who is about to set sail for Suria [Syria]. . . . he became of a mind to return through Makedonia. ⁴Sōpatros [Sopater], son of Purros [Pyrrhus], the Beroian [Berean], was accompanying him, and also Thessalonikeans [Thessalonicans] Aristarchos [Aristarchus] and Sekoundos [Secundus], and Derbaian Gaïos [Gaius of Derbe], and Timotheos [Timothy], and Asians Tuchikos [Tychicus] and Trophimos [Trophimus]. ⁵These, going ahead, were remaining for us in Trōas, ⁶and we sailed away after the Days of Flatbread [Unleavened Bread] from Philippoi [Philippi] and we came to them in Trōas after five days, where for seven days we spent time.

Good Luck sleeping during a very long night sermon

⁷On the first day of the Sabbaths we're gathered to crack bread . . . Paulos was deliberating with them (as he was about to be gone tomorrow), and he was stretching the [teaching of the] word until the middle of the night. ⁸There were adequate lamps in the upper room where we were assembled. ⁹Some young man by the name of Eutuchos [Eutychus, meaning Good Luck], sitting at the window, falling down into a deep sleep . . . Paulos's deliberating on and on . . . having fallen into the sleep, he fell down from the third floor, and he was lifted up dead. ¹⁰Descending, Paulos fell upon him and, embracing, said, "Don't be disturbed, for his self is in him." ¹¹Ascending and cracking bread and tasting [it], and sharing adequately until dawn, so he exited. ¹²They led the young servant [home] alive and they were encouraged—no small amount.

Commissioner Paulos to Milētos

¹³We, proceeding by the boat, were led [by the winds] upon Assos, from there about to take Paulos on board. For so ordering [plans], he was himself about to go by foot. ¹⁴As he was engaging us in Assos, taking him on board, we came to Mitulēnē [Mitylene], ¹⁵and from there sailing on the next day, we arrived straight out from Chios, on the next day we crossed over to Samos, and on the coming day we came to Milētos [Miletus]. ¹⁶For Paulos had judged to sail past Ephesos [Ephesus] so he might not consume time in Asia. For he was hurrying, if it might be possible for him to come to Yierosoluma [Jerusalem] for the Day of Pentēkostē [Pentecost].

Commissioner Paulos and the Elders of Ephesos

¹⁷From Milētos, sending to Ephesos, he called back the assembly's Elders. ¹⁸As they came to him, he said to them,

"You comprehend, from the first day from which I put down in Asia, how I was with you the whole time, ¹⁹slaving for the Lord with all impoverishment and tears and testings coalescing on me in the Youdaians' [Jews'] plots, ²⁰as I did not back off of what is beneficial so to announce to you and to teach you, in public and house-to-house, ²¹witnessing to both the Youdaians and Hellēnes [Greeks] about conversion to God and faith in our Lord Yēsous.
²²And now Look! I, being bound by Spirit, journey to Yierousalēm not knowing what things in it will meet me, ²³rather that the Holy Spirit's witnessing to me in city to city, saying that bonds and troubles remain for me. ²⁴But [I offer] no word to honor myself so I may finish the race and the service that I received from the Lord Yēsous, fully to witness to the gospel of God's grace.
²⁵And now Look! I know that you all will see my face no longer—among whom I passed through announcing the Empire—²⁶because I witness to you on today's day that I am clean from everyone's blood. ²⁷For I did not back off to announce to you all God's plan.
²⁸Beware among yourselves and all the flock, among whom the Holy Spirit placed you as mentors to pastor God's assembly, which he secured through his own blood. ²⁹I know that heavy wolves will enter into your presence after my departure, not sparing the flock, ³⁰and men from yourselves will rise up, speaking turn-away ideas to remove the Apprentices [to follow] after them.
³¹Therefore, be awake, remembering that for three years, night and day, I did not stop mentoring each one of you with tears. ³²And now I present you to God and to his word about grace, which is powerful to form and to give inheritance among all who are devoted. ³³I did not desire silver or gold or robe. ³⁴You know yourselves that these hands served for my needs and those who are with me. ³⁵In all, I exhibited to you that, so laboring, it's necessary to be attached to the weak, to remember the Lord Yēsous' words that he said, 'It's more in God's blessing to give than to receive.'"

³⁶Saying these things, placing his knees down with them, he prayed. ³⁷There was adequate weeping among all and, falling upon Paulos's neck, they were kissing him, ³⁸grieving especially about the word he had said, that they were about to observe his face no longer. They were sending him on into to the boat.

Commissioner Paulos travels to Yierosoluma

21 As it happened, being removed from [the people], we were led [by the winds], going a good direct way, we came into Kōs [Cos], on the next day into Rodos [Rhodes], from there into Patara. ²Finding a boat crossing through to Phoinikē [Phoenicia], putting down, we were led [by the winds]. ³Sighting Kupros [Cyprus] and abandoning it to our left, we were sailing to Suria [Syria] and we came down into Turos [Tyre], for the boat was unloading the cargo there. ⁴Discovering the Apprentices, we remained there for seven days. They were saying to Paulos [Paul] through the Spirit not to go up into Yierosoluma [Jerusalem]. ⁵When our days were prepared, exiting, we were journeying . . . all, with women and children, are sending us on as far as the outside of the city . . . and placing the knees on the shore, praying, ⁶we greeted one another and we ascended into the boat, and they returned to their own [homes].

⁷We, completing the voyage from Turos, arrived into Ptolemaïs and, greeting the siblings, we remained for one day with them. ⁸Exiting the next day, we came into Kaisareia [Caesarea] and, entering into Philippos [Philip] the gospeler's house, being one of the Seven, we remained with him. ⁹This man's four virgin daughters were prophesying. ¹⁰[We're] remaining many days . . . some prophet by the name Agabos [Agabus] came down from Youdaia [Judea] ¹¹and, coming to us and taking Paulos's belt, binding his own feet and hands, he said, "The Holy Spirit says these things, 'In Yierousalēm the Youdaians will bind the man whose this belt is, and they will give him over into the hands of the ethnic groups.'" ¹²As we heard these things, both we and the people of that place were begging him not to ascend into Yierousalēm. ¹³Then Paulos responded, "What

are you doing, wailing and shattering my heart? For I am prepared not only to be bound but also to die in Yierousalēm for the name of the Lord Yēsous."

¹⁴He's not being persuaded . . . we were silenced, saying, "May the Lord's will happen."

¹⁵After these days, getting ready, we were ascending into Yierosoluma. ¹⁶[Some] of the Apprentices from Kaisareia came with us, leading [us] to the one with whom we were to receive hospitality, Mnasōn, the Kupriot [Cypriot], an ancient Apprentice.

Commissioner Paulos advised by the siblings

¹⁷We're in Yierosoluma . . . the siblings received us gladly. ¹⁸On the next day Paulos was coming with us to Yakōbos [James], and all the Elders were along. ¹⁹Greeting them, he expounded one by one each of the things God did among the ethnic groups through his service. ²⁰The ones hearing were splendoring God and said to him,

> "You observe, sibling, how many thousands who have trusted among the Youdaians and all are zealous for the Covenant Code. ²¹They have been catechized about you, that you are teaching all the Youdaians in the ethnic groups to revolt from Mōusēs [Moses], saying they are not to circumcise the children nor to walk around in the customs. ²²What is it, then? In all ways they will hear that you have come. ²³Therefore, do this—what we say to you. There are four men among us, having for themselves a vow. ²⁴Receiving these, be devoted with them and exhaust [your resources] for them so they shave the head, and all will know that there is nothing to what they are catechized about you, but you walk the line and are yourself guarding the Code. ²⁵Concerning the ethnic groups who have trusted: We sent a letter, judging, that they are protected from what is offered to demons and blood and what is strangled and sexual infidelity."

²⁶Then Paulos, receiving the men on the coming day, was devoted with them, was coming into the temple, announcing the completion date of the devotion's days, when the contribution for each one would be presented.

Commissioner Paulos nabbed

²⁷As the seven days were about to be completed, Youdaians from Asia, observing him in the temple, confused all the crowd and tossed the hands on him, ²⁸crying, "Yisraēlitai [Israelites], help! This is the human teaching all in all places against the people and the Code and this place, and even leads Hellēnes [Greeks] into the temple and makes this holy place common." (²⁹For they had previously seen the Ephesios [Ephesian] Trophimos [Trophimus] in the city with him, whom they were thinking Paulos led into the temple.)

³⁰The whole city was moved and there was a swarm of the people and, taking hold of Paulos, they were pulling him out of the temple and immediately the gates were shut. ³¹[They're] pursuing to kill him . . . an accusation ascended to the leader of a cohort of a thousand that the whole Yierousalēm was stirred up, ³²who instantly, taking along soldiers and leaders of a hundred, ran down to them. The ones seeing the leader of a thousand and the soldiers stopped pounding Paulos. ³³Then the leader of a thousand, coming close, took hold of him and ordered [him] to be bound with two chains and inquired who he might be and what he had done. ³⁴Others in the crowd were voicing out other things. He's unable to know the certainty because of the clamor . . . he ordered him to be led into the encampment. ³⁵When he came upon the flight of steps, it coalesced [that] he was carried by the soldiers because of the crowd's force, ³⁶for the mass of the people was following, crying, "Take him!"

Commissioner Paulos addresses the crowd

³⁷Being about to be led into the encampment, Paulos says to the leader of a thousand, "Is it possible for me to say something to you?" He said, "Do you know Hellēnisti [Greek language]? ³⁸Then are you not the Aiguptos [Egyptians], the anarchist before these days, and the one who led four thousand nationalist assassins into the wilderness?" ³⁹Paulos said, "I am a human, a Youdaian, from Kilikia Tarseus [Tarsus of Cilicia], a citizen of a city—not an

unremarkable one. I plead with you, permit me to speak to the people." ⁴⁰[They're] permitting him . . . Paulos, standing on the flight of steps, gestured with the hand to the people. There's a big silence . . . he voiced out in the Hebraïs [Hebrew, or Aramaic] dialect, saying,

22

"Siblings and fathers, hear my defense before you now."

²Hearing that he was voicing out to them in the Hebraïs [Hebrew] dialect, they presented even more silence. He said,

³"I am a man, a Youdaian [Jew], being given life in Kilikian Tarsos [Tarsus of Cilicia] but being nurtured in this city, educated at Gamaliēl's feet carefully consistent with of the paternal Covenant Code, being a zealot for God just as all of you are today. ⁴I chased this Path to death, binding and giving over both men and women into prison, ⁵as also the Senior Priest and all the eldership witness about me, from whom also receiving letters to the siblings, I was journeying to the siblings in Damaskos [Damascus], and leading those bound there to Yierousalēm [Jerusalem] so they might restore our honor.

⁶It happened in my journeying and coming close to Damaskos, around midday, unexpectedly, an adequate light from heaven flashed around me, ⁷and I fell to the ground and heard a voice saying to me, 'Saoul, Saoul [Saul, Saul], why do you chase me?' ⁸I responded, 'Who are you, Lord?' He said to me, 'I am Yēsous, the Nazōraios [Nazarene], whom you are chasing.' ⁹The ones who are with me observed the light but did not hear the voice of the one speaking to me. ¹⁰I said, 'What will I do, Lord?' The Lord said to me, 'Arising, journey into Damaskos, and there it will be spoken to you about all that I have ordered for you to do.' ¹¹As I was not seeing from that light's splendor, being led by hand by the ones with me, I came into Damaskos.
¹²Some Hananias, a man of good regard consistent with the Code, being witnessed by all the Youdaian residents, ¹³coming to me and standing over [me], said to me, 'Saoul, brother, see again!' And I, at that very hour, looked again at him. ¹⁴He said, 'The God of our fathers hand-selected you to know his will and to see the Right One and to hear a voice from his mouth, ¹⁵because you will be a witness to him to all humans what you have seen and heard. ¹⁶Now, why are you delaying? Arising, be dipped and wash away your sins, calling upon his name.' ¹⁷It happened in my returning to Yierousalēm: I'm praying in the temple . . . I was in an ecstasy ¹⁸and I saw him [the Lord] saying to me, 'Hurry! Exit shortly from Yierousalēm because they will not receive your witness about me.' ¹⁹I said, 'Lord, they themselves comprehend that I was imprisoning and beating from assembly hall to assembly hall the ones who trust in you, ²⁰and when Stephanos [Stephen] your witness's blood was poured out I was myself standing over [him] and being pleased and guarding the robes of those who did away with him.' ²¹He said to me, 'Journey because I am commissioning you out to the ethnic groups far away.'"

²²They were hearing him until this word and they lifted up their voice, saying, "Lift such a person from the land, for it isn't suitable for him to live." ²³They're making a racket and flinging their robes and tossing dust into the air . . . ²⁴the leader of a thousand ordered him to be led into the encampment, saying to interrogate him with a whip so that he might perceive the cause for which they are thus voicing out against him. ²⁵As they stretched him with straps, Paulos said to the leader of a hundred standing there, "Is it observant for you to whip an unjudged Romaios [Roman] human?" ²⁶The leader of a hundred, hearing, approaching the leader of a thousand, declared, saying, "What are you about to do? For this human is a Romaios." ²⁷The leader of a thousand, approaching, said to him, "Say to me, are you a Romaios?" He said, "Yes." ²⁸The leader of a thousand responded, "I acquired this citizenship at top shelf price." Paulos said, "But I was given life [as a Romaios]." ²⁹Therefore, immediately the ones about to interrogate him removed from

him, and the leader of a thousand was scared, perceiving that he is a Romaios and that he had bound him.

Commissioner Paulos before the Central Council

³⁰On the next day, wanting to know with certainty what he is being accused for by the Youdaians, he loosened him and ordered the Senior Priests and all the Central Council to come together. Leading Paulos down, he stood [him] among them.

23 Paulos [Paul], gazing at the Central Council, said, "Siblings, I have lived my community-life before God with an all-good consciousness up to this day." ²The Senior Priest Hananias [Ananias] ordered the one standing next to him to pound his mouth. ³Then Paulos said to him, "God is about to pound you, you plastered wall! You sit judging me consistent with the Covenant Code and, acting outside the Code, order me to be pounded?" ⁴The ones standing alongside said, "Are you snubbing God's Senior Priest?" ⁵Paulos said, "I did not know, siblings, that he is the Senior Priest. For it's written that, 'You will not speak bad about your people's leader.'"

⁶Paulos, knowing that one part is Elites [Sadducees] and the other [part] Observant ones [Pharisees], cried out in the Central Council, "Siblings, I am an Observant, son of Observant ones, and I am being judged about hope and resurrection from among the dead ones." ⁷He's saying this . . . anarchy happened between the Observant ones and the Elites, and the mass was split. (⁸For the Elites say "there is no resurrection—nor envoy, nor spirit"—but the Observant ones openly agree about both.) ⁹A great shout happened and, arising, some Code scholars [scribes] of the Observant ones' part were contesting, saying, "We find nothing bad in this human. But did a spirit speak to him or an angel? [Perhaps so.]"ᶜ ¹⁰The anarchy's great . . . the leader of a thousand, being scared that Paulos might be snapped [in two] by them, ordered the troops, descending, to snatch him from their middle and to lead into the encampment.

Commissioner Paulos to Kaisareia

¹¹That night, standing over him, the Lord said, "Be courageous! For as you witnessed around about me in Yierousalēm [Jerusalem], so it's necessary for you also to witness in Rōmē."

¹²The day's come . . . the Youdaians [Jews], making a conspiracy, anathematized themselves, saying not to eat or drink until they kill Paulos. ¹³There were more than forty making this oath together ¹⁴who, approaching the Senior Priests and the Elders, said,

> "We have vowed ourselves to destruction not to taste anything until we kill Paulos. ¹⁵Now you, therefore, appear before the leader of a thousand with the Central Council so that someone lead him down to you as about to be diagnosed more carefully about the matters concerning him. But we, before his getting close, are prepared to do away with him."

¹⁶Paulos's sister's son, hearing about the ambush, appearing and entering into the encampment, declared [this] to Paulos. ¹⁷Paulos, calling one of the leaders of a hundred, said, "Lead this young man away to the leader of a thousand, for he has something to declare to him." ¹⁸Therefore, the one who took him along led [him] to the leader of a thousand and says, "The prisoner Paulos, calling me, asked me to lead this young man to you as one having something to speak to you." ¹⁹The leader of a thousand, taking hold of his hand and slipping away by themselves, was inquiring, "What is it that you have to declare to me?" ²⁰He said that

> "The Youdaians agreed to ask you tomorrow to lead Paulos down to the Central Council as about to inquire more carefully about something concerning him. ²¹You, therefore, don't be persuaded by them, for more than forty of them are lying in ambush for him—who anathematized themselves not to eat or drink until they do away with him, and now they are prepared, attending to the pledge from you."

²²Therefore, the leader of a thousand loosened the young man, ordering [him], "Speak out to no one that you make these matters apparent to me."

ᶜThis could be "What if a spirit . . . ?" or "A spirit did speak . . . [didn't it]."

²³Calling two of the leaders of a hundred, he said, "Prepare two hundred soldiers so that they may journey until Kaisareia [Caesarea]—and seventy cavalry and two hundred right-handers—from the night's third hour [9 p.m.], ²⁴and present animals that, hoisting Paulos on it, he may be delivered to Phēlix [Felix], the Governor. ²⁵Writing a letter having this type:

> ²⁶Klaudios Lusias [Claudius Lysias]
> To the Exceptional Governor Phēlix,
> Greetings!
> ²⁷This man, taken in by the Youdaians and about to be done away with by them, standing over [him] with the troop, I rescued, being apprenticed that he is a Romaios [Romans]. ²⁸Wanting to perceive the cause for which they were calling him in, I led him down to their Central Council, ²⁹whom I found being called in for disputes about their Covenant Code but having charges not deserving of death or bonds. ³⁰A plot's being divulged to me that there would be for the man . . . I instantly sent to you, ordering also the accusers to speak about these matters against him before you."

³¹Therefore, the soldiers, consistent with what was ordered for them, taking up Paulos, led [him] through the night to Antipatris. ³²On the next day, permitting the cavalry to depart with him, they returned to the encampment. ³³Who, entering into Kaisareia and handing the letter up to the Governor, they presented also Paulos to him. ³⁴Reading [the letter], and asking from which province he is, and inquiring that [he is] from Kilikia [Cilicia], ³⁵"I will hear [your case]," he said, "whenever your accusers appear here," ordering that he be guarded in Hērōdēs's [Herod's] headquarters for soldiers.

Commissioner Paulos before Phēlix

24 After five days, the Senior Priest Hananias [Ananias] descended with some Elders and an orator, some Tertullos, who appeared to the Governor against Paulos [Paul]. ²He's called . . . Tertullos began to accuse, saying,

> "Attaining much peace through you and . . . restorations happening for this ethnic group through your mindset . . . ³we welcome [this] in all ways in all places, Most Exceptional Phēlix [Felix], with all thanks. ⁴But in order that I not cut you off anymore, I encourage you to hear us briefly in your fairness. ⁵Finding this man a pestilence and a mover of anarchies for all Youdaians [Jews] in the inhabited world and first-anarchist of the Nazōraios [Nazarene] faction, ⁶who also was tempted to defile the temple, whom we also grasped,ᵈ ⁸from whom you yourself, examining all these matters, will be able to perceive [the matters about] which we accuse him."

⁹The Youdaians also added on, claiming these matters to be so.

¹⁰The Governor nodding to speak . . . Paulos responded,

> "Comprehending you as being judge for this ethnic group for many years, with good emotion I defend the matters concerning myself. ¹¹. . . You being able to perceive that there are for me not more than twelve days since I ascended, bowing down in Yierousalēm [Jerusalem] . . . ¹²they found me—neither in the temple deliberating against someone nor making a supervision over the crowd nor in the assembly halls nor throughout the city, ¹³neither are they able to present to you [a case for] the matters which they now accuse me. ¹⁴I openly agree with this for you that consistent with the Path, which they say is a faction, so I venerate the paternal God, being allegiant to everything consistent with the Covenant Code and those matters written in the Prophets, ¹⁵having hope in God—to which [hope] they themselves attend—a resurrection about to be for both the right ones and the wrongdoing ones. ¹⁶In this I myself also exercise to have a non-accusing consciousness before God and humans at all times. ¹⁷After many years, I arrived making donations to my ethnic group—and contributions, ¹⁸in which [act] they found me—devoted in the temple, neither with a crowd nor with a clamor. ¹⁹But some Youdaians

---

ᵈActs 24:7 isn't in the best manuscripts.

from Asia, who ought to be present and to accuse me before you if they possibly have something against me. [20]Or, let these themselves say what wrongdoing they found . . . I was standing before the Central Council . . . [21]or concerning this one voice that I cried out, standing among them—that 'I am being judged today before you concerning the resurrection from among the dead ones.'"

[22]But Phēlix deferred them, knowing carefully the matters concerning the Path, saying, "Whenever Lusias the leader of a thousand descends I will diagnose the matters against you [pl.]," [23]ordering the leader of a hundred to keep him and to have leisure and to prevent none of his own to serve him.

[24]After some days, Phēlix with his own woman Drousilla [Drusilla] (being Youdaian) arriving, sent back for Paulos and heard him concerning allegiance to Christos Yēsous. [25]He's deliberating about rightness and self-discipline and the judgment about to come . . . Phēlix, being in awe, responded, "Journey for the time being, taking a season, I will call back for you." ([26]At the same time, hoping that money will be given to him by Paulos, and therefore, sending back for him frequently, he was conversing with him.)

[27]Two years being filled out, Phēlix received a successor, Porkios Phēstos [Porcius Festus], and, wanting to lay down a grace for the Youdaians, Phēlix abandoned the bound Paulos.

Commissioner Paulos before Phēstos

25 Therefore, Phēstos [Festus], after three days coming upon the province, ascended into Yierosoluma [Jerusalem] from Kaisareia [Caesarea], [2]and the Senior Priests and the First Ones [chiefs] of the Youdaians [Jews] made [the case] apparent to him against Paulos [Paul] and they were encouraging him, [3]asking for a grace against him so he might send him back to Yierousalēm—an ambush [was] in the making to put him away on the path. [4]Therefore, Phēstos responded for Paulos to be kept in Kaisareia and he himself was about to journey out quickly. [5]Therefore, "the Powerful Ones among you," he says, "descending with me, if any is out-of-place with this man, let them accuse him."

[6]Spending time among them for not more than eight or ten days, descending to Kaisareia, on the next day sitting at the Bēma [judgment seat] he ordered Paulos to be led [into court]. [7]He's arriving . . . the Youdaians who had descended from Yierosoluma stood around him, bringing against him many and heavy charges, which they did not have strength to demonstrate. [8]. . . Paulos defending himself that "I have not sinned in something, neither against the Youdaians' Covenant Code, nor against the temple, nor against Kaisar [Caesar]." . . . [9]Phēstos, wanting to lay down a grace for the Youdaians, responding to Paulos, said, "Do you want, ascending to Yierosoluma, to be judged by me concerning these things there?" [10]Paulos said, "I am standing before Kaisar's Bēma, where it's necessary for me to be judged. I have not wronged in any way the Youdaians, as also you are perceiving most beautifully. [11]Therefore, if I do wrong and I have practiced something deserving death, I am not requesting an excused absence from dying. But if there is nothing of which these are accusing me, no one is able to release me to them. I call on Kaisar." [12]Then Phēstos, speaking with the Council, responded, "On Kaisar you have called, to Kaisar you will journey."

Phēstos confers with Agrippas

[13]Some days were passing . . . King Agrippas [Agrippa] and Bernikē [Bernice] arrived in Kasareia, greeting Phēstos. [14]As they were spending more days there, Phēstos laid out for the king that matters against Paulos, saying,

> "Some man was abandoned in bonds by Phēlix [Felix], [15]concerning whom . . . I was in Yierosoluma . . . the Senior Priests and the Youdaians' Elders appeared, asking a sentence against him. [16]I responded to them that it isn't a custom for Romaioi [Romans] to release some human before the one accused has face time with the accusers and takes a place of defense concerning the summons. [17]Therefore they're coming here together . . . making no delay, sitting on the next [day] at the Bēma, I ordered the man to be led [in]. [18]Concerning whom, the accusers, standing, were bringing not even one cause of evil that I was considering, [19]but they had some disputes concerning their own superstitions toward him and concerning

some dead Yēsous whom Paulos was claiming to live. [20]I, being perplexed about the dispute concerning these matters, was saying if he might want to journey to Yierosoluma to be judged there concerning these matters? [21]Paulos is calling that he be kept for a diagnosis by the Sebastos [August One] . . . I ordered him to be kept until I could send him up to Kaisar."

[22]Agrippas to Phēstos, "I was myself wanting to hear the human." "Tomorrow," he says, "you will hear him."

[23]. . . Therefore, on tomorrow Agrippas and Bernikē were coming with much pomposity and entering into the hearing room with the leader of one thousand and men who are City Prominents and Phēstos ordering . . . Paulos was led [before them]. [24]Phēstos says,

> "King Agrippas and all men who are with us, you observe this one, concerning whom the whole mass of Youdaians interceded with me, both in Yierosoluma and here, bellowing [that] it isn't necessary for him to live any longer. [25]But I prevailed that nothing that he had practiced was deserving of death. . . . He's calling on Sebastos . . . I judged to send [him]. [26]Concerning whom I don't have anything certain to write to the lord. Therefore, I first led him before you [pl.] and especially before you, King Agrippas, so that . . . he's examined . . . I may have something I may write—[27]for, sending a prisoner not also signaling a cause against him, seems unreasonable to me."

Commissioner Paulos before Agrippas

26 Agrippas [Agrippa] said to Paulos [Paul], "It's permitted for you to speak for yourself." Then Paulos, extending the hand, was defending himself:

> [2]"Concerning all the matters for which I am being called in by Youdaians [Jews], King Agrippas, I have considered myself blessed by you, being about to defend myself today, [3]especially your being knowledgeable of both all the customs and pursuits consistent with Youdaians. Thus, I plead [with you] to hear me patiently.

> [4]Therefore, my life, which from youth, which being from the beginning among my ethnicity and in Yierosoluma [Jerusalem]—all the Youdaians have known, [5]knowing me from the top [of my life], if they might want to witness, that I lived as an Observant [Pharisee] consistent with the most careful faction of our worship. [6]Now, for the hope of the pledge by God to our ancestors I stand here being judged, [7]at which our Twelve-tribe, venerating extensively night and day, is hoping to arrive, concerning which hope I am called in by Youdaians, King. [8]Why is it judged non-allegiant by you if God raises the dead ones? [9]Therefore, I thought for myself it's necessary to practice many counter-acts against Yēsous Nazōraios' name, [10]which I also did in Yierosoluma, and also many of the devoted ones I confined in prisons, receiving the authority of the Senior Priests . . . doing away with them . . . and I brought the pebble [vote] against [them]. [11]In restoring honor with them in all the assembly halls, I compelled [them] to insult [God], being exceedingly enraged with them, I even chased to outside cities.

> [12]In these acts, journeying to Damaskos [Damascus] with the Senior Priests' authority and decision, [13]at midday on the path I saw, King, from heaven, a light brighter than the sun shining around me and the ones journeying with me. [14]. . . We're all falling down on the land . . . I heard a voice saying to me in the Hebraïs [Hebrew] dialect, 'Saoul, Saoul [Saul, Saul], why do you chase me? It's harsh for you to "kick the stingers."' [15]I said, 'Who are you, Lord?' The Lord said, 'I am Yēsous whom you are chasing. [16]But arise and stand on your feet. For I have appeared to you for this: You are hand-selected as a subordinate and witness both that you saw me and of what I will have appear to you, [17]rescuing you from the people and from the ethnicities—to whom I commission you: [18]to open their eyes so to turn away from darkness to light and from Satanas's [Satan's] authority to God so they may receive

release from sins and an inheritance among the devoted by allegiance to me.' ¹⁹At which, King Agrippas, I did not become unpersuaded by the heavenly vision ²⁰but first to the ones in Damaskos and in Yierosoluma, as well as to all the Youdaian region and to the ethnicities, I declared to convert and to turn to God, practicing works deserving of conversion. ²¹Because of these [actions], Youdaians, taking me in the temple, were tempted to administer death. ²²Therefore, attaining help from God until this day, I stand witnessing to both small and great, saying nothing outside of what both the prophets and Mōüsēs [Moses] spoke regarding what is about to happen: ²³if the Christos [is] a sufferer, if the Christos [is] first of the resurrection of the dead ones, [then] he is about to announce light both to the people and to the ethnicities."

²⁴He's defending these things for himself . . . Phēstos says in a great voice, "Paulos, you are frenzied! Many letters are turning you into frenzy!" ²⁵Paulos: "I am not frenzied," he says, "Exceptional Phēstos, but I am enunciating utterances of truth and prudence. ²⁶For concerning these things the King comprehends, to whom also, being frank, I speak, for I am not persuaded in any way some of this has escaped his notice, for this has not been practiced in a corner. ²⁷Do you trust, King Agrippas, the prophets? I know you trust."

²⁸Agrippas to Paulos: "Are you persuading me to become a Christianos [Christian] with little [argument]?" ²⁹Paulos: "I formulate before God, in both little and great, not only for you but for all those hearing me today to become even such as I am—except for these bonds." ³⁰The King rose up—as well as the Governor and Bernikē [Bernice] and those sitting with them ³¹and, slipping away, they were speaking to one another, saying that "This human practices nothing deserving death or bonds." Agrippas said to Phēstos, "This human was able to be released if he had not called on Kaisar."

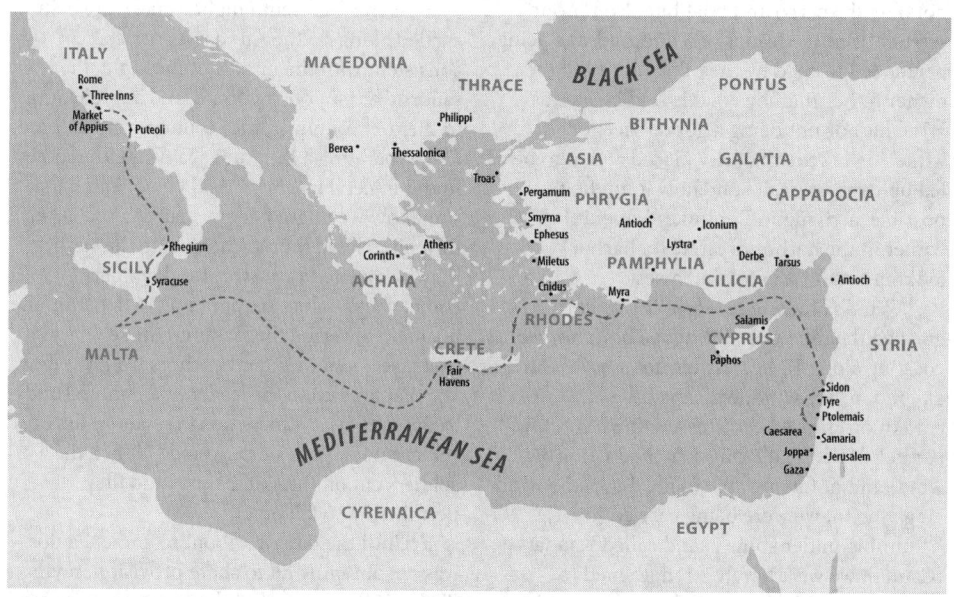

Figure 11. Paul's journey to Rome

Commissioner Paulos sails to Italia

27 As it was judged for us to sail to Italia [Italy], they were giving over Paulos [Paul] and some other prisoners to a leader of a hundred named Youlios [Julius], of Sebastos's [Augustus's] Cohort. ²Putting down in a boat from Adrammuttēnos [Adrammytium] about to sail to the places along Asia, we were led up

... Aristarchos [Aristarchus], a Thessalonikeus Makedōn [Macedonian of Thessalonica], being with us.... ³On another [day], we were led down to Sidōn, and Youlios, treating Paulos in a human-loving way, permitted journeying to friends to attain care. ⁴Being led from there, we sailed under Kupros [Cyprus] because the winds were against us. ⁵Sailing through the depths along Kilikia [Cilicia] and Pamphulia [Pamphylia], we came down into Lukia's Mura [Myra of Lycia]. ⁶There the leader of a hundred, finding an Alexandrinos [Alexandrian] boat sailing to Italia, boarded us into it. ⁷Slowly sailing in adequate days and barely getting along Knidos [Cnidus] ... the wind not permitting us ... we sailed under Krētē [Crete] along Salmōnē ⁸and barely coasting along it we came to some place called Beautiful Harbor, near to which is a city, Lasaia [Lasea].

⁹An adequate time's passing by and the sailing being already uncertain because also the fast [for the Day of Atonement] had already passed by ... Paulos advised, ¹⁰saying to them, "Men, I observe that the sailing is about to be with much assault and with much forfeit for not only the cargo and boat but also for our selves." ¹¹But the leader of a hundred was being persuaded instead by the pilot and the ship owner rather than by what is said by Paulos. ¹²The harbor not being a good place for wintering ... the majority placed a plan to be led up from there, if somehow it might be possible, arriving in Phoinikē [Phoenix] to winter in the harbor of Krētē, [a harbor] looking southwest and northwest.

¹³Wind's blowing ... thinking to have grasped the intention, lifting anchor, they were coasting along Krētē. ¹⁴After not a little while, a typhoon-like wind, which is called a "eurakulōn" [nor'easter], tossed down from it [Crete]. ¹⁵The boat being snatched with [the wind] and not being able to head into the wind ... giving in, we were being carried [by it]. ¹⁶Running under some island called Kauda [Cauda], we were barely strengthened to control the skiff, ¹⁷which, lifting, they used helps, undergirding the boat, and being scared they might fall out onto the Surtis [shallows], lowering the vessel—so they were being carried [by the wind]. ¹⁸We're being extremely winter-waves-beaten.... On the next [day] we were doing a dump-out ¹⁹and on the third [day] with their own hands they dropped the boat's vessel. ²⁰Neither sun nor stars shining for many days, a storm laying on—no small one ... all remaining hope of our being delivered was taken away.

²¹Existing without food for many days ... then, standing in their middle, Paulos said,

"It was necessary, O men, by consenting willingly to me not to have been led up from Krētē and to gain this assault and forfeit [of cargo], ²²and now I advise you to be of good emotion for there will be not one tossing away of one of your selves—except the boat! ²³For an envoy of God—whose I am and whom I venerate—was present to me this night, saying, ²⁴ 'Don't be scared, Paulos. It's necessary for you to be present to Kaisar [Caesar] and Look! God has graced you [with safety]—all the ones sailing with you.' ²⁵Therefore, be of good emotion, men, for I trust in God that it will be consistent with the manner spoken to me. ²⁶But it's necessary for us to fall out onto some island."

²⁷As the fourteenth night came, we're being carried along on the Adrias [Adriatic] ... consistent with the middle of the night, the sailors were supposing some land approaching to them. ²⁸Sounding, they found twenty fathoms and, separating a little and again sounding, they found fifteen fathoms. ²⁹And being scared that somehow we might fall out against a rocky place, dropping down four anchors from the stern, they formulated [a prayer] for day[light] to come. ³⁰The sailors are pursuing to flee from the boat and lowering the skiff into the sea, in a pretense about to extend anchors from the bow. ... ³¹Paulos said to the leader of a hundred and to the soldiers, "If these don't remain in the boat, you are not able to be delivered." ³²Then the soldiers cut off the skiff's ropes and they permitted it to fall out.

³³Until the day was about to come, Paulos was encouraging all to share provision, saying, "Today is the fourteenth day anticipating you're completing without food, receiving nothing. ³⁴Therefore, I encourage you to share provision for this exists for your deliverance, for not a hair from the head of any of you will be destroyed." ³⁵Saying these things and taking bread, he thanked God before all and, cracking,

he began to eat. ³⁶All being good in emotion, they themselves received provision. (³⁷We—all selves in the boat—were 276.) ³⁸Being satiated with provision, they lightened the boat, tossing the wheat out into the sea.

³⁹When day came, they were not perceiving the land but noticed some fold in the land having a shore into which they were wanting—if it were possible—to beach the boat. ⁴⁰Lifting away the anchors, they were permitting [them] into the sea. At the same time, loosening the rudders' cords and lifting up the sail to the blowing [of wind], they were possessing [their course] toward the shore. ⁴¹Falling into a between-the-sea [tides] place, they ran the ship into land. The bow being stuck, it remained unmoveable. The stern was loosened by the waves' vitality. ⁴²The plan of the soldiers was that they were to kill the bound ones so none, plunging into the sea to swim, could flee. ⁴³But the leader of one hundred, wanting to deliver Paulos, prevented them from their planning, and ordered the ones able to swim, jumping out first to go away to the land ⁴⁴and the others [to follow], some on boards and some on some of what came from the boat.

So it happened that all were delivered on the land.

28 Being delivered, we then perceived the island is called Melitē [Malta]. ²The Barbaroi [barbarians] were presenting to us an unexpected human-love. For lighting a fire, they welcomed all of us because of the rain above us and cold. ³Paulos's [Paul's] bringing together a mass of some sticks and placing on fire . . . a viper, exiting from the heat, latched onto his hand. ⁴As the Barbaroi saw the wild thing dangling from his hand, they were saying to one another, "By all means, this human is a murderer who, being delivered from the sea, Dikē [justice goddess] did not permit to live." ⁵Therefore, he, shaking off the wild thing into the fire, suffered nothing bad. ⁶But they were anticipating him about to swell up or fall down unexpectedly dead but . . . after they were expecting and observing nothing happening out-of-place . . . shifting, they were saying, "He is a god!"

⁷In the area around that place was a region for the First [Chief] of the Island, by the name Poplios [Publius], who, receiving us, gave courteous hospitality for three days. ⁸It happened that Poplios's father was laid out, being absorbed with a fever and dysentery, to whom Paulos, entering and praying, placing hands on him, cured him. ⁹This was happening . . . the remaining on the island, having weaknesses, were approaching and they were healed, ¹⁰who honored us with many honors and, being led up [to sail], they placed [on us] things for our needs.

¹¹After three months, we, having wintered on the island, were led in a boat, an Alexandrinos [Alexandrian] [boat], its sign being Dioskoroi [twin gods, sons of Zeus]. ¹²Being led down into Surakousai [Syracuse], we remained for three days, ¹³then, going around, we arrived in Rēgion [Rhegium]. After one day a southerly [wind] came up. . . . On the second we came into Potioloi [Puteoli], ¹⁴where, finding siblings, we were encouraged by them to remain seven days, and so we came into Rōmē. ¹⁵There the siblings hearing matters about us, came for an official reception as far as Appios's [Apius's] Forum and the Three Taverns, whom, Paulos seeing, thanking God, took heart.

Commissioner Paulos in Rōmē

¹⁶When we entered into Rōmē, it was permitted for Paulos to remain by himself with a soldier guarding him.

¹⁷It happened after three days, he called together those who were First Youdaians [leaders of the Jews]. They're gathering . . . he was saying to them,

> "Siblings, I, doing nothing against the people or the ancestors' customs, was given over into bonds from Yierosoluma [Jerusalem] into the Romaioi's [Romans'] hands, ¹⁸who, examining me, were wanting to release me because nothing being a cause of death in me. ¹⁹The Youdaians are contradicting [me] . . . I was compelled to call upon Kaisar [Caesar], not having something about which to accuse my ethnic group. ²⁰Therefore, because of this cause I begged to see and to speak to you, for because of Yisraēl's [Israel's] hope I am draped with this chain."

²¹They said to him, "We received neither a letter about you from the Youdaians nor, appearing, have any of the siblings declared or spoken something evil about you. ²²We deserve

to hear from you what you think, for concerning this faction it's known to us that it's contradicted in all places."

²³Ordering for him a day, even more came to him in his guest room, before whom he laid out, witnessing about God's Empire, and persuading them about Yēsous from Mōüsēs' [Moses'] Covenant Code and the Prophets, from early until evening. ²⁴Some were persuaded by what is being said, but others distrusted. ²⁵Disagreeing with one another, they were leaving, . . . Paulos was saying one utterance . . . that "the Holy Spirit spoke beautifully through Ēsaias [Isaiah] the prophet to your fathers, ²⁶saying,

> Journey to this people and say,
> In hearing you will hear and not understand,
> and in seeing you will see and not perceive.
> ²⁷The heart of this people has thickened
> and they heard with dull ears
> and they shut their eyes . . .
> so that in no case they may perceive with eyes
> and hear with ears
> and understand with heart
> and return . . .
> and I will cure them.

²⁸Therefore, let it be known to you that this deliverance of God has been commissioned to the ethnic groups, and they will hear."ᵉ

³⁰He remained two whole years at his own wage and he received all journeying to him, ³¹announcing God's Empire and teaching unhindered matters about the Lord Yēsous Christos with all frankness.

THE LIFE OF PAULOS

The Commissioner was a missionary, and his three missionary trips, including important surrounding events, recorded in Acts look like this:
- First Trip: Acts 13:4–14.28 (AD 47–48)
- Jerusalem Council: Acts 15:6-29 (c. 48/49)
- Second Trip: Acts 15:36–18:22 (49–52)
- Third Trip: Acts 18:23–21:16 (52–57)
- Jerusalem, Arrest, Appeal, Trials: Acts 21:17–28:20

Dating his letters in what is recorded in Acts creates numerous puzzles, some of which don't find compelling conclusions. One can distinguish three periods of writing in Paulos's biography:

(1) The early period, which is shaped in part by this question, Who's in the church? (48 to 57).
- Galatians (48)
- 1–2 Thessalonians (50)
- 1–2 Corinthians (54, 56)
- Romans (57)

Then we have letters that come from time in prison, though we have no idea how many times Paulos was imprisoned and where all of these imprisonments occurred. So, a second set of letters are from his (2) prison ministry, where one of the questions becomes, What is the church? (53–55?). Many think Paulos's prison letters all came from Rome, but this is most likely not accurate. It's reasonable to think at least Philemon and Colossians, if not Philippians, come from an Ephesian imprisonment, and perhaps Ephesians itself.
- Philemon, Colossians, Philippians (c. 53, 53, 55 or 63?)
- Ephesians (c. 55)

(3) The later period is shaped by the question, What will the church be? (60–62, perhaps 64 or later). Dating the Pastoral Letters creates lots of questions that are difficult to answer, but one view is that they were written later in Paulos's life—2 Timothy from Rome (1:16-17) but 1 Timothy seemingly from Macedonia (cf. 1 Tim 1:3). Titus assumes Paulos has been to Crete, though nothing in Acts indicates this, so perhaps that trip was unmentioned in Acts or it happened after an imprisonment in Rome.
- 1–2 Timothy, Titus (c. early 60s or later)

ᵉActs 28:29 isn't in the best manuscripts.

INTRODUCTION TO ROMANS

Paulos's mission explodes into this his most influential letter. Romans isn't abstract theology even if at times his words become heavy and the ideas dense. Few get through Romans 1–11 without taking some long breaks. Romans is in fact a letter for a specific set of house churches in a specific location at a specific time with a specific purpose. It's more timely than timeless. Paulos is most likely in Corinth or its port city Cenchreae, and he's on his way to Spain by way of Jerusalem and Rome! Written about AD 56–57, this letter brings into expression more than two decades of mission work in Asia Minor (modern Turkey) and Greece. That mission work involved seemingly constant discussions and debates on two fronts: with fellow Jews who did not believe Yēsous was Messiah and with Gentiles coming from a welter of viewpoints for whom this Jewish Messiah made no sense. Romans in many ways puts into print the topics of Paulos's mission conversations and his responses.

That mission work was put to great effect in Romans for what appears to be five house churches (or more; 16:3-16), and recent study shows these Yēsous Apprentices were located in Rome's poorest sections—in the Trastevere west of the Tiber River and along the Appian Way as it proceeds into the city of Rome. Some seem also to have lived closer to the high-status region of the Aventine Hill, an area into which high-status Romans were moving as Nero expanded his own territory in the heart of Rome.

Paulos's letters, especially Romans, have a unique style: sometimes agitated and choppy and forceful, at times artistic and poetic, at times polemical and argumentative, and always aimed at a specific congregation with specific challenges. If one reads Romans aloud, as it was originally, and I suspect by the wealthy church benefactor Phoebe (16:1-2), and if one pauses to answer each question Paulos asks, one will feel perhaps for the first time just how argumentative, direct, and piercing this letter can be. Dozens of questions are concentrated in two sections (Rom 2–4; 9–10), and they come off as a lawyer challenging someone for direct answers. They are in bold for easier visibility and also as a reminder for the reader to listen to the question and answer it before reading on. (This is what Paulos's first audiences in Rome would have done.) In Romans 5–8 Paulos's major terms (Flesh, Sin, Death, the Covenant Code [Law], Gift, Grace, etc.) have become agents, actors in the drama of redemption, and are not simply personifications. Capitalization of such terms is designed to emphasize the terms indicate an agent.

Romans is best read if one first reads Romans 12–14, where we meet two parties—the weak and the strong. The weak are Judean believers in Yēsous; the strong are Gentile believers in Rome. The weak are poor and low status and powerless, while the strong are wealthier, high status, and powerful (15:1). Starting at the end, which of course counters everything our grammar-school teachers taught us, avoids two common wrongs: neglecting the context of the letter and turning the letter into abstract theology. This letter feeds our theology, but it's a pastoral letter through and through. In fact, many wear out by the time they get to Romans 12, so it's a good place to start for that reason too. If one does begin the letter at the end, one will hear echoes of the debate among the weak and strong throughout the entire letter; if one waits, one may miss the pastoral heart of the letter.

Paulos's letter to the Romans has shaped the theology of the church universal, given it a language, a message, and a mission. The letter has four parts: (1) a long back-and-forth with his Judean believing opponents who think the Covenant Code/Law is the path of Christian victory (1:18–4:25); (2) a glorious exploration of how the Christian life actually works—death to sin, life in Christ, the power of the Spirit, the all-conquering love of God (5:1–8:39); (3) a response both to the weak and the strong in a more narrative form about God's surprisingly sovereign shifts in history to bring about redemption in the Messiah (9:1–10:10 and 10:11–11:36); and finally, (4) Paulos speaks to the contextual situation of this letter, and for that context his big plea is for both weak and strong to become more like Christ (12:1–16:27).

TO THE ROMANS

From Paulos to Rōmē

1 Paulos, slave of Christos Yēsous, a called Commissioner, isolated for God's gospel ²that was previously pledged through his prophets in the devoted writings ³about his Son,

> who consistent with the flesh was of the seed of Dauid [David],
> ⁴who consistent with the Spirit of devotion is established Son-of-God-in-power on the basis of resurrection from among the dead, our Lord Yēsous Christos,
> ⁵through whom we received a grace, that is, the commission for the obedience of faith among all the ethnic groups for his name,
> ⁶in whom you are also the called ones by Yēsous Christos . . .

⁷To all in Rōmē who are God's loved ones, called devoted ones.

Grace to you and peace from our Father-God and Lord Yēsous Christos.

Paulos thanks God for the Romaioi

⁸First, I thank my God through Yēsous Christos for all of you because your allegiance is proclaimed in the whole Kosmos. ⁹For my witness is God, whom I venerate in my spirit in the gospel about his Son, as I incessantly make memory about you, ¹⁰always in my prayers pleading—if somehow at last my path may make its way in God's plan to come to you. ¹¹For I long to see you so I might distribute to you some Spirit-prompted grace-act to support you, ¹²which is to say, to be co-encouraged by you through one another's allegiance—both yours and mine. ¹³I don't want you to be uninformed, siblings, that I often offered to come to you—and up to now I have been hindered—so I might have some fruit also among you just as among the remaining ethnic groups. ¹⁴I am a debtor both to the Hellēnes [Greeks] and Barbaroi [barbarians], both to the wise and to the brainless—¹⁵thus my intention to gospel to you who are in Rōmē.

Paulos's gospel

¹⁶For I am not degraded by the gospel for it's God's power for deliverance of all the allegiant, Youdaians [Jews] first and then Hellēnes. ¹⁷For God's rightness is apocalypsed in it—out of allegiance unto allegiance, as it's written: *The Right One will live out of allegiance.*

God and human corruption

¹⁸For God's anger is apocalypsed from heaven against all human impiety and wrongdoing, who possess the truth in wrongdoing, ¹⁹because what is known about God is apparent in them. For God made it apparent to them. ²⁰For from the creation of the Kosmos, his knowable invisibilities—that is, his eternal power and divinity—are see-able in what is made, so they are defenseless, ²¹because, knowing God, they did not splendor or thank [God] as God, but they became vain in their deliberations and their ignorant heart was darkened. ²²Claiming to be wise, they became fools ²³and they changed the imperishable God's splendor into a representation of an image of a perishable human and birds and tetrapods and reptiles.

²⁴Therefore God gave them over in the desires of their hearts to uncleanness to dishonor their bodies among themselves. ²⁵Some exchanged God's truth with a falsehood, and they reverenced and venerated creation instead of the Creator, who is Blessed to the Eras, Amēn!

²⁶Because this is true: God gave them over to dishonoring passions—for their females exchanged natural relations for the against-natural, ²⁷and likewise also the males, releasing natural relations with females, burned in their appetites for one another, males with males, effecting the shameful and receiving among themselves the penalty that was necessary for their deception.

²⁸Just as they did not judge it suitable to have God in their mind, God handed them over to a mind judged unsuitable, to do what isn't proper ²⁹—who were filled out with
> every wrongdoing,
> wickedness,
> wanting more and more,
> evil;
> full of envy,
> murder,
> strife,
> disguise,

bad character,
gossips,
30slanderers,
God-haters,
arrogant,
status-mongers,
braggarts,
devisers of badness,
rejecters of parents—
31mindless, the covenant-less, love-less, mercy-less.
32Who, perceiving the right rules of God—that those who practice such things deserve death—not only do them but also are co-pleased with those who practice them.

Interrogation of "the Judge" begins

2 Therefore, you are defenseless, O human—everyone who is the Judge, for in the matter in which you are judging another, you condemn yourself—for the Judge practices the same matters. ²We know that God's judgment is consistent with truth on those who practice such matters.

³**Do you calculate this—O human, the Judge of those who practice such things and do the same—that you will run away from God's judgment?**
⁴**Or, do you snub the wealth of his graciousness and truce and patience, not informed that God's gracefulness leads you to conversion?**

⁵You are treasuring for yourself—consistent with your sclerotic and unconverted heart—anger on the Day of Anger and of apocalypse of God's right judgment, ⁶who *will pay back to each person consistent with a person's works.*

⁷To those who, by resilience in good works, are pursuing splendor and honor and non-decay—Era Life,
⁸but to those who [act] out of status seekings and are unpersuaded by the truth, that is, ones persuaded by wrongdoing—anger and fury.

⁹Trouble and distress on every human self who effects the bad, first to the Youdaians [Jews] and then to the Hellēnes [Greeks]. ¹⁰But splendor and honor and peace to everyone who works what is the good, first to the Youdaians and then to Hellēnes. ¹¹For there is no face-favoring with God.

¹²For whoever sinned without the Covenant Code will also be destroyed without the Code; whoever sinned in the Code will be judged through the Code. ¹³For it isn't the Code-hearers who are right with God, but the Code-doers who will be righted. ¹⁴For whenever the ethnic groups, who don't have the Code, by nature do the matters of the Code—these, not having the Code, are the Code among themselves, ¹⁵who exhibit the Code's work written in their hearts—their conscious co-witnessing and reasonings back and forth accusing or even defending—¹⁶on the Day when God judges the hidden things of humans consistent with my gospel through Christos Yēsous.

Interrogation about the true Youdaian

¹⁷If you name yourself "Youdaios" and rest yourself in the Code and boast in God ¹⁸and you know the will, and judge suitable what is superior—being catechized from the Code—¹⁹having persuaded yourself to be a pathway for the sightless, light for ones in darkness, ²⁰instructor of the imprudent, teacher of children, having the form of knowledge and truth in the Code . . .

²¹Therefore, the one teaching others: Do you teach yourself?
The one announcing not to thieve: Do you thieve?
²²The one saying not to be adulterous: Do you adulterate?
The one detesting demon-idols: Do you spoil devoted sites?
²³He who boasts in the Code: Do you dishonor God through violation of the Code?

(²⁴*For God's name is insulted because of you among the ethnic groups,* just as it's written.) ²⁵For circumcision gains if you practice the Code. But if you are a violator of the Code, your circumcision becomes foreskin.

²⁶**If therefore the foreskin [people] guards the right rules of the Code, doesn't their foreskin calculate to circumcision?**

²⁷The foreskin [person] in nature who finishes the Code will judge you, the violator—through letter and circumcision—of the Code. ²⁸For one isn't manifestly a Youdaian, nor is circumcision manifest in the flesh, ²⁹but one is a hidden Youdaian, and circumcision is of the

heart, in Spirit not in letter, where the public praise isn't from humans but from God.

Interrogation regarding the exceptional

3 Therefore, what abounds about the Youdaian [Jew], or what is the benefit of circumcision?

²Much, in every manner. First: for they have been entrusted with God's sayings.

³**For what?**
Did some fail in allegiance?
Does their non-allegiance undo the allegiance of God?

⁴May that never happen! Let God be truthful and every human a falsifier, just as it's written: *So that you may be righted in your words, and you will conquer in your judging.*

⁵**If our wrongdoing affirms God's rightness, what do we say?**
Is God, who brings on anger, the one not right?

(I speak consistent with humans.)
⁶May that never happen!

How then does God judge the Kosmos?
⁷**If God's truth—in my falsifying—flows over into his splendor, why am I still being judged a sinner?**
⁸**And not: As we are insulted and as some are saying we say, "Let us do bad so the good may come?"**

(Their judgment is in the right.)

⁹**What then?**
Are we ahead?

Not in all ways. For we already accused both all Youdaians and Hellēnes [Greeks] to be under Sin, ¹⁰just as it's written that

No one is right, not even one.
¹¹*No one is an understander,*
No one is a searcher for God.
¹²*Everyone leaned away*
Together they have become useless.
No one is a doer of graciousness,
There is not even one.
¹³*Their larynx: a grave opened,*
they deceive with their tongues,
Poison of snakes: behind their lips.
¹⁴*Their mouth: full of curses and rancor,*
¹⁵*Their feet: impulsive to pour out blood,*
¹⁶*Ruin and hardship in their paths,*
¹⁷*They don't know the path of peace.*
¹⁸*There is not the awe of God before their eyes.*

¹⁹We know that whatever the Code says, it speaks to those in the Code so that every mouth may be shut and the whole Kosmos may become indicted by God. ²⁰Because, all flesh will not be righted before him from Code-works—through the Code is the perception of sin.

A parenthetical clarification

²¹Now, apart from the Code, God's rightness is made apparent—being witnessed by the Code and the prophets—²²God's rightness through Yēsous-Christos-allegiance [Jesus-Christ-faith] for everyone who is allegiant (For there is no distinction ²³for all sinned and lack God's splendor.), ²⁴being righted as a gift by his grace through the liberation that is in Christos Yēsous.

> ²⁵Whom God offered as mercy seat
> through trust in his blood
> to exhibit his rightness
> (because of his ignoring of previously
>   committed sin-acts²⁶—in God's
>   patience)
> to exhibit his rightness in the present
>   season,
> so he is right and the one who rights a
>   person on the basis of Yēsous-
>   allegiance.

Resumption of interrogation

²⁷**Therefore, where is the boasting?**

It's shut out.

By which Code? Of works?

No, but by the Code's allegiance. ²⁸For we calculate a human to be righted by allegiance apart from Code-works.

²⁹**Is God only of the Youdaians?**
Not also of the ethnic groups?

Yes, also of the ethnic groups, ³⁰since one is the God who will right the circumcision from allegiance and the foreskin [people] through allegiance.

³¹Therefore, is the Code undone through allegiance?

May that never happen!
Instead, we establish the Code.

Interrogation regarding Abra'am and circumcision

4 Therefore, what do we say Abra'am, our first father consistent with flesh, has found?

²For if Abra'am was righted from works, he has a boast but not with God.

³What does the writing say?

Abra'am trusted God and it was calculated for him for rightness. ⁴For the one who works the wage isn't calculated consistent with grace but consistent with debt, ⁵but for the one not working but trusting on the one who rights the impious, his trust is calculated for rightness.

⁶Just as Dauid [David] says about the God-blessedness of the human to whom God calculates rightness independent of works:

> ⁷*God's blessings on whose covenant-breakings are released*
> *and whose sins are covered up.*
> ⁸*God's blessing on the man to whom the Lord never calculates sin.*

⁹Therefore, this God-blessedness: on the circumcised or also upon the foreskin [people]?

For we are saying, "Trust was calculated to rightness for Abra'am."

¹⁰Therefore, how was it calculated? While in circumcision or foreskin?

Not in circumcision but in foreskin. ¹¹He accepted circumcision as the authenticating sign, as a seal of trust-rightness while in foreskin: so he is father of all the trusting ones during foreskin, so rightness can be calculated for them, ¹²and father of the circumcision, who are not just of the circumcision but also walk the line in the footprints of our father Abra'am's trust while in foreskin.

Interrogation regarding Abra'am and the pledge

¹³For it was not through Code that that pledge [was given to] Abra'am or to his seed—to be the Kosmos's heir—but through allegiance-rightness. ¹⁴For if [they are] the heirs from Code, allegiance is hollowed and the pledge is undone. ¹⁵For the Code effects anger. Where there isn't Code neither is there violation. ¹⁶Because "of allegiance" is true . . . so it might be consistent with grace, so the firm pledge is for all the seed, not only for the one of Code but also for the one of Abra'am-allegiance—who is father of us all—¹⁷just as it's written that *I placed you father of many ethnic groups,* in front of whom he gave allegiance to the God who makes life for the dead and calls things that are not to be things that are. ¹⁸Who was allegiant in hope against hope that he would be "father many ethnic groups" consistent with what has been said, *So will be your seed,* ¹⁹and was not weakening in allegiance, he pondered his own already deadened body—being about one hundred years old—and the deadness of Sarra's [Sarah's] womb. ²⁰He was not mentally wavering in anti-trust about God's pledge but was empowered in allegiance, giving splendor to God ²¹and, fully assured that what had been pledged, [God] was able also to do. ²²So *it was calculated for him to rightness.* ²³But that *it was calculated for him* was not written because of him alone ²⁴but also because of us, to whom it's about to be calculated—to those with allegiance to the one who raised our Lord Yēsous from among the dead, ²⁵who was given over because of our wrongs and was raised because of our right-making.

Life is being right with God

5 Therefore, being right from allegiance, we have peace with God through our Lord Yēsous Christos, ²through whom also we now have had access by allegiance into this grace—in which we have stood and are boasting in hope of God's splendor. ³And not only . . . but also we are boasting in the troubles, knowing that the trouble effects resilience, ⁴and resilience approval, and approval hope. ⁵Hope doesn't degrade because God's love [for us] is poured out in our hearts through the Holy Spirit, who was given to us.

⁶For Christos, while we being weak, at the right season died for the impious. ⁷For barely does someone die for a right one. For perhaps someone dares to die for the good one. ⁸But God affirmed his own love for us because, while being

sinners, Christos died for us. ⁹Therefore, now being righted by his blood, how much more will we be delivered through him from the anger! ¹⁰For, if being enemies, we were reconciled with God through his Son's death, how much more, being reconciled, we will be delivered by his life. ¹¹Not only . . . but also boasting in God through our Lord Yēsous Christos, through whom now we received reconciliation.

Life or death

¹²Because this is true: Just as through one human Sin entered the Kosmos and Death through Sin, so also Death crossed through to all humans—because all sinned . . .

> (¹³For sin was in the world until the Covenant Code but Sin isn't calculated when there is no Code, ¹⁴but Death ruled from Adam until Moüsēs [Moses] even over those who did not sin in the representation of Adam's wrong—Adam is a type of the one about to come.)

¹⁵ . . . but so the grace-act is not as the wrong.

> For if the many died by one man's wrong, how much more God's grace and the gift in grace of the one human, Yēsous Christos, flows over for the many. ¹⁶The gift isn't like the one person's sin: For judgment from one [leads] to condemnation, but the grace-act for the many wrongs [leads] to right-act. ¹⁷For if, in the wrong of one, Death ruled through the one, how much more will the ones receiving the excessive grace and gift of rightness rule in Life through the one, Yēsous Christos! ¹⁸Therefore, as one's wrong [leads] to condemnation for all humans, so also through the one's right act [leads] to Life's right-making for all humans. ¹⁹For just as through one human's disobedience the many were determined "sinners," so through the obedience of the one the many will be determined "right ones." ²⁰The Code penetrated so the wrong would be magnified, but where Sin was magnified Grace super-abounded ²¹so that, as Sin ruled in Death, so also Grace may rule through rightness into Era Life through our Lord Yēsous Christos.

Life begins with death

6 Therefore, what do we say?
Continue in sin so grace may magnify?

²May that never happen!

We who died to Sin, how will we still live in it?
³**Or are you uninformed that we who were dipped into Christos Yēsous were dipped into his death?**

⁴Therefore, we were buried with him through the dipping into the Death so that, just as Christos was raised from among the dead ones through the Father's splendor, so also we may walk around in Life's newness. ⁵For if we have become co-natured in a representation of his death—but we will also be [co-natured in a representation] of the resurrection. ⁶Knowing this: that our Ancient Human was co-crucified so that the Sin-Body may be undone, so we are no longer enslaved to Sin. ⁷For the dying one has been righted from Sin. ⁸If we died with Christos we trust that we will also live with him ⁹—knowing that Christos, being raised from among the dead ones, no longer dies—his death no longer lords. (¹⁰For what he died, he died to Sin once for all; what he lives, he lives to God.) ¹¹Thus also you calculate yourselves to be dead to Sin, but as living ones to God in Christos Yēsous. ¹²Therefore, don't let Sin rule in your mortal body—to heed its desires. ¹³Nor present your body parts as weapons of wrongdoing, but present yourselves to God as living-ones-from-the-dead-ones and your body parts to God as weapons of rightness. ¹⁴Sin doesn't lord over you, for you are not under Code but under Grace.

Life is liberation

¹⁵**What then?**
Are we to sin because we are not under Code but under Grace?

May that never happen!

¹⁶**Did you know that to whom you present yourselves as slaves to obedience—you are slaves to the one you heed—either of Sin to Death or of obedience to rightness?**

¹⁷Grace to God! Because you were slaves to Sin, but you heeded from the heart to the type of

teaching to which you were given over ¹⁸and, being liberated from Sin, you were enslaved to rightness. ¹⁹I am speaking humanly because of your flesh's weakness. For just as you presented your body parts as slaves to uncleanness and to the Covenant-breaking into more Covenant-breaking, so now present your body parts as slaves to rightness into devotion. ²⁰For when you were Sin's slaves, you were liberated from rightness.

²¹Therefore, what fruit did you have then?

(About which things you are now degraded, for their completion is Death.) ²²But now, being liberated from Sin, being enslaved to God, you have your fruit into devotion, the completion [being] Era Life. ²³Sin's fee is Death, but God's grace-act is Era Life in our Lord Christos Yēsous.

Life is not through the Covenant Code

7 Or, siblings, are you uninformed—I speak to Covenant-Code knowers—that the Code lords over a human as long as the person lives?

²For a man-attached woman is bound by the Code to the living man. But if the man dies, she's undone from the Code about the man. ³Accordingly therefore, with a living man, if she is with another man, she will be revealed as "adulteress." But if the man dies, she is liberated from the Code; she isn't an "adulteress" being with another man. ⁴So, my siblings, you died to the Code through Christos's body so you could be with another, with the one raised from among the dead ones, so you can produce fruit to God. ⁵For when we were in the Flesh, the sufferings of Sin were energized in our body parts through the Code to produce fruit for Death. ⁶But now we have been undone from the Code, dying in what possessed us, so that we slave in the Spirit's newness and not in the letter's antiquity.

⁷Therefore, what do we say?
Is the Code Sin?

May that never happen!
But I did not know sin except through the Code. For I have not known desire except the Code was saying, *You will not desire.* ⁸Sin, taking the opportunity through the order, effected in me every desire. (Apart of the Code Sin is dead.) ⁹I once was living apart from the Code but . . . the order's come . . . Sin came to life again, ¹⁰I died, and this order "for life" was found to be Death for me. ¹¹For Sin, taking the opportunity through the order, deceived me and through it killed ¹²so that the Code is devoted and the order is devoted and right and good.

¹³Therefore, did The Good become Death for me?

May that never happen!
But Sin, so it might appear as Sin, through The Good effected Death so Sin, through the order, may become "superior" Sin.

¹⁴For we know that the Code is Spirit-prompted.
I am enfleshed, sold out under Sin.
¹⁵For what I effect, I don't know.
For what I don't want, this I practice, but what I hate, this I do.
¹⁶If what I don't want, this I do, I affirm the Code, that it's beautiful.
¹⁷But now I no longer effect it, but Sin—residing in me.
¹⁸For I know that The Good doesn't reside in me—that is in my flesh.
For to want is present in me but to effect The Beautiful isn't.
¹⁹For The Good I want, that I don't do, but The Bad I don't want, that I practice.
²⁰If what I don't want, this I do, I am no longer effecting it but Sin is present with me.
²¹I find then the Code—in my wanting to do The Good—that The Bad is present with me.
²²For I take pleasure in God's Code consistent with the inner human, ²³but I see another Code in my body parts, waging war with my mind's Code and capturing me in Sin's Code, which is in my body parts.
²⁴I—a miserable human!

Who will rescue me from this Death's body?

²⁵Grace to God through our Lord Yēsous Christos. Accordingly, therefore, I myself—in the mind—slave in God's Code, but in the Flesh in Sin's Code.

Life is through the Spirit and with glory

8 Accordingly, now there is no condemnation for the ones in Christos Yēsous. ²For the Life-Spirit's Code in Christos Yēsous liberated you from Sin-and-Death's Code. ³For the Covenant Code's powerlessness, in which it was weakening through the Flesh, God—sending his own Son in the representation of Sin's Flesh—for Sin also condemned Sin-in-the-Flesh ⁴so the Code's right acts may be filled out in us who walk around not consistent with Flesh but consistent with Spirit. ⁵For the ones consistent with Flesh think about the Flesh's matters, but the ones consistent with Spirit about the Spirit's matters. ⁶Flesh's thoughts—Death; Spirit's thoughts—Life and Peace. ⁷Because the Flesh's thought is hostile to God, for it's not ordered under God's Code—for it's incapable. ⁸Ones who are in Flesh are not able to please God. ⁹You are not in Flesh but in Spirit, since God's Spirit resides in you. If someone doesn't have Christos's Spirit, this person isn't of him. ¹⁰But if Christos is in you, the body is dead through Sin, but the Spirit is Life because of rightness. ¹¹If the Spirit of the one who raised Yēsous from among the dead ones resides in you, the one who raised Yēsous from among the dead ones will also make life for your mortal bodies through his residing Spirit in you.

¹²Accordingly therefore, siblings, we are debtors—not to the Flesh to live consistent with Flesh . . . ¹³for if you live consistent with Flesh, you are about to die. But if in Spirit you kill the Body's practices, you will live. ¹⁴For whoever is led by God's Spirit—these are God's descendants! ¹⁵For you did not receive slavery's spirit again into being scared, but you received family-placement's Spirit, in whom we cry, "Abba, Father!" ¹⁶This same Spirit co-witnesses with our spirit that we are God's children. ¹⁷If children, also heirs—God's heirs, co-heirs with Christos—since we co-suffer so may we be co-splendored.

¹⁸For I calculate that the sufferings of the present season are not deserving of the coming splendor to be apocalypsed to us. ¹⁹For creation's impatient expectation awaits the apocalypse of God's descendants. ²⁰For creation was ordered under idleness—not willingly but because of The Orderer—in hope ²¹that creation itself will be liberated from decay's slavery into God's children's splendorous liberation! ²²For we know that all creation co-groans and co-labors until now, ²³but not only that but also we ourselves—ones having the Spirit as firstfruit—we ourselves groan among ourselves, impatiently waiting family-placement, our body's redemption. ²⁴For we were delivered in hope, but hope seen isn't hope—for who hopes for what one sees? ²⁵But if we hope for what we don't see, we impatiently wait through resilience. ²⁶Similarly also the Spirit assists in our weakness: For we don't know what is necessary for us to pray for? But the Spirit itself—super-aiding with wordless groanings. (²⁷The one exploring hearts knows what the Spirit's mind is: it intercedes consistent with God for the devoted ones.)

²⁸We know that [God] coworks all things for good with those who love God, with those called consistent with the intention:

²⁹Because those whom he knew before
he also predetermined those [to be]
    co-morphed-to-his-Son's-image
(so that he is the Firstborn among many
    siblings);
³⁰Those predetermined, those he also
    called;
Those called, those he also righted;
Those righted, those he also splendored.

³¹**Therefore, what are we to say about these things?**
If God is for us, who is against us?
³²**He who did not spare his own Son but gave him over for all of us—how does he not also grace all things to us with him?**
³³**Who will call in against God's elect?**

God is the one righting.

³⁴**Who is the one condemning?**

Christos, the one who died—rather, the one who was raised, who also is at God's right hand, who also intercedes for us.

³⁵**Who separates us from Christos's love? Trouble or distress or chasing, or famine or nakedness, or danger or long knife?**

³⁶Just as it's written, that:
Because of you we are killed the whole day,

We are calculated as slaughter sheep.
37But in all these things we super-conquer through the one who loved us. **38**I am persuaded that

> not Death,
> not life,
> not envoys,
> not celestial leaders,
> not things present,
> not things to come,
> not powers,
> **39**not heights,
> not depths,
> not any other creation

will be capable to separate us from God's love in Christos Yēsous our Lord.

Yisraēl's privilege and God's way of deliverance

9 I speak truth in Christos I am not falsifying . . . my consciousness is co-witnessing to me in Holy Spirit . . . **2**that pain for me is great and gapless sorrow is in my heart. **3**I was formulating for myself a vow-to-destruction from Christos over my ethnic siblings consistent with the flesh,

> **4**who are Yisraēlitai [Israelites],
> of whom is the family-placement
> and the splendor
> and the Covenants
> and the Covenant Code–placement
> and the veneration
> and the pledges,
> **5**of whom are the fathers
> and out of whom is the Christos, the
> > one consistent with flesh, who is over all God,
> Blessed to the Eras.
> Amēn!

6It isn't the case that God's Word flopped. For not all those from Yisraēl [Israel] are Yisraēl, **7**nor that all the seed of Abra'am are children, but *in Yisa'ak* [Isaac] *your seed will be called*. **8**That is, it's not the fleshly children who are God's children but the pledge's children are calculated for seed. **9**For this is the pledge-word: *consistent with this season I will come and for Sarra* [Sarah] *there will be a son*. **10**Not only, but also Rebekka [Rebecca], having coitus from one, Yisa'ak, our father. **11**. . . they had not even been given a life or practiced good or foul—so God's elective-intention

might remain **12**(not from works but from the one calling) . . . it was said to her that *the greater will be slave to the lesser*, **13**just as it's written, *I loved Yakōb* [Jacob], *but Ēsau I hated*.

14Therefore, what will we say?
Is there not wrongdoing with God?

May that never happen!

15For he says to Mōüses [Moses], *I will have compassion on whom I have compassion, and I will pity the one I pity*. **16**Accordingly, therefore, [it happens] not of the one wanting nor the one running but of the God having compassion. **17**For the writing says to Pharaō [Pharaoh] that *for this very [reason] I raised you up so that I might exhibit in you my power and so that my name might be announced in the whole land*. **18**Accordingly therefore, he shows compassion on whom he wants and he makes stubborn the one whom he wants.

19Therefore, you will say to me:

Why, therefore, still does he blame?
For who has resisted his will?

20O human, to the contrary!

Who are you?
The one responding to God?
Will the formed say to the former, "Why did you make me like this?"
21Or does the potter of clay have authority over his lump to make a utensil for honor and for dishonor?
22What if God, wanting to exhibit his anger and to make known his power, carried in much patience a utensil of anger—prepared for destruction—**23**and that he might make his splendored wealth known on a vessel of compassion that he prepared for splendor?
24Also for those he called—us—not only from Youdaians [Judeans, Jews] but also from ethnic groups?

25As also it says in Ōsēe [Hosea],

> *I will call Not My People "My People"*
> *And the Unloved the "Loved"*
> **26***and it will be in the place where it was said to them, "You are not 'My people,'" there they will be called "the living God's descendants."*

27Ēsaïas [Isaiah] cries for Yisraēl,

> If the number of Yisraēl's descendants be
> as the sea's sand, the vestige will be
> delivered.
> ²⁸For upon the land the Lord will do
> judgment—completing and cutting
> it short.

²⁹Just as Ēsaïas has said,

> If the Lord of Armies did not abandon
> seed for us,
> we would have become as Sodoma
> [Sodom]
> and compared with Gomorra.

³⁰Therefore, what will we say? That ethnic groups, the ones not chasing rightness, prevailed with rightness—a rightness that is of allegiance—³¹but Yisraēl, chasing Code rightness, did not arrive at Code [rightness]? ³²Why?

Because—not out of allegiance but as if out of works. They stumbled on the stumbling stone, ³³just as it's written:

> Look!
> I place in Siōn [Zion] *a stumbling stone
> and a tripping rock,*
> And the one allegiant to him will never be
> degraded.

10

Siblings, my heart's delight and request to God for them is deliverance. ²I witness about them, that they have zeal for God but not consistent with perception. ³For being uninformed about God's rightness and pursuing to establish their own rightness, they were not ordered under God's rightness. ⁴The completion of the Covenant Code is Christos, for rightness to everyone who is allegiant.

⁵For Mōūsēs [Moses] writes about the rightness that is from the Code, that *The human doers of these things will live in them.*

⁶But the rightness from allegiance says it like this, *Don't say in you heart, "Who will ascend into heaven?"* (That is, to lead Christos down.)

⁷Or, *Who will descend into the abyss?* (That is, to lead Christos up from among the dead ones.)

⁸But what does it say?

The utterance is close to you—in your mouth and in your heart. (That is, the allegiance-utterance that we announce.)

⁹Because if you openly agree "Yēsous as Lord" with your mouth and trust in your heart that God raised him from among the dead ones, you will be delivered. ¹⁰For in the heart one trusts for rightness; with the mouth one publicly agrees for deliverance. ¹¹For the writing says, *Every allegiant one will not be degraded.* ¹²For there is no discrimination between Youdaian [Judean, Jew] and Hellēnes [Greek]—for he is Lord over all and the one enriching for all calling upon him. ¹³For *everyone who calls upon the Lord's name will be delivered.*

¹⁴Therefore, how then do they call upon the one they didn't trust?
How do they trust the one they didn't hear?
How do they hear apart from announcing?
¹⁵How do they announce if they are not commissioned?

Just as it's written, *How blooming are the feet of ones gospeling good things!* ¹⁶But not all heed the gospel, for Ēsaïas [Isaiah] says, *Lord, who trusted our report?* ¹⁷Accordingly, allegiance—from hearing; hearing—through the Christos-utterance.

¹⁸But I say,

"Have they not heard?"

On the contrary!
*Their shout exited into the whole land
And their utterances to the ends of habitation.*

¹⁹But I say,

"Did Yisraēl [Israel] not know?"

First, Mōūsēs says,
*I will irritate you to zeal over "Not an ethnic group,"
I will anger you over an ignorant ethnic group.*
²⁰Ēsaïas emboldens and says,
*I have been found by those not pursuing me,
I have become manifest to those not questioning me.*
²¹To Yisraēl he says,
The whole day I stretched out my hands to a people unpersuaded and contradictory.

11

Therefore, I say:

"Has God repelled his people?"

May that never happen! For I, too, am an Yisraēlitēs [Israelite], From Abra'am's seed, Of Benyamin's [Benjamin's] tribe. ²*God did not repel his people* whom he knew before.

Or, did you not know what the writing says in Ēlias [Elijah], as he intercedes with God against Yisraēl [Israel]?

[3]"Lord, *they killed your prophets, they ravaged your sacrificial altars, and I alone am left and they are pursuing my self.*"

[4]**But what does the one revealing say to him?**

I left for myself seven thousand men who didn't bend a knee to the Master [Ba'al]. [5]Therefore, so also at the present season there exists some remaining consistent with elective grace. [6]If by grace, no longer from works, since grace then would become no longer grace.

[7]**What then?**

What Israel pursues, this it did not achieve, but the election achieved. The ones remaining were petrified, [8]just as it's written:

God gave them a bewildering spirit,
Eyes not to see,
Ears not to hear,
Until this day.

[9]And Dauid [David] says,

May their table become a snare and a
 trap
and a trip and reciprocation for them.
[10]*May their not-to-see-eyes be darkened*
and [you] *bend their back through it all.*

[11]Therefore I say,

"Did they stumble so they would fall?"

May that never happen!
Rather, in their wrong the deliverance [comes] for the ethnic groups so they are provoked to zeal. [12]If their wrong [becomes] wealth for the Kosmos, and their failure [becomes] riches for the ethnic groups, how much more their fullness!

Ethnic groups privilege and God's way of deliverance

[13]I say now to you, the ethnic groups.
Therefore, in that I am a Commissioner to the ethnic groups, I splendor my service, [14]if somehow I may provoke to zeal my flesh and may deliver some of them. [15]For if their tossing away [becomes] reconciling the world, what is their acceptance if not life from among the dead ones? [16]If the firstfruit is devoted, also the lump, and if the root is devoted, also the branches. [17]If some of the branches have been snapped off, you—being a wild olive shoot—were grafted into them and share a common life in the sap of the olive tree's root, [18]don't boast over the branches. If you boast over—you don't carry the root but the root you! [19]Therefore, you will say, "Branches were snapped off so I might be grafted in." [20]Beautifully! They were snapped off in their anti-trust, but you have stood in trust. Don't think high-status thoughts. Rather, be awed, [21]for if God did not spare the natural branches, perhaps he will not spare you. [22]Therefore look at both God's graciousness and snipping: snipping for the fallen, God's graciousness for you—if you remain in that graciousness, since you also can be chopped off. [23]Those, if they don't remain in anti-trust, will be grafted back in. God is powerful to graft them in again. [24]For if you have been naturally chopped off from a wild olive tree and grafted unnaturally into a beautiful olive tree, how much more will these natural ones be grafted back into their own olive tree!

[25]For I don't want you to be uninformed, siblings, about this secret—so that you may not be the "prudent" among yourselves: that a partial hardening has come to Yisraēl until the fullness of the ethnic groups enters [26]and so all Yisraēl will be delivered, just as it's written,

The Rescuer will come from Siōn [Zion],
He will turn impiety away from Yakōb
 [Jacob].
[27]*This is the Covenant with me,*
when I lift away their sins.

[28]Consistent with the gospel [they become] enemies because of you, but consistent with election [they are] loved ones because of the fathers, [29]for God's grace-acts and calling are without regret. [30]For just as you once were unpersuaded by God but now you have received compassion during their unpersuasion, [31]so also these now are unpersuaded during your compassion so that they also may now receive compassion. [32]For God has enclosed all in unpersuasion so he may show compassion on all.

⁳³O the depth of wealth and of God's
    wisdom and knowledge!
How unsearchable his judgments!
How incomprehensible his paths!

³⁴*Who knew the Lord's mind?*
Who became his adviser?
³⁵*Who gave* [a gift] *over to him*
and God would reciprocate a gift to him?

³⁶Because all things are from him and
    through him and to him.
The splendor is for him unto the Eras.
    Amēn!

Start life here

12 Therefore, I beg you, siblings, through God's sympathies to present your bodies as an offering—living, devoted, judged exceptional to God, your calculated veneration—²and don't become a model of this Era, but become remodeled by a revival of the mind so you can judge suitable what God wants—what is good, judged exceptional, and complete.

Body life

³For I say, through the grace given to me, to everyone who is among you, not to have high-status thoughts more than is necessary but to have sensible thoughts—as God split off to each a portion of the faith. ⁴For just as we have many parts in one body, and not all parts have the same practice, ⁵so we, the many, are one body in Christos, and parts one with another, ⁶having differing grace-acts consistent with the grace given to us:

    If prophecy—consistent with the faith's
        articulation;
⁷if service—in the service;
if one teaching—in the teaching;
⁸if one encouraging—in encouragement;
the one distributing—in generosity;
the one leading—in seriousness;
the one being compassionate—with glee.

Life habits

⁹Love—unmasked.[a]
Repelling the evil,
uniting to The Good;
¹⁰affectionate ones in sibling-love for
    one another;
leading in honoring one another;
¹¹not timid in seriousness;
zesty in the Spirit;
slaving to the Lord;
¹²rejoicing in the hope;
resilience in the trouble;
persisting in the prayer;
¹³sharing a common life in the needs of
    the devoted ones;
chasing foreigner-love hospitality.
¹⁴Bless those chasing you!
Bless, and don't curse!
¹⁵To rejoice with those rejoicing, to wail
    with the wailing.
¹⁶Thinking the same status with one
    another, not thinking high status
    but being carried away with the
    impoverished.
Don't become the "prudent" among
    yourselves!
¹⁷Not giving back bad for bad;
thinking first about what is beautiful for
    all humans.
¹⁸If it's possible from you, peace-ing with
    all humans.
¹⁹Not "giving a right sentence" on one
    another, loved ones, but create
    space for anger, for it's written,
    Right-making is for me, I will pay
    back, says the Lord.
²⁰Instead, *if your enemy hungers, nurse him!*
If one thirsts, give the person a drink! For,
    doing this, coals of fire are piled on
    the person's head.
²¹Don't conquer The Bad by The Bad but
    conquer The Bad by The Good.

Life in the empire

13 Let every self order oneself under the high-placed authorities! For, if not for God there is no authority—those existing have been ordered by God. ²So that the anti-orderers of the authority have resisted God's order, and the ones who have resisted will receive judgment for themselves. ³For the leaders are not scary to the good work but to the bad.

---

[a]Usually all these verbal expressions are turned into imperatives. I have left the participles in participial form and put an exclamation for each imperative so readers can see the differences.

Do you not want not to be scared of the authority?

Do The Good and you will have public praise from it. ⁴For it's God's servant for you for The Good. If you do The Bad, be scared, for it doesn't carry the long knife uselessly. For God's servant exacts right-making in anger for the one who practices The Bad. ⁵So, it's compulsory to order yourselves under [the authority], not only because of the anger but also because of consciousness.

⁶For, because this is true, also pay tribute! For they are God's public workers, persisting in this very matter. ⁷Pay back the debts to everyone! To whom tribute—tribute; to whom tax—tax; to whom awe—awe; to whom honor—honor.

A life of love

⁸Owe nothing to no one except to love one another. For the one loving the other has filled out the Covenant Code. ⁹For the [code]—*You will not be adulterous, you will not murder, you will not thieve, you will not desire*, and if there is another order—comes to a head in this one: *You will love your neighbor as yourself.* ¹⁰The love doesn't work bad to the neighbor. Therefore, the love is the fullness of the Code.

I wish we'd all been ready

¹¹And this: knowing the season, that the hour is already for you to rise up from sleep, for the deliverance is closer now than when we trusted. ¹²The night advanced, the day has come close. Therefore, let us put off the dark's works; let us put on the light's weapons. ¹³Let us walk around respectably as in the day:

not in parties and boozings,
not in coituses and flaunting sensualities,
not in strife and zeal,
¹⁴but put on the Lord Yēsous Christos!
Don't do the Flesh's mindset for desires!

Life with the powerful and powerless

14 Welcome the weak-in-the-faith—not for deliberations' distinguishings! ²One trusts eating everything, but the weak eats leafy vegetables. ³The eater isn't to devalue the non-eater, and the non-eater isn't to judge the eater, for God welcomes the person. ⁴Who are you? The Judge of an outsider's domestic? The person stands or falls with one's own lord. He will be stood up, for the Lord is able to stand him up. ⁵For one judges a day over a day, and one judges all days. Let each be fully assured in one's own mind. ⁶The one prudent about a day thinks prudently to the Lord. The eater eats to the Lord, for the person thanks God. The non-eater doesn't eat to the Lord and thanks God. ⁷For no one of us lives to oneself and no one dies to oneself. ⁸For if we so live we live to the Lord, if we die we die to the Lord. Therefore, if we live or if we die—we are the Lord's. ⁹For this reason Christos died and lived, so also he may lord over the dead and living.

¹⁰Why do you judge your sibling? Or also you, why do you devalue your sibling?

For we all will present ourselves at God's Bēma [judgment seat], ¹¹for it's written:

> *I live, says the Lord, because to me every knee will bow*
> *And every tongue will publicly acknowledge the Lord.*

¹²Accordingly therefore, each of us will give a word concerning oneself to God.

¹³Therefore, no longer let us judge one another, but instead judge this: Not to place a stumbling- or tripping-stone for a sibling. ¹⁴I have known and I am persuaded in Lord Yēsous that nothing is common in itself. Exception: to the one calculating something to be common, for that person it's common. ¹⁵For if your sibling grieves because of food, you are no longer walking around consistent with love. Don't destroy by your food that person for whom Christos died. ¹⁶Therefore, let not your Good become insulting. ¹⁷For God's Empire isn't food and drink, but rightness and peace and joy—in Holy Spirit. ¹⁸For in this the one slaving to Christ is judged exceptional by God and approved by humans. ¹⁹Accordingly, therefore, may we chase the things of peace and the things of formation for one another. ²⁰Don't demolish God's work for food. Everything is clean, but it's bad for the eating human [becoming] a stumbling-stone. ²¹It's beautiful not to eat *treif* [unclean food], not to drink wine, and not anything that trips up your sibling. ²²The allegiance you yourself have, you have before God. God's blessing on the one who doesn't judge oneself in what one judges suitable. ²³The

mentally wavering one, if one eats, has been condemned because it's not of allegiance. Everything not out of allegiance is sin.

15 We, the Powerful, ought to carry the weaknesses of the Powerless, and not to please ourselves. ²Let each of us please the neighbor—for The Good, toward formation. ³For even Christos did not please himself but just as it's written, *The degradations of the ones degrading you fell on me.* ⁴For whatever was first written was written for our teaching so, through the resilience and through the encouragement of the writings, we may have hope. ⁵May the resilience-and-encouragement-God give to you the same prudence among one another—consistent with Christos Yēsous—⁶so that in shared passion, in one mouth, you may splendor the God and Father of our Lord, Yēsous Christos.

⁷So, welcome one another just as Christos welcomed you—to God's splendor. ⁸For I say Christos became a servant of the circumcision [group] for God's truth—to assure the fathers' pledges ⁹and so the ethnic groups could splendor God for mercy, just as it's written:

Because this is true:
I will publicly acknowledge you among
    the ethnic groups
And I will accompany the strings to your
    name.

¹⁰Again it says,

Be glad, ethnic groups, with his people!

¹¹And again,

Exalt, all the ethnic groups, the Lord
And praise him, all the peoples.

¹²And again Ēsaïas [Isaiah] says,

Yessai's [Jesse's] root will be
And the one who rises up to rule the
    ethnic groups—
On him the ethnic groups will hope.

¹³May the hope-God fill you out with all joy and peace in allegiance, so you flow over in hope—in power of Holy Spirit.

The Commissioner Paulos's plans

¹⁴I am myself persuaded about you, my siblings, that you are yourselves full of goodness, filling out with all knowledge, empowering also to mentor one another. ¹⁵I wrote to you more boldly—partly reminding you through the grace given to me by God ¹⁶to be Christos Yēsous' public worker for the ethnic groups, priesting God's gospel—so the ethnic groups' contribution may be well-received, having been devoted by Holy Spirit. ¹⁷Therefore, I have a boast in Christos Yēsous about matters pertaining to God, ¹⁸for I will not dare to speak of anything that Christos did not effect through me for the ethnic groups' obedience—word or deed, ¹⁹in a power of authenticating signs and omens, in a power of God's Spirit—so that I have filled out Christos's gospel from Yierousalēm [Jerusalem] and encircling to Illurikon [Illyricum]—²⁰thus loving the honor to gospel not where Christos has been named, so I may not form on an outsider's foundation, ²¹but just as it's written,

They, to whom he has not been
    announced, will see
And they, who have not heard, will
    understand.

²²So also I was cut off many times from coming to you ²³but now, no longer having space in these environs and having a longing to come to you for many years ²⁴as I journey to Spania [Spain]. . . . For I hope, journeying through, to observe you and there to be sent on by you—if I may be first partly filled up by you. ²⁵But now I journey to Yierousalēm, serving the devoted ones. ²⁶Makedonia [Macedonia] and Achaia delighted to make some resources common for the begging devoted ones in Yierousalēm. ²⁷For they delighted and they are debtors to them. For if they had a common life with the ethnic groups in their Spirit-connected ways, they also are indebted to working publicly for them in flesh-connected ways. ²⁸Therefore, completing this, sealing this fruit for them, I will depart through you to Spania. ²⁹I have known that, coming to you, I will come in the fullness of Christos's blessing.

³⁰I beg you, siblings, through our Lord Yēsous Christos and through the Spirit's love, to co-agonize with me in prayers to God for me: ³¹that I may be rescued from the unpersuaded in Youdaia [Judea] and that my service for Yierousalēm may be well-received by the devoted ones ³²so, coming in joy to you through God's plan, I will be co-refreshed with you.

³³The Peace-God—with you all! Amēn!

Phoebe

16 I affirm our sister Phoibē [Phoebe] to you, who is a deacon of the assembly of Kenchreai [Cenchreae], ²that you attend to her, in the Lord, in a manner deserving for the devoted ones and present to her in whatever she may require of you. For she has also become a benefactor for many, and for me personally.

Rōmē's house churches[b]

³Greet Priska* and Akulas [Priscilla and Aquila],# my coworkers in Christos Yēsous, ⁴who laid down their neck for my self, whom not only I thank but also many assemblies of the ethnic groups, ⁵and [greet] the assembly in their house.

Greet Epainetos [Epenetus], my loved one, who is a firstfruit to Christos of Asia.

⁶Greet Maria* [Mary], who labored much for you.

⁷Greet Andronikos and Younia* [Andronicus and Junia], my relatives and my co-prisoners, who are distinguished in the Commissioners, and who were in Christos before me.

⁸Greet Ampliatos [Ampliatus], my loved one in Lord.

⁹Greet Ourbanos [Urbanus], our coworker in Christos, and Stachus [Stachys], my loved one.

¹⁰Greet Apellēs, approved in Christos.

Greet the ones of [the house] of Aristoboulos# [Aristobulus].

¹¹Greet Hērōdiōn, my relative.

Greet the ones of [the house] of Narkissos# [Narcissus] who are in Lord.

¹²Greet Truphaina* [Tryphena] and Truphōsa* [Tryphosa], laborers in Lord.

Greet Persis*, loved one, who labored much in Lord.

¹³Greet Rouphos [Rufus], elect in Lord, and his and my mother*.

¹⁴Greet Asunkritos [Asyncritus], Phlegōn, Hermēs, Patrobas, Hermas, and the siblings with them.#

¹⁵Greet Philologos [Philologus] and Youlia* [Julia], Nērea [Nereus] and his sister*, and Olumpas [Olympas] and all the devoted ones with them#.

¹⁶Greet one another with a devoted kiss. All Christos's assemblies greet you.

Final appeal to peace in the heart of the empire

¹⁷I beg you, siblings, to scope out the ones making divisions and trippings—against the teaching in which you were apprenticed—and lean away from them. ¹⁸For such persons are not slaving to our Lord Christos but to their own belly. Through sweet-words and blessings they deceive the hearts of the ones without badness. ¹⁹For your obedience reached out to all. Therefore, I rejoice over you, and I want you to be wise for The Good and innocent for The Bad. ²⁰The Peace-God will break the Satanas [Satan] under your feet—shortly.

The grace of our Lord Yēsous—with you!

From Paulos's circle

²¹Timotheos [Timothy], my coworker, greets you—also Loukios [Lucius] and Yasōn [Jason] and Sōsipatros [Sosipater], my relatives.

²²I, Tertios [Tertius], the one who wrote this letter, greet you in the Lord.

²³Gaios [Gaius], host to me and to the whole assembly, greets you.

Erastos [Erastus], the City Administrator [of Corinth], and Kouartos [Quartus], the sibling, greets you.

A doxology

²⁵To the one powerful to support you
    consistent with my gospel and the
    announcement of Yēsous
    Christos,
consistent with the apocalypse of the
    secret—silenced for long Eras,
²⁶but now manifested through the
    prophetic writings consistent
    with the Era-God's order,
made known to all the ethnic groups for
    the obedience of allegiance,
²⁷to the only wise God,
through Yēsous Christos.
to whom be the splendor for the Eras.
Amēn!

---

[b]The asterisk indicates a female, and the pound sign a house church.

INTRODUCTION TO THE FIRST LETTER TO CORINTH

First Corinthians is another of Paulos's [Paul's] sometimes consoling and sometimes agitating letters. While we call this letter "First" Corinthians, "I wrote to you in the letter" in 5:9 indicates he has already written at least one letter to them.

The letter was written from Ephesus (16:8) probably in AD 54 to Corinth, a prosperous, growing, and very much social-climbing city in Greece—west of Athens and sitting gently on the isthmus between the mainland and the Peloponnese. The Corinthian believers were populated with Roman wannabes, and they were comfortable in Corinth—their faith and practices seemed to have created very little tension with the Kosmos. That is, many had embraced the Roman way of life—status, power, wealth, and opportunistic sexual freedoms. They imposed such a way of life on the Christians, and Paulos battled their impositions with rhetorical force.

The letter moves from item to item, beginning at 1:10 with a focus on social-status divisions in the house churches, which leads to Paulos shadowboxing with those in Corinth who had better ideas for how to conduct the mission in Greece (1:10–4:21). He addresses in turn sexual infidelity (5:1-13), lawsuits between Christians (6:1-11), more about sexual infidelity (6:12-20), marriage and virgins (7:1-40), demon worship and food offered to demons (8:1-13; 10:1–11:1)— and interrupts these items to talk about his own ministry (9:1-27). Then he turns to worship wars about women (11:2-16), the Lord's Supper (11:17-34), spiritual gifts (12:1–14:40)—with an interruption (chap. 13) about love—the resurrection (15:1-58), and finally collection for the begging devoted ones in Jerusalem (16:1-4).

Paulos urges in this letter for the Corinthian believers to embrace an anti-Roman way of life marked by love, by unity, by mutual spiritual formation, and by holiness or a devoted way of life.

THE FIRST LETTER TO CORINTH

From Paulos to Korinthos

1 Paulos [Paul], a called Commissioner by Christos Yēsous through God's plan, and Sōsthenēs [Sosthenes], the brother, ²to God's assembly that is in Korinthos [Corinth], having been devoted in Christos Yēsous, called devoted ones, with all those calling on the name of our Lord, Yēsous Christos, in every place—theirs and ours.

³Grace to you and peace from our Father-God and Lord Yēsous Christos.

Paulos thanks God for the Corinthians

⁴I thank my God always for you at God's grace given to you in Christos Yēsous, ⁵because in everything you were enriched in him—in all word and all knowledge—⁶just as the Christos-witness was assured among you, ⁷so that you—who are impatiently waiting the apocalypse of our Lord, Yēsous Christos—don't lack in any grace-act. ⁸He will assure you until the completion [so you will be], unimpeachable on the day of our Lord, Yēsous Christos.

⁹God is allegiant—through whom you were called into common life with his Son, Yēsous Christos, our Lord.

All those for unity!

¹⁰I beg you, siblings—through the name of our Lord Yēsous Christos—that you all say the same thing and [that] there not be rips among you, but [that] you be prepared with the same mind and in the same conclusion. ¹¹For it has been divulged to me about you, my siblings, by the ones from Chloë, that there are status seekings among you. ¹²I say this: That each of you is saying, "I am of Paulos " and "I am of Apollōs" and "I am of Kēphas [Cephas]" and "I am of Christos."

**¹³Is Christos split into parts?
Was Paulos crucified for you?
Or were you dipped into the name of Paulos?**

¹⁴I thank God that I dipped none of you—except Krispos [Crispus] and Gaïos [Gaius]—¹⁵so that someone cannot say that you were dipped into my name. ¹⁶But I also dipped the house of Stephanas—beyond that I don't know if I dipped some other person. ¹⁷For Christos did not commission me to dip but to gospel—not with word-wisdom—so the cross of Christos may not be hollowed.

Cruciform preaching: Theory

¹⁸For the word that is about the cross is idiocy to those being destroyed but God's power for those being delivered. ¹⁹For it's written,

> I will destroy the "wisdom of the wise"
> And I will reject the "understanding of the understanders."

**²⁰Where is the wise?
Where the Covenant-Code scholar?
Where this Era's disputer?
Has not God turned the Kosmos' wisdom into idiocy?**

²¹For since—in God's wisdom—the Kosmos did not know God through the wisdom, God delighted through the idiocy of the announcement to deliver the allegiant ones. ²²Since Youdaians ask for authenticating signs and Hellēnes [Greeks] pursue wisdom, ²³we announce Christos crucified—to the Youdaians a trip, to the ethnic groups idiocy, ²⁴but to the ones called—both Youdaians and Hellēnes—Christos, God's power and God's wisdom. ²⁵Because "God's idiocy" is wiser than humans and "God's weakness" is stronger than humans. ²⁶For look at your calling, siblings, that not many are wise consistent with flesh, not many powerful, not many noble. ²⁷But God selected the Kosmos's idiots to degrade the wise, and God elected the Kosmos's weak to degrade the strong, ²⁸and God elected the Kosmos's ignoble and devalued—the ones who "are not"—to undo the ones who "are," ²⁹so that no flesh may boast before God. ³⁰From him [God] you are in Christos Yēsous, who became wisdom for us from God, and also rightness and devotedness and liberation, ³¹so—as it's written—*the one boasting: let the person boast in Lord.*

Cruciform preaching: Personal

2 Coming to you, siblings, I came not proclaiming God's secret to you with high-status word or wisdom. ²For I judged not to know anything among you except Yēsous Christos—and this one crucified. ³I was with you in weakness, in fear, and in much trembling, ⁴and my word and my announcement—not in wisdom's persuasive words but in a demonstration of Spirit and power, ⁵so your allegiance would not be in human wisdom but in God's power.

The apocalypse through the Spirit

⁶We speak wisdom among the complete ones, a wisdom not of this Era nor of the leaders of this Era, the undone ones. ⁷But we speak God's wisdom in secret, the hidden [wisdom], which God predetermined before the Eras for our splendor, ⁸which none of the leaders of this Era had known. (For, if they knew, they would not have crucified splendor's Lord.) ⁹But, as it's written,

> What things an eye did not see and an ear did not hear and did not rise up in a human heart,
> What things God prepared for the ones loving him.

¹⁰But God apocalypsed [it] to us through the Spirit. For the Spirit explores all things, even God's deep matters. ¹¹For who among humans has known human matters except the human spirit, which is in the person? So also no one has known God's matters except God's Spirit. ¹²We did not receive the Kosmos's spirit but the Spirit that is from God, so we may know grace-acts given to us by God. ¹³About which matters we also speak, not in words taught in human-like wisdom, but in [words] taught of Spirit—Spirit matters co-discerned by a Spirit-person. ¹⁴A selfish human doesn't receive Spirit-of-God matters, for they are idiocy to that person and the person isn't able to know because the [matters] are examined Spiritually. ¹⁵The Spirit-person examines all things, and the person is examined by no one. ¹⁶For *Who knew the Lord's mind? Who instructs him?* We have Christos's mind.

Gospel ministry

3 I, siblings, wasn't able to speak to you as to Spirit-people but as to Flesh-people, as to infants in Christos. ²I gave you milk to drink, not food. For you weren't yet able, but you aren't able even now, ³for you are still Flesh-people. For where there is zeal and strife among you—aren't you "Fleshies" and walking around consistent with a human?

⁴For whenever someone says, "I am of Paulos [Paul]" and another "I am of Apollōs," are you not [just] humans? ⁵Therefore, who is Apollōs? And who is Paulos?

Servants through whom you trusted, and to each as the Lord gave. ⁶I planted, Apollōs gave to drink, but God was causing growth ⁷so that neither the one planting is anything, nor the one giving drink, but the God who causes growth. ⁸Both the one planting and the one giving drink are one; each will receive one's own wage consistent with one's own labor, ⁹For we are God's coworkers; you are God's field, God's formation.

¹⁰Consistent with God's grace given to me, as the wise lead builder, I placed a foundation, another formed on it. Let each look how one forms on it. ¹¹For no one is able to lay a foundation other than the one that is set, who is Yēsous Christos. ¹²If someone forms on the foundation gold, silver, honorable stones, woods, grass, straw—¹³the work of each will be apparent, for the Day will divulge [it] because it will be apocalypsed with fire. The fire will judge it—what each's kind of work is. ¹⁴If the work that was formed on it remains, the person will receive a wage. ¹⁵If the work of someone will be burned up, it [the wage] will be damaged, but the person will be delivered—thus as [passing] through fire.

¹⁶Haven't you known that you are God's sanctuary and [that] God's Spirit resides among you?

¹⁷If someone abominates God's sanctuary, God will abominate the person. For God's sanctuary is a devoted one—which is what you are!

Gospel agents

¹⁸Let no one deceive oneself! If someone among you looks wise in this Era, let the person become an idiot so the person may become wise. ¹⁹For the Kosmos's wisdom is idiocy with God. For it's written, *The one who is clutching the wise ones in their [rhetorical] trickery.* ²⁰Again, *The Lord knows the "wise's" deliberations, that they*

are useless. ²¹So let no one boast in humans, for all things are yours—²²whether it's Paulos, or Apollōs, or Kēphas [Cephas], or Kosmos, or life, or death, or present matters or future matters—all things are yours, ²³and you are Christos's; Christos is God's.

4 So let a human calculate us as Christos's subordinates and administrators of God's secret. ²Now it follows [that] it pursues administrators—that the person be found allegiant. ³With me, it's small potatoes that I am examined by you or by a human day [in court], but I don't even examine myself. ⁴For I am personally aware that I am nothing, but in this [judgment] I am not made right. Anyway, the one examining me is the Lord. ⁵So, don't judge someone prior to the season [of judgment], [that is,] before the Lord comes, who will enlighten hidden matters of the Darkness and will cause to appear the plans of the hearts. Then the public praise will come to each from God.

⁶Because of you, I have reshaped these things, siblings, for myself and Apollōs so you may be apprenticed among us in this: "Nothing beyond what is written"—so you don't use your natural status—each for one against another.

[Sarcastic use of opponents' language]

⁷For who "discriminates" you?
What do you have you didn't receive?
Now if you also received, why do you boast as one "not receiving"?

⁸You are already "satiated"!
You are already "enriched"!
Without us you "ruled"!
For sure, I could wish that you ruled so also we could co-rule!
⁹For it looks like God has demonstrated us—the Commissioners—last, as death-bound, that we have become theater to the Kosmos and to envoys and humans.

[Sarcastic again] ¹⁰We are "idiots" because of Christos.
You are "prudent" in Christos.
We are "weak."
You are "strong."
You are in "splendor."
We are "dishonored."
¹¹Up to the present hour we hunger and we thirst and are shabby and slapped and destabilized ¹²and we labor, working with our own hands.

In snubbing, we bless;
in being chased, we put up [with it];
¹³in dissing, we console.
We have become like the Kosmos's trash, the compost of all—until the present.

Paulos's love for Korinthos

¹⁴Deferring, I am not writing these matters to you but mentoring as my children I love. ¹⁵For if you have innumerable educators in Christos, but you don't have many fathers. For in Christos Yēsous, through the gospel, I gave a life to you. ¹⁶Therefore, I beg you—become copies of me. ¹⁷Because this is true, I sent Timotheos [Timothy] to you, who is my loved and allegiant child in Lord, who will remember to you my ways, the ones in Christos Yēsous just as I teach in all places, in all assemblies.

¹⁸As if [I were] not coming to you, some appealed to their natural status.

¹⁹I will come to quickly to you if the Lord wants, and I will know, not the word of the ones using natural status, but the power. ²⁰For God's Empire isn't in word but in power.

²¹What do you want?
Do I come to you with stick or with both love and a spirit of meekness?

Item: Sexual infidelity

5 Sexual infidelity is actually heard among you, and the kind of sexual infidelity that isn't [practiced] among the ethnic groups—so that some man has the woman of the father. ²You are [using] your natural status and are not grieved so that the one practicing this work might be removed from the middle of you. ³⁻⁴For I, absenting in body but being present in the Spirit, have already—as being present—judged in the name of our Lord Yēsous the one who effected this [act] . . . in your being assembled together and my spirit's with you in the power of our Lord Yēsous. . . . ⁵Such a person is to be given over to the Satanas [Satan] for the Flesh's calamity so that the spirit may be delivered on the Day of the Lord.

⁶Your boasting isn't beautiful. Do you not know that "a little yeast leavens the whole batch"? ⁷Clean out the ancient yeast so you

may be a new batch—just as you are unleavened. For our Pascha [Passover lamb] has also been sacrificed—Christos. ⁸So that we celebrate, not with the ancient yeast nor with bad and evil yeast, but in the unleavenings of transparency and truth.

⁹I wrote to you in the letter not to co-mix with the sexually immoral ¹⁰(not always [in the sense of with] this Kosmos's sexually unfaithful) or with the ones wanting more and more or rapacious ones or demon worshipers— since then you would have to exit from the Kosmos. ¹¹Now I wrote you not to co-mix if someone named "sibling" is sexually immoral or one wanting more and more or a demon worshiper or snubber or boozer or rapacious— with such persons don't even co-eat. ¹²For what is it to me to judge the ones outside? Do you not judge those inside? ¹³God will judge the ones outside. *Lift out the evil from among them.*

Item: Lawsuits

6 Does someone among you, having a matter against another, dare to judge [him] before the wrongdoers and not before the devoted ones?

²Or, have you not known that the devoted ones will judge the Kosmos?
If the Kosmos is to be judged by you, are you undeserving of being tribunals for the least [of complaints]?
³Have you not known that we will judge envoys—not the least then the realities of life?
⁴If therefore you have tribunals for realities of life, do you seat these [on the tribunal], the devalued in the assembly?

⁵I say [this] to your embarrassment.

Thus, is there not one among you who is wise, who is able to discriminate one of his siblings from another?
⁶But is sibling judging sibling—and this before an anti-trusting person?

⁷Therefore, already there is total defeat for you because you have judgments with one another.

**Why not instead be wronged?
Why not instead be deprived?**

⁸But you are doing wrong and depriving, and this to siblings!

⁹Or, do you not know that the wrongdoers won't inherit God's Empire?

Don't be deceived! Neither the sexually immoral ones nor demon worshipers nor adulterers nor males being penetrated [by males] nor [males] penetrating males ¹⁰nor thieves nor the ones wanting more and more, not boozers, not snubbers, and not the rapacious will inherit God's Empire. ¹¹Some [of you] were these sorts, but you were washed, but you were made devoted, but you were righted in the name of the Lord Yēsous Christos and in our God's Spirit.

Item: Shadowboxing about sexual infidelity

¹²"All things are permissible for me," [you say].
But not all things benefit!
"All things are permissible for me."
But I will not be overpowered by someone!
¹³"Food for the belly and the belly for food" and "God will undo this and that."

But the body isn't [designed] for sexual immorality but for the Lord and the Lord for the body. ¹⁴God raised the Lord, and he will raise us up through his power.

**¹⁵Have you not known that your bodies are parts of Christos?
Therefore, lifting the body parts of Christos, will I make [them] parts of a prostitute?**

May that never happen!

¹⁶Or have you not known that the one uniting to a prostitute is one body?

(For *they will be*, it says, *the two into one flesh*.)
¹⁷But the one uniting with the Lord is one spirit.
¹⁸Flee sexual immorality! Every sin-act that a human does is outside the body. The one committing sexual immorality sins to one's own body.

¹⁹Or have you not known that your body is a sanctuary of the Holy Spirit-in-you, which you have from God, and you are not from yourselves?

²⁰For you were purchased at an honorable sum. Splendor God in your [plural] Body.

Item: Marriage, as well as status in society

7 Concerning items about which you wrote: "It's beautiful for a human not to touch a woman."

²But because of sexual immoralities, let each have his own woman and let each have her own man. ³Let the man pay the debt to the woman, and likewise also the woman [pay the debt] to the man. ⁴The woman doesn't authorize her own body but instead the man, and likewise also the man doesn't authorize his own body but instead the woman. ⁵Don't deprive one another [of sexual relations] except out of mutual agreement, for a season, to have leisure for prayer and then you may be at the same place again—so the Satanas [Satan] may not tempt you because of your absence of control. ⁶I say this consistent with concession, not consistent with an order. ⁷I want all humans to be as I am myself, but each has one's own grace-act from God—one so, another so.

⁸To the unmarried and widows, I say this: It's beautiful for them if they remain as I am. ⁹If they are not disciplined, let them marry, for it's better to marry than to be set on fire.

¹⁰To the ones who have been married, I order—not I but the Lord—a woman not to be separated from [her] man¹¹—now if she is separated, let her remain unmarried or be reconciled to [her] man—and a man isn't to release [his] woman.

¹²To the remaining, I say—not the Lord: If some sibling has an anti-trusting woman and she co-delights to reside with him, let him not release her. ¹³If some woman has an anti-trust man and he co-delights to reside with her, let her not release the man. ¹⁴For the anti-trust man has been devoted by the woman and the anti-trust woman has been devoted by the brother. (Since then your children are unclean but they are now devoted.) ¹⁵If the anti-trust one is separated, let the person separate. The brother or the sister isn't enslaved in such a case. God has called you in peace.

¹⁶**For what have you known, woman, if you will save the man?**
Or, what have you known, man, if you will save the woman?

Theory: What happens to one's status in Christ?

¹⁷Except let each so walk around as the Lord split us, as God has called each. I order thus in all the assemblies.

¹⁸**Was someone called being a circumcised person?**

Let him not be epispasm-ed.ᵃ

Has someone been called in foreskin?

Let him not be circumcised. ¹⁹Circumcision is nothing and foreskin is nothing, but instead [merely] keeping God's orders. ²⁰Let each—in the calling in which one was called—remain in that [calling]. ²¹You were called [as] a slave? Don't let it be a concern to you. But if also you are able to become liberated, rather use [the liberation]. ²²For the slave, being called by the Lord, is the Lord's liberated one; likewise, the liberated, being called, is Christos's slave. ²³You were purchased at an honorable price. Don't become slaves of humans! ²⁴Let each—in which one was called, siblings—remain in this with God.

Item: Virgins and the imminent trouble

²⁵Concerning virgins:
I don't have the Lord's order, so I give a conclusion—as one shown mercy by the Lord to be allegiant.
²⁶Therefore, I think this: It's beautiful—because of the present necessity . . . that it's beautiful for a human to be just so:

²⁷**Have you been bound to a woman?**

Don't pursue loosening.

Have you been released from a woman?

Don't pursue a woman.
²⁸Even if you married, you didn't sin. If the virgin married, she didn't sin. Such persons will have trouble in the flesh, and I am sparing you [that]. ²⁹I am saying this, siblings: the season is tightened. For what remains—so ones having women may be as ones not having [them], ³⁰and ones wailing as not wailing, and ones rejoicing as not rejoicing, and ones purchasing as not possessing, ³¹and ones using

---

ᵃ"Epispasm," derived from the Greek term *epispao*, denotes "pulling the foreskin foreword" and was done both by Jews seeking to hide their Jewishness and proselytes reversing their conversion.

the Kosmos as not fully using [it]. For this Kosmos's scheme is passing by.

³²I want you to be without disturbance.
The unmarried man is disturbed about the Lord's matters—how he might please the Lord.
³³The one married is disturbed about the Kosmos's matters—how he might please the woman—³⁴and he is split.
The unmarried woman and the virgin are disturbed about the Lord's matters so she may be devoted both in the body and in the spirit.
The one married is disturbed about the Kosmos's matters, how she might please the man.
³⁵I say this for your own benefit—not so I toss a rope on you but for an undistracted good scheme and good presence with Lord.
³⁶If someone thinks to disrespect his virgin, if he is beyond virility, and it ought to be, let him do what he wants, he isn't sinning, let them marry. ³⁷He who has stood stable in his heart, not having a necessity, and has authority over his own plan and has judged this in his own heart—to guard his virgin himself—he will do beautifully. ³⁸So that the one marrying his own virgin does beautifully, and the one not marrying will do better.
³⁹A woman is bound as long as her man lives. If the man "sleeps," she is liberated to whom she wants to be married—only in the Lord. ⁴⁰But she is more blessed by God if she remains so [as she was]—consistent with my conclusion. I seem also to have God's Spirit.

Item: Demon worship and food

8 Concerning things offered to demons: "We have known that we all have knowledge."
Knowledge enhances status. Love forms. ²If it looks like someone has known something, that person did not yet know as it's necessary to know. ³If someone loves God, that person has been known by him.
⁴Therefore, concerning food offered to demon-idols:
"We have known that a demon-idol isn't in Kosmos" and that "no one is God except one."
⁵For indeed since there are ones saying [there are] gods—whether in heaven or on the land—just as there are many gods and many lords, ⁶but for us—
[There is] one God, the Father,
From whom—all things,
And we—for him,
And one Lord, Yēsous Christos,
Through whom—all things
And we—through him.
⁷But the "knowledge" isn't in all. Some eat, in the demon-idol custom (until this moment), food as offered to demons, and their consciousness, "being weak," is stained.
⁸"Food will not present us to God."
"Neither if we don't eat, will we lack; nor if we eat, will we flow over."
⁹Now see that this authority of yours doesn't become a stumbling stone for the weak. ¹⁰For if someone sees you, who has "knowledge," reclining in a demon temple, will not the person's consciousness—being weak—be formed to eat food offered to demons? ¹¹For the weak is destroyed by your "knowledge," the sibling because of whom Christos died. ¹²Thus, sinning against the siblings and pounding their weak consciousness, you sin against Christos.
¹³Summarily: if food trips my sibling, I will never eat *treif* [unclean food] until the Era [to Come] so I may not trip my sibling.

Interrogating those who question Paulos's mission life

9 Am I not liberated?
Am I not a Commissioner?
Have I not seen Yēsous, our Lord?
Are you not my work in the Lord?

²If I am not a Commissioner to others, but at least I am to you. For you are my commissioning seal in the Lord. ³This is my defense for the ones examining me.

⁴**Don't we have authority to eat and drink?**

[No]

⁵**Don't we have authority to lead around a sibling woman [wife] as the remaining Commissioners, the Lord's [physical?] siblings, and Kēphas [Cephas] do?**

[No]

⁶**Or, is it I alone and Bar-Nabas [Barnabas]—that we don't have the authority not to work?**
⁷**Who soldiers one time, paying his own fee? Who plants a vineyard and doesn't eat its fruit?**

Or, who shepherds a flock and doesn't eat from the flock's milk?
⁸Do I speak these things in a human way?

[No]

Or, does the Covenant Code not also say these things?

[Yes]

(⁹For in Mōüsēs' [Moses'] Code of it's written, *You will not nosebag a threshing ox.*)

Can it be that God's care is for the oxen ¹⁰or is he speaking entirely because of us?

[No]

(For because of us it was written that *It's obligated for the one plowing to plow in hope and the one threshing to share in hope.*)

¹¹If we sowed Spirit-prompted matters for you, [is it] a great [matter] if we harvest your fleshly matters? ¹²If others share your authority, do we not even more?

[Yes]

But we did not use this authority, but we endure all things so we might not give someone an obstacle to the Christos's gospel.

¹³Have you not known that the temple workers eat things from the temple, [that] ones assisting at the sacrificial altar share in the altar's sacrifices?

¹⁴So also the Lord ordered the ones proclaiming the gospel to live from the gospel.
¹⁵I have not used any of these matters. I did not write these things so that it might thus be [the case] for me. For it's beautiful for me rather to die than . . . no one will hollow out my boast! ¹⁶For if I am gospeling, a boast is not for me. For it's a necessity laid on me. For Oy! on me if I don't gospel. ¹⁷For if I on my own practice this, I have a wage; if I not on my own [practice this], I'm trusted with a management. ¹⁸Therefore, what is my wage? That, gospeling, I might place the gospel without a fee so not to utilize my authority in the gospel.

The principle of Paulos's mission life

¹⁹For being liberated from all I enslaved myself to all so I may have an advantage with even more. ²⁰I became to Youdaians [Judeans, Jews] as a Youdaian so I might have an advantage with Youdaians. To those under the Covenant Code, as one under Code—not being myself under Code—so I might have an advantage with those under Code. ²¹To the non-covenanted [to the Code], as one non-covenanted—not being God's non-covenanted but Christos's "non-covenanted" that I might gain the non-covenanted. ²²I became a weak to the weak so I might have an advantage with the weak. I have become all things to all [humans] so I might in all ways deliver some. ²³I do all things because of the gospel so I might have its common life.

²⁴Have you not known that the ones running in a stadium all run, but one takes the prize?

Run in such a way that you prevail! ²⁵Every contesting person controls oneself in all matters—they, therefore, so they might take a perishable crown but, we, an imperishable. ²⁶I then run in such a way as [one] not confused, I punch in such a way as one not beating air. ²⁷Instead, I pound my body and enslave [it], so that, announcing to others, I myself might not be judged unsuitable.

Learning allegiant worship from Israel's story

10 For I don't want you to be uninformed, siblings, that:

All our fathers were under the cloud,
All crossed through the sea,
²All were dipped into Mōüsēs [Moses]
 in the cloud and the sea.
³All ate the same Spirit-prompted food
⁴All drank the same Spirit-prompted
 drink.
(For they were drinking from the
 Spirit-prompted rock following
 [them]. The rock was Christos.)

⁵But God was not delighted with most of them, for they were scattered out in the wilderness. ⁶These have become types for us so we are not desirers of bad, as they desired.
⁷Don't become demon worshipers as some of them, just as it's written, *The people sat to eat and drink and they rose up to play.* ⁸Let us not engage in sexual immorality, as some of them committed sexual immorality and twenty-three thousand fell on one day. ⁹Let us not test out the Christos as some of them tested and were

destroyed by snakes. ¹⁰Don't grumble, as some of them grumbled and were destroyed by the destroyer. ¹¹These were coalescing for them as types; it was written to mentor us—for whom the Ends of the Eras have arrived. ¹²So, the one who looks to be standing—let the person watch so as not to fall. ¹³Testing has not come to you except as is human-like. God is allegiant, who will not allow you to be tested above what you are able but with the test will also make an outcome: to enable [you] to carry on.

¹⁴Summarily, my loved ones, flee demon worship! ¹⁵I say as to the prudent: you judge what I am saying. ¹⁶The blessing cup that we bless—

is it not common life with Christos's blood?

[Yes] The bread that we crack—

is it not common life with Christos's body?

[Yes] ¹⁷Because there is one bread, we (the many) are one body, for we (the all) share from the one bread. ¹⁸Look at Yisraēl [Israel] consistent with flesh:

Are not the ones eating the sacrifice sharing a common life with the sacrificial altar?

[Yes]

¹⁹Therefore, what am I saying? That demon offering is something, or that a demon-idol is something?

²⁰But that what they sacrifice, they sacrifice to demons and not to God. I don't want you to become common lifers with demons. ²¹You aren't able to drink the Lord's cup and demons' cup; you aren't able share the Lord's table and demons' table.

²²Or, are we provoking the Lord to zeal? Are we stronger than he?

[No]

> ²³"All things are observant."
> But not all benefit!
> "All things are observant."
> But not all from [us]!

²⁴Let no one pursue what is of oneself but what is of the other. ²⁵Eat everything that is sold in the market, not examining because of the consciousness ²⁶*for the land and its fullness are of the Lord.* ²⁷If someone of the anti-trust calls you and you want to journey, eat everything presented before you, not examining because of the consciousness. ²⁸If someone says to you, "This is temple-sacrificed," don't eat because of that divulging person and [because of] the consciousness. ²⁹I say "consciousness"—not my own but that of the other. For why is my liberation judged by another's consciousness? ³⁰If I share in grace, why am I insulted for what I give thanks?

³¹Therefore, whether you eat or drink or do something, do everything for God's splendor. ³²Be not accused by Youdaians [Judeans, Jews] and Hellēnes [Greeks] and God's assembly, ³³just as I please all in all ways, not pursuing my own benefits but what [benefits] the many, so they may be delivered.

11

Become copies of me just as I am of Christos.

Item: Back-and-forth about women worshiping

²I praise you that you have remembered me in everything and, just as I gave over to you, you possess the conventions.ᵇ

³[Paulos:] I want you to know that:
The head of every man is Christos,
The head of a woman is the man,
The head of Christos is God.

⁴[Male opponents:] "Every man praying or prophesying, having [a veil] over the head, degrades his head.

⁵Every woman praying or prophesying with an unveiled head degrades her head.
For it's one and the same with being shaved."

⁶[Paulos:] For if a woman isn't veiled, let her [hair] also be clipped.
If it's degrading for a woman to be clipped or shaved, let her be veiled.

⁷[Male opponents:] "For a man ought not have a head veiled—being God's image and splendor.
The woman is the man's splendor.

ᵇThe text of 1 Corinthians 11:2-16 is notoriously complicated to sort out what Paulos is saying, and some statements are in deep tensions with others. Verses 11-12 are in tension with what is said in verses 8-10, where the opposite seems to be stated. One reading, represented here, is to see Paulos quoting male proponents at Korinthos [Corinth] and responding.

⁸For a man isn't from a woman but a woman from a man. ⁹For man was not created because of the woman but a woman because of the man. ¹⁰Because this is true: a woman ought to have authority on the head because of the envoys."

¹¹[Paulos:] However: neither a woman is without a man nor a man without a woman in Lord. ¹²For just as the woman is from the man, so also the man is through the woman. All things are from God. ¹³Judge among yourselves:

Is it appropriate for a woman to pray unveiled to God?
¹⁴[Male opponents:] **"But doesn't nature itself teach you that a man, if he long-hairs it, is a dishonor to himself?"**
¹⁵[Paulos:] **But [if] a woman long-hairs it, is it a splendor for her?**

Because her long hair is given to her instead of a covering.
¹⁶If someone looks to be argumentative, we don't have any such custom [about this], and neither do God's assemblies.

Item: Status-mongering when assembling

¹⁷Ordering this, I'm not praising because you assemble not for the better but for the worse. ¹⁸For first . . . you're assembling in an assembly . . . I hear rips exist among you and in part I believe it. ¹⁹For it's even necessary that factions are among you so the ones tested may become apparent among you.

²⁰Therefore . . . you're assembling at the same place . . . it isn't to eat a Lord-type banquet ²¹for, in the eating, each takes one's own supper early, and one hungers and one boozes.

²²**For do you not have houses for eating and drinking?**
Or, do you snub God's assembly?
Do you degrade those who don't have?
What do I say to you?
Am I to praise you?

In this, I am not praising.

²³For I received from the Lord what I give over to you, that:
The Lord Yēsous, on the night in which he was given over, took bread ²⁴and, thanking [God], cracked [it] and said, "This is my body which is for you. Do this to remember me." ²⁵Similarly also the cup, after the dining, saying, "This cup is the new covenant in my blood. Do this, whenever you drink, to remember me." ²⁶For whenever you eat this bread and drink this cup, you proclaim the Lord's death—until he comes.

²⁷So that: whoever eats the bread or drinks the Lord's cup undeservingly, will be guilty for the Lord's body and blood. ²⁸Let a human judge oneself suitable and so let the person eat from the bread and drink from the cup. ²⁹For the one eating and the one drinking eats and drinks judgment for oneself, not discriminating the body [of Christ?]. ³⁰Because this is true, many among you are weak and ill, and [an] adequate [number] are "sleeping." ³¹If we discriminate among ourselves, then we wouldn't be judged. ³²In being judged by the Lord, we are disciplined so we will not be condemned with the Kosmos.

³³So that: my siblings, in assembling to eat, wait for one another. ³⁴If someone hungers, let the person eat in house so you don't assemble for judgment.

About the remaining matters, I will provide orders whenever I might come.

Item: Worship wars about Spirit-prompted graces

12 Concerning Spirit-(gifted)-persons, siblings:

I don't want you to be uninformed. ²You have known that when you were (classed as) ethnic groups, being led away toward voiceless demon-idols—whenever you were being led. ³Therefore, I make known to you that no one speaking in God's Spirit says, "Yēsous is vowed-to-destruction!" No one is able to say

> "Yēsous is Lord!" unless in Holy Spirit.
> ⁴There are distributions of grace-acts
>   [Spirit-prompted gifts] but the
>   same Spirit.
> ⁵And distributions of services, but the
>   same Lord.
> ⁶And distributions of energies, but the
>   same God, who energizes all
>   things in all ways.

⁷The Spirit-manifestation is given to each for the common benefit.

⁸For to one a word of wisdom is given
through the Spirit,
to another a word of knowledge
consistent with the same Spirit,
⁹to another faith by the same Spirit,
to another grace-acts of curing by the
one Spirit,
¹⁰to another energies of power,
to another prophecy,
to another distinguishing spirits,
to another kinds of tongues,
to another interpretation of tongues.

¹¹All of these are energized by the one and same Spirit, assigning to each individually as [the Spirit] decides. ¹²For just as there is one body and has many parts, all the body's parts, being many, there is one body—so also Christos. ¹³For also in one Spirit we were all dipped into one body—whether Youdaians [Judeans, Jews] or Hellēnes [Greeks] or slaves or liberated—and all drank one Spirit. ¹⁴For also the body isn't one part but many.

¹⁵If the foot were to say, "Because I am not a hand, I am not of the body," is it really [the case] that it is not-of-the-body? ¹⁶If the ear were to say, "Because I am not an eye, I am not of the body," is it really [the case] that it is not-of-the-body? ¹⁷If the whole body is an eye, where is the hearing? If the whole [is] hearing, where is the smelling?

¹⁸But now God has placed the parts, each one of them in the body as God wants.

¹⁹If the all [parts] were one part, where is the body?

²⁰Now [there are] many parts but one body.

²¹The eye isn't able to say to the hand, "I don't have a need of you," or again the head—to the feet, "I don't have a need for you." ²²Instead, all the more: the parts of the body that look to be weaker are necessary, ²³and [parts] of the body we look on as dishonorable, these are draped with abounding honor, and our unpresentables have all the more good presentation—²⁴our presentables don't have a need [for presentation].

But God blended the body, giving excessive honor to the lacking [parts] ²⁵so there may not be rips in the body but the parts are "disturbed" the same about one another. ²⁶When one part suffers, all parts co-suffer; when one part is splendored, all parts co-rejoice.

²⁷You are Christos's body, and each playing its part. ²⁸The ones whom God located in the assembly are:

first, commissioners,
second, prophets,
third, teachers;
then powers,
then grace-acts of cures,
aids,
administrations,
kinds of tongues.

²⁹All are not apostles, are they?

[No]

All are not prophets, are they?

[No]

All are not teachers, are they?

[No]

All are not powers, are they?

[No]

³⁰All don't have grace-acts of cures, do they?

[No]

All don't speak in tongues, do they?

[No]

All don't interpret, do they?

[No]

³¹Be zealous for the greater grace-acts and, yet, I exhibit to you a superior path.

Love is the superior path

13 If I speak in human tongues and of envoys but I don't have love, I have become noisy bronze or an off-beat cymbal. ²If I have prophecy and I see all secrets and all knowledge, and if I have all trust so to remove mountains, and I don't have love, I am nothing. ³And if I gave away all my possessions as food and if I gave over my body so I may be burned but I don't have love, I gain nothing.

⁴Love patiences, love graces,
doesn't zeal, doesn't parade oneself
around, doesn't appeal to status, ⁵doesn't
devalue, doesn't pursue self-matters,
doesn't provoke, doesn't calculate the

bad, ⁶and doesn't rejoice over wrongdoing but co-rejoices in truth. ⁷[Love] resists all, trusts all, hopes all, is resilient in all.
⁸Love never falls.
If there are prophecies, they will be undone.
If there are tongues, they will cease.
If there is knowledge, it will be undone.
⁹For we know in part and prophesy in part, ¹⁰but when the completion comes, the in part will be undone.
¹¹When I was an infant, I was speaking as an infant,
I was prudent as an infant,
I was calculating as an infant.
When I became a man, I became undone with infant-matters.

¹²For we now see through a mirror, in an enigma, but then face to face. Now I know in part, but then I will perceive as I am perceived. ¹³Now allegiance, hope, love remain—these three—the greatest of these is love.

Spirit-prompted gifts, some more on worship wars

14 Chase love, be zealous for the Spirit-prompted gifts, but especially that you may prophesy.
²For the one speaking in tongues doesn't speak to humans but to God, for no one hears; the person is speaking secrets in spirit.
³The one prophesying speaks formation and encouragement and what soothes to humans.
⁴The one speaking in tongues forms oneself.
The one prophesying forms an assembly.
⁵I want all of you to speak in tongues, but more that you may prophesy. The one prophesying is greater than the one speaking in tongues—except when it's interpreted, so the assembly may receive formation.
⁶Now, siblings, if I come to you speaking in tongues, how do I gain for you unless I speak to you in an apocalypse or in a tongue or in a prophecy or in a teaching? ⁷Similar to lifeless [instruments] that give a sound—whether an aulos [reed instrument] or cithara [string instrument]—if they don't give a distinct tone, how is the aulist or the citharist to be known?

⁸**For if the trumpet gives an indistinct sound, how is one prepared for war?** ⁹**So also you: if you don't give a distinct word through the tongue, how can what is spoken be known?**

(For you will be speaking into air.) ¹⁰There are, perhaps, kinds of sounds in the Kosmos, but none is soundless. ¹¹Therefore, if I don't know the sound's power, I will be to the one speaking a barbarian and the one speaking a barbarian to me. ¹²So also you, since you are zealous for the Spirit-prompted, pursue that you may flow over for the the assembly's formation.
¹³Therefore, let one speaking in tongues pray that it may be interpreted. ¹⁴For if I pray in a tongue, my spirit prays but my mind is fruitless.

¹⁵**Therefore, which is it?**

I will pray in the Spirit, and also pray in mind. I will play the strings in the Spirit, and I will also play the strings in the mind. ¹⁶Since if you bless in spirit, the one-filling-the-place-of-the-novice—how does that person say "Amen!" to your thanks? (Since the person doesn't know what you are saying.) ¹⁷For you are thanking [God] beautifully, but the other isn't formed. ¹⁸I thank God [that] I speak in tongues more than all of you. ¹⁹But in assembly I want to speak five words with my mind so I also catechize others, than [to speak] innumerable words in a tongue.

²⁰Siblings, don't be children in comprehension but be an infant in what is bad. Be complete in comprehension.

²¹[Opponents:] In the Covenant Code it's written that,
I will speak to this people in other-tongues and with the lips of others,
And, they will not thus *listen to me,* says the Lord.
²²So that: Tongues are a sign, not for the allegiant but for the anti-trusters, and prophecy—not for the anti-trusters but for the allegiant.

²³[Paulos] Therefore, if the whole assembly assembles in the same place and all speak in tongues, and the novices or anti-trusters enter, will they not say that you are frenzied? ²⁴If all prophesy, and if some anti-truster or novice enters, the person is convinced by all, is

examined by all, ²⁵the secrets of the person's heart become apparent and thus, falling down on the face, bows down to God, declaring that *God really is among you.*

²⁶Therefore, which is it, siblings?

When you assemble, each has a string-accompanied song, has a teaching, has an apocalypse, has a tongue, has an interpretation. Let all matters be for formation. ²⁷If someone speaks in a tongue, let two or at most three speak in turn and let one interpret. ²⁸If there isn't an interpreter, let the person be silent in assembly; let the person speak to oneself and to God. ²⁹Let the prophets—two or three—speak and let others discriminate. ³⁰If one "apocalypses" to a seated person, let the first one be silent. ³¹For you are all by person able to prophesy—so all may be apprenticed and all be encouraged. ³²Spirits of prophets are to be ordered under the prophets. ³³For [he is the] God, not of anarchy, but of peace, as in all the devoted ones' assemblies.ᶜ

³⁶Or, does God's word exit from you?
Or, to you alone does it arrive?

³⁷⁻³⁸If someone looks to be like a prophet or Spirit-person, let the person perceive what matters I write to you: that it's the Lord's order. If someone ignores, [the person] is to be ignored. ³⁹So that, my siblings: Be zealous to prophesy and to speak, and don't hinder tongues. ⁴⁰Let all things be done respectably and consistent with order.

Item: Gospel resurrection (1)

15 I make known to you, siblings, the gospel that I gospeled to you, which you also received, in which you also stand, ²through which you also are delivered, (For what reason did I gospel you?)— if you possess [it], unless you trusted in a hollow manner. ³For I have given over to you in first matters what I also received, that: Christos died for our sins consistent with the writings, ⁴and that he was buried and that he was raised on the third day consistent with the writings, ⁵and that he appeared to Kēphas [Cephas], then to the Twelve. ⁶Then he appeared to more than five hundred siblings at once, among whom the majority remain until now but some have fallen "asleep." ⁷Then he appeared to Yakōbos [James], then to all the Commissioners. ⁸Last of all, he appeared also to me—as in some kind of "traumatic birth."ᵈ

(⁹For I am the least of the Commissioners, [I am one] who is inadequate to be called "Commissioner" because I chased God's assembly. ¹⁰I am what I am by God's grace, and his grace-to-me did not become hollow, but I labored excessively beyond all of them—not I but God's grace-with-me. ¹¹Therefore, whether it's I or they, we thus announce and thus you trusted.)

Resurrection Q&A

¹²If Christos is announced, that he has been raised from among the dead ones, how do they say among you that "There isn't a resurrection [from among the] dead ones"?

¹³If there isn't a resurrection from among the dead ones, neither has Christos been raised.

ᶜSome manuscripts don't contain verses 34-35, and we think they were not written by Paulos. If they were, perhaps they are quoting the male opponents of Paulos at Corinth, and thus verses 33-38 could be translated as follows:
   ³³For [he is the] God, not of anarchy, but of peace.
   [Male opponents:] "As in all the devoted ones' assemblies, ³⁴let the women in the assemblies be silent. For it's not permitted for them to speak but let them be ordered under—just as the Covenant Code says. ³⁵If she wants to learn, let them question their own man at home. For It's degrading for a woman to speak in assembly."
   ³⁶Or, does God's word exit from you? Or, to you alone does it arrive?
   ³⁷If someone looks to be like a prophet or Spirit-person, let the person perceive what matters I write to you: that it's Lord's order. ³⁸If someone ignores [v. 37], [the person] is to be ignored.
ᵈIt's likely Paulos is here using terms of his critics in Corinth.

¹⁴If Christos has not been raised, our announcement is then hollow and your allegiance is hollow. ¹⁵We are found [to be] God's false witnesses because we witnessed—against God!—that he raised the Christos, who did not arise if then dead ones are not raised. ¹⁶For if dead ones are not raised, neither has Christos been raised. ¹⁷If Christos has not been raised, your allegiance is useless, you are still in your sins, ¹⁸and then the ones "sleeping" in Christos are destroyed. ¹⁹If in this life we have hoped only in Christos, we are the most to be pitied of all humans.

Gospel resurrection (2)

²⁰Now, Christos has been raised from among the dead ones, the firstfruit of those who have been "asleep." ²¹For since death is through a human so also resurrection from among the dead ones is through a human. ²²For as in Adam all die, so also in the Christos all will have a life remade. ²³Each in one's own order:

Christos the firstfruit;
then those of the Christos at his Parousia [coming];

²⁴then the completion, whenever he may give over the Empire to God and Father, whenever all [corrupted] celestial leadership and all authority and power may be undone. ²⁵For it's necessary for him to rule until *he places* all *the enemies under his feet.* ²⁶Death—last enemy—is undone. ²⁷For *he ordered all things under his feet.* Whenever he says that "all things are ordered under," it's clear that this excludes the one ordering all things under. ²⁸Whenever all things are ordered under him, then also the Son himself will be ordered under the one who ordered all things under him, so God may be the all in all.

Questions about gospel resurrection

²⁹Since what will the dippers-for-the-dead do?
If the dead are totally not raised, why also are they dipped for them?
³⁰Why also are we endangered every hour?

³¹I die daily. Indeed, [I swear by my] boast about you, siblings, that I have in Christos Yēsous [Jesus], our Lord.

³²If consistent with a human I warred with wild things in Ephesos [Ephesus], what benefit is it to me?

If the dead are not raised, *Let us eat and drink, for tomorrow we die.* ³³Don't be deceived! "Bad gangs abominate gracious habits." ³⁴Sober up rightly and don't sin, for some have God-ignorance. I speak [this] to your embarrassment.

³⁵But someone will say, "How are the dead ones raised?
With kind of body do they come?"

³⁶Imprudent one! What you plant isn't made alive unless it dies. ³⁷And what you plant . . . you don't plant the body of what is to be but naked grain—perhaps wheat or some remaining [produce]. ³⁸God gives it a body just as he wanted, and to each of the seeds its own body. ³⁹Not all flesh is the same flesh but one flesh for humans, another flesh for animals, another flesh for the birds, and another for fishes. ⁴⁰Heavenly bodies, earthy bodies, or instead, one splendor of the heavenlies, another splendor of the earthies. ⁴¹One splendor for sun, and another splendor for moon, and another splendor for stars, for one star is superior in splendor to [another] star.

Gospel resurrection (3)

⁴²Thus, also [is] the resurrection from among the dead ones:

It's planted in decay, it's raised non-decayable;
⁴³It's planted without honor, it's raised in splendor;
It's planted in weakness, it's raised in power;
⁴⁴It's planted a selfish body, it's raised a Spirit-prompted [*pneumatikon*] body.

If there is a selfish [*psychikon*] body, there is also a Spirit-prompted [*pneumatikon*]. ⁴⁵Thus also it's written,

> *The* first *human*, Adam, *a living self*, the last Adam a life-making Spirit.

⁴⁶But the first—not the Spirit-prompted [*pneumatikon*] but the selfish [*psychikon*], then the Spirit-prompted [*pneumatikon*]. ⁴⁷The first human—of earth; the second human—of heaven. ⁴⁸As the earthy one—[so] those earthy ones;

As the Heavenly One—so those heavenly ones.

⁴⁹Just as we carried the earthy one's image, so we will carry the Heavenly One's.

⁵⁰I say this, siblings, that flesh-and-blood isn't able to inherit God's Empire, nor does the decay inherit the non-decayable. ⁵¹Look! I speak a secret to you: We will not all be put to "sleep," but we will all be changed. ⁵²In an instant, in a blink of an eye, in the last trumpet. For he will trumpet and the dead ones will be raised non-decayable and we will be changed. ⁵³For it's necessary for this decayable to put on non-decayable and this mortality to put on immortality. ⁵⁴Whenever this decayable puts on non-decayable and this mortality [puts on] immortality, then the written word will happen,

> Death has been guzzled in victory.
> ⁵⁵Where, Death, is your victory?
> Where, Death, is your sting?

⁵⁶Death's sting is sin, the Covenant Code is sin's power. ⁵⁷Grace to God, who gives to us of the victory through our Lord Yēsous Christos.

⁵⁸So that my loved siblings: Be stable, unmoved, always flowing over in the Lord's work, knowing that your labor isn't hollow in the Lord.

Item: Funds for the devoted ones

16
Concerning the collection for the devoted ones:

Just as I ordered the assemblies in Galatia, so also you should do. ²Consistent with the first [day] of the Sabbath [week], let each of you place to one's side, treasuring up whatever profit has made a good path to you, so whenever I come there may not then be collections. ³Whenever I arrive, I will send those judged suitable through letters to carry your grace to Yierousalēm [Jerusalem]. ⁴If it seems deserving for me also to journey, they will journey with me.

Plans of Paulos

⁵I will come to you whenever I cross through Makedonia [Macedonia], for I am crossing through Makedonia, ⁶perhaps I will remain with you or even spend the winter, so you can send me ahead where I may journey. ⁷For I don't want now to see you in passing, for I hope to remain for some time with you if the Lord permits. ⁸I will remain in Ephesos [Ephesus] until Pentēkostē [Pentecost], ⁹for a great and energizing door has opened for me—and [there are] many opposers.

¹⁰If Timotheos [Timothy] comes, see that he is fearless with you, for he is working the Lord's work as I am. ¹¹Therefore, don't let someone devalue him. Send him ahead in peace, so he may come to me. For I welcome him with the siblings.

¹²Concerning Apollōs, the sibling: I begged him many times to come to you with the siblings, and he was always not wanting to come now. He will come whenever the time is good.

¹³Be awake!
Stand in allegiance!
Be manly [brave]!
Be strong!
¹⁴Let all things be [done] in love!

¹⁵I beg you, siblings: You have known Stephanas's household, that it's Achaia's firstfruit and they ordered themselves in the service to the devoted ones, ¹⁶so you also order yourselves under such persons and under all coworkers and laborers. ¹⁷I rejoice at the arrival of Stephanas and Phortounatos [Fortunatus] and Achaïkos [Achaicus], that these filled up your lack. ¹⁸For they rested my spirit and yours. Therefore, recognize such persons.

¹⁹The Asian assemblies greet you.

Akulas [Aquila] and Priska [Priscilla] greet you many times in the Lord with the assembly in their home.

²⁰All the siblings greet you.

Greet one another with a devoted kiss.

²¹The greeting is in my hand—Paulos [Paul].

²²If someone doesn't love the Lord, let him be vowed-to-destruction!

Marana tha! [Our Lord, come!]

²³The Lord Yēsous' grace be with you!

²⁴My love be with all of you in Christos Yēsous!

INTRODUCTION TO THE SECOND LETTER TO CORINTH

Someone, or make that a number of someones, spoiled the church at Korinthos's [Corinth's] confidence in Commissioner Paulos [Paul]. He spent the better part of a decade in back and forths with a disgruntled, denouncing, and disaffected set of house churches. Their issues with Paulos, which can be heard behind the lines and between the words of nearly every verse in this letter, concerned his disapproval of their desire for status, their criticism of his (non)eloquence, and their feeling shamed by his peculiar refusal to accept funds from them. He won't accept pay for his ministry, his practice seems to indicate, until they grow up to his satisfaction. When this refusal is combined with his pleading with them to give him money for the begging Youdaian [Judean, Jewish] believers in Yierousalēm [Jerusalem], they were thoroughly confused by what he was teaching about giving. He, on the other hand, believed he got it right. They expected a man of his status to boast in his status-shaping accomplishments: he refused to boast like that but turned the tables and boasted in what was for them all the wrong "accomplishments" in suffering. Back and forth, accusation and defense. Welcome to his second letter to the churches in Korinthos.

This second letter is but one of several letters Paulos wrote to them. It takes some imagination and effort to put together the scattered comments, but this seems reasonable: Letter A is mentioned in 1 Corinthians 5:9-13, and it has to do with how the believers were to associate or not with nonbelievers in Corinth. A prompts a response in Letter B, which is mentioned in 1 Corinthians 1:11; 5:1; 16:15-17. Letter C is our 1 Corinthians and is a response to both Letter B (and probably A). Paulos then makes plans to visit Korinthos (1 Cor 16:5-8, 10-11; Acts 19:22), but first Timotheos [Timothy] visits and reports back to Paulos, which leads to what is called Paulos's "painful visit" (2 Cor 2:1, 5-8; 7:8-13; 11:4). Evidently at this time opposition to Paulos arose in Korinthos, and we read between the lines about this in 2 Corinthians 10-13. Paulos returns to Ephesus and, out of his own pastoral anxiety, sends Titus with Letter D, the tearful letter (2 Cor 2:3-9; 7:8-12; 8:6). His anxiety over the response in Korinthos (2 Cor 2:12-13) leads him to searching for good news from Titus upon his return, which good news is found 2 Corinthians 7:6-13. During this time Paulos has been pleading for money for the saints, the so-called collection (seen in 2 Cor 8-9). He plans to visit again (2 Cor 2:3; 9:5; 12:20-13:1) and sends Letter E (our 2 Corinthians).

There are in 2 Corinthians (Letter E) three major parts: chapters 1-7, 8-9, and 10-13. Add some introduction and a conclusion, and we have the letter. One can read 2 Corinthians as a single letter drafted over months with long gaps between sections or as a stitching together of two or three or more separate letters. The first section extends from chapter 1 through chapter 7, but it has separable units (1:1-2:13 and 7:5-6, and 2:14-6:13 and 6:14-7:1). The second is about the collection, found in chapters 8-9, while the third is found in chapters 10-13.

No letter is more revealing of Paulos's heart, his passion, his vulnerabilities, his irritableness, his loves, and his frustrations. His prose is choppy at times—he's quoting his Corinthian critics and responding, and it's not always easy to know when he's quoting and when he's responding. I put in quotations those words I think are reasonably clearly coming from his critics. There are many more examples, but we'll have to live with suspicions as we watch Paulos defend the gospel and himself and criticize his critics all in the same breath. This, then, is *the* pastoral letter of the Second Testament, far eclipsing the letters gathered in that name (1-2 Timothy, Titus). In this letter we hear Paulos describe gospel ministry and gospel agents and we watch him act pastorally with his troubled house churches sitting comfortably and proudly at the isthmus that could carry people and products by boat toward the capitol of the empire or back east on the Mediterranean.

THE SECOND LETTER TO CORINTH

From Paulos to Korinthos

1 Paulos [Paul], Commissioner of Christos Yēsous through God's will, and Timotheos [Timothy], the sibling.

To God's assembly that is in Korinthos [Corinth], with all the devoted ones who are in the whole of Asia.

²Grace to you and peace from our Father-God and [from our] Lord Yēsous Christos.

Paulos thanks God for the Korinthioi

³Blessed is God and Father of our Lord Yēsous Christos, the Father of sympathies and God of all encouragement, ⁴the one encouraging us in all our trouble so we might be able to encourage the ones in all trouble through the encouragement, in which we ourselves are encouraged by God. ⁵Because, just as Christos's sufferings flow over for us, so through Christos our encouragement flourishes. ⁶If then we are troubled—for your encouragement and deliverance; if we are encouraged—for your encouragement from what is working in resilience of the very sufferings that we also are suffering. ⁷Our hope is firm for you, knowing that as you have common life with of [our] sufferings, so also of [our] encouragement.

⁸For we don't want you to be uninformed, siblings, about our trouble that happened in Asia, because we were depressed—excessively, beyond ability—so that we despaired even of living. ⁹But we ourselves had among ourselves the death sentence so we might not be persuaded in ourselves but in God, the one who raises the dead ones, ¹⁰who rescued and will rescue us out of such great deaths, in whom we have hoped that he will also still rescue. ¹¹. . . Your co-operating in [prayer] request for us . . . so, from many faces the grace-act-to-us may be thanked for us by many.

Travel plans of Paulos (1)

¹²For this is our boast, our consciousness's witness: that we were behaving in the Kosmos (aboundingly so toward you) with God's generosity and transparency, and not with fleshy wisdom but with God's grace. ¹³For I am not writing other matters to you other than what you read or even perceive. I hope that you will perceive in completion ¹⁴just as you also perceived us in part, because we are your boast just as also you are ours on the Day of our Lord Yēsous.

¹⁵In this persuasion, I was deciding to come to you first so you might have double grace ¹⁶and through you to cross through into Makedonia [Macedonia], and again from Makedonia to come to you and to be sent ahead by you into Youdaia [Judea].

¹⁷**Therefore, deciding this, was I then "making light" [the decision]?**
Or, am I deciding what-I-am-deciding consistent with Flesh?
So with me it might be the "Yes-Yes and the No-No"?

¹⁸God is allegiant because our word, the one to you, isn't "Yes-and-No." ¹⁹For God's Son, Yēsous Christos, who was announced among you through us—through me and Silouanos [Silvanus] and Timotheos—did not become Yes-and-No but has become Yes-in-him! ²⁰For as many as [there are] God's pledges, in him [they are] the Yes! Thus also, through him the Amēn! [is said] to God for splendor through us.

> ²¹The one who firms us up with you in Christos
> and christened us,
> is God,
> ²²who also is the one who sealed us
> and the one who gave the Spirit-pledge
> in our hearts.

²³I call on God as witness about my self, that sparing you I have not yet come to Korinthos. ²⁴Not that we lord over your allegiance, but we are coworkers for your joy, for you have stood in allegiance.

2 For I judged this myself: not to come to you again in pain. ²For if I pained you, who is the one making me glad? Only the one pained by me? ³I wrote this very matter so, coming, I might not have pain from those who ought to bring me joy, fully persuaded about all of you that my joy is all of yours. ⁴For out of much trouble and heart-anguish I wrote through many tears, not so you may be pained but so you may know the love that I have aboundingly for you.

Releasing offenders from their failures

⁵If someone was pained, the person has not pained me but in part—so that I do not overload (this point)—[he has pained] all of you. ⁶This "dishonoring," which is by the many, is adequate for this person, ⁷so that, on the contrary, you are rather to be gracious and to encourage, so somehow such a person not be guzzled with abounding pain. ⁸Thus, I beg you to ratify love for the person. ⁹For I wrote also for this, so I may know your approval—if you are obedient in all matters. ¹⁰To whomever you show grace, I too. For what I have shown grace—if I have shown grace about something—[is] because of you in Christos's face, ¹¹so we may not be outwitted by the Satanas [Satan]. For we are not uninformed about his mentalities.

Travel plans of Paulos (2)

¹²Coming into Trōas for the Christos-gospel and having a door opened for me in Lord, ¹³I did not have leisure in my spirit in not finding Titos [Titus], my sibling, but, saying farewell to them, I exited to Makedonia [Macedonia].

¹⁴But grace to God, the one always parading us in the Christos and [always] through us manifesting the fragrance of knowing him in every place. ¹⁵Because we are Christos's good aroma to God among ones being delivered and among ones being destroyed. ¹⁶To some, the fragrance of Death to Death, to some the fragrance of Life to Life. Who is adequate to these things? ¹⁷For we are not like the many hucksters of God's word but we speak as from transparency, as from God in front of God in Christos.

Covenant gospel agents (1)

3 Are we beginning to "affirm ourselves again"?
Or, do we require—as some [do]—"Affirmation Letters" to you or from you?

²You are our letter, having been written in our hearts, having been known and read by all humans, ³manifesting that you are Christos's letter, served by us, having been written not with black ink but with God's living Spirit, not on stone tablets but on fleshy, heart tablets.

⁴We have such a persuasion with God through Christos. ⁵We are not adequate from ourselves to calculate something as from ourselves, but our adequacy is from God, ⁶who made us adequate as the new covenant's servants, not of letter but of Spirit—for the letter kills, the Spirit makes life.

> ⁷*If* the Death-service, in letters, having been etched on stones, came in splendor—so that Yisraēl's descendants were unable to gaze into Mōūsēs' [Moses'] face because of his face's splendor—which is [now] undone—⁸how much more won't the Spirit's service be in splendor!
> ⁹For *if* a splendor was in a condemning service, how much more does the rightness service flow over! ¹⁰For what had been splendored hasn't been splendored in this case because of the excessive splendor.
> ¹¹For *if* the undone [came] through splendor, how much more [does] the remaining [come] in splendor!

¹²Therefore, having such hope, we use much frankness, ¹³and not as Mōūsēs—he was placing a veil over his face so Yisraēl's descendants did not gaze at the completion of what is being undone. ¹⁴But their mentalities were petrified. For up to today the same veil remains at the reading of the ancient covenant, [the veil] has not been unveiled because it's undone in Christos. ¹⁵But until today whenever Mōūsēs is read, a veil is laid on their heart, ¹⁶but *whenever a person returns to Lord, the veil is lifted away.* ¹⁷The Lord is the Spirit. Where the Lord's Spirit [is, there is] liberation. ¹⁸We all, having an unveiled face, reflecting the Lord's splendor, are metamorphosed into the same image—from [one] splendor to [another] splendor—just as [we are] from the Lord, who is the Spirit.

Covenant gospel agents (2)

4 Because this is true, having this service, just as we were shown compassion, we don't become negligent ²but we repudiate shameful, hidden matters, not walking around in trickery nor disguising God's word but, in manifesting truth, affirming ourselves to every human consciousness before God. ³If indeed our gospel is covered, it's covered for those being destroyed, ⁴among whom this Era's god blinded the anti-trusting ones' mentalities so not to illuminate [for them] the Christos's splendored-gospel-light, who is God's image. ⁵For we don't announce ourselves but "Yēsous Christos [is] Lord," and ourselves [as] your slaves because of Yēsous, ⁶because [it's] the God who said "Light shines out of darkness" who shone in our hearts to illuminate [us] to know God's splendor in the face of Yēsous Christos.

⁷We have this treasure chest in terracotta vessels so the power's excess may be God's and not from us.

> ⁸In every way, [we are] ones being
> troubled but not distressed;
> ones perplexed but not overperplexed,
> ⁹ones being chased but not abandoned,
> ones being tossed down but not
> destroyed,

¹⁰always carrying around in our body Yēsous' dying so Yēsous' life may also be apparent in our body. ¹¹For we, the living ones, are always being given over to death because of Yēsous so also Yēsous' life may be apparent in our mortal flesh. ¹²So that Death is working in us but Life in you.

¹³Having the same allegiance-Spirit, consistent with what is written, "I trusted, so I spoke"—we also trust, so we also speak, ¹⁴knowing that the one who raised the Lord Yēsous will also raise us with Yēsous and will present us with you. ¹⁵For all matters are because of you, so the grace, magnifying through the many, will flow the thanks over for God's splendor.

¹⁶Thus we don't become negligent. But even if also our outer-human is being corroded, our inner[-human] is being renewed day by day. ¹⁷For our momentary, light trouble is effecting for us—excessive times excess—the Era's weight of splendor ¹⁸. . . our scoping isn't on the visibles but on the invisibles. For the visibles are temporary, but the invisibles are for the Eras.

Gospel confidence

5 For we know that, if our earthy tent-house is demolished, we have a formation from God, a house made not from human hands for the Era in the heavens. ²For even in this we groan, longing to be over-clothed with our abode, the one from heaven—³assuming, once over-clothed, we will not be found naked. ⁴For we—ones in the tent—also groan, being depressed, since we don't want to be off-clothed but over-clothed so the mortal may be guzzled by the Life. ⁵The one who prepared us for this very state is God, who gave us the Spirit-pledge.

⁶Therefore, being confident always and knowing that being at home in the body we are out-of-home from the Lord. ⁷For we walk around by allegiance, not by appearance. ⁸Moreover, we are confident and we are delighted even more to be out-of-home from the body and in-home with the Lord. ⁹Therefore also we love the honor, whether being in-home or out-of-home, of being judged exceptional. ¹⁰For it's necessary for all of us to be apparent before Christos's Bēma [judgment seat] so each may obtain what was practiced through the body, whether good or foul.

Covenant gospel agents (3)

¹¹Therefore, knowing awe before the Lord, we persuade humans. We have become apparent before God. I also hope to become apparent before your moral faculties. ¹²We are not again affirming ourselves to you but giving you an opportunity for boasting about us so you may have something against ones boasting in face but not in heart. ¹³For if we lost our mind—for God; if we are sensible—for you! ¹⁴For Christos-love absorbs us, judging this: that one died for all, therefore all died, ¹⁵and he died for all so one living might no longer live for themselves but for the one who died and was raised for them. ¹⁶So that, from now on, we know no person consistent with Flesh. Even if we have known Christos consistent with Flesh, but we now no longer know [him like that]. ¹⁷So if someone is in Christos—new creation. The ancient matters pass away. Look! New matters have come. ¹⁸All matters are from God, the one who reconciled us to himself through Christos and gave to us the reconciling service—¹⁹as God was in Christos reconciling the Kosmos to himself, not calculating their wrongs for them and placed among us the reconciling word. ²⁰Therefore, we mediate for Christos . . . God is begging through us. We plead for Christos—be

reconciled to God. ²¹He made the one who did not know sin [to be] sin so we might become God's rightness in him.

Covenant gospel agents (4)

6 Coworking then [with God], we beg you not to receive God's grace in a hollow way. ²For it says,

> At the receptive season I heard you,
> On the day of deliverance I helped you.

Look! Now is a good receptive season.
Look! Now is day of deliverance.
³Giving no one in any way a stumbling stone so the service may not be censured, ⁴but in all ways affirming ourselves as God's servants,

> in all resilience,
> in troubles
> in necessities
> in distresses
> ⁵in plagues
> in prisons
> in anarchies
> in labors
> in sleepless nights
> in fastings
> ⁶in devotedness
> in knowledge
> in patience
> in graciousness
> in Holy Spirit
> in unmasked love
> ⁷in a word about truth
> in God's power.
> Through rightness's weapons—for the right and left hand
> ⁸through splendor and dishonor
> through bad report and good report.
> As "deceivers" and true ones
> ⁹as "uninformed" and perceiving ones
> as "dying" and—Look!—we live
> as "disciplined" and not being ones put to death
> ¹⁰as ones always pained and rejoicing
> as beggars but enriching many
> as not having and possessing all things.

Paulos appeals to the Korinthioi (1)

¹¹Our mouth has opened to you, Korinthioi [Corinthians]. Our heart is widened. ¹²You are not "distressed by us"; you are distressed in your empathies. ¹³With the same exchange—I say as to children—you be widened [for us]!

Kosmos at work in Korinthos

¹⁴Don't become cross-harnessed with anti-trusting ones!

For what partnership for rightness and covenant-breaking?
Or what common life for light with darkness?
¹⁵What symphony for Christos with Beliar [Belial]?
Or what part for allegiance with anti-trust?
¹⁶What concord for God's sanctuary with demon-idols?

For we are God's living sanctuary, just as God said that,

> I will reside in them and I will walk around [among them],
> I will be their God and they will be my people.
> ¹⁷"Therefore exit from among them and be isolated," says the Lord,
> "and don't touch unclean things.
> I will welcome you.
> ¹⁸And I will be to you as Father
> and you will be to me as sons and daughters,"
> says Lord All-Powerful.

7 Therefore, having these pledges, loved ones, let us clean ourselves from every stain from flesh and spirit, completing devotedness in awe of God.

Paulos appeals to the Korinthioi (2)

²Make space for us! We didn't wrong anyone, we abominated no one, we outwitted no one. ³I am not saying [this] for condemnation. For I have said that you are in our hearts—to die with and to live with. ⁴For me [there is] much frankness toward you; for me [there is] much boasting about you. I am filled out with encouragement; I am uber-flourishing in joy in all our trouble.

Paulos's appeal to the Korinthioi is heard!

⁵For our coming into Makedonia [Macedonia] . . . our flesh did not have any

leisure but troubling in every way: battles outside, scares inside. ⁶But the one encouraging the impoverished, God, encouraged us in Titos's [Titus's] arrival. ⁷Not only in his arrival but also in the encouragement in which he was encouraged about you, announcing to us your longing, your laments, your zeal for me so that I rejoiced even more. ⁸Because even if I "pained" you in my letter, I don't experience regret. Even if I were experiencing regret—for I see that that letter pained you, even if for an hour—⁹now I rejoice, not because you were pained but because you were pained into conversion. For you were pained consistent with God, so you were not in one matter damaged from us. ¹⁰For a consistent-with-God pain works conversion to an unregrettable deliverance, but the Kosmos's pain effects Death. ¹¹For Look! This same consistent-with-God pain effected so much seriousness for you:

But also what defense [of yourselves]!
... what indignation!
... what awe!
... what longing!
... what zeal!
... what right-making!

In everything you affirmed yourselves to be devoted in the matter.

¹²Therefore if I also wrote to you not because of the one who did wrong nor because of the one done wrong, but because your seriousness for us would be apparent to you before God. ¹³ᵃBecause this is true we have been encouraged.

¹³ᵇAt our encouragement, we rather aboundingly rejoiced at Titos's joy because his spirit was rested by all of you. ¹⁴Because if I had boasted about something to him about you, I was not degraded, but as we spoke all matters to you in truth, so also our boast to Titos has become the truth. ¹⁵His empathies are aboundingly for you, remembering all your obedience, as you received him with awe and trembling. ¹⁶I rejoice in everything because I am confident in you.

Gospel generosity

8 We are making known to you, siblings, God's grace that has been given among the Makedonian [Macedonian] assemblies, ²that in the trouble's great test of approval their joy's excess and their poverty's depth flowed over into their generosity's wealth, ³because consistent with [their] power—I witness—and beyond [their] power as volunteers ⁴with much encouragement, pleading with us for the grace and common life [of sharing funds] in the service to the devoted ones. ⁵And not as we hoped but they first gave themselves to Lord and to us through God's will ⁶so we could encourage Titos [Titus]—that just as he previously began so also that he might complete this grace in you also. ⁷But just as you flow over in all matters—in allegiance and in word and in knowledge and in all seriousness and in the love from us [at work] among you— so may you flow over in this grace also! ⁸I say [this] not consistent with an order but judging suitable the genuineness of your love in comparison with others' seriousness [about the funds for the devoted ones]. ⁹For you know our Lord's, Yēsous Christos's, grace, that because of you, he, being rich, was impoverished, so you might be enriched by his poverty.

¹⁰In this I gave my conclusion: For this benefits you who a year back began not only to do but also to want [to do]—¹¹now also complete the doing so that, just as the ardor [of your] wanting, so also the completion from [your] having. ¹²For if the ardor is present, [it's] acceptable in accordance with what one has, not in accordance with what one doesn't have. ¹³For [this giving] isn't so [financial] leisure [comes] to others [with] trouble for you, but that [the result may be] on the basis of equity. ¹⁴In the present season, your overflow [may meet] their lack, so their overflow may come to your lack—so that there may be equity. ¹⁵Just as it's written: *The one [with] much did not magnify and the one [with] little did not diminish.*

¹⁶Grace to God who gave in Titos's heart the same seriousness [we have] for you, ¹⁷because he received the encouragement then, as one who is very serious, as a volunteer exited [to come] to you. ¹⁸We sent with him the brother, who is publicly praised in the gospel through all the assemblies, ¹⁹not only that but also, having had the assemblies' hands laid on him to be our fellow traveler with this grace being served by us to the Lord's splendor and our ardor, ²⁰avoiding this: that no one may censure us in this lavishness, which is being

served by us. ²¹For we are thinking first about what is beautiful, not only before the Lord but also before humans. ²²We sent with them our brother, who is serious, whom we judged suitable often in many ways, but now much more serious in his much persuasion about you. ²³Whether [it's] for Titos—my common life and coworker for you or for our siblings, Commissioners of the assemblies, [may there be] splendor for Christos! ²⁴Therefore, exhibiting your love's exhibition and our boast for you to them in the face of the assemblies.

9 Writing to you concerning the service for the devoted ones abound beyond [what's needed], ²for I know your ardor about which I boast for you to the Makedōnians [Macedonians]—that Achaīa was prepared a year ago and your zeal incited the many. ³I sent the brothers so our boast for you may not be hollow in this part so that—just as I said—you would be prepared, ⁴so if somehow Makedonians should come with me and find you unprepared, we would be shamed (not that I say "you" [would be shamed]) in this substance. ⁵Therefore, I considered it necessary to encourage the brothers that they come ahead to you and that they first prepare your prepledged blessing, so this would be prepared, thus as a blessing and not as wanting more and more.

⁶And this: The one planting skimpily harvests skimpily, and the one planting on the basis of blessings harvests on the basis of blessings. ⁷Each as one has previously decided in the heart, not out of pain or out of necessity, for God loves a gleeful giver. ⁸God is able to flow over every grace for you, so in every way, always, having all self-sufficiency you may flow over into every good work, ⁹just as it's written:

> He scattered, he gave to indigent ones,
> His rightness remains to the Era.

¹⁰The one supplying *seed for the one planting and bread for food* will supply and make your seed abundant, and your rightness-produce will grow. ¹¹In every way, being enriched for all generosity, which, through us, effects thanks to God. ¹²Because this public work's service isn't only amply replenishing what the devoted ones lack, but [is] flowing over through many thanks to God. ¹³Through this service's approval, [you will be] splendoring God in your ordering [yourselves]

under the public agreement of the Christos-gospel and in the generosity of common resources for them and for all. ¹⁴. . . They're longing in their prayer request for you because of God's extreme grace upon you. . . .

¹⁵Grace to God for his unexplainable gift.

Gospel ministry: Accusations and responses

10 I myself, Paulos [Paul], beg you through Christos's meekness and fairness—"[I] who when face-to-face am impoverished among you, when away I am confident toward you." ²Yes, I plead [with you that] I, being present, [will not have to] be bold in the persuasion by which I calculate [that I will] dare to [use] with some who calculate us as "walking around in the flesh." ³For, "walking around in the flesh," we don't soldier consistent with the flesh. ⁴Our soldiering's weapons are not fleshy but able in God to demolish fortresses, demolishing reasonings ⁵and every high-status place raising itself against knowing God, and capturing every mentality for Christos-obedience ⁶and having preparation to make right every disobedience whenever your obedience is filled out.

⁷Look at matters in the face! If someone is persuaded in oneself to be "of Christos," let this person calculate again for oneself: that just as one is "of Christos" so also are we! ⁸For if I "boast a bit excessively about our authority," which the Lord gave for your formation and not for demolition, I am not shamed, ⁹so I look somehow to be scaring you through the letters. ¹⁰That is: "The letters," they say, "are heavy and strong, yet his body's arrival is weak and the word devalued." ¹¹Let this person calculate this: that who we are in word through letters (being away), that is who we are also in work (being present).

¹²For we don't dare to classify or compare ourselves with some who affirm themselves but they, measuring themselves among themselves and comparing themselves to themselves, don't understand. ¹³We will not "boast" to the point beyond the measure but consistent with the assigned area's measure—which God measured as a measure for us, to reach even as far as you. ¹⁴For "we did not overreach ourselves"—as though [we were] not [to be] reaching you, for we arrived as far as even you with the Christos-gospel, ¹⁵not "boasting" beyond the measure "in

outsiders' labors," yet having hope . . . your allegiance's growing . . . to be magnified to excess [in gospel work] among you consistent with our assigned area, ¹⁶to gospel beyond you, not to "boast" in "an outsider's already-accomplished [work] assigned area." ¹⁷*The one boasting, let the person boast in Lord.* ¹⁸For [it's] not the one affirming self who is approved, but the one the Lord affirms.

11 Wishing that you were putting up with me for a little bit of imprudence. Even so, put up with me! ²For I am zealous for you with God's zeal, for I coupled you to one man, a devout virgin, to present [you] to the Christos. ³I fear that somehow, as the snake deceived Heua [Eve] in its trickery, your mentalities may be abominated from the generosity and devotion that are for the Christos. ⁴For if the one coming announces another Yēsous whom we did not announce, or you take a different spirit that you did not take, or another gospel that you did not receive, you put up [with these] beautifully!

⁵For I calculate [that I] "lack" nothing compared to the "superlative" Commissioners. ⁶Even if [I am] a "self-taught in word" . . . but I'm not in knowledge, but in every way becoming apparent in all things to you.

**⁷Or, did I "sin," impoverishing myself so your status might be raised?
Because I gospeled to you God's gospel "as a gift"?**

⁸I "plundered" other assemblies, taking a fee, to serve to you. ⁹And, being present with you and lacking, I did not burden anyone. For the siblings, coming from Makedonia [Macedonia], amply replenished the matters I lacked and in every way I kept—and will keep myself—from being a load. ¹⁰Christos's truth is in me—that "this boast" will not be shut down in me in the environs of Achaïa.

**¹¹Why?
Because "I don't love you"?**

God has known.

¹²What I do I will also do so I might chop off the opportunity of the ones wanting an opportunity so they may be found "just like us" in which they may boast. ¹³For such are false Commissioners, deceitful workers, reshaping themselves into Christos's Commissioners. ¹⁴It is not stunning! For Satanas [Satan] himself reshapes into a light-envoy. ¹⁵No biggie, therefore, if even his servants reshape themselves as rightness-servants—whose completion will be consistent with their works!

Give it up for boasting!

¹⁶I say again, let no one think of me as "an imprudent one." But if you think otherwise, receive me as an imprudent one so I may also boast a little bit. ¹⁷What I am speaking, I am not speaking—in "this boasting's substance"—consistent with Lord but as "in imprudence." ¹⁸Since many boast consistent with flesh, I also will boast.

¹⁹For you, being prudent ones, put up with pleasure the "imprudent ones."
²⁰For you put up if someone enslaves you,
if someone gobbles [you] up,
if someone takes [you],
if someone elevates [one's status],
if someone beats your face.
²¹I say this consistent with dishonor, because we have been "weakened." In which [confident boasting], if someone dares—I speak in imprudence—I also dare:
²²Are they "Hebraioi [Hebrews]"? I am also.
Are they "Yisraēlitai [Israelites]"? I am also.
Are they "Abra'am's seed"? I am also.
²³Are they "Christos's servants"? (I speak contrary to prudence.) I am more:
aboundingly in labors,
aboundingly in prisons,
excessively in plagues,
often in deaths.
²⁴By Youdaians [Judeans, Jews], five times I received forty-minus-one [lashes].
²⁵Three times I was flogged.
Once I was stoned.
Three times I was shipwrecked.
For a night and a day I was rolling in the deep [sea].
²⁶Often on journeys,
in dangers of rivers,
in dangers of bandits,
in dangers from [my own] ethnic group,
in dangers from ethnic groups,
in dangers in a city,
in dangers in a desert,
in dangers in a sea,

in dangers with false siblings, ²⁷in labor and fatigue,
often in sleeplessnesses,
in hunger and thirst,
often in fastings,
in cold and nakedness.

²⁸Apart from the exceptions [to the above] [there is] my daily supervision, [that is], the anxiety for all the assemblies.

²⁹Who weakens and I don't weaken? Who trips and I am not set on fire?

³⁰If it's necessary to boast, I will boast about my weaknesses.

(³¹The God and Father of the Lord Yēsous has known—who is blessed into the Eras—that I am not falsifying.)

³²In Damaskos [Damascus], Aretas the king's ethnarch was guarding the city of Damaskos to catch me, ³³and through a window, in a basket, I was lowered through the wall, and I fled from his hands.

A little more boasting

12 It's necessary to "boast." Of course, it not being beneficial, but I will go on to visions and apocalypses of the Lord.

²I know a human in Christos, fourteen years ago—whether in body I don't know, out of the body I don't know, God knows—such a human was snatched up to third heaven. ³I know such a human—whether in body, or whether apart from the body I don't know, God knows—⁴that he was snatched up into Paradise and he heard unutterable utterances that are not permissible for a human to speak.

⁵I will boast for such a human, but I will not boast for myself—except in the "weaknesses." ⁶For if I wanted to boast, I won't be "an imprudent one," for I would be saying truth. But I am sparing [you], so no one may calculate about me beyond what the person sees in me or hears something from me, even [calculating] the apocalypses' superiority!

⁷Therefore, so I may not raise my status, a thorn-piercing-the-flesh was given to me, a Satanas[Satan]-envoy, to punch me, so I would not raise my status. ⁸Three times I begged the Lord about this—to remove [it] from me. ⁹And he has said to me, "My grace is enough for you, for the power is completed in weakness." Therefore, instead I will boast with pleasure in my weaknesses so Christos's power might camp on me. ¹⁰Therefore, I take delight
in weaknesses,
in assaults,
in necessities,
in chases and distresses,
for Christos.

For whenever I am weakened, then I am empowered.

¹¹I have become an imprudent one, but you compelled me. For I ought to have been affirmed by you, for I lacked nothing compared to the "superlative" Commissioners—even if I am "nothing." ¹²The Commissioner's authenticating signs were effected among you in all resilience—in authenticating signs, as well as omens and powers.

¹³For how were you "lowered in status beyond the remaining assemblies"? If not that I myself did not burden you?

(Grace me this "injustice"!)

¹⁴Look! This [is] the third time I have prepared to come to you, and I will not burden [you]. For I don't pursue your resources but you. For the children are not obligated to treasure [provisions] for parents but parents for the children. ¹⁵I will, with pleasure, exhaust [my resources] and be exhausted for your selves.

If I aboundingly love you, am I "loved worse"?

¹⁶Let it be: I did not overload you. But, "being tricky, I took you in deceit."

**¹⁷I did not "outwit you" through him, did I, through any of those I have commissioned to you?
¹⁸I encouraged Titos [Titus] and with him I commissioned the brother.
Titos did not outwit you, did he?
Did we not walk around in the same spirit?
Did we not [walk around] in the same steps?**

¹⁹Have you been thinking all this time that "we are defending ourselves to you." We are speaking before God in Christos. All these

matters, loved ones, [have been] for your formation. ²⁰For I fear that somehow, coming,

> I will find you not how I want,
> and "I will be found to you not how you want"—
> somehow [there will be]:
> strife,
> zeal,
> anger,
> status seekings,
> slanders,
> gossipings,
> using natural status,
> anarchies.

²¹I'm coming again . . . somehow God may impoverish me before you, and I may grieve over many who have previously sinned and were not converted from impurity and sexual immorality and flaunting sensuality, which they practiced.

13

This [is the] third time I am coming to you: *Every utterance will be established in the mouth of two or three witnesses.* ²I have said before and I say in advance—when present a second time and now absent—to those who previously sinned and to all the remaining, that if I come again I will not spare [you], ³since you pursue approval of the Christos speaking in me, who isn't weakening but is empowering among you. ⁴For indeed he was crucified out of weakness but lives out of God's power. For indeed we are weakened in him but we will live with him for you out of God's power.

⁵Test yourselves if you are in the faith. Judge yourselves suitable.

Do you not perceive yourselves that Yēsous Christos [is] in you? If [so], you are not unapproved, are you!?

⁶I hope that you will know that we are not unapproved. ⁷We formulate a prayer to God not to do anything bad, not so we may appear approved but so you may do the beautiful and we may be as the unapproved. ⁸For we aren't able [to do] something against the truth but for the truth. ⁹For we rejoice whenever we are weakened but whenever you are powerful. We formulate a prayer also for this: your restoration. ¹⁰Because this is true: I, being away, am writing these things so, being present, I may not act cuttingly consistent with the authority that the Lord gave me for formation and not for demolition.

¹¹What remains, siblings, rejoice! Be prepared! Be encouraged! Be prudent about the same thing! Be peaceful! And the love-and-peace-God will be with you.

¹²Greet one another with a devoted kiss! All the devoted ones greet you.

¹³The Lord Yēsous Christos' grace and God's love and the Holy Spirit's common life [be] with all of you!

INTRODUCTION TO GALATIANS

The letter of Paulos [Paul] to the house-church assemblies in Galatia is probably his earliest surviving letter and in important ways anticipates the fuller exposition of its dominant themes in his letter to the Romans. Dating his letters is fraught with hypotheses often difficult to prove, but a date from the mid- to late 40s is reasonable.

Galatia refers to two regions in central and south-central modern Turkey, and the south-central cities were gospeled somewhat successfully (though not always convincingly) by Paulos and his associates as recorded in Acts 14. Perhaps most notable in this letter, and this anticipates what is found in every location Paulos did gospel work, is fierce disagreement with him over the place of Covenant Code [Mosaic Torah, law] for the ethnic groups [Gentiles] who turned over their lives to Yēsous, Yisraēl's Christos. In this letter the defensive tone is best explained by the success of his rival missioners who believe a complete conversion to the gospel requires commitment to the Covenant Code. To counter their somewhat successful counter-missionary work, Paulos contends Abra'am's [Abraham's] pledge is by faith/allegiance and not by Code's works and that rightness with God is established by faith. This rightness is available both to Youdaioi [Judeans, Jews] and the ethnic groups, and that makes all the believers accepted with God and therefore siblings in Christos. Any kind of compelling the non-Youdaioi to embrace circumcision, the principal act of Code fidelity, distorts the gospel and divorces a person from Christos and his redemptive work.

The letter has three major divisions: Chapters 1–2 are more or less an autobiographical defense of the gospel preached by Paulos, a gospel that is theologically articulated in yet another defensive form in chapters 3–4. The intent of this letter is to establish for the allegiant ones in Galatia a life of liberation from sin, from systemic evil, from the Kosmos, and from imposing the Code on those following Yēsous from among the ethnic groups. That life of liberation, one marked by moving away from the flesh and living instead in the Spirit, is sketched with particular concerns for the Galatian churches in chapters 5–6, where we hear about fleshy patterns of division, of some powerful leaders imposing circumcision, and of life in the Spirit called the "Spirit's fruit." Love is the heart of it all.

TO THE GALATIANS

1 Paulos [Paul], Commissioner—not from humans nor through humans but through Yēsous Christos and Father-God, who raised him from among the dead ones—²and all the siblings with me.

To the assemblies of Galatia.

³Grace to you, and peace from our Father-God and Lord Yēsous Christos, ⁴who gave himself for our sins so that he might lift us out of this present evil Era consistent with our God and Father's plan,

⁵to whom [be] the splendor unto the Eras of the Eras.

Amēn!

Stunned by Galatian behaviors

⁶I am stunned that you are so quickly shifting from the one who called you in Christos's grace to another gospel ⁷(which isn't another, but some are agitating you and wanting to twist the Christos-gospel). ⁸But even if we or an envoy from heaven were to gospel you against what we gospeled to you—let the person be vowed-to-destruction! ⁹As we have said before I say now again—if someone gospels you against what you received—let the person be vowed-to-destruction!

Accusation leading to . . .

¹⁰For am I persuading humans or God? Am I pursuing to please humans?

If I were still pleasing humans, I would not be Christos's slave.

. . . defensive autobiography

¹¹For I make known to you, siblings, the gospel gospeled by me, that it isn't "consistent with a human." ¹²For I neither received it from a human nor was I taught it, but through an apocalypse of Yēsous Christos.

¹³For you have heard of my behavior once in Youdaïsmos [Judaism], that I was extensively chasing God's assembly and devastating it, ¹⁴and I was advancing in Youdaïsmos beyond many peers in my ethnic group—being aboundingly zealous for my fathers' conventions. ¹⁵When God—the one who isolated me from my mother's womb and called me through his grace—delighted ¹⁶to apocalypse his Son in me that I might gospel him among the ethnic groups, immediately I did not consult "flesh and blood" ¹⁷nor did I ascend into Yierosoluma [Jerusalem] to the ones who were Commissioners before me, but I departed into Arabia and again I returned to Damaskos [Damascus]. ¹⁸Then, after three years, I ascended into Yierosoluma to inquire of Kēphas [Cephas] and I remained with him fifteen days. ¹⁹I did not see another of the Commissioners except Yakōbos [James], the Lord's brother. ²⁰The matters I am writing to you—Look! Before God I am not falsifying. ²¹Then I came into the environs of Suria [Syria] and of Kilikia [Cilicia]. ²²I was unknown by face to the Youdaian [Judean, Jewish] assemblies who are in Christos. ²³Only, they were hearing that "Our one-time chaser now gospels the faith that he was once devastating." ²⁴They splendored God in me.

2 Then after fourteen years I again ascended into Yierosoluma [Jerusalem] with Bar-Nabas [Barnabas], taking along also Titos [Titus]. ²I ascended consistent with an apocalypse and I laid out for them the gospel that I announce among the ethnic groups—by myself to the Reputables in the event I am running or was running into a hollow. ³But, not even Titos, who was with me, being a Hellēn [Greek], was compelled to be circumcised. ⁴Because of the furtive false siblings, who penetrated to reconnoiter our liberty that we have in Christos Yēsous—so they might subdue us to slavery—⁵to whom we did not concede for even an hour in under-ordering so the gospel's truth would persist with you. ⁶From the Reputables who are something—what they once were to me doesn't make them superior. (God doesn't receive human face.) For the Reputables added nothing to me, ⁷but on the contrary, seeing that I had been trusted with the gospel for the foreskin [people] just as Petros [Peter] for the circumcised, ⁸for the one who energized in Petros for a commission to the circumcised energized also in me for the ethnic groups ⁹and, knowing the grace given to me, Yakōbos [James] and Kēphas [Cephas] and Yōannēs [John], the ones reputing to be pillars, gave a right hand of common life to me and to Bar-Nabas—so we [could go] to the ethnic groups and they to the circumcised. ¹⁰Only—that we might remember the begging ones, which I committed to do this very thing.

Paulos squares off with Kēphas

¹¹When Kēphas came to Antiocheia [Antioch] I resisted him face to face because he was knowably wrong. ¹²For, before some persons from Yakōbos came he was eating with the ethnic groups, but when they came, he was backing off and isolating himself, being scared of the circumcision [people]. ¹³The remaining Youdaians [Judeans, Jews] co-performed the same mask-wearing with him so that even Bar-Nabas was led away with them in wearing the mask.

¹⁴But when I saw that they were not walking the line of the gospel's truth, I said to Kēphas before all, "If you, being a Youdaian, live like the ethnic groups and not like the Youdaians, how do you compel the ethnic groups to Youdaīze [Judaize]?"

¹⁵We, by nature are Youdaians and not sinners from the ethnic groups, ¹⁶knowing that a human isn't righted from Covenant Code's works but through Yēsous-Christos-allegiance, and we became allegiant to Christos Yēsous so we might be righted from Christos-allegiance and not from Code's works (because from Code's works no flesh is righted.)

¹⁷If, pursuing to be righted in Christos, we were found also to be sinners ourselves, is then Christos Sin's servant?

May that never happen! ¹⁸For, if I form again these things I demolished, I affirm myself as a violator. ¹⁹For I died to Code through Code so I might live to God. I have been co-crucified with Christos. ²⁰I no longer live, Christos lives in me. What I now live in flesh I live in allegiance to God's Son, the one who loved me and the one who gave himself for me. ²¹I don't reject God's grace. For if rightness [were] through Code, then Christos died as a [wasted] gift.

Five pointed questions

3 O brainless Galatai [Galatians]!

Who enchanted you—to whose eyes Yēsous Christos was first inscribed as [the] crucified one?

²I want only to be apprenticed in this from you:

Did you receive the Spirit from Covenant Code's works or from allegiant's hearing? ³So, are you brainless—beginning in Spirit, are you now completing yourselves in flesh? ⁴Did you suffer these things in a hollow manner? (If it was in a hollow manner.) ⁵Therefore, did the one supplying you the Spirit and the one energizing powers among you [do such] out of Code's works or allegiant hearing?

Abra'am's allegiance versus Covenant Code

⁶Just as Abra'am *was allegiant to God and it was calculated for him as rightness.* ⁷You know then that the allegiant ones, these are Abra'am's descendants. ⁸The writing, knowing first that God rights the ethnic groups out of allegiance, first gospeled to Abra'am that *In you all the ethnic groups will be God-blessed.* ⁹So that the allegiant ones are God-blessed with allegiant Abra'am.

¹⁰For whoever is from Code's works are under God's curse. For it's written that *Cursed is everyone who doesn't remain in everything written in the Book of the Code—to do them.* ¹¹Because by Code no one is righted with God—that's clear, because *the right one will live out of allegiance.* ¹²The Code isn't out of allegiance but *one who does these will live in them.* ¹³Christos purchased us out from the Code's curse, becoming a curse for us (because it's written, *Cursed is everyone suspended on a tree*) ¹⁴so Abra'am's blessing might be for the ethnic groups in Christos Yēsous, so we might receive the pledge, that is, the Spirit, through allegiance.

Pledge, covenant, Covenant Code, inheritance

¹⁵Siblings, I say this consistent with a human: Nonetheless, no one rejects or rearranges a human-ratified covenant. ¹⁶The pledges were said to Abra'am and to his seed. It doesn't say, "And to his seeds"—as for many

but as for one—*And to your seed*, who is Christos. ¹⁷I say this: The Code, having come after 430 years, doesn't reject a God-ratified covenant to void the pledge. ¹⁸For if the inheritance [is] of the Code, it's no longer of pledge. God has graced Abra'am through a pledge.

¹⁹Why then the Code?

It was added because of violations until the seed to whom it was pledged came, being ordered through envoys, in a mediator's hand. (²⁰The mediator isn't one, but God is one.)

²¹Is therefore the Code against God's pledges?

May it never be! For if a Code, one able to make life, was given, rightness would really be of the Code. ²²But, the writing enclosed all things under Sin so the pledge might be given to the allegiant, from Yēsous-Christos-allegiance. ²³Before the Faith came we were guarded by Code, enclosed until the about-to-come Faith was apocalypsed, ²⁴so that the Code became our educator to Christos so we might be righted from allegiance. ²⁵. . . Faith's come . . . we are no longer under the pedagogue. ²⁶For you are all God's descendants through the allegiance in Christos Yēsous. ²⁷For all who were dipped into Christos put on Christos. ²⁸There is neither Youdaian [Judean, Jew] nor Ellēn [Greek], neither slave nor liberated, there isn't *male and female*. For you all are one in Christos Yēsous. ²⁹If you are of Christos, then you are Abra'am's seed, heirs consistent with pledge.

4 I am saying: As long as the heir is an infant he—being lord over all—isn't superior to a slave ²but is under supervisors and administrators until the time determined by the father. ³So also we, when we were infants, we were enslaved by the Kosmos's categories, ⁴but when the period's fullness came, God commissioned his Son—being from a woman, being under Code—⁵to purchase ones under Code so we might receive family-placement. ⁶Because you are descendants, God commissioned out his Son's Spirit into our hearts, crying, "Abba! (Father)." ⁷So that you are no longer a slave but a descendant. If a descendant, also an heir through God.

Exhortations for the Galatai

⁸But then, not knowing God, you were slaves to objects not being gods by nature.

⁹But now, knowing God—or rather being known by God—how do you return again to the weak and beggarly categories? Do you again want to be enslaved from above to them?

¹⁰You observe days and months and seasons and years. ¹¹I am scared for you that somehow I have labored for you in a hollow manner.

¹²Become as I am because I am as you are, siblings—I am pleading with you. You didn't wrong me. ¹³You know that I gospeled to you the first time because of the flesh's weakness ¹⁴and during your test in my flesh you did not devalue or spit out but you welcomed me as God's envoy, as Christos Yēsous.

¹⁵Therefore, where is your God-blessing?

For I testify to you that, if possible, digging out your eyes, you would have given [them] to me!

¹⁶So that, have I, truthing to you, become your enemy?

¹⁷They are zealous for you—not beautifully, but they want to shut you out so you are zealous for them. ¹⁸It's beautiful to be zealed-for always in beauty and not only in my presence with you. ¹⁹My children, for whom again I am groaning in birth until Christos is morphed in you, ²⁰I was wanting to be present with you now and to alter my voice because I am perplexed with you.

An allegory on the Covenant Code

²¹Say to me, [you] who are wanting to be under Covenant Code, do you hear the Code?

²²For it's written that Abra'am had two sons, one from the young servant [woman] and from the liberated [woman]. ²³But the one from the young servant was given life consistent with flesh and the one from the liberated woman through a pledge.

²⁴Which elements being allegorized:
For these are two covenants—one from Mount Sina [Sinai], giving life to slavery, which is Hagar. ²⁵The Hagar is Mount Sina in Arabia. She categorizes to the present Yierousalēm [Jerusalem], for she slaves with her children. ²⁶The Yierosalēm above is liberated, which is our mother. ²⁷For it's written:

> Be glad, sterile [woman] who isn't birthing,
> Break down and bellow out, she who isn't groaning in birth,
> Because the desert's children are many
> More than the one having the man.

²⁸But you, siblings, are children consistent with Yisa'ak's [Isaac's] pledge. ²⁹But, just as then the one given life consistent with flesh chased the one consistent with Spirit, so also now. ³⁰But what does the writing say? *Toss out the young servant [woman] and her son. For the young servant's son will not inherit with* the liberated [woman's] *son.* ³¹Therefore, siblings, we are not children of the young servant but of the liberated [woman].

Liberated for liberation, not consumption

5 Christos liberated us for liberation. Therefore, stand and don't have it in again for slavery's yoke.
²Look! I Paulos [Paul] say to you that if you are circumcised, Christos gains you nothing. ³I witness again to every circumcised human that he is a debtor to do the whole Covenant Code.
⁴You have been undone from Christos!
You are being "righted by Code"!
You fell from grace!
⁵For, in the Spirit, from allegiance, we impatiently wait for the rightness's hope. ⁶For in Christos Yēsous neither circumcision nor foreskin has any strength but allegiance being energized through love.
⁷You were running beautifully.

Who cut you off not to be persuaded by the truth?

⁸The persuasion isn't from the one who calls you. ⁹A little yeast leavens the whole batch. ¹⁰I have been persuaded for you in Lord that you will be prudent for no other thing. The one agitating you will carry the judgment, whoever it may be.

¹¹I, siblings, if I am still announcing circumcision, why am I still being chased?

Then the cross's tripping has been undone. ¹²I wish the ones causing anarchy for you would cut [it] off!

¹³For you were called to liberation, siblings—only not liberation for an opportunity for the flesh, but be a slave for one another through love. ¹⁴For the whole Code is filled out in one word, in this: *You will love your neighbor as yourself.* ¹⁵If you bite and gobble one another . . . see that you are not consumed by one another.

Flesh versus Spirit

¹⁶I say, walk around in Spirit and you will not complete flesh's desire. ¹⁷For the flesh desires against the Spirit, and the Spirit against the flesh, these things oppose one another so—whatever you want—these things you don't do. ¹⁸If you are led in Spirit, you aren't under Code.
¹⁹The flesh's works are apparent, which are
sexual immorality,
impurity,
flaunting sensuality,
²⁰demon-idol worship,
drug-induced sorcery,
enemy-makings,
strife,
zeal,
fury,
status seekings,
divisions,
factions,
²¹envies,
boozings,
parties . . .
and things comparable to these,
which I say in advance to you, just as I said before, that the ones practicing these things will not inherit God's Empire.
²²The Spirit's fruit is
love,
joy,
peace,
patience,
graciousness,
goodness,
allegiance,
²³meekness,
self-discipline.

Against such things there is no Code. ²⁴The ones of Christos Yēsous crucified the flesh with the passions and desires. ²⁵If we live in Spirit, let us walk the line in Spirit. ²⁶Let us not become airheads, calling out one another, envying one another.

Caring for one another

6 Siblings, if a human is taken early in some wrong, you Spirit-people prepare such [a human] in a meek spirit, scoping yourself so you are not tempted.

²Carry one another's burdens and so you will fill up Christos's [Christ's] Code.

³If someone seems to be something [special], not being anything, the person deceives oneself. ⁴Let each judge suitable his own work and then only he will have the boast in himself and not in another person. ⁵Each carries one's own load.

⁶Let the one catechized in the word have common life with the catechist in all good things. ⁷Don't be deceived! God isn't snorted at. For whatever a human plants, this a person will also harvest. ⁸Because the one who plants to one's own flesh will harvest decay from the flesh, but the one who plants to the Spirit will harvest Era Life from the Spirit.

⁹Let us not be negligent doing The Beautiful, for we will harvest in its season, not fainting.

¹⁰Accordingly therefore, as we have season, let us work The Good for all, especially for the allegiant's household.

Finishing the letter

¹¹Look! I wrote to you in large letters in my hand.

¹²Whoever wants to have a good face in flesh, these are compelling you to be circumcised—only so they may not be chased for Christos's cross. ¹³For not even the ones being circumcised guard the Code themselves but want you to be circumcised so they may boast in your flesh. ¹⁴For, may it never be for me to boast except in our Lord Yēsous Christos's cross, through whom Kosmos has been crucified to me and I to Kosmos. ¹⁵For neither circumcision is something—nor foreskin, but new creation. ¹⁶Whoever walks the line with this rule, peace and mercy on them and God's Yisraēl [Israel].

¹⁷For the remaining: Let no one present labors to me, for I carry in my body Yēsous' scars.

¹⁸Our Lord Yēsous Christos's grace—with your spirit, siblings.

Amēn!!

INTRODUCTION TO EPHESIANS

Ephesos [Ephesus], a magnificent city still on display today on the western edge of modern Turkey as one of the world's great archaeological sites, was one of the major cities in the Roman Empire. Paulos [Paul] centered the second part of his mission (after Antioch) there as he evangelized today's western coast of Turkey and the eastern coast of Greece down to Athēnai [Athens] and Korinthos [Corinth]. Vignettes of his ministry in Ephesos can be seen in Acts 19–20. Turkey [or Asia Minor or Anatolia] was the heart of first-century Christianity, and Ephesos was also well-known for its own religions, including especially its temple to Artemis.

The letter to the Ephesians is in some ways a crystallization of Paulos's major themes in church [assembly] theology. That theology begins with a redemption that elicits unbridled worship of God (1:3-14) and rich prayer for spiritual maturity (1:15-23) of those who have moved from spiritual death into life (2:1-10). The assembly is for all the redeemed, Youdaioi [Judeans, Jews] or the ethnic groups [Gentiles] (2:11-22), and that mission of redemption is Paulos's calling (3:1-13). He returns to a prayer and to the theme of unity (3:14-21 and 4:1-16) before he delineates more about what the Christian life looks like (4:17–6:9), finishing with a well-known description of the cosmic battle (6:10-18).

This is the only letter of Paulos's whose addressee isn't entirely clear. Some early and good manuscripts have only "to the devoted ones in . . ." with "in Ephesos" omitted. Some have suggested, accordingly, that this was a letter sent by Paulos to Ephesos but it was also a circular letter for all the churches in Paulos's orbit in the area and when the reader got to "in _____" it was filled with the location's name. Others counter that this was sent to a specific church on a specific occasion, not least a problem with the worship of Artemis. The letter is directed at converts from the ethnic groups (2:11; 3:1; 4:17), but at the same time the message is that in Christos (a favorite theme of Paulos) the believers in Christos are now one body (2:11-22). The prose at times reaches extensive sentence lengths: Ephesians 1:3-14 is 202 words long, and 1:15-23 is 170 words long. Each starts in one place, clarifies with subordinations and side notes, yet ends up with a singular flow in thought. Dating Ephesians, which is connected in some way to the letter to the Colossians, is difficult, and any proposal must remain far from certain, but one suggestion is that it was written as a circular letter from Paulos's imprisonment in Ephesos in the early 50s. Others date it to the early 60s from Rome.

TO THE EPHESIANS

From Paulos to Ephesos

1 Paulos [Paul], Commissioner of Christos Yēsous through God's plan,
to the devoted ones in _____ and to the allegiant ones in Christos Yēsous.
²Grace to you and peace from our Father-God and from the Lord Yēsous Christos.

One long blessing

³Blessed is the God and Father of our Lord Yēsous Christos,
the one who blessed us with every Spirit-prompted blessing, in the heavenly places, in Christos,
⁴just as God selected us in him before the Kosmos's origin so we would be devoted and inerrant before him in love,
⁵[the one] who predetermined us for family-placement to himself through Yēsous Christos, consistent with his plan's delight,
⁶to his grace's splendor's public praise, which grace he graced us in the one he has loved.
⁷In whom we have liberation through his blood, the release from the wrongs, consistent with his grace's wealth,
⁸which flowed over to you in all wisdom and prudence,
⁹making known to you his plan's secret, consistent with his delight that he offered in him ¹⁰for the management of the seasons' fullness, for all matters to be recapitulated in the Christos—matters in the heavens and matters in the land in him,
¹¹in whom also we received an inheritance, predetermining consistent with the energizing one's intention, consistent with his plan's decision ¹²for us to be for his splendor's public praise, [for us] the ones who have first hoped in the Christos,
¹³in whom also you, hearing the truth-word, your deliverance's gospel,
in whom also, trusting, you were sealed with the pledged Holy Spirit, ¹⁴who is our inheritance's pledge for the acquisition of liberation—for his splendor's public praise.

Paulos prays for them

¹⁵Because this is true, I also, hearing about your allegiance in the Lord Yēsous and the love for all the devoted ones—¹⁶I don't stop thanking [God] for you, making memory in my prayers, ¹⁷so that the God of our Lord Yēsous Christos, the splendorous Father, may give to you the Spirit of wisdom and apocalypse in perception of God, ¹⁸having your heart's eyes enlightened so you know

what is his calling's hope,
what is his inheritance's spendorous wealth among the devoted ones,
¹⁹and what is his power's great excess for us allegiant ones consistent with his strong grip's energy,

²⁰which he energized in Christos, raising him from among the dead ones and seating him at his right hand in the heavenlies ²¹above all celestial leadership and authority and power and lordship and [above] every name being named, not only in this Era but in the coming [Era], ²²and *he ordered all things under his feet* and gave him [to be] head over the whole assembly, ²³which is his body, the fullness of the one filling all things in all ways.

Once dead, now living

2 You, being dead in your wrongs and sins, ²in which you once walked around consistent with this Kosmos's Era, consistent with the air's authoritative leader—the spirit now energizing among unpersuasion's descendants, ³among whom also we all once behaved in our flesh's desires, doing the things the flesh and intelligence want, and we were by nature anger's children—as are also the remaining.

⁴But God, being wealthy in mercy, because of all his love with which he loved us⁵—we being dead ones in our wrongs, [God] made a life for us with Christos—you have been delivered by grace—⁶and [God] co-raised and co-seated us in the heavenlies in Christos Yēsous, ⁷to exhibit in the coming Eras his grace's excessive wealth in graciousness for us in Christos Yēsous. ⁸For by grace you are delivered through allegiance—this isn't from you; it's God's gift—⁹not from works so someone might not boast. ¹⁰We are his compositions, being created in Christos Yēsous for good works, for which God previously prepared so we might walk around in them.

Formerly divided, now united

¹¹Therefore, remember that you *once* [were] the ethnic groups in flesh, the ones being called "foreskin" by those being called "circumcision"—in the flesh, handmade—¹²because you were away from Christos in that season, rendered as "others" from Yisraēl's [Israel's] communal-life and foreigners of the pledge's covenants, not having hope and atheists in the Kosmos. ¹³*Now*, in Christos Yēsous, you who were *once* far away have come near by the Christos's blood. ¹⁴For he is our peace, making both groups one and loosened the dividing barrier, the wall, the enemy, by his flesh, ¹⁵undoing the Covenant Code of orders in rulings, so he might create in himself the two into one new human, making peace ¹⁶and reconciling both in one body to God through the cross, killing the enemy in it. ¹⁷Coming, he gospeled peace to you, to the far, and peace to the near. ¹⁸Because, through him we both have access, in one Spirit, to the Father.

¹⁹Accordingly, therefore, you are no longer foreigners and resident aliens but you are the devoted ones' co-citizens and God's house members, ²⁰being formed on the Comissioners-and-prophets' foundation . . . Christos Yēsous himself's the cornerstone . . . ²¹in whom the whole formation, being joined together, grows into a sanctuary, devoted in the Lord, ²²in whom also you are co-formed into God's dwelling in the Spirit.

Paulos's secret and prayer

3 Because of this, I Paulos [Paul], Christos Yēsous' prisoner for you ethnic groups—²if indeed you heard about the management of God's grace, [a management] given to me for you, ³that, consistent with an apocalypse, the secret was made known to me, just as I wrote previously in a few [words], ⁴which you are able, reading, to know my understanding in the Christos-secret, ⁵which [the secret that] was not made known to other generations of human descendants as now it has been apocalypsed to his devoted Commissioners and prophets in the Spirit, ⁶[that] the ethnic groups are the pledge's co-inheritors and co-bodies and co-sharers, in Christos Yēsous through the gospel, ⁷of which I became a servant consistent with God's grace-act given to me consistent with his power's energy.

⁸To me, the least of all devoted ones, this grace was given: to gospel Christos's incomprehensible wealth to the ethnic groups ⁹and to enlighten all [about] what [is] the mystery's management that has been hidden from the Eras in God, the one who created all things, ¹⁰so God's multivaried wisdom might be made known now to the celestial leaders and authorities in the heavenlies through the assembly, ¹¹consistent with the Era's intention, which he made in our Lord Christos Yēsous, ¹²in whom we have frankness and access, with persuasion, through his allegiance. ¹³Therefore, I ask not to be negligent in my troubles for you, which is your splendor.

¹⁴Because of this, I bend my knees to the Father, ¹⁵from whom every paternity in heavens and on earth is named, ¹⁶so he might give to you, consistent with his splendorous wealth, power to be strengthened through his Spirit in the inner human, ¹⁷for the Christos to reside through allegiance in your hearts, rooted and founded in love, ¹⁸that you, with all the devoted ones, may be strengthened to grasp what is the width and length and height and depth, ¹⁹indeed, to know the excessiveness of knowing Christos-love, so you may be filled out in all of God's fullness.

²⁰To the one empowered to do beyond all things uber-abundantly more than what we ask or think, consistent with the power energizing in you, ²¹to him [be] the splendor in the assembly and in Christos Yēsous for all the Era of Era's generations. Amēn!

Gifts for the assembly's growth

4 Therefore, I, a prisoner in the Lord, beg you to walk deservingly of the calling to which you were called, ²with all impoverishment and meekness, with patience, putting up with one another in love, ³committing to observe the Spirit's oneness in a peace-bond.

⁴There is one body and one Spirit,
just as you were called in your calling's
one hope.
⁵One Lord,
one allegiance,
one dipping,
⁶one God and Father of all,
who is over all and through all and in all.

⁷To each of us was given the grace consistent with the measure of the Christos's gift. ⁸Therefore it says,

*Ascending to the height,
he captured captives,
He gave gifts to humans.*

⁹This *he ascended*, what is it except that he also descended into the lower regions of the land? ¹⁰The one descending is also the same one *ascending* way above all heavens so he might fill out all things. ¹¹He gave some to be Commissioners, some to be prophets, some to be gospelers, some to be pastors and teachers: ¹²for preparing the devoted ones, for service-works, for Christos-body formation, ¹³until all of us arrive unto allegiance's oneness and perception of God's Son, unto a complete adulthood, unto a measure—the height of Christos's fullness—¹⁴so we may no longer be infants, wave-tossed and carried around by every wind of teaching, [done] by human "rolling of the dice," by trickery, in line with the device of deception, ¹⁵truthing in love, that we may grow into him in all matters, who is the head, Christos, ¹⁶from whom the whole body, joined and held together through every supplying joint, consistent with the measured energy of each one's part, makes the body's growth for formation of itself in love.

The no-longer life of the ethnic groups

¹⁷Therefore, I say this and I witness in Lord: You are no longer to walk around as the ethnic groups are walking around in the idleness of their perception, ¹⁸being darkened in intelligence, being "othered" from God's life because of ignorance among themselves, because of their heart's hardening, ¹⁹who having become insensible gave themselves over to flaunting sensuality for working every impurity in wanting more and more.

²⁰You were not apprenticed to Christos like that, ²¹if indeed you heard him and you were taught in him as is truth in Yēsous:

²²you are to *put off* consistent with your
former behavior the ancient
human, the one abominating
consistent with deceit's desires,
²³and be new-minded by the Spirit of
your mind,
²⁴and *put on* the new human who, being
created consistent with God['s
image] in truth's rightness and piety.

Some do's and don'ts

²⁵Therefore, putting off the falsehood, *each of you speak truth with one's neighbor* because we are parts of one another.

²⁶*Be angry and don't sin.*
Let not the sun set on your anger,
²⁷nor create space for the Accuser.

²⁸The thief—let him thieve no longer but instead let him labor, working the good with his own hands, so he may have [something good] to distribute to the one having need.

²⁹Don't let any diseased word journey out from your mouth, but if something is good [let it be] for the formation [of the one in] need—so it may give grace to the ones hearing.

³⁰Don't pain God's Holy Spirit, in which you were sealed for deliverance day.

³¹Let every bitterness and wrath and anger and shouting and insult be lifted from you with every evil.

³²Be gracious to one another, commiserating, gracing one another just as God has graced you in Christos.

5 Therefore, be copies of God as loved children.

²Walk around in love as the Christos loved us and gave himself for us, a contribution and sacrifice to God for a good-aroma fragrance.

³Let not sexual immorality and any impurity or wanting more and more even be

named among you, just as it's appropriate for the devoted ones, ⁴and [also] vulgarity and moronic words and jocularity, which things are not proper, but instead—thanks.

⁵For, know this: knowing that every person prostituting or impure or wanting-more-and-more—which is demon worship—doesn't have inheritance in the Christos-and-God's Empire.

⁶Let no one deceive you with hollow words. For because of these matters God's anger comes on unpersuasion's descendants. ⁷Therefore, don't become their coparticipants.

⁸For you were once darkness but now light in the Lord. Walk around as light's children—⁹for the light's fruit [grows] in all goodness and rightness and truth—¹⁰judging suitable what is judged beautiful by the Lord.

¹¹Don't have common life with darkness's unfruitful works, but instead even convince [them]. ¹²For the matters done in secret by them are degrading even to say. ¹³All the matters that convince [of the truth] are made apparent by the light, ¹⁴for everything that is apparent is light. Therefore it says,

Arise, sleeping one,
And rising up from among the dead
    ones,
The Christos will shine on you.

¹⁵Therefore, look carefully how you walk around, not as unwise but as wise, ¹⁶purchasing the season because the days are evil. ¹⁷Because this is true, don't be imprudent but understand what the Lord's will is. ¹⁸Don't booze it up with wine, in which is dissolution, but be filled up in Spirit [by]: ¹⁹speaking to yourselves in string-accompanied songs and hymns and spiritual odes, singing and playing the strings in your heart to the Lord, ²⁰always thanking for everything (in our Lord Yēsous Christos's name) the Father-God, ²¹ordering yourselves under one another in awe of Christos:

²²*Women* [ordering under] your own men as to the Lord, ²³because man is women's head as also the Christos is the assembly's head—he is the Body's Deliverer—²⁴but as the assembly orders itself under the Christos so also women to men in all things.

²⁵*Men*, love your women just as also the Christos loved the assembly and gave himself over for it, ²⁶so he might devote it, purifying by water's lustration in utterance, ²⁷so he might present the assembly to himself in splendor, not having a stain or crease or any such thing, but *so* the assembly might be devoted and inerrant. ²⁸In such a way men ought to love their own women as their own bodies. The one who loves his own woman, loves himself. ²⁹For no one once hated one's own flesh but nurtures and warms it, just as the Christos [does] the assembly, ³⁰because we are parts of his Body. ³¹*Because of this a human will leave father and mother and will be joined to his woman, and they will be two in one flesh*. ³²This secret is great: I speak about Christos and the assembly. ³³However, also you individually: let each love his own woman as himself and the woman: that she might awe the man.

6 *Children*, heed your parents in Lord, for this is right. ²*Honor your father and mother*, which is the first order with a pledge, ³*so it may be good for you and you may have macro-duration on the land*.

⁴And *fathers*, don't irritate your children but nurture them in Lord's education and mentoring.

⁵*Slaves*, heed your fleshy lords, with awe and trembling, in your heart's generosity, as [you heed] Christos, ⁶not consistent with eye-slaving—as human-pleasing—but as Christos's slaves, doing God's will from the self, ⁷slaving with a good mind as to the Lord and not to humans, ⁸knowing that each one, if one does what is good, this one will obtain from Lord, whether slave or free.

⁹*Lords*, do the same things to them, abandoning the threat, knowing that their and your Lord is in heavens, and there is no face-favoring with him.

God's protective armor

¹⁰What remains: be empowered in the Lord and in his might's grip. ¹¹Put on God's panoply of weapons so you are powered to stand against the Accuser's devices ¹²because for us the wrestling-match isn't against blood and flesh but against the celestial leaders, against the

authorities, against this darkness's Kosmos-strength, against evil's spiritual beings in the heavenlies. ¹³Because this is true, take up God's panoply of weapons so you are powered to resist in the evil day and, effecting all these things, [powered] to stand.

¹⁴Therefore stand:
wrapping truth around your waist,
putting on rightness's breastplate,
¹⁵binding your feet with preparation [to announce] the peace gospel,
¹⁶in all ways, taking up faith's shield,
with which you will be powered to snuff out all the evil one's fiery arrows.
¹⁷Receive salvation's helmet
and the Spirit's long knife, which is God's utterance.

¹⁸Praying through every prayer and request in every season in the Spirit, and for this, being alert in all persistence and request for all the devoted ones ¹⁹and for me, that a word may be given to me in opening my mouth to make known with frankness the gospel's secret, ²⁰for which I mediate in chains, that I may be given frankness as it's necessary for me to speak.

²¹Tuchikos [Tychicus]—the loved brother and allegiant servant in Lord—will make known all matters to you so you may know the matters about me—what I practice, ²²whom I sent to you for this reason so you may know the matters about us and [that he might] encourage your hearts.

²³Peace to the siblings and love with allegiance from Father-God and Lord Yēsous Christos. ²⁴Grace be with all the lovers of our Lord Yēsous Christos—in non-decayability.

INTRODUCTION TO PHILIPPIANS

One reads Paulos's [Paul's] letters best when one reads the last sections of the letter first. We get the social realities that way, and they inform our reading of the letter itself. Those sections often tell us about persons and events, and in his letter to the Philippians we learn about two women, Euodia and Suntuchē [Syntyche] (4:2) and about a man named Klēmēs [Clement] (4:3). A few paragraphs later we read about how the Philippians had contributed provisions to Paulos when he was in Thessalonikē [Thessalonica] (4:15-16). In the middle of the letter is another section that opens the lid on the assemblies: we learn about Timotheos [Timothy] (2:19-24) and Epaphroditos [Epaphroditus] (2:25-30; 4:18), the latter who was sent with the letter and the former whom Paulos planned to send (and perhaps accompany him).

There was some issue between the two women, and it's futile to speculate what it was, but what we learn about them is that they needed to "think the same in the Lord" and Paulos needed support from his "genuine partner." As the sentence moves on we learn that Euodia and Suntuchē were co-competitors with Paulos in gospel work and they were in the inner circle of his coworkers. The issue, then, is about unity in the assemblies [churches] of Christos in his first "European" mission location for Paulos the Lord's Commissioner.

Paulos's prayer and thanksgiving are simultaneously ethical vision statements: his desire is that their common life and fellowship and love and perception and insight can lead to moral discernment and rightness (1:3-11). His own imprisonment, which is why a letter is sent instead of him being personally present, is both an opportunity for him to embody gospel suffering and the opportunity for them to provide for him (1:12-26). His wonderful exhortations to unity and common life, or fellowship, then become the prominent themes in the letter, and this unity was embodied in Christos's self-denying surrender for others, and that very way of thinking was to be the paradigm for the Philippians (2:1-11). The way of Christos is the way for the Philippians. Notice in reading this letter how often Paulos in a variety of ways encourages them to think in a new way (see 2:2, 5).

There are problem people, as there always were in the assemblies of Paulos, and these seemingly claim to preach the true way of biblical faith (2:15-18). Against these Paulos turns in chapter 3 to call them "dogs" and "evil workers" and "incisionists" (3:2), while he claims it's the people of Christos who are the true "circumcision(ists)" (3:3). Paulos's claims are deep, yet he presses on in Christos for the final day of reckoning.

This letter, while distinct because it was for one community's assemblies, typifies Paulos's letters in its style, its apparent agitation at times, and its quick shifts to other topics. Running throughout this letter are contextual problems and theological acuteness (about God and about redemption in Christos), but in the end his deepest concern is how these people are to live in Christos—especially with one another in a common life in unity.

TO THE PHILIPPIANS

From Paulos and Timotheos to Philippoi

1 Paulos [Paul] and Timotheos [Timothy], Christos Yēsous' slaves,
to all the devoted ones in Christos Yēsous who are in Philippoi [Philippi], with mentors and deacons.
²Grace to you and peace from our Father-God and Lord Yēsous Christos.

Paulos prays for Philippoi

³I thank my God at every memory of you, ⁴always in my every request for all of you, making the request with joy, ⁵for your common life in the gospel from the first day until now, ⁶fully persuaded of this very matter, that the one beginning the good work in you will complete [it] until the Day of Christos Yēsous, ⁷just as it's right for me to think this about all of you because I have you in my heart, in my imprisonment and in my defense and in the gospel's confirmation, all of you being in common life with me in the grace. ⁸For God is my witness: How I long for all of you in Christos Yēsous' empathies. ⁹I am praying this: that your love may overflow more and more in perception and all insight ¹⁰so you may judge superior matters suitable, so you may be transparent with nothing noticeable at Christos's Day, ¹¹filled out with rightness's fruit, through Yēsous Christos, to God's splendor and public praise.

Paulos called to prison ministry

¹²I want you to know, siblings, that my matters have come rather for the gospel's advance ¹³so that my bonds become apparent in Christos to the whole soldiers' headquarters and to all the remaining ones ¹⁴and [so that] most of the siblings, having been persuaded in the Lord by my bonds, dare aboundingly to speak the word fearlessly. ¹⁵Some because of envy and strife and others because of delight announce Christos. ¹⁶These [announce Christos] out of love, knowing that I am laid here for the gospel's defense, ¹⁷but those out of strife proclaim the Christos, without devotion, imagining to raise trouble in my bonds. ¹⁸For what? However—that in every manner, whether in pretense or in truth, Christos is proclaimed, and in this I rejoice.

But I also will rejoice: ¹⁹For I know that this will result in deliverance for me, through your requests and [through] Yēsous Christos's Spirit's supply ²⁰consistent with my impatient expectation and hope, that I will not be shamed in anything but in all frankness—as always, also now—Christos will be magnified in my body, whether through life or whether through death. ²¹For—for me—to live is Christos and to die is gain. ²²If to live in the flesh, this for me is work's fruit, and which [one] I choose I don't know. ²³I am absorbed between the two, having the desire to leave and to be with Christos, for that is much better, ²⁴but to remain in the flesh is more necessary because of you. ²⁵Having been persuaded of this: I know that I will remain and closely remain with all of you for your advancement and allegiance's joy ²⁶so your boast about me will overflow in Christos Yēsous through my arrival again with you.

Gospel competitors

²⁷Only, live your community-life deservingly of the Christos-gospel so—whether coming and seeing you, or being away—I hear matters about you: that you stand in one Spirit, co-training with one self in the gospel-allegiance, ²⁸not being terrified in any way by the opposers, which is destruction's exhibition for them but deliverance for you, and this from God, ²⁹because [the suffering] for Christos has been graced to you, not only to be allegiant to him but also to suffer for him, ³⁰having the same contest that you saw in me and now you hear in me.

Unity through humility

2 Therefore,
if [there is] any encouragement in Christos,
if any of love's comfort,
if any of the Spirit's common life,
if any empathies and sympathies,
²[then] fill out my joy so you may
think the same,
having the same love,
co-selves,
thinking one thing,

³not [acting] consistent with strife, not consistent with airheadedness,

but, in impoverishment, considering one
  another superior to themselves,
⁴each person not scoping out
  matters for themselves but each
  of you [scoping out] matters for
  the others.

⁵Think this among you, which is also in Christos Yēsous,

⁶Who, being in God's form,
Did not consider being equal with God
  [a status to be] seized,
⁷but hollowed himself,
taking a slave's form,
becoming representation of humans;
and, being found in a scheme like a
  human,
⁸he impoverished himself,
becoming obedient all the way to death
(death on a cross).
⁹Therefore also, God exalted him in
  status,
and graced him with the name above
  every name,
¹⁰so at Yēsous' name every knee would
  bend,
in the heavens,
on the earth,
and in the underworld,
¹¹and every tongue openly agrees that
  Yēsous Christos is Lord,
  to Father-God's splendor.

God's infallible, inerrant children

¹²So that, my loved ones, just as you always heeded me, not only in my arrival but now even more in my absence, and with awe and trembling, effect your deliverance, ¹³for God is the one energizing in you, both to want and to energize for the sake of delight.

¹⁴Do all things apart from grumbling and deliberations ¹⁵so you may be infallible and innocent, God's inerrant children in the middle of a crooked and distorted generation, among whom you appear as stars in the Kosmos, ¹⁶clinging to Life's word—for me to boast on Christos's Day: that I did not run hollow, nor did I labor hollow. ¹⁷But even if I am poured out on the sacrifice and your faith's public work, I rejoice and co-rejoice with all of you, ¹⁸and in the same way you also rejoice and co-rejoice with me.

Timotheos and Epaphroditos

¹⁹I hope, in the Lord Yēsous, quickly to send Timotheos [Timothy] to you so I too may be revived, knowing matters about you. ²⁰For I have no equal-self, who genuinely is disturbed about matters concerning you. ²¹For all pursue matters for themselves, not matters for Yēsous Christos, ²²but you know his approval: that he slaved for the gospel with me as a child with a father. ²³Therefore, I hope to send this person immediately, as soon as I determine matters about me. ²⁴I am persuaded in the Lord that I also will come to you quickly.

²⁵I considered it necessary to send to you Epaphroditos [Epaphroditus] (the brother and coworker and my co-soldier, and your Commissioner-and-public-worker for my need), ²⁶since he was longing for all of you and being discomforted because you heard that he was weakened. ²⁷For he was even weakened approaching death, but God showed compassion to him, not to him alone but also to me so I might not have pain upon pain. ²⁸Therefore, with commitment I sent him so, seeing him, you again may rejoice and I may be pain-free. ²⁹Therefore, attend to him in the Lord with all joy and have public honor for such persons ³⁰because for Christos's work he closed in on death, putting his self at risk so he might fill up what you lack in public work for me.

3 What remains: My siblings, rejoice in Lord!

To write these same matters to you isn't timidity for me but certainty for you.

Incisionists, circumcisionists, and rightness

²Look at the dogs!
Look at the bad workers!
Look at the incisionists!

³For we are the circumcision(ists), ones venerating in God's Spirit and boasting in Christos Yēsous and not having been persuaded in flesh, ⁴even though I, also having a persuasion in the flesh. If another person looks like he has been persuaded in the flesh, I [have] more:

⁵Eighth day for circumcision,
from Yisraēl's [Israel's] ethnic group,
tribe of Benyamin [Benjamin],

Hebraios of Hebraioi [Hebrew of Hebrews]
Observant [Pharisee] consistent with Covenant Code,
⁶chasing the assembly consistent with zeal,
being infallible consistent with rightness in Code.

⁷But those matters that were a gain for me—these matters I have considered forfeit because of Christos. ⁸But then even more: I consider all matters to be a forfeit because of the higher status of knowing Christos Yēsous my Lord, because of whom I have forfeited all matters and I consider them to be feces so I may gain Christos ⁹and that I may be found in him, not having my rightness from Code but rightness through Christos-allegiance, God's rightness on the basis of allegiance, ¹⁰to know him and his resurrection's power and his suffering's common life, being co-morphed to his death, ¹¹if somehow I may arrive at the reinvigoration from among the dead ones.

We are not yet there

¹²Not that I already received [*lambanō*] [the prize] or already have completed. Rather, I am chasing so that I might also prevail [*katalambanō*]—for which also I was prevailed [*katalambanō*] by Christos Yēsous. ¹³Siblings, I don't calculate myself to have prevailed. But one thing [I do is] forgetting the matters behind and stretching out to those matters in front, ¹⁴I am chasing consistent with the scope: God's upper calling prize in Christos Yēsous. ¹⁵Therefore, whoever is complete, let the person think this. If someone thinks differently, God will also apocalypse this to you. ¹⁶However, at [the level] we have arrived, walk the line at that level.

¹⁷Become my co-copies, siblings, and scope out those who so walk around just as you have us as a type. ¹⁸For many walk around—about whom I was often speaking to you but now I, wailing, speak—as Christos-cross's enemies,

¹⁹whose completion is destruction,
whose God is the belly,
and the splendor is in their shame,
who are earthy-thinkers.

²⁰For our community-life exists in the heavens, from which we also impatiently wait a Deliverer, Lord Yēsous Christos, ²¹who will reshape our impoverished body to be co-morphed to his splendorous body consistent with the energy that empowers him also to order all things under him.

4 So that, my siblings—loved and longed for, my joy and crown, so stand in the Lord, siblings.

Euodia and Syntyche

²I beg Euodia [Ms. Good Path] and I beg Suntuchē [Syntyche] [Ms. Fortune] to think the same in the Lord. ³Yes, and I ask you [sg.], genuine partner [male] . . . co-assisting them . . . who have co-trained with me in the gospel and with Klēmēs [Clement] and my remaining coworkers, whose names are in Life's Book.

Unity as habit

⁴Rejoice in Lord always! Again I say, Rejoice!

⁵May your meekness be known to all humans.

The Lord is close.

⁶Don't be disturbed but, in everything in prayer and in requests—with thanks—let your asks be made known to God.

⁷God's peace, which is superior to all perception, will guard your hearts and your mentalities in Christos Yēsous.

⁸What remains: siblings, whatever is true,
whatever is deserving of respect,
whatever is right,
whatever is devoted,
whatever is friendly,
whatever is well-stated—
if there is any virtue,
if there is any public praise—calculate these matters.

⁹And the matters in which you were apprenticed and received and heard and knew in me: practice these, and the Peace-God will be with you.

Paulos and the Philippoi

¹⁰I have been greatly joyed in the Lord because now at last you blossomed into thinking about me, about whom indeed you were thinking but you lacked opportunity. ¹¹I am not speaking consistent with a lack, for I

am apprenticed to be self-sufficient with what I have. ¹²I know [what it is] to be impoverished and I know also [what it is] to flow over. In all matters and in all ways I am initiated: to be satisfied and to hunger, to flow over and to lack. ¹³I am strong in all [these] matters in the one who empowers me. ¹⁴However, you did beautifully, sharing a common life in my troubles.

¹⁵You also have known, Philippēsioi [Philippians], that in the gospel's beginning, when I exited from Makedonia [Macedonia], no assembly shared commonly with me in an account of giving and receiving except you alone, ¹⁶because even in Thessalonikē [Thessalonica], once and twice you sent for my need. ¹⁷Not that I pursue the gift but I pursue the fruit that magnifies to your account. ¹⁸I have all things and I flow over. I am filled out, receiving from Epaphroditos [Epaphroditus] the items from you, a good-aroma fragrance, a receivable sacrifice, judged beautiful by God.

¹⁹My God will fill out all your need consistent with his wealth in splendor in Christos Yēsous. ²⁰May the splendor be to our Father-God unto the Eras of Eras.

Amēn!

²¹Greet all the devoted in Christos Yēsous. The siblings with me greet you.

²²All the devoted ones (especially the ones in Kaisar's [Caesar's] house) greet you.

²³The Lord Yēsous Christos's grace be with your spirit.

INTRODUCTION TO COLOSSIANS

Dating Paulos's [Paul's] letters requires patience and caution. We use the information that surfaces in his letters, compare them, and then sort them out along with what is said in the Acts of the Apostles—and then approximate. I date Colossians, along with Philēmon, to the early 50s, perhaps AD 53–55, when Paulos is in prison—in what may well be Ephesos [Ephesus] (not Rōmē).

The founder of the churches of the Lycus Valley—Kolossai [Colossae], Laodikeia [Laodicea], Hierapolis (each visible today, but Kolossai remains nothing but a large grassy mound that has yet to be excavated)—was not Paulos, for he tells us in 2:1 that these assemblies have not yet met him face to face. The founder was the fellow Colossian Epaphras, a young convert of Paulos's about whom Paulos glows with words of commendation (1:7-8; 4:12-13). Evidently, and here we have to offer a suggestion, Epaphras's training with Paulos was inadequate for responding to some in Kolossai who had combined Jewish law and rulings with mystical experiences (2:8-23). Paulos saw this teaching as dangerous and not sufficiently anchored in Christos (2:19), and it's reasonable to think the amazing hymn-like words of Colossians 1:15-20 are also designed to offer the proper teaching on Christos.

That teaching about Christos is that he is Creator, redeemer, and nothing less than the origin and goal of all creation! In Yēsous the fullness of what makes God *God* dwells in bodily form, and yet that incarnate one is truly both Creator and goal of all creation—he sustains and directs all toward reconciliation. God's reconciliation of all things in Christos includes the Colossians, and this reconciliation by God's grace generates a new life of living in Christos (2:6-7), which itself manifests itself in any number of specifics, some of which are expressed in various exhortations in the letter (see 2:20–4:6). One of the distinguishing features of this letter, along with Ephesians, is Paulos's instructions for how the believers are to live in the context of their households (3:18–4:1), a major feature of which is those more powerful using that status for the empowerment of others (husbands for wives, fathers for children, and masters for slaves). Life in the Lord transformed all relationships. This section in the letter turns the Roman way of life, that is, power and status, on its head.

It's noticeable that the letter carrier seems to be either Tuchikos [Tychicus] or, perhaps, both Tuchikos and Onēsimos, the runaway slave, whom we will meet again in Paulos's letter to Philēmon, a householder in Kolossai (see 4:7-9; Philemon).

TO THE COLOSSIANS

Paulos and Timotheos to Kolossai

1 Paulos [Paul], Christos Yēsous' Commissioner through God's plan, and Timotheos [Timothy], the brother, ²to the devoted and allegiant siblings in Christos in Kolossai [Colossae].

Grace to you and peace from our Father-God.

Paulos prays for Kolossai

³We always thank the Father-God of our Lord Yēsous Christos, praying for you, ⁴hearing about your allegiance in Christos Yēsous and the love that you have for all the devoted ones ⁵because of the hope deposited for you in the heavens, which you previously heard in truth's word, the gospel, ⁶which being present to you, just as also in the whole Kosmos it [gospel] is fruit-producing and growing, so also among you, from the day you heard and perceived God's grace in truth—⁷just as you were apprenticed from Epaphras, our loved co-slave, who is Christos's allegiant servant for you, ⁸and also the one who divulged to us your love in the Spirit.

⁹Because this is true, we also, since the day we heard, don't stop praying and asking for you, that you may be filled out with perception of his plan in all wisdom and Spirit-prompted understanding, ¹⁰to walk around deserving of the Lord in all pleasing, producing good fruit in every good work and growing in perceiving God, ¹¹in all power empowering in a manner consistent with his splendorous grip for all resilience and patience. With joy ¹²thanking the Father who made us adequate us for the devoted ones' part in the inheritance in the light,

Digression on reconciliation in Christos

¹³who rescued us from the Darkness's authority and removed [us] into his loved Son's Empire, ¹⁴in whom we have the liberation, release from the sins . . .

¹⁵who is the invisible God's image,
all Creation's Firstborn,
¹⁶because in him all things were created,
in the heavens and on the land,
the visibles and the invisibles,
whether thrones or lordships,
whether leaders or authorities.
all things were created through him and
    for him.
¹⁷He is before all things
and in him all things co-exist.
¹⁸He is the head of the Body, the
    assembly.
Who is beginning,
Firstborn from among the dead ones,
so he might in all things become the
    preeminenting one.
¹⁹Because in him all the fullness was
    delighted to reside,
²⁰and through him to reconcile all
    things to him,
making peace through his cross's blood,
through him,
whether things on the land
or things in the heavens.

Digression continues: Their reconciliation in Christos

²¹You, who were once othered and enemies in [your] intelligence—in the evil works—²²but [you] he now reconciled in his flesh's body through the death to present you devoted and inerrant and unimpeachable before him—²³if you remain in allegiance, being founded and stabilized and not shifting from the hope of the gospel that you heard, that was announced in all creation that is under the heaven, of which I, Paulos, became a servant.

My story and your story

²⁴I now rejoice in the sufferings for you and I fill up the lacks in Christos's troubles in my flesh for his body, which is the assembly [church], ²⁵of which I became a servant consistent with God's management that was given to me for you to fill out God's word, ²⁶the secret that has been hidden from the Eras and from the generations—but now has become apparent to his devoted ones, ²⁷to whom God wanted to make known what is this secret's splendorous wealth among the ethnic groups, which is Christos in you, the splendor's hope, ²⁸whom we proclaim, mentoring every human and teaching every human in all wisdom, so we might present every human complete in

Christos, ²⁹for which I also labor, contesting in a manner consistent with his energy that is energizing in me with power.

2 For I want you to know how great of a contest I have for you and for those in Laodikeia [Laodicea]—and whoever has not seen my fleshly face—²so their hearts may be encouraged, being instructed in love and in understanding's wealth of full assurance, in perception of God's secret, that is, Christos, ³in whom all of wisdom's and knowledge's treasures are hidden.

⁴I say this so no one will deceive you in a persuasive word. ⁵For even if I am absent in the flesh, but I am with you in the Spirit, rejoicing and seeing your order and the firmness of your allegiance in Christos.

Heart of the Exhortation

⁶Therefore, as you received the Christos Yēsous, the Lord, walk around in him, ⁷being rooted and formed up in him and being assured in the faith just as you were taught, flowing over in thanks.

Correcting false religion

⁸See that there will be no one who plunders you through philosophy and hollow deceit consistent with humans' convention, consistent with Kosmos's categories and not consistent with Christos, ⁹because all the divine fullness resides in him bodily, ¹⁰and you have been filled out in him,

Who is the head over all rule and
    authority.
¹¹In him also you were circumcised with
    a non-hand-performed
    circumcision,
in the stripping away of your flesh's body,
in the Christos-circumcision,
¹²being co-buried with him in the
    dipping,
in which also you were co-raised
    through trusting God's energy,
    who raised him up from among
    the dead ones.

¹³You, being dead in your wrongs and in your flesh's foreskin . . . God made a life for you with him, gracing us all our wrongs, ¹⁴wiping out the handwritten bill that was against us (with its rulings), which was opposed to us, and he lifted it [bill] from the midst, nailing it to the cross. ¹⁵Stripping the leaders and authorities, he exhibited [them] with frankness, parading them in it.

¹⁶Therefore, let no one judge you in food or in drink or with regard to a feast, a new moon, or the Sabbaths—¹⁷which practices are a shadow of coming events, but the body is of the Christos. ¹⁸Don't let any deprive you, wanting "impoverishment" and "angel-like worship," entering into what they have seen—[such a person is] appealing to natural status vainly by his fleshy mind ¹⁹and not grabbing the Head, from whom the whole body, being supplied and being knit together by the connections and bonds, grows God's growth.

True religion

²⁰If you died with Christos from the Kosmos's categories, why do you make rules yourself as living in the Kosmos? ²¹"Don't touch! Don't taste! Don't handle"—²²all of which practices are [headed] to decay by consumption, consistent with humans' ordinances and teachings, ²³which things having a "word of wisdom" in "self-shaped worship" and "impoverishment" and "body severity" [but gain] no honor for the flesh's satiety.[a]

3 Therefore, if you have been co-raised with Christos, pursue upper matters, where the Christos is sitting at God's right. ²Think about upper matters, not on-the-land matters, ³for you died and your life has been hid with the Christos in God. ⁴Whenever the Christos becomes apparent, [who is] your life, then also you with him will become apparent in splendor.

Expanding the exhortation: Old and new

⁵Therefore, deaden the on-the-land parts—

sexual immorality,
impurity,
passion,
bad desire,
and wanting more and more, which is
    demon worship,

---

[a] The words in quotation marks are most likely quotations of those whom Paul is opposing.

⁶because of which God's anger comes upon the unpersuaded's descendants. ⁷Among whom also you once walked around when you were living in those [sins]. ⁸But now you also put off all these ways—

> anger,
> fury,
> badness,
> insult,
> shaming speech from your mouth.

⁹Don't falsify to one another,
having stripped away the ancient human with its practices ¹⁰and having put on the new [human], who is being renewed in perception consistent with the image of the one who created it, ¹¹where there isn't Hellēn [Greek] and Youdaios [Judean, Jew], circumcision and foreskin, barbarian, Skuthēs [Scythian], slave, liberated . . . but Christos is all matters and in all.

> ¹²Therefore, put on—as God's elect,
>   devoted and loved—
> empathies of sympathy,
> graciousness,
> impoverishment,
> meekness,
> patience,
> ¹³putting up with one another
> and gracing each other if someone has a
>   grievance toward someone—just
>   as also the Lord graced you, so
>   also you [grace others].
> ¹⁴On all these: love, which is
>   completeness's bond.
> ¹⁵Let Christos's peace umpire in your
>   hearts, to which also you were
>   called in one body.
> Be thankful.
> ¹⁶Let Christos's word reside among you
>   richly, in all wisdom teaching and
>   mentoring each other—in
>   string-accompanied songs, hymns,
>   and Spirit-prompted odes, in grace
>   singing in your hearts to God.

Exhortations about life "in the Lord"

¹⁷Whatever you do in word or in work, [do] all in Lord Yēsous' name, thanking the Father-God through him.

¹⁸*Women*, order yourselves under the men as is proper in the Lord.

¹⁹*Men*, love the women and don't become poisonous toward them.

²⁰*Children*, heed your parents consistent with all ways, for this is pleasing in the Lord.

²¹*Fathers*, don't pick fights with your children so they may not be deflated.

²²*Slaves*, heed your fleshy lords, not while [there's] an eye-on-the-slave, human-pleasing [manner] but with a generous heart, fearing the Lord. ²³Whatever you do, work from the self as to the Lord and not to humans, ²⁴knowing that you will receive from the Lord the inheritance-reward.

Slave to the Lord Christos!

²⁵For the one doing wrong will obtain what one wronged, and there is no face-favoring.

4 *Lords*, present to the slaves rightness and equality, knowing that you also have the Lord in heaven.

Exhortations for the church

²Persist in the prayer, being awake in it in thanks, ³praying then also for us so God may open for us the word's door to speak the secret, the Christos—because of which [secret] I have also been bound—⁴so I may make it apparent as it's for me necessary to speak.

⁵Walk around in wisdom toward those outside, purchasing the season.

⁶Let your word [be] always in grace, flavored with salt, so you may know how it's necessary to respond to each one.

Letter carriers

⁷Tuchikos [Tychicus], the loved brother and allegiant servant and co-slave in Lord, will make known to you all matters about me. ⁸I sent him to you for this very reason—that you may know the matters concerning us and he may encourage your hearts—⁹with Onēsimos [Handyman], the allegiant and loved brother, who is of you. They will make all the matters here known to you.

These greet you

¹⁰Aristarchos [Aristarchus], my co-prisoner, greets you, and [so does] Markos [Mark], Bar-Nabas's [Barnabas's] cousin (concerning whom you received orders: if he comes to you, receive him), ¹¹and [so does] Yēsous, the one called Youstos [Justus]—ones being of the circumcision, these only [are]

coworkers in God's Empire, who have become consolers for me. ¹²Epaphras, who is of you, Christos Yēsous' slave, always contesting for you in the prayers that you may stand complete and fully assured in all God's will—greets you. ¹³For I witness for him that he has much pain for you and ones in Laodikeia [Laodicea] and ones in Hierapolis. ¹⁴Loukas [Luke], the doctor who is loved, greets you, and [so does] Dēmas.

Please greet these

¹⁵You greet the siblings in Laodikeia and Numpha [Nympha] and the assembly that [meets] at her house.

Read this letter elsewhere

¹⁶Whenever the letter has been read for you, do [the same] also that it may be read in the assembly of Laodikeia, and also [do the same] that you also read the letter from Laodikeia.

¹⁷Say to Archippos [Archippus]: "See the service that you received in the Lord, that you fill it out."

¹⁸Paulos's greeting in my hand.
Remember my bonds.
The grace be with you.

INTRODUCTION TO THE FIRST LETTER TO THE THESSALONIANS

Paulos [Paul] along with Silouanos [Silvanus] founded assemblies in this major port city on the Egnatian Way. Thessaloniki [Thessalonica] is also today a major European city in modern northern Greece. Because of opposition instigated by fellow Youdaians [Judeans, Jews], they were not in Thessalonikē (pronounced Thes-SAL-ah-nee-kee) long, as Acts 17 shows, even though this letter reveals Paulos worked night and day and converted Gentiles. Noticeably, this opposition formed into the accusation that Paulos and Silouanos defied the Kaisar's [Caesar's] decrees by claiming another king, namely, Yēsous Christos.

Not long after Paulos and Silouanos departed Thessalonikē they arrived in Athenai [Athens], from which location Paulos sent Timotheos [Timothy] (3:1-5) back to Thessalonikē. Paulos then moved to Korinth [Corinth], where Timotheos and Silouanos caught up with him. From there Paulos sent this personally warm letter (probably) in AD 50. So, we have a letter to a relatively new assembly of Christians where already some problems need to be addressed, including a batch of lazy believers who may well have stopped working because they thought the Parousia [coming] was at hand—a theme addressed intensely in 4:13–5:11. There is a strong tone of apocalyptic eschatology in both of the letters sent to the believers in Thessalonikē.

Socially, there is tension between believers and nonbelievers in the city according to Acts 17:1-9, and the expression "much trouble" in 1:6, the suffering at 2:14, and the emphasis in chapter 5 on loving one another and getting along with leaders make one think social peace was not yet achieved. Remarkably, there is no emphasis in this letter on the common problem faced in the Pauline mission: how the ethnic groups were to live with respect to the Covenant Code laid out by Moses. Perhaps most of the converts in this city were Gentiles. Yet, there does seem to be opposition to Paulos's mission (cf. 2:14-16).

THE FIRST LETTER TO THE THESSALONIANS

From Paulos, Silouanos, and Timotheos to Thessalonikē

1 Paulos [Paul] and Silouanos [Silvanus] and Timotheos [Timothy] to the Thessalonians' assembly in Father-God and in the Lord Yēsous Christos. Grace to you and peace.

Thanking God for them

²We thank God always for all of you, making memory in our prayers, incessantly ³remembering your allegiance's work and your love's labor and the resilence's hope in our Lord Yēsous Christos—[all prayed] before our God and Father—⁴knowing, loved-by-God-siblings, your election, ⁵that our gospel did not come to you in word only but also in power and in the Holy Spirit and in much full assurance, just as you know what kind of persons we became among you for you. ⁶You became copies of us and the Lord, receiving the word in much trouble with the Holy Spirit's joy, ⁷so that you became a type for all the allegiant ones in Makedonia [Macedonia] and in Achaia, ⁸for the Lord's word echoes out from you not only in Makedonia and in Achaia but in every place your allegiance toward God has exited out so that we don't have a need to speak about it. ⁹For about us they declare what kind of path-entry we had to you, and how you returned to God from demon-idols to be a slave for the living and true God ¹⁰and to wait for his Son from the heavens, whom he raised from among the dead ones, Yēsous—the one who rescued us from the coming anger.

Paulos and Thessalonikē

2 For you yourselves know, siblings, our path-entry to you—that it did not become hollow ²but, previously suffering and being assaulted, as you know, in Philippoi [Philippi], in our God we frankly spoke God's gospel to you in a great contest. ³For our encouragement isn't out of deception nor out of impurity nor in disguise ⁴but, just as we have been judged suitable by God to be entrusted with the gospel, so we speak, not as pleasing humans but [pleasing] God, who approves our hearts. ⁵For not even once were we with a word of flattery (just as you know) or with pretense of wanting more and more (God is witness), ⁶or pursuing splendor from humans—neither from you nor from others—⁷being empowered weightily to be [received] as Christos-Commissioners—but we were as infants in your midst, as if a nurse nurturing her own children; ⁸so, yearning for you, we were delighted to distribute to you not only God's gospel but our own selves because you were loved ones to us. ⁹For you remember, siblings, our labor and fatigue: night and day working not to overload any of you, we announced to you God's gospel. ¹⁰You are witnesses and also God—how piously and rightly and infallibly we were with you allegiant ones, ¹¹just as you know, as to each one of you, as a father to his children, ¹²encouraging you and soothing and witnessing for you to walk around deservingly of the God who called you into his Empire and splendor.

¹³Because this is true, we also thank God incessantly that, receiving God's word you heard from us, you welcomed it not as a human word but (as it's truly) God's word, who is also energizing among you who are allegiant. ¹⁴For you became copies, siblings, of God's assemblies [churches] who are in Youdaia [Judea] in Christos Yēsous, that you suffered the same things—you from your own tribe as they from the Youdaians [Judeans, Jews] ¹⁵(the ones who also killed the Lord Yēsous and the prophets)—and chased us out, and not pleasing God and being against all humans, ¹⁶hindering us to speak to the ethnic groups so they may be delivered—always to fill up their sins. The anger has arrived on them to completion.

¹⁷We, siblings, being orphaned from you for an hour's season—by face, not heart—we abundantly committed to see your face with much desire. ¹⁸Because we wanted to come to you, I Paulos [Paul] once and twice, and Satanas [Satan] cut us off. ¹⁹For who is our hope and joy and boast's crown—or is it not indeed you—before our Lord Yēsous at his Parousia [coming]? ²⁰For you are our splendor and joy.

3 Therefore, resisting no longer, we were delighted to be abandoned in Athēnai [Athens] alone ²and we sent Timotheos [Timothy], our brother and God's coworker in the Christos gospel, to support you and to encourage [you] about your allegiance ³so that no one is wagged back and forth by these troubles. For you yourselves know that we are laid out for this. ⁴For indeed when we were with you, we previously said to you that we are about to be troubled just as it happened and you know. ⁵Because this is true I also, no longer resisting, sent to know about your allegiance, so you wouldn't be tempted by the one who tempts and our labor might become hollow.

⁶But now . . . Timothy's come to us from you and he's gospeling to us about your allegiance and your love and that you always have a good memory about us, longing to see us just as also we you. . . . ⁷Because this is true we have been encouraged about you, siblings—during all our necessity and trouble—through your allegiance ⁸because now we live if you stand in the Lord. ⁹For what thanks are we empowered to pay God back for you in all joy in which we rejoice because of you before our God, ¹⁰night and day uber-abundantly pleading to see your face and to prepare what is lacking in your allegiance?

A prayer

¹¹May our Father-God himself and our Lord Yēsous straighten our path to you. ¹²May the Lord magnify and make you flow over in love for one another and for all just as we [have love] for you, ¹³to support your hearts as infallible in devotedness before our God-Father at the Lord Yēsous' Parousia with all his envoys, Amēn.

Some Don'ts and Dos

4 Therefore, what remains: siblings, we ask you and encourage [you] in the Lord Yēsous that—just as you received from us how it's necessary for you to walk around and to please God, and just as you are walking around—that you flow over more. ²For you know what orders we gave to you through the Lord Yēsous.

³For this is God's plan—your devotion: to stay away from sexual immorality, ⁴for each of you to know how to acquire [control] of one's own "vessel" [body] in devotion and honor, ⁵not in desire's passion as it is with the ethnic groups that have not known God, ⁶not to exceed and want more and more from his sibling in this matter because the Lord is prosecutor about all these matters, just as we also previously told you and we bore witness. ⁷For God did not call us to impurity but in devotion. ⁸Therefore, accordingly, the one rejecting isn't rejecting a human but God, who gives his Spirit, the holy one, to you.

⁹Concerning sibling-love: you have no need [for us] to write to you, for you yourselves are God-taught into loving one another, ¹⁰for indeed you do this to all the siblings in the whole Makedonia [Macedonia]. We encourage you, siblings, to flow over more ¹¹and to love the honor of living quietly and to practice one's own manners and to work with your own hands, just as we ordered you, ¹²so you may walk around respectably toward those outside and have need of nothing.

The Lord's Parousia

¹³We don't want you to be uninformed, siblings, about those who are "sleeping" so you may not be pained as are the remaining not having hope. ¹⁴For if we believe that Yēsous died and rose up, so also, through Yēsous, God will lead with him the ones who have "slept." ¹⁵For we say this to you in a word of the Lord: That we, the living who are remaining to the Lord's Parousia [coming], will never arrive before the "sleepers." ¹⁶Because the Lord himself

in a summons,
in a ruling envoy's voice
and in God's trumpet,

will descend from heaven and the dead ones in Christos will rise up first, ¹⁷then we, the living ones who remain, will be snatched with them in the clouds to the Lord's official reception in the air. And so we will be always with Lord. ¹⁸So that you encourage one another with these words.

5 Concerning the times and seasons, siblings, you don't have a need [for something] to be written to you, ²for you yourselves know carefully that the Lord's Day so comes as a thief-in-the-night. ³Whenever they say "Peace! Security!" then unexpected calamity comes upon them—just as labor pains [come unexpectedly upon] having a child in the womb—and they can never run away. ⁴But you, siblings, are not in Darkness so that the Day will prevail over you as a thief. ⁵For you are all Light's descendants and Day's descendants. We are not [descendants] of the Night or of Darkness. ⁶Therefore then let us not sleep as the remaining ones but let us be awake and be temperate. ⁷For the ones sleeping sleep at night and the boozers booze at night. ⁸But we, being of the Day, are temperate, putting on allegiance-and-love's breastplate and a head-covering of deliverance's hope ⁹because God did not place us for anger but for acquisition of deliverance through our Lord Yēsous Christos, ¹⁰who died for us—so whether we are awake or we sleep we may live together with him. ¹¹Therefore, encourage one another and form [one another] one by one, just as you also do.

Do's and don'ts

¹²We ask you, siblings, to know the ones laboring among you and ones leading you in the Lord and the ones mentoring you ¹³and consider them uber-abundantly in love because of their work.

> Be peaceful among them!
> ¹⁴We encourage you, siblings:
> Mentor the disorderly!
> Soothe the discouraged!
> Stick to the weak!
> Be patient toward all!

¹⁵See that no one pays back to someone bad with bad, but always chase the Good to one another and to all! ¹⁶Always rejoice! ¹⁷Pray incessantly! ¹⁸Give thanks in everything! For this is God's plan in Christos Yēsous for you. ¹⁹Don't snuff out the Spirit! ²⁰Don't devalue prophecies! ²¹Judge all things suitable! Possess The Beautiful! ²²Stay away from evil's every appearance! ²³May the Peace-God himself devote you uber-completely, and may your uber-connected spirit and self and body be infallibly kept in our Lord Yēsous Christos's Parousia [coming]. ²⁴The one who calls you is allegiant; he will do it. ²⁵Siblings, pray also for us. ²⁶Greet all the siblings with a devoted kiss.

In Paulos's hand

²⁷I make you swear by the Lord that you will have this letter read to all the siblings! ²⁸Our Lord Yēsous Christos's grace [be] with you.

INTRODUCTION TO THE SECOND LETTER TO THE THESSALONIANS

It's more difficult to know when Paulos [Paul] wrote this letter, though many would say it was soon after writing the first letter, that is, about AD 50. The emphasis in the first letter on apocalyptic eschatology gets a boost in this letter in 2:1-12, where we meet the Possessor and the Non-Covenant One, in other words, end-time opponents of the gospel. Furthermore, if 1 Thessalonians revealed that the Lord could return anytime, 2 Thessalonians comes to terms with some who are convinced the Lord has already returned.

Another new face in this letter is those whom Paulos calls "disorderly," which appears to be a term for people who among other things refuse to work. One may connect intense eschatological expectations with refusal to work—"after all," such persons have always reasoned, "the Lord is about to return." The harsh words about God's judgment in 1:5-12, which fit the emphasis in these letters on eschatology, threaten God's judgment on those who are troubling the believers in Thessalonikē [Thessalonica].

One will notice a few moments where the prose is momentarily interrupted for a parenthetical gloss as well. Notice, too, that if the first letter had an abundance of references to God (about eight per chapter), the second emphasizes the Lord Yēsous Christos.

THE SECOND LETTER TO THE THESSALONIANS

Paulos, Silouanos, and Timotheos to Thessalonikē

1 Paulos [Paul] and Silouanos [Silvanus] and Timotheos [Timothy] to the Thessalonian assembly in our Father-God and the Lord Yēsous Christos. ²Grace to you and peace from Father-God and the Lord Yēsous Christos.

Thanking God and praying for the Thessalonikeis

³We ought to thank God always for you, siblings, as it's deserving because your allegiance uber-grows and your love—each of all of you for one another—magnifies ⁴so that we ourselves boast in you among God's assemblies for your resilience and your allegiance in all your chasings and troubles, which you have put up with—⁵an exhibition of God's right judgment to make you deserving of God's Empire, for which also you suffer, ⁶since it's right with God to pay back trouble to those who trouble you ⁷and [to pay back] leisure to you, troubled ones, with us, at the Lord Yēsous' apocalypse from heaven with his powerful envoys ⁸in flaming fire, giving right-making to ones who don't know God and to ones who don't heed our Lord Yēsous' gospel, ⁹who will pay a right penalty: Era calamity from the Lord's face and from his strength's splendor ¹⁰whenever he comes to be fully splendored among his devoted ones and to be stunning among all the allegiant ones—because our witness about you has been trusted—on that Day. ¹¹For which also we always pray for you, that our God may make you deserving of the call and fill out every delight in goodness and allegiance's work in power, ¹²so that our Lord Yēsous' name may be fully splendored among you, and you in him, consistent with our God's and Lord Yēsous Christos's grace.

The Parousia

2 We ask you, siblings—about our Lord Yēsous Christos's Parousia [coming] and your assembly to him—²not to be quickly shaken from the mind nor to be alarmed—whether by spirit or by word or by letter "through us"—as that the Lord's Day is present. ³Don't let someone deceive you in any manner because unless the revolt comes first and the Covenant-breaking human is apocalypsed, the destruction's descendant, ⁴the one opposing and exalting over everything called "God" or "objects of worship"—so that he sits in God's sanctuary, demonstrating himself that he is God. (⁵Do you not remember that I was saying these things to you while being with you?)

⁶You know what is now possessing [him]—so he may be apocalypsed in his season. ⁷For the secret of the one breaking the Covenant Code is already energizing, [but] only until the one possessing now is moved from the middle. ⁸Then the Covenant-breaking one will be apocalypsed, whom the Lord Yēsous will put away with his mouth's Spirit and will undo at his [the non-Covenant-one's] parousia's appearance, ⁹whose parousia corresponds to Satanas's [Satan's] energy—in power and signs and false omens ¹⁰and in every deceitful wrongdoing among the ones being destroyed because they did not receive the love of truth so they would be delivered. ¹¹Because this is true, God sends to them deception's energy so they would believe the falsehood, ¹²that all not trusting the truth but delighting in wrongdoing may be judged.

¹³We ought to thank God always for you, siblings loved by Lord, that God lifted you as firstfruit for deliverance in the Spirit's devotion and allegiance to the truth, ¹⁴for which [God] called you through our gospel to our Lord Yēsous Christos's acquisition of splendor.

¹⁵Therefore then, siblings, stand and grab the conventions that you were taught—whether through word or through our letter.

¹⁶May our Lord Yēsous Christos himself and our Father-God, who loved us and gave Era-encouragement and good hope in grace, ¹⁷encourage your hearts and support [you] in every good work and word.

Pray for us as we pray for you

3 What remains: siblings, pray for us that the Lord's word may run and be splendored just as also [it was] with you ²and that we may be rescued from out-of-place and evil humans. For the Faith isn't for all. ³The

Lord is allegiant, who will support you and guard you from the evil one. ⁴We have been persuaded in the Lord, about you, that you do and will do the matters we order. ⁵May the Lord straighten your hearts to God's love and to Christos-resilience.

Regarding the disorderly ones

⁶We order that you, siblings, in name of our Lord Yēsous Christos, that you avoid every sibling walking around in a disorderly manner and not consistent with the convention that you received from us. ⁷For you yourselves know how it's necessary to copy us, that we were not disorderly among you, ⁸nor did we eat bread from someone as a gift but working in labor and fatigue night and day so not to overload any of you. ⁹Not that we don't have authority, but so we may give ourselves as a type so to copy us.

¹⁰For even when we were with you . . . we order you this: "That if anyone doesn't want to work, let that person not eat!" ¹¹For we hear some are walking around among you in a disorderly manner—not working but working around working. ¹²We order such persons and encourage in Lord Yēsous Christos that, working quietly, they may eat their own bread. ¹³You, siblings, don't neglect in doing beauty.

¹⁴If anyone doesn't heed our word through the letter, assign that person "Not to intermingle with the person" that he may be in deference. ¹⁵Don't consider that [person] as an enemy but mentor as a sibling.

¹⁶May the Peace-Lord himself give to you the peace through all [time] in every manner.

The Lord [be] with all of you.

¹⁷The greeting of Paulos in my hand, which is a sign in every letter. So I write.

¹⁸The grace or our Lord Yēsous Christos [be] with all of you.

THE PASTORAL EPISTLES

Apart from discovering an archaeological record of table talk between Paulos [Paul] and all his coworkers in the gospel, which isn't likely to happen, the best we've got on how Paulos pastored and how Paulos expected his fellow gospel workers to pastor is the Pastoral Epistles (PEs: 1–2 Timothy, Titus). A noticeable feature, then, of the PEs is a record of Paulos talking to Timotheos [Timothy] and Titos [Titus] while Paulos is also at the same speaking to the churches they pastor.

One of the key terms in the PEs is translated "godliness" in many translations, but translating *eusebeia* is a challenge. What we find in the PEs is a kind of public spirituality, a respectable religion, so we translate the term with "civilized piety." In this we borrow from current scholars on the evocations of this Greek term in the locations to which Paulos writes. This term captures the essence of Paulos's agenda for Timotheos, Titos, and their churches. He wants his leaders and the congregants of these churches to behave in socially respectable ways.

Speaking of "Paulos" here opens up a problem for many. The Greek of the PEs simply isn't the Greek of Romans or of Colossians, letters that themselves differ somewhat from one another. But the difference with the PEs is far more noticeable. Some have suggested that Paulos therefore did not write the PEs; but this is too simplistic because by Paulos's own admission, he did not "write" any of his letters. Tertios [Tertius], for instance, wrote Romans (cf. Rom 16:22), so the style of that letter is his. If one were to guess, perhaps one could conclude that the author of Acts is the one who put quill to papyrus in the PEs, though that is hardly certain.

When were these letters written? Traditionally they are dated to after Paulos's release from prison in the early 60s, but that's not easily demonstrable. When Paulos wrote Titus, Paulos was in Nikopolis [Nicopolis] (Titus 3:12), and he was no doubt there more than once, and Titos is on the beautiful island of modern-day Crete. We don't know when he was there. Timotheos is in Ephesos [Ephesus], where Paulos spent many months, and Paulos is on his way to Makedonia [Macedonia] (northern Greece). It isn't possible to locate these life events with certainty. It's possible Paulos was released from prison in Rōmē, and it's possible he was not. It's possible, then, that the letters were written after that imprisonment, and it's possible they were written before or during. As for the order of the letters themselves: the order in our Bible is by length, not chronology. We don't know exactly, but it's possible that Titus was first, and then later 1 and then 2 Timothy.

What we do know is that Paulos is facing opponents to his gospel through the leadership of Timotheos and Titos, and the opponents pop up throughout these letters (e.g., 1 Tim 1:3-7, 18-20; 4:1-10; 6:2-10, 20-21; 2 Tim 2:14-26; 3:1-9; 4:1-5; Titus 1:9-16; 3:9-11). It appears his opponents were, as was often his experience, his fellow Youdaians [Judeans, Jews] (cf. 1 Tim 1:7); there is some wealth problem (1 Tim 6:3-10; Titus 1:11); there is moral and faith failure (1 Tim 4:1-2). At times the letter's language becomes polemical about false teachers, even while Paulos instructs these leaders to conduct themselves respectfully and lovingly in their engagements.

These challenges led Paulos to focus on leaders for the households of God, and he uses these terms: *episkopos* (bishops, which we translate as "mentors"), *presbyteros*, and *diakonos* (elders and deacons, or assistants). Their qualifications are listed, but the lists are not the same, so one must see the various items in 1 Timothy 3:1-13; Titus 1:5-9 as symptoms of a good character rather than as rigid requirements. In the context of these leaders Paulos also addresses women, and he sees them both as needing to be "good teachers" or "teachers of what is good" (Titus 2:3), but he also restricts, until they are better taught, from teaching (1 Tim 2:11-15). The author of the PEs, then, doesn't think women are banned from teaching altogether.

Overall there is a tone for the pastor here of leading by example, of teaching healthy theology, and of passing on the faith to the next generation. That, Paulos knew at that time, was the mission of pastoral leadership.

INTRODUCTION TO THE FIRST LETTER TO TIMOTHY

Paulos [Paul] is in Makedonia [Macedonia] and appoints Timotheos [Timothy], his closest coworker, to care for the various house churches in Ephesos [Ephesus]. Paulos's instructions combine direct teaching to Timotheos on what he should do and instructions through Timotheos to the assemblies on how to resolve their problems, especially of false teachings impacting the health of the churches. Fitting 1 Timothy into the life of Paulos has been a challenge, though it is not insurmountable. Attributing this letter to the Comissioner Paulos requires that Paulos be released from prison after his arrest and trial in the 60s, and that he then carried on mission work subsequent to what is recorded in the book of Acts.

THE FIRST LETTER TO TIMOTHY

1 Paulos [Paul], Christos Yēsous' Commissioner consistent with the order of God, our Deliverer, and Christos Yēsous, our hope.

²To Timotheos [Timothy], a genuine child in allegiance.

Grace, mercy, peace from our Father-God and the Lord Yēsous Christos.

Commissioner Paulos warns about false Covenant-Code teachers

³As I, journeying to Makedonia [Macedonia], encouraged you to be attached in Ephesos [Ephesus], so you might order some not to teach other teachings ⁴nor to be absorbed by myths and unending life-records that present intense pursuits rather than God's management that is by allegiance. ⁵The order's completion is love from a clean heart and a good consciousness and unmasked allegiance, ⁶from which some, not walking the line, deviated into vain-words, ⁷wanting to be Covenant-Code teachers—not knowing the matters they say or [the matters] about which they are assured. ⁸We know that the Code is beautiful if someone uses it in a Covenant-Code manner: ⁹knowing this, that the Code isn't laid down for the right one but for the non-Code and disordered people, for the impious and sinful ones, for the unsaintly and profane, for the father- and mother-killers, for men-murderers, ¹⁰for sexually immoral, for [males] penetrating males, for men-snatchers [kidnappers], for falsifiers, for false oathtakers—and if any other [person] opposes healthy teachings ¹¹consistent with the gospel of the splendored-blessed-God, with which I have been trusted.

Commissioner Paulos's sinful past

¹²I have grace for Christos Yēsous our Lord, the one who empowered me, that he considered me allegiant, placing [me] into service, ¹³being formerly an insulter [of God's Christos] and chaser and arrogant, but I was shown compassion because, being uninformed, I did [such actions] in anti-trust. ¹⁴But our Lord's grace was uber-magnified with allegiance and love that are in Christos Yēsous. ¹⁵The word is allegiant and deserving of complete reception, that "Christos Yēsous came into the Kosmos to deliver sinners" (of whom I am first!). ¹⁶But, because this is true, I was shown compassion so in me first Christos Yēsous might exhibit complete patience as a model for ones who are about to trust in him for Era Life.

¹⁷To the King of the Eras, unperishable, invisible only God, [be] honor and splendor for the Era of Eras. Amēn!

Commissioner Paulos for Timotheos

¹⁸I present this order to you, child Timotheos, consistent with the previous prophecies on you, that you soldier in them with beautiful soldiering, ¹⁹having allegiance and a good consciousness, which some, repelling, shipwrecked concerning the faith, ²⁰of whom is Humenaios [Hymenaeus] and Alexandros [Alexander], whom I gave over to the Satanas [Satan] so they may be disciplined not to insult [God].

Commissioner Paulos instructs about gatherings

2 Therefore, I encourage, first of all, that requests, prayers, intercessions, thanks be made for all humans, ²for kings and all in high status, so we may lead a quiet and gentle life in all civilized piety and respect. ³This is beautiful and acceptable before our Deliverer, God, ⁴who wants all humans to be delivered and to come to perception of truth.

⁵For there is one God,
and one mediator of God and humans,
the human Christos Yēsous,
⁶who gave himself as a ransom for all,
the witness in its own seasons.

⁷For this I was placed as an announcer and Commissioner—I say the truth, I don't falsify—a teacher of ethnic groups in the faith and the truth.

⁸Therefore, I want the men to pray in every place, lifting up saintly hands without anger and deliberation.

⁹Likewise, also, [I want] women to decorate themselves in garments of decorum with modesty and prudence, not in plaited hair and gold or pearls or a costly robe, ¹⁰but (what is appropriate for women pledging God-reverence) through good works. ¹¹Let a woman, in silence, be apprenticed in complete under-ordering. ¹²It

isn't appropriate for a woman to teach, nor to overwhelm a man, but to be [learning] in silence.

(¹³For Adam was formed first, then Heua [Eve], ¹⁴and Adam was not deceived but the woman, being deceived, was in violation, ¹⁵but she will be delivered through giving-a-child-a-life if they remain in the faith and in love and in devotion with prudence.)

Commissioner Paulos's instructions about mentors

3 This word is allegiant:
If someone aspires to a mentorship, the person desires a beautiful work.
²Therefore, it's necessary for the mentor to be above reproach:

a one-woman's man,
temperate,
moderate,
decorous,
hospitable,
teachable;
³not addicted to wine,
not a bully but gentle,
non-warrior,
non-lover-of-silver;
⁴leading beautifully one's own house, having children who are under-ordered with all respect
⁵(if someone doesn't know [how] to lead one's own house, how will that person care for God's assembly?);
⁶not a neophyte so the person, being puffed up, may fall into the Accuser's judgment. ⁷It's necessary, too, to have a beautiful witness from ones outside so the person doesn't fall into the Accuser's reproach and trap.

Commissioner Paulos's instructions about deacons

⁸[It's necessary for] deacons, likewise, to be respected,
not double-worded,
not absorbed with much wine,
not avaricious;
⁹having the faith's secret with a clean consciousness.
¹⁰Let these first be judged suitable, then let them serve, being unimpeachable.

¹¹[It's necessary] for women, likewise, to be respected,
not accusers,
moderate,
allegiant in all ways.
¹²Let the deacons be
one-woman's men,
leading children and their own houses beautifully.
¹³(For those deacon-ing beautifully secure for themselves a beautiful status and much frankness in the faith that is in Christos Yēsous.)

Commissioner Paulos's plans

¹⁴I write these matters to you, hoping to come to you quickly. ¹⁵If I delay: [I write these matters to you] so you may know how it's necessary to behave in God's house, which is the living God's assembly, truth's pillar and support. ¹⁶In open agreement, great is civilized piety's secret:
Who was apparent in flesh,
righted in Spirit,
seen by envoys,
announced in ethnic groups,
trusted in the Kosmos,
taken up in splendor.

Commissioner Paulos's instructions about gospel opponents

4 The Spirit says oratorically that in the later seasons some will remove themselves from the faith, absorbing deceiving spirits and demons' teachings ²in the mask-wearing of false words: having burned their own consciousness, ³preventing to marry, [teaching them] to stay away from foods that God created for participation with thanks by the allegiant ones and by the ones who perceive the truth, ⁴because every creation by God is beautiful and nothing received with thanks is tossed away. (⁵For it's devoted through God's word and intercession.)

COMMISSIONER PAULOS'S INSTRUCTIONS FOR ASSEMBLY LIFE

Timotheos

⁶Laying these things down for the siblings, you will be a beautiful servant of Christos

Yēsous, being nourished by the faith's words and the beautiful teachings that you have closely followed. ⁷Request an absence from populist and old-woman myths. Exercise yourself toward civilized piety, ⁸for "embodied exercise is a profit for little but civilized piety is a profit for everything," having pledge for life now and for the coming [life]. ⁹That word is allegiant and deserving of complete reception. ¹⁰For we labor and are contestants for this, because we have hoped in the living God who is Deliverer of all humans, especially [for] the allegiant.

¹¹Order and teach these matters. ¹²Let no one snub your youth, but become a type of allegiance in word, in behavior, in love, in allegiance, in devotion. ¹³Until I come, absorb [yourself] in reading, in encouragement, in teaching. ¹⁴Don't neglect the grace-act in you that was given to you through prophecy with the eldership placing on the hands. ¹⁵Focus on these matters, be in them, so your advancement may be apparent to all. ¹⁶Hold on to yourself and the teaching, remain in them for, doing this, you will deliver both yourself and the ones hearing you.

Age Groups

5 Don't scold an older man but encourage [him] as a father,
[encourage] young men as brothers,
²older women as mothers,
younger women as sisters—in all devotion.

Widows

³Honor widows who really are widows. ⁴If some widow has children or grandchildren, let them first be apprenticed to civilized piety for their own house and to pay back a repayment to the parents. For this is acceptable before God. ⁵The real widow also, having been alone, has hoped in God and is attached to requests and prayers night and day, but ⁶the indulgent [widow], living, has died. ⁷Order these matters so they may be above reproach. ⁸If someone doesn't think first of one's own and especially of those in the household—he has denied the faith and is worse than the anti-trust one.

⁹Let a widow be enumerated:
being not less than sixty years,
a one-man woman,
¹⁰being witnessed by beautiful works,
if she has nourished children,
if she housed strangers,
if she washed the feet of the devoted,
if she aided the troubled,
if she followed on in every good work.

¹¹Request absence for young widows for whenever they have strong impulses against the Christos, they want to marry, ¹²having judgment because they rejected the first allegiance. ¹³Accordingly, they are apprenticed [to be] workless, going around to houses, and not only workless but also conveying bad ideas and practicing marginal deeds, speaking matters not necessary. ¹⁴Therefore, I want younger [ones]:

to marry,
to nourish children,
to control the house,
to give no opportunity to the opposing one for slander.

¹⁵For already some have deviated after the Satanas [Satan].

¹⁶If some allegiant woman has widows [under her care], let her aid them and let the assembly not be depressed so it may aid those who are real widows.

Elders

¹⁷Let the elders leading beautifully be deserving of double honor [pay], especially the ones laboring in word and teaching. ¹⁸For the writing says,

Don't silence a threshing ox.

And

The worker deserves his wage.

¹⁹Don't receive a category [of accusation] against an elder unless [there are] *two or three witnesses*. ²⁰Convince the one sinning before all so the remaining may have awe. ²¹I witness before God and Christos Yēsous and the elect envoys that you guard these matters without prejudice, not doing anything consistent with bias.

Timotheos

²²Place hands on no one quickly.
Don't form common life with outsiders' sins.
Keep yourself devoted.

²³Hydrate no longer with just water, but use a little wine because of the stomach and your frequent weaknesses.

²⁴The sins of some humans are obvious, leading to judgment; but for others [the sins] even follow [them]. ²⁵Likewise, also, the beautiful works are obvious and the ones that are otherwise are not able to be hidden.

Slaves

6 Let those who are slaves under a yoke consider their own masters deserving of complete honor so God's name and the teaching may not be insulted. ²Let the ones having allegiant masters not snub [them] because they are siblings, but instead they are to slave [for them], because ones connecting to their good work are allegiant and loved ones. These matters—teach and encourage.

Commissioner Paulos's instructions about bad leaders and money problems

³If someone teaches other teachings and doesn't approach the healthy words of our Lord Yēsous Christos and with teaching consistent with civilized piety, ⁴they have become puffed up, understanding nothing but, being ill for disputes and word-wars, from which come

> envy,
> strife,
> insults,
> conjectures,
> evils,

⁵brawling by humans corroding the mind and depriving the truth, thinking civilized piety to be cash.

⁶Now civilized piety is great cash—with self-sufficiency, ⁷for we carried nothing into the Kosmos because neither are we able to carry anything out. ⁸Having sustenance and protection—with these we will be content. ⁹The ones wanting to be rich fall into temptation and trap and many brainless and damaging desires that plunge humans into calamity and destruction. ¹⁰For the root of all badnesses is silver-love, which some, craving, have wandered from the faith and pierced themselves with many sorrows.

Commissioner Paulos's instructions for Timotheos

¹¹You, O human of God, flee these things!

Chase rightness, civilized piety, allegiance, love, resilience, mildness!

¹²Be a contestant for the faith's beautiful contest!

Take hold of Era Life, for which you were called and openly agreed to the beautiful open agreement before many witnesses!

¹³I encourage you—before the God who keeps all things alive and before Christos Yēsous, who, witnessing before Pontios Pilatos [Pontius Pilate] the beautiful open agreement—¹⁴that you observe the order non-blamed, above reproach until our Lord Yēsous Christos's Appearance, ¹⁵which he will show in its own seasons,

> the God-blessed and only Dynast,
> the King of all the ones ruling as kings,
> and Lord of all the ones lord-ing.

¹⁶The only one having immortality,
the one residing in unapproachable light,
whom no human saw nor is able to see,
to whom is honor and Era-strength,
Amēn!

Commissioner Paulos: Back to the rich

¹⁷Order the rich in this Era not to "highbrow" nor to have hope in uncertain riches but in God, who presents to us richly with all things for pleasure, ¹⁸to work the good, to be enriched in beautiful works, to be good-distributors, common lifers, ¹⁹treasuring for themselves a beautiful foundation for what is to come, so they may take hold of the real Life.

Commissioner Paulos's instructions to Timotheos

²⁰O Timotheos, guard the deposit, deviating from populist empty voices and contradictions of falsely named knowledge ²¹that some, pledging [as experts], did not walk the faith's line.

Grace [be] with you!

INTRODUCTION TO THE SECOND LETTER TO TIMOTHY

See the introduction to the Pastoral Epistles before 1 Timothy.

Paulos's second letter to Timotheos [Timothy] is more personal (1:15-18; 4:9-13, 19-21) and has less concern about opponents (cf. 2:14-18; 3:1-9; 4:14-15) and more instruction for Timotheos than is found in 1 Timothy. More names are mentioned in this letter than in 1 Timothy. He is called to a life of faithfulness in both practice and theology as he teaches Scripture in the household of God (3:10-17; 4:2). His second letter also contains some personal information suggesting Paulos has been in court on trial awaiting a decision, but his confidence in God is unwavering (2 Tim 4:6, 16-18). The date of the letter depends on identifying the date of trial in chapter 4.

THE SECOND LETTER TO TIMOTHY

1 Paulos [Paul], Commissioner of Christos Yēsous through God's will consistent with Life's pledge that is in Christos Yēsous, ²To Timotheos [Timothy], loved child, Grace, mercy, peace from Father-God and our Lord Christos Yēsous.

Commissioner Paulos's pastoral care for Timotheos

³I have grace to God, whom I venerate, originating with [my] ancestors, in a clean consciousness, as I have gapless memory about you in my requests night and day, ⁴longing to see you—remembering your tears—so that I may be filled out with joy, ⁵taking a reminder of the unmasked allegiance in you, which resided first in your grandmama Lōïs and in your mother Eunikē [Eunice], and I am persuaded that [it] is also in you.

⁶For which cause I remind you to ignite God's grace-act that is in you through the laying on of my hands, ⁷for God did not give to us the cowardice-spirit but power and love and moderation. ⁸Therefore, don't be degraded about our Lord's witness nor about me, his prisoner, but co-suffer bad things for the gospel consistent with God's power,

> ⁹who delivered us
> and called us with a devout calling,
> not consistent with our works,
> but consistent with his own intention
>   and grace
> that was given to us in Christos Yēsous
> before times of the Eras.
> ¹⁰But now being apparent
> through our Deliverer, Christos Yēsous'
>   Appearance,
> who undid death,
> and enlightened Life and non-decay
>   through the gospel.

¹¹For which I was placed as an announcer and Commissioner and teacher, ¹²because of which cause I also suffer these things. But I am not degraded for I know in whom I have trusted and am persuaded that he is powerful to guard my deposit for that Day. ¹³Have a model of healthy words, which you heard from me, in allegiance and love that are in Christos Yēsous. ¹⁴Guard the beautiful deposit through the Holy Spirit who resides in us.

¹⁵You know this: that all who are in Asia have been turned away from me—of whom is Phugelos and Hermogenēs. ¹⁶May the Lord give compassion to Onēsiphoros's house because he often revived me and was not degraded at my chains ¹⁷but, being in Rōmē, pursued me with commitment and found [me]. ¹⁸May the Lord give to him to find compassion from the Lord on that Day. How much he served in Ephesos [Ephesus]—you know better.

Commissioner Paulos's instructions for Timotheos

2 You, therefore, my child, be empowered in the grace that is in Christos Yēsous ²and, what you heard from me through many witnesses, these things present to allegiant humans who will be adequate also to teach others. ³Co-suffer bad things as Christos Yēsous' beautiful soldier.

⁴No one soldiering gets oneself braided with life's pragmatics so one may please the soldier enlister.

⁵If also someone competes, one isn't crowned unless one competes by the code.

⁶It's necessary for the laboring farmer to share the fruit first.

⁷Know what I say, for the Lord will give to you understanding in all matters.

⁸Remember Yēsous Christos: having been raised from among the dead ones, from Dauid's [David's] seed—consistent with my gospel, ⁹in which I suffer bad things—as far as chains as [if] a worker of bad things, but God's word isn't bound. ¹⁰Because this is true: I am resilient [in] all matters because of the elect so they also may attain deliverance that is in Christos Yēsous with Era's splendor. ¹¹The word is allegiant:

> For if we co-died, we will also co-live;
> ¹²if we are co-resilient, we will also
>   co-rule;
> if we deny, that one will deny us;
> ¹³if we anti-trust, that one remains
>   allegiant,
> for he isn't able to deny himself.

¹⁴Remind about these matters, witnessing before God not to word-war: useful for nothing, for subjugation of the ones listening. ¹⁵Commit to present yourself to God as judged suitable, an unashamed worker, cutting the word of truth for a straight path. ¹⁶Go around populist empty voices, for uncivilized piety is advancing abundantly ¹⁷and their word will come as a spreading gangrene. (Of whom is Humenaios [Hymenaeus] and Philētos, ¹⁸who did not walk the line concerning truth, saying the resurrection had already happened, and they overturn the allegiance of some.) ¹⁹Nevertheless, God's firm foundation stands, having this seal: *The Lord knew who are his* and *Let everyone naming the Lord's name remove from wrongdoing.* ²⁰In a great house there are not only vessels of gold and silver but also of wood and clay, some [are] for honor and some for dishonor. ²¹Therefore, if someone cleans oneself out from these, the vessel will be for honor, devoted, of good use to the master, having been prepared for every good work.

²²Flee youthful desires!

Chase rightness, allegiance, love, peace with those calling on the Lord from a clean heart!

²³Request absence from idiotic and uninstructed disputes, knowing that they give life to battles. ²⁴It isn't necessary for the Lord's slave to war but to be calm toward all, able to teach, above bad actions, ²⁵disciplining contradicters in meekness. Perhaps God will give to them conversion to truth-perception ²⁶and they may become sober again from the Accuser's trap, having been captured by him for that one's will.

Commissioner Paulos's instructions on people in the last days

3 Know this, that in the last days dangerous seasons will be present. ²For the humans will be . . .

self-lovers,
silver-lovers,
braggarts,
status-mongers,
insulters,
unpersuaded by parents,
ungracious,
unsaintly,
³unloving,
unrelenting,
accusers,
uncontrolled,
untamed,
unfriendly-with-good,
⁴traitors,
precipitous,
puffed up,
lovers-of-pleasure rather than lovers-of-God,
⁵having civilized piety's form but
 denying its power.
 Turn away from these!

⁶For of such persons are the ones creeping into houses and capturing little women, having been piled up with sins, being led by many desires, ⁷always being apprenticed and never being able to come to perception of truth. ⁸As with the manner of Yannēs [Jannes] and Yambrēs [Jambres] who resisted Mōüsēs [Moses], so also these are resisting the truth, humans having corrupted the mind, judged unsuitable concerning the faith, ⁹but they will not advance any more, for their ignorance will be very clear to all—as also the [ignorance] of these men became [clear].

Commissioner Paulos's further instructions for Timotheos

¹⁰Now you followed along with my teaching, my guidance, my intention, my allegiance, my patience, my love, my resilience, ¹¹my chases, my sufferings—what happened to me in Antiocheia [Antioch], in Yikonion [Iconium], in Lustra [Lystra]—what kind of chases I shouldered, and the Lord rescued me from all. ¹²All those wanting to live in a civilized-piety-manner in Christos Yēsous will be chased. ¹³Evil humans and charlatans will advance to the worse, deceiving and being deceived, ¹⁴but you remain in the matters in which you were apprenticed and have been committed to, knowing from whom you were apprenticed, ¹⁵and that from infancy you have known the sacred writings, the matters able to wisen you to deliverance through allegiance that is in Christos Yēsous. ¹⁶Every scripture is God-spirited and useful for teaching, for convicting, for straightening out, for education that is in rightness, ¹⁷so God's human may be fit, outfitted for every good work.

4 I witness before God and Christos Yēsous, who is about to judge the living and the dead, and [I witness] to his Appearance and his Empire:

> ²Announce the word!
> Superintend in good season and bad season!
> Convince!
> Rebuke!
> Encourage!
> [All these] in all patience and teaching!

³For there will be a season when they will not put up with healthy teaching but pile up for themselves teachers consistent with their own desires, their hearing being tickled, ⁴and they will turn away the hearing from the truth and will deviate onto myths.

> ⁵But you, be sober in all matters!
> Suffer bad things!
> Do the gospeler's work!
> Be fully assured about your service!

Commissioner Paulos talks about himself

⁶For I am already poured out [as a drink offering], and my release's season has stood over [me]. ⁷I am a contestant in the beautiful contest, I have completed the course, I have observed the faith. ⁸What remains: the crown of rightness is laid out for me, which the Lord will pay back to me on that Day, the right judge, not only for me but also for all who have loved his Appearance.

⁹Be committed to come to me quickly. ¹⁰For Dēmas abandoned me, loving the now-Era, and journeyed to Thessalonikē [Thessalonica]; Krēskēs [Crescens] to Galatia; Titos [Titus] to Dalmatia; ¹¹Loukas [Luke] alone is with me. Taking up Markos [Mark], lead him with you, for he is of good-use to me in service. ¹²I commissioned Tuchikos [Tychicus] to Ephesos [Ephesus]. ¹³Coming, carry the jacket (that I left behind in Trōas with Karpos [Carpus]) and the books, especially the parchments. ¹⁴Alexandros [Alexander] the coppersmith exhibited many bad actions to me. The Lord will pay him back consistent with his works. ¹⁵Whom you too must guard, for he strongly resisted our words.

¹⁶In my first defense no one appeared alongside me but all abandoned me. May it not be calculated to them. ¹⁷The Lord was present with me and he empowered me so that through me the announcement was fully assured and that all the ethnicities may hear, and I was rescued from the lion's mouth. ¹⁸The Lord will rescue me from all evil work and will deliver [me] into his heavenly Empire.

To whom be splendor to the Eras of Eras. Amēn.

¹⁹Greet Priska [Prisca] and Akulas [Aquila] and Onēsiphoros's [Onesiphorus's] house.

²⁰Erastos [Erastus] remained in Korinthos [Corinth], but Trophimos [Trophimus] I left, weakening, in Milētos [Miletus].

²¹Commit to come before the stormy season.

Euboulos [Eubulus] greets you, [as] also [do] Poudēs [Pudens] and Linos [Linus] and Klaudia [Claudia] and all the siblings.

²²The Lord [be] with your spirit.
The grace [be] with you.

INTRODUCTION TO TITUS

Titos [Titus] was another of Paulos's [Paul's] co-missioners in Mediterranean cities. In particular, with Paulos in Nikopolis, a personal letter (cf. 3:12-15) is sent to Titos, Paulos's child (1:4), whom Paulos left in Krētē (Crete), so he would know how to care for the assemblies on that island. He instructs Titos to set the place in order and to appoint leaders who have good character and the skills to guide the churches (1:5-9), and as with both 1 and 2 Timothy, there are problem people and theologies at work on the island. As with the other Pastoral Epistles, how the believers conduct themselves in the public sphere matters intensely to Paulos (3:1-11).

TO TITUS

1 Paulos [Paul], God's slave, Yēsous Christos's Commissioner, consistent with the allegiance of God's elect ones and perception of truth that is consistent with civilized piety, ²in hope of Era's life, which the unfalsifying God pledged before the Eras' times, ³but, in his own seasons, made apparent his word in the announcement, with which I was trusted consistent with God our Deliverer's order,

⁴To Titos [Titus], my genuine child consistent with a common faith,

Grace and peace from Father-God and our Deliverer Christos Yēsous.

Commissioner Paulos's instructions for elders/mentors

⁵For this I abandoned you in Krētē [Crete] so you can make straight what remains and determine elders by city, as I ordered you:

⁶If someone is unimpeachable,
one-woman's man,
having allegiant children not in the category of dissolution or disorder.
⁷For it's necessary for the mentor to be unimpeachable as God's administrator,
not self-regarding,
not angerly,
not addicted to wine,
not a bully,
not avaricious,
⁸but hospitable,
a lover of the good,
moderate,
right,
saintly,
self-disciplined,
⁹sticking to the allegiant word consistent with the teaching so the one may be empowered to encourage in healthy teaching and convince the contradictors.

Commissioner Paulos's warnings about false teachers

¹⁰For many are disordered, demagogues and mind-deceivers, especially the ones of the circumcision, ¹¹whom it's necessary to stopper the mouth, who overturn whole houses, teaching matters not necessary for the sake of avaricious profit. ¹²Someone of them, one of their own prophets, said,

Krēs [Cretans] are always falsifiers,
Bad beasts,
Workless guts.

¹³This witness is true, for this reason convince them cuttingly so they may be healthy in the faith, ¹⁴not absorbing Youdaïkan [Jewish] myths and humans' orders, turning away from the truth. ¹⁵For the clean, all things are clean, but for the soiled and anti-trusters nothing is clean but even their mind and consciousness has been soiled. ¹⁶They openly agree to know God; they deny in their works, being abominated and unpersuaded and judged unsuitable for any good work.

COMMISSIONER PAULOS'S INSTRUCTIONS ABOUT HOUSEHOLD LIVING

2 You, speak what is appropriate for healthy teaching.

Older Men

²The older men to be sober, respected, moderate, healthy in the faith, in love, in resilience.

Older Women

³The older women, likewise, to be sacred in demeanor, not accusing, not enslaved to much wine, teachers of beauty ⁴so they may moderate the young women to be man-lovers, children-lovers, ⁵moderate, devoted, house-workers, good, ordered under their own men—so God's word may not be insulted.

Younger Men

⁶Exhort the younger men, likewise, to be sensible ⁷in all matters, presenting yourself as a model of beautiful works, in teaching—integrity, respect, ⁸not knowably wrong with a healthy word—so the one against you may be in deference, not having anything foul concerning us.

Slaves

⁹The slaves to order themselves under their own masters in all matters, to be good-pleasers, not contradicting, ¹⁰not purloining, but exhibiting every allegiance [in doing] good so they may decorate in all ways the teaching that is from God our Deliverer.

All

¹¹For God's grace has appeared, deliverance for all humans, ¹²disciplining us so, denying uncivilized piety and world-decorated desires, we may live in this Era moderately, rightly, and with civilized piety, ¹³waiting the blessed hope and Appearance of the splendorous great God and our Deliverer Yēsous Christos, ¹⁴who gave himself for us so he might liberate us from all covenant-breaking and clean for himself a special people, zealous for beautiful works. ¹⁵Speak these matters and encourage and convince with all orderliness. Let no one think circles around you.

3 Remind them to order themselves under the leaders, authorities, to consent willingly, to be prepared for every good work, ²insulting no one, to be non-warriors, gentle, exhibiting all meekness toward all humans. ³For we were once also brainless, unpersuaded, deceived, slaving to desires and various pleasures, passing [life] in badness and envy, loathing, hating one another.

⁴But when the graciousness and the human-love of God our Deliverer appeared,

⁵not of works that are in rightness that
    we did,
but consistent with his compassion
he delivered us
through life-again-lustration and Holy
    Spirit revival,
⁶whom he poured out on us richly,
through Yēsous Christos our Deliverer,
⁷so being righted by that grace,
we might become heirs consistent with
    Era Life hope.
⁸The word is allegiant.

⁸ᵇI want you to be assured concerning these matters so that the ones who have trusted in God may ponder leading themselves with beautiful works. This is beautiful and useful for humans. ⁹Make your way around from idiotic disputes and genealogies and strifes and Covenant-Code battles, for they are unuseful and useless. ¹⁰Request absence from a factional human with one and two mentorings, ¹¹knowing that such a person is warped and sins, being self-condemned.

Commissioner Paulos closes

¹²Whenever I send Artemas or Tuchikos [Tychicus] to you, commit to come to me to Nikopolis [Nicopolis], for I have judged to winter there. ¹³Send ahead with commitment Zēnas the Covenant-Code expert and Apollōs so that there is nothing lacking for them. ¹⁴Let those who are ours be apprenticed to lead with beautiful works for necessary needs so they may not be fruitless.

¹⁵All those with me greet you.
Greet the ones loving us with allegiance.
Grace [be] with all of you.

INTRODUCTION TO PHILEMON

There is nothing like this letter in the rest of the Second Testament, as it's a short personal letter about a personal matter. That personal matter is that a slave named Onēsimus has evidently run away to find freedom, or he ran away to persuade Paulos [Paul] to be his advocate with his slaveowner—either way, he has been converted, his giftedness for the mission is evident, and the Commissioner Paulos sends him back to restore relations with his slaveowner.

The letter is an act of rhetorical persuasion, and Paulos both strokes the back of Philēmōn and presses him to do what Paulos wants—namely, to welcome Onēsimos back as a sibling in Christos, which transcends their social relation of slaveowner and slave. There is no sign that Paulos thought Onēsimos ["Handyman"] ought to be emancipated or that he thought slavery was morally wrong. Yet, the potency of "no longer as a slave but better than a slave, as a loved brother" in verse 16 could have been and has become a foundation for undoing slavery.

Dating this letter requires that we know where Paulos is in prison, and we don't know that for sure: a common answer puts him in Rōmē's prison, and thus the letter was written in the early to mid-60s; a more likely view is that he is in prison in Ephesos [Ephesus], and thus the letter was written about a decade earlier.

TO PHILEMON

¹Paulos [Paul], Christos Yēsous' prisoner, and Timotheos [Timothy], the brother, ²to the loved and our coworker Philēmōn, and to Ap-phia, the sister, and to Archippos [Archippus], our co-soldier, and to the assembly in your [sg.] house.

³Grace to you [pl.] and peace from our Father-God and the Lord Yēsous Christos.

⁴I thank my God, always making memory of you [sg.] in my prayers, ⁵hearing of your love and your allegiance that you have for the Lord Yēsous, and [the love you have] for all the devoted ones, ⁶so that your faith's common life may become an energy in the perception of every good thing that [is] among us in Christos. ⁷Because of your love I have much joy and encouragement, that is, the empathies have come to rest on the devoted ones through you, sibling.

⁸Therefore, having much frankness in Christos to order you [about] what is proper, ⁹I encourage you instead because of love—being such [a person] as Paulos, an old man and now even a Christos-Yēsous-prisoner¹⁰—I encourage you about my child, to whom I gave life in bonds, Onēsimos [Handyman], ¹¹who was once useless to you but now of good use to you and to me, ¹²whom I sent back to you, him—who is my empathies—¹³whom I was deciding to possess [keep] for myself so he might serve me for you in gospel-bonds, ¹⁴but I wanted to do nothing without your conclusion so that your good [action] might not be consistent with compulsion but consistent with voluntary [action].

¹⁵For perhaps because of this he was separated for an hour so you might possess him for Era, ¹⁶no longer as a slave but, above a slave, as a loved brother, especially for me but even more for you, both in the flesh and in the Lord. ¹⁷Therefore, if you share a common life with me, receive him as me. ¹⁸If he wronged you or owes anything, calculate this to me.

¹⁹*I Paulos wrote [this last line] in my hand, I will pay back.*

. . . so I don't say to you that "You even owe yourself to me!" ²⁰Yes, brother, may I benefit from you in the Lord: Rest my empathies in Christos!

²¹Being persuaded of your heeding, I wrote to you, knowing that you will do above what I say. ²²At the same time also, prepare hospitality for me, for I hope that, through your prayers, I may be graced to you.

²³Epaphras, my co-prisoner in Christos Yēsous, greets you—²⁴Markos [Mark], Aristarchos [Aristarchus], Dēmas, Loukas [Luke], my coworkers [also greet you].

²⁵The grace of the Lord Yēsous Christos [be] with your spirit.

INTRODUCTION TO HEBREWS

The theology of this sophisticated book magnifies comparisons of Yēsous with envoys [angels], priests, the temple, Mōüsēs [Moses], the first covenant's sacrificial system, and Yisraēl [Israel] itself. Redemption is so much better in the second covenant, the author presses home. In ways that anticipated the Christian belief in God as Trinity, the author assigns personal voices—Father, Son, Spirit—at times to citations from the First Testament (see 2:12-13; 3:7; 4:3; 5:5-6; 7:17, 20-22; 10:5-7; etc). The letter's focus is on the centrality of Yēsous as the redemptive agent in God's plan for the world, and the author cannot center him enough.

The letter moves from profound theological reflections and comparisons to rather sudden and strong warnings to the audience five different times, some of which have caused many to quake in fear. The author's concern is with those who have intentionally and consciously abandoned redemption in Christos. As such, the author's moral focus is on allegiance or faithful following of Yēsous and a common life with other followers of him.

We don't know who wrote this beautiful early Christian "encouragement-word" (13:22), but it seems probable the person both was in Italy (13:24) and, at the time of writing, was with Timotheos [Timothy], who had himself been in prison (13:23). It seems possible, too, that the author of this letter was himself in prison. Not knowing who wrote this letter, perhaps we are wiser to say "himself" or "herself" for this reason: if this letter is from Italia, and thus too from Rōmē, we know the main leaders of the house churches of Rōmē at this time were Priska [Prisca] and Akula [Aquila] (Rom 16:3-5), and thus if this letter is from Rōmē at that time, it would have had to pass through the approval of both of them. What could add to this dual-authorship theory is that Hebrews 13:18 uses the term *we*, while the very next verse uses *I*. One could infer this was composed by two (or more) persons. The author received the gospel from those who heard the Lord personally (2:3), putting the author in the earliest circle of believers. The style, the theological orientation, and the vocabulary are not the Commissioner Paulos's [Paul's], hence the letter originates in Paulos's circle but was not from him. Perhaps it was the highly educated Apollos, though we cannot be sure. The date can only be determined by the author, and thus we can't be sure of either.

TO THE HEBREWS

1 ¹God,
in many places and in many patterns,
in the past,
speaking to the patriarchs in the prophets,
²at the last of these days,
spoke to us in the Son,
whom he placed heir of all,
through whom also he made the Eras,
³who, being the Splendor's radiance and his Reality's representation,
and carrying all things by his Power's utterance,
making a cleansing from sins,
sat on the right of the Majesty in the heights,
⁴becoming so much better than the envoys
as the Name he has inherited carries so much more weight than theirs.

Envoys and the Son

⁵For to which of the envoys did he once say,

My son you are,
I have given life to you today?

and again,

I will be to him for Father,
And he will be to me for Son?

⁶Again, whenever he leads the Firstborn into the inhabited world, he says,

Let all God's envoys bow down to him.

⁷and to the envoys he says,

The one who makes his envoys spirits
and his workers fire-flame.

⁸but to the Son,

Your throne, God, is unto Era of the Era,
and the staff of straightness is your
Empire's staff.
⁹*You loved rightness and you hated*
covenant-breaking.
Because this is true: God, your God,
christened you with over-joy's oil
beyond your associates.

¹⁰and,

You, Lord, at the beginnings founded the
land,
the heavens are your hands' works,
¹¹*they will be destroyed, but you remain,*
and all will be aged like a robe.
¹²*And you will roll them up as a covering,*
as a robe they will also be changed.
But you are the same one and your years
will not eclipse.

¹³To which of the envoys has he once spoken:

Sit from my right,
Until I place your enemies as a footstool
for your feet?

¹⁴Are not all workers spirits commissioned for service because of those about to inherit deliverance?

Warning one

2 Because this is true: It's all the more necessary for us to absorb what we have heard so that we may not drift away. ²For if a word spoken through envoys became firm, and every violation and disobedience received the right payback, ³how will we flee away, neglecting such a great deliverance, which, being received at first to have been spoken through the Lord, was confirmed for us by those who heard ⁴. . . God co-witnessing in both authenticating signs and omens and diverse powers and partings of the Holy Spirit consistent with his will?

Envoys and the Son again

⁵For God did order the coming inhabited world under envoys, concerning which [coming world] we speak. ⁶Someone somewhere witnessed, saying,

> What is a human that you remember one,
> Or a son of humanity that you care for one?
> ⁷You diminished one for some while below the envoys,
> You crowned one with splendor and honor,
> ⁸You ordered all things under one's feet.

For in this ordering-everything-under, he released nothing not ordered under *him*, but now we see all things not yet ordered under *him*. ⁹But we see Yēsous—some while diminished below the envoys—because of death's suffering crowned with splendor and honor so that by God's grace he might taste death for all.

¹⁰For it's appropriate for him [God]—because of whom all things and through whom all things [are]—leading many siblings to splendor, to complete the Originator of their deliverance through sufferings. ¹¹For the one who devotes and the ones devoted are all from one. Because of which reason he was not degraded to call them siblings, ¹²saying,

> I declare my name to my siblings,
> In the middle of the assembly I sing a hymn to you.

¹³and again,

> I will be persuaded in him,

and again,

> Look! I and the children that God gave to me.

¹⁴Therefore, since the children have had blood and flesh in common, and he himself shared equally in the same, so through death he might undo the one having Death's grip, that is, the Accuser, ¹⁵and he might liberate them—whoever, in awe of death, were slavery's subject through all their living. ¹⁶For surely he doesn't take hold of envoys but he takes hold of Abra'am's seed. ¹⁷For which reason he was obligated to be made like his siblings consistent in all ways so he might become a mercy-giving and allegiant Senior Priest for God's matters so to be propitious for the people's sins. ¹⁸For in which, being tested, he has suffered, he is able to help ones being tested.

Mōüsēs and the Son

3 For which reason, devoted siblings, associates in a heavenly calling, ponder our open agreement's Commissioner and Senior Priest, Yēsous, ²being allegiant to the one who made him just as *Mōüsēs* [Moses] [was] *in his* [God's] *whole house*. ³For this one has deserved greater splendor than Mōüsēs, just as the preparer of a house has so much greater honor than the house. ⁴For every house is prepared by someone, but God is the preparer of all things. ⁵Mōüsēs [was] allegiant in his [God's] whole house as an attendant for a witness of what will be spoken, ⁶but Christos as Son over his [God's] house. We are his house, if only we possess frankness and hope's boast.

Warning two

⁷Therefore, just as the Holy Spirit says,

> Today, if you hear his voice,
> ⁸don't make your hearts stubborn as in the argument,
> consistent with the day of testing in the wilderness,
> ⁹where your ancestors tested [me] in an Examination,
> and they saw my works ¹⁰for forty years.
> Therefore, I was indignant with that generation
> and I said, "Always they wander in the heart,
> and they did not know my paths,
> ¹¹as I made an oath in my anger:
> 'If they will not enter into my resting place.'"

¹²See, siblings, that there will not be in some of you anti-trust's evil heart in removing from the living God, ¹³but encourage yourselves consistent with each day, as long as it's called "Today" so that someone of you not become stubborn in sin's deceit—¹⁴for we have become Christos-associates only if we possess firmly the reality's beginning until the completion—¹⁵in being said,

> Today, if you hear his voice
> don't make your hearts stubborn as in the Argument.

¹⁶For who, hearing, argued? But was it not all the ones who exited from Aiguptos [Egypt] through Mōüsēs? ¹⁷With whom was he indignant for forty years? Was it not the sinners, whose limbs fell in the wilderness? ¹⁸To whom did he make an oath "not to enter into his resting place" if not to those who were unpersuaded?

¹⁹We see that they were not able to enter because of anti-trust.

4 Therefore, let us be afraid so that ... the pledge to enter into his resting place being abandoned ... someone of you seem to have lacked [allegiance]. ²For we are gospeled just as also they. But the word they heard was not a gain for them, not having been blended with allegiance for the ones who heard. ³For we, the allegiant ones, enter into the resting place just as it has been said,

> As I made an oath in my anger:
> "If they will not enter into my resting place."

... Even though *the works* are done from Kosmos's origin.... ⁴For he [God] has said somewhere about the seventh [day] this: *And God rested in the seventh day from all his works,* ⁵and again in this [passage]: *"If they will not enter into my resting place."* ⁶Therefore, since it's left open for some to enter into it, and the former gospeled ones did not enter because of un-persuasion, ⁷again he makes an oath for some day, *Today,* saying in Dauid [David], after such time, just as it has been previously said,

> Today, if you hear his voice
> don't make your hearts stubborn.

⁸For if Yēsous [Joshua] rested them, he [God] would not have spoken of another day after these [events]. ⁹Therefore a sabbatical is left open for God's people. ¹⁰For the one who enters into his resting place also rested from his works as God [rested] from his own.

¹¹Therefore let us commit to enter into that resting place so one may not fall into the same kind of un-persuasion model. ¹²For God's word [is]

> living,
> and energetic,

and sharper than any two-edged long knife,
and piercing until a parting of self and spirit,
of both joints and marrow,
and judge of a heart's musings and notions;
¹³and there isn't a creation unapparent before him [God],
but everything is naked and bare-necked to his eyes,
to whom, for us, the word [is given].

Senior Priest and the Son

¹⁴Therefore, having a great Senior Priest who has gone through the heavens, Yēsous God's Son, let us grab the open agreement. ¹⁵For we don't have a Senior Priest unable to co-suffer with our weaknesses, but having been tested consistent with all things, consistent with comparison, apart from sin. ¹⁶Therefore, let us approach with frankness Grace's throne so we may receive compassion and we may find grace for good-timed help.

5 For every Senior Priest, being taken from humans, is established for humans about matters pertaining to God so he may offer both gifts and sacrifices for sins, ²being able to moderate passions for the uninformed and wandering since he also is draped with weakness ³and, because of it, is obligated—as for the people so also for himself—to offer [sacrifices] for sins. ⁴Someone doesn't take this honor for himself but, being called by God, just as Aarōn [was].

⁵So also the Christos did not splendor himself to become a Senior Priest but the one who spoke to him,

> My Son you are,
> Today I have given life to you.

⁶Just as also in another [location] says,

> You are a priest into the Era consistent
>   with Melchisedek's order.

⁷Who, in his flesh's days, offering requests and appeals to the one able to deliver him from death, with a strong cry and tears, and, being heard from his reverence. ⁸Although being Son, he was apprenticed to heeding from what he suffered ⁹and, being completed, he became the cause of Era-deliverance for all who heed

him, ¹⁰having been saluted by God as Senior Priest *consistent with Melchisedek's order*.

Warning three

¹¹Concerning which the word for us is much, and tough-interpretation to say, since you have become sluggish in hearings. ¹²For being obligated to be teachers because of time, you have need again for someone to teach you the first categories of God's sayings and have become [ones] having need of milk and not firm provision. ¹³For everyone who shares milk is untested in rightness's word, for the person is an infant. ¹⁴Firm provision is for the complete ones, for those who, because of practice, have exercised sensibilities—for distinguishing both beautiful and bad.

6 Therefore, releasing the Christos-origination word, let us carry on toward completeness, not throwing down again a foundation of conversion:

> from dead works and trust in God,
> ²teaching about dippings,
> laying on hands,
> resurrection from among the dead ones
> and Era judgment.

³And this we will do if indeed God permits.
⁴For one is powerless for those
who once have once been illumined,
who tasted the heavenly gift,
who have become associates in the Holy Spirit
⁵who tasted God's beautiful utterance
and the coming Era's powers,
⁶and who fall off [the path],
to renew them again to conversion
re-crucifying for themselves God's Son
and making him a public exhibition.

⁷For land, drinking the water coming on it often and giving birth to plants well-placed for whom it's farmed, shares a blessing from God. ⁸But, [land] carrying out thorns and thistles—unapproved and close to [being] cursed—whose completion is for burning.

⁹We have been persuaded concerning you, loved ones, of the better things and coming deliverance, even if we speak like this. ¹⁰For God [does] not [do] what is wrong to forget your works and love that you exhibited in his name, when you served the devoted and are serving. ¹¹We desire each of you to exhibit the same seriousness toward hope's full assurance until the completion ¹²so you may not become sluggish but copies of the pledges' inheritors through allegiance and patience.

¹³For God, pledging to Abra'am, since he had no one greater consistent with whom to make an oath, made an oath consistent with himself, ¹⁴saying,

> *If, surely, blessing, I will bless you*
> *and, abounding, I will make you abound.*

¹⁵And so, being patient, he achieved the pledge. ¹⁶For humans make an oath consistent with one greater, and the oath for firmness [is] beyond every contradiction for them. ¹⁷In which God—much more wanting to exhibit to the pledge-inheritors the unchangeableness of his will—mediated with an oath ¹⁸so through two unchangeable matters—in which it's powerless for God to falsify—we who fled may have a strong encouragement to grab the preceding hope, ¹⁹which we have as a self-anchor, both certain and firm, and entering into the interior, the inner curtain, ²⁰where the forerunner, Yēsous, entered for us, becoming a Senior Priest into the Era consistent with Melchisedek's order.

High priests and the Son

7 For this Melchisedek, *king of Salēm, the Highest God's priest*, the one *meeting Abra'am returning from cutting down kings, and blessing him*, ²*to whom Abra'am also parted a tenth of everything*. First, [his name "Melchisedek"] being interpreted [is] "King of Rightness," and then he is also *king of Salēm*, which is "King of Peace": ³no father, no mother, no genealogy; not a beginning of days nor having a completion of life—comparable to God's Son, he remains a priest in perpetuity.

⁴Observe how great this one is, *to whom also Abra'am* the patriarch *gave a tenth* from the plunder. ⁵Those of Leui's [Levi's] descendants, receiving priesthood, have an order to collect a tithe from the people consistent with the Covenant Code—this is from their siblings—although also having come out from Abra'am's waist. ⁶But the one who doesn't have a genealogy from them has collected a tithe from Abra'am and he has blessed the one

having the pledges. ⁷Without any contradiction, the lesser is blessed by the greater. ⁸Here humans, dying, receive tithes, but there [Scripture] witnesses that he lives. ⁹It could be said that "through Abra'am" even Leui receiving tithes has paid a tithe, ¹⁰for he was still in his father's waist when Melchisedek met him.

¹¹Therefore, if completion was through the Leuitikos [Levitical] priesthood—for the people were Covenant-Coded on the basis of it—what further need is there for another priest to be raised consistent with Melchisedek's order, and not to be said consistent with Aarōn's order? ¹²For shifting the priesthood of a necessity becomes a Code shift. ¹³For about whom these matters are said has participated in another tribe, from which no one has officiated at the sacrificial altar. ¹⁴For [it's] obvious that our Lord has risen up from Youda [Judah], about which tribe Mōūsēs [Moses] spoke nothing concerning priests. ¹⁵It's all the more obvious if another priest arises consistent with comparison to Melchisedek, ¹⁶who has become [a priest] not consistent with the Code's fleshly order but consistent with a power of an indestructible life. ¹⁷For it's witnessed that,

> You are a priest into the Era consistent
> with Melchisedek's order.

¹⁸For, on the one hand, the previous order is displaced because of its weakness and unusefulness—¹⁹for the Covenant Code completed nothing—and, on the other, [because it's] the lead-in of a better hope through which we come close to God. ²⁰And, consistent to how much [it's established] not without an oath: For the priests have become [priests] without an oath, ²¹but he with an oath through the one saying to him,

> The Lord has made an oath and will not
> be regretful.
> "You are a priest into the Era."

²²Consistent with this, Yēsous has also become the guarantor of a better covenant. ²³And the priests had become many because [they] were hindered remaining by death, ²⁴but because he remains unto the Era he has a priesthood inviolably, ²⁵and so he is able to deliver completely the ones approaching God through him, living always to intercede for them.

²⁶For such a Senior Priest is appropriate for us: saintly, without evil, without stain, separated from sinners, being exalted in status over the heavens, ²⁷who did not have a daily necessity as the Senior Priests—first, to offer up sacrifices for his own sins, then for those of the people. For he did this once for all, offering up himself. ²⁸For the Code is established for humans who are Senior Priests having a weakness, but the oath's word, which is after the Code, [establishes] a Son having been completed unto the Era.

Covenant and the Son

8 The header upon what is being said: We have such a Senior Priest who sat in the heavens at the Majesty's Throne's right, ²a worker of the devoted [places] and of the true tent, which the Lord, not a human, pitched. ³For every Senior Priest is established to offer both gifts and sacrifices so it's a necessity for this person to have something that he may offer. ⁴Therefore, if he were on land, he would not be a priest . . . [there] being offerers of gifts consistent with the Covenant Code . . . ⁵who venerate in a model and shadow of the heavenly [realities] just as it was revealed to Mōūsēs [Moses], about to complete the tent, for *See*! it says, *You will make all things consistent with the type that has been exhibited to you on the mountain*. ⁶But now he has attained a much better public work, as much as he is the Mediator of a better covenant, which was Covenant-Coded on better pledges.

⁷For if that first [covenant] were infallible, there would not have been a place for pursuing a second. ⁸For, blaming, he [God] says to them,

> Look! Days are coming, says the Lord,
> and I will fully complete for Yisraēl's
>   [Israel's] house and for Youda's
>   [Judah's] house a new covenant,
> ⁹not consistent with the covenant that I
>   made with their ancestors,
> . . . on the day I took hold of [them] by
>   their hand . . .
> to lead them out from Aiguptos [Egypt]
>   land,
> because they did not remain in my
>   covenant,
> and I neglected them, says the Lord.
> ¹⁰Because this is the covenant that I will
>   arrange with Yisraēl's house

*after those days, says the Lord.
Giving my Code into their minds,
and on their hearts I will inscribe them,
and I will be God for them,
and they will be people for me.*
11*Each [of them] will never teach his citizen,
and each his sibling, saying, "Know the
        Lord,"
because all will have known me,
from smallest to their greatest,*
12*because I will be merciful on their
        wrongdoings
and their sins I will never ever remember.*

13In saying *new [covenant]* he has made the first ancient, and what is made ancient and old [is] close to vanishing.

The Covenant Code, the kosmic devoted place, and the Christos

9 Therefore, the first (on the one hand) was having right rules for veneration and for the kosmic devoted [place]. **2**For a tent was prepared, the first [section] in which were the lampstand and the table and the presence bread, which is called "devoted." **3**After the second inner curtain, a tent that is called "devoted of the devoted," **4**having a golden incense altar and the Covenant chest, having been covered on all sides in gold, in which [was] a golden urn having the manna and Aarōn's staff that sprouted and Covenant's tablets, **5**and above it splendorous cherubs overshadowing the mercy seat—concerning these now isn't [the place] to speak part by part. **6**These being so prepared . . . the priests always go into the first tent, completing the venerations, **7**but into the second, once in a year only the Senior Priest [goes], not without blood that he offers for himself and for the ignorances of the people . . . **8**the Holy Spirit divulging this . . . the path into the devoted [places] wasn't yet apparent, having the first tent still in force, **9**which is an analogy for the present-existing season, consistent with their offering both gifts and sacrifices that are not able to complete the consciousness for the ones venerating. (**10**[Dealing] only with food and drink and various dippings, imposing the flesh's right rules until the reformation's season.)

11But (on the other hand) Christos appearing as Senior Priest for the good things that happened through the greater and more complete tent, not handmade (that is, not of this creation), **12**and not through blood of goats and calves but through his own blood he entered once for all into the devoted [places], having found liberation for the Era. **13**For if the blood of goats and bulls and a heifer's ashes, sprinkling the ones made common, devotes for cleaning the flesh, **14**how much more will Christos's blood, who through the Era's Spirit offered himself inerrant to God, clean our consciousness from dead works for venerating the living God!

15Because this is true: He is Mediator of a new covenant so that . . . death occurring for the liberation from the violations at the [time of] first covenant . . . the ones who have been called may receive the pledge, the Era's inheritance. **16**For where [there is] a covenant, [it's] necessary to carry the death of the covenant-arranger. **17**For a covenant [is] firm on the basis of dead ones since it's never strong when the covenant-arranger lives. **18**Thus, not even the first [covenant] was made new without blood. **19**. . . For every order having been spoken consistent with Covenant Code by Mōüsēs [Moses] to all the people . . . taking the blood of calves [and of goats] with water and scarlet wool and hyssop, he sprinkled both the book itself and all the people, **20**saying, *This [is] the Covenant-blood that God ordered for you,* **21**and likewise he sprinkled with blood both the tent and all the veneration's vessels. **22**Indeed, almost everything is cleaned with blood consistent with the Code, and without blood-pouring there is no release [from sins].

23Therefore, [it was] necessary for the models of the [items] in the heavenlies to be cleaned by these [sacrifices] but the heavenlies themselves by better sacrifices than these. **24**For Christos did not enter into handmade devoted [places]—reproductions of the true [places]— but into heaven itself, now to become apparent to God's face for us. **25**Nor may he offer himself many times, just as the Senior Priest enters into the devoted [places] yearly with the blood of an outsider, **26**since it would be necessary for him to suffer many times from the Kosmos's origin. But now, once, at the Eras' completion, he has become apparent for sin's displacement through sacrifice of himself. **27**As much as it's laid down for humans to die once—after this a judgment—²⁸so also the Christos, being offered once to lift up sins for many, will appear a second time without [a concern for] sin for those impatiently waiting for him for deliverance.

10

For the Covenant Code—having a shadow of the good things to come, not the image itself of the matters—is never able, through the same sacrifices that they offer in perpetuity year by year, to complete the presenters—²since, would they [sacrifices] not have stopped being offered, because the venerators, once having been cleaned, would not still have any consciousness of sins? ³But in these [sacrifices] is a year-by-year remembrance of sins. ⁴For the blood of bulls and goats are powerless to carry away sins. ⁵Therefore, entering into the Kosmos, he says,

> *A sacrifice and an offering you did not want,*
> *but a body you prepared for me.*
> ⁶*with burnt offerings and [offerings] for sins you are not delighted.*
> ⁷*Then I said, "Look! I have come—*
> *At the header of the book it's written about me—*
> *to do your will, God."*

⁸Saying above that,

> *Sacrifices and offerings* and *burning offerings and [offerings] for sins,*
> *I did not want nor [in them] am I delighted*—

which are offered consistent with the Code, ⁹then he has said,

> *Look! I have come to do your will.*

He lifts away the first in order so he may establish the second—¹⁰in which will we are made devoted through the offering of Yēsous Christos's body once for all.

¹¹Every priest has stood daily venerating and often offering the same sacrifices that never once are able to take away sins, ¹²but he, one time, offering a sacrifice for sins, sat at God's right in perpetuity, ¹³finally waiting until his enemies can be placed under his feet. ¹⁴For by one offering he has completed for perpetuity the ones being devoted. ¹⁵The Holy Spirit also witnesses to us, for after it was said,

> ¹⁶"*This [is] the covenant that I will arrange a covenant for them after those days,"*
> The Lord says.
> "*Giving my Code on their hearts and on their minds I will write them.*
> ¹⁷*And their sins* and their Covenant-breaking *I will no longer remember.*"

¹⁸Where there is release from these there is no longer an offering for sins.

Warning four

¹⁹Therefore, siblings, having frankness for the path-entry of the devoted [places] by Yēsous' blood, ²⁰which made new for us a fresh and living path through the inner veil (which is his flesh) ²¹and [having] a great priest at God's house, ²²let us approach with true hearts in allegiance's full assurance, having the hearts sprinkled from an evil consciousness and the body being washed with clean water. ²³May we possess the open agreement's hope without leaning, for the one who pledged is allegiant, ²⁴and may we ponder one another for an incitement of love and beautiful works, ²⁵not abandoning the assembly of ourselves, as [is] custom for some, but encouraging, and all the more as you see the day coming close.

²⁶ . . . We're sinning willingly after receiving perception of the truth . . . [there is] no longer a sacrifice for sins left, ²⁷but some fear-inducing of an expected judgment and zealous fire about to eat up the opponents. ²⁸Someone rejecting Mōüsēs' [Moses'] Covenant Code *dies without mercies on the basis of two or three witnesses.* ²⁹How much worse of an evaluation do you think one deserves who trampled on God's Son, who considered the covenant-blood common (by which the person was devoted), and who assaulted the grace-Spirit? ³⁰For we know the one who said, *Right-making is for Me, I will pay back,* and again, *The Lord will judge his people.*

³¹[It's] fear-inducing to fall into the living God's hands.

³²Remember the former days, in which, being illumined, you were resilient in a hard contest of sufferings, ³³sometimes publicly exposed to degradations and troubles, and sometimes having a common life with those

being treated in such a manner. ³⁴For you sympathized with the prisoners and you welcomed the plundering of your possessions with joy, knowing you yourselves have a greater and remaining possession. ³⁵Therefore, don't toss away your frankness, which has a great payback. ³⁶For you have need for resilience so that, doing God's will, you may receive the pledge.

> ³⁷For yet *in very little while*
> *the Coming One will come and will not take a long time,*
> ³⁸*My Right One will live from allegiance,*
> And *if someone backs off, my self doesn't delight in the person.*

³⁹But we are not of the backers-off into destruction but of the allegiance for the acquisition of [one's] self.

The allegiant ones

11 Allegiance is the reality of things hoped for, conviction in matters not seen. ²For in this [allegiance] the elders were witnessed. ³In allegiance we know the Eras to be prepared by God's utterance, so that what is seen has not come from what appears.

⁴In allegiance Habel [Abel] offered to God the better sacrifice than Kaïn [Cain], through which it was witnessed to be right . . . God witnessing about his gifts . . . and, dying, through it [allegiance] still speaks.

⁵In allegiance Henōch [Enoch] was shifted not to see death, and *he was not found because God shifted him.* For before the shift he was witnessed to have delighted God. (⁶Without allegiance one is powerless to delight [God] for it's necessary for the one who approaches God to be allegiant to the God that is and the payer-back for those who pursue him.)

⁷In allegiance Nōe [Noah], being revealed about things not yet seen, being pious, prepared a chest for the deliverance of his house, through which he condemned the Kosmos, and became an heir of rightness consistent with allegiance.

⁸In allegiance Abra'am, being called, heeded to exit to a place that he was about to receive for inheritance, and he exited not knowing where he is going. ⁹In allegiance he inhabited the pledged land as an outsider, residing in tents with Yisa'ak [Isaac] and Yakōb [Jacob], co-heirs of the same pledge. ¹⁰For he was waiting for a city having foundations, whose Artisan and Producer is God. ¹¹In allegiance, even Sarra [Sarah] herself sterile, [Abra'am] received a power for seed-origins—and beyond her season—since he considered the one pledging allegiant. ¹²Therefore, from one [man]—these things from one having been "dead"—they were given life, as the heaven's stars in mass and as the sand, which is along the sea's lip, which is innumerable.

¹³Consistent with allegiance these all died, not receiving the pledges but seeing them and greeting from a distance, and openly agreeing that they are outsiders and temporary residents on the land. ¹⁴For the ones saying these things make apparent that they pursue one's ancestral village. ¹⁵If they were remembering that [city] from which they went out, they would have had a season to return, ¹⁶but now they aspire for a better [city], that is heavenly. Therefore, God isn't degraded to be called their God, for he prepared a city for them.

¹⁷In allegiance Abra'am, being tested, had offered Yisa'ak—and he was offering his only son—[Abra'am] the one who accepted the pledges, ¹⁸to him it was said that *In Yisa'ak a seed will be called for you,* ¹⁹calculating that God was powerful even to raise from among the dead ones, from which [calculation] he even received him analogously.

²⁰In allegiance also Yisa'ak blessed Yakōb and Ēsau about matters to come.

²¹In allegiance Yakōb, dying, blessed each of Yōsēf's [Joseph's] sons and *he bowed down on his staff's top.*

²²In allegiance Yōsēf, ending life, remembered the Yisraēl's [Israel's] sons' exodus and gave orders about his bones.

²³In allegiance Mōüsēs [Moses], having been given life, was hidden for three months by his fathers because they saw the child [was] attractive and they were not scared of the king's edict. ²⁴In allegiance Mōüsēs, becoming great, denied being spoken of as "Pharaō's [Pharaoh's] daughter's son," ²⁵rather, choosing to be co-treated-badly with God's people than to have a pleasure season of sin, ²⁶considering Christos-degradations greater wealth than Aiguptos's [Egypt's] treasures, for he was looking out for the payback. ²⁷In allegiance he abandoned Aiguptos, not being scared of the

king's fury, for he endured as one seeing the invisible one. ²⁸In allegiance he has done the Pascha [Passover lamb] and the blood spattering so that the one destroying the firstborn would not touch them.

²⁹In allegiance they crossed through the Red Sea as through stiff land, [in] which [sea], the Aiguptioi [Egyptians], taking the attempt [to cross through], were swallowed.

³⁰In allegiance Yiericho's [Jericho's] walls fell, having been encircled for seven days.

³¹In allegiance, Ra'ab [Rahab] the prostitute was not destroyed with the unpersuaded ones, receiving the reconnoiterers with peace.

³²What still can I say? For time fails for my narrating about Gedeōn [Gideon], Barak, Sampsōn, Yiefthae [Jephthah], Dauid [David] and Samouēl [Samuel] and the prophets—³³who through allegiance contested kingdoms, effected rightness, obtained pledges, shut lions' mouths, ³⁴snuffed out fire's power, fled a long knife's mouth, were empowered from weakness, became strong in war, flattened outsiders' encampments. ³⁵Women received their dead ones from a resurrection. Others were beaten, not welcoming liberation so they could obtain a greater resurrection. ³⁶Others took the mockings-and-afflictions test, and even more bonds and prison. ³⁷They were stoned, sawn in two, died in knife-murder, they went around in sheepskins, in goat hides—lacking, being troubled, being maltreated—³⁸of whom the Kosmos wasn't deserving—wandering in wildernesses and mountains and caves and land lairs.

³⁹All these, being witnessed through allegiance, did not receive the pledge ⁴⁰. . . God foreseeing something better for us . . . so without us they would not be completed.

Warning five

12 Accordingly we, having such a cloud of witnesses surrounding us, laying aside every encumbrance and enticing sin, let us run with resilience the contest laying ahead of us, ²looking away to the allegiance's Originator and Completer, Yēsous, who for the joy laying ahead for him was resilient on a cross, snubbing the degradation, and has sat down at the right of God's throne. ³For you are to calculate the one who has been resilient through so much contradiction against himself by sinners so you may not be wearied in your selves, fainting.

⁴You have not yet, contesting against sin, combated to the point of blood. ⁵Have you completely forgotten the encouragement, which deliberates with you as children?

> *My child, don't make little the Lord's education,*
> *nor faint, being convinced by him,*
> ⁶*For the Lord educates the one he loves,*
> *and lashes every child he receives.*

⁷Be resilient in education, as God presents you as children, for what child [is there] that a father doesn't educate? ⁸If you are without education (in which all have become associates), then you are illegitimate and not children. ⁹Then we had our fleshly fathers as educators and we were deferring to them. Should we not much more be ordered under the Father of spirits and live? ¹⁰For they were educating for a few days consistent with what seemed [right] to them, but [God] in the benefit of sharing his devotedness. ¹¹Every education, in the present, doesn't seem to be a joy but a pain but later pays back a peace-fruit of rightness for those trained by it.

¹²Therefore, straighten up your dropped hands and your paralyzed knees, ¹³and make straight lanes for your feet so the "lame" may not deviate but rather be cured. ¹⁴Chase peace and devotion with all, without which [devotion] no one will see the Lord, ¹⁵mentoring, so no one is lacking God's grace, so *some bitter root does not grow up with disturbance* and through it many become soiled, ¹⁶so that there isn't some sexually immoral or profane person, like Ēsau, who in exchange for one food gave back his firstborn rights. ¹⁷For you know that afterwards, wanting to inherit the blessing, he was rejected, for he did not find place of conversion even though pursuing it with tears.

¹⁸For you have not approached what is felt, to a flaming fire, to a darkness, to a gloom, to a hurricane, ¹⁹to a trumpet echo and to an uttering voice, from which the ones hearing wanted absence so there would not be another word added. (²⁰For they were not carrying what was ordered: "if even a beast touches the mountain, let it be stoned" ²¹and so fear-inducing was the spectacle that Mōüsēs [Moses] said, "*I am scared* and trembling.")

²²But you have approached
to Mount Siōn [Zion], to the Living
  God's city, to heavenly
  Yierousalēm [Jerusalem],
and to myriads of envoys, to a festival,
²³and to a firstborn assembly who are
  inscribed in heavens,
and to a judge, God of all,
and to spirits of right ones made
  complete,
²⁴and to Yēsous, Mediator of a new
  covenant,
and to a sprinkling-blood that speaks
  better than Habel [Abel].

²⁵See that you are not absent from the one speaking. For if they did not escape, making themselves absent from the one who revealed on land, how much more will we, the ones turning away from the one [revealing] from the heavens, [not escape]. ²⁶His voice then shook the land, but now he has pledged, saying,

Yet once for all I will shake not only *the*
  land,
but *also the heaven.*

²⁷The *Yet once for all* divulges the shift of the shaken elements (as made things) so the unshaken elements may remain. ²⁸Therefore, let us, receiving an unshakable Empire, have grace, by which let us venerate God acceptably with reverence and respect, ²⁹for our *God is a devouring fire.*

Exhortations

13 Let sibling-love remain. ²Don't forget stranger-love, for through this some "forgot" [their] being hospitable to envoys. ³Remember the bonds as ones being co-bonded; the ones being mistreated as yourselves being [mistreated] in the body. ⁴Let marriage be honored by all and the [marital] bed unstained [by sin], for God will judge the sexually immoral and adulterers. ⁵Let your manner be non-silver-loving, being content with your possessions, for he has said, *I will never leave you nor will I ever abandon you,* ⁶so being confident to say to you,

The Lord is helper to me,
I will not be scared,
What will a human do to me?

⁷Remember the ones leading you, who spoke God's word to you: observing clearly their behavior's outcome, copy their allegiance. ⁸Yēsous Christos, yesterday and today, is the same—and into the Era. ⁹Do not be carried away with divergent and strange teachings, for it's beautiful for the heart to be firmed up by grace, not by foods in which those walking around are not benefited. ¹⁰We have a sacrificial altar from which the ones venerating in the tent don't have authority to eat. ¹¹For the blood of the living animals for sins is carried into the devoted [places] by the Senior Priest, the bodies of those [animals] are burned up outside the encampment. ¹²Therefore also Yēsous, so he can devote the people by his own blood, suffered outside the gate. ¹³So then let us exit to him outside the encampment, carrying his degradation. ¹⁴For we don't have here a remaining city but we pursue the coming [city]. ¹⁵Through him, therefore, let us always carry up a praise-sacrifice to God—that is, the fruit of lips openly agreeing with his name. ¹⁶Don't forget doing good and a common life, for in such sacrifices God is well-pleased. ¹⁷Be persuaded by your leading ones and yield [to them], for they are alert for your selves, and giving back a word [to God], so with joy they do this, and not groaning—for this is of no value for you.

¹⁸Pray for us. For we are persuaded that we have a beautiful consciousness, wanting to behave beautifully in all things. ¹⁹I encourage you all the more to do this so I may be restored to you quicker.

²⁰May the peace-God, who led up our Lord Yēsous from among the dead ones, the great shepherd of the sheep, by the Era's covenant-blood, ²¹strengthen you in all good so you do his will, doing among us what is pleasing before him through Yēsous Christos, to whom be the splendor into the Eras of Eras, Amēn! ²²I encourage you, siblings: put up with the encouragement-word, for I wrote to you briefly. ²³Know [that] our brother Timotheos [Timothy] has been released, with whom, if he comes quickly, I will see you.

²⁴Greet all your leading ones and all the devoted ones.

Those from Italia [Italy] greet you.

²⁵The grace be with all of you.

INTRODUCTION TO THE LETTER OF JAMES

The name "James" is an Anglicized version of the Hebrew name *Ya'akov*, which transliterated into Greek, as in the Second Testament, is Yakōbos. One could easily suggest that all along we might have called this the letter of Jacob, and in the process we would have realized the man was named after one of Yisraēl's [Israel's] patriarchs in Genesis.

This small letter was sent to Youdaian [Judean, Jewish] believers who lived outside the land of Yisraēl in what the letter calls "the Diaspora" (1:1), and the letter's focus is on conduct consistent with the way of Yēsous, though he is barely mentioned in the letter (1:1; 2:1). As such, the letter is a window on early Youdaian Christianity or, perhaps better, Christian Judaism. The author is most likely the "brother" of Yēsous. If so, the expression of 1:27 ("orphans and widows") opens a door into life in the home of Yakōbos in Nazara [Nazareth].

A number of themes emerge as important for Jewish believers outside the land: learning to live with tests, which indicates they are suffering—and the kind of suffering in this letter is mostly exploitation of the poor by the rich; learning to hear and do and not just hear the word of God; learning how to avoid prejudice in favor of the wealthy against the poor; learning that true faith is an allegiance marked by works. There appears to be a section focused on teachers (3:1–4:12) that zeroes in on the tongue, on wisdom, on dissensions and on slandering one another. The wealthy who oppress the poor seem somehow to be connected as well to the assembly of Christians, for Yakōbos expresses severe warnings about presumption and oppression, and he finishes with advice for how the assembly should respond (4:13–5:11).

The Greek of Yakōbos's letter is sophisticated, on par with Acts and Hebrews and the Pastoral Letters, but the letter is punchier and more epigrammatic. Style aside, the letter speaks volumes into churches throughout the history of the church. Noticeable in this letter is a focus on works and faith, and one can assume that somehow Yakōbos has heard something distorted about Commissioner Paulos's [Paul's] teachings, and so 2:14-26 appears to bring the distorters back in line: true faith is a kind of allegiance that has works, and workless faith is simply not genuine. It's unfortunate that Yakōbos's teaching on faith/allegiance has made so many nervous, for that nervousness is a sign that Paulos himself has not been comprehended well.

THE LETTER OF JAMES

1 Yakōbos [James], God's and the Lord Yēsous Christos's slave,
To the twelve tribes that are in the Diaspora,
Greetings!

Tests

²Consider [it] all joy, my siblings, whenever you fall into divergent tests, ³knowing that the testing of your allegiance effects resilience. ⁴Let resilience have its complete work so you may be complete and wholly intact, lacking nothing.

⁵If someone of you lacks wisdom, let the person ask from the God who gives to all generously, and not degrading, and it will be given to the person. ⁶Let the person ask in trust, not mentally wavering, for the mental waverer is comparable to a sea-wave, wind-driven and tossed. ⁷For let not that human think that one might receive anything from the Lord, ⁸a double-self man, an anarchist in all one's paths.

⁹Let the impoverished sibling boast in one's high status, ¹⁰but the wealthy in one's impoverishment, because the person will pass away as a grass's flower. ¹¹For the sun, with the burning, rose up, and it withered the grass and its flower fell off and its face's good looks were destroyed. So also the wealthy one, in one's business journeys, will be wasted.

¹²God blesses the man who is resilient in a test because he, judged suitable, will receive life's crown that was pledged to the ones loving him. ¹³May no one being tested say that "I am tested from God." For God isn't testable by bad things, and he tests no one. ¹⁴For each person is tested by one's own desires, being enticed and lured. ¹⁵Then desire, conceiving, births sin, and sin, being full completed, brings forth death.

¹⁶Don't be deceived, my loved siblings: ¹⁷Every good act of giving and every complete gift is from above, descending from the Father of lights, with whom there is no variation or shadow of change. ¹⁸Being wanted, he brings us forth by the truth-word so we are some firstfruits of his creatures.

Exhortations

¹⁹Know [this], my loved siblings: Let every human be quick to listen, slow to speak, slow to anger. ²⁰For a man's anger doesn't effect God's rightness. ²¹Therefore, laying aside every filthiness and excessive badness, receive in meekness the implanted word that is powerful to deliver your selves.

²²Be doers of the word and not only hearers, deceiving yourselves. ²³Because, if someone is a hearer of the word and not a doer, this person is comparable to a man pondering his creation-face in a mirror, ²⁴for he ponders himself and has gone away and immediately he forgets what he was like. ²⁵The one peering into the complete Covenant Code that is of liberation and remains, not becoming a forgetful hearer but a work doer, this person God will bless in one's doing.

²⁶If someone seems to be a worshiper, not restraining one's tongue but deceiving one's heart—such a person's worship is useless. ²⁷Worship [that is] clean and unstained with the God and Father is this: to care for orphans and widows in their trouble, to keep oneself non-blamed by the Kosmos.

Partiality

2 My siblings, don't have our splendorous Lord Yēsous Christos's allegiance with face-favoring. ²For if a gold-ringed man in radiant clothing entered into your assembly hall and a poor [man] in filthy clothing entered, ³and [if] you look upon the one carrying radiant clothing and say, "You should sit here beautifully," and to the poor one you say, "You should stand there or sit under my footstool," ⁴have you not discriminated among yourselves and become judges with deliberating evil thoughts? ⁵Listen, my loved siblings: Has not God elected the poor in the Kosmos [to be] wealthy ones in allegiance and heirs of the Empire that he pledged to the ones loving him? ⁶You dishonored the poor. Are not the wealthy over-dominating you and pulling you into tribunals? ⁷Are not they insulting the beautiful name that has been called upon you?

⁸If indeed you complete the royal Covenant Code consistent with the writing, *You will love your neighbor as yourself,* you do beautifully. ⁹If you favor faces, you work sin, being convinced by the Code as a violator. ¹⁰For whoever observes the whole Code but stumbles on one

[code], has become guilty for all. ¹¹For the one saying, *Don't adulterate*, said also, *Don't murder*. If you don't adulterate but murder, you have become a Code-violator.

¹²So speak and so do as about to be judged through liberty's Code. ¹³For judgment has no compassion for the one not doing compassion. Compassion boasts against judgment.

Faith and works

¹⁴**What is the benefit, my siblings, if someone says to have faith but doesn't have works? Is faith not able to deliver him? ¹⁵If a brother or sister are naked and lacking ephemeral provision ¹⁶and someone of you says to them, "Depart in peace! Be warmed! Be satisfied!" but doesn't give to them the body's necessities, what is the benefit?**

¹⁷So also faith by itself, if it doesn't have works, is dead.

¹⁸But someone will say, "You have faith and I have works."

YAKŌBOS'S RESPONSE

Exhibit to me your faith without works and I will exhibit to you faith from my works.

¹⁹**You believe that God is one?**

You do beautifully. Even the demons believe and shudder.

²⁰**Do you want to know, O hollow human, that faith without works is workless? ²¹Abra'am our father—was he not righted from works, offering up Yisa'ak [Isaac] his son on the sacrificial altar?**

²²You see that faith coworked with his works, and faith was completed from his works. ²³And the writing was filled out that says, *Abra'am trusted in God and it was calculated for him as rightness*, and he was called "God's friend." ²⁴You see that a human is righted from works and not from faith alone.

²⁵**Likewise, also Ra'ab [Rahab], the prostitute—was she not righted from works, welcoming the envoys and tossing them out another path?**

²⁶For as the body without spirit is dead, so also faith without works is dead.

The tongue

3 Not many [of you] should become teachers, my siblings, knowing that we will receive the greater judgment. ²For we all stumble in many ways. If someone doesn't stumble in a word, this man is complete, able to restrain also the whole body. ³If we toss restrainers into the mouths of horses so they may be persuaded by us, we guide their whole body. ⁴Look also at boats that, being so large and driven by harsh winds, are guided by a very small rudder where the director's surge wants, ⁵so also the tongue is a small part and brags great things. Look! What size a forest is kindled by what size a fire! ⁶The tongue is a fire:

> The wrongdoing Kosmos,
> the tongue is appointed among our parts,
> the one staining the whole body,
> igniting the cycle of origins,
> and ignited by the Valley of Destructive Fire [Gehenna].

⁷For every nature [species], both beasts and birds, both reptiles and sea creatures, is tamed and has been tamed by human nature [species], ⁸but no one is able to tame humans' tongue, a bad anarchy, full of death-carrying poison. ⁹By it we bless the Lord and Father and by it we curse humans who have been made consistent with God's likeness, ¹⁰from the same mouth exit both blessing and cursing. This ought not to be so, my siblings!

¹¹**Does a spring, from the same opening, pour forth sweet and bitter? ¹²A fig tree, my siblings, isn't able to do olives, is it? Or, a grapevine figs?**

Nor is saltwater [able to] do sweet.

Wisdom

¹³**Who is wise and knowledgeable among you?**

Let the person exhibit from one's beautiful behavior one's works with wisdom's meekness. ¹⁴If you have bitter zeal and strife in your [pl.] heart, don't boast and falsify the truth. ¹⁵This "wisdom" isn't coming down from above, but is earthy, selfish, demonic. ¹⁶For where there is zeal and strife, there is anarchy and every foul practice. ¹⁷Wisdom from above is first devout, then peaceful, gentle, persuadable, full of compassion and good fruits, non-biased, unmasked. ¹⁸Rightness's fruit is planted in peace by the ones doing peace.

Dissensions

4 From where do wars and from where do battles among you come from? Is it not from within, from your pleasures that soldier among your body parts?

²You desire and you don't have, you murder and you are zealous and you are not able to obtain, you battle and you war, you don't have because you don't ask. ³You ask and you don't receive because you ask badly so you may exhaust [them] on your pleasures.

⁴**Adulteresses! Do you not know that Kosmos-friendship is God-enmity?**

Therefore, whoever wants to be Kosmos's friend is appointed God's enemy.

⁵**Or, do you think that the writing hollowly says, "The spirit that resides in us longs toward envy"?**

⁶But [God] gives greater grace. Because it says,

> God resists the status-mongers
> but gives grace to the impoverished ones.

⁷Therefore, order yourselves under God and resist the Accuser, and he will flee from you.
⁸Get close to God and he will get close to you.
Clean the hands, sinners!
Devote the hearts, double-self people!
⁹Be devastated and grieve and wail!
Let your laughter change into grief, and the joy into dejection!
¹⁰Be impoverished before the Lord, and God will raise your status!

¹¹Don't slander one another, siblings! The sibling-slanderer or the sibling-judger slanders the Covenant Code and judges the Covenant Code. If you judge the Code, you are not the Code-doer but the Code-judge. ¹²There is one Code-giver and Judge, the one able to deliver and to destroy.

Who are you, the one judging the neighbor?

Presumption and oppression

¹³Come now, ones who say: "Today or tomorrow we will journey into such city and we will do [business] there for a year, and we will conduct business and we will gain [a profit]." ¹⁴Whoever [you are], you don't know tomorrow.

What is your life?

For you are a mist appearing for a little while, and then disappearing. ¹⁵Instead you are to say, "If the Lord wants, we will live and we will do this or that." ¹⁶But now you boast in your braggings. All such boasting is evil. ¹⁷Therefore, for the one knowing to do the beautiful thing and not doing, for that person it's sin.

5 Come now, wealthy ones: Wail, howling for the devastations coming upon you! ²Your wealth has rotted and your robes have become moth-eaten, ³your gold and silver are rusted, and their poison will be a witness to you and it will eat your fleshes like fire. You treasured for the last days. ⁴Look! The workers' wages who mowed your fields—[the wages] deprived by you—cry out, and the harvesters' bellows have entered *into the Lord Sabaōth's ears*. ⁵You luxuriated on the land and indulged, you nurtured your hearts *on the Day of Slaughter*. ⁶You condemned, you murdered the Right One; he did not resist you.

⁷Therefore, siblings, be patient until the Lord's Parousia [coming]. Look! The farmer waits it out for the land's fruit-price, being patient for it until it receives early and late rains. ⁸You also be patient! Support your hearts because the Lord's Parousia has come close. ⁹Don't groan, siblings, against one another so you will not be judged. Look! The Judge has stood before the doors. ¹⁰Receive as a model, siblings, the bad-suffering and patient prophets, who spoke in the Lord's name. ¹¹Look! We bless the resilient ones. Listen to Yiōb's [Job's] resilience and you know the Lord's completion, that the Lord is multi-empathizing and sympathetic.

Exhortations

¹²Before all, my siblings, don't agree to an oath, neither by heaven nor by the land nor by

any other oath. Let your Yes be Yes and your No be No, so you don't fall under judgment.

[13]Who is suffering bad things among you? Let the person pray. Who feels good? Let the person sing playing the strings. [14]Who is weak among you? Let the person call the assembly's elders and let them pray over the person, oiling with olive oil in the Lord's name. [15]The faith-vow will deliver the one wearied and the Lord will raise the person. If it be someone who has done sins, it will be released for the person. [16]Therefore, openly agree about sins with one another and formulate prayers for one another so you may be cured. The right-one's energized request is strong. [17]Ēlias [Elijah] was a human of comparable feelings to us and he prayed a prayer for it not to rain, and it did not rain on the land for three years and six months. [18]He prayed again, and the heaven gave rain and the land sprouted its fruit.

[19]My siblings, if someone among you wanders from the truth and someone returns the person, [20]let the person know that the one who returns a sinner from one's wandering path delivers the person's self from death *and will cover a mass of sins.*

INTRODUCTION TO THE FIRST LETTER OF PETER

This letter echoes at times the theology and language of Paulos [Paul] but in other ways takes a different approach. The location of the ministry for this letter is the upper parts of Asia Minor (today's northwest Turkey), the assemblies are apparently mostly from the ethnic groups outside Youdaia [Judea], and they are challenged by opposition to the gospel, which entails clear threats to their own livelihood.

The future for the assemblies to which he writes is "salvation," or "deliverance," and it's noticeable that for Petros [Peter] deliverance is a future final verdict and state (e.g, 1:5, 9; 2:2; 4:18). This doesn't mean believers are not yet saved but that salvation isn't fully complete until the final Empire of God. Thus, the believer has been inaugurated into a salvation that will be completed at the coming (here called "apocalypse") of Christos.

Petros calls them "exiles and temporary residents" (2:11-12), and these terms don't spiritualize life on earth as a pilgrimage but describe the social condition of displaced Christians. Petros's problem, if we can call it that, was how believers were to relate to the powers of the Roman Empire. Hence, there is here an emphasis on suffering, with Christos as the pure model, but Petros operates with a clear strategy. The assemblies under his and the elders' care are to become people who "do good," a strong theme that indicates public benevolence through either financial support or public service. This call to public service runs right through all their social networks and institutions: from government to each household, and surely one strategy is leading others to Christos (3:1-6), but another is public reputation that will preserve the believers from further attacks. The rather cavalier assumption of abusive power in 2:10–4:19 and how to deal with it troubles readers today, but Petros lived in a Roman Empire against which there was not even a possibility of group resistance. Resistance, then, had to be by way of life that witnessed to a kingdom reality rather than armed rebellion or public protest.

The letter is written from Rome, for that is what "Babulōn" [Babylon] means in 5:13. The Greek of 1 Petros bristles with brilliant syntax and careful choice of vocabulary and ranks as one of the "higher" styles of the Second Testament.

THE FIRST LETTER OF PETER

1 Petros [Peter], Yēsous Christos's Commissioner,
To the elect temporary residents of the Diaspora—in Pontos, Galatia, Kappadokia [Cappadocia], Asia, and Bithunia—

²[Elect] consistent with Father-God's foreknowledge,
in the Spirit's devotion,
for heeding and Yēsous Christos's blood-sprinkling,

Grace to you and peace be abounding.

God's deliverance

³Blessed be the God and Father of our Lord Yēsous Christos, [the Father] who gave us life again consistent with his much mercy for a living hope through Yēsous Christos's resurrection from among the dead ones, ⁴for an unperishable, unstained, unfading inheritance, having been kept in the heavens for you ⁵who are being guarded by God's power through allegiance for a deliverance prepared to be apocalypsed in the last season, ⁶in which [season] you are overjoyed, [even] if for a little while it's necessary to be pained by divergent testings ⁷so that your allegiance's testing—more precious than gold that is being destroyed and being tested by fire—may be found for public praise and splendor and honor at Yēsous Christos's apocalypse. ⁸Whom, not seeing, you love, in whom now not seeing, but trusting you are overjoyed with inexpressible and splendored joy, ⁹receiving your allegiance's completion, deliverance of your selves.
¹⁰Concerning which deliverance prophets (who prophesied about the grace for you) pursued and deeply inquired, ¹¹inquiring into whom or what season the Christos-Spirit in them was divulging, witnessing in advance about the sufferings for Christos and the splendor after these. ¹²To whom it was apocalypsed that they were serving these things not for themselves but for you, which things now are being announced to you through the ones who gospeled you in the Holy Spirit commissioned from heaven—into which things the envoys desire to peer.

Hope, devotion, awe

¹³Therefore, surrounding your mental waist [with your robe], being sober, completely hope in the grace being carried to you at Yēsous Christos's apocalypse. ¹⁴As heeding children, not being remodeled by the desires of your former ignorance ¹⁵but consistent with the Devoted One who called you, you yourselves become devoted in all your behavior, ¹⁶because it's written that *You will be devoted because I am Devoted*. ¹⁷If you call on the "Father," the one who judges without face-favoring consistent with each person's work, behave during the time of your exile in awe, ¹⁸knowing that you were liberated not by perishable things—silver and gold—from your useless behavior passed on from your fathers, ¹⁹but by Christos's priceless blood, as of an inerrant, unstained lamb, ²⁰who being known before the Kosmos's origins, but become apparent at the last times for you, ²¹who, through him, are allegiant to the God who raised him from among the dead ones and who gave him splendor, so that your allegiance and hope are in God.

Love

²²Having had your selves devoted by heeding the truth for an unmasked sibling-love, love one another stretchingly, from clean hearts, ²³having been given a new life, not from a perishable seed but from an imperishable [seed], through the living and remaining God's word. ²⁴Because

> *All flesh is as grass,*
> *and all its splendor as a flower of grass,*
> *the grass withers and the flower falls off*
> ²⁵*but the Lord's utterance remains to the*
>   *Era.*

This is the utterance that was gospeled to you.

Growing up

2 Therefore, putting off all badness and all disguise and mask-wearing and envies and all slanders, ²as new-life infants, long for undisguised word-shaped milk so you may grow into deliverance, ³since you tasted that *the*

Lord is gracious. **4**Approaching to him, a living stone that has been rejected by humans but an honorable election to God, **5**and you yourselves, as living stones, are formed [as] a Spirit-shaped house into a devoted priesthood to offer Spirit-shaped sacrifices with good acceptance by God through Yēsous Christos. **6**Because it's contained in the writing,

> Look! I place in Siōn [Zion] *a stone, a cornerstone,*
> *an honorable-elect* [stone]
> *and the one allegiant to him will never be degraded.*

7Therefore, to you allegiant ones [he is] honorable, for the anti-trusting ones *a stone the formers rejected, this one has become the corner's head* **8**and *a stumbling stone and a tripping rock.* They stumble, being unpersuaded at the word—to which they also were placed.

New people

9You are a chosen family, an imperial priesthood, a devoted ethnic group, an *acquired* people—so that you may declare *the virtues* of the one who called you out of darkness into his stunning light.

> **10**The ones once: *not people* but now: God's people,
> the ones *not shown compassion* now have been shown compassion.

Social groups: General principles

11Loved ones, I encourage [you] as exiles and temporary residents to stay away from fleshy desires that soldier against the self. **12**Having your conduct beautiful among the ethnic groups so that in that which they slander you as bad-doers, on the basis of your beautiful works, watching [you], they may splendor God *on the day of mentorship.*

Roman government

13Be ordered under every human-shaped creation because of the Lord: if to the Emperor, as under one having high status; **14**if to Governors, as ones sent by him for making it right for bad-doers but public praise for good-doers. **15**Because so is God's will: in doing good to silence the ignorance of imprudent humans—**16**[being ordered under] as liberated ones, and not [as] having liberty as a cover-up for badness, but as God's slaves.

17Honor everyone,
love the siblingship,
awe God,
honor the Emperor.

Slaves

18Domestics being ordered under the masters in all awe, not only to the good and kind but also to the rascals. **19**For this is grace: if because of consciousness of God someone bears under pains, suffering wrongly. **20**For what credit is it if you are resilient—sinning and are beaten? But if, doing good and suffering, you are resilient, this is grace with God. **21**For to this you have been called:

> That Christos also suffered for you,
> leaving behind an outline,
> so you could follow in his steps,
> **22***who did not sin nor was disguise found in his mouth,*
> **23**who, being beaten, was not beating back,
> suffering, was not threatening,
> but was giving himself over to the one who judges rightly,
> **24**who himself carried up our sins
> in his body on the tree,
> so, being absent from sins,
> we might live for rightness,
> by whose *bruises you are cured.*
> **25**For you were *wandering as sheep,*
> but you have now turned back to the Shepherd
> and Mentor of your selves.

Women

3 Likewise, the women, ordering under their own men so even if some are not persuaded by the word, through the behavior of the women, without a word, may be gained, **2**watching out for your devout behavior in awe. **3**Let not their external world of braiding hair and wearing gold or putting on of robes [be your decoration], **4**but the heart's hidden human, in the imperishable [way] of meekness and quiet spirit, which is high-priced before God. **5**For so once also the devoted women who hoped in God decorated themselves, ordering under their own men, **6**as Sarra

[Sarah] heeded Abra'am, calling him "lord"—of whom you have become children, doing good and not being in awe of any dread.

Men

⁷Likewise, the men, residing consistent with knowledge with the women-folk, as with a weaker vessel, assigning honor [to them] as also co-heirs of life's grace—so your prayers are not cut off.

Everyone

⁸The completion: all [of you be] one-minded, sympathetic, sibling-loving, good empathies, impoverished, ⁹not paying back bad for bad or beating for beating. Instead, blessing because to this you were called so you may inherit blessing. ¹⁰For

> The one who wants to love life
> and to see good days,
> let the person stop the tongue from bad
> and the lips not to speak disguise.
> ¹¹Let the person turn away from bad and do good,
> Let the person pursue peace and chase it.
> ¹²Because the Lord's eyes are on the right ones,
> And his ears to their request,
> And the Lord's face is on those doing bad.

¹³And who is the one who will do bad to you if you become zealots for the good? ¹⁴But if you also were to suffer because of rightness, you are blessed by God. *Don't be scared of their scare nor be agitated,* ¹⁵but *devote* the Christos *as Lord* in your hearts, always prepared for a defense to everyone who asks you a word about the hope in you, ¹⁶but with meekness and awe, having a good consciousness so that, in what matter you are slandered, the mistreaters of your good behavior in Christos may be degraded. ¹⁷For it's better to suffer for doing good—if this be God's will—than for doing bad.

Christos, the outline

> ¹⁸Because Christos also suffered, once for all for sins.
> The right one for the wrongdoing ones, so he might lead you to God,
> having died in flesh,
> being made alive in spirit.

¹⁹In which [spirit] also, journeying to the spirits in prison, he announced, ²⁰who were once unpersuaded when God's patience was waiting it out in Nōe's [Noah's] days . . . the ark's prepared, in which a few (that is, eight selves) were delivered through water . . . ²¹which, dipping, also, as an anti-type, now delivers you—not putting off the dirty flesh but a solemn pledge to God of a good consciousness, through Yēsous Christos's resurrection, ²²who is at God's right, having journeyed into heaven, ordering under himself envoys and authorities and powers.

Your life has changed

4 Christos suffered in flesh . . . therefore, you too be armed with the same notion because the one who suffered in flesh has stopped sins ²so no longer to live the remaining time in flesh in human desires but in God's will. ³For the time that has passed is adequate to effect the ethnic groups' will, having journeyed in flaunting sensualities, desires, wine-soaking, parties, symposia bashes, and nonobservant idolatries, ⁴in which they consider it foreign you aren't running with them into the same dissolution-flood, insulting—⁵who will pay back a word to the One prepared to judge the living and the dead. ⁶For this it was gospeled to the dead ones so that they might be judged in flesh consistent with humans but in spirit consistent with God.

Assembly life

⁷The completion of all has come close. Therefore, have sensible thoughts and be sober in prayers. ⁸Before everything having a stretched love for one another because *love covers a mass of sins,* ⁹being hospitable to one another without grumbling. ¹⁰As each received a grace-act, serving it to one another as good as beautiful administrators of God's diverse grace. ¹¹If someone speaks—as God's sayings; if someone serves—as from a strength that God supplies: so God may be splendored in all ways through Yēsous Christos, to whom be the splendor and the grip into the Eras of Eras, Amēn!

Suffering

¹²Loved ones, don't think the fire, coming among you to test you, is a foreign thing

coalescing upon you, ¹³but as you have a common life in Christos's sufferings, rejoice so you may rejoice, overjoying, at his splendorous apocalypse. ¹⁴If you are degraded in Christos's name, you are God-blessed because the splendorous Spirit, *God's Spirit, is resting* upon you. ¹⁵For don't let someone of you suffer as a murderer or a thief or bad-doer or as a snoop—¹⁶if as a "Christian," let the person not be shamed but let the person splendor God in this name ¹⁷because [it's] the season to begin judgment from God's house. If first from us, what is the completion for the ones not persuaded by God's gospel? ¹⁸*If the right one is barely delivered, where will the impious and sinner appear?* ¹⁹So, let the ones suffering consistent with God's will present their selves with good deeds to the allegiant Creator.

Leaders

5 Therefore, I, a co-elder and witness to Christos's sufferings and one who also has a common life in the splendor about to be apocalypsed, encourage the elders among you. ²Pastor God's flock among you, mentoring,

> not from necessity but willingly, consistent with God,
> not for shameful gain but emotionally, ³not as ruling over the part [assigned to you] but becoming models for the flock.
> ⁴The First Shepherd's appeared . . . you will receive an unfadeable, splendorous crown.

⁵ᵃLikewise, younger men, order yourselves under the elders.

Everyone now

⁵ᵇAll [of you], fasten impoverishment to one another because God *resists the high-status ones and gives grace to the impoverished ones.* ⁶Therefore, be impoverished under God's gripping hand so he may raise your status in season, ⁷throwing all your anxieties on him because he cares for you.

⁸Be sober!
Be awake!

Your adversary, the Accuser, walks around *as a roaring lion* pursuing someone to swallow up. ⁹Resist him, firm in allegiance, knowing the same [sorts of] sufferings are being completed by your siblingship in the Kosmos.

¹⁰The God of all grace who called you into his Era-splendor in Christos Yēsous, suffering a little while, will himself prepare, support, strengthen, found [you]. ¹¹To him be the grip into the Eras, Amēn!

Details

¹²I wrote briefly to you through Silouanos [Silvanus], our allegiant brother (as I calculate), encouraging and witnessing this to be God's true grace: Stand in it.

¹³The co-elect [lady] in "Babulōn [Babylon]" greets you, and Markos [Mark], my son.

¹⁴Greet one another with a loving kiss.
Peace [be] to you all in Christos.

INTRODUCTION TO THE SECOND LETTER OF PETER

A feature of this letter, along with Jude, is its vituperative rhetoric against false teachers for fomenting false theology. The uppermost issues are denial of the second coming or Parousia (1:16-18; 3:4-10) and moral degeneracy (2:2, 10, 13, 18-22; 3:2, 15-16), and one might suspect weak Christology as well (2:1, 10). With false teaching looming for the audience, the focus of Petros [Peter] is on a firmly founded allegiance (1:12-21; 3:1-2).

Because the author, "Sumeōn Petros," knows he is on the verge of dying (1:14), many read this short letter as a last will and testament and, as such, as connected in some ways to similar writings in the Judean world (such as the pseudonymous *2 Baruch* 78–86 or the *Testaments of the Twelve Patriarchs*). Authorship questions aside, the testamentary nature of the letter gives the reader a fresh approach. The style of Greek in 2 Peter isn't the same as in 1 Peter, so different that it's reasonable to say whoever wrote 1 Petros (Silounas) did not write 2 Petros. Such an observation can be explained in various ways. Second Peter 2 seems dependent on Jude (cf. vv. 4-16) rather than the reverse.

THE SECOND LETTER OF PETER

1 Sumeōn Petros [Simon Peter], Yēsous Christos's slave and Commissioner,
To the ones designated with an equally-honorable-for-us allegiance in the rightness of our God and Deliverer, Yēsous Christos,
²May grace to you and peace abound in perceiving God and our Lord Yēsous.

A calling to allegiance's virtue

³... As his divine power has granted to us all things toward life and civilized piety, through perceiving the One who called us in his own splendor and virtue, ⁴through these he has granted the honorable and great pledges to us so through these you might be common-life participants with the divine nature, fleeing the decay in desire in the Kosmos ...
⁵[Concerning] this same thing, having brought along all seriousness, supply:
in your allegiance virtue,
in your virtue knowledge,
⁶in your knowledge self-discipline,
in your self-discipline resilience,
in your resilience civilized piety,
⁷in your civilized piety sibling-love,
In your sibling-love love.
⁸For these items, existing and magnifying among you, establish you as neither workless nor fruitless for perceiving our Lord Yēsous Christos. ⁹For the one in whom these things are not present is sightless, that is, close-eyed, taking forgetfulness of the cleansing of one's ancient sins. ¹⁰Therefore, instead, siblings, seriously commit to make your calling and election firm for, doing these things, you will never once stumble. ¹¹For so the path-entry into the Era Empire of our Lord and Deliverer, Yēsous Christos, will be wealthily supplied for you.

Looking to the future

¹²Therefore, I will always be about to remind you about these things, though you have known and are supported in the present truth. ¹³I consider it right as long as I am in this tent to raise you up in memory, ¹⁴having known that the laying aside of my tent is soon-ish, just as our Lord Yēsous Christos divulged to me. ¹⁵I will be serious [about this] so you after my exodus have [opportunity] to make memory at any time of these things.
¹⁶For we didn't make known to you the power and Parousia [coming] of our Lord Yēsous Christos by following out "enwisened" myths but by becoming eyewitnesses of that magnificence. ¹⁷For, receiving honor and splendor from Father-God ... a voice like this being carried to him by the Magnificent Splendor, "My royal Son, my loved one, this one is [the one] in whom I delighted" ... ¹⁸we also listened to this voice being carried from heaven, being with him on devoted mountain. ¹⁹We have the firmest prophetic word, to which you do beautifully in absorbing as a lamp appearing in a bleak place, until day dawns and a morning star arises in your hearts, ²⁰knowing this first that every prophetic writing doesn't come about from one's own explanation, ²¹for a prophecy has not once been carried by human will, but humans, being carried by the Holy Spirit, spoke from God.

False teachers

2 There were false prophets among the people as also there will be false teachers among you, who penetrate furtively to destructive factions, denying the Master who purchased them, leading themselves away to soon-ish destruction, ²and many will follow after them for flaunting sensualities, because of whom the truth's path will be insulted, ³and, in wanting more and more, they will "conduct business" with you with fabricated words, for whom the judgment [indicated] long ago isn't workless and their destruction isn't sleeping.
⁴For if God did not spare the envoys who sinned but gave them over, tossing them into Tartaros in chains of gloom, being kept for judgment,
⁵and [if God] did not spare the ancient Kosmos but guarded an eighth [person], Nōe [Noah], announcer of rightness, bringing a cataclysm for the Kosmos on the impious,
⁶and [if God], ash-ing the cities of Sodoma [Sodom] and Gomorra [Gomorrah], condemned [them] to catastrophe as a model placed for things to come for the impious,

⁷and [then God] rescued right Lōt, being exhausted by the illicit ones' flaunting sensual behavior (⁸for, in the see-able and hear-able, the right one—residing among them day after day as a right self—was tormented by their anti-Covenant-Code works),

⁹[then] the Lord knows to rescue the civilized pious from testing, but [knows also] to keep chastising the wrongdoers for Judgment Day, ¹⁰ᵃespecially the ones journeying after the flesh in polluting desire and snubbing lordship.

¹⁰ᵇSelf-regarding bold ones! They don't tremble at the splendors, insulting, ¹¹where envoys, being greater in strength and power, don't carry against them an insulting judgment from the Lord.

¹²These are like wordless living things—given life by nature for capturing and decay, in which things they are uninformed, insulting, in their decay they will be decayed, ¹³being wronged as the wage of wrongdoing, considering luxury in daytime to be pleasure.

[These are] stains and blots! Luxuriating in their deceits, feasting with you, ¹⁴having eyes full of adultery and unstoppable sins, luring firmless selves, having a heart fully trained with [greed] for more and more.

God-cursed children! ¹⁵Abandoning the straight path, they wander away, following after the path of Bala'am, son of Bosor, who loved wrongdoing's wage. ¹⁶He got a conviction for his own Covenat-Code-lessness—a voiceless donkey uttering in a human voice prohibited the prophet's Code-lessness.

¹⁷These are waterless springs and mists driven by whirlwinds, for whom the darkness's gloom has been kept ¹⁸for, uttering idle exaggerations, they lure by flaunting sensuality's fleshy desires the ones barely fleeing away from the ones behaving in deceit, ¹⁹pledging liberty for them—these being themselves decay's slaves. For by what someone has been defeated, to this one is enslaved. ²⁰For if, fleeing from the Kosmos's blots by perceiving our Lord and Deliverer, Yēsous Christos, they are defeated by them, being entangled again, [then] the last things have become worse than the first things. ²¹For it would be better for them not to have perceived rightness's path than, perceiving, to turn away from the devout order that has been given over to them. ²²The true proverb has coalesced for them: "A dog returning to its own vomit" and "A sow, being washed, [returning] to rolling in muck."

The Parousia

3 I now write this second letter to you, loved ones, in which I raise up in memory your sincere mind ²to remember the previously spoken utterances by the devoted prophets and the order of your Commissioners of the Lord and Deliverer. ³Knowing this first, that on the last days scoffers will come in scoffing, journeying consistent with their own desires ⁴and saying, "Where is his Parousia's [coming's] pledge? For since the ancestors were put to sleep, all things remain just so from creation's beginning!" ⁵For this is forgotten for them, who want it so, that the heavens were long ago, and land being established from water and through water by God's word, ⁶through which the Kosmos once, being deluged with water, was destroyed. ⁷But now, by the same word, the heavens and the land are treasured up for fire, being kept for Judgment Day and destruction for impious humans.

⁸Don't forget this one thing, loved ones, that one day with the Lord is as a thousand years and a thousand years as one day. ⁹The pledge's Lord isn't slow, as some are led by slowness, but [the Lord] is patient for you, not wanting some to be destroyed but for all to find space for conversion. ¹⁰The Day of the Lord will come like a thief, on which [Day] the heavens will pass away with roaring and the first categories, burning up, will be loosened and the land and the works in it will be found. ¹¹. . . All these are being so loosened . . . so what kind of persons is it necessary for you to be in devoted behavior and civilized piety, ¹²anticipating and hurrying the Parousia of God's Day (because of which the heavens, set on fire, will be loosened and the first categories, burning up, melt)? ¹³We anticipate *a new heavens and a new land* consistent with his pledge, in which rightness resides.

Exhortations

¹⁴Therefore, loved ones, anticipating these things, be serious to be found by him in peace, unstained and inerrant. ¹⁵Consider our Lord's patience to be deliverance, just as also our

loved brother Paulos [Paul], consistent with the wisdom given to him, wrote to you, ¹⁶as also in all letters, speaking in them about these matters, in which some things are difficult to understand, which the unapprenticed and unstable twist, as also [they do to] the remaining writings, to their own destruction.

¹⁷You, therefore, loved ones, knowing in advance, guard yourselves that you are not deceived by the illicit ones; [that you] being carried off, fall away from one's own firmness. ¹⁸Grow in grace and knowledge about our Lord and Deliverer Yēsous Christos.

To him be the splendor, both now and into Era's Day.

Amēn!

INTRODUCTION TO THE FIRST LETTER OF JOHN

The author of 1–3 John is the same, and in the second and third letter calls himself the "Elder" so we refer to the author as the Elder Yōannēs [John]. Whether the Elder Yōannēs and the apostle/Commissioner Yōannēs are the same is disputed. The first of his letters may well have been a circular letter that was passed from church to church in Yōannēs's circle of churches, which would have been western Asia Minor (see the seven churches of Rev 2–3). Many think the letter was written sometime in the later decades of the first century AD. The style involves simple grammar and vocabulary appearing frequently (*truth, love, life*, and *light* with *falsity, hate, death*, and *darkness*, as well as *Father* and *Son*), but the effect of this style is a profound clarity and depth of thought. When these terms refer to agents that seem to act on humans, I capitalize them.

There are tensions lurking behind this letter. They concern what one is to believe about Yēsous Christos (2:19; 4:2-3): Has he come in the flesh? Is he Israel's true Messiah (Christos)? Yōannēs robustly defends an affirmation of both and pronounces judgment on those who deny these truths. There is also very serious tension, evidently, between believers in the churches connected to this letter. The constant theme of loving one's siblings emerges from siblings not loving one another.

The ethic of 1 John requires a good ear: the Elder believes believers are changed by grace and the gospel into becoming people who love, who walk in the light, and who do what is right. There is a zero-sum game played in this letter: either you do God's will or you don't, and it can lead at times to some mistakenly thinking the Elder believed in sinless perfection. But the reality of both sin and confession makes clear that sinlessness isn't an assumption or expectation (cf. 1:9; 5:17). The theme is that God is love, and those born of God are to become loving humans, loving both God and one another.

THE FIRST LETTER OF JOHN

1 ¹What was from the beginning,
what we have heard,
what we have seen with our eyes,
what we observed and our hands felt,
about the Logos of Life:
(²The Life was made apparent,
and we have seen
and we witness
and we declare to you the Era Life
that was with the Father and has become apparent to us.)
³What we have seen and have heard
we declare also to you
so you also may have a common life with us.
(The common Life that is ours is with the Father
and with his Son, Yēsous Christos.)
⁴We write these so our joy may be filled out.

If we say . . .

⁵This is the announcement that we have heard from him and we announce to you: That God is Light and there is no Darkness in him at all.

⁶If we say that we have a common life with him and walk around in Darkness, we falsify and we don't do the Truth.

⁷If we walk around in the Light as he is in the Light, we have a common life with one another and Yēsous his Son's blood cleans us from all sins.

⁸If we say that we don't have sin, we deceived ourselves and the Truth isn't in us.

⁹If we openly agree [with God] about our sins, he is allegiant and right so that he releases us from our sins and cleans us from all wrongdoing.

¹⁰If we say that we have not sinned, we make him a falsifier and his Logos isn't in us.

Knowing we are in him

2 My children, I write these things to you so you may not sin. If someone sins, we have an Illuminator [Paraklētos] with the Father, Yēsous Christos, the Right One. ²He is the means of mercy for our sins, not for ours only but for the whole Kosmos.

³In this we know that we have known him, if we observe his orders.

⁴The one who says that "I have known him" and who doesn't observe his orders is a falsifier, and the Truth isn't in this person,

⁵but whoever observes his word, God's love is truly completed in this person.

In this we know that we are in him.

⁶The one who says to remain in him is obligated to walk around just as that one walked around.

New order, old order

⁷Loved ones, I don't write to you a new order but an ancient order that you had from the beginning. The order that is ancient is the word that you heard.

⁸Again, I write to you a new order, which is true in him and in you, that the Darkness is passing away and the true Light is already appearing.

⁹The one who says to be in the Light and hates one's sibling is until now in the Darkness.

¹⁰The one who loves one's sibling remains in the Light, and there is no tripping in the person.

¹¹The one who hates one's sibling is in the Darkness and walks around in the Darkness and doesn't know where one is going away because the Darkness made the person's eyes sightless.

I write to you

¹²I write to you, children [teknia], because the sins have been released from you because of his name.

¹³I write to you, fathers, because you have known the One from the beginning.

I write to you, young ones, because you have conquered the Evil One.

[14]I wrote to you, children [*paidia*], because you have known the Father.

I wrote to you, fathers, because you have known the One from the beginning.

I wrote to you, young ones, because you are strong and God's Logos remains in you and you have conquered the Evil One.

Kosmos love and its falsifier

[15]Don't love the Kosmos nor the things in the Kosmos. If someone loves the Kosmos, loving the Father isn't in the person [16]because everything that is in the Kosmos—the Flesh's desire, the eyes' desire, and wanting more and more out of life—isn't from the Father but is from the Kosmos. [17]The Kosmos passes away and its desire, but the one who does God's will remains to the Era.

[18]Children [*paidia*], this is last hour, and just as you heard that the Anti-Christos [Antichrist] comes, and now many Antichristoses have come, from this you know that this is last hour. [19]They exited from us, but they were not from us. For if they are from us, they would have remained with us. But [they exited] so they may be apparent, that they are not all from us. [20]You have a charism from the Holy One and you all know.

[21]I did not write to you because you don't know the Truth but because you know it and every falsehood isn't from the Truth.

> [22]Who is the falsifier if not the denier who says "Yēsous isn't the Christos"? This is the Anti-Christos, the denier of the Father and the Son.
> [23]Everyone who denies the Son doesn't have the Father.
> The one who openly agrees about the Son has the Father.

[24]You: what you heard from the beginning, let it remain in you. If what you heard from the beginning remains in you—you will remain in the Son and in the Father. [25]This is the pledge that he pledged to you: the Era Life.

The charism

[26]I wrote these things to you about the ones deceiving you. [27]You: the charism that you received from him remains in you, and you have no need that someone teach you. But as his charism teaches you about all things—and

it's true and it isn't a falsifier—just as it taught you, remain in him.

[28]Now, children [*teknia*], remain in him so if he becomes apparent, we may have frankness and not be shamed by him in his Parousia. [29]If you know that he is the Right One, you know that everyone who does rightness has been given life from him.

God's children

3 Look at how much love the Father has given to us so we may be called "God's children." And we are! Because of this, the Kosmos doesn't know us, because it did not know him. [2]Loved ones, now we are God's children, and it has not yet appeared what we will be. We know that if he appears, we will be comparable to him because we will see him as he is.

> [3]Everyone who has this hope in him devotes oneself, just as he is devout.
> [4]Everyone who does sin, does Covenant-Code breaking, and sin is Code-breaking. [5]You know that he has become apparent so he may lift away sins, and sin isn't in him.
> [6]Everyone who remains in him doesn't sin. Everyone who sins has not seen him and has not known him.
> [7]Children [*teknia*], let no one deceive you.
> The one who does rightness is right, just as he is right.
> [8]The one who does sin is of the Accuser, because the Accuser sins from the beginning.
> For this God's Son became apparent: to loosen the Accuser's works.
> [9]Everyone who has been given life from God doesn't do sin because his seed remains in him and is unable to sin because the person has been given life from God.
> [10]In this God's children and the Accuser's children are apparent: everyone who doesn't do rightness isn't from God—and the one who doesn't love one's sibling.

Loving your siblings

[11]Because this is the announcement that you heard from the beginning, that we love one

another, ¹²not as Kaïn [Cain], who was of the Evil One and slayed his brother. For what reason did he slay him? Because his words were evil but his brother's [works were] right.

¹³Don't be stunned, siblings, if the Kosmos hates you. ¹⁴We know that we have shifted from Death into Life because we love the siblings. The one who doesn't love remains in Death. ¹⁵Everyone who hates one's sibling is a human-killer, and you know that every human-killer doesn't have Era Life remaining in oneself. ¹⁶In this we have known love, that he placed his self for us, and we ought to place [our] selves for the siblings. ¹⁷Whoever has Kosmos's life and observes one's sibling having need and shuts one's empathies from the person—how does God's love remain in the person? ¹⁸Children [teknia], don't love in word or tongue but in work and truth.

We are of the Truth

¹⁹In this we will know that we are of the Truth, and we will persuade our heart before him, ²⁰that if our heart is knowably wrong, that God is greater than our heart and knows all things. ²¹Loved ones, if our heart isn't knowably wrong, we have frankness before God, ²²and whatever we ask we receive from him because we observe his orders and we do pleasing acts before him.

²³This is his order, that we trust in the name of his Son, Yēsous Christos, and we love one another, as he gave to us an order. ²⁴The one who observes his orders remains in him, and he in the person. In this we know that he remains in us: from the Spirit whom he gave to us.

Know the Spirit and the spirits

4 Loved ones, don't believe every spirit, but approve the spirits if they are from God, because many false prophets have exited into the Kosmos. ²In this you know God's Spirit: Every spirit that openly agrees that Yēsous Christos has come in flesh is from God, ³and every spirit that doesn't openly agree about Yēsous isn't from God. This is the [spirit] of the Anti-Christos, which you have heard comes, and now is already in the Kosmos.

We are from God

⁴You are of God, children [teknia], and you have conquered them because greater is the One in you than the one in the Kosmos. ⁵These are of the Kosmos because this is true: they speak from the Kosmos and the Kosmos hears them. ⁶We are from God. The one who knows God hears us, the one not from God doesn't hear us. From this we know Truth's Spirit and deceit's spirit.

⁷Loved ones, let us love one another, because love is from God.
Everyone who loves has been given life from God and knows God.
⁸The one who doesn't love didn't know God because God is love.
⁹In this God's love became apparent among us: that God has commissioned his only Son into the Kosmos so we might live through him.
¹⁰In this is love: not that we have loved God but that he loved us and commissioned his Son as the means of mercy for our sins.

Love, love, love

¹¹Loved ones, if God so loved us, we ought to love one another. ¹²No one has once observed God. If we love one another, God remains in us and his love is fully completed in us.

¹³In this we know that we remain in him and he in us: that he has given to us from his Spirit.

¹⁴We have observed and witness that the Father has commissioned the Son as the Kosmos's Deliverer. ¹⁵Whoever openly agrees that Yēsous is God's Son, God remains in the person and the person in God. ¹⁶We have known and we have trusted the love that God has in us.

God is love, and the one who remains in love remains in God and God remains in the person.

¹⁷In this love has been completed with us so we may have frankness in the Judgment Day, because just as he is [so also] we are in this Kosmos. ¹⁸There is no fear in love but complete love tosses out fear because fear has chastisement, but the one who fears has not been completed in love. ¹⁹We love because he first loved us. ²⁰If someone says that "I love God" and hates one's sibling, the person is a falsifier. For the one who doesn't love one's

sibling, whom one has seen, is unable to love God, whom one has not seen. ²¹We have this order from him: that the one who loves God loves also one's sibling.

Love obeys God

5 Everyone who trusts that Yēsous is the Christos has been given life from God—and everyone who loves the One who gave life loves also the one given life from him. ²In this we know that we love God's children: whenever we love God and do his orders. ³For this is God's love, that we observe his orders, and his orders are not heavy. ⁴Because everyone who has been given life from God conquers the Kosmos. And this is the conquest that conquers the Kosmos: our allegiance.

God's witness

⁵Who is the one who conquers the Kosmos except the one who trusts that Yēsous is God's Son? ⁶This is the one who came through water and blood, Yēsous Christos, not in water only but in the water and the blood. The Spirit is the one who witnesses because the Spirit is the Truth. ⁷Because three are witnessers: ⁸the Spirit, the water, and the blood, and the three are one. ⁹If we receive humans' witness, God's witness is greater because this is God's witness that he has witnessed about his Son.

> ¹⁰The one who trusts in God's Son has the witness in oneself,
> the one who doesn't trust in God has made him a falsifier because one has not trusted in the witness that God has witnessed about his Son.
> ¹¹This is the witness: that God gave to us Era Life, and this Life is in his Son.

¹²The one who has the Son has the Life. The one who doesn't have God's Son doesn't have the Life.

So you may know

¹³I wrote these to you so you may know that you have Era Life, [you] who trust in God's Son's name. ¹⁴This is the frankness that we have toward him that, whatever we ask consistent with his will, he hears us ¹⁵and, if we know that he hears us about whatever we ask, we know that we have the requests that we have asked from him.

When not to pray for a sibling

¹⁶If someone sees one's sibling sinning a sin not toward Death, the one will ask and will give Life to him—for the ones sinning not toward Death. There is a sin toward Death. I am not saying that you request about that. ¹⁷Every wrongdoing is sin, and there is sin not toward Death.

We know

¹⁸We know that everyone who has been given life from God doesn't sin, but the one who has been given life from God observes oneself, and the Evil One doesn't touch the person.
¹⁹We know we are from God and the whole Kosmos lies in the Evil One.
²⁰We know that God's Son has come and has given to us understanding so we may know the truthfulness, and we are in the truthfulness, in Yēsous Christos his Son. This one is the true God and Era Life.
²¹Children [*teknia*], guard yourselves from demon-idols.

INTRODUCTION TO THE SECOND LETTER OF JOHN

As with 1 John and 3 John, the tests for genuine faith include believing in the Truth and walking in Love, and the Truth is about Yēsous Christos come in the flesh while the Love is about living consistently according to the teachings of Yēsous about love, which in these letters is called an "order" (or a commandment). The wandering and Anti-Christos [antichrist] folks deny the Truth about Christos and don't walk in Love.

Here the author is stated to be "the Elder," as in 3 John. The letter's style is enough like 1 John to make the Elder John the author of all three letters.

This brief letter opens a door into an early Christian house church that appears to be led by a female church leader ("lady-lord" in our translation below). It's unlikely the "lady-lord" of verse 1 and "her children" immediately after "lady-lord" are one and the same. It is, however, possible that "lady-lord" refers to a local church to which this letter is sent (as found in 1 Pet 5:13), and some have seen a fellow sister-church in 2 John 13, though once again this may refer to the lady-lord's actual sister.

We would have to guess to determine the location, but Yōannēs's ministry was in and around Ephesos [Ephesus], so one would be safest to suggest there or a surrounding location. We don't know the date.

THE SECOND LETTER OF JOHN

¹The Elder,
To the elect lady-lord and to her children, whom I love in Truth and not only I but all those who have known the Truth, ²because of the Truth remaining in us and with us will be unto the Era. ³Grace, mercy, peace from Father-God and from the Father's Son, Yēsous Christos, will be with us in truth and love.

The order from the beginning: Love one another

⁴I was greatly joyed because I have found [some] of your children walking around in Truth just as we received an order from the Father. ⁵Now I request you, lady-lord, not writing to you as a new order but which we have had from the beginning, that we love one another. ⁶This is Love, that we walk around consistent with his order. This is the order, just as you heard from the beginning, that we walk around in it.

Wanderers

⁷Because many wanderers exited into the Kosmos, those not openly agreeing about Yēsous Christos coming in the flesh. This is the Wanderer and the Anti-Christos [Antichrist]. ⁸Watch yourselves so you don't destroy what we have effected but so you may receive back a full wage.

⁹Everyone who goes ahead, and doesn't remain in the teaching about Christos, doesn't have God.
The one who remains in the teaching, this person has both the Father and the Son.

¹⁰If someone comes to you and doesn't carry this teaching, don't receive the person into a house and don't say a greeting to the person. ¹¹For the one who says to greet the person makes common life with the person's evil deeds.

Closing

¹²Having many things to write to you, I did not choose [to communicate much] through paper and ink, but I hope to come to you and to speak mouth to mouth, so our joy may be completed.

¹³The children of your elect sister greet you.

INTRODUCTION TO THE THIRD LETTER OF JOHN

Third John is another door opened to an early house church, this one with a narcissistic problem person named Diotrephēs who doesn't recognize Yōannēs [John] as a church leader, opposes him, prevents people from recognizing him, and boots out of the local assembly those who do recognize Yōannēs. Another person, perhaps the letter carrier or someone representing Yōannēs, named Dēmētrios [Demetrius], does recognize Yōannēs, and thus all the reverse is probably accurate: supports Yōannēs, encourages others to recognize Yōannēs, and welcomes people with hospitality into the assembly who support Yōannēs. We have then a battle of power that Yōannēs sees as one-sided: one person in the right and one person usurping authority. Yōannēs thus writes to a Gaïos [Gaius], who appears to be the leader of the assembly. He can guide the assembly in a way consistent with the teachings of Yōannēs.

As with the other letters of Yōannēs, the emphasis is on walking around in the Love and the Truth of the gospel about Yēsous Christos. Allegiance to the gospel for this letter involves whom to receive with hospitality and whom not to receive, as hospitality embodies one's allegiance to the gospel.

THE THIRD LETTER OF JOHN

¹The Elder

To the loved Gaïos [Gaius], whom I love in truth.

The good path of Truth

²Loved one, in many ways I formulate a prayer for you for to make a good path and to be healthy, just as your self is on a good path. ³For I was greatly joyed . . . brothers coming and witnessing your Truth . . . just as you walk around in Truth. ⁴I have no greater joy than this, that I hear my children walking around in the Truth.

Hospitality for siblings

⁵Loved one, you do allegiantly with whatever you work for the siblings and [doing] this for foreigners, ⁶who witnessed your love before the assembly; you were doing beautifully sending [them] ahead as God-deserving. ⁷For they exited for the name [of Christos], not receiving [provisions] from the ethnic groups. ⁸Therefore, we are obligated to take up such persons so we may become coworkers in the Truth.

The chatterbox

⁹I wrote something to the assembly. But Diotrephēs, who loves first place for himself, doesn't recognize us. ¹⁰Because this is true: if I come, I will remind him about the works that he does, chatterboxing with evil words about us. Not being content with these, nor does he recognize the siblings and prohibits those wanting [to recognize] and tosses [them] from the assembly.

The good-doer

¹¹Loved one, don't copy the evil but the good.

The good-doer is from God,
the bad-doer has not seen God.
¹²Dēmētrios is witnessed by all and by the Truth itself, and we also witness [about him], and you know that our witness is true.

Closing

¹³I had many things to write to you but I don't want to write to you through ink and reed. ¹⁴I hope to see you immediately, and we will speak mouth to mouth.

¹⁵Peace to you!

The friends greet you.

Greet the friends name consistent with a name.

INTRODUCTION TO THE LETTER OF JUDE

The author of this short and heated apocalyptic letter of sorts is a man named Youdas [Jude], the brother of Yakōbos [James], who is the "brother" of Yēsous. Like his brother Yakōbos, he was named after a patriarch. Youdas's letter, which in some ways is very similar to 2 Peter (and 2 Peter is dependent on Youdas), is filled with warnings about false teachers. The manner of discourse is a going back and forth from describing the false teachers to examples in Jewish history as Youdas warns those whom he pastors. I have indicated the examples he is using by indenting them. Though used only one time, the word *dreamer* is popular in this letter because it's implied with the word "these" (vv. 8, 10, 12, 14, 16, 19).

The date is impossible to fix with certainty; the location is just as disputable, though a brother of Yēsous is most likely to have been living in the land of Israel and writing to believers in that location. The style of this letter is educated and elevated, and it would have been composed to be read aloud by someone who knew how to perform it with skill. As such it was designed to bring believers in line with the faith and warn them about arrogant, divisive, fleshly, and false teachers. Noticeably, verses 14-15 quote the pseudepigraphal source *1 Enoch* 1:9.

THE LETTER OF JUDE

¹Youdas [Jude], Yēsous Christos's slave and Yakōbos's [James's] brother,
To the called ones—loved in Father-God and kept by Yēsous Christos:
²Mercy to you and peace and love be abounding.

The story about false teachers

³Loved ones, making all seriousness to write to you about our common deliverance, I had a necessity to write to you, encouraging [you] to wage a contest for the faith once for all given over to the devoted ones. ⁴For some humans furtively penetrated, [humans] who were written about long ago for this, the judgment—impious ones!—shifting our God's grace into flaunting sensuality, and denying our only Master and Lord, Yēsous Christos.

⁵I want you to remember, knowing all things, that the Lord once delivering a people from the land of Aiguptos [Egypt], a second time destroyed those who were not allegiant,
⁶and he has kept the envoys—who, not keeping their rule but abandoning their own abode—in eternal bonds under gloom for the Great Day's judgment,
⁷as Sodoma [Sodom] and Gomorra [Gomorrah] and the cities around them, in a comparable manner as these, being sexually immoralized and departing after other flesh, laid before a model of Era-fire, undergoing right penalty.

⁸Likewise indeed also these dreamers: they soil flesh, reject lordships, insult splendors.

⁹Michaēl, the Ruling Envoy, when disputing with the Accuser, was deliberating about Mōüsēs' [Moses'] body, did not dare to bring a judgment of insult but said, "May the Lord rebuke you!"

¹⁰But these [dreamers] insult whatever they don't know, and whatever they understand naturally—as wordless living things—by these they are abominated. ¹¹Oy to them!

Because they journeyed on Kaïn's [Cain's] path
and are poured out in Bala'am's deceit—for a wage,
and are destroyed in Kore's [Korah's] contradiction.
¹²These [dreamers] are stains in your love [feasts], feasting with you, fearlessly pastoring themselves!
Waterless clouds carried along by winds!
Autumnal trees, fruitless, dying twice, uprooted!
¹³Wild sea waves, foaming their own shame!
Wandering stars, for whom darkness's gloom has been kept for the Era!
¹⁴Henōch [Enoch], seventh from Adam, also prophesied about these [dreamers], saying, "Look! The Lord came with a myriad of his devoted ones ¹⁵to do judgment against all and to convict all selves about all works of their impiety, which they impiously did and for the hardnesses which impious sinners spoke against him."

¹⁶These [dreamers] are grumblers, censorious, journeying consistent with their own desires, and their mouth speaks exaggerations, stunning faces for the sake of [their own] benefit.

Not you

¹⁷But you, loved ones, remember the utterances that were spoken previously by our Lord Yēsous Christos's Commissioners ¹⁸that were saying to you, "That at the last of time there will be scoffers journeying consistent with their own desires of impieties." ¹⁹These are the dividers, selfish, not having the Spirit.
²⁰But you, loved ones, forming yourselves on your most devout faith, praying in the Holy Spirit, ²¹keep yourselves in God's love, attending to our Lord Yēsous Christos's mercy for Era Life. ²²Be compassionate to those mentally wavering, ²³delivering them, snatching from fire, be compassionate on those in awe, hating even that robe stained from the flesh.
²⁴To the one able to guard you from stumbling and to stand [you] before his splendor inerrant in over-joy, ²⁵to our only Deliverer-God, through our Lord Yēsous Christos [be] splendor, majesty, grip, and authority before every Era, now, and into all Eras, Amēn!

INTRODUCTION TO THE APOCALYPSE OF JOHN

The Apocalypse of Yōannēs [John] is the most unusual book of the Second Testament, the book most often misread in the history of the church, and perhaps the book that brings the most consolation to Christians longing for a wider, deeper, and better justice in the world. It's misread until it's read backward—starting with chapter 17, where God's design for this world comes into view, beginning with the eradication of evil and sin and death and ending with the New Yierousalēm's [New Jerusalem's] utopian city. Everything in the Apocalypse is on a journey toward that city, with a Marvel Cinematic Universe–like imagination required.

The Apocalypse is a letter (1:4-8; 2–3; 22), a prophecy in that it speaks God's word to God's people about God's world, and an apocalypse in that it's an unveiling of what is otherwise unknown, an unveiling occurring through visions. The reader of the Apocalypse will encounter "I saw" many times. What was seen was a cornucopia of arresting images and metaphors, which are not meant to be taken literally but understood as images pointing the readers toward God's view of the world and how God's Lamb will soon rule God's world. As such, the reader is invited to come to terms with the major players on the stage in this book—for example, God, the Lamb, the assemblies, and envoys [angels] who are in an epic, Lord of the Rings–like battle with the Satanas [Satan] and the Wild Thing [Beast] and Babulōn [Babylon]/Rōmē. All of this is staged on the land [earth, world].

The Apocalypse—as letter, prophecy, apocalypse—was designed for seven first-century churches on the western edge of modern-day Turkey (then Anatolia, the Rising of the Sun, or the East), and is about those churches and the troubles they are facing. It's a mistake to think the Apocalypse was written in the first century but only pertains to a much later age (ours!). It was written then and was for those churches then, though it has powerful theological potential for us.

What is written to the seven assemblies in Asia Minor (2–3) is expanded by visions of God's Throne room (4–5), and then those visions are expanded by a series of visions of God's judgment on a power- and money- and sex- and violence-drunk empire, which is nothing other than the Roman Empire. The visions of chapters 6–16 then are designed for the assemblies of chapters 2–3, who are themselves in need of turning their hearts toward full devotion. The chapters of judgments (seals, trumpets, shallow bowls; chaps. 6–16) are crystallized in the incredibly good news for those assemblies that Rōmē (depicted in language taken from the First Testament's take on Babulōn) will be judged by God and the unjust treatment of God's people will be reversed (17–18). Those who listen to God and follow the Lamb will rule in the New Yierousalēm (19–22). Thus, judgment against sins and judgment against Rōmē are followed by the establishment of a splendorous world of love, peace, and justice. One can see, then, that this book is not for idle speculation about who does what or who is who in the Apocalypse, but a prophetic warning of judgment on evil empire ideology. Thus, this book is divine political theology. Yet, we must not sit in some kind of *Schadenfreude* delighting in someone else's judgment: the book urges the assemblies to turn from their own sins, and it holds out the hope and expectation that the ethnic groups of this world who are mixed in with Rōmē will repent and worship God and the Lamb.

The style of the Apocalypse is unusual at times. A notable instance is that sometimes the author has plural nouns with a singular verb, or he might switch tenses in the middle of a sentence or use case or gender in an uncommon manner. Many explanations have been offered for the oddities of grammar in the Apocalypse, some of them convincing, but the best explanation is that this is how Yōannēs wrote. It's what it is. The style of the Apocalypse is not the same as the Gospel of Yōannēs but is close enough to draw this book into the circle of that book's author, though it is unlikely that the author of the Apocalypse was the same as the one who wrote the epistles or the Gospel.

THE APOCALYPSE OF JOHN

1 The Yēsous Christos apocalypse that God gave to him to exhibit to his slaves the events necessary to happen quickly, and he signified [it], commissioning [it] through his envoy to his slave Yōannēs [John], ²who witnessed God's word and the Yēsous Christos witness—whatever he saw. ³God's blessing for the reader and the hearers of the prophecy's words, and observing the matters written in it—for the time is close.

⁴Yōannēs to the seven assemblies that are in Asia:

> Grace to you and peace from "the One who is and the One who was and the Coming One," and from the Seven Spirits that are before his Throne ⁵and from Yēsous Christos, the witness, the allegiant one, the firstborn from among the dead ones and the leader over the land's kings.
> To the One who loves us and who loosened us from our sins by his blood, ⁶and made us an Empire, priests for his Father-God,
> To him be splendor and grip into the Era of Eras.
> Amēn.
> ⁷*Look!* he comes with the clouds,
> And every eye *will see him*,
> even the ones who *pierced* him.
> *And all the land's tribes will strike themselves over him.*
> Yes, Amēn.

⁸I am the Alpha and the Omega, says the Lord God, "the One who is and who was and the Coming One," the All-Powerful.

Yōannēs sees Yēsous

⁹I, Yōannēs (your sibling and companion in the trouble and the Empire and resilience in Yēsous) was on the island called Patmos because of God's word and the Yēsous witness. ¹⁰I was in Spirit on the Lord's Day and I heard behind me a great voice—like a trumpet—¹¹saying, "What you see, write in a book and send to the seven assemblies: to Ephesos [Ephesus] and to Smurna [Smyrna] and to Pergamos [Pergamum] and to Thuateira [Thyatira] and to Sardeis [Sardis] and to Philadelpheia [Philadelphia] and to Laodikeia [Laodicea]."

¹²I turned around to see the voice that was speaking with me and, turning around, saw seven golden lampstands ¹³and in the middle of the lampstands—like Son of Humanity:

> clothed in a long robe and wrapped around the breasts a golden belt.
> ¹⁴His head and his hairs were white as white wool, as snow,
> and his eyes as a fire-flame
> ¹⁵and his feet like refined bronze as having been fired in a furnace,
> and his voice as voice of many waters,
> ¹⁶and having in his right hand seven stars and from his mouth journeyed out a sharp, two-edged sword,
> and his visage as the sun appearing in its power.

¹⁷When I saw him, I fell to his feet as a dead man, and he placed his right [hand] on me, saying, "Do not be afraid. I am the First and the Last ¹⁸and the one living. I was dead and Look! I am living into the Era of Eras and I have Death's and Hades's keys. ¹⁹Therefore, write what you saw and what events are and what events are about to happen after these events. ²⁰The secret of the seven stars that you saw in my right [hand] and the seven golden lampstands: the seven stars are the envoys of the seven assemblies and the seven lampstands are the seven assemblies.

To the seven assemblies

EPHESOS

2 To the envoy of the assembly in Ephesos [Ephesus] write:

These are what the one gripping the seven stars in his right, the one walking around in middle of the seven lampstands, says:

²I know your works and your labor and your resilience and that you are unable to carry the bad ones, and you tested the ones who say they are Commissioners and they are not and you found them falsifiers, ³and you have resilience and you carried [the load] because of my name and have not become labored.

⁴But I have against you: That you have released your first love.

⁵Therefore, remember from where you have fallen and convert and do the first works. If not, I come to you and will move your lampstand from its place—if you do not convert.

⁶But you have this, that you hate the works of the Nikolaïtes [Nicolaitans] that I also hate.

⁷The one having ears, let the person hear what the Spirit says to the assemblies. I will give to the one conquering to eat from the Life's tree, which is in God's Paradise.

SMURNA

⁸To the envoy of the assembly in Smurna [Smyrna] write:

These are what the First and the Last, who was dead and lived, says:

⁹I know your trouble and your poverty (but you are wealthy) and the insult from the ones saying of themselves they are Youdaians [Judeans, Jews] and are not but are Satanas's [Satan's] assembly hall.

¹⁰Do not be afraid of things you are about to suffer. Look! The Accuser is about to toss [some] of you into prison so you may be tested and you will have trouble for ten days. Be allegiant to death, and I will give to you the Life's crown.

¹¹The one having ears, let the person hear what the Spirit says to the assemblies. The one conquering will never be wronged by the second death.

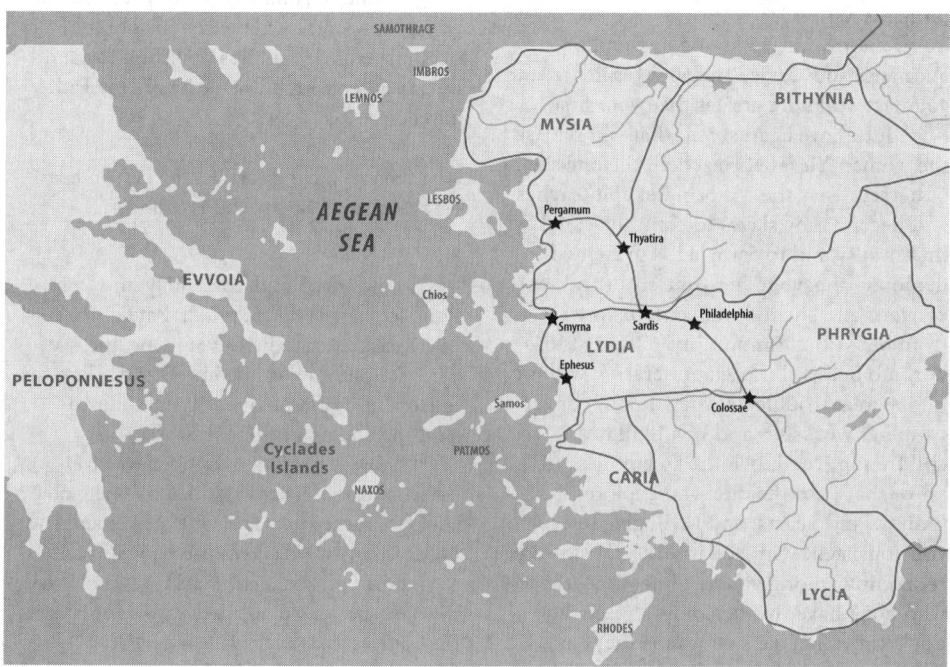

Figure 12. Map of the seven churches

PERGAMOS

¹²To the envoy of the assembly in Pergamos [Pergamum], write:

These are what the one having the sharp, two-edged sword says:

¹³I know where you reside, where the Satanas's throne [is], and you grip my name and did not deny my allegiance—even in the days of Antipas, my witness, my allegiant one, who was killed among you, where Satanas resides.

¹⁴But I have some things against you, that: You have there the ones gripping Bala'am's teaching, who taught Balak to toss a tripping-stone before Yisraēl's [Israel's] children to eat what is presented to demons and to commit

sexual immorality. **15**So, you have also ones gripping Nikolaïtan teaching likewise.

16Therefore, convert. If not, I come to you quickly and I will war with them with my mouth's sword.

17The one having ears, let the person hear what the Spirit says to the assemblies. I will give to the one conquering manna that has been hidden and I will give to him a white pebble, and on the pebble written a new name that no one knew except the one receiving.

THUATEIRA

18To the envoy of the assembly in Thuateira [Thyatira], write:

These are what God's Son, the one having his eyes as a fire-flame and his feet like refined bronze, says:

19I know your works and love and allegiance and service and your resilience, and your last works are greater than your first. **20**But I have against you that you release the woman Yiezabel [Jezebel], the one saying of herself [that she's] a prophet and teaches and deceives my slaves to commit sexual immorality and to eat what is presented to demons. **21**I gave to her time so she might convert, and she did not want to convert from her sexual immorality. **22**Look! I toss her into bed and those adulterating with her into a great trouble—if they do not convert from her works—**23**and I will kill her children in Death. All the assemblies will know that I am the one who explores kidneys and hearts, and I will give to each of you consistent with your works. **24**I say to the remaining among you in Thuateira—those who don't have this teaching, those who don't know Satanas's depth (as they say). I don't toss on you another deep thing. **25**However, what you have, grip until I come.

26The one conquering and observing my works until the completion, I will give to him authority over the ethnic groups **27**and *he will pastor them with an iron staff as clay vessels are broken,* **28**as also I have received from my Father, and I will give to the person the morning star.

29The one having ears, let the person hear what the Spirit says to the assemblies.

SARDEIS

3 To the envoy of the assembly in Sardeis [Sardis], write:

These are what the one who has God's Seven Spirits and seven stars says:

I know your works that you have a name that you live, and you are dead. **2**Be watching and strengthen what remains that were about to die, for I have not found your works filled out before my God. **3**Therefore, remember how you have received and heard, and observe and convert!

Therefore, if you are not awake, I will come as a thief, and you will never know what hour I will come upon you. **4**But you have a few names in Sardeis who didn't soil their robes, and they walk around with me in whites because they are deserving.

5The one so conquering will wrap oneself in white robes and I will never wipe out the person's name from Life's Book and I will openly agree with his name before my Father and before his envoys.

6The one having ears, let the person hear what the Spirit says to the assemblies.

PHILADELPHEIA

7To the envoy of the assembly in Philadelpheia [Philadelphia], write:

These are what the Devout One, the True One, the one having Dauid's [David's] key, the one opening and no one will shut, the one shutting and no one opens, says:

8I know your works. Look! I have given before you an opened door that no one is able to shut it because you have a little power and you observed my word and didn't deny my name.

9Look! I give Satanas's [Satan's] assembly hall, the ones speaking of themselves to be Youdaians [Judeans, Jews], and they are not but they falsify—Look! I will make them, that they will come and they will bow down before your feet and they may know that I loved you **10**because you observed the word of my resilience, and I will keep you from the testing's hour that is about to come upon the whole inhabited earth to test the one residing on the land. **11**I come quickly. Grip what you have so no one takes your crown.

12The one conquering I will make him a pillar in my God's sanctuary and the person will never exit outside ever and I will write on the person my God's name and my God's city's name, the New Yierousalēm [Jerusalem] that descends from the heaven from my God, and my new name.

¹³The one having ears, let the person hear what the Spirit says to the assemblies.

LAODIKEIA

¹⁴To the envoy of the assembly in Laodikeia [Laodicea], write:

These are what the Amēn, the allegiant and true witness, the Origin of God's creation, says:

¹⁵I know your works that you are neither cold nor boiling—wishing that you were cold or boiling. ¹⁶Thus, because you are lukewarm and neither boiling or cold, I am about to emit you from my mouth ¹⁷because you say that 'I am rich and have been enriched and I have need of nothing,' and you don't know that you are miserable and pitied and a beggar and sightless and naked, ¹⁸I counsel you to purchase from me fired-in-fire gold so you may be enriched, and white robes so you may wrap yourself and your nakedness's shame not appear, and salve to anoint your eyes so you may see. ¹⁹I convince and discipline as many as I love. Therefore, be zealous and convert! ²⁰Look! I stood at the door and I knock. If someone hears my voice and opens the door, and I will enter into the person and I will dine with the person and the person with me. ²¹The one conquering I will give to the person to sit with me on my Throne, as I conquered and sat with my Father on his Throne.

²²The one having ears, let the person hear what the Spirit says to the assemblies."

Worship in heaven

4 After these events I saw and Look! An opened door in the heaven, and the first voice that I heard as a trumpet speaking with me, saying, "Ascend here! I will exhibit to you the events necessary to happen after these things."

²Immediately I was in Spirit. Look! A Throne was laid out in heaven, and [one] sitting on the Throne, ³and the one sitting in a vision like jasper and carnelian, and a rainbow encircling the Throne in a vision like emerald. ⁴Encircling the Throne [I saw] twenty-four thrones, and on the twenty-four thrones elders sitting wrapped in white robes and on their heads gold crowns.

⁵From the Throne journeyed out lightnings and voices and thunders, and seven lampstands flaming lamps before the Throne, which are God's Seven Spirits, ⁶and before the Throne as a glassy sea like crystal.

In the middle of the Throne and circling the Throne, four Living Things full of eyes before and behind. ⁷The first Living Thing was like a lion and the second Living Thing like an ox and the third Living Thing having the face as a human and the fourth Living Thing like a flying eagle. ⁸The four Living Things—one by one—each having six wings, they are full of eyes encircling and inside, they do not have refreshment day and night, saying,

> "*Devoted, devoted, devoted is the Lord
>   God, the Almighty.* Who was and
>   Who is and the Coming One."

⁹Whenever the Living Things will give splendor and honor and thanks to the one sitting on the Throne, who lives into the Era of Eras, ¹⁰the twenty-four elders will fall before the one sitting on the Throne and they will bow down to the Living One into the Era of Eras and they will toss their crowns before the Throne, saying,

> ¹¹"You are deserving, our Lord and God,
>   to receive splendor and honor and
>   power,
>   because you created all things,
>   and because of your will they were and
>   have been created."

5 I saw at the right [hand] of the one sitting on the Throne a book written inside and on the back, having been sealed with seven seals. ²I saw a strong envoy announcing in a great voice, "Who is deserving to open the book and to loosen its seals?" ³No one was able in heaven or upon the land nor below the land either to open the book or to see it. ⁴I was wailing much because no one was found deserving either to open the book or to see it. ⁵One of the elders says to me, "Do not wail! Look! The Lion—who is from Youda [Judah] tribe, Dauid's [David's] root—conquered to open the book and its seven seals."

⁶I saw in the middle of the Throne and the four Living Things and in the middle of the elders a Lamb, having stood as slain, having seven horns and seven eyes that are God's Seven Spirits commissioned to the whole land.

⁷He came and has received [the book] from the right [hand] of the one sitting on the Throne. ⁸When he took the book, the four Living Things and twenty-four elders fell before the Lamb, each one having a kithara[a] and gold bowls filled with incense (which represents the prayers of the devoted), ⁹and they sing a new ode, saying,

> "Deserving are you to receive the book
>   and to open its seals,
> because you were slain, and you
>   purchased—for God, by your
>   blood—
> people from every tribe and language
>   and people and ethnic group
> ¹⁰and made them into an Empire and
>   priests for our God,
> and they will rule on the land."

¹¹I saw, and I heard a voice of many envoys circling the Throne and the Living Things and the elders, and their number was myriads of myriads and chiliads of chiliads, ¹²saying in a great voice,

> "Deserving is the Lamb that was slain
> to receive power and riches and wisdom
>   and strength and honor and splendor
>   and blessing."

¹³Every creature that is in heaven and on
>   the land and under the land and
>   on the sea—and all things in
>   them—I heard saying,
> "To the one sitting on the Throne and to
>   the Lamb:
> Blessing and honor and splendor and grip
>   into the Era of Eras."

¹⁴The four Living Things were saying, "Amēn." The elders fell and bowed down.

Seven seals

FIRST SEAL

6 Then I saw when the Lamb opened the first of the seven seals, and I heard one of the four Living Things, saying as a thunderous voice, "Come!" ²I saw and Look! A white horse and the one sitting on it having a bow, and a crown was given to him, and he exited conquering and so he might conquer.

SECOND SEAL

³When he opened the second seal, I heard the second Living Thing saying, "Come!" ⁴Another horse, fire-red, exited, and it was given to the one sitting on it to take peace from the land and so they might slay one another and a great long knife was given to him.

THIRD SEAL

⁵When he opened the third seal, I heard the third Living Thing saying, "Come!" I saw and Look! A black horse and the one sitting on it having a balancing scale in his hand. ⁶I heard as a voice in the middle of the four Living Things, saying, "A quart of wheat for a dēnarion and three quarts of barley for a dēnarion and do not wrong the olive oil and the wine."

FOURTH SEAL

⁷When he opened the fourth seal, I heard a voice of the fourth Living Thing, saying, "Come!" ⁸I saw, and Look! An ashen horse, and the one sitting upon it—a name for him: Death, and Hades was following with him, and authority over one fourth of the land was given to them to kill with a sword and with famine and with death and by the Wild Things of the land.

FIFTH SEAL

⁹When he opened the fifth seal, I saw under the sacrificial altar the selves of ones slain because of God's word and because of the witness that they were having. ¹⁰They cried out in a great voice, saying, "Until when, O devout and true Emperor? Do you not judge and make right our blood taken by the ones residing on the land?" ¹¹To each was given to them a white stole, and it was said to them that they will rest for a little while longer until both their co-slaves and their siblings (the ones about to be killed as they are) will be filled out.

SIXTH SEAL

¹²I saw when he opened the sixth seal, and a great earthquake happened and the sun became black as hairy sackcloth and the whole moon became as blood. ¹³The heaven's stars fell into the land as a fig tree shaken by a great wind tosses her wild figs. ¹⁴The heaven was separated as a book rolling up, and every mountain and island was moved from their

---

[a] A stringed instrument.

places. ¹⁵The land's kings and magnates and leaders of a thousand and wealthy ones and strong ones and every slave and free person hid themselves in caves and in mountainous rocks ¹⁶*and saying to the mountains and rocks, "Fall on us* and *hide us* from the face of the one sitting on the Throne and from the Lamb's anger ¹⁷because the great day of their anger came and who is able to stand up?"

INTERLUDE

7 After this I saw four envoys standing at the land's four corners, gripping the land's four winds so the wind may neither blow on the land or on the sea or on any tree. ²I saw another envoy ascending from the sun's rising [Anatolia, the East] having a seal of the Living God, and it cried out in a great voice to the four envoys to whom it has been given to them to wrong the land and the sea, ³saying, "Do not wrong either the land or the sea or the trees until we seal our God's slaves on their foreheads."

⁴I heard the sealed ones' number—144,000—having been sealed from every tribe of the children of Yisraēl [Israel]:

⁵From the tribe of Youda [Judah]—12,000,
from the tribe of Roubēn [Reuben]—12,000,
from the tribe of Gad—12,000,
⁶from the tribe of Asēr [Asher]—12,000,
from the tribe of Nephthalim [Naphtali]—12,000,
from the tribe of Manassēs [Manasseh]—12,000,
⁷from the tribe of Sumeōn [Simeon]—12,000,
from the tribe of Leui [Levi]—12,000,
from the tribe of Issachar—12,000,
⁸from the tribe of Zaboulōn [Zebulon]—12,000,
from the tribe of Yōsēf [Joseph]—12,000,
from the tribe of Benyamin [Benjamin]—12,000.

⁹After these things I saw, and Look! A great crowd that no one was able to count from every ethnic group and tribe and people and tongue standing before the Throne and before the Lamb, having been wrapped with white stoles and date-palm branches in their hands, ¹⁰and crying out in a great voice, saying, "Deliverance [belongs] to our God who sits on the Throne and to the Lamb!"

¹¹All the envoys had been standing circling the Throne and the elders and the four Living Things, and they fell before the Throne on their faces and bowed down to God, saying,

¹²"Amēn!
Blessing and splendor and wisdom and
    thanks and honor and power and
    strength
[belong] to our God into the Era of Eras.
    Amēn!"

¹³One of the elders responded, saying to me, "Who are these wrapped with white stoles and where have they come from?"

¹⁴I have said to him, "My lord, you
    know." He said to me,
"These are the ones coming from the
    Great Trouble,
they rinsed their stoles,
they whitened them in the Lamb's blood.
¹⁵Because this is true: they are before
    God's Throne,
they venerate him day and night in his
    sanctuary,
the one sitting on the Throne pitches a
    tent over them.
¹⁶*They will not hunger* any longer *nor*
    will they thirst any longer,
Nor will the sun fall on them or any *heat.*
¹⁷Because the Lamb that is in the middle
    of the Throne will pastor them,
and he will make a path for them to
    Life's water-springs,
and God will wipe off every tear from
    their eyes."

SEVENTH SEAL

8 Whenever he opened the seventh seal, there was silence in the heaven about one half-hour.

Seven trumpets

²I saw the seven envoys, the ones who stood before God, and seven trumpets were given to them.

Back to heaven

³Another envoy came and was stood on the sacrificial altar having a golden censer, and many incenses were given to it [the envoy] so it

will give all the devoted ones' prayers at the golden sacrificial altar that is before the Throne. ⁴The incense's smoke ascended with the devoted ones' prayers from the envoy's hand before God. ⁵The envoy had received the censer and filled it from the sacrificial altar's fire and tossed [it] into the land, and there were thunders and voices and lightnings and an earthquake.

Seven trumpets (resumed)

⁶The seven envoys, the ones having the seven trumpets, prepared them so they might trumpet.

FIRST TRUMPET

⁷The first trumpeted. There was hail and fire having been mixed with blood, and it was tossed into the land, and a third of the land was burned up and a third of the trees was burned up and all the green grass was burned up.

SECOND TRUMPET

⁸The second envoy trumpeted, and as a great mountain burning in fire was tossed into the sea, and a third of the sea became blood ⁹and a third of the creatures in the sea (the ones having selves) died, and a third of the boats were abominated.

THIRD TRUMPET

¹⁰The third envoy trumpeted, and a great star, burning as a lamp, fell from the heaven and fell on a third of the rivers and on water-springs, ¹¹and the star's name is called "Wormwood," and a third of the waters became wormwood, and many humans died from the waters that had been embittered.

FOURTH TRUMPET

¹²The fourth envoy trumpeted, and a third of the sun and a third of the moon and a third of the stars were knocked so a third of them was darkened and the day did not appear—a third of it, and the night likewise.

INTERLUDE

¹³I saw, and I heard one eagle flying in midheaven, saying in a great voice,

"Oy! Oy! Oy! to the ones residing on the land from the remaining trumpet voices of the three envoys about to trumpet!"

FIFTH TRUMPET (AND FIRST OY!)

9 The fifth envoy trumpeted, and I saw a star from the heaven fallen into the land, and the key to the abyss's cistern was given to it [the star] ²and it opened the abyss's cistern, and smoke ascended from the cistern as smoke from a great furnace, and the sun and the air were darkened from the cistern's smoke. ³From the smoke locusts exited into the land, and authority was given to them as the land's scorpions have authority. ⁴It was said to them that they not wrong the land's grass nor anything green nor any tree, except [they could wrong] the humans who don't have God's mark on the foreheads. ⁵It was given to them that they may not kill them, but they may be tortured for five months, and their torment [was] as a scorpion's torment whenever one hits a human. ⁶In those days humans will pursue death and they will never find it, and they will desire to die and death flees from them.

⁷The representations of the locusts were like horses prepared for war, and on their heads—as crowns like gold, their faces—as faces of humans, ⁸and they were having hairs—as hairs of women, and their teeth—as they were of lions, ⁹and they were having breastplates—as iron breastplates, and the voice of their wings—as the voice of chariots with many horses running into war, ¹⁰and they have tails like scorpions and stingers, and in their tails their authority to wrong humans for five months, ¹¹they have over them a king, the Abyss's Envoy, a name for him in Hebraïsti [Hebrew] is "Abaddōn," and in Hellenikos [Greek] has a name "Apolluōn [Apollyon]."

¹²The first Oy! departed. Look! Two more Oys! come after these.

SIXTH TRUMPET (AND SECOND OY!)

¹³The sixth envoy trumpeted, and I heard one voice from the four horns of the golden sacrificial altar before God, ¹⁴saying to the sixth envoy—the one having the trumpet: "Loosen the four envoys who have been bound at the great Euphratēs River." ¹⁵The four envoys were loosened—who have been prepared for the hour and day and month and year—so they could kill one-third of the humans. ¹⁶The number of the horse-riding troop was two myriads times myriads [twenty thousand times ten thousand]. I heard their number.

¹⁷So I saw the horses in my vision and the ones sitting on them, having fire-red, sapphirey and sulfury breastplates, and horses' heads—as heads of lions, and from their mouths journeyed out fire and smoke and sulfur. ¹⁸From these three plagues a third of the humans were killed: from the fire and the smoke and the sulfur journeying out from their mouths. ¹⁹For horses' authority is in their mouth and in their tails, for their tails are like snakes having heads and with them they do wrong.

²⁰The remaining humans who were not killed in these plagues, neither converted from the works of their hands so they may not bow down to demons and to golden and silver and bronze and stone and wooden idols— which aren't able either to see or to hear or to walk around—²¹and they did not convert from their murders or from their potions or from their sexual immoralities or from their thefts.

INTERLUDE: EATING A LITTLE SCROLL

10 I saw another strong envoy descending from the heaven wrapped in a cloud, and the halo on its head and its face as the sun and its feet as fire-pillars,
²and having in his hand a little book opened.
It placed its right foot on the sea,
the left on the land,
³and it cried out in a great voice as a lion roaring.
When it cried out, the seven thunders spoke their own voices.
⁴When the seven thunders spoke, I was about to write, and I heard a voice from the heaven saying, "Seal what the seven thunders spoke, and do not write them."
⁵The envoy that I saw standing on the sea and the land,
lifted its right hand to the heaven
⁶and made an oath with the one living into the Era of Eras
(who created the heaven and the things in it,
and the land and the things in it,
and the sea and things in it)
that there will be no more time [left],
⁷but in the days of the seventh envoy's voice,
whenever it's about to trumpet,
and God's secret has been completed,
as he gospeled to his slaves, the prophets.

⁸The voice that I heard from heaven speaking with me again and saying,
"Depart! Take the opened book in the envoy's hand,
the one standing on the sea and the land."
⁹I departed to the envoy, saying to it to give the little book to me.
It says to me,
"Take and gobble it down!
It will embitter your stomach but will be sweet as honey in your mouth."
¹⁰I took the little book from the envoy's hand and gobbled it down,
and it was sweet as honey in my mouth
and when I ate it my stomach was embittered.
¹¹They say to me, "It's necessary for you again to prophesy
against peoples and the ethnic groups and the tongues and many kings."

INTERLUDE: TWO WITNESSES

11 A reed like a staff was given to me, saying,
"Arise and measure God's sanctuary and the sacrificial altar
and the ones bowing down in it,
²and the enclosure outside the sanctuary,
toss outside and don't measure it because it has been given to the ethnic groups,
and the devoted city will be walked on for forty-two months.
³I will give my two witnesses
and they will prophesy 1,260 days wrapped in sackcloth."
⁴These are the two olive trees and the two lampstands
who have been standing before the Lord over the land.
⁵If someone wants to wrong them,
fire journeys out from their mouth and gobbles up their enemies.
If someone may want to wrong them,
it's necessary for the person so to be killed.
⁶These have the authority to shut the heaven
so it doesn't rain water during their prophecy's days,
and they have authority over the waters to turn them into blood
and to beat the land with every plague—as often as they may want.

⁷Whenever they complete their witness,

the Wild Thing [Beast] ascending from the abyss will make war with them
and he will conquer them and he will kill them.
⁸Their corpse [will lie] on the great city's plaza, which is called spiritually "Sodoma [Sodom] and Aiguptos [Egypt]"
(where their Lord was crucified).
⁹[Some] from the peoples and the tribes and the tongues and the ethnic groups
see their corpses for three and a half days,
and their corpses are not released to be placed in a tomb.
¹⁰The ones residing on the land rejoice over them
and are glad
and send gifts to one another
because these two prophets tormented the ones residing on the land.

¹¹After the three and a half days *Life's Spirit* from God *entered in them and they stood on their feet,*
and great fear fell on the ones observing them.
¹²They heard a great voice from heaven saying to them, "Ascend here!"
They ascended into heaven in the cloud, and their enemies observed them.
¹³In that hour there was a great earthquake
and a tenth of the city fell and seven thousand names of humans were killed,
and the remaining were full of fear and gave splendor to heaven's God.
¹⁴The second Oy! departs. Look! The third Oy! comes quickly.

SEVENTH TRUMPET (AND THIRD OY!)

¹⁵The seventh envoy trumpeted. There were great voices in heaven, saying,

> "The Kosmos's Empire has become our Lord's and his Christos's,
> and he will rule into the Era of Eras."

¹⁶The twenty-four elders who are sitting on their thrones before God fell on their faces and bowed down to God, ¹⁷saying,

> "We thank you, Lord God the Almighty,
> who is and who was,
> because you have received your great power and you ruled.

¹⁸The ethnic groups are angered,
and your anger came
and the season for the dead to be judged
and to give the wage to your slaves,
to the prophets, and to the devoted ones
and to the ones in awe of your name,
both to the small and great,
and to abominate the ones abominating the land."

¹⁹God's sanctuary was opened, the one in heaven, and his Covenant's chest [ark] was seen in his sanctuary, and there were lightnings and voices and thunders and an earthquake and great hail.

The cosmic battle

THE WOMAN AND THE DRAGON 1

12 ¹A great authenticating sign was seen in heaven, a woman having been wrapped with the sun, and the moon under her feet and a twelve-star crown on her head, ²and having a child in the womb, she cries out groaning in birth and being tormented to give birth.

³Another authenticating sign was seen in heaven, and Look! A great fire-red sea Dragon, having seven heads and ten horns and on his head seven diadems, ⁴and his tail drags a third of heaven's stars and he tossed them into the land. The Dragon has stood before the woman who is about to birth so whenever the child is birthed, he could gobble it down.

⁵She birthed a man-son, who is about to pastor all the ethnic groups with an iron staff. Her child was snatched to God and to his Throne. ⁶The woman fled into the wilderness, where she had there a place prepared from God so there they may nurture her 1,260 days.

A COSMIC BATTLE

⁷A war happened in heaven, Michaēl and his envoys warring with the Dragon. The Dragon and his envoys warred back, ⁸and he was neither strong nor was a place found any longer for them in heaven. ⁹The Dragon, the great one, was tossed, the ancient snake, the one called "Accuser" and "the Satanas [Satan]," the deceiver of the whole inhabited world, was tossed into the land, and his envoys were tossed with him. ¹⁰I heard a great voice in heaven saying,

"Now has come the deliverance and the
    power,
And our God's Empire,
And his Christos's authority,
Because the category [for prosecution]
        against our siblings has been
        tossed out,
    the one bringing a category [of
        prosecution] against them before
        our God day and night.
¹¹They conquered him because of the
    Lamb's blood
And because their witness's word,
And they did not love their self until
    death.
¹²Because this is true: be glad, heavens
    and those pitching a tent in them!
Oy! to the land and the sea,
Because the Accuser descended to you,
Having great fury,
Knowing that he has a little season."

THE WOMAN AND THE DRAGON 2

¹³When the Dragon saw that he had been tossed into the land, he chased the woman who birthed the man. ¹⁴The two wings of a great eagle were given to the woman so she could fly into the wilderness, into her place (where she is nurtured there for a season and seasons and half a season) from the snake's face. ¹⁵The snake tossed water as a river from its mouth after the woman so he might make a tsunami over her. ¹⁶The land helped the woman and the land opened its mouth and swallowed the river that the Dragon tossed from its mouth. ¹⁷The Dragon was angered at the woman and departed to make war with the remainders of her seed, the ones observing God's orders and having the Yēsous witness.

¹⁸It was stood on the sea's shore.

THE DRAGON'S TWO WILD THINGS

13 I saw a Wild Thing [beast] ascending from the sea, having ten horns and seven heads and on its horns ten diadems and on its heads insulting names. ²The Wild Thing that I saw was comparable to a leopard and its feet as a bear's and its mouth as a lion's mouth. The Dragon gave to it its power and its throne and great authority. ³One of its heads [was] as having been slain to death, and its death-plague was healed. The whole land was stunned after the Wild Thing ⁴and they bowed down to the Dragon because it gave authority to the Wild Thing, and they bowed down to the Wild Thing, saying, "Who is comparable to the Wild Thing and who is able to war with it?"

⁵A mouth speaking great things and insults was given to it, and to it was given to make authority for forty-two months. ⁶It opened its mouth for insults toward God to insult his name and his tent, [toward] the ones pitching a tent in heaven. ⁷It was given to it to make war with the devoted ones and to conquer them, and authority was given to it over every tribe and people and tongue and ethnic group. ⁸All the ones residing on the land bowed down to it, of whom its name is not written in Lamb's life-book, [the Lamb] who has been slain from Kosmos's origin.

⁹If someone has ears, let the person hear.
¹⁰If someone [takes] into captivity, the
    person departs into captivity.
If someone is put to death with a long
    knife, the person is to be put to death
    with a sword.
Here is the devoted ones' resilience and
    allegiance.

¹¹I saw another Wild Thing ascending from the land, and it was having two horns comparable to a Lamb and it was speaking as the Dragon. ¹²It makes all the authority of the first Wild Thing before it, and it makes the land and the ones residing in it so they will bow down to the first Wild Thing, of whom its death-plague was healed. ¹³It did great authenticating signs so that it even makes fire descend from heaven into the land before the humans, ¹⁴and it deceives the ones residing on the land because of the authenticating signs that have been given it to do before the Wild Thing, saying to the ones residing on the land to make an image for the Wild Thing, who has the knife's-plague and lived.

¹⁵It was given to it to give a spirit to the Wild Thing's image so that the Wild Thing's image may even speak and may make whoever does not bow down to the Wild Thing's image that they may die. ¹⁶It makes all, the small ones and the great ones, and the wealthy and the beggars, and the free ones and the slaves that they give to them a mark on their right hand or on their forehead, ¹⁷and that no one is able to purchase or sell if not having the Wild Thing's name's mark or its name's number.

¹⁸Here is wisdom.
The one having a mind, let the person
   estimate the Wild Thing's number.
(For it's a human's number. Its number is 666.)

The allegiant ones

14 I saw and Look! The Lamb standing on Mount Siōn [Zion] and with him 144,000 having his name and his Father's name having been written on their foreheads. ²I heard a voice from heaven as a voice of many waters and as a voice great thunder, and the voice that I heard as of kitharists kitharing on their kitharas. ³They are singing a new ode before the Throne and before the four Living Things and the elders, and no one was able to be apprenticed to the ode except the 144,000, the ones who have been purchased from the land.

⁴These are those who were not soiled with women, for they are virgins, these who follow the Lamb wherever he goes away. These were purchased from humans, firstfruits to God and to the Lamb, ⁵and *in their mouth was not found a falsification*—they are inerrant.

Be allegiant!

⁶I saw another envoy flying in midheaven having an Era-gospel to gospel the ones sitting on the land and every ethnic group and tribe and tongue and people, ⁷saying in a great voice, "Be in awe of God and give to him splendor because his judgment hour came, and bow down to the one who made heaven and the land and the sea and springs of waters."

⁸Another envoy, a second, followed, saying, "It fell, it fell: the great Babulōn [Babylon], who has given all the ethnic groups to drink of the wine of her sexual immorality's fury."

⁹Another envoy, a third, followed them, saying in a great voice, "If someone bows down to the Wild Thing and its image and receives the mark on one's forehead or on one's hand, ¹⁰the person will also drink the wine of God's fury, mixed unmixed in the cup of his anger, and the person will be tormented in fire and sulfur before the devout envoys and before the Lamb. ¹¹Their torment's smoke ascends into the Era of Eras and the ones bowing down to the Wild Thing and its image don't have refreshment day and night—if someone receives its name's mark."

¹²Here is the devoted ones' resilience, the ones observing God's orders and Yēsous-allegiance.

¹³I heard a voice from heaven saying, "Write: God's blessing for the ones dying in the Lord from now on." "Yes," says the Spirit, "they will be refreshed from their labors, for their works follow with them."

Judgment

¹⁴I saw, and Look! A white cloud and sitting on the cloud one comparable to the Son of Humanity, having a gold crown on his head and in his hand a sharp sickle.

¹⁵Another envoy exited from the sanctuary crying out in a great voice to the one sitting on the cloud, "Send your sickle and harvest, because the hour to harvest came, because the land's harvest has withered."

¹⁶The one sitting on the cloud tossed his sickle on the land and the land was harvested.

¹⁷Another envoy exited from the sanctuary that is in heaven, also having itself a sharp sickle.

¹⁸Another envoy exited from the sacrificial altar, one having authority over fire, and it voiced in a great voice to the one having the sharp sickle, saying,

> Send your sharp sickle and collect the
>   clusters of the land's vine because
>   her bunches ripened.

¹⁹The envoy tossed its sickle into the land and collected the land's vine and tossed [it] into the great winepress of God's fury. ²⁰The winepress was trampled outside the city, and blood from the winepress exited up to the horses' bridles for about sixteen hundred stades [184 miles].

Seven bowls of seven plagues

15 I saw another authenticating sign in heaven—great and stunning, seven envoys having the seven last plagues, because in them God's fury is completed.

INTERLUDE: THE CONQUERORS

²I saw as a glassy sea having been mixed with fire and the ones conquering the Wild Thing [Beast] and its image and its name's number—standing on the glassy sea having God's kitharas. ³They sing the ode of Mōüsēs

[Moses], God's slave, and the ode of the Lamb, saying,

> Great and stunning are your works,
> O Lord God Almighty,
> right and true are your paths,
> the King over the ethnic groups.
> ⁴Who may never fear, Lord,
> and splendor your name?
> Because [you] alone [are] Saintly,
> because *all the ethnic groups will come
> and bow down before you,*
> because your right actions will become apparent.

SEVEN PLAGUES OF THE SHALLOW BOWLS INTRODUCED

⁵After these things I saw, and the witness-tent's sanctuary in heaven was opened, ⁶and the seven envoys having the seven plagues exited from the sanctuary, having put on clean, shiny linen and wrapped around the breasts with golden belts. ⁷One of the four Living Things gave to the seven envoys seven gold shallow bowls filled with the fury from the God who lives into the Era of Eras. ⁸The sanctuary was filled with smoke from God's splendor and from his power, and no one was able to enter into the sanctuary until the seven plagues of the seven envoys are completed.

16

I heard a great voice from the sanctuary saying to the seven envoys, "Depart and pour out the seven shallow bowls of God's fury into the land."

FIRST SHALLOW BOWL

²The first exited and poured out its shallow bowl into the land, and a bad and evil sore came upon the humans having the Wild Thing's [Beast's] mark and upon those who bowed down to its image.

SECOND SHALLOW BOWL

³The second poured its shallow bowl into the sea, and it became blood as of a dead one, and every living self died that was in the sea.

THIRD SHALLOW BOWL

⁴The third poured out its shallow bowl into the rivers and the springs of waters, and it became blood. ⁵I heard the waters' envoy, saying,

> You are right, the one who is and who was, the Saintly One,
> because you judged these things,
> ⁶because they poured out devoted ones'
>   and prophets' blood,
> you have given blood for them to drink.
> They are deserving.

⁷I heard the sacrificial altar, saying,

> Yes, Lord God, the Almighty One,
> Your judgments are true and right.

FOURTH SHALLOW BOWL

⁸The fourth poured out its shallow bowl on the sun, and it was given to it to scorch humans with fire. ⁹The humans were scorched with great scorch and they insulted God's name (the one having authority over these plagues) and they did not convert to give splendor to him.

FIFTH SHALLOW BOWL

¹⁰The fifth poured out its shallow bowl on the Wild Thing's throne, and his empire was darkened, and they chewed their tongues from the pain, ¹¹and they insulted the God of heaven from their pain and from their sores and they did not convert from their works.

SIXTH SHALLOW BOWL

¹²The sixth poured out its shallow bowl on the great river Euphratēs, its water withered so that the path for the kings from the sun's rising [Anatolia, the East] was prepared. ¹³I saw three contaminating spirits, as frogs, from the Dragon's mouth and from the Wild Thing's mouth and from the false prophet's mouth. ¹⁴For they are demon-spirits doing authenticating signs, [spirits] that journey out on the whole inhabited world's kings to assemble them into the war of the Great Day of God, the Almighty One. ¹⁵("Look! I come as a thief. God's blessing for the one watching and observing one's robes, so one may not walk around naked and they see one's shame.") ¹⁶The [spirits] assembled them in the place that is called in Hebraïsti [Hebrew] "Mountain of Megiddo" [*Har-magedōn*, Armageddon].

SEVENTH SHALLOW BOWL

¹⁷The seventh poured out its shallow bowl on the air, and a great voice exited from the sanctuary from the Throne, saying, "It has happened." ¹⁸Lightnings and voices and thunders happened and a great earthquake happened, such as had not happened from [the

time] which a human happened to be on the land—such a great earthquake, so great. ¹⁹The great city happened into three parts and the ethnic groups' cities fell. The great Babulōn [Babylon] was remembered before God—to give to her the cup of the wine of the fury of his anger. ²⁰Every island fled and mountains were not found. ²¹A great hailstone as a talent [100 pounds] descends from heaven upon humans, and the humans insulted God from the hailstone's plague, because its plague was extremely great.

Babulōn! Babulōn!
THE REAL BABULŌN REVEALED

17 One of the seven envoys having the seven shallow bowls came and spoke with me, saying, "Come! I will exhibit for you the judgment on the great prostitute sitting upon many waters, ²with whom the land's kings prostituted and [with whom] the ones residing on the land were boozed up from her sexual immorality's wine."

³It carried me off into the wilderness in the Spirit.

I saw a woman sitting on a scarlet Wild Thing, filled with insult's names, having seven heads and ten horns. ⁴The woman was wrapped in purple and scarlet, and goldened with gold and a precious stone and pearls, having in her hand a gold cup full of abominations and her sexual immorality's contaminations, ⁵and on her forehead a name was written:

> A secret:
> The great Babulōn [Babylon], the
>   mother of prostitutes
> and the land's abominations.

⁶I saw the woman boozed up from the blood of the devoted ones and from the blood of the Yēsous-witnesses. I was stunned with a great stunning seeing her.

⁷The envoy said to me, "Why were you stunned? I will tell you the secret about this woman and the Wild Thing carrying her who has the seven heads and the ten horns:

> ⁸The Wild Thing that you saw was and is not and is about to ascend from the abyss and depart into destruction. The ones residing on the land (whose name is not written on Life's Book from Kosmos's origin) will be stunned seeing the Wild Thing that was and is not and will be.

⁹Here is the mind having wisdom: The seven heads and seven mountains, where the woman sits on them. They are seven emperors. ¹⁰Five fell, the one is, the other has not yet come, and whenever he comes it's necessary for him to remain a little while. ¹¹The Wild Thing that was and is not, he is both eighth and is of the seven, and he departs into destruction.

¹²The ten horns that you saw are ten emperors who have not yet received an empire but they receive authority as kings for one hour with the Wild Thing. ¹³These have one mind, and they give their power and their authority to the Wild Thing. ¹⁴These will war with the Lamb and the Lamb will conquer them because he is Lord of lords and Emperor of emperors, and the ones with him are the called ones and elected ones and allegiant ones."

¹⁵He says to me,

> "The waters that you saw where the prostitute sits are peoples and crowds and ethnic groups and tongues. ¹⁶The ten horns that you saw and the Wild Thing—these will hate the prostitute and they will make her a wilderness and naked and they will eat her fleshes and burn her up with fire. (¹⁷For God gave into their hearts to do his mind—to do one mind—and to give their empire to the Wild Thing until God's words will be completed.) ¹⁸The woman that you saw is the great city, the one having an empire over the land's kings."

RESPONDING TO BABULŌN'S DESTRUCTION

18 After these things, I saw another envoy descending from heaven having great authority, and the land was illumined from its splendor. ²It cried out in a strong voice, saying,

> "It fell. It fell. The great Babulōn!
> It became a residence for demons
> and a prison for every contaminating
>   spirit

and a prison for every contaminating
    bird
and a prison for every contaminating
    and hated Wild Thing
[3]because all the ethnic groups have
    drunk from the wine of her
    sexual immorality's fury,
and the land's kings prostituted with her
and the land's conductors of business got
    rich from her sensuality's power."

[4]I heard another voice from heaven, saying,

"Exit from her, my people, so you may not share a common life in her sins, and [exit] from her plagues so you may not receive [them] [5]because her sins have been united up to heaven and God remembered her wrongdoings. [6]Pay her back as she paid back, and double the doubles of her works, in the cup in which she mixed you mix double to her, [7]to the degree she splendored herself and sensualized, to that same degree give to her torment and grief. Because in her heart she says that 'I sit as a queen, and I am not a widow, and I will never see grief.' [8]Because this is true: in one day her plagues will come—death and grief and famine—and she will be burned up with fire because the God who judges her is a strong Lord.

[9]The land's kings, who prostituted and sensualized with her, will wail and strike themselves over her whenever they see her fire's smoke, [10]having stood far away because they're afraid of her torment, saying,

'Oy! Oy! The great city,
Babulōn, the strong city,
because in one hour your judgment came.'
[11]The land's ones conducting business
    wail and grieve over her because
    no one buys their cargo any
    longer:
[12]cargo of gold and silver and precious
    stone and pearls
and fine linen and purple and silk and
    scarlet,
and every citron wood and every ivory
    vessel and every vessel from
    costly wood
and brass and iron and marble,
[13]and cinnamon and spice and incenses
    and ointment and frankincense
and wine and olive oil and flour and
    wheat
and cattle and sheep,
and horses and chariots,
and [enslaved] bodies and selves of
    humans.
[14]'The fruit of your self's desire departed
    from you,
And all your delicacies and bling
    destroyed from you,
And they will never find these any
    longer.'

[15]The ones conducting business of these items, who became rich from her, will stand from afar because they're afraid of her torment, wailing and grieving, [16]saying,

'Oy! Oy! the great city,
the one wrapped in fine linen and
    purple and scarlet
and goldened in gold and precious stone
    and pearl,
[17]because in one hour such riches
    become a wilderness.'

Every pilot and everyone sailing over a place and sailors and whoever works the sea, they stood from afar [18]and were crying out, seeing her fire's smoke, saying, 'Who is comparable to the great city?' [19]They tossed dust on their heads and were crying out, wailing and grieving, saying,

'Oy! Oy! the great city,
in which all the ones having boats in the
    sea were made rich from her
    costliness,
because in one hour she has become a
    wilderness.'

[20]Be glad about her, heaven, and devoted ones and commissioners and prophets!
    Because God judged her judgment of you.
[21]One strong envoy lifted a stone as a great grinding-stone and tossed [it] into the sea, saying,

'With such force Babulōn, the great city,
    will be tossed,
and it will never be found ever.

²²A voice of kitharists and musicians
and persons playing recorders
and trumpeters
will never be heard in you ever,
and every artisan of every art will never
be found in you ever,
and a voice of a grinding-stone will
never be heard in you ever,
²³a lamp light will never appear in you
ever,
a voice of a bridegroom and a bride will
never be heard in you ever—
because the ones conducting your
business were the land's magnates,
because in your drug-induced sorcery
all the ethnic groups were
deceived,
²⁴and in her the blood of prophets and
devoted ones was found
and all the ones slain on the land."

Beyond Babulōn

CELEBRATING GOD'S VICTORY

19 After these events, I heard as a great voice of a big crowd in heaven, saying,

"Hallēlouïa!
The deliverance and the splendor and
the power of God!
²Because his judgments are true and
right,
Because he judged the great prostitute
who abominated the land with her
sexual immorality
And he made it right for his slaves' blood
from her hand."

³A second time they have said,
"Hallēlouïa!
Her smoke ascends into the Era of Eras."
⁴The twenty-four elders and the four Living Things fell and they bowed down to God who sits on the Throne, saying, "Amēn Hallēlouïa!"
⁵A voice from the Throne exited, saying,

"Praise our God,
All his slaves and the ones in awe of
him—the small ones and the
great ones."

⁶I heard as a voice of a big crowd and as a voice of many waters and as voice of strong thunders, saying,

"Hallēlouïa!
Because our Lord God, the Almighty
One, ruled.
⁷Let us rejoice and let us be overjoyed
and let us give splendor to him,
Because Lamb's marriage came and his
woman prepared herself."

(⁸It was given to her to wrap herself in fine linen, bright, clean; for the fine linen is the right actions of the devoted ones.)
⁹It says to me, "Write! God's blessing for the ones who have been called to the Lamb's marriage supper!" It says to me, "These are God's true words." ¹⁰I fell before his feet to bow down to him. It says to me, "See [that you] not [do this]! I am a co-slave and [one of] your siblings having the Yēsous-witness. Bow down to God! For the Yēsous-witness is prophecy's Spirit."

THE WHITE HORSE AND ITS RIDER

¹¹I saw heaven opened, and Look! A white horse and one sitting on it, called "Allegiant and True," and he judges and makes war in rightness. ¹²His eyes as a fire-flame and on his head many diadems, having a name written that no one knows except he, ¹³and wrapped with a robe having been dipped in blood, and his name was called "The Logos of God."
¹⁴The troops in heaven, having put on fine linen, white clean, were following him on the white horses. ¹⁵From his mouth a sharp sword journeys out so he can beat the ethnic groups with it, and he will pastor them with an iron staff, and he tramples the winepress of the wine of the fury of the wrath of God, the Almighty One, ¹⁶and he has on the robe and on his thigh a name written, "Emperor of emperors and Lord of lords."

CONQUERING THE WILD THING

¹⁷I saw one envoy standing in the sun and cried out in a great voice, saying to all the birds flying in midheaven, "Come! Be assembled to the God's great supper ¹⁸so you may eat kings' flesh and leaders of a thousands' flesh and strong ones' flesh and horses' flesh and the ones sitting on them, and everyone's flesh— both free ones and slaves, both small ones and great ones."

¹⁹I saw the Wild Thing and land's emperors and their troops having been assembled to

make war with the one sitting on the horse and with his army. ²⁰The Wild Thing was caught, and with it the false prophet who did authenticating signs before it, by which he deceived the ones receiving the Wild Thing's mark and the ones bowing down to its image. Living, the two were tossed into the lake of fire burning with sulfur. ²¹The remaining ones were killed with the sword (that exits from his mouth) of the one sitting on the horse, and all the birds were satisfied from their fleshes.

CONQUERING THE DRAGON

20 I saw an envoy descending from heaven having the abyss's key and a great chain in its hand. ²It gripped the Dragon, the ancient snake, who is the Accuser and the Satanas [Satan], and it bound it for a thousand years. ³It tossed it into the abyss and shut and sealed over it so it may no longer deceive the ethnic groups until a thousand years are completed. After these events it's necessary to loosen him for a little time.

THE CONQUERORS

⁴I saw thrones and they sat on them and judgment was given for them, and [I saw] the selves who had been beheaded because of the Yēsous-witness and because of God's word and who did not bow down to the Wild Thing nor to its image and did not receive the mark on the forehead and on their hand. They lived and they ruled with the Christos for a thousand years. ⁵The remaining of the dead ones did not live until a thousand years was completed.

This is the first resurrection. ⁶God's blessing and devoted is the one having part in the first resurrection. Upon these the second death does not have authority, but they will be priests for God and the Christos, and they will rule with him for a thousand years.

CONQUERING THE SATANAS

⁷Whenever the thousand years are completed, the Satanas will be loosened from his prison ⁸and he will exit to deceive the ethnic groups that are in the land's four corners—Gōg and Magōg—to assemble them into the war, whose number is as sea's sand. ⁹It ascended to the land's plain and encircled the devoted ones' encampment and the loved city, *and fire descended from heaven and gobbled them up.* ¹⁰The Accuser deceiving them was tossed into the lake of fire and sulfur, where also the Wild Thing and false prophet are, and they will be tormented day and night into the Era of Eras.

ALL THE DEAD JUDGED

¹¹I saw a great white Throne and one sitting on it, from whose face the land and the heaven fled, and a place was not found for them. ¹²I saw the dead ones, both great ones and small ones, standing before the Throne. Books were opened, and another book was opened, which is Life's [Book], and the dead were judged from what was written in the books consistent with their works. ¹³The sea gave the dead who [are] in it and Death and Hadēs gave the dead who [are] in them, and each was judged consistent with their works. ¹⁴Death and Hadēs were tossed into the lake of fire.

This is the second death: the lake of fire.

¹⁵If someone was not found in Life's Book the person was tossed into the lake of fire.

Beyond the Beyond

THE PEOPLE

21 I saw a new heaven and a new land. The first heaven and the first land departed, and the sea is no longer. ²I saw the devoted city, New Yierousalēm [Jerusalem], descending from heaven from God, prepared as bride, decorated for her man. ³I heard a great voice from the Throne, saying,

"Look! God's tent is with humans,
he will pitch his tent with them,
they will be his people and God himself
    will be their God with them,
⁴*and he will wipe off all the tears from*
    their eyes,
and Death will be no more,
nor grieving nor wailing nor pain will
    be any longer,
because the first things departed."

⁵The one seated on the Throne said, "Look! I make all things new," and says, "Write: These words are allegiant and true." ⁶He said to me, "It has happened. I am the Alpha and the Omega, the Beginning and the Completion. I will give to the one thirsting from Life's water's spring as a gift. ⁷The one conquering will inherit these things and *I will be God for the person and the person will be child for me.* ⁸To

the cowards and the anti-trusters and the detestables and murderers and prostituters and drug-induced sorcerers and demon worshipers and all the falses—their part [will be] in the lake burning with fire and sulfur, which is the Second Death."

NEW YIEROUSALĒM

⁹One of the seven envoys having seven shallow bowls filled with the seven last plagues came and spoke with me, saying, "Come! I will exhibit for you the bride, the Lamb's woman." ¹⁰It lifted me away in the Spirit onto a great and high mountain, and exhibited for me the devoted city, Yierousalēm, descending from heaven from God, ¹¹having God's splendor, her radiance comparable to a precious stone—as jasper crystallizing, ¹²having a great and high wall, having twelve gates and the gates twelve envoys, and names had been written that are the names of Yisraēl's [Israel's] sons' twelve names. ¹³From the sun's rising [Anatolia, the East] three gates and from the north three gates and from the south three gates and from the west three gates. ¹⁴The city's wall having twelve foundations and on them the Lamb's twelve Commissioners' twelve names.

¹⁵The one speaking with me was having a gold measuring reed so that it could measure the city and her gates and her wall. ¹⁶The city laid out as a square and her length the same as the width, and it measured the city with the reed at 12,000 stadia [1,500 miles], the length and width and height equal. ¹⁷It measured [the thickness of] her wall at 144,000 cubits [216 feet], a human's measure, which is an envoy's [measure]. ¹⁸Her wall's material was jasper and the city clean gold comparable to clean glass. ¹⁹The city wall's foundations decorated with every precious stone:

  First, jasper;
  second, sapphire;
  third, agate;
  fourth, emerald;
  ²⁰fifth, sadonyx;
  sixth, carnelian;
  seventh, chrysolite;
  eighth, beryl;
  ninth, topaz;
  tenth, chrysoprase;
  eleventh, jacinth;
  twelfth, amethyst.

²¹The twelve gates are twelve pearls, each one of the gates was from one pearl. The city's plaza is clean gold as transparent as glass.

WHAT AND WHO IS IN THE NEW YIEROUSALĒM?

²²I did not see a sanctuary in it, for her sanctuary is Lord God, the Almighty One, and the Lamb. ²³The city has no need of sun nor of moon to shine in her, for God's splendor illumines her, and the Lamb is her lamp. ²⁴The ethnic groups will walk around through her light, and the land's kings will carry their splendor to her, ²⁵and her gates may never be closed by day, for night will not be there, ²⁶and they will carry the ethnic groups' splendor and honor to her. ²⁷Anything common and one doing detestable acts and a falsehood will never enter into her, but only the ones written in the Lamb's Life Book.

ITS RIVER

22 It exhibited for me the River of Life's Water, shining as crystal, journeying out from God's and the Lamb's Throne ²in her plaza's and the river's middle, here and there is Life's Tree, making twelve fruits, paying back each month its fruit, and the tree's leaves are for healing the ethnic groups. ³Anything cursed will not be any longer. God's and the Lamb's Throne will be in her and his slaves will venerate him ⁴and they will see his face, and his name will be on their foreheads. ⁵Night will not be there any longer and they do not have a need for a lamp's light and sun's light because the Lord God will illumine them, and they will rule into the Era of Eras.

The End

⁶The envoy said to me,

"These words are allegiant and true, and
  the Lord God of the prophets'
  spirits commissioned his envoy to
  exhibit to his slaves what events
  are necessary to happen—quickly.
⁷Look! I come quickly.
God's blessing on the one observing the
  words of this book's prophecy."

⁸I, Yōannēs [John]—the one hearing and seeing these things.

When I heard and saw, I fell to bow down before the envoy's feet, the one exhibiting these events for me. ⁹It says to me, "See [that you] not [do this]! I am your co-slave and your siblings' and the prophets' and the ones observing this book's words. Bow down to God!"

¹⁰It says to me, "Do not seal the words of this book's prophecy, for the season is close. ¹¹Let the one doing wrong still do wrong, and let the filthy one still do the filthy, and let the right one still do the right, and let the devoted one still be devoted."

¹²Look! I come quickly. My wage is with me to pay back to each as is the person's work. ¹³I am the Alpha and the Omega, the First and the Last, the Beginning and the Completion.

¹⁴God's blessing for the ones rinsing their stoles so their authority will be for Life's Tree and they may enter by the gates into the city. ¹⁵Outside are the dogs and drug-induced sorcerers and the prostituters and the murders and the demon worshipers and anyone loving and doing falsehood.

¹⁶I, Yēsous [Jesus], sent my envoy to witness these things to you for the assemblies. I am Dauid's [David's] root and family, the early morning shining star.

¹⁷The Spirit and the bride say, "Come!"
Let the one hearing say, "Come!"
Let the one thirsting come.
Let the one wanting take Life's water as a gift.
¹⁸I testify to everyone who hears the words of this book's prophecy:

If anyone places on these things, God will place on the person the plagues written in this book,

¹⁹and if anyone lifts away from the words of this prophecy's book, God will lift away the person's part from Life's Tree and from the devoted city, which are written about in this book.

²⁰The one witnessing these events says, "Yes, I come quickly."

Amēn. Come, Lord Yēsous!
²¹The Lord Yēsous' grace be with all.

GLOSSARY

Translators choose one term over another in order to convey sense. Sometimes words are so common and familiar to readers that they slip through our minds without thought. I have often chosen terms meant to slow the reader down and cause them to think about what the sense is. *The Second Testament* avoids religiously and theologically familiar terms, just as it, following the pattern of *The First Testament*, transliterates the original names of persons (such as Yōannēs for John, or Yēsous for Jesus). It is not always possible to use the same English term for the same Greek term in each instance, but consistency from Greek to English has been attempted.

Analogy, analogies. Usually translated "parable." The Greek word has the sense of tossing down something alongside something else. Hence, an analogy. Some are simple two or three line analogies, others are longer and become stories or fables.

apocalypse, to apocalypse. God reveals redemption in Jesus Christ in the power of the Spirit. To reveal in such a manner is to apocalypse because it is a history-altering act of revelation.

Apprentices [disciples]. Those following Jesus, those being conformed to the life of Jesus, and those being trained to extend the kingdom to others.

Bēma [judgment seat]. A specific legal court location on which sat the judge and before him a person appeared to hear a verdict. It was in some cases a platform and in others, say in Corinth, a large, elevated, enclosed edifice.

Central Council [Sanhedrin]. The central court (most often) in Jerusalem, functioning more or less like the Supreme Court in the US.

Christos. Transliteration of the Greek word for "Christ" or "Messiah."

Commissioner [apostle]. An officially sent person by Jesus.

Common life. Fellowship or communion with or in.

Covenant Code [law of Moses]. The law of Moses was a covenantal arrangement by God with the people of Israel. This code of conduct expected of them was not the same as law in the Roman world or what law means to us today. It is a revelation of God's will for God's covenant people but requires ongoing interpretation and adjustments.

Covenant Code scholars [scribes]. A specialist in reading and interpreting the Covenant Code [law of Moses], and thus responsible for the ongoing interpretations of the Covenant Code. They are behind what is sometimes called the "tradition of the elders," the more or less official interpretation of the Code for observant Jews.

Covenant Code experts [lawyers]. Much the same as Covenant Code scholars, with more emphasis on the legal and public side of interpreting and applying the Code.

dip, dipper. Baptize or baptizer; hence, Yōannēs the Dipper is John the Baptist. The "baptism" here is a dipping, or plunging, or immersing into the water.

Elites [Sadducees]. A group in Judaism, especially in Jerusalem, who were the upper class, politically ruling leaders and responsible for the rules, maintenance, and worship in the temple in Jerusalem.

Empire [kingdom]. The word *basileia* evokes the rule and domination of Rome, and hence it evokes an empire.

Era. The Greek term *aiōnios* translates the Hebrew term *olam*, which means a period of time, like a century or an epoch or a longer period of time. Its common translation "eternal" suggests that it always means forever and ever, but it does not. It refers most often to the period of the coming kingdom of God, which also has endless duration. Thus, "Era Life" means "Life pertaining to the final Era."

faith, believe. The English translations "faith" and "believe" and "trust" translate the Greek words *pistis* and *pisteuō*. When referring to faith in general, that is, what we believe (our faith), I use "faith." When it means a singular act of faith, I use "trust," and when it refers to a longer sense of trusting over time, I use "allegiance." I have purposely varied the translation in order to keep all three in mind, especially trust and allegiance, because a difference is not always clear in the context.

Flatbread. Unleavened bread, the Flatbreads Day being the Day of Unleavened Bread on the Jewish calendar.

Kosmos [world]. A term used for the system of this earthly life more than a planet or a globe; it also often conveys a sense of the "cosmic."

masked, masked ones. Those wearing a mask, and hence often translated "hypocrite."

My Greatness. Rabbi, which means "my Great one" or "my Greatness."

Observant [Pharisees]. *Pharisee* has become a public, universal pejorative term for a hypocrite. Pharisees were observant of the interpretations of the Covenant Code called the "tradition of the elders." They conformed their behaviors to the interpretation. Among the various groups of Jews at the time of Jesus, they were perhaps closest to Jesus in their overall concern to make a radical commitment to the will of God (as they understood it).

Oy! [woe]. The term is a warning to someone but not a curse or damnation of someone.

Paraklētos. Illuminator. The Spirit continuing and splendoring the work of Yēsous as illuminator, mediator, revealer, teacher, helper, advocate, witness, and convicting agent.

Parousia. An appearing, a return; hence, the Parousia of Christ refers to his appearing or Second Coming.

Pascha. Passover.

path-entry. The path of redemption revealed in Jesus.

police. Used for the guards or law enforcement in the temple courts.

Praitōrion [Praetorium]. A place where special, upper-level military gathered for counsel, and the Praitōrion guards were the special military personnel who specially protected the emperor of Rome.

restoration. When God wraps up all the divine plan for history on earth and restores everything to its proper place.

right, to right, rightness [justify, justification, righteousness]. The core sense of the Greek term *dikaio-* is what is right, what is made right in God's salvation, what is declared right, and what is just and establishing justice.

scaly-skin [leprosy]. The term refers to more than Hansen's disease. It describes a breakout in the skin.

self, selves [*psychē*]. One of the more difficult terms to translate. *Psychē* refers to the inner self, the self, the mere living-ness of the self, or the human-ward dimension of who we are, while *pneuma*, "spirit," refers to the God-ward dimension of who we are.

siblings. Used instead of "brothers" or "brothers and sisters" when it refers both to women and men.

splendor, splendoring [glory, glorifying]. (Greek *doxa, doxazō*). Often translated as "glory" or "glorify," the word *splendor* emphasizes the magnificence, brightness, grandeur, and glorious appearance, goodness, love, grace, and holiness of God.

Valley of Destructive Fire [Gehenna, hell]. A valley southwest of the walls and city of Jerusalem, famous for a place not only at one time for child sacrifice but also as a trope for the place where God would judge a sinful people. It was not a garbage dump at the time of Jesus. It was distinguished from "hades," which translates the Hebrew *she'ol*, which refers to the place of all the dead, both the righteous and unrighteous.